NON SANZ DROICT.

William Shakespeare

Four Great Tragedies

Hamlet
Othello
King Lear
Macbeth

WITH AN INTRODUCTION BY
Sylvan Barnet

A SIGNET CLASSIC

SIGNET CLASSIC
Published by New American Library, a division of
Penguin Putnam Inc., 375 Hudson Street, New York, New York 10014, U.S.A.
Penguin Books Ltd, 27 Wrights Lane, London W8 5TZ, England
Penguin Books Australia Ltd, Ringwood, Victoria, Australia
Penguin Books Canada Ltd, 10 Alcorn Avenue, Toronto, Ontario, Canada M4V 3B2
Penguin Books (N.Z.) Ltd, 182–190 Wairau Road, Auckland 10, New Zealand

Penguin Books Ltd, Registered Offices: Harmondsworth, Middlesex, England

First Printing, May 1982
First Printing (Revised Edition), June 1998
10   9   8   7   6   5

Hamlet, Othello, King Lear, and *Macbeth* are also available as separate volumes
in the Signet Classic Shakespeare editions.

Ⅽ   REGISTERED TRADEMARK—MARCA REGISTRADA

Library of Congress Catalog Card Number: 81-85146

Printed in the United States of America

Introduction

Hundreds of books have been written about tragedy (indeed hundreds have been written about Shakespeare's tragedies), and it is fairly usual for them to begin by saying that there is no such thing as tragedy—there are only *tragedies*. We get the point; each play is different and ought not to be forced into a Procrustean bed, its special features lopped off or stretched so that it may be neatly confined within a label.

Still, Shakespeare's contemporaries certainly thought there was such a thing as tragedy; they used the word in talking about literature, and they defined it in their dictionaries. Here are some definitions. Thomas Cooper in 1568 (Shakespeare was four years old) defined tragedy as "a kind of plays representing personages of great estate, and matters of much trouble." The redundantly named Thomas Thomas, writing a dictionary at about the time that Shakespeare was probably beginning his theatrical career, i.e., the late 1580's, said that tragedy is

> a lofty kind of poetry, and representing personages of great state and matter of much trouble, a great broil or stir: it beginneth prosperously, it endeth unfortunately and doubtfully, contrary to comedy.

And, finally, a definition by John Florio, three of whose books Shakespeare undoubtedly knew—and he may have known Florio himself, since Florio tutored the man to whom Shakespeare dedicated *Venus and Adonis* (1593) and *The Rape of Lucrece* (1594). In his Italian-English dictionary of 1598 Florio defines tragedy thus:

> A tragedy or mournful play being a lofty kind of poetry and representing personages of great state and matter of much trouble, a great broil or stir: it beginneth prosperously and endeth unfortunately or sometimes doubtfully, and is contrary to comedy.

v

These and similar definitions (to say nothing of the plays themselves) allow us to assert that the Elizabethans regarded a tragedy as a "lofty" play showing "personages of great state" engaged or caught up in a "lamentable" action that "beginneth prosperously and endeth unfortunately." The terms apply well to Shakespeare's tragedies; the only modification needed is that *Hamlet* does not begin prosperously, for Hamlet's father has already been killed, and his mother (in his view) has ignobly remarried. But the three other plays begin with the hero riding high on Fortune's wheel. Othello, the chief prop of Venice, is married to his heart's joy; Lear, full of years and power, is surrounded by an attentive court; Macbeth, victorious in battle, is given new honors by his grateful and gracious king. And of course all four of these tragic heroes will, in the course of the plays, go through nearly unendurable agonies and will, in the fifth act, die.

Behind the figures in Renaissance drama who fall from high place are medieval nondramatic tragedies, that is, narrative poems telling of the insubstantiality of high place in a world governed by Fortune. Chaucer's Monk knows a hundred such stories and recites fifteen of them to his fellow pilgrims before the Knight, bored stiff, interrupts him. The one interesting thing about the Monk's tedious narratives is that although he instances his tragic figures (correctly enough) as people deserted by Fortune, they are a mixed bag. King Peter of Cyprus is totally innocent—indeed, he is slain merely out of envy—yet Lucifer, on the other hand, "fel . . . for his synne," and Adam lost Paradise because of his "mysgovernaunce." So there are two explanations for the fall: capricious fortune, and man's vice. If we go beyond the four plays in this volume and look at the whole range of Shakespeare's tragedies, we can say that at one pole are Romeo and Juliet, attractive young people who are "star-crossed," i.e., who have bad luck and who can be regarded almost as sacrificial victims, and at the other pole is Macbeth, who knowingly embarks on a career of murder and who is, for his "mysgovernaunce," justly punished. Rejecting the view that Fortune governs capriciously or malevolently, Macbeth sees that "even-handed justice / Commends th' ingredients of our poisoned chalice / To our own lips" (1.7.10–12).

We can say, then, that for Shakespeare there was such a thing as tragedy (people in high estate fall into intense suffering and finally into death), and yet every play is unique; Shakespeare never repeated himself, but always filled the old bottles with new wine. The plays differ in countless ways: *Hamlet* and *Lear* are rich in pervasive bitter comedy but *Othello* has only two short, witless comic scenes; *Hamlet* is almost twice the length of *Macbeth*; Lear is unique in having a subplot (Gloucester and his sons) running parallel to the main plot

(Lear and his daughters); the source of *Othello* is a short story that runs only a few pages, but the sources of *Lear* include an old play (in which, by the way, the king is restored to the throne) and a monstrously long prose romance, and the source of *Macbeth* is a long prose historical account. And, to return to the chief point, the degree of guilt of the tragic figures ranges greatly—from Hamlet, who initially finds himself in a wretched situation not at all of his own making, to Lear, who indeed bungles by giving his kingdom to two villainous daughters (but here his intentions are good, and, considering the hideous treatment he later receives, he can fairly say that he is "more sinned against than sinning"), to Othello, who is duped into murdering his wife, to Macbeth, who knows what is right but who nevertheless kills in order to gain the crown.

In 1615, four years after Shakespeare had retired from the theater, one John Greene published a blast against the theatrical profession. He took a survey of what he had seen and read—and although he does not name Shakespeare, there is no reason to assume that he was exempting Shakespeare—and he set down his thoughts.

> The matter of tragedies is haughtiness, arrogancy, ambition, pride, injury, anger, wrath, envy, hatred, contention, war, murder, cruelty, rapine, incest, rovings, depradations, piracies, spoils, robberies, rebellions, treasons, killing, hewing, stabbing, dagger-drawing, fighting, butchery, treachery, villainy, etc. and all kind of heroic evils whatever.

There is a good deal of redundancy here, but on the whole it is true. *Hamlet* (probably written 1600–01), to take the earliest play in our group, fits the description nicely, except perhaps for "rapine" (plunder). "Haughtiness, arrogancy": Hamlet bitterly speaks of the "insolence of office," perhaps thinking of the usurper Claudius. "Ambition, pride": somewhat oddly, Hamlet characterizes himself as ambitious and proud, and in any case in 3.3.55 Claudius specifically refers to the "ambition" that prodded him to kill for a crown and a queen. "Injury, anger, wrath, envy, hatred, contention": these need scarcely to be documented. "War": the play is full of talk of war between Norway and Denmark, and at the end the Norwegian prince takes possession of Denmark. There is, too, the battle between Hamlet and Claudius ("mighty opposites," in Hamlet's words). "Murder, cruelty": we need hardly point out examples, but we should note that Hamlet himself is, in various ways and for various reasons, "cruel." For example, he says to his mother, "I must be cruel, only to be kind"; his cruelty to Rosencrantz and

Guildenstern (he kills them) is understandable, for he is, in effect, at war, but perhaps less understandable is his almost joyful contemplation of the trick by which he dispatches them. "Incest": Hamlet is deeply disturbed that his mother has posted to "incestuous sheets," i.e., married her former brother-in-law, an incestuous act by Elizabethan standards. We need not go through the rest of John Greene's catalog except to mention that even "piracies" is present in *Hamlet*, for he escapes from the ship bearing him to death in England by the fortunate appearance of a pirate vessel, which he boards. And yet Greene's blast against tragedies, so right in all its details, is somehow all wrong. One is reminded of the story that Mark Twain's very proper wife, to cure him of his habit of cursing, once repeated one of his foul outbursts word for word. He listened, thought for a moment, and then patiently explained to her that she had the words right but she didn't have the intonation. Greene argued that because tragedy is concerned with evil, it corrupts the spectators. What he didn't see was the vision behind the plays; we can almost say "the moral vision." Hamlet, for example, *is* partly corrupted by the corrupt world around him; but heroically, and almost miraculously, he finally accomplishes the stern task imposed upon him by the ghost of his murdered father ("Revenge his foul and most unnatural murder"), and he accomplishes it nobly, not by any base scheme but by stabbing the murderer with a poisoned foil that Laertes, Claudius's tool, had treacherously prepared to use against Hamlet, and by forcing Claudius to drink a cup of poison that Claudius had prepared for Hamlet. Hamlet has been sorely tried, and he has done things that no decent person willingly does, but (despite the school of criticism that sees him as a weakling who invents excuses for not getting on with the job) on the whole and finally he behaves heroically, meriting the military funeral that he is given at the end. When the cannon pay final tribute to him, we are audibly reminded that he has been a warrior and that against all odds he has done his duty. Indeed, our memories need not be especially keen to recall, when we hear this closing military salute, that earlier in the play cannon were used to salute Claudius as he downed his wine (1.4.6–12); here, at the end of the play, they are put to fitter use, providing Hamlet with "the soldiers' music," in tribute to his tragic victory in a just cause.

This brief introduction has not touched on the two questions that many people think are central to *Hamlet*: Why does Hamlet delay? and, Is Hamlet mad or only pretending to be? Nor will it touch on them, except to say that they do not arise when one is deeply immersed in reading the play or in seeing it on the stage. Rather than go into these tedious matters, the limited space at hand will be used (before glancing at the three other tragedies printed in this book) to talk briefly about the languages of drama, drawing examples chiefly from *Hamlet*. Elizabeth Bowen has said that in fiction, *dialogue* is what the characters *do* to each other. A very shrewd observation. But a play is people moving about on the stage—engaging in dialogue, of course, but also wearing costumes, picking up props, making gestures, hearing sound effects—matters to keep in mind while we read the play.

Take the business of costumes: Hamlet at the start is dressed (according to his own words) in an "inky cloak," and this garment doubtless sets him apart from the opulently dressed court in 1.2. That is, the costume *says* something. It says that Hamlet is in mourning, and (by contrast with all the other courtly costumes) it says that he is isolated. And it also marks him as a figure of death, for we cannot overlook the fact that he deals in death: Rosencrantz and Guildenstern, Polonius, Laertes, and Claudius all meet death at his hands, and he bears some responsibility for Ophelia's death too. (This is not to say that he is a villain—that role is clearly reserved for Claudius—but only that this "sweet prince," forced into the role of avenger, is dressed accordingly.) Later, in his description of his activities while sailing for England, he speaks of wearing his "sea gown," and it may well be that when we first see him after the voyage (in the churchyard, in 5.1.) he is dressed in this gown, the change in costume indicating a change within, for from this point he is confirmed in his purpose.

When we turn to theatrical props, we think first perhaps of the prayerbook that Polonius, that meddlesome stage-manager, thrusts into Ophelia's hands, but we should also remember such things as the throne on which the usurping Claudius sits, the poisoned chalice, and, most important of all, the sword that Hamlet doubtless wears throughout the play—reminding us that he is in combat. We have already noticed the chief sound effects, the roar of cannon, but we should also recall the "flourish" of trumpets announcing the entry of Claudius, in 1.2.1 and elsewhere, and the "trumpets and kettledrums" that precede the dumbshow in 3.2.92.

But of course a play—especially a play by Shakespeare—chiefly makes use of words, and something must be said about Shakespeare's prose and verse. We think of Shakespeare primarily as a poetic dramatist, but only two of his plays (*Richard II* and *King John*) are written entirely in poetry. About half of the other plays are at least one-fourth in prose. Almost one-third of *Hamlet,* for example, is in prose, and the same is true of *King Lear*. It is sometimes said that in Shakespeare's tragedies the noble characters speak verse and the lower characters speak prose, but this generalization is far too simple, even when modified by such an amendment as the assertion that noble characters when mad speak prose. The fact is, Shakespeare's noble characters use prose in a wide variety of situations. Hamlet, for example, uses it in greeting his old school friends Rosencrantz and Guildenstern (2.2), in princely reflections on "What a piece of work is a man" (also 2.2), and in meditative comments on the impending duel with Laertes (5.2). Let's look briefly at these passages. First, a sample of Hamlet with Rosencrantz and Guildenstern. When he sees them he says, "My excellent good friends! How dost thou, Guildenstern? Ah, Rosencrantz! Good lads, how do you both?" A moment earlier Hamlet had been taunting Polonius—in witty prose—but now, seeing his old schoolfriends, his genial nature and his sense of courtesy revive, and he expresses in simple language his heartfelt joy at their presence. But almost immediately he suspects that Claudius has sent them to spy on him, and his prose begins to hammer at them:

> Were you not sent for? Is it your own inclining? Is it a free visitation? Come, come, deal justly with me. Come, come; nay, speak.
> (2.2.280–83)

When they confess that the king sent for them, Hamlet, secure in knowing that he has their number, can turn his thoughts away from them and to himself, and we get a speech that, although addressed to Rosencrantz and Guildenstern, sounds almost like a soliloquy:

> I have of late, but wherefore I know not, lost all my mirth, forgone all custom of exercises; and indeed, it goes so heavily with my disposition that this goodly frame, the earth, seems to me a sterile promontory; this most excellent canopy, the air, look you, this brave o'erhanging firmament, this majestical roof fretted with golden fire: why, it appeareth nothing to me but a foul and pestilent congregation of vapors. What a piece of work is a man, how noble in reason, how infinite in faculties, in form and moving how express and admirable, in action how like an angel, in apprehension how like a god: the beauty of the world, the paragon of animals; and yet to me, what is this quintessence of dust? Man delights not me; nor woman neither, though by your smiling you seem to say so.
> (303–19)

Only in the last part of the last sentence (from "nor woman, neither") does the prose again become a weapon to use against the two spies.

Finally, let's look at Hamlet's response to Horatio's offer to make excuses if Hamlet wishes to avoid dueling with Laertes:

> Not a whit, we defy augury. There is special providence in the fall of a sparrow. If it be now, 'tis not to come; if it be not to come, it will be now; if it be not now, yet it will come. The readiness is all. Since no man of aught he leaves knows, what is't to leave betimes? Let be. (5.2.220–25)

Of the sixty-two words in the speech, all but seven are monosyllabic. On the whole the diction is colloquial (e.g. "Not a whit"), but there is a solemn echo of the Bible ("special providence in the fall of a sparrow"), and the clauses are balanced. The speech is simple and meditative, yet strong-willed in the final "Let be."

Now for an equally brief discussion of the poetry. Some of the poetry is rhymed, but most is unrhymed, written in blank verse. We shall consider blank verse in a moment, but first we will dispose of the rhymed poetry. Sometimes the end of a blank verse speech is given emotional heightening by a couplet (a pair of rhyming lines). A particularly interesting variation of this device occurs in *Hamlet*, where, after conversing with the ghost, Hamlet rejoins his fellows, speaks blank verse, and then uses a couplet which (however bitter) seems by virtue of the rhyme emphatic or forceful—but then Hamlet adds a short unrhymed line; the effect of this addition is not only to indicate Hamlet's need for companionship (that is the gist or content of the line) but to indicate his exhaustion:

> Rest, rest, perturbèd spirit. So, gentlemen,
> With all my love I do commend me to you,
> And what so poor a man as Hamlet is
> May do t'express his love and friending to you,
> God willing, shall not lack. Let us go in together,
> And still your fingers on your lips, I pray.
> The time is out of joint. O cursèd spite,
> That ever I was born to set it right!
> Nay, come, let's go together. (1.4.182–90)

Couplets are also sometimes used to end a scene or an act, to wrap it up before a new group of characters enters. Long speeches in rhyme may be used to indicate that these speeches are not normal discourse, for in the play, normal discourse is chiefly unrhymed poetry, or prose. An obvious example in *Hamlet* is the play-within-the-play in 3.2. And of course there are other uses for rhyme, such as Ophelia's mad songs in 4.5 and Hamlet's poem in his letter to Ophelia in 2.2.

Having said that Shakespeare makes dramatic use of prose and of rhyme, we must of course recognize that his chief medium is blank verse, unrhymed iambic pentameter. In a mechanically exact line there are five iambic feet (each foot consisting of an unstressed syllable followed by a stressed syllable), so of the ten syllables every second is stressed. But the stresses are not all of equal weight, and in any case Shakespeare often departs from the pattern. One reads a passage according to the sense, not according to a fixed idea of meter. In the following passage, Claudius rather formally addresses his court:

> Though yet of Hamlet our dear brother's death
> The memory be green, and that it us befitted
> To bear our hearts in grief, and our whole kingdom
> To be contracted in one brow of woe,
> Yet so far hath discretion fought with nature
> That we with wisest sorrow think on him
> Together with remembrance of ourselves.   (1.2.1–7)

But Claudius does not always sound so poised and kingly. To get an idea of the range of Shakespeare's blank verse, and of the ways in which it creates or reveals character, we can compare this speech with another passage from the same scene, where Claudius puts aside, to some degree, the ceremonious manner we have just heard, and speaks more intimately to Laertes:

> And now, Laertes, what's the news with you?
> You told us of some suit. What is't, Laertes?
> You cannot speak of reason to the Dane
> And lose your voice. What wouldst thou beg, Laertes,
> That shall not be my offer, not thy asking?   (42–46)

Intimacy is here created not only by the shift from the royal "us" in the second line to the more human "my" in the last, and by the ingratiating repetition of "Laertes," but also by the short sentences: we get five sentences in five lines, as opposed to the single sentence seven lines long quoted in the previous example.

These comments on Shakespeare's language (nonverbal as well as verbal) have only scratched the surface, but they may serve to alert the reader to some of the subtleties and complexities of Shakespeare's art. On each rereading one will see and hear more, but this is not to say that on an initial encounter with a play one should worry about whether a passage is in rhyme, blank verse, or prose. Merely read the play carefully (it's no use speed-reading the speeches as though they are items in a newspaper), if not aloud at least so that they sound in the mind's ear, and they will do their work, or at least much of it. Once you are familiar with the plot and the characters, and indeed with Shakespeare's language, you can reread, paying closer attention to the artistry and thereby deriving yet greater pleasure from it. There is scarcely a speech which, if read aloud two or three times, will not in some way grow richer—perhaps funnier, perhaps more pathetic, perhaps more harrowing. Listening to good recordings of the plays (most libraries have them) will also greatly deepen understanding and enjoyment.

After writing *Hamlet*, Shakespeare probably wrote *The Merry Wives of Windsor*, *Troilus and Cressida*, and *All's Well that Ends Well*, and then, in 1604, *Othello*, the tragedy that next concerns us. *Hamlet* is a revenge play, which means that its structure is that of action and reaction, an eye for an eye, a tooth for a tooth. The initial action—the murder of Hamlet's father—took place before the play begins, but when Hamlet learns who the murderer is, his course of action, or, so to speak, his reaction, is clear, and from this point onward Hamlet and Claudius engage in a barely concealed battle. But in *Othello* we get a play with a different structure, largely because Othello does not clearly know, until the final scene, that he is being acted upon. This play, like *King Lear* and *Macbeth*, is indebted to a late medieval genre called the morality play (the most famous example is *Everyman*), specifically to the kind of morality play that shows a man tempted into sin. Iago is the tempter here, a sort of devil (he himself appeals to hell for inspiration in devising his scheme); at the other side of Othello stands "the divine Desdemona," a sort of good angel. Shakespeare derived his plot from a rather unimpressive story that would occupy about ten pages in this book, and he turned it into a play that is at once intensely human and yet rich in reverberations of mysterious powers. We have no ghost, as in *Hamlet*, and no witches, as in *Macbeth*; rather, we have only suggestions of mysterious powers, chiefly through imagery of angelic goodness on the one hand and diabolical evil on the other. Iago offers several motives for hating Othello—Othello has not promoted Iago, Iago suspects Othello has been to bed with Iago's wife, etc.—but the best comment on Iago's search for a motive is Coleridge's: "the motive-hunting of motiveless malignity." Why this malignity? As well ask why Judas betrayed Christ. Indeed, perhaps this gives us a clue: a mere hatred of the good. In any case Iago says of Cassio, another of his victims,

"He hath a daily beauty in his life / That makes me ugly. . . ." (5.1.19–20).

But we can ask, To what degree is Othello himself at fault? His are the hands, after all, that kill Desdemona. And so critics have sought to find Othello's "tragic flaw." "The noble Moor" (thus he is characterized in the play) is said to be guilty of jealousy, or of stupidity, or of African barbarism covered with only a veneer of European civilization. Some evidence can be adduced in support of these charges; for example, although Othello often speaks nobly and behaves heroically, after Iago has poisoned his mind with the suggestion that Desdemona has slept with Cassio, Othello is capable of such barbarously crude utterances as "I will chop her into messes" and "I'll tear her all to pieces." This, from the man who has spoken with dignity and with splendor, as when (to take a very brief example) he said to old Brabantio, who was accompanied by an armed band prepared to attack Othello:

> Keep up your bright swords, for the dew will rust them.
> Good signior, you shall more command with years
> Than with your weapons. (1.2.58–60)

Still, the idea of hunting for a flaw in Othello is misguided, for it puts the emphasis in the wrong place. Exactly what is it that leads to the terrible tragedy of Othello killing the thing he most values? It is not a weakness but a virtue, as Iago himself tells us, and here he is no deceiver. The Moor, he says, is "of a free and open nature / That thinks men honest that but seem to be so. . . ." (1.3.390–91), and so Iago knows that Othello will not suspect him. (We might note, that Hamlet meets his death not because of a flaw but because he is high-minded. Laertes can with impunity use a poisoned foil in what is supposed to be a game because he knows that Hamlet, being "free from all contriving / Will not peruse the foils.") Iago knows, too, that he can turn Desdemona's "virtue into pitch, / And out of her own goodness make the net / That shall enmesh them all" (2.3.360–62). Nobility or excellence, paradoxically, is by its nature vulnerable, and it is this fact as much as any other that causes tragedy to arouse (in the words of Shakespeare's slightly earlier contemporary, Sir Philip Sidney) "admiration [i.e. wonder] and commiseration." Wonder and pity. But, finally, at the end of the play there is more than wonder and pity; there is almost—we might say—joy at the end, for although Othello suffers beyond endurance when he learns that he has murdered his innocent wife, the news of her innocence is not simply the worst news he could hear; it is also the best news, reestablishing his belief in goodness. And so, in a long, dignified, beautiful speech he sums up his career, judges his horrible action scrupulously (he says he, "Like the base Judean, threw a pearl away/Richer than all his tribe"), and goes on to pronounce justice on himself. He speaks of an infidel, an enemy to the state, whom he killed, and so he now, once again, kills the infidel, himself. Iago has not, after all, destroyed Othello's moral sense. T. S. Eliot oddly said that in this moving speech Othello is adopting a sentimental attitude toward himself, "endeavoring to escape reality," and is "cheering himself up." Helen Gardner much more astutely suggests that Othello, by affirming the values by which he lived, is cheering *us* up.

In *King Lear* (1605–06) Shakespeare is again indebted to the morality pattern (Lear is flanked by the virtuous Cordelia and Kent on one side, and the wicked Goneril and Regan on the other), but the play is utterly unlike *Othello*. In this play the tragic action—Lear's banishment of the loving Cordelia and his entrusting of himself to the care of Goneril and Regan—takes place in the first scene. Goneril and Regan are monstrous hypocrites, but the action is clearly Lear's alone. The banishment of Cordelia brings immediate protests from Lear's true friend, Kent; Lear cannot claim later that he was a victim. We can wish that Cordelia had spoken more gently (though we cannot blame her for lacking the "glib and oily art" of her fawning sisters), and we can scarcely blame an eighty-year-old man who wishes to retire, but the foolish deed is Lear's. The upshot is that Lear suffers terribly for his egotism at the beginning, and, through suffering, comes to value the loving Cordelia, whom he had brutally rejected. We cannot say—and do not want to say—that through his trials Lear is purified and finally dies worthy of entering heaven. We need not say, with the great critic A. C. Bradley, that the play might be called "The Redemption of King Lear," but surely at the end of the play Lear is better and wiser. Perhaps he is happier, too, and this point is worth discussing.

Bradley says that Lear dies overcome with joy in the belief that Cordelia is alive, but the text is ambiguous. Holding Cordelia in his arms, Lear dies with these words:

> Do you see this? Look on her. Look, her lips.
> Look there, look there.   (5.3.312–13)

What does Lear see on her lips? Breath and motion, or lifelessness? It will not do to assert dogmatically that Lear, madly thinking Cordelia is alive, dies joyfully, or, on the other hand, that he dies full of outrage that the virtuous Cordelia has been murdered. But we can say this: earlier in the speech the agonized Lear, aware in a lucid moment that the innocent Cordelia is dead, asks, "Why should a dog, a horse, a rat have life,/And thou no breath at all?" Lear does not formulate an answer, but our answer must be, "Because a human being, but not a lower animal, can choose (as Cordelia chooses) to act out of love rather than out of self-interest." The monstrous unfairness remains, but nothing further needs to be said, and Lear, having already experienced the most intense suffering (as well as the most intense joy when, however briefly, he is reconciled with Cordelia) can scarcely go on living. It is surely preposterous to say, with a recent critic, that Lear's "final retreat to madness . . . makes it impossible to retain *any* concept of an ordered universe." At the end of the play, as at the beginning, Lear is wrong about some facts (his infirm mind seems not to grasp, for example, the fact that the loyal Kent has served him in disguise as Caius), but he is right about Cordelia's love, and whether he dies outraged at the fact of her death or overjoyed (surely the more meaningful interpretation) in the mistaken belief that she is alive matters less than that Cordelia loved him, that he comes to see this, and that he is reunited with her. We joy in her love, and we are immensely relieved that he is at last released from "the rack of this tough world." We can note, too, without unctuously suggesting that all's right with the world, that all of the villains are dead and that their deaths are not accidental or casual but supremely appropriate: the villainous Regan dies at the hand of her former partner in wickedness and now her rival, the villainous Goneril; Goneril dies by her own hand; Edmund dies by the hand of the brother whom he wronged.

With *Macbeth* (1605–06) we come to the last of our four great tragedies, though Shakespeare went on to write two more (*Antony and Cleopatra* and *Coriolanus*) as well as several comedies. It is Shakespeare's shortest tragedy, and the one most clearly indebted to the structure and indeed the obvious morality of the morality play. Macbeth, a sort of heroic Everyman, is tempted (his wife, and the witches); although he has at his side images of virtue (the noble King Duncan, Banquo), and he knows that he is doing wrong, he yields to temptation and then learns that he must pay the terrible price. Notice: he "knows" that he is doing wrong, but he must still "learn" that he must pay the price. And what is this price? Not simply death, but a loss of all sense of the value of life. In the fifth act he sees clearly the irony of his tragic action: he killed Duncan in order to increase his happiness, but he finds that he has lost all happiness, all of what was represented by Duncan's world:

> My way of life
> Is fall'n into the sear, the yellow leaf,
> And that which should accompany old age,
> As honor, love, obedience, troops of friends,
> I must not look to have; but, in their stead,
> Curses, not loud, but deep. . . .   (5.3.22–27)

This speech only states explicitly what spectators of the play see: they see, for example, that after Macbeth, encouraged by his wife, murders Duncan, Macbeth becomes gradually isolated even from her, his accomplice in this first crime. In 3.2 he keeps from her his plan to murder Banquo and Fleance. She has already noticed his isolation, and she asks him, "Why do you keep alone,/Of sorriest fancies your companions making?" and he replies by saying that he is tormented by the thought that Banquo and Fleance still live. To her question, "What's to be done?" he answers only, "Be innocent of the knowledge, dearest chuck;" the affection in "dearest chuck" (i.e., chick) and the desire to shield her from further evildoing only underscore the pain of the separation from the woman who earlier was his "dearest partner of greatness." After 4.1 Macbeth is never again seen in the play with any of his former associates, not even Lady Macbeth, who dies offstage in 5.6 and whose death evokes from him only the dead words, "She should have died hereafter;/There would have been a time for such a word." Whether these words mean, "She would have died sometime anyway" or "She ought to have died at a more opportune moment" does not much matter; it is clear from the view expressed in the lines that follow—Macbeth's, not Shakespeare's—that life is now meaningless:

> Tomorrow, and tomorrow, and tomorrow
> Creeps in this petty pace from day to day,
> To the last syllable of recorded time;
> And all our yesterdays have lighted fools
> The way to dusty death. Out, out, brief candle!
> Life's but a walking shadow, a poor player
> That struts and frets his hour upon the stage
> And then is heard no more. It is a tale
> Told by an idiot, full of sound and fury
> Signifying nothing.   (5.5.19–28)

Aristotle in his *Poetics* (composed almost two thousand years before *Macbeth*) was the first to tell us that tragedy evokes "pity" and "terror," and here, at the end of our brief discussion of four great tragedies, we can see how these terms apply to this play. The terror is obvious enough: that Macbeth, receiver of Duncan's bounty, should murder his benefactor, is terrifying. That he should go on to a career of slaughter, killing not only those who are obviously his enemies but even the utterly innocent Lady Macduff and her child, suggests that we live in a world where no one is safe from the reaches of a madman. Terror, too, that *we,* like Macbeth, might yield to temptations if the prize seemed within easy reach, and terror that we would suffer Macbeth's fate. And this gets us to the matter of pity, not only the obvious pity for Macbeth's victims but even for Macbeth himself, for it is strange but true that although he is monstrous he nevertheless evokes a degree of pity. Why do we feel any pity for this man who, unlike all of Shakespeare's earlier tragic heroes, knowingly does evil? A few answers may be suggested. (1) It is pitiful that a brave warrior who is, at first, a savior of his nation should become the enemy of his nation. (2) He is in some degree the victim of the Witches and of Lady Macbeth, i.e., of some destructive power-seeking force that permeates the world. (3) Knowing that his deeds are evil, he is tormented by his conscience. His punishment, as has already been suggested, is not merely that he dies but that his conscience afflicts him with fear and guilt, with "terrible dreams/That shake us nightly" (3.2.18–19). (4) Finally, at the end of the play he fights strongly, and we can only recall sadly that, in contrast with the report of his courage and patriotism in 1.1, he now fights for a wicked cause.

No reader of this introduction to four tragic masterpieces will be more aware than the writer that its assertions are too simple and that its omissions are great. Even if much more space were available it would be inadequate to these plays, which, on the page and in the theater, evoke infinitely complicated responses. I can only with the words of Shakespeare's two fellow actors who wrote the preface to the first collection (1623) of Shakespeare's plays: "And so we leave you to other of his friends, whom if you need can be your guides. If you need them not, you can lead yourselves, and others. And such readers we wish him."

—SYLVAN BARNET
Tufts University

The Tragedy of Hamlet
Prince of Denmark

Hamlet, Prince of Denmark, son of the late king and of Gertrude
Claudius, King of Denmark, Hamlet's uncle
Ghost of the late king, Hamlet's father
Gertrude, Queen of Denmark, widow of the late king, now wife of Claudius
Polonius, councillor to the king
Laertes, son of Polonius
Ophelia, daughter of Polonius
Reynaldo, servant of Polonius
Horatio, Hamlet's friend and fellow student
Rosencrantz } courtiers, former school friends of Hamlet
Guildenstern }
Voltemand } Danish ambassadors to Norway
Cornelius }
Osric, a foppish courtier
Marcellus }
Barnardo } soldiers
Francisco }
English ambassadors
Fortinbras, prince of Norway
Captain, in Fortinbras's army
Players, performing the roles of Prologue, King, Queen, and Lucianus
A Priest
Two Clowns—a Grave-digger and his companion
Lords, Ladies, Soldiers, Sailors, Messengers, Attendants

Scene: In and around the court at Elsinore]

The Tragedy of Hamlet
Prince of Denmark

[ACT 1

Scene 1. *A guard platform of the castle.*]

Enter Barnardo and Francisco, two sentinels.

Barnardo. Who's there?

Francisco. Nay, answer me. Stand and unfold°¹ yourself.

Barnardo. Long live the King!°

Francisco. Barnardo?

Barnardo. He.   5

Francisco. You come most carefully upon your hour.

Barnardo. 'Tis now struck twelve. Get thee to bed,
Francisco.

---

¹The degree sign (°) indicates a footnote, which is keyed to the text by
the line number. Text references are printed in **boldface** type; the annotation follows in roman type.
1.1.2 **unfold** disclose   3 **Long live the King** (perhaps a password, perhaps a greeting)

3

Francisco. For this relief much thanks. 'Tis bitter cold,
And I am sick at heart.

Barnardo. Have you had quiet guard?

10 *Francisco.* Not a mouse stirring.

Barnardo. Well, good night.
If you do meet Horatio and Marcellus,
The rivals° of my watch, bid them make haste.

Enter Horatio and Marcellus.

Francisco. I think I hear them. Stand, ho! Who is
there?

Horatio. Friends to this ground.

15 *Marcellus.* And liegemen to the Dane.°

Francisco. Give you° good night.

Marcellus. O, farewell, honest soldier.
Who hath relieved you?

Francisco. Barnardo hath my place.
Give you good night. *Exit Francisco.*

Marcellus. Holla, Barnardo!

Barnardo. Say——
What, is Horatio there?

Horatio. A piece of him.

20 *Barnardo.* Welcome, Horatio. Welcome, good Marcellus.

Marcellus. What, has this thing appeared again tonight?

Barnardo. I have seen nothing.

Marcellus. Horatio says 'tis but our fantasy,
And will not let belief take hold of him
25 Touching this dreaded sight twice seen of us;
Therefore I have entreated him along
With us to watch the minutes of this night,
That, if again this apparition come,
He may approve° our eyes and speak to it.

---

13 **rivals** partners   15 **liegemen to the Dane** loyal subjects to the King
of Denmark   16 **Give you** God give you   29 **approve** confirm

Horatio. Tush, tush, 'twill not appear.

Barnardo.　　　　　　　　　　Sit down awhile,　　30
And let us once again assail your ears,
That are so fortified against our story,
What we have two nights seen.

Horatio.　　　　　　　　　　Well, sit we down,
And let us hear Barnardo speak of this.

Barnardo. Last night of all,　　　　　　　35
When yond same star that's westward from the
　pole°
Had made his course t' illume that part of heaven
Where now it burns, Marcellus and myself,
The bell then beating one——

Enter Ghost.

Marcellus. Peace, break thee off. Look where it comes
again.　　　　　　　　　　　　　　40

Barnardo. In the same figure like the king that's dead.

Marcellus. Thou art a scholar; speak to it, Horatio.

Barnardo. Looks 'a not like the king? Mark it, Horatio.

Horatio. Most like: it harrows me with fear and wonder.

Barnardo. It would be spoke to.

Marcellus.　　　　　　　　　Speak to it, Horatio.　　45

Horatio. What art thou that usurp'st this time of night,
Together with that fair and warlike form
In which the majesty of buried Denmark°
Did sometimes march? By heaven I charge thee,
　speak.

Marcellus. It is offended.

Barnardo.　　　　　　　See, it stalks away.　　50

Horatio. Stay! Speak, speak. I charge thee, speak.
　　　　　　　　　　　　　　　Exit Ghost.

36 **pole** polestar　48 **buried Denmark** the buried King of Denmark

Marcellus. 'Tis gone and will not answer.

Barnardo. How now, Horatio? You tremble and look
    pale.
Is not this something more than fantasy?
55 What think you on't?

Horatio. Before my God, I might not this believe
    Without the sensible and true avouch°
    Of mine own eyes.

Marcellus.   Is it not like the King?

Horatio. As thou art to thyself.
60   Such was the very armor he had on
    When he the ambitious Norway° combated:
    So frowned he once, when, in an angry parle,°
    He smote the sledded Polacks° on the ice.
    'Tis strange.

Marcellus. Thus twice before, and jump° at this dead
65   hour,
    With martial stalk hath he gone by our watch.

Horatio. In what particular thought to work I know
       not;
    But, in the gross and scope° of my opinion,
    This bodes some strange eruption to our state.

Marcellus. Good now, sit down, and tell me he that
70   knows,
    Why this same strict and most observant watch
    So nightly toils the subject° of the land,
    And why such daily cast of brazen cannon
    And foreign mart° for implements of war,

---

57 **sensible and true avouch** sensory and true proof   61 **Norway** King
of Norway   62 **parle** parley   63 **sledded Polacks** Poles in sledges
65 **jump** just   68 **gross and scope** general drift   72 **toils the subject**
makes the subjects toil   74 **mart** trading

Why such impress° of shipwrights, whose sore task   *75*
Does not divide the Sunday from the week,
What might be toward° that this sweaty haste
Doth make the night joint-laborer with the day?
Who is't that can inform me?

Horatio.   That can I.
At least the whisper goes so: our last king,   *80*
Whose image even but now appeared to us,
Was, as you know, by Fortinbras of Norway,
Thereto pricked on by a most emulate pride,
Dared to the combat; in which our valiant Hamlet
(For so this side of our known world esteemed him)   *85*
Did slay this Fortinbras, who, by a sealed compact
Well ratified by law and heraldry,°
Did forfeit, with his life, all those his lands
Which he stood seized° of, to the conqueror;
Against the which a moiety competent°   *90*
Was gagèd° by our King, which had returned
To the inheritance of Fortinbras,
Had he been vanquisher, as, by the same comart°
And carriage of the article designed,°
His fell to Hamlet. Now, sir, young Fortinbras,   *95*
Of unimprovèd° mettle hot and full,
Hath in the skirts° of Norway here and there
Sharked up° a list of lawless resolutes,°
For food and diet, to some enterprise
That hath a stomach in't;° which is no other,   *100*
As it doth well appear unto our state,
But to recover of us by strong hand
And terms compulsatory, those foresaid lands
So by his father lost; and this, I take it,
Is the main motive of our preparations,   *105*

---

75 **impress** forced service   77 **toward** in preparation   87 **law and heraldry** heraldic law (governing the combat)   89 **seized** possessed
90 **moiety competent** equal portion   91 **gagèd** engaged, pledged
93 **comart** agreement   94 **carriage of the article designed** import of
the agreement drawn up   96 **unimprovèd** untried   97 **skirts** borders
98 **Sharked up** collected indiscriminately (as a shark gulps its prey)
98 **resolutes** desperadoes   100 **hath a stomach in't** i.e., requires
courage

The source of this our watch, and the chief head°
Of this posthaste and romage° in the land.

Barnardo. I think it be no other but e'en so;
Well may it sort° that this portentous figure
110 Comes armèd through our watch so like the King
That was and is the question of these wars.

Horatio. A mote it is to trouble the mind's eye:
In the most high and palmy state of Rome,
A little ere the mightiest Julius fell,
115 The graves stood tenantless, and the sheeted dead
Did squeak and gibber in the Roman streets;°
As stars with trains of fire and dews of blood,
Disasters° in the sun; and the moist star,°
Upon whose influence Neptune's empire stands,
120 Was sick almost to doomsday with eclipse.
And even the like precurse° of feared events,
As harbingers° preceding still° the fates
And prologue to the omen° coming on,
Have heaven and earth together demonstrated
125 Unto our climatures° and countrymen.

Enter Ghost.

But soft, behold, lo where it comes again!
I'll cross it,° though it blast me.—Stay, illusion.
                         It spreads his° arms.
If thou hast any sound or use of voice,
Speak to me.
130 If there be any good thing to be done
That may to thee do ease and grace to me,
Speak to me.
If thou art privy to thy country's fate,
Which happily° foreknowing may avoid,

---

106 **head** fountainhead, origin   107 **romage** bustle   109 **sort** befit   116 **Did squeak . . . Roman streets** (the break in the sense which
follows this line suggests that a line has dropped out)   118 **Disasters**
threatening signs   118 **moist star** moon   121 **precurse** precursor, fore-
shadowing   122 **harbingers** forerunners   122 **still** always   123 **omen**
calamity   125 **climatures** regions   127 **cross it** (1) cross its path, confront it (2) make the sign of the cross in front of it   127 s.d. **his** i.e., its,
the ghost's (though possibly what is meant is that Horatio spreads his
own arms, making a cross of himself)   134 **happily** haply, perhaps

O, speak!　　　　　　　　　　　　　　　　　　　*135*
Or if thou hast uphoarded in thy life
Extorted° treasure in the womb of earth,
For which, they say, you spirits oft walk in death,
　　　　　　　　　　　　　　The cock crows.
Speak of it. Stay and speak. Stop it, Marcellus.

Marcellus. Shall I strike at it with my partisan?°　　　*140*

Horatio. Do, if it will not stand.

Barnardo.　　　　　　　　　　'Tis here.

Horatio.　　　　　　　　　　　　　　　'Tis here.

Marcellus. 'Tis gone.　　　　　　　　　*Exit Ghost.*
We do it wrong, being so majestical,
To offer it the show of violence,
For it is as the air, invulnerable,　　　　　　　　*145*
And our vain blows malicious mockery.

Barnardo. It was about to speak when the cock crew.

Horatio. And then it started, like a guilty thing
Upon a fearful summons. I have heard,
The cock, that is the trumpet to the morn,　　　　*150*
Doth with his lofty and shrill-sounding throat
Awake the god of day, and at his warning,
Whether in sea or fire, in earth or air,
Th' extravagant and erring° spirit hies
To his confine; and of the truth herein　　　　　*155*
This present object made probation.°

Marcellus. It faded on the crowing of the cock.
Some say that ever 'gainst° that season comes
Wherein our Savior's birth is celebrated,
This bird of dawning singeth all night long,　　　*160*
And then, they say, no spirit dare stir abroad,
The nights are wholesome, then no planets strike,°
No fairy takes,° nor witch hath power to charm:
So hallowed and so gracious is that time.

Horatio. So have I heard and do in part believe it.　*165*

---

137 **Extorted** ill-won　140 **partisan** pike (a long-handled weapon)
154 **extravagant and erring** out of bounds and wandering　156 **probation** proof　158 **'gainst** just before　162 **strike** exert an evil influence
163 **takes** bewitches

But look, the morn in russet mantle clad
Walks o'er the dew of yon high eastward hill.
Break we our watch up, and by my advice
Let us impart what we have seen tonight
170   Unto young Hamlet, for upon my life
This spirit, dumb to us, will speak to him.
Do you consent we shall acquaint him with it,
As needful in our loves, fitting our duty?

Marcellus. Let's do't, I pray, and I this morning know
175   Where we shall find him most convenient.   *Exeunt.*

[Scene 2. *The castle.*]

*Flourish.° Enter Claudius, King of Denmark, Gertrude
the Queen, Councilors, Polonius and his son Laertes,
Hamlet, cum aliis° [including Voltemand and Cor-
nelius].*

King. Though yet of Hamlet our dear brother's death
The memory be green, and that it us befitted
To bear our hearts in grief, and our whole kingdom
To be contracted in one brow of woe,
5   Yet so far hath discretion fought with nature
That we with wisest sorrow think on him
Together with remembrance of ourselves.
Therefore our sometime sister,° now our Queen,
Th' imperial jointress° to this warlike state,
10   Have we, as 'twere, with a defeated joy,
With an auspicious° and a dropping eye,
With mirth in funeral, and with dirge in marriage,
In equal scale weighing delight and dole,
Taken to wife. Nor have we herein barred
15   Your better wisdoms, which have freely gone

1.2.s.d. **Flourish** fanfare of trumpets   s.d. **cum aliis** with others (Latin)
8 **our sometime sister** my (the royal "we") former sister-in-law
9 **jointress** joint tenant, partner   11 **auspicious** joyful

With this affair along. For all, our thanks.
Now follows that you know young Fortinbras,
Holding a weak supposal of our worth,
Or thinking by our late dear brother's death
Our state to be disjoint and out of frame,°   20
Colleaguèd with this dream of his advantage,°
He hath not failed to pester us with message,
Importing the surrender of those lands
Lost by his father, with all bands of law,
To our most valiant brother. So much for him.   25
Now for ourself and for this time of meeting.
Thus much the business is: we have here writ
To Norway, uncle of young Fortinbras—
Who, impotent and bedrid, scarcely hears
Of this his nephew's purpose—to suppress   30
His further gait° herein, in that the levies,
The lists, and full proportions° are all made
Out of his subject;° and we here dispatch
You, good Cornelius, and you, Voltemand,
For bearers of this greeting to old Norway,   35
Giving to you no further personal power
To business with the King, more than the scope
Of these delated articles° allow.
Farewell, and let your haste commend your duty.

Cornelius, Voltemand. In that, and all things, will we
     show our duty.   40

King. We doubt it nothing. Heartily farewell.
                   Exit Voltemand and Cornelius.
And now, Laertes, what's the news with you?
You told us of some suit. What is't, Laertes?
You cannot speak of reason to the Dane
And lose your voice.° What wouldst thou beg,
     Laertes,   45
That shall not be my offer, not thy asking?
The head is not more native° to the heart,

20 **frame** order   21 **advantage** superiority   31 **gait** proceeding   32 **proportions** supplies for war   33 **Out of his subject** i.e., out of old Norway's subjects and realm   38 **delated articles** detailed documents 45 **lose your voice** waste your breath   47 **native** related

The hand more instrumental to the mouth,
Than is the throne of Denmark to thy father.
What wouldst thou have, Laertes?

50 *Laertes.*   My dread lord,
Your leave and favor to return to France,
From whence, though willingly I came to Denmark
To show my duty in your coronation,
Yet now I must confess, that duty done,
55 My thoughts and wishes bend again toward France
And bow them to your gracious leave and pardon.

King. Have you your father's leave? What says Polonius?

Polonius. He hath, my lord, wrung from me my slow
leave
By laborsome petition, and at last
60 Upon his will I sealed my hard consent.°
I do beseech you give him leave to go.

King. Take thy fair hour, Laertes. Time be thine,
And thy best graces spend it at thy will.
But now, my cousin° Hamlet, and my son——

Hamlet. [*Aside*] A little more than kin, and less than
65 kind!°

King. How is it that the clouds still hang on you?

Hamlet. Not so, my lord. I am too much in the sun.°

Queen. Good Hamlet, cast thy nighted color off,
And let thine eye look like a friend on Denmark.
70 Do not forever with thy vailèd° lids
Seek for thy noble father in the dust.
Thou know'st 'tis common; all that lives must die,
Passing through nature to eternity.

60 **Upon his ... hard consent** to his desire I gave my reluctant
consent   64 **cousin** kinsman   65 **kind** (pun on the meanings "kindly"
and "natural"; though doubly related—**more than kin**—Hamlet asserts
that he neither resembles Claudius in nature nor feels kindly toward
him)   67 **sun** sunshine of royal favor (with a pun on "son")   70 **vailèd**
lowered

Hamlet. Ay, madam, it is common.°

Queen.   If it be,
  Why seems it so particular with thee?   *75*

Hamlet. Seems, madam? Nay, it is. I know not "seems."
  'Tis not alone my inky cloak, good mother,
  Nor customary suits of solemn black,
  Nor windy suspiration° of forced breath,
  No, nor the fruitful river in the eye,   *80*
  Nor the dejected havior of the visage,
  Together with all forms, moods, shapes of grief,
  That can denote me truly. These indeed seem,
  For they are actions that a man might play,
  But I have that within which passes show;   *85*
  These but the trappings and the suits of woe.

King. 'Tis sweet and commendable in your nature,
      Hamlet,
  To give these mourning duties to your father,
  But you must know your father lost a father,
  That father lost, lost his, and the survivor bound   *90*
  In filial obligation for some term
  To do obsequious° sorrow. But to persever
  In obstinate condolement° is a course
  Of impious stubbornness. 'Tis unmanly grief.
  It shows a will most incorrect to heaven,   *95*
  A heart unfortified, a mind impatient,
  An understanding simple and unschooled.
  For what we know must be and is as common
  As any the most vulgar° thing to sense,
  Why should we in our peevish opposition   *100*
  Take it to heart? Fie, 'tis a fault to heaven,
  A fault against the dead, a fault to nature,
  To reason most absurd, whose common theme
  Is death of fathers, and who still hath cried,
  From the first corse° till he that died today,   *105*
  "This must be so." We pray you throw to earth

74 **common** (1) universal (2) vulgar   79 **windy suspiration** heavy sighing   92 **obsequious** suitable to obsequies (funerals)   93 **condolement** mourning   99 **vulgar** common   105 **corse** corpse

This unprevailing° woe, and think of us
As of a father, for let the world take note
You are the most immediate to our throne,
110   And with no less nobility of love
Than that which dearest father bears his son
Do I impart toward you. For your intent
In going back to school in Wittenberg,
It is most retrograde° to our desire,
115   And we beseech you, bend you° to remain
Here in the cheer and comfort of our eye,
Our chiefest courtier, cousin, and our son.

Queen. Let not thy mother lose her prayers, Hamlet.
I pray thee stay with us, go not to Wittenberg.

120   *Hamlet.* I shall in all my best obey you, madam.

King. Why, 'tis a loving and a fair reply.
Be as ourself in Denmark. Madam, come.
This gentle and unforced accord of Hamlet
Sits smiling to my heart, in grace whereof
125   No jocund health that Denmark drinks today,
But the great cannon to the clouds shall tell,
And the King's rouse° the heaven shall bruit° again,
Respeaking earthly thunder. Come away.
                    Flourish. Exeunt all but Hamlet.

Hamlet. O that this too too sullied° flesh would melt,
130   Thaw, and resolve itself into a dew,
Or that the Everlasting had not fixed
His canon° 'gainst self-slaughter. O God, God,
How weary, stale, flat, and unprofitable
Seem to me all the uses of this world!
135   Fie on't, ah, fie, 'tis an unweeded garden
That grows to seed. Things rank and gross in nature
Possess it merely.° That it should come to this:
But two months dead, nay, not so much, not two,

---

107 **unprevailing** unavailing   114 **retrograde** contrary   115 **bend
you** incline   127 **rouse** deep drink   127 **bruit** announce noisily
129 **sullied** (Q2 has **sallied,** here modernized to **sullied,** which makes
sense and is therefore given; but the Folio reading, **solid,** which fits better with **melt,** is quite possibly correct)   132 **canon** law   137 **merely**
entirely

So excellent a king, that was to this
Hyperion° to a satyr, so loving to my mother   *140*
That he might not beteem° the winds of heaven
Visit her face too roughly. Heaven and earth,
Must I remember? Why, she would hang on him
As if increase of appetite had grown
By what it fed on; and yet within a month—   *145*
Let me not think on't; frailty, thy name is woman—
A little month, or ere those shoes were old
With which she followed my poor father's body
Like Niobe,° all tears, why, she—
O God, a beast that wants discourse of reason°   *150*
Would have mourned longer—married with my
    uncle,
My father's brother, but no more like my father
Than I to Hercules. Within a month,
Ere yet the salt of most unrighteous tears
Had left the flushing° in her gallèd eyes,   *155*
She married. O, most wicked speed, to post°
With such dexterity to incestuous° sheets!
It is not, nor it cannot come to good.
But break my heart, for I must hold my tongue.

Enter Horatio, Marcellus, and Barnardo.

Horatio. Hail to your lordship!

Hamlet.   I am glad to see you well.   *160*
    Horatio—or I do forget myself.

Horatio. The same, my lord, and your poor servant
    ever.

Hamlet. Sir, my good friend, I'll change° that name
    with you.
    And what make you from Wittenberg, Horatio?
    Marcellus.   *165*

140 **Hyperion** the sun god, a model of beauty 141 **beteem** allow
149 **Niobe** (a mother who wept profusely at the death of her children)
150 **wants discourse of reason** lacks reasoning power 155 **left the flushing** stopped reddening 156 **post** hasten 157 **incestuous** (canon law considered marriage with a deceased brother's widow to be incestuous) 163 **change** exchange

Marcellus. My good lord!

Hamlet. I am very glad to see you. [*To Barnardo*]
    Good even, sir.
But what, in faith, make you from Wittenberg?

Horatio. A truant disposition, good my lord.

170 *Hamlet.* I would not hear your enemy say so,
Nor shall you do my ear that violence
To make it truster° of your own report
Against yourself. I know you are no truant.
But what is your affair in Elsinore?
175 We'll teach you to drink deep ere you depart.

Horatio. My lord, I came to see your father's funeral.

Hamlet. I prithee do not mock me, fellow student.
I think it was to see my mother's wedding.

Horatio. Indeed, my lord, it followed hard upon.

180 *Hamlet.* Thrift, thrift, Horatio. The funeral baked
    meats
Did coldly furnish forth the marriage tables.
Would I had met my dearest° foe in heaven
Or ever I had seen that day, Horatio!
My father, methinks I see my father.

Horatio. Where, my lord?

185 *Hamlet.*   In my mind's eye, Horatio.

Horatio. I saw him once. 'A° was a goodly king.

Hamlet. 'A was a man, take him for all in all,
I shall not look upon his like again.

Horatio. My lord, I think I saw him yesternight.

190 *Hamlet.* Saw? Who?

Horatio. My lord, the King your father.

Hamlet.   The King my father?

Horatio. Season your admiration° for a while
With an attent ear till I may deliver
Upon the witness of these gentlemen

172 **truster** believer   182 **dearest** most intensely felt   186 **'A** he
192 **Season your admiration** control your wonder

    This marvel to you.

Hamlet.   For God's love let me hear!   *195*

Horatio. Two nights together had these gentlemen,
    Marcellus and Barnardo, on their watch
    In the dead waste and middle of the night
    Been thus encountered. A figure like your father,
    Armèd at point exactly, cap-a-pe,°   *200*
    Appears before them, and with solemn march
    Goes slow and stately by them. Thrice he walked
    By their oppressed and fear-surprisèd eyes,
    Within his truncheon's length,° whilst they, distilled°
    Almost to jelly with the act° of fear,   *205*
    Stand dumb and speak not to him. This to me
    In dreadful° secrecy impart they did,
    And I with them the third night kept the watch,
    Where, as they had delivered, both in time,
    Form of the thing, each word made true and good,   *210*
    The apparition comes. I knew your father.
    These hands are not more like.

Hamlet.   But where was this?

Marcellus. My lord, upon the platform where we
    watched.

Hamlet. Did you not speak to it?

Horatio.   My lord, I did;
    But answer made it none. Yet once methought   *215*
    It lifted up it° head and did address
    Itself to motion like as it would speak:
    But even then the morning cock crew loud,
    And at the sound it shrunk in haste away
    And vanished from our sight.

Hamlet.   'Tis very strange.   *220*

Horatio. As I do live, my honored lord, 'tis true,
    And we did think it writ down in our duty
    To let you know of it.

200 **cap-a-pe** head to foot   204 **truncheon's length** space of a short
staff   204 **distilled** reduced   205 **act** action   207 **dreadful** terrified
216 **it** its

Hamlet. Indeed, indeed, sirs, but this troubles me.
　　Hold you the watch tonight?

225 *All.*　　　　　　　　　　　We do, my lord.

Hamlet. Armed, say you?

All. Armed, my lord.

Hamlet. From top to toe?

All.　　　　　　　　My lord, from head to foot.

Hamlet. Then saw you not his face.

230 *Horatio.* O, yes, my lord. He wore his beaver° up.

Hamlet. What, looked he frowningly?

Horatio. A countenance more in sorrow than in anger.

Hamlet. Pale or red?

Horatio. Nay, very pale.

Hamlet.　　　　　　　　And fixed his eyes upon you?

Horatio. Most constantly.

235 *Hamlet.*　　　　　　　　　I would I had been there.

Horatio. It would have much amazed you.

Hamlet. Very like, very like. Stayed it long?

Horatio. While one with moderate haste might tell° a
　　hundred.

Both. Longer, longer.

Horatio. Not when I saw't.

240 *Hamlet.*　　　　　　　　His beard was grizzled,° no?

Horatio. It was as I have seen it in his life,
　　A sable silvered.°

Hamlet.　　　　　　I will watch tonight.
　　Perchance 'twill walk again.

Horatio.　　　　　　　I warr'nt it will.

Hamlet. If it assume my noble father's person,

230 **beaver** visor, face guard　238 **tell** count　240 **grizzled** gray
242 **sable silvered** black mingled with white

I'll speak to it though hell itself should gape   *245*
And bid me hold my peace. I pray you all,
If you have hitherto concealed this sight,
Let it be tenable° in your silence still,
And whatsomever else shall hap tonight,
Give it an understanding but no tongue;   *250*
I will requite your loves. So fare you well.
Upon the platform 'twixt eleven and twelve
I'll visit you.

All.   Our duty to your honor.

Hamlet. Your loves, as mine to you. Farewell.
                         Exeunt [all but Hamlet].
My father's spirit—in arms? All is not well.   *255*
I doubt° some foul play. Would the night were come!
Till then sit still, my soul. Foul deeds will rise,
Though all the earth o'erwhlem them, to men's eyes.
                                        Exit.

[Scene 3. *A room.*]

Enter Laertes and Ophelia, his sister.

Laertes. My necessaries are embarked. Farewell.
    And, sister, as the winds give benefit
    And convoy° is assistant, do not sleep,
    But let me hear from you.

Ophelia.   Do you doubt that?

Laertes. For Hamlet, and the trifling of his favor,   *5*
    Hold it a fashion and a toy° in blood,
    A violet in the youth of primy° nature,
    Forward,° not permanent, sweet, not lasting,
    The perfume and suppliance° of a minute,

248 **tenable** held   256 **doubt** suspect 1.3.3 **convoy** conveyance   6 **ᴛoy**
idle fancy   7 **primy** springlike   8 **Forward** premature   9 **suppliance**
diversion

No more.

Ophelia.   No more but so?

10 *Laertes.*   Think it no more.
   For nature crescent° does not grow alone
   In thews° and bulk, but as this temple° waxes,
   The inward service of the mind and soul
   Grows wide withal. Perhaps he loves you now,
15 And now no soil nor cautel° doth besmirch
   The virtue of his will; but you must fear,
   His greatness weighed,° his will is not his own.
   For he himself is subject to his birth.
   He may not, as unvalued° persons do,
20 Carve for himself; for on his choice depends
   The safety and health of this whole state;
   And therefore must his choice be circumscribed
   Unto the voice and yielding of that body
   Whereof he is the head. Then if he says he loves you,
25 It fits your wisdom so far to believe it
   As he in his particular act and place
   May give his saying deed, which is no further
   Than the main voice of Denmark goes withal.
   Then weigh what loss your honor may sustain
30 If with too credent° ear you list his songs,
   Or lose your heart, or your chaste treasure open
   To his unmastered importunity.
   Fear it, Ophelia, fear it, my dear sister,
   And keep you in the rear of your affection,
35 Out of the shot and danger of desire.
   The chariest maid is prodigal enough
   If she unmask her beauty to the moon.
   Virtue itself scapes not calumnious strokes.
   The canker° galls the infants of the spring
40 Too oft before their buttons° be disclosed,
   And in the morn and liquid dew of youth
   Contagious blastments are most imminent.

---

11 **crescent** growing   12 **thews** muscles and sinews   12 **temple** i.e.,
the body   15 **cautel** deceit   17 **greatness weighed** high rank considered   19 **unvalued** of low rank   30 **credent** credulous   39 **canker**
cankerworm   40 **buttons** buds

Be wary then; best safety lies in fear;
Youth to itself rebels, though none else near.

Ophelia. I shall the effect of this good lesson keep   45
As watchman to my heart, but, good my brother,
Do not, as some ungracious° pastors do,
Show me the steep and thorny way to heaven,
Whiles, like a puffed and reckless libertine,
Himself the primrose path of dalliance treads   50
And recks not his own rede.°

                    Enter Polonius.

Laertes.   O, fear me not.
I stay too long. But here my father comes.
A double blessing is a double grace;
Occasion smiles upon a second leave.

Polonius. Yet here, Laertes? Aboard, aboard, for
    shame!   55
The wind sits in the shoulder of your sail,
And you are stayed for. There—my blessing with
    thee,
And these few precepts in thy memory
Look thou character.° Give thy thoughts no tongue,
Nor any unproportioned° thought his act.   60
Be thou familiar, but by no means vulgar.
Those friends thou hast, and their adoption tried,
Grapple them unto thy soul with hoops of steel,
But do not dull thy palm with entertainment
Of each new-hatched, unfledged courage.° Beware   65
Of entrance to a quarrel; but being in,
Bear't that th' opposèd may beware of thee.
Give every man thine ear, but few thy voice;
Take each man's censure,° but reserve thy judgment.
Costly thy habit as thy purse can buy,   70
But not expressed in fancy; rich, not gaudy,
For the apparel oft proclaims the man,
And they in France of the best rank and station

---

47 **ungracious** lacking grace   51 **recks not his own rede** does not heed
his own advice   59 **character** inscribe   60 **unproportioned** unbal-
anced   65 **courage** gallant youth   69 **censure** opinion

Are of a most select and generous, chief in that.°
75 Neither a borrower nor a lender be,
    For loan oft loses both itself and friend,
    And borrowing dulleth edge of husbandry.°
    This above all, to thine own self be true,
    And it must follow, as the night the day,
80 Thou canst not then be false to any man.
    Farewell. My blessing season this° in thee!

Laertes. Most humbly do I take my leave, my lord.

Polonius. The time invites you. Go, your servants
    tend.°

Laertes. Farewell, Ophelia, and remember well
    What I have said to you.

85 *Ophelia.*   'Tis in my memory locked,
    And you yourself shall keep the key of it.

Laertes. Farewell.   *Exit Laertes.*

Polonius. What is't, Ophelia, he hath said to you?

Ophelia. So please you, something touching the Lord
    Hamlet.

90 *Polonius.* Marry,° well bethought.
    'Tis told me he hath very oft of late
    Given private time to you, and you yourself
    Have of your audience been most free and bounte-
    ous.
    If it be so—as so 'tis put on me,
95 And that in way of caution—I must tell you
    You do not understand yourself so clearly
    As it behooves my daughter and your honor.
    What is between you? Give me up the truth.

Ophelia. He hath, my lord, of late made many tenders°
100 Of his affection to me.

---

74 **Are of . . . in that** show their fine taste and their gentlemanly instincts more in that than in any other point of manners (Kittredge)
77 **husbandry** thrift 81 **season this** make fruitful this (advice)
83 **tend** attend 90 **Marry** (a light oath, from "By the Virgin Mary")
99 **tenders** offers (in line 103 it has the same meaning, but in line 106
Polonius speaks of **tenders** in the sense of counters or chips; in line
109 **Tend'ring** means "holding," and **tender** means "give," "present")

Polonius. Affection pooh! You speak like a green girl,
  Unsifted° in such perilous circumstance.
  Do you believe his tenders, as you call them?

Ophelia. I do not know, my lord, what I should think.

Polonius. Marry, I will teach you. Think yourself a
      baby   *105*
  That you have ta'en these tenders for true pay
  Which are not sterling. Tender yourself more dearly,
  Or (not to crack the wind of the poor phrase)
  Tend'ring it thus you'll tender me a fool.°

Ophelia. My lord, he hath importuned me with love   *110*
  In honorable fashion.

Polonius. Ay, fashion you may call it. Go to, go to.

Ophelia. And hath given countenance to his speech, my
      lord,
  With almost all the holy vows of heaven.

Polonius. Ay, springes to catch woodcocks.° I do know,   *115*
  When the blood burns, how prodigal the soul
  Lends the tongue vows. These blazes, daughter,
  Giving more light than heat, extinct in both,
  Even in their promise, as it is a-making,
  You must not take for fire. From this time   *120*
  Be something scanter of your maiden presence.
  Set your entreatments° at a higher rate
  Than a command to parley. For Lord Hamlet,
  Believe so much in him that he is young,
  And with a larger tether may he walk   *125*
  Than may be given you. In few, Ophelia,
  Do not believe his vows, for they are brokers,°
  Not of that dye° which their investments° show,
  But mere implorators° of unholy suits,
  Breathing like sanctified and pious bonds,°   *130*
  The better to beguile. This is for all:

102 **Unsifted** untried   109 **tender me a fool** (1) present me with a fool
(2) present me with a baby   115 **springes to catch woodcocks** snares to
catch stupid birds   122 **entreatments** interviews   127 **brokers** procur-
ers   128 **dye** i.e., kind   128 **investments** garments   129 **implorators**
solicitors   130 **bonds** pledges

I would not, in plain terms, from this time forth
Have you so slander° any moment leisure
As to give words or talk with the Lord Hamlet.
135 Look to't, I charge you. Come your ways.

Ophelia. I shall obey, my lord.   *Exeunt.*

[Scene 4. *A guard platform.*]

Enter Hamlet, Horatio, and Marcellus.

Hamlet. The air bites shrewdly;° it is very cold.

Horatio. It is a nipping and an eager° air.

Hamlet. What hour now?

Horatio.   I think it lacks of twelve.

Marcellus. No, it is struck.

Horatio. Indeed? I heard it not. It then draws near the
5   season
Wherein the spirit held his wont to walk.
           A flourish of trumpets, and two pieces go off.
What does this mean, my lord?

Hamlet. The King doth wake° tonight and takes his
       rouse,°
Keeps wassail, and the swagg'ring upspring° reels,
10   And as he drains his draughts of Rhenish° down
The kettledrum and trumpet thus bray out
The triumph of his pledge.°

Horatio.   Is it a custom?

---

133 **slander** disgrace 1.4.1 **shrewdly** bitterly   2 **eager** sharp   8 **wake**
hold a revel by night   8 **takes his rouse** carouses   9 **upspring** (a
dance)   10 **Rhenish** Rhine wine   12 **The triumph of his pledge** the
achievement (of drinking a wine cup in one draught) of his toast

Hamlet. Ay, marry, is't,
    But to my mind, though I am native here
    And to the manner born, it is a custom   15
    More honored in the breach than the observance.
    This heavy-headed revel east and west
    Makes us traduced and taxed of° other nations.
    They clepe° us drunkards and with swinish phrase
    Soil our addition,° and indeed it takes   20
    From our achievements, though performed at height,
    The pith and marrow of our attribute.°
    So oft it chances in particular men
    That for some vicious mole° of nature in them,
    As in their birth, wherein they are not guilty,   25
    (Since nature cannot choose his origin)
    By the o'ergrowth of some complexion,°
    Oft breaking down the pales° and forts of reason,
    Or by some habit that too much o'erleavens°
    The form of plausive° manners, that (these men,   30
    Carrying, I say, the stamp of one defect,
    Being nature's livery, or fortune's star°)
    Their virtues else, be they as pure as grace,
    As infinite as man may undergo,
    Shall in the general censure° take corruption   35
    From that particular fault. The dram of evil
    Doth all the noble substance of a doubt,
    To his own scandal.°

Enter Ghost.

Horatio.   Look, my lord, it comes.

Hamlet. Angels and ministers of grace defend us!
    Be thou a spirit of health° or goblin damned,   40
    Bring with thee airs from heaven or blasts from hell,
    Be thy intents wicked or charitable,

18 **taxed of** blamed by   19 **clepe** call   20 **addition** reputation (literally, "title of honor")   22 **attribute** reputation   24 **mole** blemish   27 **complexion** natural disposition   28 **pales** enclosures   29 **o'erleavens** mixes with, corrupts   30 **plausive** pleasing   32 **nature's livery, or fortune's star** nature's equipment (i.e., "innate"), or a person's destiny determined by the stars   35 **general censure** popular judgment   36–38 **The dram . . . own scandal** (though the drift is clear, there is no agreement as to the exact meaning of these lines)   40 **spirit of health** good spirit

Thou com'st in such a questionable° shape
That I will speak to thee. I'll call thee Hamlet,
45   King, father, royal Dane. O, answer me!
Let me not burst in ignorance, but tell
Why thy canonized° bones, hearsèd in death,
Have burst their cerements,° why the sepulcher
Wherein we saw thee quietly interred
50   Hath oped his ponderous and marble jaws
To cast thee up again. What may this mean
That thou, dead corse, again in complete steel,
Revisits thus the glimpses of the moon,
Making night hideous, and we fools of nature
55   So horridly to shake our disposition°
With thoughts beyond the reaches of our souls?
Say, why is this? Wherefore? What should we do?
                              Ghost beckons Hamlet.

Horatio. It beckons you to go away with it,
As if it some impartment° did desire
To you alone.

60   *Marcellus.*   Look with what courteous action
It waves you to a more removèd ground.
But do not go with it.

Horatio.   No, by no means.

Hamlet. It will not speak. Then I will follow it.

Horatio. Do not, my lord.

Hamlet.   Why, what should be the fear?
65   I do not set my life at a pin's fee,
And for my soul, what can it do to that,
Being a thing immortal as itself?
It waves me forth again. I'll follow it.

Horatio. What if it tempt you toward the flood, my
         lord,
70   Or to the dreadful summit of the cliff

43 **questionable** (1) capable of discourse (2) dubious   47 **canonized**
buried according to the canon or ordinance of the church   48 **cerements** waxed linen shroud   55 **shake our disposition** disturb us
59 **impartment** communication

That beetles° o'er his base into the sea,
And there assume some other horrible form,
Which might deprive your sovereignty of reason°
And draw you into madness? Think of it.
The very place puts toys° of desperation, *75*
Without more motive, into every brain
That looks so many fathoms to the sea
And hears it roar beneath.

Hamlet.   It waves me still.
Go on; I'll follow thee.

Marcellus. You shall not go, my lord.

Hamlet.   Hold off your hands. *80*

Horatio. Be ruled. You shall not go.

Hamlet.   My fate cries out
And makes each petty artere° in this body
As hardy as the Nemean lion's nerve.°
Still am I called! Unhand me, gentlemen.
By heaven, I'll make a ghost of him that lets° me! *85*
I say, away! Go on. I'll follow thee.
                              Exit Ghost, and Hamlet.

Horatio. He waxes desperate with imagination.

Marcellus. Let's follow. 'Tis not fit thus to obey him.

Horatio. Have after! To what issue will this come?

Marcellus. Something is rotten in the state of Denmark. *90*

Horatio. Heaven will direct it.

Marcellus.   Nay, let's follow him.   *Exeunt.*

---

71 **beetles** juts out   73 **deprive your sovereignty of reason** destroy the
sovereignty of your reason   75 **toys** whims, fancies   82 **artere** artery
83 **Nemean lion's nerve** sinews of the mythical lion slain by Hercules
85 **lets** hinders

[Scene 5. *The battlements.*]

Enter Ghost and Hamlet.

Hamlet. Whither wilt thou lead me? Speak; I'll go no
     further.

Ghost. Mark me.

Hamlet.   I will.

Ghost.   My hour is almost come,
     When I to sulf'rous and tormenting flames
     Must render up myself.

Hamlet.   Alas, poor ghost.

5   *Ghost.* Pity me not, but lend thy serious hearing
     To what I shall unfold.

Hamlet.   Speak. I am bound to hear.

Ghost. So art thou to revenge, when thou shalt hear.

Hamlet. What?

Ghost. I am thy father's spirit,
10   Doomed for a certain term to walk the night,
     And for the day confined to fast in fires,
     Till the foul crimes° done in my days of nature
     Are burnt and purged away. But that I am forbid
     To tell the secrets of my prison house,
15   I could a tale unfold whose lightest word
     Would harrow up thy soul, freeze thy young blood,
     Make thy two eyes like stars start from their
        spheres,°
     Thy knotted and combinèd locks to part,
     And each particular hair to stand an end

1.5.12 **crimes** sins   17 **spheres** (in Ptolemaic astronomy, each planet
was fixed in a hollow transparent shell concentric with the earth)

Like quills upon the fearful porpentine.° 20
But this eternal blazon° must not be
To ears of flesh and blood. List, list, O, list!
If thou didst ever thy dear father love——

Hamlet. O God!

Ghost. Revenge his foul and most unnatural murder. 25

Hamlet. Murder?

Ghost. Murder most foul, as in the best it is,
But this most foul, strange, and unnatural.

Hamlet. Haste me to know't, that I, with wings as swift
As meditation° or the thoughts of love, 30
May sweep to my revenge.

Ghost.   I find thee apt,
And duller shouldst thou be than the fat weed
That roots itself in ease on Lethe wharf,°
Wouldst thou not stir in this. Now, Hamlet, hear.
'Tis given out that, sleeping in my orchard, 35
A serpent stung me. So the whole ear of Denmark
Is by a forgèd process° of my death
Rankly abused. But know, thou noble youth,
The serpent that did sting thy father's life
Now wears his crown.

Hamlet.   O my prophetic soul! 40
My uncle?

Ghost. Ay, that incestuous, that adulterate° beast,
With witchcraft of his wits, with traitorous gifts—
O wicked wit and gifts, that have the power
So to seduce!—won to his shameful lust 45
The will of my most seeming-virtuous queen.
O Hamlet, what a falling-off was there,
From me, whose love was of that dignity
That it went hand in hand even with the vow
I made to her in marriage, and to decline 50

20 **fearful porpentine** timid porcupine   21 **eternal blazon** revelation
of eternity   30 **meditation** thought   33 **Lethe wharf** bank of the river
of forgetfulness in Hades   37 **forgèd process** false account   42 **adulter-
ate** adulterous

Upon a wretch whose natural gifts were poor
To those of mine.
But virtue, as it never will be moved,
Though lewdness° court it in a shape of heaven,
55 So lust, though to a radiant angel linked,
Will sate itself in a celestial bed
And prey on garbage.
But soft, methinks I scent the morning air;
Brief let me be. Sleeping within my orchard,
60 My custom always of the afternoon,
Upon my secure° hour thy uncle stole
With juice of cursed hebona° in a vial,
And in the porches of my ears did pour
The leperous distillment, whose effect
65 Holds such an enmity with blood of man
That swift as quicksilver it courses through
The natural gates and alleys of the body,
And with a sudden vigor it doth posset°
And curd, like eager° droppings into milk,
70 The thin and wholesome blood. So did it mine,
And a most instant tetter° barked about
Most lazarlike° with vile and loathsome crust
All my smooth body.
Thus was I, sleeping, by a brother's hand
75 Of life, of crown, of queen at once dispatched,
Cut off even in the blossoms of my sin,
Unhouseled, disappointed, unaneled,°
No reck'ning made, but sent to my account
With all my imperfections on my head.
80 O, horrible! O, horrible! Most horrible!
If thou hast nature in thee, bear it not.
Let not the royal bed of Denmark be
A couch for luxury° and damnèd incest.
But howsomever thou pursues this act,
85 Taint not thy mind, nor let thy soul contrive

---

54 **lewdness** lust   61 **secure** unsuspecting   62 **hebona** a poisonous plant   68 **posset** curdle   69 **eager** acid   71 **tetter** scab   72 **lazarlike** leperlike   77 **Unhouseled, disappointed, unaneled** without the sacrament of communion, unabsolved, without extreme unction   83 **luxury** lust

Against thy mother aught. Leave her to heaven
And to those thorns that in her bosom lodge
To prick and sting her. Fare thee well at once.
The glowworm shows the matin° to be near
And 'gins to pale his uneffectual fire.   *90*
Adieu, adieu, adieu. Remember me.   *Exit.*

Hamlet. O all you host of heaven! O earth! What else?
And shall I couple hell? O fie! Hold, hold, my heart,
And you, my sinews, grow not instant old,
But bear me stiffly up. Remember thee?   *95*
Ay, thou poor ghost, whiles memory holds a seat
In this distracted globe.° Remember thee?
Yea, from the table° of my memory
I'll wipe away all trivial fond° records,
All saws° of books, all forms, all pressures° past   *100*
That youth and observation copied there,
And thy commandment all alone shall live
Within the book and volume of my brain,
Unmixed with baser matter. Yes, by heaven!
O most pernicious woman!   *105*
O villain, villain, smiling, damnèd villain!
My tables—meet it is I set it down
That one may smile, and smile, and be a villain.
At least I am sure it may be so in Denmark. [*Writes.*]
So, uncle, there you are. Now to my word: *110*
It is "Adieu, adieu, remember me."
I have sworn't.

Horatio and Marcellus. (*Within*) My lord, my lord!

       Enter Horatio and Marcellus.

Marcellus.   Lord Hamlet!

Horatio.   Heavens secure him!

Hamlet. So be it!

Marcellus. Illo, ho, ho,° my lord!   *115*

Hamlet. Hillo, ho, ho, boy! Come, bird, come.

89 **matin** morning   97 **globe** i.e., his head   98 **table** tablet, notebook
99 **fond** foolish   100 **saws** maxims   100 **pressures** impressions   115 **Illo,
ho, ho** (falconer's call to his hawk)

Marcellus. How is't, my noble lord?

Horatio.   What news, my lord?

Hamlet. O, wonderful!

Horatio. Good my lord, tell it.

Hamlet.   No, you will reveal it.

Horatio. Not I, my lord, by heaven.

120 *Marcellus.*   Nor I, my lord.

Hamlet. How say you then? Would heart of man once
    think it?
    But you'll be secret?

Both.   Ay, by heaven, my lord.

Hamlet. There's never a villain dwelling in all Denmark
    But he's an arrant knave.

Horatio. There needs no ghost, my lord, come from the
125   grave
    To tell us this.

Hamlet.   Why, right, you are in the right;
    And so, without more circumstance° at all,
    I hold it fit that we shake hands and part:
    You, as your business and desire shall point you,
130   For every man hath business and desire
    Such as it is, and for my own poor part,
    Look you, I'll go pray.

Horatio. These are but wild and whirling words, my
    lord.

Hamlet. I am sorry they offend you, heartily;
    Yes, faith, heartily.

135 *Horatio.*   There's no offense, my lord.

Hamlet. Yes, by Saint Patrick, but there is, Horatio,
    And much offense too. Touching this vision here,
    It is an honest ghost,° that let me tell you.
    For your desire to know what is between us,
140   O'ermaster't as you may. And now, good friends,

127 **circumstance** details   138 **honest ghost** i.e., not a demon in his father's shape

As you are friends, scholars, and soldiers,
Give me one poor request.

Horatio. What is't, my lord? We will.

Hamlet. Never make known what you have seen tonight.

Both. My lord, we will not.

Hamlet.   Nay, but swear't.

Horatio.   In faith,   *145*
My lord, not I.

Marcellus.   Nor I, my lord—in faith.

Hamlet. Upon my sword.

Marcellus.   We have sworn, my lord, already.

Hamlet. Indeed, upon my sword, indeed.
                    Ghost cries under the stage.

Ghost. Swear.

Hamlet. Ha, ha, boy, say'st thou so? Art thou there,
truepenny?°   *150*
Come on. You hear this fellow in the cellarage.
Consent to swear.

Horatio.   Propose the oath, my lord.

Hamlet. Never to speak of this that you have seen.
Swear by my sword.

Ghost. [*Beneath*] Swear.   *155*

Hamlet. Hic et ubique?° Then we'll shift our ground;
Come hither, gentlemen,
And lay your hands again upon my sword.
Swear by my sword
Never to speak of this that you have heard.   *160*

Ghost. [*Beneath*] Swear by his sword.

Hamlet. Well said, old mole! Canst work i' th' earth so
fast?
A worthy pioner!° Once more remove, good friends.

150 **truepenny** honest fellow   156 **Hic et ubique** here and everywhere
(Latin)   163 **pioner** digger of mines

Horatio. O day and night, but this is wondrous strange!

165 *Hamlet.* And therefore as a stranger give it welcome.
    There are more things in heaven and earth, Horatio,
    Than are dreamt of in your philosophy.
    But come:
    Here as before, never, so help you mercy,
170   How strange or odd some'er I bear myself
    (As I perchance hereafter shall think meet
    To put an antic disposition° on),
    That you, at such times seeing me, never shall
    With arms encumb'red° thus, or this headshake,
175   Or by pronouncing of some doubtful phrase,
    As "Well, well, we know," or "We could, an if we
       would,"
    Or "If we list to speak," or "There be, an if they
       might,"
    Or such ambiguous giving out, to note
    That you know aught of me—this do swear,
180   So grace and mercy at your most need help you.

Ghost. [*Beneath*] Swear.   [*They swear.*]

Hamlet. Rest, rest, perturbèd spirit. So, gentlemen,
    With all my love I do commend me° to you,
    And what so poor a man as Hamlet is
185   May do t' express his love and friending to you,
    God willing, shall not lack. Let us go in together,
    And still your fingers on your lips, I pray.
    The time is out of joint. O cursèd spite,
    That ever I was born to set it right!
190   Nay, come, let's go together.   *Exeunt.*

---

172 **antic disposition** fantastic behavior   174 **encumb'red** folded
183 **commend me** entrust myself

[ACT 2

Scene 1. *A room.*]

Enter old Polonius, with his man Reynaldo.

Polonius. Give him this money and these notes, Reynaldo.

Reynaldo. I will, my lord.

Polonius. You shall do marvell's° wisely, good Rey-
naldo,
Before you visit him, to make inquire
Of his behavior.

Reynaldo.　　　　My lord, I did intend it.　　　　　5

Polonius. Marry, well said, very well said. Look you
sir,
Inquire me first what Danskers° are in Paris,
And how, and who, what means, and where they
keep,°
What company, at what expense; and finding
By this encompassment° and drift of question　　　10
That they do know my son, come you more nearer
Than your particular demands° will touch it.
Take you as 'twere some distant knowledge of him,
As thus, "I know his father and his friends,
And in part him." Do you mark this, Reynaldo?　　15

Reynaldo. Ay, very well, my lord.

2.1.3 **marvell's** marvelous(ly)　7 **Danskers** Danes　8 **keep** dwell
10 **encompassment** circling　12 **demands** questions

35

Polonius. "And in part him, but," you may say, "not
    well,
    But if't be he I mean, he's very wild,
    Addicted so and so." And there put on him
20   What forgeries° you please; marry, none so rank
    As may dishonor him—take heed of that—
    But, sir, such wanton, wild, and usual slips
    As are companions noted and most known
    To youth and liberty.

Reynaldo.   As gaming, my lord.

Polonius. Ay, or drinking, fencing, swearing, quarrel-
25   ing,
    Drabbing.° You may go so far.

Reynaldo. My lord, that would dishonor him.

Polonius. Faith, no, as you may season it in the charge.
    You must not put another scandal on him,
30   That he is open to incontinency.°
    That's not my meaning. But breathe his faults so
    quaintly°
    That they may seem the taints of liberty,
    The flash and outbreak of a fiery mind,
    A savageness in unreclaimèd blood,
    Of general assault.°

35 *Reynaldo.*   But, my good lord——

Polonius. Wherefore should you do this?

Reynaldo.   Ay, my lord,
    I would know that.

Polonius.   Marry, sir, here's my drift,
    And I believe it is a fetch of warrant.°
    You laying these slight sullies on my son
40   As 'twere a thing a little soiled i' th' working,
    Mark you,
    Your party in converse, him you would sound,

---

20 **forgeries** inventions   26 **Drabbing** wenching   30 **incontinency** ha-
bitual licentiousness   31 **quaintly** ingeniously, delicately   35 **Of general assault** common to all men   38 **fetch of warrant** justifiable device

Having ever seen in the prenominate crimes°
The youth you breathe of guilty, be assured
He closes with you in this consequence:°   45
"Good sir," or so, or "friend," or "gentleman"—
According to the phrase or the addition°
Of man and country—

Reynaldo.   Very good, my lord.

Polonius. And then, sir, does 'a° this—'a does—
What was I about to say? By the mass, I was about   50
to say something! Where did I leave?

Reynaldo. At "closes in the consequence," at "friend
or so," and "gentleman."

Polonius. At "closes in the consequence"—Ay, marry!
He closes thus: "I know the gentleman;   55
I saw him yesterday, or t'other day,
Or then, or then, with such or such, and, as you say,
There was 'a gaming, there o'ertook in's rouse,
There falling out at tennis"; or perchance,
"I saw him enter such a house of sale,"   60
Videlicet,° a brothel, or so forth.
See you now—
Your bait of falsehood take this carp of truth,
And thus do we of wisdom and of reach,°
With windlasses° and with assays of bias,°   65
By indirections find directions out.
So, by my former lecture and advice,
Shall you my son. You have me, have you not?

Reynaldo. My lord, I have.

Polonius.   God bye ye, fare ye well.

Reynaldo. Good my lord.   70

Polonius. Observe his inclination in yourself.°

---

43 **Having . . . crimes** if he has ever seen in the aforementioned crimes
45 **He closes . . . this consequence** he falls in with you in this conclusion
47 **addition** title 49 **'a** he 61 **Videlicet** namely 64 **reach** far-
reaching awareness (?) 65 **windlasses** circuitous courses 65 **assays of
bias** indirect attempts (metaphor from bowling; **bias** = curved course)
71 **in yourself** for yourself

Reynaldo. I shall, my lord.

Polonius. And let him ply his music.

Reynaldo.   Well, my lord.

Polonius. Farewell.   *Exit Reynaldo.*

          Enter Ophelia.

          How now, Ophelia, what's the matter?

75 *Ophelia.* O my lord, my lord, I have been so affrighted!

Polonius. With what, i' th' name of God?

Ophelia. My lord, as I was sewing in my closet,°
     Lord Hamlet, with his doublet all unbraced,°
     No hat upon his head, his stockings fouled,
80   Ungartered, and down-gyvèd° to his ankle,
     Pale as his shirt, his knees knocking each other,
     And with a look so piteous in purport,°
     As if he had been loosèd out of hell
     To speak of horrors—he comes before me.

Polonius. Mad for thy love?

85 *Ophelia.*   My lord, I do not know,
     But truly I do fear it.

Polonius.   What said he?

Ophelia. He took me by the wrist and held me hard;
     Then goes he to the length of all his arm,
     And with his other hand thus o'er his brow
90   He falls to such perusal of my face
     As 'a would draw it. Long stayed he so.
     At last, a little shaking of mine arm,
     And thrice his head thus waving up and down,
     He raised a sigh so piteous and profound
95   As it did seem to shatter all his bulk
     And end his being. That done, he lets me go,
     And, with his head over his shoulder turned,
     He seemed to find his way without his eyes,

77 **closet** private room   78 **doublet all unbraced** jacket entirely un-
laced   80 **down-gyvèd** hanging down like fetters   82 **purport** expression

For out o' doors he went without their helps,
And to the last bended their light on me.   *100*

Polonius. Come, go with me. I will go seek the King.
This is the very ecstasy° of love,
Whose violent property fordoes° itself
And leads the will to desperate undertakings
As oft as any passions under heaven   *105*
That does afflict our natures. I am sorry.
What, have you given him any hard words of late?

Ophelia. No, my good lord; but as you did command,
I did repel his letters and denied
His access to me.

Polonius.   That hath made him mad.   *110*
I am sorry that with better heed and judgment
I had not quoted° him. I feared he did but trifle
And meant to wrack thee; but beshrew my jealousy.°
By heaven, it is as proper° to our age
To cast beyond ourselves° in our opinions   *115*
As it is common for the younger sort
To lack discretion. Come, go we to the King.
This must be known, which, being kept close, might
   move
More grief to hide than hate to utter love.°
Come.   *Exeunt.* *120*

---

102 **ecstasy** madness   103 **property fordoes** quality destroys 112 **quoted**
noted   113 **beshrew my jealousy** curse on my suspicions   114 **proper**
natural   115 **To cast beyond ourselves** to be overcalculating
117–19 **Come, go ... utter love** (the general meaning is that while
telling the King of Hamlet's love may anger the King, more grief would
come from keeping it secret)

[Scene 2. *The castle.*]

Flourish. Enter King and Queen, Rosencrantz, and Guildenstern [with others].

King. Welcome, dear Rosencrantz and Guildenstern.
Moreover that° we much did long to see you,
The need we have to use you did provoke
Our hasty sending. Something have you heard
5 Of Hamlet's transformation: so call it,
Sith° nor th' exterior nor the inward man
Resembles that it was. What it should be,
More than his father's death, that thus hath put him
So much from th' understanding of himself,
10 I cannot dream of. I entreat you both
That, being of so° young days brought up with him,
And sith so neighbored to his youth and havior,°
That you vouchsafe your rest° here in our court
Some little time, so by your companies
15 To draw him on to pleasures, and to gather
So much as from occasion you may glean,
Whether aught to us unknown afflicts him thus,
That opened° lies within our remedy.

Queen. Good gentlemen, he hath much talked of you,
20 And sure I am, two men there is not living
To whom he more adheres. If it will please you
To show us so much gentry° and good will
As to expend your time with us awhile
For the supply and profit of our hope,
25 Your visitation shall receive such thanks
As fits a king's remembrance.

Rosencrantz.   Both your Majesties

2.2.2 **Moreover that** beside the fact that   6 **Sith** since   11 **of so** from
such   12 **youth and havior** behavior in his youth   13 **vouchsafe your
rest** consent to remain   18 **opened** revealed   22 **gentry** courtesy

Might, by the sovereign power you have of us,
Put your dread pleasures more into command
Than to entreaty.

Guildenstern.   But we both obey,
And here give up ourselves in the full bent°   30
To lay our service freely at your feet,
To be commanded.

King. Thanks, Rosencrantz and gentle Guildenstern.

Queen. Thanks, Guildenstern and gentle Rosencrantz.
And I beseech you instantly to visit   35
My too much changèd son. Go, some of you,
And bring these gentlemen where Hamlet is.

Guildenstern. Heavens make our presence and our
     practices
Pleasant and helpful to him!

Queen.   Ay, amen!
     *Exeunt Rosencrantz and Guildenstern [with some
                              Attendants].*

               Enter Polonius.

Polonius. Th' ambassadors from Norway, my good
     lord,   40
Are joyfully returned.

King. Thou still° hast been the father of good news.

Polonius. Have I, my lord? Assure you, my good liege,
I hold my duty, as I hold my soul,
Both to my God and to my gracious king;   45
And I do think, or else this brain of mine
Hunts not the trail of policy so sure°
As it hath used to do, that I have found
The very cause of Hamlet's lunacy.

King. O, speak of that! That do I long to hear.   50

Polonius. Give first admittance to th' ambassadors.
My news shall be the fruit to that great feast.

---

30 **in the full bent** entirely (the figure is of a bow bent to its capacity)   42 **still** always   47 **Hunts not . . . so sure** does not follow clues of political doings with such sureness

King. Thyself do grace to them and bring them in.
[*Exit Polonius.*]

55   He tells me, my dear Gertrude, he hath found
The head and source of all your son's distemper.

Queen. I doubt° it is no other but the main,°
His father's death and our o'erhasty marriage.

King. Well, we shall sift him.

Enter Polonius, Voltemand, and Cornelius.

Welcome, my good friends.
Say, Voltemand, what from our brother Norway?

60   *Voltemand.* Most fair return of greetings and desires.
Upon our first,° he sent out to suppress
His nephew's levies, which to him appeared
To be a preparation 'gainst the Polack;
But better looked into, he truly found
65   It was against your Highness, whereat grieved,
That so his sickness, age, and impotence
Was falsely borne in hand,° sends out arrests
On Fortinbras; which he, in brief, obeys,
Receives rebuke from Norway, and in fine,°
70   Makes vow before his uncle never more
To give th' assay° of arms against your Majesty.
Whereon old Norway, overcome with joy,
Gives him threescore thousand crowns in annual fee
And his commission to employ those soldiers,
75   So levied as before, against the Polack,
With an entreaty, herein further shown,
[*Gives a paper.*]
That it might please you to give quiet pass
Through your dominions for this enterprise,
On such regards of safety and allowance°
As therein are set down.

80   *King.*   It likes us well;
And at our more considered time° we'll read,
Answer, and think upon this business.

56 **doubt** suspect   56 **main** principal point   61 **first** first audience
67 **borne in hand** deceived   69 **in fine** finally   71 **assay** trial   79 **re-**
gards of safety and allowance i.e., conditions   81 **considered time**
time proper for considering

Meantime, we thank you for your well-took labor.
Go to your rest; at night we'll feast together.
Most welcome home!   *Exeunt Ambassadors.*

Polonius.   This business is well ended.   85
My liege and madam, to expostulate°
What majesty should be, what duty is,
Why day is day, night night, and time is time,
Were nothing but to waste night, day, and time.
Therefore, since brevity is the soul of wit,°   90
And tediousness the limbs and outward flourishes,
I will be brief. Your noble son is mad.
Mad call I it, for, to define true madness,
What is't but to be nothing else but mad?
But let that go.

Queen.   More matter, with less art.   95

Polonius. Madam, I swear I use no art at all.
That he's mad, 'tis true: 'tis true 'tis pity,
And pity 'tis 'tis true—a foolish figure.°
But farewell it, for I will use no art.
Mad let us grant him then; and now remains   100
That we find out the cause of this effect,
Or rather say, the cause of this defect,
For this effect defective comes by cause.
Thus it remains, and the remainder thus.
Perpend.°   105
I have a daughter: have, while she is mine,
Who in her duty and obedience, mark,
Hath given me this. Now gather, and surmise.
                    [*Reads*] *the letter.*
"To the celestial, and my soul's idol, the most
beautified Ophelia"—   110
That's an ill phrase, a vile phrase; "beautified" is a
vile phrase. But you shall hear. Thus:
"In her excellent white bosom, these, &c."

Queen. Came this from Hamlet to her?

Polonius. Good madam, stay awhile. I will be faithful.   115
          "Doubt thou the stars are fire,

86 **expostulate** discuss   90 **wit** wisdom, understanding   98 **figure** figure of rhetoric   105 **Perpend** consider carefully

Doubt that the sun doth move;
Doubt° truth to be a liar,
But never doubt I love.

120 O dear Ophelia, I am ill at these numbers.° I have
not art to reckon my groans; but that I love thee
best, O most best, believe it. Adieu.

   Thine evermore, most dear lady, whilst this
   machine° is to him, HAMLET."

125 This in obedience hath my daughter shown me,
And more above° hath his solicitings,
As they fell out by time, by means, and place,
All given to mine ear.

King.   But how hath she
Received his love?

Polonius.   What do you think of me?

130 *King.* As of a man faithful and honorable.

Polonius. I would fain prove so. But what might you
   think,
When I had seen this hot love on the wing
(As I perceived it, I must tell you that,
Before my daughter told me), what might you,
135 Or my dear Majesty your Queen here, think,
If I had played the desk or table book,°
Or given my heart a winking,° mute and dumb,
Or looked upon this love with idle sight?
What might you think? No, I went round to work
140 And my young mistress thus I did bespeak:
"Lord Hamlet is a prince, out of thy star.°
This must not be." And then I prescripts gave her,
That she should lock herself from his resort,
Admit no messengers, receive no tokens.
145 Which done, she took the fruits of my advice,
And he, repellèd, a short tale to make,

---

118 **Doubt** suspect   120 **ill at these numbers** unskilled in verses
124 **machine** complex device (here, his body)   126 **more above** in addition   136 **played the desk or table book** i.e., been a passive recipient of
secrets   137 **winking** closing of the eyes   141 **star** sphere

Fell into a sadness, then into a fast,
Thence to a watch,° thence into a weakness,
Thence to a lightness,° and, by this declension,
Into the madness wherein now he raves,   *150*
And all we mourn for.

King.   Do you think 'tis this?

Queen. It may be, very like.

Polonius. Hath there been such a time, I would fain know that,
That I have positively said " 'Tis so,"
When it proved otherwise?

King.   Not that I know.   *155*

Polonius. [*Pointing to his head and shoulder*] Take this from this, if this be otherwise.
If circumstances lead me, I will find
Where truth is hid, though it were hid indeed
Within the center.°

King.   How may we try it further?

Polonius. You know sometimes he walks four hours together   *160*
Here in the lobby.

Queen.   So he does indeed.

Polonius. At such a time I'll loose my daughter to him.
Be you and I behind an arras° then.
Mark the encounter. If he love her not,
And be not from his reason fall'n thereon,   *165*
Let me be no assistant for a state
But keep a farm and carters.

King.   We will try it.

Enter Hamlet reading on a book.

Queen. But look where sadly the poor wretch comes reading.

Polonius. Away, I do beseech you both, away.
                    Exit King and Queen.

---

148 **watch** wakefulness   149 **lightness** mental derangement   159 **center** center of the earth   163 **arras** tapestry hanging in front of a wall

170   I'll board him presently.° O, give me leave.
    How does my good Lord Hamlet?

Hamlet. Well, God-a-mercy.

Polonius. Do you know me, my lord?

Hamlet. Excellent well. You are a fishmonger.°

175 *Polonius.* Not I, my lord.

Hamlet. Then I would you were so honest a man.

Polonius. Honest, my lord?

Hamlet. Ay, sir. To be honest, as this world goes, is to
    be one man picked out of ten thousand.

180 *Polonius.* That's very true, my lord.

Hamlet. For if the sun breed maggots in a dead dog,
    being a good kissing carrion°—— Have you a
    daughter?

Polonius. I have, my lord.

185 *Hamlet.* Let her not walk i' th' sun. Conception° is a
    blessing, but as your daughter may conceive, friend,
    look to't.

Polonius. [*Aside*] How say you by that? Still harping
    on my daughter. Yet he knew me not at first. 'A said
190   I was a fishmonger. 'A is far gone, far gone. And
    truly in my youth I suffered much extremity for
    love, very near this. I'll speak to him again.—What
    do you read, my lord?

Hamlet. Words, words, words.

195 *Polonius.* What is the matter, my lord?

Hamlet. Between who?

Polonius. I mean the matter° that you read, my lord.

---

170 **board him presently** accost him at once   174 **fishmonger** dealer
in fish (slang for a procurer). (The joke is in the inappropriateness. Although many editors say that *fishmonger* is slang for a procurer, such usage is undocumented)   182 **a good kissing carrion** (perhaps the
meaning is "a good piece of flesh to kiss," but many editors emend *good*
to *god,* taking the word to refer to the sun)   185 **Conception** (1) understanding (2) becoming pregnant   197 **matter** (Polonius means "subject
matter," but Hamlet pretends to take the word in the sense of "quarrel")

Hamlet. Slanders, sir; for the satirical rogue says here that old men have gray beards, that their faces are wrinkled, their eyes purging thick amber and plum- 200 tree gum, and that they have a plentiful lack of wit, together with most weak hams. All which, sir, though ·I most powerfully and potently believe, yet I hold it not honesty° to have it thus set down; for you yourself, sir, should be old as I am if, like a 205 crab, you could go backward.

Polonius. [*Aside*] Though this be madness, yet there is method in't. Will you walk out of the air, my lord?

Hamlet. Into my grave.

Polonius. Indeed, that's out of the air. [*Aside*] How 210 pregnant° sometimes his replies are! A happiness° that often madness hits on, which reason and sanity could not so prosperously be delivered of. I will leave him and suddenly contrive the means of meeting between him and my daughter.—My lord, 215 I will take my leave of you.

Hamlet. You cannot take from me anything that I will more willingly part withal—except my life, except my life, except my life.

Enter Guildenstern and Rosencrantz.

Polonius. Fare you well, my lord. 220

Hamlet. These tedious old fools!

Polonius. You go to seek the Lord Hamlet? There he is.

Rosencrantz. [*To Polonius*] God save you, sir!
                                    [*Exit Polonius.*]

Guildenstern. My honored lord! 225

Rosencrantz. My most dear lord!

Hamlet. My excellent good friends! How dost thou, Guildenstern? Ah, Rosencrantz! Good lads, how do you both?

204 **honesty** decency   211 **pregnant** meaningful   211 **happiness** apt turn of phrase

230 *Rosencrantz.* As the indifferent° children of the earth.

Guildenstern. Happy in that we are not overhappy.
    On Fortune's cap we are not the very button.

Hamlet. Nor the soles of her shoe?

Rosencrantz. Neither, my lord.

235 *Hamlet.* Then you live about her waist, or in the middle
    of her favors?

Guildenstern. Faith, her privates° we.

Hamlet. In the secret parts of Fortune? O, most true!
    She is a strumpet. What news?

240 *Rosencrantz.* None, my lord, but that the world's
    grown honest.

Hamlet. Then is doomsday near. But your news is not
    true. Let me question more in particular. What
    have you, my good friends, deserved at the hands of
245 Fortune that she sends you to prison hither?

Guildenstern. Prison, my lord?

Hamlet. Denmark's a prison.

Rosencrantz. Then is the world one.

Hamlet. A goodly one, in which there are many
250 confines, wards,° and dungeons, Denmark being
    one o' th' worst.

Rosencrantz. We think not so, my lord.

Hamlet. Why, then 'tis none to you, for there is nothing
    either good or bad but thinking makes it so. To me
255 it is a prison.

Rosencrantz. Why then your ambition makes it one.
    'Tis too narrow for your mind.

Hamlet. O God, I could be bounded in a nutshell and
    count myself a king of infinite space, were it not
260 that I have bad dreams.

Guildenstern. Which dreams indeed are ambition, for

---

230 **indifferent** ordinary   237 **privates** ordinary men (with a pun on
"private parts")   250 **wards** cells

the very substance of the ambitious is merely the
shadow of a dream.

Hamlet. A dream itself is but a shadow.

Rosencrantz. Truly, and I hold ambition of so airy and   265
light a quality that it is but a shadow's shadow.

Hamlet. Then are our beggars bodies, and our
monarchs and outstretched heroes the beggars'
shadows.° Shall we to th' court? For, by my fay,°
I cannot reason.   270

Both. We'll wait upon you.

Hamlet. No such matter. I will not sort you with the
rest of my servants, for, to speak to you like an
honest man, I am most dreadfully attended. But in
the beaten way of friendship, what make you at   275
Elsinore?

Rosencrantz. To visit you, my lord; no other occasion.

Hamlet. Beggar that I am, I am even poor in thanks,
but I thank you; and sure, dear friends, my thanks
are too dear a halfpenny.° Were you not sent for?   280
Is it your own inclining? Is it a free visitation?
Come, come, deal justly with me. Come, come;
nay, speak.

Guildenstern. What should we say, my lord?

Hamlet. Why anything—but to th' purpose. You were   285
sent for, and there is a kind of confession in your
looks, which your modesties have not craft enough
to color. I know the good King and Queen have
sent for you.

Rosencrantz. To what end, my lord?   290

Hamlet. That you must teach me. But let me conjure
you by the rights of our fellowship, by the con-
sonancy of our youth, by the obligation of our ever-

267–69 **Then are ... beggars' shadows** i.e., by your logic, beggars
(lacking ambition) are substantial, and great men are elongated shadows
269 **fay** faith   280 **too dear a halfpenny** i.e., not worth a halfpenny

preserved love, and by what more dear a better
295   proposer can charge you withal, be even and direct
with me, whether you were sent for or no.

Rosencrantz. [*Aside to Guildenstern*] What say you?

Hamlet. [*Aside*] Nay then, I have an eye of you.—If
you love me, hold not off.

300   *Guildenstern.* My lord, we were sent for.

Hamlet. I will tell you why; so shall my anticipation
prevent your discovery,° and your secrecy to the
King and Queen molt no feather. I have of late, but
wherefore I know not, lost all my mirth, forgone all
305   custom of exercises; and indeed, it goes so heavily
with my disposition that this goodly frame, the
earth, seems to me a sterile promontory; this most
excellent canopy, the air, look you, this brave
o'erhanging firmament, this majestical roof fretted°
310   with golden fire: why, it appeareth nothing to me
but a foul and pestilent congregation of vapors.
What a piece of work is a man, how noble in reason,
how infinite in faculties, in form and moving how
express° and admirable, in action how like an angel,
315   in apprehension how like a god: the beauty of the
world, the paragon of animals; and yet to me, what
is this quintessence of dust? Man delights not me;
nor woman neither, though by your smiling you
seem to say so.

320   *Rosencrantz.* My lord, there was no such stuff in my
thoughts.

Hamlet. Why did ye laugh then, when I said "Man
delights not me"?

Rosencrantz. To think, my lord, if you delight not in
325   man, what lenten° entertainment the players shall
receive from you. We coted° them on the way, and
hither are they coming to offer you service.

---

302 **prevent your discovery** forestall your disclosure   309 **fretted**
adorned   314 **express** exact   325 **lenten** meager   326 **coted** overtook

Hamlet. He that plays the king shall be welcome; his
Majesty shall have tribute of me; the adventurous
knight shall use his foil and target;° the lover shall 330
not sigh gratis; the humorous man° shall end his
part in peace; the clown shall make those laugh
whose lungs are tickle o' th' sere;° and the lady shall
say her mind freely, or° the blank verse shall halt°
for't. What players are they? 335

Rosencrantz. Even those you were wont to take such
delight in, the tragedians of the city.

Hamlet. How chances it they travel? Their residence,
both in reputation and profit, was better both ways.

Rosencrantz. I think their inhibition° comes by the 340
means of the late innovation.°

Hamlet. Do they hold the same estimation they did
when I was in the city? Are they so followed?

Rosencrantz. No indeed, are they not.

Hamlet. How comes it? Do they grow rusty? 345

Rosencrantz. Nay, their endeavor keeps in the wonted
pace, but there is, sir, an eyrie° of children, little
eyases, that cry out on the top of question° and are
most tyrannically° clapped for't. These are now
the fashion, and so berattle the common stages° (so 350
they call them) that many wearing rapiers are afraid
of goosequills° and dare scarce come thither.

Hamlet. What, are they children? Who maintains 'em?
How are they escoted?° Will they pursue the

---

330 **target** shield   331 **humorous man** i.e., eccentric man (among
stock characters in dramas were men dominated by a "humor" or odd
trait)   333 **tickle o' th' sere** on hair trigger (*sere* = part of the gunlock)
334 **or** else   334 **halt** limp   340 **inhibition** hindrance   341 **innovation** (probably an allusion to the companies of child actors that had become popular and were offering serious competition to the adult actors)
347 **eyrie** nest   348 **eyases, that ... of question** unfledged hawks that
cry shrilly above others in matters of debate   349 **tyrannically** violently   350 **berattle the common stages** cry down the public theaters
(with the adult acting companies)   352 **goosequills** pens (of satirists
who ridicule the public theaters and their audiences)   354 **escoted** fi-
nancially supported

355 quality° no longer than they can sing? Will they not say afterwards, if they should grow themselves to common players (as it is most like, if their means are no better), their writers do them wrong to make them exclaim against their own succession?°

360 *Rosencrantz.* Faith, there has been much to-do on both sides, and the nation holds it no sin to tarre° them to controversy. There was, for a while, no money bid for argument° unless the poet and the player went to cuffs in the question.

365 *Hamlet.* Is't possible?

Guildenstern. O, there has been much throwing about of brains.

Hamlet. Do the boys carry it away?

Rosencrantz. Ay, that they do, my lord—Hercules and 370 his load° too.

Hamlet. It is not very strange, for my uncle is King of Denmark, and those that would make mouths at him while my father lived give twenty, forty, fifty, a hundred ducats apiece for his picture in little.
375 'Sblood,° there is something in this more than natural, if philosophy could find it out.

A flourish.

Guildenstern. There are the players.

Hamlet. Gentlemen, you are welcome to Elsinore. Your hands, come then. Th' appurtenance of wel-
380 come is fashion and ceremony. Let me comply° with you in this garb,° lest my extent° to the players (which I tell you must show fairly outwards) should more appear like entertainment than yours. You are welcome. But my uncle-father and aunt-mother are
385 deceived.

---

355 **quality** profession of acting   359 **succession** future   361 **tarre** incite   363 **argument** plot of a play   369–70 **Hercules and his load** i.e., the whole world (with a reference to the Globe Theatre, which had a sign that represented Hercules bearing the globe)   375 **'Sblood** by God's blood   380 **comply** be courteous   381 **garb** outward show   381 **extent** behavior

Guildenstern. In what, my dear lord?

Hamlet. I am but mad north-northwest:° when the wind is southerly I know a hawk from a handsaw.°

Enter Polonius.

Polonius. Well be with you, gentlemen.

Hamlet. Hark you, Guildenstern, and you too; at each ear a hearer. That great baby you see there is not yet out of his swaddling clouts. 390

Rosencrantz. Happily° he is the second time come to them, for they say an old man is twice a child.

Hamlet. I will prophesy he comes to tell me of the players. Mark it.—You say right, sir; a Monday morning, 'twas then indeed. 395

Polonius. My lord, I have news to tell you.

Hamlet. My lord, I have news to tell you. When Roscius° was an actor in Rome—— 400

Polonius. The actors are come hither, my lord.

Hamlet. Buzz, buzz.°

Polonius. Upon my honor——

Hamlet. Then came each actor on his ass——

Polonius. The best actors in the world, either for tragedy, comedy, history, pastoral, pastoral-comical, historical-pastoral, tragical-historical, tragical-comi-cal-historical-pastoral; scene individable,° or poem unlimited.° Seneca° cannot be too heavy, nor Plautus° too light. For the law of writ and the liberty,° these are the only men. 405 410

---

387 **north-northwest** i.e., on one point of the compass only   388 **hawk from a handsaw** (hawk can refer not only to a bird but to a kind of pickax; **handsaw**—a carpenter's tool—may involve a similar pun on "hernshaw," a heron)   393 **Happily** perhaps   400 **Roscius** (a famous Roman comic actor)   402 **Buzz, buzz** (an interjection, perhaps indicating that the news is old)   408 **scene individable** plays observing the unities of time, place, and action   408–09 **poem unlimited** plays not restricted by the tenets of criticism   409 **Seneca** (Roman tragic dramatist)   410 **Plautus** (Roman comic dramatist)   410–11 **For the law of writ and the liberty** (perhaps "for sticking to the text and for improvising"; perhaps "for classical plays and for modern loosely written plays")

Hamlet. O Jeptha, judge of Israel,° what a treasure
hadst thou!

Polonius. What a treasure had he, my lord?

415 *Hamlet.* Why,
> "One fair daughter, and no more,
>   The which he lovèd passing well."

Polonius. [*Aside*] Still on my daughter.

Hamlet. Am I not i' th' right, old Jeptha?

420 *Polonius.* If you call me Jeptha, my lord, I have a
daughter that I love passing well.

Hamlet. Nay, that follows not.

Polonius. What follows then, my lord?

Hamlet. Why,

425
> "As by lot, God wot,"
and then, you know,
> "It came to pass, as most like it was."
The first row of the pious chanson° will show you
more, for look where my abridgment° comes.

Enter the Players.

430 You are welcome, masters, welcome, all. I am glad
to see thee well. Welcome, good friends. O, old
friend, why, thy face is valanced° since I saw thee
last. Com'st thou to beard me in Denmark? What,
my young lady° and mistress? By'r Lady, your
435 ladyship is nearer to heaven than when I saw you
last by the altitude of a chopine.° Pray God your
voice, like a piece of uncurrent gold, be not cracked
within the ring.°—Masters, you are all welcome.
We'll e'en to't like French falconers, fly at any-

---

412 **Jeptha, judge of Israel** (the title of a ballad on the Hebrew judge
who sacrificed his daughter; see Judges 11)   428 **row of the pious
chanson** stanza of the scriptural song   429 **abridgment** (1) i.e., enter-
tainers, who abridge the time (2) interrupters   432 **valanced** fringed
(with a beard)   434 **young lady** i.e., boy for female roles   436 **chopine**
thick-soled shoe   437–38 **like a piece . . . the ring** (a coin was unfit for
legal tender if a crack extended from the edge through the ring enclosing
the monarch's head. Hamlet, punning on *ring,* refers to the change of
voice that the boy actor will undergo)

thing we see. We'll have a speech straight. Come, 440
give us a taste of your quality. Come, a passionate
speech.

Player. What speech, my good lord?

Hamlet. I heard thee speak me a speech once, but it
was never acted, or if it was, not above once, for 445
the play, I remember, pleased not the million; 'twas
caviary to the general,° but it was (as I received it,
and others, whose judgments in such matters cried
in the top of° mine) an excellent play, well digested
in the scenes, set down with as much modesty as 450
cunning.° I remember one said there were no
sallets° in the lines to make the matter savory;
nor no matter in the phrase that might indict the
author of affectation, but called it an honest method,
as wholesome as sweet, and by very much more 455
handsome than fine.° One speech in't I chiefly loved.
'Twas Aeneas' tale to Dido, and thereabout of it
especially when he speaks of Priam's slaughter. If
it live in your memory, begin at this line—let me
see, let me see: 460
   "The rugged Pyrrhus, like th' Hyrcanian
      beast°——"
'Tis not so; it begins with Pyrrhus:
   "The rugged Pyrrhus, he whose sable° arms,
   Black as his purpose, did the night resemble
   When he lay couchèd in th' ominous horse,°   465
   Hath now this dread and black complexion
      smeared
   With heraldry more dismal.° Head to foot
   Now is he total gules, horridly tricked°
   With blood of fathers, mothers, daughters, sons,
   Baked and impasted° with the parching streets,   470

447 **caviary to the general** i.e., too choice for the multitude   449 **in the top of** overtopping   450–51 **modesty as cunning** restraint as art   452 **sallets** salads, spicy jests   455–56 **more handsome than fine** well-proportioned rather than ornamented   461 **Hyrcanian beast** i.e., tiger (Hyrcania was in Asia)   463 **sable** black   465 **ominous horse** i.e., wooden horse at the siege of Troy   467 **dismal** ill-omened   468 **total gules, horridly tricked** all red, horridly adorned   470 **impasted** encrusted

That lend a tyrannous and a damnèd light
To their lord's murder. Roasted in wrath and fire,
And thus o'ersizèd° with coagulate gore,
With eyes like carbuncles, the hellish Pyrrhus
475 Old grandsire Priam seeks."
      So, proceed you.

Polonius. Fore God, my lord, well spoken, with good
accent and good discretion.

Player.   "Anon he finds him,
480 Striking too short at Greeks. His antique sword,
Rebellious to his arm, lies where it falls,
Repugnant to command.° Unequal matched,
Pyrrhus at Priam drives, in rage strikes wide,
But with the whiff and wind of his fell sword
485 Th' unnervèd father falls. Then senseless Ilium,°
Seeming to feel this blow, with flaming top
Stoops to his base,° and with a hideous crash
Takes prisoner Pyrrhus' ear. For lo, his sword,
Which was declining on the milky head
490 Of reverend Priam, seemed i' th' air to stick.
So as a painted tyrant° Pyrrhus stood,
And like a neutral to his will and matter°
Did nothing.
But as we often see, against° some storm,
495 A silence in the heavens, the rack° stand still,
The bold winds speechless, and the orb below
As hush as death, anon the dreadful thunder
Doth rend the region, so after Pyrrhus' pause,
A rousèd vengeance sets him new awork,
500 And never did the Cyclops' hammer fall
On Mars's armor, forged for proof eterne,°
With less remorse than Pyrrhus' bleeding sword
Now falls on Priam.
Out, out, thou strumpet Fortune! All you gods,
505 In general synod° take away her power,

473 **o'ersizèd** smeared over   482 **Repugnant to command** disobedient
485 **senseless Ilium** insensate Troy   487 **Stoops to his base** collapses
(*his* = its)   491 **painted tyrant** tyrant in a picture   492 **matter** task
494 **against** just before   495 **rack** clouds   501 **proof eterne** eternal
endurance   505 **synod** council

Break all the spokes and fellies° from her wheel,
And bowl the round nave° down the hill of
  heaven,
As low as to the fiends."

Polonius. This is too long.

Hamlet. It shall to the barber's, with your beard.— 510
  Prithee say on. He's for a jig or a tale of bawdry,
  or he sleeps. Say on; come to Hecuba.

Player. "But who (ah woe!) had seen the mobled°
  queen——"

Hamlet. "The mobled queen"?

Polonius. That's good. "Mobled queen" is good. 515

Player. "Run barefoot up and down, threat'ning the
  flames
With bisson rheum;° a clout° upon that head
Where late the diadem stood, and for a robe,
About her lank and all o'erteemèd° loins,
A blanket in the alarm of fear caught up— 520
Who this had seen, with tongue in venom steeped
'Gainst Fortune's state would treason have pro-
  nounced.
But if the gods themselves did see her then,
When she saw Pyrrhus make malicious sport
In mincing with his sword her husband's limbs, 525
The instant burst of clamor that she made
(Unless things mortal move them not at all)
Would have made milch° the burning eyes of
  heaven
And passion in the gods."

Polonius. Look, whe'r° he has not turned his color, 530
  and has tears in's eyes. Prithee no more.

Hamlet. 'Tis well. I'll have thee speak out the rest of
  this soon. Good my lord, will you see the players
  well bestowed?° Do you hear? Let them be well

506 **fellies** rims   507 **nave** hub   513 **mobled** muffled   517 **bisson rheum** blinding tears   517 **clout** rag   519 **o'erteemèd** exhausted with childbearing   528 **milch** moist (literally, "milk-giving")   530 **whe'r** whether   534 **bestowed** housed

535 used, for they are the abstract and brief chronicles
of the time. After your death you were better have
a bad epitaph than their ill report while you live.

Polonius. My lord, I will use them according to their
desert.

540 *Hamlet.* God's bodkin,° man, much better! Use every
man after his desert, and who shall scape whipping?
Use them after your own honor and dignity. The
less they deserve, the more merit is in your bounty.
Take them in.

545 *Polonius.* Come, sirs.

Hamlet. Follow him, friends. We'll hear a play tomorrow. [*Aside to Player*] Dost thou hear me, old
friend? Can you play *The Murder of Gonzago*?

Player. Ay, my lord.

550 *Hamlet.* We'll ha't tomorrow night. You could for a
need study a speech of some dozen or sixteen lines
which I would set down and insert in't, could you
not?

Player. Ay, my lord.

555 *Hamlet.* Very well. Follow that lord, and look you
mock him not. My good friends, I'll leave you till
night. You are welcome to Elsinore.

          Exeunt Polonius and Players.

Rosencrantz. Good my lord.

        Exeunt [Rosencrantz and Guildenstern].

Hamlet. Ay, so, God bye to you.—Now I am alone.

560 O, what a rogue and peasant slave am I!
Is it not monstrous that this player here,
But in a fiction, in a dream of passion,°
Could force his soul so to his own conceit°
That from her working all his visage wanned,

565 Tears in his eyes, distraction in his aspect,
A broken voice, and his whole function° suiting

---

540 God's bodkin by God's little body **562 dream of passion** imaginary emotion 563 **conceit** imagination 566 **function** action

With forms° to his conceit? And all for nothing!
For Hecuba!
What's Hecuba to him, or he to Hecuba,
That he should weep for her? What would he do   570
Had he the motive and the cue for passion
That I have? He would drown the stage with tears
And cleave the general ear with horrid speech,
Make mad the guilty and appall the free,°
Confound the ignorant, and amaze indeed   575
The very faculties of eyes and ears.
Yet I,
A dull and muddy-mettled° rascal, peak
Like John-a-dreams,° unpregnant of° my cause,
And can say nothing. No, not for a king,   580
Upon whose property and most dear life
A damned defeat was made. Am I a coward?
Who calls me villain? Breaks my pate across?
Plucks off my beard and blows it in my face?
Tweaks me by the nose? Gives me the lie i' th' throat   585
As deep as to the lungs? Who does me this?
Ha, 'swounds,° I should take it, for it cannot be
But I am pigeon-livered° and lack gall
To make oppression bitter, or ere this
I should ha' fatted all the region kites°   590
With this slave's offal. Bloody, bawdy villain!
Remorseless, treacherous, lecherous, kindless° villain!
O, vengeance!
Why, what an ass am I! This is most brave,°
That I, the son of a dear father murdered,   595
Prompted to my revenge by heaven and hell,
Must, like a whore, unpack my heart with words
And fall a-cursing like a very drab,°

---

567 **forms** bodily expressions   574 **appall the free** terrify (make pale?) the guiltless   578 **muddy-mettled** weak-spirited   578–79 **peak/Like John-a-dreams** mope like a dreamer   579 **unpregnant of** unquickened by   587 **'swounds** by God's wounds   588 **pigeon-livered** gentle as a dove   590 **region kites** kites (scavenger birds) of the sky   592 **kindless** unnatural   594 **brave** fine   598 **drab** prostitute

A scullion!° Fie upon't, foh! About,° my brains.
600 Hum——
I have heard that guilty creatures sitting at a play
Have by the very cunning of the scene
Been struck so to the soul that presently°
They have proclaimed their malefactions.
605 For murder, though it have no tongue, will speak
With most miraculous organ. I'll have these players
Play something like the murder of my father
Before mine uncle. I'll observe his looks,
I'll tent° him to the quick. If 'a do blench,°
610 I know my course. The spirit that I have seen
May be a devil, and the devil hath power
T' assume a pleasing shape, yea, and perhaps
Out of my weakness and my melancholy,
As he is very potent with such spirits,
615 Abuses me to damn me. I'll have grounds
More relative° than this. The play's the thing
Wherein I'll catch the conscience of the King.   *Exit.*

---

599 **scullion** low-ranking kitchen servant, noted for foul language
599 **About** to work   603 **presently** immediately   609 **tent** probe
609 **blench** flinch   616 **relative** (probably "pertinent," but possibly
"able to be related plausibly")

[ACT 3

Scene 1. *The castle*.]

*Enter King, Queen, Polonius, Ophelia, Rosencrantz,
Guildenstern, Lords.*

King. And can you by no drift of conference°
　Get from him why he puts on this confusion,
　Grating so harshly all his days of quiet
　With turbulent and dangerous lunacy?

Rosencrantz. He does confess he feels himself dis-
　tracted,　　　　　　　　　　　　　　　　　　　5
　But from what cause 'a will by no means speak.

Guildenstern. Nor do we find him forward to be
　sounded,°
　But with a crafty madness keeps aloof
　When we would bring him on to some confession
　Of his true state.

Queen.　　　　　　　　Did he receive you well?　　10

Rosencrantz. Most like a gentleman.

Guildenstern. But with much forcing of his disposi-
　tion.°

Rosencrantz. Niggard of question,° but of our demands
　Most free in his reply.

3.1.1 **drift of conference** management of conversation　7 **forward to
be sounded** willing to be questioned　12 **forcing of his disposition** effort　13 **Niggard of question** uninclined to talk

61

Queen.   Did you assay° him
15   To any pastime?

Rosencrantz. Madam, it so fell out that certain players
        We o'erraught° on the way; of these we told him,
        And there did seem in him a kind of joy
        To hear of it. They are here about the court,
20   And, as I think, they have already order
        This night to play before him.

Polonius.   'Tis most true,
        And he beseeched me to entreat your Majesties
        To hear and see the matter.

King. With all my heart, and it doth much content me
25   To hear him so inclined.
        Good gentlemen, give him a further edge
        And drive his purpose into these delights.

Rosencrantz. We shall, my lord.
                    Exeunt Rosencrantz and Guildenstern.

King.   Sweet Gertrude, leave us too,
        For we have closely° sent for Hamlet hither,
30   That he, as 'twere by accident, may here
        Affront° Ophelia.
        Her father and myself (lawful espials°)
        Will so bestow ourselves that, seeing unseen,
        We may of their encounter frankly judge
35   And gather by him, as he is behaved,
        If't be th' affliction of his love or no
        That thus he suffers for.

Queen.   I shall obey you.
        And for your part, Ophelia, I do wish
        That your good beauties be the happy cause
40   Of Hamlet's wildness. So shall I hope your virtues
        Will bring him to his wonted way again,
        To both your honors.

Ophelia.   Madam, I wish it may.
                                    [*Exit Queen.*]

---

14 **assay** tempt   17 **o'erraught** overtook   29 **closely** secretly   31 **Affront** meet face to face   32 **espials** spies

Polonius. Ophelia, walk you here.—Gracious, so please
　　you,
　We will bestow ourselves. [*To Ophelia*] Read on this
　　book,
　That show of such an exercise may color°   45
　Your loneliness. We are oft to blame in this,
　'Tis too much proved, that with devotion's visage
　And pious action we do sugar o'er
　The devil himself.

King.   [*Aside*] O, 'tis too true.
　How smart a lash that speech doth give my con-
　　science!   50
　The harlot's cheek, beautied with plast'ring art,
　Is not more ugly to the thing that helps it
　Than is my deed to my most painted word.
　O heavy burden!

Polonius. I hear him coming. Let's withdraw, my lord.   55
　　　　　　　　[*Exeunt King and Polonius.*]
　　　　　　Enter Hamlet.

Hamlet. To be, or not to be: that is the question:
　Whether 'tis nobler in the mind to suffer
　The slings and arrows of outrageous fortune,
　Or to take arms against a sea of troubles,
　And by opposing end them. To die, to sleep—   60
　No more—and by a sleep to say we end
　The heartache, and the thousand natural shocks
　That flesh is heir to! 'Tis a consummation
　Devoutly to be wished. To die, to sleep—
　To sleep—perchance to dream: ay, there's the rub,°   65
　For in that sleep of death what dreams may come
　When we have shuffled off this mortal coil,°
　Must give us pause. There's the respect°
　That makes calamity of so long life:°
　For who would bear the whips and scorns of time,   70

45 **exercise may color** act of devotion may give a plausible hue to (the
book is one of devotion)　65 **rub** impediment (obstruction to a bowler's
ball)　67 **coil** (1) turmoil (2) a ring of rope (here the flesh encircling the
soul)　68 **respect** consideration　69 **makes calamity of so long life** (1)
makes calamity so long-lived (2) makes living so long a calamity

Th' oppressor's wrong, the proud man's contumely,
The pangs of despised love, the law's delay,
The insolence of office, and the spurns
That patient merit of th' unworthy takes,
75　When he himself might his quietus° make
With a bare bodkin?° Who would fardels° bear,
To grunt and sweat under a weary life,
But that the dread of something after death,
The undiscovered country, from whose bourn°
80　No traveler returns, puzzles the will,
And makes us rather bear those ills we have,
Than fly to others that we know not of?
Thus conscience° does make cowards of us all,
And thus the native hue of resolution
85　Is sicklied o'er with the pale cast° of thought,
And enterprises of great pitch° and moment,
With this regard° their currents turn awry,
And lose the name of action.—Soft you now,
The fair Ophelia!—Nymph, in thy orisons°
Be all my sins remembered.

90　*Ophelia.*　　　　　　　　　　　Good my lord,
How does your honor for this many a day?

Hamlet. I humbly thank you; well, well, well.

Ophelia. My lord, I have remembrances of yours
That I have longèd long to redeliver.
I pray you now, receive them.

95　*Hamlet.*　　　　　　　　　　　No, not I,
I never gave you aught.

Ophelia. My honored lord, you know right well you
did,
And with them words of so sweet breath composed
As made these things more rich. Their perfume lost,
100　Take these again, for to the noble mind

---

75 **quietus** full discharge (a legal term)　76 **bodkin** dagger　76 **fardels**
burdens　79 **bourn** region　83 **conscience** (1) self-consciousness, in-
trospection (2) inner moral voice　85 **cast** color　86 **pitch** height (a
term from falconry)　87 **regard** consideration　89 **orisons** prayers

Rich gifts wax poor when givers prove unkind.
There, my lord.

Hamlet. Ha, ha! Are you honest?°

Ophelia. My lord?

Hamlet. Are you fair?   105

Ophelia. What means your lordship?

Hamlet. That if you be honest and fair, your honesty
should admit no discourse to your beauty.°

Ophelia. Could beauty, my lord, have better commerce
than with honesty?   110

Hamlet. Ay, truly; for the power of beauty will sooner
transform honesty from what it is to a bawd° than
the force of honesty can translate beauty into his
likeness. This was sometime a paradox, but now
the time gives it proof. I did love you once.   115

Ophelia. Indeed, my lord, you made me believe so.

Hamlet. You should not have believed me, for virtue
cannot so inoculate° our old stock but we shall relish
of it.° I loved you not.

Ophelia. I was the more deceived.   120

Hamlet. Get thee to a nunnery. Why wouldst thou be
a breeder of sinners? I am myself indifferent honest,°
but yet I could accuse me of such things that it were
better my mother had not borne me: I am very
proud, revengeful, ambitious, with more offenses at   125
my beck° than I have thoughts to put them in,
imagination to give them shape, or time to act them
in. What should such fellows as I do crawling between earth and heaven? We are arrant knaves all;
believe none of us. Go thy ways to a nunnery.   130
Where's your father?

---

103 **Are you honest** (1) are you modest (2) are you chaste (3) have you
integrity   107–08 **your honesty ... to your beauty** your modesty
should permit no approach to your beauty   112 **bawd**° procurer
118 **inoculate** graft   118–19 **relish of it** smack of it (our old sinful nature)   122 **indifferent honest** moderately virtuous   126 **beck** call

Ophelia. At home, my lord.

Hamlet. Let the doors be shut upon him, that he may
play the fool nowhere but in's own house. Farewell.

135 *Ophelia.* O help him, you sweet heavens!

Hamlet. If thou dost marry, I'll give thee this plague
for thy dowry: be thou as chaste as ice, as pure as
snow, thou shalt not escape calumny. Get thee to a
nunnery. Go, farewell. Or if thou wilt needs marry,
140 marry a fool, for wise men know well enough what
monsters° you make of them. To a nunnery, go,
and quickly too. Farewell.

Ophelia. Heavenly powers, restore him!

Hamlet. I have heard of your paintings, well enough.
145 God hath given you one face, and you make yourselves another. You jig and amble, and you lisp;
you nickname God's creatures and make your
wantonness your ignorance.° Go to, I'll no more
on't; it hath made me mad. I say we will have no
150 moe° marriage. Those that are married already—all
but one—shall live. The rest shall keep as they are.
To a nunnery, go.   *Exit.*

Ophelia. O what a noble mind is here o'erthrown!
The courtier's, soldier's, scholar's, eye, tongue, sword,
155 Th' expectancy and rose° of the fair state,
The glass of fashion, and the mold of form,°
Th' observed of all observers, quite, quite down!
And I, of ladies most deject and wretched,
That sucked the honey of his musicked vows,
160 Now see that noble and most sovereign reason
Like sweet bells jangled, out of time and harsh,
That unmatched form and feature of blown° youth
Blasted with ecstasy.° O, woe is me
T' have seen what I have seen, see what I see!

Enter King and Polonius.

141 **monsters** horned beasts, cuckolds   147–48 **make your wantonness your ignorance** excuse your wanton speech by pretending ignorance   150 **moe** more   155 **expectancy and rose** i.e., fair hope
156 **The glass ... of form** the mirror of fashion, and the pattern of excellent behavior   162 **blown** blooming   163 **ecstasy** madness

King. Love? His affections° do not that way tend,   *165*
   Nor what he spake, though it lacked form a little,
   Was not like madness. There's something in his soul
   O'er which his melancholy sits on brood,
   And I do doubt° the hatch and the disclose
   Will be some danger; which for to prevent,   *170*
   I have in quick determination
   Thus set it down: he shall with speed to England
   For the demand of our neglected tribute.
   Haply the seas, and countries different,
   With variable objects, shall expel   *175*
   This something-settled° matter in his heart,
   Whereon his brains still beating puts him thus
   From fashion of himself. What think you on't?

Polonius. It shall do well. But yet do I believe
   The origin and commencement of his grief   *180*
   Sprung from neglected love. How now, Ophelia?
   You need not tell us what Lord Hamlet said;
   We heard it all. My lord, do as you please,
   But if you hold it fit, after the play,
   Let his queen mother all alone entreat him   *185*
   To show his grief. Let her be round° with him,
   And I'll be placed, so please you, in the ear
   Of all their conference. If she find him not,°
   To England send him, or confine him where
   Your wisdom best shall think.

King.   It shall be so.   *190*
   Madness in great ones must not unwatched go.
                                        Exeunt.

165 **affections** inclinations   169 **doubt** fear   176 **something-settled** somewhat settled   186 **round** blunt   188 **find him not** does not find him out.

[Scene 2. *The castle.*]

Enter Hamlet and three of the Players.

Hamlet. Speak the speech, I pray you, as I pronounced
it to you, trippingly on the tongue. But if you mouth
it, as many of our players do, I had as lief the town
crier spoke my lines. Nor do not saw the air too much
5   with your hand, thus, but use all gently, for in the
very torrent, tempest, and (as I may say) whirlwind
of your passion, you must acquire and beget a temperance that may give it smoothness. O, it offends
me to the soul to hear a robustious periwig-pated°
10   fellow tear a passion to tatters, to very rags, to split
the ears of the groundlings,° who for the most part
are capable of° nothing but inexplicable dumb
shows° and noise. I would have such a fellow
whipped for o'erdoing Termagant. It out-herods
15   Herod.° Pray you avoid it.

Player. I warrant your honor.

Hamlet. Be not too tame neither, but let your own discretion be your tutor. Suit the action to the word, the
word to the action, with this special observance, that
20   you o'erstep not the modesty of nature. For anything
so o'erdone is from° the purpose of playing, whose
end, both at the first and now, was and is, to hold,
as 'twere, the mirror up to nature; to show virtue
her own feature, scorn her own image, and the very
25   age and body of the time his form and pressure.°

3.2.9 **robustious periwig-pated** boisterous wig-headed   11 **groundlings** those who stood in the pit of the theater (the poorest and presumably most ignorant of the audience)   12 **are capable of** are able to
understand   12–13 **dumb shows** (it had been the fashion for actors
to preface plays or parts of plays with silent mime)   14–15 **Termagant ... Herod** (boisterous characters in the old mystery plays)
21 **from** contrary to   25 **pressure** image, impress

Now, this overdone, or come tardy off, though it
makes the unskillful laugh, cannot but make the
judicious grieve, the censure of the which one must
in your allowance o'erweigh a whole theater of
others. O, there be players that I have seen play,   *30*
and heard others praise, and that highly (not to
speak it profanely), that neither having th' accent of
Christians, nor the gait of Christian, pagan, nor
man, have so strutted and bellowed that I have
thought some of Nature's journeymen° had made   *35*
men, and not made them well, they imitated humanity so abominably.

Player. I hope we have reformed that indifferently°
with us, sir.

Hamlet. O, reform it altogether! And let those that   *40*
play your clowns speak no more than is set down
for them, for there be of them that will themselves
laugh, to set on some quantity of barren spectators to
laugh too, though in the meantime some necessary
question of the play be then to be considered. That's   *45*
villainous and shows a most pitiful ambition in the
fool that uses it. Go make you ready.

                              Exit Players.
   Enter Polonius, Guildenstern, and Rosencrantz.

How now, my lord? Will the King hear this piece of
work?

Polonius. And the Queen too, and that presently.   *50*

Hamlet. Bid the players make haste.   *Exit Polonius.*
Will you two help to hasten them?

Rosencrantz. Ay, my lord.   *Exeunt they two.*

Hamlet. What, ho, Horatio!

       Enter Horatio.

Horatio. Here, sweet lord, at your service.   *55*

Hamlet. Horatio, thou art e'en as just a man

---

35 **journeymen** workers not yet masters of their craft   38 **indifferently**
tolerably

As e'er my conversation coped withal.°

Horatio. O, my dear lord——

Hamlet.   Nay, do not think I flatter.
For what advancement° may I hope from thee,
60 That no revenue hast but thy good spirits
To feed and clothe thee? Why should the poor be
    flattered?
No, let the candied° tongue lick absurd pomp,
And crook the pregnant° hinges of the knee
Where thrift° may follow fawning. Dost thou hear?
65 Since my dear soul was mistress of her choice
And could of men distinguish her election,
S' hath sealed thee° for herself, for thou hast been
As one, in suff'ring all, that suffers nothing,°
A man that Fortune's buffets and rewards
70 Hast ta'en with equal thanks; and blest are those
Whose blood° and judgment are so well com-
    meddled°
That they are not a pipe for Fortune's finger
To sound what stop she please. Give me that man
That is not passion's slave, and I will wear him
75 In my heart's core, ay, in my heart of heart,
As I do thee. Something too much of this—
There is a play tonight before the King.
One scene of it comes near the circumstance
Which I have told thee, of my father's death.
80 I prithee, when thou seest that act afoot,
Even with the very comment° of thy soul
Observe my uncle. If his occulted° guilt
Do not itself unkennel in one speech,
It is a damnèd ghost that we have seen,
85 And my imaginations are as foul
As Vulcan's stithy.° Give him heedful note,
For I mine eyes will rivet to his face,

57 **coped withal** met with   59 **advancement** promotion   62 **candied** sugared, flattering   63 **pregnant** (1) pliant (2) full of promise of good fortune   64 **thrift** profit   67 **S' hath sealed thee** she (the soul) has set a mark on you   68 **As one . . . nothing** Shakespeare puns on *suffering*: Horatio *undergoes* all things, but is *harmed* by none   71 **blood** passion   71 **commeddled** blended   81 **very comment** deepest wisdom   82 **occulted** hidden   86 **stithy** forge, smithy

And after we will both our judgments join
In censure of his seeming.°

Horatio.   Well, my lord.
If 'a steal aught the whilst this play is playing,   90
And scape detecting, I will pay the theft.

*Enter Trumpets and Kettledrums, King, Queen,
Polonius, Ophelia, Rosencrantz, Guildenstern,
and other Lords attendant with his Guard carrying
torches. Danish March. Sound a Flourish.*

Hamlet. They are coming to the play: I must be idle;°
Get you a place.

King. How fares our cousin Hamlet?

Hamlet. Excellent, i' faith, of the chameleon's dish;°   95
I eat the air, promise-crammed; you cannot feed
capons so.

King. I have nothing with this answer, Hamlet; these
words are not mine.

Hamlet. No, nor mine now. [*To Polonius*] My lord, you   101
played once i' th' university, you say?

Polonius. That did I, my lord, and was accounted a good
actor.

Hamlet. What did you enact?

Polonius. I did enact Julius Caesar. I was killed i' th'   105
Capitol; Brutus killed me.

Hamlet. It was a brute part of him to kill so capital a
calf there. Be the players ready?

Rosencrantz. Ay, my lord. They stay upon your patience.   110

Queen. Come hither, my dear Hamlet, sit by me.

Hamlet. No, good mother. Here's metal more attractive.°

---

89 **censure of his seeming** judgment on his looks   92 **be idle** play the
fool   95 **the chameleon's dish** air (on which chameleons were thought
to live)   112–13 **attractive** magnetic

Polonius. [*To the King*] O ho! Do you mark that?

115 *Hamlet.* Lady, shall I lie in your lap?

> [*He lies at Ophelia's feet.*]

Ophelia. No, my lord.

Hamlet. I mean, my head upon your lap?

Ophelia. Ay, my lord.

Hamlet. Do you think I meant country matters?°

120 *Ophelia.* I think nothing, my lord.

Hamlet. That's a fair thought to lie between maids' legs.

Ophelia. What is, my lord?

Hamlet. Nothing.

125 *Ophelia.* You are merry, my lord.

Hamlet. Who, I?

Ophelia. Ay, my lord.

Hamlet. O God, your only jig-maker!° What should a man do but be merry? For look you how cheerfully
130 my mother looks, and my father died within's two hours.

Ophelia. Nay, 'tis twice two months, my lord.

Hamlet. So long? Nay then, let the devil wear black, for I'll have a suit of sables.° O heavens! Die two
135 months ago, and not forgotten yet? Then there's hope a great man's memory may outlive his life half a year. But, by'r Lady, 'a must build churches then, or else shall 'a suffer not thinking on, with the hobby-horse,° whose epitaph is "For O, for O, the hobby-
140 horse is forgot!"

The trumpets sound. Dumb show follows:

---

119 **country matters** rustic doings (with a pun on the vulgar word for the pudendum)   128 **jig-maker** composer of songs and dances (often a Fool, who performed them)   134 **sables** (pun on "black" and "luxurious furs")   138–39 **hobbyhorse** mock horse worn by a performer in the morris dance

Enter a King and a Queen very lovingly, the Queen em-
bracing him, and he her. She kneels; and makes show
of protestation unto him. He takes her up, and declines
his head upon her neck. He lies him down upon a bank
of flowers. She, seeing him asleep, leaves him. Anon
come in another man: takes off his crown, kisses it,
pours poison in the sleeper's ears, and leaves him. The
Queen returns, finds the King dead, makes passionate
action. The poisoner, with some three or four, come in
again, seem to condole with her. The dead body is car-
ried away. The poisoner woos the Queen with gifts; she
seems harsh awhile, but in the end accepts love.

                                          Exeunt.

Ophelia. What means this, my lord?

Hamlet. Marry, this is miching mallecho;° it means
    mischief.

Ophelia. Belike this show imports the argument° of
    the play.   145

                   Enter Prologue.

Hamlet. We shall know by this fellow. The players
    cannot keep counsel; they'll tell all.

Ophelia. Will 'a tell us what this show meant?

Hamlet. Ay, or any show that you will show him. Be
    not you ashamed to show, he'll not shame to tell you 150
    what it means.

Ophelia. You are naught,° you are naught; I'll mark
    the play.

Prologue. For us, and for our tragedy,
           Here stooping to your clemency,   155
           We beg your hearing patiently.   [*Exit.*]

Hamlet. Is this a prologue, or the posy of a ring?°

Ophelia. 'Tis brief, my lord.

Hamlet. As woman's love.

142 **miching mallecho** sneaking mischief   144 **argument** plot
152 **naught** wicked, improper   157 **posy of a ring** motto inscribed in
a ring.

Enter [two Players as] King and Queen.

Player King. Full thirty times hath Phoebus' cart° gone
160   round
      Neptune's salt wash° and Tellus'° orbèd ground,
      And thirty dozen moons with borrowed sheen
      About the world have times twelve thirties been,
      Since love our hearts, and Hymen did our hands,
165   Unite commutual in most sacred bands.

Player Queen. So many journeys may the sun and
      moon
      Make us again count o'er ere love be done!
      But woe is me, you are so sick of late,
      So far from cheer and from your former state,
170   That I distrust° you. Yet, though I distrust,
      Discomfort you, my lord, it nothing must.
      For women fear too much, even as they love,
      And women's fear and love hold quantity,
      In neither aught, or in extremity.°
175   Now what my love is, proof° hath made you know,
      And as my love is sized, my fear is so.
      Where love is great, the littlest doubts are fear;
      Where little fears grow great, great love grows there.

Player King. Faith, I must leave thee, love, and shortly
      too;
180   My operant° powers their functions leave to do:
      And thou shalt live in this fair world behind,
      Honored, beloved, and haply one as kind
      For husband shalt thou——

Player Queen.   O, confound the rest!
      Such love must needs be treason in my breast.
185   In second husband let me be accurst!
      None wed the second but who killed the first.

---

160 **Phoebus' cart** the sun's chariot   161 **Neptune's salt wash** the sea
161 **Tellus** Roman goddess of the earth   170 **distrust** am anxious
about   173–74 **And women's . . . in extremity** (perhaps the idea is that
women's anxiety is great or little in proportion to their love. The previous line, unrhymed, may be a false start that Shakespeare neglected to
delete)   175 **proof** experience   180 **operant** active

Hamlet. [Aside] That's wormwood.°

Player Queen. The instances° that second marriage move°
  Are base respects of thrift,° but none of love.
  A second time I kill my husband dead
  When second husband kisses me in bed.   190

Player King. I do believe you think what now you speak,
  But what we do determine oft we break.
  Purpose is but the slave to memory,
  Of violent birth, but poor validity,°   195
  Which now like fruit unripe sticks on the tree,
  But fall unshaken when they mellow be.
  Most necessary 'tis that we forget
  To pay ourselves what to ourselves is debt.
  What to ourselves in passion we propose,   200
  The passion ending, doth the purpose lose.
  The violence of either grief or joy
  Their own enactures° with themselves destroy:
  Where joy most revels, grief doth most lament;
  Grief joys, joy grieves, on slender accident.   205
  This world is not for aye, nor 'tis not strange
  That even our loves should with our fortunes change,
  For 'tis a question left us yet to prove,
  Whether love lead fortune, or else fortune love.
  The great man down, you mark his favorite flies;   210
  The poor advanced makes friends of enemies;
  And hitherto doth love on fortune tend,
  For who not needs shall never lack a friend;
  And who in want a hollow friend doth try,
  Directly seasons him° his enemy.   215
  But, orderly to end where I begun,
  Our wills and fates do so contrary run
  That our devices still are overthrown;
  Our thoughts are ours, their ends none of our own.

---

187 **wormwood** a bitter herb   188 **instances** motives   188 **move** induce   189 **respects of thrift** considerations of profit   195 **validity** strength   203 **enactures** acts   215 **seasons him** ripens him into

220   So think thou wilt no second husband wed,
       But die thy thoughts when thy first lord is dead.

Player Queen. Nor earth to me give food, nor heaven
       light,
       Sport and repose lock from me day and night,
       To desperation turn my trust and hope,
225   An anchor's° cheer in prison be my scope,
       Each opposite that blanks° the face of joy
       Meet what I would have well, and it destroy:
       Both here and hence pursue me lasting strife,
       If, once a widow, ever I be wife!

230   *Hamlet.* If she should break it now!

Player King. 'Tis deeply sworn. Sweet, leave me here
       awhile;
       My spirits grow dull, and fain I would beguile
       The tedious day with sleep.

Player Queen.   Sleep rock thy brain,
                                   [*He*] *sleeps.*
       And never come mischance between us twain!   *Exit.*

235   *Hamlet.* Madam, how like you this play?

Queen. The lady doth protest too much, methinks.

Hamlet. O, but she'll keep her word.

King. Have you heard the argument?° Is there no
       offense in't?

240   *Hamlet.* No, no, they do but jest, poison in jest; no
       offense i' th' world.

King. What do you call the play?

Hamlet. The Mousetrap. Marry, how? Tropically.°
       This play is the image of a murder done in Vienna:
245   Gonzago is the Duke's name; his wife, Baptista. You
       shall see anon. 'Tis a knavish piece of work, but
       what of that? Your Majesty, and we that have free°

225 **anchor's** anchorite's, hermit's   226 **opposite that blanks** adverse
thing that blanches   238 **argument** plot   243 **Tropically** figuratively
(with a pun on "trap")   247 **free** innocent

souls, it touches us not. Let the galled jade winch;° our withers are unwrung.

Enter Lucianus.

This is one Lucianus, nephew to the King.   250

Ophelia. You are as good as a chorus, my lord.

Hamlet. I could interpret° between you and your love, if I could see the puppets dallying.

Ophelia. You are keen,° my lord, you are keen.

Hamlet. It would cost you a groaning to take off mine   255 edge.

Ophelia. Still better, and worse.

Hamlet. So you mistake° your husbands.—Begin, murderer. Leave thy damnable faces and begin. Come, the croaking raven doth bellow for revenge.   260

Lucianus. Thoughts black, hands apt, drugs fit, and time agreeing,
    Confederate season,° else no creature seeing,
    Thou mixture rank, of midnight weeds collected,
    With Hecate's ban° thrice blasted, thrice infected,
    Thy natural magic and dire property°   265
    On wholesome life usurps immediately.

              Pours the poison in his ears.

Hamlet. 'A poisons him i' th' garden for his estate. His name's Gonzago. The story is extant, and written in very choice Italian. You shall see anon how the murderer gets the love of Gonzago's wife.   270

Ophelia. The King rises.

Hamlet. What, frighted with false fire?°

Queen. How fares my lord?

Polonius. Give o'er the play.

---

248 **galled jade winch** chafed horse wince   252 **interpret** (like a show-man explaining the action of puppets)   254 **keen** (1) sharp (2) sexually aroused   258 **mistake** err in taking   262 **Confederate season** the opportunity allied with me   264 **Hecate's ban** the curse of the goddess of sorcery   265 **property** nature   272 **false fire** blank discharge of firearms

275 *King.* Give me some light. Away!

Polonius. Lights, lights, lights!

> *Exeunt all but Hamlet and Horatio.*

Hamlet. Why, let the strucken deer go weep,
> The hart ungallèd play:
> For some must watch, while some must sleep;
280 > Thus runs the world away.
Would not this, sir, and a forest of feathers°—if the rest of my fortunes turn Turk° with me—with two Provincial roses° on my razed° shoes, get me a fellowship in a cry° of players?

285 *Horatio.* Half a share.

Hamlet. A whole one, I.
> For thou dost know, O Damon dear,
> This realm dismantled was
> Of Jove himself; and now reigns here
290 > A very, very—pajock.°

Horatio. You might have rhymed.°

Hamlet. O good Horatio, I'll take the ghost's word for a thousand pound. Didst perceive?

Horatio. Very well, my lord.

295 *Hamlet.* Upon the talk of poisoning?

Horatio. I did very well note him.

Hamlet. Ah ha! Come, some music! Come, the recorders!°
> For if the King like not the comedy,
300 > Why then, belike he likes it not, perdy.°
Come, some music!

> *Enter Rosencrantz and Guildenstern.*

Guildenstern. Good my lord, vouchsafe me a word with you.

---

281 **feathers** (plumes were sometimes part of a costume) 282 **turn Turk** i.e., go bad, treat me badly   283 **Provincial roses** rosettes like the roses of Provence (?)   283 **razed** ornamented with slashes   284 **cry** pack, company   290 **pajock** peacock   291 **You might have rhymed** i.e., rhymed "was" with "ass"   297–98 **recorders** flutelike instruments 300 **perdy** by God (French: *par dieu*)

Hamlet. Sir, a whole history.

Guildenstern. The King, sir——   305

Hamlet. Ay, sir, what of him?

Guildenstern. Is in his retirement marvelous distemp'red.

Hamlet. With drink, sir?

Guildenstern. No, my lord, with choler.°   310

Hamlet. Your wisdom should show itself more richer to signify this to the doctor, for for me to put him to his purgation would perhaps plunge him into more choler.

Guildenstern. Good my lord, put your discourse into   315
some frame,° and start not so wildly from my affair.

Hamlet. I am tame, sir; pronounce.

Guildenstern. The Queen, your mother, in most great affliction of spirit hath sent me to you.

Hamlet. You are welcome.   320

Guildenstern. Nay, good my lord, this courtesy is not of the right breed. If it shall please you to make me a wholesome answer, I will do your mother's commandment: if not, your pardon and my return shall be the end of my business.   325

Hamlet. Sir, I cannot.

Rosencrantz. What, my lord?

Hamlet. Make you a wholesome° answer; my wit's diseased. But, sir, such answer as I can make, you shall command, or rather, as you say, my mother.   330
Therefore no more, but to the matter. My mother, you say——

Rosencrantz. Then thus she says: your behavior hath struck her into amazement and admiration.°

---

310 **choler** anger (but Hamlet pretends to take the word in its sense of "biliousness") 316 **frame** order, control 328 **wholesome** sane 334 **admiration** wonder

335 *Hamlet.* O wonderful son, that can so stonish a mother!
    But is there no sequel at the heels of this mother's
    admiration? Impart.

Rosencrantz. She desires to speak with you in her
    closet ere you go to bed.

340 *Hamlet.* We shall obey, were she ten times our mother.
    Have you any further trade with us?

Rosencrantz. My lord, you once did love me.

Hamlet. And do still, by these pickers and stealers.°

Rosencrantz. Good my lord, what is your cause of dis-
345   temper? You do surely bar the door upon your own
    liberty, if you deny your griefs to your friend.

Hamlet. Sir, I lack advancement.°

Rosencrantz. How can that be, when you have the
    voice of the King himself for your succession in
350   Denmark?

Enter the Players with recorders.

Hamlet. Ay, sir, but "while the grass grows"—the
    proverb° is something musty. O, the recorders. Let
    me see one. To withdraw° with you—why do you
    go about to recover the wind° of me as if you would
355   drive me into a toil?°

Guildenstern. O my lord, if my duty be too bold, my
    love is too unmannerly.°

Hamlet. I do not well understand that. Will you play
    upon this pipe?

360 *Guildenstern.* My lord, I cannot.

Hamlet. I pray you.

Guildenstern. Believe me, I cannot.

Hamlet. I pray you.

Guildenstern. Believe me, I cannot.

343 **pickers and stealers** i.e., hands (with reference to the prayer; "Keep
my hands from picking and stealing")   347 **advancement** promotion   352 **proverb** ("While the grass groweth, the horse starveth")
353 **withdraw** speak in private   354 **recover the wind** get on the wind-
ward side (as in hunting)   355 **toil** snare   356–57 **if my duty . . . too
unmannerly** i.e., if these questions seem rude, it is because my love for
you leads me beyond good manners.

Hamlet. I do beseech you.

Guildenstern. I know no touch of it, my lord.

Hamlet. It is as easy as lying. Govern these ventages°   365
with your fingers and thumb, give it breath with your
mouth, and it will discourse most eloquent music.
Look you, these are the stops.

Guildenstern. But these cannot I command to any
utt'rance of harmony; I have not the skill.   370

Hamlet. Why, look you now, how unworthy a thing
you make of me! You would play upon me; you
would seem to know my stops; you would pluck
out the heart of my mystery; you would sound me
from my lowest note to the top of my compass;°   375
and there is much music, excellent voice, in this little
organ,° yet cannot you make it speak. 'Sblood, do
you think I am easier to be played on than a pipe?
Call me what instrument you will, though you can
fret° me, you cannot play upon me.   380

Enter Polonius.

God bless you, sir!

Polonius. My lord, the Queen would speak with you,
and presently.

Hamlet. Do you see yonder cloud that's almost in
shape of a camel?   385

Polonius. By th' mass and 'tis, like a camel indeed.

Hamlet. Methinks it is like a weasel.

Polonius. It is backed like a weasel.

Hamlet. Or like a whale.

Polonius. Very like a whale.   390

Hamlet. Then I will come to my mother by and by.

---

365 **ventages** vents, stops on a recorder   375 **compass** range of voice
377 **organ** i.e., the recorder   380 **fret** vex (with a pun alluding to the
frets, or ridges, that guide the fingering on some stringed instruments)

    [*Aside*] They fool me to the top of my bent.°—I
will come by and by.°

Polonius. I will say so.   *Exit.*

395 *Hamlet.* "By and by" is easily said. Leave me, friends.
                      [*Exeunt all but Hamlet.*]
    'Tis now the very witching time of night,
    When churchyards yawn, and hell itself breathes out
    Contagion to this world. Now could I drink hot
      blood
    And do such bitter business as the day
400 Would quake to look on. Soft, now to my mother.
    O heart, lose not thy nature; let not ever
    The soul of Nero° enter this firm bosom.
    Let me be cruel, not unnatural;
    I will speak daggers to her, but use none.
405 My tongue and soul in this be hypocrites:
    How in my words somever she be shent,°
    To give them seals° never, my soul, consent!   *Exit.*

[Scene 3. *The castle.*]

Enter King, Rosencrantz, and Guildenstern.

King. I like him not, nor stands it safe with us
    To let his madness range. Therefore prepare you.
    I your commission will forthwith dispatch,
    And he to England shall along with you.
5 The terms° of our estate may not endure
    Hazard so near's° as doth hourly grow
    Out of his brows.

Guildenstern.   We will ourselves provide.

---

392 **They fool . . . my bent** they compel me to play the fool to the
limit of my capacity   393 **by and by** very soon   402 **Nero** (Roman
emperor who had his mother murdered)   406 **shent** rebuked   407 **give
them seals** confirm them with deeds   3.3.5 **terms** conditions   6 **near's**
near us

Most holy and religious fear it is
To keep those many many bodies safe
That live and feed upon your Majesty.   10

Rosencrantz. The single and peculiar° life is bound
With all the strength and armor of the mind
To keep itself from noyance,° but much more
That spirit upon whose weal depends and rests
The lives of many. The cess of majesty°   15
Dies not alone, but like a gulf° doth draw
What's near it with it; or it is a massy wheel
Fixed on the summit of the highest mount,
To whose huge spokes ten thousand lesser things
Are mortised and adjoined, which when it falls,   20
Each small annexment, petty consequence,
Attends° the boist'rous ruin. Never alone
Did the King sigh, but with a general groan.

King. Arm° you, I pray you, to this speedy voyage,
For we will fetters put about this fear,   25
Which now goes too free-footed.

Rosencrantz.   We will haste us.
                              Exeunt Gentlemen.

                    Enter Polonius.

Polonius. My lord, he's going to his mother's closet.°
Behind the arras I'll convey myself
To hear the process.° I'll warrant she'll tax him
    home,°
And, as you said, and wisely was it said,   30
'Tis meet that some more audience than a mother,
Since nature makes them partial, should o'erhear
The speech of vantage.° Fare you well, my liege.
I'll call upon you ere you go to bed
And tell you what I know.

King.   Thanks, dear my lord.   35
                              Exit [Polonius].

11 **peculiar** individual, private   13 **noyance** injury   15 **cess of majesty** cessation (death) of a king   16 **gulf** whirlpool   22 **Attends** waits on, participates in   24 **Arm** prepare   27 **closet** private room   29 **process** proceedings   29 **tax him home** censure him sharply   33 **of vantage** from an advantageous place

O, my offense is rank, it smells to heaven;
It hath the primal eldest curse° upon't,
A brother's murder. Pray can I not,
Though inclination be as sharp as will.
40 My stronger guilt defeats my strong intent,
And like a man to double business bound
I stand in pause where I shall first begin,
And both neglect. What if this cursèd hand
Were thicker than itself with brother's blood,
45 Is there not rain enough in the sweet heavens
To wash it white as snow? Whereto serves mercy
But to confront° the visage of offense?
And what's in prayer but this twofold force,
To be forestallèd ere we come to fall,
50 Or pardoned being down? Then I'll look up.
My fault is past. But, O, what form of prayer
Can serve my turn? "Forgive me my foul murder"?
That cannot be, since I am still possessed
Of those effects° for which I did the murder,
55 My crown, mine own ambition, and my queen.
May one be pardoned and retain th' offense?
In the corrupted currents of this world
Offense's gilded hand may shove by justice,
And oft 'tis seen the wicked prize itself
60 Buys out the law. But 'tis not so above.
There is no shuffling;° there the action lies
In his true nature, and we ourselves compelled,
Even to the teeth and forehead of our faults,
To give in evidence. What then? What rests?°
65 Try what repentance can. What can it not?
Yet what can it when one cannot repent?
O wretched state! O bosom black as death!
O limèd° soul, that struggling to be free
Art more engaged!° Help, angels! Make assay.°
70 Bow, stubborn knees, and, heart with strings of steel,

---

37 **primal eldest curse** (curse of Cain, who killed Abel)   47 **confront**
oppose   54 **effects** things gained   61 **shuffling** trickery   64 **rests** remains   68 **limèd** caught (as with birdlime, a sticky substance spread on
boughs to snare birds)   69 **engaged** ensnared   69 **assay** an attempt

  Be soft as sinews of the newborn babe.
  All may be well.   *[He kneels.]*

Enter Hamlet.

Hamlet. Now might I do it pat, now 'a is a-praying,
  And now I'll do't. And so 'a goes to heaven,
  And so am I revenged. That would be scanned.° 75
  A villain kills my father, and for that
  I, his sole son, do this same villain send
  To heaven.
  Why, this is hire and salary, not revenge.
  'A took my father grossly, full of bread,° 80
  With all his crimes broad blown,° as flush° as May;
  And how his audit° stands, who knows save heaven?
  But in our circumstance and course of thought,
  'Tis heavy with him; and am I then revenged,
  To take him in the purging of his soul, 85
  When he is fit and seasoned for his passage?
  No.
  Up, sword, and know thou a more horrid hent.°
  When he is drunk asleep, or in his rage,
  Or in th' incestuous pleasure of his bed, 90
  At game a-swearing, or about some act
  That has no relish° of salvation in't—
  Then trip him, that his heels may kick at heaven,
  And that his soul may be as damned and black
  As hell, whereto it goes. My mother stays. 95
  This physic° but prolongs thy sickly days. *Exit.*

King. *[Rises]* My words fly up, my thoughts remain
  below.
  Words without thoughts never to heaven go. *Exit.*

---

75 **would be scanned** ought to be looked into 80 **bread** i. e., worldly
gratification 81 **crimes broad blown** sins in full bloom 81 **flush** vigorous 82 **audit** account 88 **hent** grasp (here, occasion for seizing)
92 **relish** flavor 96 **physic** (Claudius' purgation by prayer, as Hamlet
thinks in line 85)

[Scene 4. *The Queen's private chamber.*]

Enter [Queen] Gertrude and Polonius.

Polonius. 'A will come straight. Look you lay home°
  to him.
  Tell him his pranks have been too broad° to bear
  with,
  And that your Grace hath screened and stood between
  Much heat and him. I'll silence me even here.
5 Pray you be round with him.

Hamlet. (*Within*) Mother, Mother, Mother!

Queen. I'll warrant you; fear me not. Withdraw; I hear
  him coming.   [*Polonius hides behind the arras.*]

Enter Hamlet.

Hamlet. Now, Mother, what's the matter?

10 *Queen.* Hamlet, thou hast thy father much offended.

Hamlet. Mother, you have my father much offended.

Queen. Come, come, you answer with an idle° tongue.

Hamlet. Go, go, you question with a wicked tongue.

Queen. Why, how now, Hamlet?

Hamlet.   What's the matter now?

Queen. Have you forgot me?

15 *Hamlet.*   No, by the rood,° not so!
  You are the Queen, your husband's brother's wife,
  And, would it were not so, you are my mother.

Queen. Nay, then I'll set those to you that can speak.

Hamlet. Come, come, and sit you down. You shall not
  budge.

3.4.1 **lay home** thrust (rebuke) him sharply 2 **broad** unrestrained
12 **idle** foolish 15 **rood** cross

You go not till I set you up a glass°   20
Where you may see the inmost part of you!

Queen. What wilt thou do? Thou wilt not murder me?
Help, ho!

Polonius. [*Behind*] What, ho! Help!

Hamlet. [*Draws*] How now? A rat? Dead for a ducat,
dead!   25
[*Thrusts his rapier through the arras and*] *kills Polonius.*

Polonius. [*Behind*] O, I am slain!

Queen.   O me, what hast thou done?

Hamlet. Nay, I know not. Is it the King?

Queen. O, what a rash and bloody deed is this!

Hamlet. A bloody deed—almost as bad, good Mother,
As kill a king, and marry with his brother.   30

Queen. As kill a king?

Hamlet.   Ay, lady, it was my word.
          [*Lifts up the arras and sees Polonius.*]
Thou wretched, rash, intruding fool, farewell!
I took thee for thy better. Take thy fortune.
Thou find'st to be too busy is some danger.—
Leave wringing of your hands. Peace, sit you down   35
And let me wring your heart, for so I shall
If it be made of penetrable stuff,
If damnèd custom have not brazed° it so
That it be proof° and bulwark against sense.°

Queen. What have I done that thou dar'st wag thy
          tongue   40
In noise so rude against me?

Hamlet.   Such an act
That blurs the grace and blush of modesty,
Calls virtue hypocrite, takes off the rose
From the fair forehead of an innocent love,
And sets a blister° there, makes marriage vows   45

20 **glass** mirror   38 **brazed** hardened like brass   39 **proof** armor
39 **sense** feeling   45 **sets a blister** brands (as a harlot)

As false as dicers' oaths. O, such a deed
As from the body of contraction° plucks
The very soul, and sweet religion makes
A rhapsody° of words! Heaven's face does glow
50 O'er this solidity and compound mass
With heated visage, as against the doom
Is thoughtsick at the act.°

Queen.   Ay me, what act,
That roars so loud and thunders in the index?°

Hamlet. Look here upon this picture, and on this,
55 The counterfeit presentment° of two brothers.
See what a grace was seated on this brow:
Hyperion's curls, the front° of Jove himself,
An eye like Mars, to threaten and command,
A station° like the herald Mercury
60 New lighted on a heaven-kissing hill—
A combination and a form indeed
Where every god did seem to set his seal
To give the world assurance of a man.
This was your husband. Look you now what follows.
65 Here is your husband, like a mildewed ear
Blasting his wholesome brother. Have you eyes?
Could you on this fair mountain leave to feed,
And batten° on this moor? Ha! Have you eyes?
You cannot call it love, for at your age
70 The heyday° in the blood is tame, it's humble,
And waits upon the judgment, and what judgment
Would step from this to this? Sense° sure you have,
Else could you not have motion, but sure that sense
Is apoplexed,° for madness would not err,
75 Nor sense to ecstasy° was ne'er so thralled
But it reserved some quantity of choice

---

47 **contraction** marriage contract   49 **rhapsody** senseless string
49–52 **Heaven's face . . . the act** i.e., the face of heaven blushes over
this earth (compounded of four elements), the face hot, as if Judgment
Day were near, and it is thoughtsick at the act   53 **index** prologue   55
counterfeit presentment represented image   57 **front** forehead   59
station bearing   68 **batten** feed gluttonously   70 **heyday** excitement
72 **Sense** feeling   74 **apoplexed** paralyzed   75 **ecstasy** madness

To serve in such a difference. What devil was't
That thus hath cozened you at hoodman-blind?°
Eyes without feeling, feeling without sight,
Ears without hands or eyes, smelling sans° all,　　　80
Or but a sickly part of one true sense
Could not so mope.°
O shame, where is thy blush? Rebellious hell,
If thou canst mutine in a matron's bones,
To flaming youth let virtue be as wax　　　　　　85
And melt in her own fire. Proclaim no shame
When the compulsive ardor° gives the charge,
Since frost itself as actively doth burn,
And reason panders will.°

Queen.　　　　　　　　　　　O Hamlet, speak no more.
Thou turn'st mine eyes into my very soul,　　　　90
And there I see such black and grainèd° spots
As will not leave their tinct.°

Hamlet.　　　　　　　　　　　Nay, but to live
In the rank sweat of an enseamèd° bed,
Stewed in corruption, honeying and making love
Over the nasty sty——

Queen.　　　　　　　　　　　O, speak to me no more.　　95
These words like daggers enter in my ears.
No more, sweet Hamlet.

Hamlet.　　　　　　　　　　A murderer and a villain,
A slave that is not twentieth part the tithe°
Of your precedent lord, a vice° of kings,
A cutpurse of the empire and the rule,　　　　　100
That from a shelf the precious diadem stole
And put it in his pocket——

Queen.　　　　　　　　　　　No more.

---

78 **cozened you at hoodman-blind** cheated you at blindman's buff
80 **sans** without　82 **mope** be stupid　87 **compulsive ardor** com-
pelling passion　89 **reason panders will** reason acts as a procurer
for desire　91 **grainèd** dyed in grain (fast dyed)　92 **tinct** color　93
enseamèd (perhaps "soaked in grease," i.e., sweaty; perhaps "much
wrinkled")　98 **tithe** tenth part　99 **vice** (like the Vice, a fool and
mischief-maker in the old morality plays)

Enter Ghost.

Hamlet. A king of shreds and patches—
    Save me and hover o'er me with your wings,
    You heavenly guards! What would your gracious
105   figure?

Queen. Alas, he's mad.

Hamlet. Do you not come your tardy son to chide,
    That, lapsed in time and passion, lets go by
    Th' important acting of your dread command?
110   O, say!

Ghost. Do not forget. This visitation
    Is but to whet thy almost blunted purpose.
    But look, amazement on thy mother sits.
    O, step between her and her fighting soul!
115   Conceit° in weakest bodies strongest works.
    Speak to her, Hamlet.

Hamlet.   How is it with you, lady?

Queen. Alas, how is't with you,
    That you do bend your eye on vacancy,
    And with th' incorporal° air do hold discourse?
120   Forth at your eyes your spirits wildly peep,
    And as the sleeping soldiers in th' alarm
    Your bedded hair° like life in excrements°
    Start up and stand an end.° O gentle son,
    Upon the heat and flame of thy distemper
125   Sprinkle cool patience. Whereon do you look?

Hamlet. On him, on him! Look you, how pale he
      glares!
    His form and cause conjoined, preaching to stones,
    Would make them capable.°—Do not look upon
      me,
    Lest with this piteous action you convert
130   My stern effects.° Then what I have to do
    Will want true color; tears perchance for blood.

Queen. To whom do you speak this?

115 **Conceit** imagination   119 **incorporal** bodiless   122 **bedded hair** hairs laid flat   122 **excrements** outgrowths (here, the hair)   123 **an end** on end   128 **capable** receptive   129–30 **convert/My stern effects** divert my stern deeds

Hamlet.   Do you see nothing there?

Queen. Nothing at all; yet all that is I see.

Hamlet. Nor did you nothing hear?

Queen.   No, nothing but ourselves.

Hamlet. Why, look you there! Look how it steals away!   *135*
    My father, in his habit° as he lived!
    Look where he goes even now out at the portal!

                               Exit Ghost.

Queen. This is the very coinage of your brain.
    This bodiless creation ecstasy
    Is very cunning in.

Hamlet.   Ecstasy?   *140*
    My pulse as yours doth temperately keep time
    And makes as healthful music. It is not madness
    That I have uttered. Bring me to the test,
    And I the matter will reword, which madness
    Would gambol° from. Mother, for love of grace,   *145*
    Lay not that flattering unction° to your soul,
    That not your trespass but my madness speaks.
    It will but skin and film the ulcerous place
    Whiles rank corruption, mining° all within,
    Infects unseen. Confess yourself to heaven,   *150*
    Repent what's past, avoid what is to come,
    And do not spread the compost° on the weeds
    To make them ranker. Forgive me this my virtue.
    For in the fatness of these pursy° times
    Virtue itself of vice must pardon beg,   *155*
    Yea, curb° and woo for leave to do him good.

Queen. O Hamlet, thou hast cleft my heart in twain.

Hamlet. O, throw away the worser part of it,
    And live the purer with the other half.
    Good night—but go not to my uncle's bed.   *160*
    Assume a virtue, if you have it not.

---

136 **habit** garment (Q1, though a "bad" quarto, is probably correct in saying that at line 102 the ghost enters "in his nightgown," i.e., dressing gown) 145 **gambol** start away 146 **unction** ointment 149 **mining** undermining 152 **compost** fertilizing substance 154 **pursy** bloated 156 **curb** bow low

That monster custom, who all sense doth eat,
Of habits devil, is angel yet in this,
That to the use° of actions fair and good
165 He likewise gives a frock or livery°
That aptly is put on. Refrain tonight,
And that shall lend a kind of easiness
To the next abstinence; the next more easy;
For use almost can change the stamp of nature,
170 And either° the devil, or throw him out
With wondrous potency. Once more, good night,
And when you are desirous to be blest,
I'll blessing beg of you.—For this same lord,
I do repent; but heaven hath pleased it so,
175 To punish me with this, and this with me,
That I must be their° scourge and minister.
I will bestow° him and will answer well
The death I gave him. So again, good night.
I must be cruel only to be kind.
180 Thus bad begins, and worse remains behind.
One word more, good lady.

Queen.   What shall I do?

Hamlet. Not this, by no means, that I bid you do:
Let the bloat King tempt you again to bed,
Pinch wanton on your cheek, call you his mouse,
185 And let him, for a pair of reechy° kisses,
Or paddling in your neck with his damned fingers,
Make you to ravel° all this matter out,
That I essentially am not in madness,
But mad in craft. 'Twere good you let him know,
190 For who that's but a queen, fair, sober, wise,
Would from a paddock,° from a bat, a gib,°
Such dear concernings hide? Who would do so?
No, in despite of sense and secrecy,

---

164 **use** practice 165 **livery** characteristic garment (punning on "habits" in line 163) 170 **either** (probably a word is missing after *either*; among suggestions are "master," "curb," and "house"; but possibly *either* is a printer's error for *entertain*, i.e. "receive"; or perhaps *either* is a verb meaning "make easier") 176 **their** i.e., the heavens' 177 **bestow** stow, lodge 185 **reechy** foul (literally "smoky") 187 **ravel** unravel, reveal 191 **paddock** toad 191 **gib** tomcat

Unpeg the basket on the house's top,
Let the birds fly, and like the famous ape,   *195*
To try conclusions,° in the basket creep
And break your own neck down.

Queen. Be thou assured, if words be made of breath,
And breath of life, I have no life to breathe
What thou hast said to me.   *200*

Hamlet. I must to England; you know that?

Queen.   Alack,
I had forgot. 'Tis so concluded on.

Hamlet. There's letters sealed, and my two school-
fellows,
Whom I will trust as I will adders fanged,
They bear the mandate;° they must sweep my way   *205*
And marshal me to knavery. Let it work;
For 'tis the sport to have the enginer
Hoist with his own petar,° and 't shall go hard
But I will delve one yard below their mines
And blow them at the moon. O, 'tis most sweet   *210*
When in one line two crafts° directly meet.
This man shall set me packing:
I'll lug the guts into the neighbor room.
Mother, good night. Indeed, this counselor
Is now most still, most secret, and most grave,   *215*
Who was in life a foolish prating knave.
Come, sir, to draw toward an end with you.
Good night, Mother.
          [*Exit the Queen. Then*] *exit Hamlet, tugging in*
                                        Polonius.

---

196 **To try conclusions** to make experiments · 205 **mandate** command
208 **petar** bomb   211 **crafts** (1) boats (2) acts of guile, crafty schemes

[ACT 4

Scene 1. *The castle.*]

Enter King and Queen, with Rosencrantz and
Guildenstern.

King. There's matter in these sighs. These profound
  heaves
  You must translate; 'tis fit we understand them.
  Where is your son?

Queen. Bestow this place on us a little while.
          [*Exeunt Rosencrantz and Guildenstern.*]
5 Ah, mine own lord, what have I seen tonight!

King. What, Gertrude? How does Hamlet?

Queen. Mad as the sea and wind when both contend
  Which is the mightier. In his lawless fit,
  Behind the arras hearing something stir,
10 Whips out his rapier, cries, "A rat, a rat!"
  And in this brainish apprehension° kills
  The unseen good old man.

King.   O heavy deed!
  It had been so with us, had we been there.
  His liberty is full of threats to all,
15 To you yourself, to us, to every one.
  Alas, how shall this bloody deed be answered?
  It will be laid to us, whose providence°

4.1.11 **brainish apprehension** mad imagination   17 **providence** fore-
sight

94

Should have kept short, restrained, and out of haunt°
This mad young man. But so much was our love
We would not understand what was most fit,   20
But, like the owner of a foul disease,
To keep it from divulging, let it feed
Even on the pith of life. Where is he gone?

Queen. To draw apart the body he hath killed;
O'er whom his very madness, like some ore   25
Among a mineral° of metals base,
Shows itself pure. 'A weeps for what is done.

King. O Gertrude, come away!
The sun no sooner shall the mountains touch
But we will ship him hence, and this vile deed   30
We must with all our majesty and skill
Both countenance and excuse. Ho, Guildenstern!

> *Enter Rosencrantz and Guildenstern.*

Friends both, go join you with some further aid:
Hamlet in madness hath Polonius slain,
And from his mother's closet hath he dragged him.   35
Go seek him out; speak fair, and bring the body
Into the chapel. I pray you haste in this.
          [*Exeunt Rosencrantz and Guildenstern.*]
Come, Gertrude, we'll call up our wisest friends
And let them know both what we mean to do
And what's untimely done . . .°   40
Whose whisper o'er the world's diameter,
As level as the cannon to his blank°
Transports his poisoned shot, may miss our name
And hit the woundless° air. O, come away!
My soul is full of discord and dismay.   *Exeunt.*   45

---

18 **out of haunt** away from association with others   25–26 **ore/Among
a mineral** vein of gold in a mine   40 **done** . . . (evidently something has
dropped out of the text. Capell's conjecture, "So, haply slander," is usually printed)   42 **blank** white center of a target   44 **woundless** invulnerable

[Scene 2. *The castle.*]

Enter Hamlet.

Hamlet. Safely stowed.

Gentlemen. (Within) Hamlet! Lord Hamlet!

Hamlet. But soft, what noise? Who calls on Hamlet?
O, here they come.

Enter Rosencrantz and Guildenstern.

Rosencrantz. What have you done, my lord, with the
5   dead body?

Hamlet. Compounded it with dust, whereto 'tis kin.

Rosencrantz. Tell us where 'tis, that we may take it
thence
And bear it to the chapel.

Hamlet. Do not believe it.

10 *Rosencrantz.* Believe what?

Hamlet. That I can keep your counsel and not mine
own. Besides, to be demanded of° a sponge, what
replication° should be made by the son of a king?

Rosencrantz. Take you me for a sponge, my lord?

15 *Hamlet.* Ay, sir, that soaks up the King's countenance,°
his rewards, his authorities. But such officers do the
King best service in the end. He keeps them, like an
ape, in the corner of his jaw, first mouthed, to be
last swallowed. When he needs what you have
20 gleaned, it is but squeezing you and, sponge, you
shall be dry again.

Rosencrantz. I understand you not, my lord.

Hamlet. I am glad of it: a knavish speech sleeps in a
foolish ear.

4.2.12 **demanded of** questioned by   13 **replication** reply   15 **countenance** favor

Rosencrantz. My lord, you must tell us where the body   25
   is and go with us to the King.

Hamlet. The body is with the King, but the King is not
   with the body.° The King is a thing——

Guildenstern. A thing, my lord?

Hamlet. Of nothing. Bring me to him. Hide fox, and   30
   all after.°   *Exeunt.*

[Scene 3. *The castle.*]

Enter King, and two or three.

King. I have sent to seek him and to find the body:
   How dangerous is it that this man goes loose!
   Yet must not we put the strong law on him:
   He's loved of the distracted° multitude,
   Who like not in their judgment, but their eyes,
   And where 'tis so, th' offender's scourge is weighed,
   But never the offense. To bear° all smooth and even,   5
   This sudden sending him away must seem
   Deliberate pause.° Diseases desperate grown
   By desperate appliance are relieved,
   Or not at all.

   Enter Rosencrantz, [Guildenstern,] and all the rest.   10

               How now? What hath befall'n?

Rosencrantz. Where the dead body is bestowed, my
   lord,
   We cannot get from him.

King.   But where is he?

Rosencrantz. Without, my lord; guarded, to know your
   pleasure.

27–28 **The body . . . the body** (an allusion to a contemporary theory of
kingship that distinguished between the king's two bodies, the Body
Natural and the Body Politic. The king [Claudius] has a body, but the
Body Politic [the kingship of Denmark] is not inherent in that body)
30–31 **Hide fox, and all after** (a cry in a game such as hide-
and-seek; Hamlet runs from the stage) 4.3.4 **distracted** bewildered,
senseless   7 **bear** carry out   9 **pause** planning

King. Bring him before us.

15 *Rosencrantz.*   Ho! Bring in the lord.

                    They enter.

King. Now, Hamlet, where's Polonius?

Hamlet. At supper.

King. At supper? Where?

Hamlet. Not where he eats, but where 'a is eaten. A
20   certain convocation of politic° worms are e'en at
    him. Your worm is your only emperor for diet. We
    fat all creatures else to fat us, and we fat ourselves
    for maggots. Your fat king and your lean beggar is
    but variable service°—two dishes, but to one table.
25   That's the end.

King. Alas, alas!

Hamlet. A man may fish with the worm that hath eat of
    a king, and eat of the fish that hath fed of that worm.

King. What dost thou mean by this?

30 *Hamlet.* Nothing but to show you how a king may
    go a progress° through the guts of a beggar.

King. Where is Polonius?

Hamlet. In heaven. Send thither to see. If your mes-
    senger find him not there, seek him i' th' other
35   place yourself. But if indeed you find him not
    within this month, you shall nose him as you go
    up the stairs into the lobby.

King. [*To Attendants*] Go seek him there.

Hamlet. 'A will stay till you come.

                    [*Exeunt Attendants.*]

40 *King.* Hamlet, this deed, for thine especial safety,
    Which we do tender° as we dearly grieve
    For that which thou hast done, must send thee hence
    With fiery quickness. Therefore prepare thyself.

---

20 **politic** statesmanlike, shrewd   24 **variable service** different courses
31 **progress** royal journey   41 **tender** hold dear

The bark is ready and the wind at help,
Th' associates tend,° and everything is bent   *45*
For England.

Hamlet.   For England?

King. .   Ay, Hamlet.

Hamlet.   Good.

King. So is it, if thou knew'st our purposes.

Hamlet. I see a cherub° that sees them. But come, for
England! Farewell, dear Mother.

King. Thy loving father, Hamlet.   *50*

Hamlet. My mother—father and mother is man and
wife, man and wife is one flesh, and so, my mother.
Come, for England!   *Exit.*

King. Follow him at foot;° tempt him with speed
aboard.
Delay it not; I'll have him hence tonight.   *55*
Away! For everything is sealed and done
That else leans° on th' affair. Pray you make haste.
                    [*Exeunt all but the King.*]
And, England, if my love thou hold'st at aught—
As my great power thereof may give thee sense,
Since yet thy cicatrice° looks raw and red   *60*
After the Danish sword, and thy free awe°
Pays homage to us—thou mayst not coldly set
Our sovereign process,° which imports at full
By letters congruing to that effect
The present° death of Hamlet. Do it, England,   *65*
For like the hectic° in my blood he rages,
And thou must cure me. Till I know 'tis done,
Howe'er my haps,° my joys were ne'er begun.
                                        Exit.

45 **tend** wait 48 **cherub** angel of knowledge 54 **at foot** closely
57 **leans** depends 60 **cicatrice** scar 61 **free awe** uncompelled sub-
mis-sion 62–63 **coldly set/Our sovereign process** regard slightly
our royal command 65 **present** instant 66 **hectic** fever 68 **haps**
chances, fortunes

[Scene 4. *A plain in Denmark.*]

Enter Fortinbras with his Army over the stage.

Fortinbras. Go, Captain, from me greet the Danish
    king.
  Tell him that by his license Fortinbras
  Craves the conveyance of° a promised march
  Over his kingdom. You know the rendezvous.
5 If that his Majesty would aught with us,
  We shall express our duty in his eye;°
  And let him know so.

Captain.   I will do't, my lord.

Fortinbras. Go softly° on.

                 [*Exeunt all but the Captain.*]
      Enter Hamlet, Rosencrantz, &c.

Hamlet. Good sir, whose powers° are these?

10 *Captain.* They are of Norway, sir.

Hamlet. How purposed, sir, I pray you?

Captain. Against some part of Poland.

Hamlet. Who commands them, sir?

Captain. The nephew to old Norway, Fortinbras.

15 *Hamlet.* Goes it against the main° of Poland, sir,
  Or for some frontier?

Captain. Truly to speak, and with no addition,°
  We go to gain a little patch of ground
  That hath in it no profit but the name.
20 To pay five ducats, five, I would not farm it,
  Nor will it yield to Norway or the Pole
  A ranker° rate, should it be sold in fee.°

4.4.3 **conveyance of** escort for 6 **in his eye** before his eyes (i.e., in his
presence) 8 **softly** slowly 9 **powers** forces 15 **main** main part 17
with no addition plainly 22 **ranker** higher 22 **in fee** out-right

Hamlet. Why, then the Polack never will defend it.

Captain. Yes, it is already garrisoned.

Hamlet. Two thousand souls and twenty thousand
 ducats   25
 Will not debate° the question of this straw.
 This is th' imposthume° of much wealth and peace,
 That inward breaks, and shows no cause without
 Why the man dies. I humbly thank you, sir.

Captain. God bye you, sir.   [*Exit.*]

Rosencrantz.   Will't please you go, my lord? 30

Hamlet. I'll be with you straight. Go a little before.
         [*Exeunt all but Hamlet.*]
 How all occasions do inform against me
 And spur my dull revenge! What is a man,
 If his chief good and market° of his time
 Be but to sleep and feed? A beast, no more. 35
 Sure he that made us with such large discourse,°
 Looking before and after, gave us not
 That capability and godlike reason
 To fust° in us unused. Now, whether it be
 Bestial oblivion,° or some craven scruple 40
 Of thinking too precisely on th' event°—
 A thought which, quartered, hath but one part wis-
  dom
 And ever three parts coward—I do not know
 Why yet I live to say, "This thing's to do,"
 Sith I have cause, and will, and strength, and means 45
 To do't. Examples gross° as earth exhort me.
 Witness this army of such mass and charge,°
 Led by a delicate and tender prince,
 Whose spirit, with divine ambition puffed,
 Makes mouths at the invisible event,° 50
 Exposing what is mortal and unsure
 To all that fortune, death, and danger dare,

---

26 **debate** settle   27 **imposthume** abscess, ulcer   34 **market** profit
36 **discourse** understanding   39 **fust** grow moldy   40 **oblivion** forgetfulness   41 **event** outcome   46 **gross** large, obvious   47 **charge** expense   50 **Makes mouths at the invisible event** makes scornful faces
(is contemptuous of) the unseen outcome

Even for an eggshell. Rightly to be great
Is not° to stir without great argument,°
55   But greatly° to find quarrel in a straw
When honor's at the stake. How stand I then,
That have a father killed, a mother stained,
Excitements° of my reason and my blood,
And let all sleep, while to my shame I see
60   The imminent death of twenty thousand men
That for a fantasy and trick of fame°
Go to their graves like beds, fight for a plot
Whereon the numbers cannot try the cause,
Which is not tomb enough and continent°
65   To hide the slain? O, from this time forth,
My thoughts be bloody, or be nothing worth!   *Exit.*

[Scene 5. *The castle.*]

Enter Horatio, [Queen] Gertrude, and a Gentleman.

Queen. I will not speak with her.

Gentleman. She is importunate, indeed distract.
Her mood will needs be pitied.

Queen.   What would she have?

Gentleman. She speaks much of her father, says she
hears
There's tricks i' th' world, and hems, and beats her
5   heart,
Spurns enviously at straws,° speaks things in doubt°
That carry but half sense. Her speech is nothing,
Yet the unshapèd use of it doth move

---

54 **not** (the sense seems to require "not not")   54 **argument** reason
55 **greatly** i.e., nobly   58 **Excitements** incentives   61 **fantasy and
trick of fame** illusion and trifle of reputation   64 **continent** receptacle,
container   4.5.6 **Spurns enviously at straws** objects spitefully to in-
significant matters   6 **in doubt** uncertainly

The hearers to collection;° they yawn° at it,
And botch the words up fit to their own thoughts,   10
Which, as her winks and nods and gestures yield
    them,
Indeed would make one think there might be
    thought,
Though nothing sure, yet much unhappily.

Horatio. 'Twere good she were spoken with, for she
    may strew
Dangerous conjectures in ill-breeding minds.   15

Queen. Let her come in.   [*Exit Gentleman.*]
    [*Aside*] To my sick soul (as sin's true nature is)
Each toy seems prologue to some great amiss;°
So full of artless jealousy° is guilt
It spills° itself in fearing to be spilt.   20

          Enter Ophelia [*distracted.*]°

Ophelia. Where is the beauteous majesty of Denmark?

Queen. How now, Ophelia?

Ophelia. (*She sings.*) How should I your truelove know
                    From another one?
                By his cockle hat° and staff   25
                    And his sandal shoon.°

Queen. Alas, sweet lady, what imports this song?

Ophelia. Say you? Nay, pray you mark.
                He is dead and gone, lady,   (*Song*)
                He is dead and gone;   30
                At his head a grass-green turf,
                    At his heels a stone.
    O, ho!

Queen. Nay, but Ophelia——

Ophelia. Pray you mark.   35

8–9 **Yet the . . . to collection** i.e., yet the formless manner of it moves her
listeners to gather up some sort of meaning 9 **yawn** gape (?) 18 **amiss**
misfortune 19 **artless jealousy** crude suspicion 20 **spills** destroys 20
s.d. the First Quarto says "Enter Ophelia playing on a lute, and her hair
down, singing." 25 **cockle hat** (a cockleshell on the hat was the sign of
a pilgrim who had journeyed to shrines overseas. The association of
lovers and pilgrims was a common one) 26 **shoon** shoes

[*Sings.*] White his shroud as the mountain snow——

Enter King.

Queen. Alas, look here, my lord.

Ophelia.   Larded° all with sweet flowers (*Song*)
                Which bewept to the grave did not go
40   With truelove showers.

King. How do you, pretty lady?

Ophelia. Well, God dild° you! They say the owl was a
  baker's daughter.° Lord, we know what we are, but
  know not what we may be. God be at your table!

45 *King.* Conceit° upon her father.

Ophelia. Pray let's have no words of this, but when
  they ask you what it means, say you this:
                Tomorrow is Saint Valentine's day.° (*Song*)
                All in the morning betime,
50   And I a maid at your window,
                To be your Valentine.

                Then up he rose and donned his clothes
                And dupped° the chamber door,
                Let in the maid, that out a maid
55   Never departed more.

King. Pretty Ophelia.

Ophelia. Indeed, la, without an oath, I'll make an end
  on't:
                [*Sings.*] By Gis° and by Saint Charity,
                Alack, and fie for shame!
60   Young men will do't if they come to't,
                By Cock,° they are to blame.
                Quoth she, "Before you tumbled me,
                You promised me to wed."

---

38 **Larded** decorated   42 **dild** yield, i.e., reward   43 **baker's daughter** (an allusion to a tale of a baker's daughter who begrudged bread to
Christ and was turned into an owl)   45 **Conceit** brooding   48 **Saint
Valentine's day** Feb. 14 (the notion was that a bachelor would become
the truelove of the first girl he saw on this day)   53 **dupped** opened (did
up)   58 **Gis** (contraction of "Jesus")   61 **Cock** (1) God (2) phallus

He answers:

> "So would I 'a' done, by yonder sun,   65
>   An thou hadst not come to my bed."

King. How long hath she been thus?

Ophelia. I hope all will be well. We must be patient, but I cannot choose but weep to think they would lay him i' th' cold ground. My brother shall know   70 of it; and so I thank you for your good counsel. Come, my coach! Good night, ladies, good night. Sweet ladies, good night, good night.   *Exit.*

King. Follow her close; give her good watch, I pray you.   [*Exit Horatio.*]

O, this is the poison of deep grief; it springs   75
All from her father's death—and now behold!
O Gertrude, Gertrude,
When sorrows come, they come not single spies,
But in battalions: first, her father slain;
Next, your son gone, and he most violent author   80
Of his own just remove; the people muddied,°
Thick and unwholesome in their thoughts and whispers
For good Polonius' death, and we have done but greenly°
In huggermugger° to inter him; poor Ophelia
Divided from herself and her fair judgment,   85
Without the which we are pictures or mere beasts;
Last, and as much containing as all these,
Her brother is in secret come from France,
Feeds on his wonder,° keeps himself in clouds,
And wants not buzzers° to infect his ear   90
With pestilent speeches of his father's death,
Wherein necessity, of matter beggared,°
Will nothing stick° our person to arraign
In ear and ear. O my dear Gertrude, this,

---

81 **muddied** muddled   83 **greenly** foolishly   84 **huggermugger** secret haste   89 **wonder** suspicion   90 **wants not buzzers** does not lack tale-bearers   92 **of matter beggared** unprovided with facts   93 **Will nothing stick** will not hesitate

95 Like to a murd'ring piece,° in many places
Gives me superfluous death.   *A noise within.*

Enter a Messenger.

Queen.   Alack, what noise is this?

King. Attend, where are my Switzers?° Let them
     guard the door.
What is the matter?

Messenger.   Save yourself, my lord.
The ocean, overpeering of his list,°
100 Eats not the flats with more impiteous haste
Than young Laertes, in a riotous head,°
O'erbears your officers. The rabble call him lord,
And, as the world were now but to begin,
Antiquity forgot, custom not known,
105 The ratifiers and props of every word,
They cry, "Choose we! Laertes shall be king!"
Caps, hands, and tongues applaud it to the clouds,
"Laertes shall be king! Laertes king!" *A noise within.*

Queen. How cheerfully on the false trail they cry!
110 O, this is counter,° you false Danish dogs!

Enter Laertes with others.

King. The doors are broke.

Laertes. Where is this king?—Sirs, stand you all
     without.

All. No, let's come in.

Laertes.   I pray you give me leave.

All. We will, we will.

Laertes. I thank you. Keep the door. [*Exeunt his
115   Followers.*] O thou vile King,
Give me my father.

Queen.   Calmly, good Laertes.

---

95 murd'ring piece (a cannon that shot a kind of shrapnel)   97
Switzers Swiss guards   **99 list** shore   **101 in a riotous head** with a rebellious force   **110 counter** (a hound runs counter when he follows the
scent backward from the prey)

Laertes. That drop of blood that's calm proclaims me
    bastard,
    Cries cuckold° to my father, brands the harlot
    Even here between the chaste unsmirchèd brow
    Of my true mother.

King.   What is the cause, Laertes,   *120*
    That thy rebellion looks so giantlike?
    Let him go, Gertrude. Do not fear° our person.
    There's such divinity doth hedge a king
    That treason can but peep to° what it would,
    Acts little of his will. Tell me, Laertes,   *125*
    Why thou art thus incensed. Let him go, Gertrude.
    Speak, man.

Laertes. Where is my father?

King.   Dead.

Queen.   But not by him.

King. Let him demand his fill.

Laertes. How came he dead? I'll not be juggled with.   *130*
    To hell allegiance, vows to the blackest devil,
    Conscience and grace to the profoundest pit!
    I dare damnation. To this point I stand,
    That both the worlds I give to negligence,°
    Let come what comes, only I'll be revenged   *135*
    Most throughly for my father.

King.   Who shall stay you?

Laertes. My will, not all the world's.
    And for my means, I'll husband them° so well
    They shall go far with little.

King.   Good Laertes,
    If you desire to know the certainty   *140*
    Of your dear father, is't writ in your revenge
    That swoopstake° you will draw both friend and foe,
    Winner and loser?

---

118 **cuckold** man whose wife is unfaithful   112 **fear** fear for   124
peep to i.e., look at from a distance   134 **That both ... to negligence**
i.e., I care not what may happen (to me) in this world or the next
138 **husband them** use them economically   142 **swoopstake** in a clean
sweep

Laertes. None but his enemies.

King.   Will you know them then?

Laertes. To his good friends thus wide I'll ope my
145   arms
And like the kind life-rend'ring pelican°
Repast° them with my blood.

King.   Why, now you speak
Like a good child and a true gentleman.
That I am guiltless of your father's death,
150 And am most sensibly° in grief for it,
It shall as level to your judgment 'pear
As day does to your eye.
         A noise within: "Let her come in."

Laertes. How now? What noise is that?

         Enter Ophelia.

O heat, dry up my brains; tears seven times salt
155 Burn out the sense and virtue° of mine eye!
By heaven, thy madness shall be paid with weight
Till our scale turn the beam.° O rose of May,
Dear maid, kind sister, sweet Ophelia!
O heavens, is't possible a young maid's wits
160 Should be as mortal as an old man's life?
Nature is fine° in love, and where 'tis fine,
It sends some precious instance° of itself
After the thing it loves.

Ophelia. They bore him barefaced on the bier (*Song*)
165   Hey non nony, nony, hey nony
          And in his grave rained many a tear——
Fare you well, my dove!

Laertes. Hadst thou thy wits, and didst persuade re-
      venge,
It could not move thus.

170 *Ophelia.* You must sing "A-down a-down, and you call

---

146 **pelican** (thought to feed its young with its own blood)   147 **Repast**
feed 150 **sensibly** acutely 155 **virtue** power 157 **turn the beam**
weigh down the bar (of the balance) 161 **fine** refined, delicate
162 **instance** sample

him a-down-a." O, how the wheel° becomes it! It is
the false steward, that stole his master's daughter.

Laertes. This nothing's more than matter.°

Ophelia. There's rosemary, that's for remembrance.
Pray you, love, remember. And there is pansies, 175
that's for thoughts.

Laertes. A document° in madness, thoughts and remembrance fitted.

Ophelia. There's fennel° for you, and columbines.
There's rue for you, and here's some for me. We 180
may call it herb of grace o' Sundays. O, you must
wear your rue with a difference. There's a daisy. I
would give you some violets, but they withered all
when my father died. They say 'a made a good end.
[*Sings*]   For bonny sweet Robin is all my joy. 185

Laertes. Thought and affliction, passion, hell itself,
She turns to favor° and to prettiness.

Ophelia.   And will 'a not come again?   (*Song*)
                  And will 'a not come again?
                      No, no, he is dead, 190
                      Go to thy deathbed,
                  He never will come again.

                  His beard was as white as snow,
                  All flaxen was his poll.°
                      He is gone, he is gone, 195
                      And we cast away moan.
                  God 'a' mercy on his soul!
And of all Christian souls, I pray God. God bye you.
                                              [*Exit.*]

171 **wheel** (of uncertain meaning, but probably a turn or dance of Ophelia's, rather than Fortune's wheel)   173 **This nothing's more than
matter** this nonsense has more meaning than matters of consequence   177 **document** lesson   179 **fennel** (the distribution of flowers
in the ensuing lines has symbolic meaning, but the meaning is disputed.
Perhaps **fennel,** flattery; **columbines,** cuckoldry; **rue,** sorrow for Ophelia and repentance for the Queen; **daisy,** dissembling; **violets,** faithful-
ness. For other interpretations, see J. W. Lever in *Review of English
Studies,* New Series 3 [1952], pp. 123–29)   187 **favor** charm, beauty
194 **All flaxen was his poll** white as flax was his head

    Laertes. Do you see this, O God?

200 *King.* Laertes, I must commune with your grief,
     Or you deny me right. Go but apart,
     Make choice of whom your wisest friends you will,
     And they shall hear and judge 'twixt you and me.
     If by direct or by collateral° hand
205   They find us touched,° we will our kingdom give,
     Our crown, our life, and all that we call ours,
     To you in satisfaction; but if not,
     Be you content to lend your patience to us,
     And we shall jointly labor with your soul
     To give it due content.

210 *Laertes.*   Let this be so.
     His means of death, his obscure funeral—
     No trophy, sword, nor hatchment° o'er his bones,
     No noble rite nor formal ostentation°—
     Cry to be heard, as 'twere from heaven to earth,
     That I must call't in question.

215 *King.*   So you shall;
     And where th' offense is, let the great ax fall.
     I pray you go with me.   *Exeunt.*

[Scene 6. *The castle.*]

Enter Horatio and others.

Horatio. What are they that would speak with me?

Gentleman. Seafaring men, sir. They say they have
    letters for you.

Horatio. Let them come in.   [*Exit Attendant.*]
5   I do not know from what part of the world
     I should be greeted, if not from Lord Hamlet.

---

204 **collateral** indirect   205 **touched** implicated   212 **hatchment** tablet bearing the coat of arms of the dead   213 **ostentation** ceremony

Enter Sailors.

Sailor. God bless you, sir.

Horatio. Let Him bless thee too.

Sailor. 'A shall, sir, an't please Him. There's a letter
for you, sir—it came from th' ambassador that was   10
bound for England—if your name be Horatio, as
I am let to know it is.

Horatio. [*Reads the letter.*] "Horatio, when thou shalt
have overlooked° this, give these fellows some
means to the King. They have letters for him. Ere   15
we were two days old at sea, a pirate of very warlike
appointment° gave us chase. Finding ourselves too
slow of sail, we put on a compelled valor, and in
the grapple I boarded them. On the instant they
got clear of our ship; so I alone became their   20
prisoner. They have dealt with me like thieves of
mercy, but they knew what they did: I am to do a
good turn for them. Let the King have the letters
I have sent, and repair thou to me with as much
speed as thou wouldest fly death. I have words to   25
speak in thine ear will make thee dumb; yet are they
much too light for the bore° of the matter. These
good fellows will bring thee where I am. Rosencrantz and Guildenstern hold their course for England. Of them I have much to tell thee. Farewell.   30
              He that thou knowest thine, HAMLET."
Come, I will give you way for these your letters,
And do't the speedier that you may direct me
To him from whom you brought them.   *Exeunt.*

4.6.14 **overlooked** surveyed   17 **appointment** equipment   27 **bore**
caliber (here, "importance")

[Scene 7. *The castle.*]

Enter King and Laertes.

King. Now must your conscience my acquittance seal,
And you must put me in your heart for friend,
Sith you have heard, and with a knowing ear,
That he which hath your noble father slain
Pursued my life.

5 *Laertes.*   It well appears. But tell me
Why you proceeded not against these feats
So criminal and so capital° in nature,
As by your safety, greatness, wisdom, all things else,
You mainly° were stirred up.

King.   O, for two special reasons,
10 Which may to you perhaps seem much unsinewed,°
But yet to me they're strong. The Queen his mother
Lives almost by his looks, and for myself—
My virtue or my plague, be it either which—
She is so conjunctive° to my life and soul,
15 That, as the star moves not but in his sphere,
I could not but by her. The other motive
Why to a public count° I might not go
Is the great love the general gender° bear him,
Who, dipping all his faults in their affection,
20 Would, like the spring that turneth wood to stone,°
Convert his gyves° to graces; so that my arrows,
Too slightly timbered° for so loud a wind,
Would have reverted to my bow again,
And not where I had aimed them.

4.7.7 **capital** deserving death   9 **mainly** powerfully   10 **unsinewed** weak   14 **conjunctive** closely united   17 **count** reckoning   18 **general gender** common people   20 **spring that turneth wood to stone** (a spring in Shakespeare's county was so charged with lime that it would petrify wood placed in it)   21 **gyves** fetters; G.R. Hibbard's emendation to *guilts* is attractive   22 **timbered** shafted

Laertes. And so have I a noble father lost,   25
   A sister driven into desp'rate terms,°
   Whose worth, if praises may go back again,°
   Stood challenger on mount of all the age
   For her perfections. But my revenge will come.

King. Break not your sleeps for that. You must not
   think   30
   That we are made of stuff so flat and dull
   That we can let our beard be shook with danger,
   And think it pastime. You shortly shall hear more.
   I loved your father, and we love ourself,
   And that, I hope, will teach you to imagine——   35

       Enter a Messenger with letters.

   How now? What news?

Messenger.   Letters, my lord, from Hamlet:
   These to your Majesty; this to the Queen.

King. From Hamlet? Who brought them?

Messenger. Sailors, my lord, they say; I saw them not.
   They were given me by Claudio; he received them   40
   Of him that brought them.

King.   Laertes, you shall hear them.—
   Leave us.   *Exit Messenger.*
   [*Reads.*] "High and mighty, you shall know I am set
   naked° on your kingdom. Tomorrow shall I beg
   leave to see your kingly eyes; when I shall (first   45
   asking your pardon thereunto) recount the occasion
   of my sudden and more strange return.

                         HAMLET."
   What should this mean? Are all the rest come back?
   Or is it some abuse,° and no such thing?   50

Laertes. Know you the hand?

King.   'Tis Hamlet's character.° "Naked"!

---

26 **terms** conditions   27 **go back again** revert to what is past   44
naked destitute   50 **abuse** deception   51 **character** handwriting

And in a postscript here, he says "alone."
Can you devise° me?

Laertes. I am lost in it, my lord. But let him come.
55   It warms the very sickness in my heart
That I shall live and tell him to his teeth,
"Thus did'st thou."

King.   If it be so, Laertes
(As how should it be so? How otherwise?),
Will you be ruled by me?

Laertes.   Ay, my lord,
60   So you will not o'errule me to a peace.

King. To thine own peace. If he be now returned,
As checking at° his voyage, and that he means
No more to undertake it, I will work him
To an exploit now ripe in my device,
65   Under the which he shall not choose but fall;
And for his death no wind of blame shall breathe,
But even his mother shall uncharge the practice°
And call it accident.

Laertes.   My lord, I will be ruled;
The rather if you could devise it so
That I might be the organ.

70 *King.*   It falls right.
You have been talked of since your travel much,
And that in Hamlet's hearing, for a quality
Wherein they say you shine. Your sum of parts
Did not together pluck such envy from him
75   As did that one, and that, in my regard,
Of the unworthiest siege.°

Laertes.   What part is that, my lord?

King. A very riband in the cap of youth,
Yet needful too, for youth no less becomes
The light and careless livery that it wears
80   Than settled age his sables and his weeds,°
Importing health and graveness. Two months since

---

53 **devise** advise   62 **checking at** turning away from (a term in falconry)   67 **uncharge the practice** not charge the device with treachery
76 **siege** rank   80 **sables and his weeds** i.e., sober attire

Here was a gentleman of Normandy.
I have seen myself, and served against, the French,
And they can° well on horseback, but this gallant
Had witchcraft in't. He grew unto his seat,   *85*
And to such wondrous doing brought his horse
As had he been incorpsed and deminatured
With the brave beast. So far he topped my thought
That I, in forgery° of shapes and tricks,
Come short of what he did.

Laertes.   A Norman was't?   *90*

King. A Norman.

Laertes. Upon my life, Lamord.°

King.   The very same.

Laertes. I know him well. He is the brooch° indeed
   And gem of all the nation.

King. He made confession° of you,   *95*
   And gave you such a masterly report,
   For art and exercise in your defense,
   And for your rapier most especial,
   That he cried out 'twould be a sight indeed
   If one could match you. The scrimers° of their
      nation   *100*
   He swore had neither motion, guard, nor eye,
   If you opposed them. Sir, this report of his
   Did Hamlet so envenom with his envy
   That he could nothing do but wish and beg
   Your sudden coming o'er to play with you.   *105*
   Now, out of this——

Laertes.   What out of this, my lord?

King. Laertes, was your father dear to you?
   Or are you like the painting of a sorrow,
   A face without a heart?

Laertes.   Why ask you this?

King. Not that I think you did not love your father,   *110*

84 **can** do   89 **forgery** invention   92 **Lamord** (the name suggests *la mort*, i.e. death [French])   93 **brooch** ornament   95 **confession** report 100 **scrimers** fencers

But that I know love is begun by time,
And that I see, in passages of proof,°
Time qualifies° the spark and fire of it.
There lives within the very flame of love

115 A kind of wick or snuff° that will abate it,
And nothing is at a like goodness still,°
For goodness, growing to a plurisy,°
Dies in his own too-much. That we would do
We should do when we would, for this "would" changes,

120 And hath abatements and delays as many
As there are tongues, are hands, are accidents,
And then this "should" is like a spendthrift sigh,°
That hurts by easing. But to the quick° of th' ulcer—
Hamlet comes back; what would you undertake

125 To show yourself in deed your father's son
More than in words?

Laertes.   To cut his throat i' th' church!

King. No place indeed should murder sanctuarize;°
Revenge should have no bounds. But, good Laertes,
Will you do this? Keep close within your chamber.

130 Hamlet returned shall know you are come home.
We'll put on those° shall praise your excellence
And set a double varnish on the fame
The Frenchman gave you, bring you in fine° together
And wager on your heads. He, being remiss,

135 Most generous, and free from all contriving,
Will not peruse the foils, so that with ease,
Or with a little shuffling, you may choose
A sword unbated,° and, in a pass of practice,°
Requite him for your father.

Laertes.   I will do't,

112 **passages of proof** proved cases   113 **qualifies** diminishes   115 **snuff** residue of burnt wick (which dims the light)   116 **still** always   117 **plurisy** fullness. excess   122 **spendthrift sigh** (sighing provides ease, but because it was thought to thin the blood and so shorten life it was spendthrift)   123 **quick** sensitive flesh   127 **sanctuarize** protect   131 **We'll put on those** we'll incite persons who   133 **in fine** finally   138 **unbated** not blunted   138 **pass of practice** treacherous thrust

And for that purpose I'll anoint my sword.   *140*
I bought an unction of a mountebank,°
So mortal that, but dip a knife in it,
Where it draws blood, no cataplasm° so rare,
Collected from all simples° that have virtue°
Under the moon, can save the thing from death   *145*
That is but scratched withal. I'll touch my point
With this contagion, that, if I gall him slightly,
It may be death.

King.   Let's further think of this,
Weigh what convenience both of time and means
May fit us to our shape.° If this should fail,   *150*
And that our drift look through° our bad per-
          formance,
'Twere better not assayed. Therefore this project
Should have a back or second, that might hold
If this did blast in proof.° Soft, let me see.
We'll make a solemn wager on your cunnings—   *155*
I ha't!
When in your motion you are hot and dry—
As make your bouts more violent to that end—
And that he calls for drink, I'll have prepared him
A chalice for the nonce,° whereon but sipping,   *160*
If he by chance escape your venomed stuck,°
Our purpose may hold there.—But stay, what noise?

                Enter Queen.

Queen. One woe doth tread upon another's heel.
So fast they follow. Your sister's drowned, Laertes.

Laertes. Drowned! O, where?   *165*

Queen. There is a willow grows askant° the brook,
That shows his hoar° leaves in the glassy stream:
Therewith° fantastic garlands did she make
Of crowflowers, nettles, daisies, and long purples,

---

141 **mountebank** quack   143 **cataplasm** poultice   144 **simples** medicinal herbs   144 **virtue power** (to heal)   150 **shape** role   151 **drift look through** purpose show through   154 **blast in proof** burst (fail) in performance   160 **nonce** occasion   161 **stuck** thrust   166 **askant** aslant   167 **hoar** silver-gray   168 **Therewith** i.e., with willow twigs

170   That liberal° shepherds give a grosser name,
        But our cold maids do dead men's fingers call them.
        There on the pendent boughs her crownet° weeds
        Clamb'ring to hang, an envious sliver° broke,
        When down her weedy trophies and herself
175   Fell in the weeping brook. Her clothes spread wide,
        And mermaidlike awhile they bore her up,
        Which time she chanted snatches of old lauds,°
        As one incapable° of her own distress,
        Or like a creature native and indued°
180   Unto that element. But long it could not be
        Till that her garments, heavy with their drink,
        Pulled the poor wretch from her melodious lay
        To muddy death.

   Laertes.   Alas, then she is drowned?

   Queen. Drowned, drowned.

185   *Laertes.* Too much of water hast thou, poor Ophelia,
        And therefore I forbid my tears; but yet
        It is our trick;° nature her custom holds,
        Let shame say what it will: when these° are gone,
        The woman° will be out. Adieu, my lord.
190   I have a speech o' fire, that fain would blaze,
        But that this folly drowns it.   *Exit.*

   King.   Let's follow, Gertrude.
        How much I had to do to calm his rage!
        Now fear I this will give it start again;
        Therefore let's follow.   *Exeunt.*

---

170 **liberal** free-spoken, coarse-mouthed   172 **crownet** coronet   173
envious sliver malicious branch   177 **lauds** hymns   178 **incapable** un-
aware   179 **indued** in harmony with   187 **trick** trait, way   188 **these**
the tears he is shedding   189 **woman** i.e., womanly part of me

[ACT 5

Scene 1. *A churchyard.*]

Enter two Clowns.°

Clown. Is she to be buried in Christian burial when she willfully seeks her own salvation?

Other. I tell thee she is. Therefore make her grave straight.° The crowner° hath sate on her, and finds it Christian burial.   5

Clown. How can that be, unless she drowned herself in her own defense?

Other. Why, 'tis found so.

Clown. It must be *se offendendo*;° it cannot be else. For here lies the point: if I drown myself wittingly, 10 it argues an act, and an act hath three branches— it is to act, to do, to perform. Argal,° she drowned herself wittingly.

Other. Nay, but hear you, Goodman Delver.

Clown. Give me leave. Here lies the water—good. 15 Here stands the man—good. If the man go to this water and drown himself, it is, will he nill he,° he goes; mark you that. But if the water come to him and drown him, he drowns not himself. Argal, he

---

5.1.s.d. **Clowns** rustics (the first clown is a grave-digger) 4 **straight** straightway 4 **crowner** coroner 9 **se offendendo** (blunder for *se defendendo,* a legal term meaning "in self-defense") 12 **Argal** (blunder for Latin *ergo,* "therefore") 17 **will he nill he** will he or will he not (whether he will or will not)

119

20   that is not guilty of his own death, shortens not his
      own life.

Other. But is this law?

Clown. Ay marry, is't—crowner's quest° law.

Other. Will you ha' the truth on't? If this had not been
25   a gentlewoman, she should have been buried out
      o' Christian burial.

Clown. Why, there thou say'st. And the more pity
      that great folk should have count'nance° in this
      world to drown or hang themselves more than their
30   even-Christen.° Come, my spade. There is no an-
      cient gentlemen but gard'ners, ditchers, and grave-
      makers. They hold up° Adam's profession.

Other. Was he a gentleman?

Clown. 'A was the first that ever bore arms.°

35 *Other.* Why, he had none.

Clown. What, art a heathen? How dost thou under-
      stand the Scripture? The Scripture says Adam
      digged. Could he dig without arms? I'll put another
      question to thee. If thou answerest me not to the
40   purpose, confess thyself——

Other. Go to.

Clown. What is he that builds stronger than either the
      mason, the shipwright, or the carpenter?

Other. The gallowsmaker, for that frame outlives a
45   thousand tenants.

Clown. I like thy wit well, in good faith. The gallows
      does well. But how does it well? It does well to those
      that do ill. Now thou dost ill to say the gallows
      is built stronger than the church. Argal, the gallows
50   may do well to thee. To't again, come.

Other. Who builds stronger than a mason, a ship-
      wright, or a carpenter?

---

23 **quest** inquest   28 **count'nance** privilege   30 **even-Christen** fellow
Christian   32 **hold up** keep up   34 **bore arms** had a coat of arms (the
sign of a gentleman)

Clown. Ay, tell me that, and unyoke.°

Other. Marry, now I can tell.

Clown. To't.   55

Other. Mass,° I cannot tell.

       Enter Hamlet and Horatio afar off.

Clown. Cudgel thy brains no more about it, for your
  dull ass will not mend his pace with beating. And
  when you are asked this question next, say "a gravemaker." The houses he makes lasts till doomsday.   60
  Go, get thee in, and fetch me a stoup° of liquor.
                       [*Exit Other Clown.***]**

  In youth when I did love, did love,   (*Song*)
    Methought it was very sweet
  To contract—O—the time for—a—my behove,°
    O, methought there—a—was nothing—a—meet.   65

Hamlet. Has this fellow no feeling of his business? 'A
  sings in gravemaking.

Horatio. Custom hath made it in him a property of
  easiness.°

Hamlet. 'Tis e'en so. The hand of little employment   70
  hath the daintier sense.°

Clown.   But age with his stealing steps   (*Song*)
      Hath clawed me in his clutch,
    And hath shipped me into the land,
      As if I had never been such.   75
                   [*Throws up a skull.***]**

Hamlet. That skull had a tongue in it, and could sing
  once. How the knave jowls° it to the ground, as if
  'twere Cain's jawbone, that did the first murder!
  This might be the pate of a politician, which this

---

53 **unyoke** i.e., stop work for the day   56 **Mass** by the mass   61 **stoup**
tankard   64 **behove** advantage   68–69 **in him a property of easiness**
easy for him   71 **hath the daintier sense** is more sensitive (because it
is not calloused)   77 **jowls** hurls

80 ass now o'erreaches,° one that would circumvent
God, might it not?

Horatio. It might, my lord.

Hamlet. Or of a courtier, which could say "Good
morrow, sweet lord! How dost thou, sweet lord?"
85 This might be my Lord Such-a-one, that praised
my Lord Such-a-one's horse when 'a went to beg
it, might it not?

Horatio. Ay, my lord.

Hamlet. Why, e'en so, and now my Lady Worm's,
90 chapless,° and knocked about the mazzard° with a
sexton's spade. Here's fine revolution, an we had
the trick to see't. Did these bones cost no more
the breeding but to play at loggets° with them?
Mine ache to think on't.

95 *Clown.*   A pickax and a spade, a spade,   *(Song)*
             For and a shrouding sheet;
             O, a pit of clay for to be made
             For such a guest is meet.

                              [*Throws up another skull.*]

Hamlet. There's another. Why may not that be the
100 skull of a lawyer? Where be his quiddities° now, his
quillities,° his cases, his tenures,° and his tricks?
Why does he suffer this mad knave now to knock
him about the sconce° with a dirty shovel, and will
not tell him of his action of battery? Hum! This
105 fellow might be in's time a great buyer of land, with
his statutes, his recognizances, his fines,° his double
vouchers, his recoveries. Is this the fine° of his fines,
and the recovery of his recoveries, to have his fine
pate full of fine dirt? Will his vouchers vouch him

---

80 **o'erreaches** (1) reaches over (2) has the advantage over   90 **chapless** lacking the lower jaw   90 **mazzard** head   93 **loggets** (a game in
which small pieces of wood were thrown at an object)   100 **quiddities**
subtle arguments (from Latin *quidditas,* "whatness")   101 **quillities**
fine distinctions   101 **tenures** legal means of holding land   103 **sconce**
head   106 **his statutes, his recognizances, his fines** his documents
giving a creditor control of a debtor's land, his bonds of surety, his documents changing an entailed estate into fee simple (unrestricted owner-
ship)   107 **fine** end

no more of his purchases, and double ones too, than   *110*
the length and breadth of a pair of indentures?°
The very conveyances° of his lands will scarcely
lie in this box, and must th' inheritor himself have no
more, ha?

Horatio. Not a jot more, my lord.   *115*

Hamlet. Is not parchment made of sheepskins?

Horatio. Ay, my lord, and of calveskins too.

Hamlet. They are sheep and calves which seek out
assurance° in that. I will speak to this fellow. Whose
grave's this, sirrah?   *120*

Clown. Mine, sir.
    [*Sings.*]   O, a pit of clay for to be made
                  For such a guest is meet.

Hamlet. I think it be thine indeed, for thou liest in't.

Clown. You lie out on't, sir, and therefore 'tis not   *125*
yours. For my part, I do not lie in't, yet it is mine.

Hamlet. Thou dost lie in't, to be in't and say it is
thine. 'Tis for the dead, not for the quick;° therefore thou liest.

Clown. 'Tis a quick lie, sir; 'twill away again from   *130*
me to you.

Hamlet. What man dost thou dig it for?

Clown. For no man, sir.

Hamlet. What woman then?

Clown. For none neither.   *135*

Hamlet. Who is to be buried in't?

Clown. One that was a woman, sir; but, rest her soul,
she's dead.

Hamlet. How absolute° the knave is! We must speak by
the card,° or equivocation° will undo us. By the   *140*

---

111 **indentures** contracts   112 **conveyances** legal documents for the
transference of land   119 **assurance** safety   128 **quick** living
139 **absolute** positive, decided   139–40 **by the card** by the compass
card, i.e., exactly   140 **equivocation** ambiguity

Lord, Horatio, this three years I have took note of
it, the age is grown so picked° that the toe of the
peasant comes so near the heel of the courtier he
galls his kibe.° How long hast thou been a grave-
145   maker?

Clown. Of all the days i' th' year, I came to't that day
that our last king Hamlet overcame Fortinbras.

Hamlet. How long is that since?

Clown. Cannot you tell that? Every fool can tell that. It
150   was that very day that young Hamlet was born—
he that is mad, and sent into England.

Hamlet. Ay, marry, why was he sent into England?

Clown. Why, because 'a was mad. 'A shall recover his
wits there; or, if 'a do not, 'tis no great matter there.

155 *Hamlet.* Why?

Clown. 'Twill not be seen in him there. There the men
are as mad as he.

Hamlet. How came he mad?

Clown. Very strangely, they say.

160 *Hamlet.* How strangely?

Clown. Faith, e'en with losing his wits.

Hamlet. Upon what ground?

Clown. Why, here in Denmark. I have been sexton
here, man and boy, thirty years.

165 *Hamlet.* How long will a man lie i' th' earth ere he rot?

Clown. Faith, if 'a be not rotten before 'a die (as we
have many pocky corses° nowadays that will scarce
hold the laying in), 'a will last you some eight year
or nine year. A tanner will last you nine year.

170 *Hamlet.* Why he, more than another?

Clown. Why, sir, his hide is so tanned with his trade

---

142 **picked** refined   144 **kibe** sore on the back of the heel   167 **pocky
corses** bodies of persons who had been infected with the pox (syphilis)

that 'a will keep out water a great while, and your
water is a sore decayer of your whoreson dead body.
Here's a skull now hath lien you i' th' earth three and
twenty years.   *175*

Hamlet. Whose was it?

Clown. A whoreson mad fellow's it was. Whose do you
think it was?

Hamlet. Nay, I know not.

Clown. A pestilence on him for a mad rogue! 'A poured   *180*
a flagon of Rhenish on my head once. This same
skull, sir, was, sir, Yorick's skull, the King's jester.

Hamlet. This?

Clown. E'en that.

Hamlet. Let me see. [*Takes the skull.*] Alas, poor   *185*
Yorick! I knew him, Horatio, a fellow of infinite
jest, of most excellent fancy. He hath borne me on
his back a thousand times. And now how abhorred
in my imagination it is! My gorge rises at it. Here
hung those lips that I have kissed I know not how   *190*
oft. Where be your gibes now? Your gambols, your
songs, your flashes of merriment that were wont to
set the table on a roar? Not one now to mock your
own grinning? Quite chapfall'n°? Now get you to my
lady's chamber, and tell her, let her paint an inch   *195*
thick, to this favor° she must come. Make her laugh
at that. Prithee, Horatio, tell me one thing.

Horatio. What's that, my lord?

Hamlet. Dost thou think Alexander looked o' this
fashion i' th' earth?   *200*

Horatio. E'en so.

Hamlet. And smelt so? Pah!   [*Puts down the skull.*]

Horatio. E'en so, my lord.

---

194 **chapfall'n** (1) down in the mouth (2) jawless   196 **favor** facial
appearance

Hamlet. To what base uses we may return, Horatio!
205   Why may not imagination trace the noble dust of
Alexander till 'a find it stopping a bunghole?

Horatio. 'Twere to consider too curiously,° to consider
so.

Hamlet. No, faith, not a jot, but to follow him thither
210   with modesty enough,° and likelihood to lead it; as
thus: Alexander died, Alexander was buried, Alexander returneth to dust; the dust is earth; of earth
we make loam; and why of that loam whereto he was
converted might they not stop a beer barrel?
215   Imperious Caesar, dead and turned to clay,
Might stop a hole to keep the wind away.
O, that that earth which kept the world in awe
Should patch a wall t' expel the winter's flaw!°
But soft, but soft awhile! Here comes the King.

*Enter King, Queen, Laertes, and a coffin, with Lords
attendant [and a Doctor of Divinity].*

220   The Queen, the courtiers. Who is this they follow?
And with such maimèd° rites? This doth betoken
The corse they follow did with desp'rate hand
Fordo it° own life. 'Twas of some estate.°
Couch° we awhile, and mark. [*Retires with Horatio.*]

Laertes. What ceremony else?

225 *Hamlet.*   That is Laertes,
A very noble youth. Mark.

Laertes. What ceremony else?

Doctor. Her obsequies have been as far enlarged
As we have warranty. Her death was doubtful,°
230   And, but that great command o'ersways the order,
She should in ground unsanctified been lodged
Till the last trumpet. For charitable prayers,

---

207 **curiously** minutely   210 **with modesty enough** without exaggera-
tion   218 **flaw** gust   221 **maimèd** incomplete   223 **Fordo it** destroy
its   223 **estate** high rank   224 **Couch** hide   229 **doubtful** suspicious

Shards,° flints, and pebbles should be thrown on her.
Yet here she is allowed her virgin crants,°
Her maiden strewments,° and the bringing home   235
Of bell and burial.

Laertes. Must there no more be done?

Doctor.   No more be done.
We should profane the service of the dead
To sing a requiem and such rest to her
As to peace-parted souls.

Laertes.   Lay her i' th' earth,   240
And from her fair and unpolluted flesh
May violets spring! I tell thee, churlish priest,
A minist'ring angel shall my sister be
When thou liest howling!

Hamlet.   What, the fair Ophelia?

Queen. Sweets to the sweet! Farewell.   245
                           [*Scatters flowers.*]
I hoped thou shouldst have been my Hamlet's wife.
I thought thy bride bed to have decked, sweet maid,
And not have strewed thy grave.

Laertes.   O, treble woe
Fall ten times treble on that cursèd head
Whose wicked deed thy most ingenious sense°   250
Deprived thee of! Hold off the earth awhile,
Till I have caught her once more in mine arms.
                           Leaps in the grave.
Now pile your dust upon the quick and dead
Till of this flat a mountain you have made
T'o'ertop old Pelion° or the skyish head   255
Of blue Olympus.

Hamlet.   [*Coming forward*] What is he whose grief

---

233 **Shards** broken pieces of pottery   234 **crants** garlands   235 **strewments** i.e., of flowers   250 **most ingenious sense** finely endowed mind 255 **Pelion** (according to classical legend, giants in their fight with the gods sought to reach heaven by piling Mount Pelion and Mount Ossa on Mount Olympus)

Bears such an emphasis, whose phrase of sorrow
Conjures the wand'ring stars,° and makes them
    stand
Like wonder-wounded hearers? This is I,
Hamlet the Dane.

260 *Laertes.*   The devil take thy soul!
                              [*Grapples with him.*]°

Hamlet. Thou pray'st not well.
    I prithee take thy fingers from my throat,
    For, though I am not splenitive° and rash,
    Yet have I in me something dangerous,
265   Which let thy wisdom fear. Hold off thy hand.

King. Pluck them asunder.

Queen.   Hamlet, Hamlet!

All. Gentlemen!

Horatio.   Good my lord, be quiet.
                              [*Attendants part them.*]

Hamlet. Why, I will fight with him upon this theme
    Until my eyelids will no longer wag.

270 *Queen.* O my son, what theme?

Hamlet. I loved Ophelia. Forty thousand brothers
    Could not with all their quantity of love
    Make up my sum. What wilt thou do for her?

King. O, he is mad, Laertes.

275 *Queen.* For love of God forbear him.

Hamlet. 'Swounds, show me what thou't do.
    Woo't weep? Woo't fight? Woo't fast? Woo't tear
        thyself?
    Woo't drink up eisel?° Eat a crocodile?

---

258 **wand'ring stars** planets   260 s.d. **Grapples with him** (Q1, a bad
quarto, presumably reporting a version that toured, has a previous direction saying "Hamlet leaps in after Laertes." Possibly he does so, somewhat hysterically. But such a direction—absent from the two good texts,
Q2 and F—makes Hamlet the aggressor, somewhat contradicting his
next speech. Perhaps Laertes leaps out of the grave to attack Hamlet)   263 **splenitive** fiery (the spleen was thought to be the seat of
anger)   278 **eisel** vinegar

I'll do't. Dost thou come here to whine?
To outface me with leaping in her grave?   280
Be buried quick with her, and so will I.
And if thou prate of mountains, let them throw
Millions of acres on us, till our ground,
Singeing his pate against the burning zone,°
Make Ossa like a wart! Nay, an thou'lt mouth,   285
I'll rant as well as thou.

Queen.   This is mere madness;
And thus a while the fit will work on him.
Anon, as patient as the female dove
When that her golden couplets are disclosed,°
His silence will sit drooping.

Hamlet.   Hear you, sir.   290
What is the reason that you use me thus?
I loved you ever. But it is no matter.
Let Hercules himself do what he may,
The cat will mew, and dog will have his day.

King. I pray thee, good Horatio, wait upon him.   295
                    Exit Hamlet and Horatio.
[*To Laertes*] Strengthen your patience in our last
    night's speech.
We'll put the matter to the present push.°
Good Gertrude, set some watch over your son.
This grave shall have a living° monument.
An hour of quiet shortly shall we see;   300
Till then in patience our proceeding be.   *Exeunt.*

---

284 **burning zone** sun's orbit · 289 **golden couplets are disclosed** (the dove lays two eggs, and the newly hatched [**disclosed**] young are covered with golden down)   297 **present push** immediate test   299 **living** lasting (with perhaps also a reference to the plot against Hamlet's life)

[Scene 2. *The castle.*]

Enter Hamlet and Horatio.

Hamlet. So much for this, sir; now shall you see the
        other.
    You do remember all the circumstance?

Horatio. Remember it, my lord!

Hamlet. Sir, in my heart there was a kind of fighting
5   That would not let me sleep. Methought I lay
       Worse than the mutines in the bilboes.° Rashly
       (And praised be rashness for it) let us know,
       Our indiscretion sometime serves us well
       When our deep plots do pall,° and that should learn
           us
10   There's a divinity that shapes our ends,
       Rough-hew them how we will.

Horatio.   That is most certain.

Hamlet. Up from my cabin,
       My sea gown scarfed about me, in the dark
       Groped I to find out them, had my desire,
15   Fingered° their packet, and in fine° withdrew
       To mine own room again, making so bold,
       My fears forgetting manners, to unseal
       Their grand commission; where I found, Horatio—
       Ah, royal knavery!—an exact command,
20   Larded° with many several sorts of reasons,
       Importing Denmark's health, and England's too,
       With, ho, such bugs and goblins in my life,°
       That on the supervise,° no leisure bated,°
       No, not to stay the grinding of the ax,

5.2.6 **mutines in the bilboes** mutineers in fetters   9 **pall** fail   15 **Fin-gered** stole   15 **in fine** finally   20 **Larded** enriched   22 **such bugs and goblins in my life** such bugbears and imagined terrors if I were al-lowed to live   23 **supervise** reading   23 **leisure bated** delay allowed

   My head should be struck off.

Horatio.   Is't possible?   25

Hamlet. Here's the commission; read it at more leisure.
   But wilt thou hear now how I did proceed?

Horatio. I beseech you.

Hamlet. Being thus benetted round with villains,
   Or° I could make a prologue to my brains,   30
   They had begun the play. I sat me down,
   Devised a new commission, wrote it fair.
   I once did hold it, as our statists° do,
   A baseness to write fair,° and labored much
   How to forget that learning, but, sir, now   35
   It did me yeoman's service. Wilt thou know
   Th' effect° of what I wrote?

Horatio.   Ay, good my lord.

Hamlet. An earnest conjuration from the King,
   As England was his faithful tributary,
   As love between them like the palm might flourish,   40
   As peace should still her wheaten garland wear
   And stand a comma° 'tween their amities,
   And many suchlike as's of great charge,°
   That on the view and knowing of these contents,
   Without debatement further, more or less,   45
   He should those bearers put to sudden death,
   Not shriving° time allowed.

Horatio.   How was this sealed?

Hamlet. Why, even in that was heaven ordinant.°
   I had my father's signet in my purse,
   Which was the model° of that Danish seal,   50
   Folded the writ up in the form of th' other,
   Subscribed it, gave't th' impression, placed it safely,
   The changeling never known. Now, the next day
   Was our sea fight, and what to this was sequent
   Thou knowest already.   55

---

30 **Or** ere   33 **statists** statesmen   34 **fair** clearly   37 **effect** purport
42 **comma** link   43 **great charge** (1) serious exhortation (2) heavy burden (punning on *as's* and "asses")   47 **shriving** absolution   48 **ordinant** ruling   50 **model** counterpart

Horatio. So Guildenstern and Rosencrantz go to't.

Hamlet. Why, man, they did make love to this employ-
          ment.
    They are not near my conscience; their defeat
    Does by their own insinuation° grow.
60 'Tis dangerous when the baser nature comes
    Between the pass° and fell incensèd points°
    Of mighty opposites.

Horatio.   Why, what a king is this!

Hamlet. Does it not, think thee, stand me now upon°—
    He that hath killed my king, and whored my mother,
65 Popped in between th' election° and my hopes,
    Thrown out his angle° for my proper life,°
    And with such coz'nage°—is't not perfect con-
          science
    To quit° him with this arm? And is't not to be
          damned
    To let this canker of our nature come
70 In further evil?

Horatio. It must be shortly known to him from England
    What is the issue of the business there.

Hamlet. It will be short; the interim's mine,
    And a man's life's no more than to say "one."
75 But I am very sorry, good Horatio,
    That to Laertes I forgot myself,
    For by the image of my cause I see
    The portraiture of his. I'll court his favors.
    But sure the bravery° of his grief did put me
    Into a tow'ring passion.

80 *Horatio.*   Peace, who comes here?

              Enter young Osric, a courtier.

Osric. Your lordship is right welcome back to Den-
          mark.

59 insinuation meddling **61 pass** thrust **61 fell incensèd points**
fiercely angry rapiers **63 stand me now upon** become incumbent upon
me **65 election** (the Danish monarchy was elective) **66 angle** fishing
line **66 my proper life** my own life **67 coz'nage** trickery (and with a
pun on *cousinage,* kinship) **68 quit** pay back **79 bravery** bravado

Hamlet. I humbly thank you, sir. [*Aside to Horatio*]
  Dost know this waterfly?°

Horatio. [*Aside to Hamlet*] No, my good lord.

Hamlet. [*Aside to Horatio*] Thy state is the more gra-   85
  cious, for 'tis a vice to know him. He hath much
  land, and fertile. Let a beast be lord of beasts, and
  his crib shall stand at the king's mess.° 'Tis a
  chough,° but, as I say, spacious° in the possession
  of dirt.   90

Osric. Sweet lord, if your lordship were at leisure, I
  should impart a thing to you from his Majesty.

Hamlet. I will receive it, sir, with all diligence of spirit.
  Put your bonnet to his right use. 'Tis for the head.

Osric. I thank your lordship, it is very hot.   95

Hamlet. No, believe me, 'tis very cold; the wind is
  northerly.

Osric. It is indifferent cold, my lord, indeed.

Hamlet. But yet methinks it is very sultry and hot for
  my complexion.°   100

Osric. Exceedingly, my lord; it is very sultry, as 'twere—
  I cannot tell how. But, my lord, his Majesty bade
  me signify to you that 'a has laid a great wager on
  your head. Sir, this is the matter——

Hamlet. I beseech you remember.   105
  [*Hamlet moves him to put on his hat.*]

Osric. Nay, good my lord; for my ease, in good faith.
  Sir, here is newly come to court Laertes—believe
  me, an absolute gentleman, full of most excellent
  differences,° of very soft society and great showing.
  Indeed, to speak feelingly° of him, he is the card°   110
  or calendar of gentry; for you shall find in him the
  continent° of what part a gentleman would see.

83 **waterfly** (Osric's costume—perhaps a hat with plumes—suggests an
insect's wings)   88 **mess** table   89 **chough** jackdaw (here, chatterer)
89 **spacious** well off   100 **complexion** temperament   109 **differences**
distinguishing characteristics   110 **feelingly** justly   110 **card** chart
112 **continent** summary

Hamlet. Sir, his definement° suffers no perdition° in
   you, though, I know, to divide him inventorially
115   would dozy° th' arithmetic of memory, and yet but
   yaw neither in respect of his quick sail.° But, in the
   verity of extolment, I take him to be a soul of great
   article,° and his infusion° of such dearth and rare-
   ness as, to make true diction° of him, his semblable°
120   is his mirror, and who else would trace him, his um-
   brage,° nothing more.

Osric. Your lordship speaks most infallibly of him.

Hamlet. The concernancy,° sir? Why do we wrap the
   gentleman in our more rawer breath?

125 *Osric.* Sir?

Horatio. Is't not possible to understand in another
   tongue? You will to't,° sir, really.

Hamlet. What imports the nomination of this gentleman?

130 *Osric.* Of Laertes?

Horatio. [*Aside to Hamlet*] His purse is empty already.
   All's golden words are spent.

Hamlet. Of him, sir.

Osric. I know you are not ignorant——

135 *Hamlet.* I would you did, sir; yet, in faith, if you did, it
   would not much approve° me. Well, sir?

Osric. You are not ignorant of what excellence Laertes
   is——

Hamlet. I dare not confess that, lest I should compare
140   with him in excellence; but to know a man well were
   to know himself.

---

113 **definement** description   113 **perdition** loss   115 **dozy** dizzy
115–16 **and yet . . . quick sail** i.e., and yet only stagger despite all (**yaw
neither**) in trying to overtake his virtues   118 **article** (literally, "item,"
but here perhaps "traits" or "importance")   118 **infusion** essential quality   119 **diction** description   119 **semblable** likeness   120–21 **um-
brage** shadow   123 **concernancy** meaning   127 **will to't** will get there
136 **approve** commend

Osric. I mean, sir, for his weapon; but in the imputa-
tion° laid on him by them, in his meed° he's un-
fellowed.

Hamlet. What's his weapon?   145

Osric. Rapier and dagger.

Hamlet. That's two of his weapons—but well.

Osric. The King, sir, hath wagered with him six Barbary horses, against the which he has impawned,° as
I take it, six French rapiers and poniards, with their   150
assigns,° as girdle, hangers,° and so. Three of the
carriages,° in faith, are very dear to fancy, very re-
sponsive° to the hilts, most delicate carriages, and
of very liberal conceit.°

Hamlet. What call you the carriages?   155

Horatio. [*Aside to Hamlet*] I knew you must be edified
by the margent° ere you had done.

Osric. The carriages, sir, are the hangers.

Hamlet. The phrase would be more germane to the
matter if we could carry a cannon by our sides. I   160
would it might be hangers till then. But on! Six Barbary horses against six French swords, their assigns,
and three liberal-conceited carriages—that's the
French bet against the Danish. Why is this all impawned, as you call it?   165

Osric. The King, sir, hath laid, sir, that in a dozen
passes between yourself and him he shall not exceed
you three hits; he hath laid on twelve for nine, and
it would come to immediate trial if your lordship
would vouchsafe the answer.   170

Hamlet. How if I answer no?

Osric. I mean, my lord, the opposition of your person
in trial.

142–43 **imputation** reputation   143 **meed** merit   149 **impawned** wagered   151 **assigns** accompaniments   151 **hangers** straps hanging the
sword to the belt   152 **carriages** (an affected word for hangers)
152–53 **responsive** corresponding   154 **liberal conceit** elaborate design   57 **margent** i.e., marginal (explanatory) comment

Hamlet. Sir, I will walk here in the hall. If it please
175   his Majesty, it is the breathing time of day with me.°
      Let the foils be brought, the gentleman willing, and
      the King hold his purpose, I will win for him an I
      can; if not, I will gain nothing but my shame and
      the odd hits.

180 *Osric.* Shall I deliver you e'en so?

Hamlet. To this effect, sir, after what flourish your
      nature will.

Osric. I commend my duty to your lordship.

Hamlet. Yours, yours. [*Exit Osric.*] He does well to
185   commend it himself; there are no tongues else for's
      turn.

Horatio. This lapwing° runs away with the shell on his
      head.

Hamlet. 'A did comply, sir, with his dug° before 'a
190   sucked it. Thus has he, and many more of the
      same breed that I know the drossy age dotes on,
      only got the tune of the time and, out of an habit of
      encounter,° a kind of yeasty° collection, which
      carries them through and through the most fanned
195   and winnowed opinions; and do but blow them to
      their trial, the bubbles are out.°

Enter a Lord.

Lord. My lord, his Majesty commended him to you by
      young Osric, who brings back to him that you
      attend him in the hall. He sends to know if your
200   pleasure hold to play with Laertes, or that you will
      take longer time.

Hamlet. I am constant to my purposes; they follow the

---

175 **breathing time of day with me** time when I take exercise   187 **lapwing** (the new-hatched lapwing was thought to run around
with half its shell on its head)   189 **'A did comply, sir, with his dug** he
was ceremoniously polite to his mother's breast   192–93 **out of an
habit of encounter** out of his own superficial way of meeting and conversing with people   193 **yeasty** frothy   196 **the bubbles are out** i.e.,
they are blown away (the reference is to the "yeasty collection")

King's pleasure. If his fitness speaks, mine is ready;
now or whensoever, provided I be so able as now.

Lord. The King and Queen and all are coming down.   205

Hamlet. In happy time.°

Lord. The Queen desires you to use some gentle enter-
tainment° to Laertes before you fall to play.

Hamlet. She well instructs me.   [*Exit Lord.*]

Horatio. You will lose this wager, my lord.   210

Hamlet. I do not think so. Since he went into France
I have been in continual practice. I shall win at the
odds. But thou wouldst not think how ill all's here
about my heart. But it is no matter.

Horatio. Nay, good my lord——   215

Hamlet. It is but foolery, but it is such a kind of gain-
giving° as would perhaps trouble a woman.

Horatio. If your mind dislike anything, obey it. I will
forestall their repair hither and say you are not fit.

Hamlet. Not a whit, we defy augury. There is special   220
providence in the fall of a sparrow.° If it be now,
'tis not to come; if it be not to come, it will be now;
if it be not now, yet it will come. The readiness is
all. Since no man of aught he leaves knows, what
is't to leave betimes?° Let be.   225

*A table prepared. [Enter] Trumpets, Drums, and
Officers with cushions; King, Queen, [Osric,] and
all the State, [with] foils, daggers, [and stoups
of wine borne in]; and Laertes.*

King. Come, Hamlet, come, and take this hand from
me.

      [*The King puts Laertes' hand into Hamlet's.*]

---

206 **In happy time** It is an opportune time   207–08 **to use some gentle
entertainment** to be courteous   217 **gaingiving** misgiving   221 **the
fall of a sparrow** (cf. Matthew 10:29 "Are not two sparrows sold for a
farthing? and one of them shall not fall on the ground without your Father")   225 **betimes** early

Hamlet. Give me your pardon, sir. I have done you
    wrong,
    But pardon't, as you are a gentleman.
    This presence° knows, and you must needs have
      heard,
230   How I am punished with a sore distraction.
    What I have done
    That might your nature, honor, and exception°
    Roughly awake, I here proclaim was madness.
    Was't Hamlet wronged Laertes? Never Hamlet.
235   If Hamlet from himself be ta'en away,
    And when he's not himself does wrong Laertes,
    Then Hamlet does it not, Hamlet denies it.
    Who does it then? His madness. If't be so,
    Hamlet is of the faction° that is wronged;
240   His madness is poor Hamlet's enemy.
    Sir, in this audience,
    Let my disclaiming from a purposed evil
    Free me so far in your most generous thoughts
    That I have shot my arrow o'er the house
    And hurt my brother.

245 *Laertes.*   I am satisfied in nature,
    Whose motive in this case should stir me most
    To my revenge. But in my terms of honor
    I stand aloof, and will no reconcilement
    Till by some elder masters of known honor
250   I have a voice and precedent° of peace
    To keep my name ungored. But till that time
    I do receive your offered love like love,
    And will not wrong it.

Hamlet.   I embrace it freely,
    And will this brother's wager frankly play.
    Give us the foils. Come on.

255 *Laertes.*   Come, one for me.

Hamlet. I'll be your foil,° Laertes. In mine ignorance

---

229 **presence** royal assembly   232 **exception** disapproval   239 **faction**
party, side   250 **voice and precedent** authoritative opinion justified by
precedent   256 **foil** (1) blunt sword (2) background (of metallic leaf)
for a jewel

　　Your skill shall, like a star i' th' darkest night,
　　Stick fiery off° indeed.

Laertes.　　　　　　　　You mock me, sir.

Hamlet. No, by this hand.

King. Give them the foils, young Osric. Cousin Hamlet,　　260
　　You know the wager?

Hamlet.　　　　　　　　Very well, my lord.
　　Your grace has laid the odds o' th' weaker side.

King. I do not fear it, I have seen you both;
　　But since he is bettered,° we have therefore odds.

Laertes. This is too heavy; let me see another.　　　265

Hamlet. This likes me well. These foils have all a
　　length?

　　　　　　　　　　　　　　　　Prepare to play.

Osric. Ay, my good lord.

King. Set me the stoups of wine upon that table.
　　If Hamlet give the first or second hit,
　　Or quit° in answer of the third exchange,　　　270
　　Let all the battlements their ordnance fire.
　　The King shall drink to Hamlet's better breath,
　　And in the cup an union° shall he throw
　　Richer than that which four successive kings
　　In Denmark's crown have worn. Give me the cups,　　275
　　And let the kettle° to the trumpet speak,
　　The trumpet to the cannoneer without,
　　The cannons to the heavens, the heaven to earth,
　　"Now the King drinks to Hamlet." Come, begin.
　　　　　　　　　　　　　　Trumpets the while.
　　And you, the judges, bear a wary eye.　　　280

Hamlet. Come on, sir.

Laertes.　　　　　　Come, my lord.　　　*They play.*

Hamlet.　　　　　　　　　　One.

Laertes.　　　　　　　　　　　　No.

258 **Stick fiery off** stand out brilliantly　264 **bettered** has improved (?)
is regarded as better by the public (?)　270 **quit** repay, hit back
273 **union** pearl　276 **kettle** kettledrum

Hamlet.   Judgment?

Osric. A hit, a very palpable hit.
   Drum, trumpets, and shot. Flourish; a piece goes off.

Laertes.   Well, again.

King. Stay, give me drink. Hamlet, this pearl is thine.
   Here's to thy health. Give him the cup.

285 *Hamlet.* I'll play this bout first; set it by awhile.
   Come. [*They play.*] Another hit. What say you?

Laertes. A touch, a touch; I do confess't.

King. Our son shall win.

Queen.   He's fat,° and scant of breath.
   Here, Hamlet, take my napkin, rub thy brows.
290 The Queen carouses to thy fortune, Hamlet.

Hamlet. Good madam!

King.   Gertrude, do not drink.

Queen. I will, my lord; I pray you pardon me. [*Drinks.*]

King. [*Aside*] It is the poisoned cup; it is too late.

Hamlet. I dare not drink yet, madam—by and by.

295 *Queen.* Come, let me wipe thy face.

Laertes. My lord, I'll hit him now.

King.   I do not think't.

Laertes. [*Aside*] And yet it is almost against my conscience.

Hamlet. Come for the third, Laertes. You do but dally.
   I pray you pass with your best violence;
300 I am sure you make a wanton° of me.

Laertes. Say you so? Come on.   [*They*] *play.*

Osric. Nothing neither way.

Laertes. Have at you now!
           In scuffling they change rapiers, [*and both are
                                          wounded*].

___

288 **fat** (1) sweaty (2) out of training   300 **wanton** spoiled child

King.   Part them. They are incensed.

Hamlet. Nay, come—again!   [*The Queen falls.*]

Osric.   Look to the Queen there, ho!

Horatio. They bleed on both sides. How is it, my lord?   *305*

Osric. How is't, Laertes?

Laertes. Why, as a woodcock to mine own springe,° Osric.
    I am justly killed with mine own treachery.

Hamlet. How does the Queen?

King.   She sounds° to see them bleed.

Queen. No, no, the drink, the drink! O my dear Hamlet!   *310*
    The drink, the drink! I am poisoned.   [*Dies.*]

Hamlet. O villainy! Ho! Let the door be locked.
    Treachery! Seek it out.   [*Laertes falls.*]

Laertes. It is here, Hamlet. Hamlet, thou art slain;
    No med'cine in the world can do thee good.   *315*
    In thee there is not half an hour's life.
    The treacherous instrument is in thy hand,
    Unbated and envenomed. The foul practice°
    Hath turned itself on me. Lo, here I lie,
    Never to rise again. Thy mother's poisoned.   *320*
    I can no more. The King, the King's to blame.

Hamlet. The point envenomed too?
    Then, venom, to thy work.   *Hurts the King.*

All. Treason! Treason!

King. O, yet defend me, friends. I am but hurt.   *325*

Hamlet. Here, thou incestuous, murd'rous, damnèd Dane,
    Drink off this potion. Is thy union° here?
    Follow my mother.   *King dies.*

Laertes.   He is justly served.

307 **springe** snare   309 **sounds** swoons   318 **practice** deception
327 **union** (1) the pearl put into the drink in 5.2.273; (2) the King's
poisonous (incestuous) marriage

It is·a poison tempered° by himself.
330   Exchange forgiveness with me, noble Hamlet.
Mine and my father's death come not upon thee,
Nor thine on me!   *Dies.*

Hamlet. Heaven make thee free of it! I follow thee.
I am dead, Horatio. Wretched Queen, adieu!
335   You that look pale and tremble at this chance,
That are but mutes° or audience to this act,
Had I but time (as this fell sergeant,° Death,
Is strict in his arrest) O, I could tell you—
But let it be. Horatio, I am dead;
340   Thou livest; report me and my cause aright
To the unsatisfied.°

Horatio.   Never believe it.
I am more an antique Roman° than a Dane.
Here's yet some liquor left.

Hamlet.   As th' art a man,
Give me the cup. Let go. By heaven, I'll ha't!
345   O God, Horatio, what a wounded name,
Things standing thus unknown, shall live behind me!
If thou didst ever hold me in thy heart,
Absent thee from felicity° awhile,
And in this harsh world draw thy breath in pain,
To tell my story.   *A march afar off.* [*Exit Osric.*]
350   What warlike noise is this?

                                  Enter Osric.

Osric. Young Fortinbras, with conquest come from
    Poland,
To th' ambassadors of England gives
This warlike volley.

Hamlet.   O, I die, Horatio!
The potent poison quite o'ercrows° my spirit.
355   I cannot live to hear the news from England,

---

329 **tempered** mixed   336 **mutes** performers who have no words to
speak   337 **fell sergeant** dread sheriff's officer   341 **unsatisfied** unin-
formed   342 **antique Roman** (with reference to the old Roman fashion
of suicide)   348 **felicity** i.e., the felicity of death   354 **o'ercrows** over-
powers (as a triumphant cock crows over its weak opponent)

But I do prophesy th' election lights
On Fortinbras. He has my dying voice.
So tell him, with th' occurrents,° more and less,
Which have solicited°—the rest is silence.　　　*Dies.*

Horatio. Now cracks a noble heart. Good night, sweet
　　Prince,　　　　　　　　　　　　　　　　　360
And flights of angels sing thee to thy rest.

　　　　　　　　　　　　　　　　　[March within.]
Why does the drum come hither?

　　　Enter Fortinbras, with the Ambassadors with
　　　　　　Drum, Colors, and Attendants.

Fortinbras. Where is this sight?

Horatio.　　　　　　　　　　What is it you would see?
If aught of woe or wonder, cease your search.

Fortinbras. This quarry° cries on havoc.° O proud
　　Death,　　　　　　　　　　　　　　　　　365
What feast is toward° in thine eternal cell
That thou so many princes at a shot
So bloodily hast struck?

Ambassador.　　　　　　　　The sight is dismal;
And our affairs from England come too late.
The ears are senseless that should give us hearing　370
To tell him his commandment is fulfilled,
That Rosencrantz and Guildenstern are dead.
Where should we have our thanks?

Horatio.　　　　　　　　　　　Not from his° mouth,
Had it th' ability of life to thank you.
He never gave commandment for their death.　　375
But since, so jump° upon this bloody question,
You from the Polack wars, and you from England,
Are here arrived, give order that these bodies
High on a stage° be placèd to the view,
And let me speak to th' yet unknowing world　　380
How these things came about. So shall you hear

358 **occurrents** occurrences　359 **solicited** incited　365 **quarry** heap
of slain bodies　365 **cries on havoc** proclaims general slaughter
366 **toward** in preparation　373 **his** (Claudius')　376 **jump** precisely
379 **stage** platform

Of carnal, bloody, and unnatural acts,
Of accidental judgments, casual° slaughters,
Of deaths put on by cunning and forced cause,
385 And, in this upshot, purposes mistook
Fall'n on th' inventors' heads. All this can I
Truly deliver.

Fortinbras.   Let us haste to hear it,
And call the noblest to the audience.
For me, with sorrow I embrace my fortune.
390 I have some rights of memory° in this kingdom,
Which now to claim my vantage doth invite me.

Horatio. Of that I shall have also cause to speak,
And from his mouth whose voice will draw on°
      more.
But let this same be presently performed,
Even while men's minds are wild, lest more mis-
395   chance
On° plots and errors happen.

Fortinbras.   Let four captains
Bear Hamlet like a soldier to the stage,
For he was likely, had he been put on,°
To have proved most royal; and for his passage°
400 The soldiers' music and the rite of war
Speak loudly for him.
Take up the bodies. Such a sight as this
Becomes the field,° but here shows much amiss.
Go, bid the soldiers shoot.

Exeunt marching; after the which a peal of ordnance
are shot off.

FINIS

383 **casual** not humanly planned, chance   390 **rights of memory** remembered claims   393 **voice will draw on** vote will influence
396 **On** on top of   398 **put on** advanced (to the throne)   399 **passage**
death   403 **field** battlefield

A Note on the Texts of *Hamlet*

Probably the most famous line in Western literature is "To be or not to be, that is the question," from Hamlet's soliloquy in 3.1.56–90. But in fact this soliloquy exists in three forms—in a text published in 1603, a text published in 1604–1605, and a text published in 1623. First, let's look at the beginning of the 1603 version. This book is a quarto (a fairly small book whose pages were made by folding a sheet of paper twice, producing four leaves, or eight pages); this edition is called Q1 because it is the first quarto version of *Hamlet*. If you are at all familiar with the speech, the Q1 version may strike you as comic, almost a parody. (Spelling and punctuation are modernized in the three versions given here.)

> To be or not to be, aye, there's the point
> To die, to sleep; is that all? Aye, all.
> No, to sleep, to dream, aye, marry, there it goes,
> For in that dream of death, when we awake,
> And borne before an everlasting judge,
> From whence no passenger ever returned,
> The undiscovered country, at whose sight
> The happy smile, and the accursed damned.
> But for this, the joyful hope of this.
> Who'd bear the scorns and flattery of the world,
> Scorned by the right rich, the rich cursed of the poor?
> The widow being oppressed, the orphan wronged,
> The taste of hunger, or a tyrant's reign. . . .

No, we did not mistakenly omit "That is the question." And even if this version were quoted in full, you would not find such familiar phrases as "the slings and arrows of outrageous fortune," or "take arms against a sea of troubles."

Before we comment on Q1, let's look at the beginning of the next version, from Q2 (i.e., the second quarto version), published in 1604–1605. This version will strike you as familiar. Line numbers keyed to the Signet text are added.

> To be or not to be: that is the question:
> Whether 'tis nobler in the mind to suffer
> The slings and arrows of outrageous fortune,
> Or to take arms against a sea of troubles,
> And by opposing end them. To die, to sleep—   60
> No more—and by a sleep to say we end
> The heartache, and the thousand natural shocks
> That flesh is heir to! 'Tis a consummation
> Devoutly to be wished. To die, to sleep—
> To sleep—perchance to dream: ay, there's the rub,   65
> For in that sleep of death what dreams may come
> When we have shuffled off this mortal coil,
> Must give us pause. There's the respect
> That makes calamity of so long life:
> For who would bear the whips and scorns of time,   70
> Th' oppressor's wrong, the proud man's contumely,
> The pangs of despised love, the law's delay. . . .
>
>   (3.1.56–72)

The third version, almost the same as the second, appears in the collection of Shakespeare's plays called the First Folio, printed in 1623. (A folio consists of pages made by folding a large sheet only once rather than twice, thereby producing two leaves or four pages, instead of a quarto's four leaves and eight pages.) In the original printings, the second and third versions (Q2 and F) often differ in spelling and punctuation—for instance, in the first line of the Folio version, the word "question" is capitalized and it is followed by a colon, whereas in Q2 "question" is not capitalized and it is followed by a comma—but despite such differences the two versions of the speech are very close to each other.

Putting aside spelling and punctuation, the two chief differences in the quoted passage are "proud" (Q2) versus "poor" (F) in line 71, and "despised" (Q1) versus "disprized," i.e. "undervalued" (F) in line 72.

Let's now look at the three texts in some detail.

The First Quarto (Q1, 1603).

Only two copies of Q1 are extant. This version has 2,154 lines, which is to say that it is much shorter than Q2 (about 3,764 lines), and than F (about 3,535 lines). (Methods of counting lines differ, so you may find slightly different figures in some other source.) In this version, for example, Laertes's speech to Ophelia in 1.3, warning her against Hamlet (5–44), is less than half the length it is in Q2 and F. The Player's speech about Pyrrhus at 2.2.461–529 is twenty lines shorter, and Hamlet's praise of Horatio at 3.2.58–89 is a dozen lines shorter. In the nineteenth century Q1 was commonly regarded either as a stage version of the pre-Shakespearean *Hamlet* or as the early play with some revisions by Shakespeare, i.e. as a sort of first version of Shakespeare's *Hamlet*. Today almost everyone agrees that, partly because many speeches are much shorter than in Q2 and F, and partly because a fair amount of the text is banal and some passages are close to nonsense, whereas some other passages show Shakespeare at the top of his form, it is not a pre-Shakespearean play and it is not an early version by Shakespeare; rather, it is an actor's garbled memory of what Shakespeare wrote. A still-unexplained feature of this version, however, is the fact that Polonius is called Corambis—something that cannot be attributed to a faulty memory. Adding to the mystery is a German play on the Hamlet story, in which the character corresponding to Polonius is called Corambus. The German version presumably is derived from an English version brought to Germany by English players on tour in the seventeenth century, but why Corambis or Corambus became Polonius, or the other way around, is unclear.

Probably an actor who had performed in an abridged version of the play—maybe a version created for a company that toured the provinces—provided the printer with the copy. Such a text is characterized as a "reported text" or a "post-performance" text or a "memorial reconstruction"—something based on the memory of an actor or actors.

In this instance, it is all but certain that the actor who gave the copy to the printer had played Marcellus. Why Marcellus? Because his lines in Q1 correspond very closely with the two other texts, and indeed the lines of characters who are on stage at the same time as Marcellus correspond pretty well, whereas many other passages depart widely and wildly—presumably because the actor was offstage and he was more or less forced to invent speeches he only vaguely recalled. On the other hand, because Lucianus's six-line speech in 3.2.261–66 is perfect—and because Voltemand's long speech in 2.2.60–79 corresponds closely with the other texts, it is likely that the actor who played Marcellus doubled in these other roles.

Texts that are not derived from Shakespeare's manuscript, or from a scribe's clean copy of either the manuscript or from a prompt book prepared for the company, are called "bad" quartos. Early in the twentieth century, the word "bad" suggested not only that the text was inaccurate but also that the actor who provided it had betrayed his company by selling his memory to an unscrupulous printer. Such a book was said to be "pirated"—but in fact we do not know that treachery or piracy were involved. The title page of Q1 bears the initials of one publisher and the name of a second, which suggests that there was nothing illegitimate in the publication.

What value can such a text have? Only a little, but especially in recent years, when there has been an emphasis on the play as a *performance* rather than as a text, claims have been made that whereas the two other versions are "literary," the Q1 version gives us the play as it was actually produced on the stage. It is thus supposedly closer to the real *Hamlet*, the *Hamlet* that the Elizabethans saw, than are the other texts, which are said in any case to be impossibly long. Thus, Graham Holderness and Bryan Loughrey say in their introduction to a reprint (1992) of Q1, "What we can assume with reasonable confidence is that this text comes closer than the other texts to actual Jacobean stage practice" (page 14). But we *cannot* say that this text gives us the play as it was performed. The title page says that the play "hath beene diuerse times acted by his Highnesse seruants in the Cittie of London: as also in the two Vniuersities of Cambridge and Oxford, and else-where," but this is a statement about the play, not about this particular text; and in any case it is an advertisement, not a document whose truth is beyond question. At best Q1 gives us the play as one actor or perhaps a few actors *remembered* it. Further, we don't have direct access to their memories, but only to the compositor's version, filled with printer's errors. For instance, old Norway in Q1 is said to be "impudent" ("impudent / And bed-rid"), but in Q2 (1.2.29) he is "impotent" ("impotent and bedred"). The context (whether "bed-rid" or "bedred") clearly calls for Q2's "impotent," not Q1's "impudent." Whether the actor's memory failed or the compositor misread the handwriting or the compositor's mind wandered we cannot know, but one hardly wants to say that because Q1 has "impudent," this is the word that was spoken in production, much less that it therefore is quite as legitimate as whatever Shakespeare wrote in his lost manuscript.

On the other hand, we can value Q1 for at least two reasons. First, it includes some stage directions not found in the other texts that do indeed seem to give us a sense of how the play was staged. For instance, Q1 has a stage direction, *"Enter Ofelia playing on a Lute, and her haire downe singing"* (4.5.20 s.d.) where Q2 has merely *"Enter Ophelia,"* and the Folio text (1623) has merely *"Enter Ophelia distracted."* A second example of an interesting stage direction in Q1: only Q1 tells us that Hamlet leaps into Ophelia's grave in 5.1.260: *"Hamlet leapes in after Leartes"* (sic). (This stage direction, by the way, causes uneasiness among some editors because it makes Hamlet the aggressor. See the footnote on the passage.) Again, this is not to say that these stage directions are Shakespeare's; the most that we can say is that they help to give us a glimpse of what an Elizabethan audience may have seen.

The second value that editors find in Q1 is this: It may clarify puzzling passages in Q2 and F. For instance, in one of his soliloquies, "O, what a rogue and peasant slave am I" (2.2.560), in Q2 Hamlet speaks of himself (incoherently?) as "the sonne of a deere murthered," and in F he similarly speaks of himself as "the Sonne of the Deere murthered." In Q1, however, he speaks of himself as "The sonne of my deare father." Editors (including the present editor) who believe that Q2 and F—probably because of a compositor's error—do not make sense, and who believe that Hamlet must be speaking of his "dear murdered father" or "dear father murthered," are glad to find the word "father" in the corresponding passage in Q1, and they use the reading in Q1 to justify their emendation of either Q2 or F. It should be mentioned, however, that Philip Edwards, the editor of *Hamlet* in the New Cambridge Shakespeare (1985), rejects this emendation. Edwards, staying with the Folio, prints "the dear murderèd"; in a footnote he glosses the expression as meaning "the loved victim."

In short, despite those enthusiastic amateur theater groups who occasionally stage Q1 and who say that it plays well on the stage—of course they say it does, since they wouldn't have produced it, nonsense and all, if they didn't think it would play well—the uses of Q1 are extremely limited.

The Second Quarto (Q2, 1604–1605).

Q2, the second published version, printed in 1604 and 1605, contains about 3,764 lines. It is the longest of Shakespeare's texts (it is almost twice as long as *Macbeth*), and it claims to be "Newly imprinted and enlarged to almost as much againe as it was, according to the true and perfect Coppie." (The title page, which makes this claim, is reproduced as our frontispiece.) Despite its length, however, it omits some material that is found in the third text, the Folio, which we will look at later.

There is much dispute about exactly what "the true and perfect Coppie" was, but it may well have been Shakespeare's manuscript—sheets that scholars customarily call "foul papers," as opposed, for instance, to a neat scribal copy (a "fair copy"), or a scribal copy with later annotations that would serve as a prompt copy for actors. A brief reminder is called for at this point: When we speak of Shakespeare's "completed manuscript" or his "final version" we may be talking about something that never existed. No Shakespeare play survives in manuscript; we do not know how he worked, and we do not know if he thought of the play as finished when he turned over a manuscript, or—a very different thing—when the play was in some degree reworked during rehearsal. And we do not know if, after the early productions, he revised the play for later productions. Fifty years ago almost no one talked of the possibility that Shakespeare revised plays after they had been staged, but today some scholars argue that the texts of *Hamlet*, *The Second Part of Henry IV*, *Troilus and Cressida*, *Othello*, and *King Lear* all show evidence of revision, i.e. there are (some people say) two authentic versions for each play.

Now to return to Q2 as "foul papers." At the beginning of 2.1 we get a stage direction: *"Enter old Polonius, with his man or two."* Such a direction suggests foul papers rather than a prompt copy; Shakespeare, in the process of beginning the scene, was not yet entirely sure about how the scene would go—maybe he would need two servants, and maybe he wouldn't. As it turns out, only one servant, Reynaldo, is needed. Presumably in a copy prepared for a stage production (a promptbook), such a direction would be corrected to something like *"Enter Polonius, and Reynaldo,"* and (if we may briefly get ahead of our story) that is exactly what we do find in the next version we will look at, the Folio version, which surely is a text based on a manuscript that reflects a production.

Of course *"with his man or two"* might survive from Shakespeare's manuscript into a clean copy that a scribe prepared for the theatrical company, but additional evidence that the source of Q2 was Shakespeare's manuscript is the fact that Q2 prints many words that are obvious misreadings of handwriting, or guesses as to what the writer intended. Thus, in 3.2.366 it gives *"the vmber"* where the sense requires *"thumb"* (Hamlet is talking about fingering a musical instrument), and in 4.7.6 it gives *"the King"* where the sense requires *checking.*"

Further, Q2 seems to include some material that Shake-speare intended to delete. Consider this passage from the Player Queen's speech in 3.2:

> For women feare too much, euen as they loue,
> And womens feare and loue hold quantitie,
> Eyther none, in neither ought, or in extremitie. . . .   (172–74)

Now, the fact that the first line does not rhyme, in a speech in which all of the other lines rhyme in pairs, is immediately a cause for suspicion. Something is wrong here. In his thoughtful Arden edition, Harold Jenkins suggests that the second quoted line seems to be a restatement of the first line, a fresh start, but the first (unrhymed) line was mistakenly printed. Further, in the third line, "Eyther none" probably was a false start that was replaced by "In neither," but, again, the compositor mistakenly printed words that should have been deleted.

In addition to working from some sort of manuscript, the compositors of Q2 made occasional use of a printed text, Q1; especially in the first five scenes there are otherwise inexplicable similarities in typography and layout. Apparently the compositors of Q2 consulted Q1 when they were puzzled by something in their manuscript.

The Folio (1623).

The third early printed version (3,535 lines), in the posthumous First Folio entitled *Mr. William Shakespeares Comedies, Histories, & Tragedies,* is a little shorter than Q2. The title page says the plays are "Published according to the True Originall Copies," but exactly what the printer's copy was for *Hamlet* is uncertain. Most students of the problem believe the compositor worked from a heavily annotated copy of Q2—the text in F contains some of Q2's errors as well as some new errors, and it also contains some of Q2's unusual spellings—but G. R. Hibbard in his Oxford edition of *Hamlet* (1987) offers strong arguments against his view. Still, even if the compositors of F did not use Q2 (or the 1611 reprint of it, Q3) as printer's copy, they may have consulted it on occasion, when their manuscript was unclear.

In any case, although F is slightly shorter than Q2, it is not simply a shortened version; it contains about eighty lines *not* found in Q2. Consider this small example. In the scene with the grave diggers, in Q2 the grave digger (in the speech prefixes he is called a clown) identifies the skull of Yorick, and we then (5.1.183–85) get this dialogue:

> *Ham.* This?
> *Clow.* Een that.
> *Ham.* Alas poore *Yoricke,* I knew him *Horatio.* . . .

But in the Folio text, Hamlet's second speech is different:

> *Ham.* Let me see. Alas poore *Yorick,* I knew him *Horatio.* . . .

The Folio's addition of "Let me see" is very interesting. Probably the words were not in Shakespeare's foul papers (Q2); we can strongly suspect that "Let me see"—words indicating that Hamlet takes the skull from the grave digger— was a bit of dialogue added during the course of producing the play.

True, some of the lines that appear only in F may have been in the manuscript for Q2 and were accidentally omitted when Q2 was printed, but some of the F-only material must be additions. Additions by whom? Are they revisions that actors made as they worked and reworked the play? Or are they revisions that Shakespeare himself made, perhaps after he saw the early productions of the play? Here are some examples of small additions which to most editors sound like the sorts of things that actors might add. In 2.2.217, where in Q2 Hamlet says, "You cannot take from me . . . ," in F he says, "You cannot, sir, take from me . . ." In Hamlet's second soliloquy, "O, what a rogue and peasant slave am I," in an extended passage of blank verse (unrhymed lines of ten syllables) we get a line that consists only of "O, vengeance" (593). A third example, and the most interesting, concerns Hamlet's last words in 5.2.359. In both Q2 and F they are, "the rest is silence," but F goes on to add, as his utterance, "O, o, o, o." This string of *o*'s probably is meant to represent a sigh, and it may well be something that an actor added to Shakespeare's text.

Consider a slightly longer but still a brief example of an addition in F. In Q2, after Rosencrantz and Guildenstern tell Hamlet he must go with them and inform the king where Polonius's body is, Hamlet says, "Bring me to him." But in F, Hamlet adds to these words, "Hide fox, and all after" (4.2.30–31)—presumably the cry from a game like hide-and-seek—and he probably runs off. Is this an authorial revision, adding liveliness to the scene and also perhaps suggesting (at least to Rosencrantz and Guildenstern) that Hamlet is a bit mad? Or is it, on the other hand, despite its theatrical effectiveness, a showy bit added by actors, and in fact *less* effective as an exit line than the simple "Bring me to him"? Or is it a revision—maybe for the worse—by Shakespeare himself?

Even if we grant that many of the small additions found in F probably are the work of actors, we should remember that Shakespeare was an actor, a member of the company that bought his plays, and we should not be too quick to dismiss the changes as unauthorized additions by meddlesome actors.

What of the longer passages found only in F, notably the thirty-odd lines in 2.2 concerning what is conventionally called The War of the Theaters, lines about the competition that companies of children were offering to the adult companies? No one doubts that the passage is authentic Shakespeare, but is it evidence that Shakespeare revised the play after it had already been on the stage? That is, was this passage absent from the manuscript behind Q2 and added in the manuscript behind F, or was it present in the Q2 ms but omitted from the printed version (perhaps because it seemed to be an undramatic digression), in which case it was not so much *added* to F as it was *restored* by F? The short answer is that inconclusive arguments have been offered on both sides. Similarly, take the passage in 5.2.57—

which is found only in F—where Hamlet, talking to Horatio, says of Rosencrantz and Guildenstern,

> Why, man, they did make love to this employment.

Did Q2 accidentally omit this line, or did Shakespeare add
it, in the course of revising the play, in order to further reveal Hamlet's character, specifically to show him justifying
the action by which he sends these two men to their deaths?

The 220-odd lines *not* in F also raise questions. For instance, the soliloquy beginning "How all occasions do inform against me" (4.4.32), present in Q2, is not in F. Does
its omission let us glimpse Shakespeare revising the play?
Did Shakespeare come to think (as some readers and viewers think) that the speech is redundant? Or did he decide to
alter the character of Hamlet, in this case by revealing less
of his thoughts? Or is the omission due merely to the company's attempt to shorten the performance time of the play?
The same questions can be asked of another passage not in
F, Hamlet's comment to his mother about Rosencrantz and
Guildenstern:

> There's letters sealed, and my two schoolfellows,
> Whom I will trust as I will adders fanged,
> They bear the mandate; they must sweep my way
> And marshal me to knavery. Let it work;
> For 'tis sport to have the enginer
> Hoist with his own petar, and 't shall go hard
> But I will delve one yard below their mines
> And blow them to the moon. O, 'tis most sweet
> When in one line two crafts directly meet.   (3.4.203–11)

Did Shakespeare have second thoughts, some time after
the play had been on the stage, and decide to delete this
passage, perhaps because it showed an unattractive cast
to Hamlet's thinking? Or perhaps because it is inconsistent
with Hamlet's later speech, when he tells Horatio that
during the voyage to England he was suddenly inspired in
a moment of "rashness" to forge the papers that send

Rosencrantz and Guildenstern to their deaths? If so, in the course of removing the passage he deleted what was to become one of his most famous phrases, "Hoist with his own petar."

In short, in F, some omissions of material that is present in Q2 are very brief, and may be accidental; other omissions are longer, and must be deliberate cuts, but we do not know if the cuts were made by Shakespeare or by someone or some group of actors charged with preparing a text for production. (It is uncertain how a manuscript became a promptbook.) Conceivably, some omissions are due to Shakespeare, some to the company, and some to carelessness.

There are also several hundred small differences—variants—between Q2 and F, such as the famous "too too solid flesh" of F, versus the "sallied" (i.e. sullied) flesh of Q2. Similarly, in 1.4.49, speaking to the ghost, Hamlet says in Q2 that its bones were "quietly interr'd," but in F he says they were "quietly enurn'd." Did Shakespeare in the course of revising think that "interred" was a bit bland, and therefore substitute "inurned"? Or did an actor make the change—or did a compositor misread the manuscript? Whether such differences are due to Shakespeare revising, actors altering the text, or compositors blundering (perhaps the word was the same in both manuscripts, but one compositor got it right and one got it wrong), cannot be established. Possibly some are authorial revisions, some are alterations made by actors, and some are errors made by compositors; everyone agrees, however, that in *some* instances (as when Q2 gives the nonsensical *"the vmber"* and F gives the meaningful *"thumb"*), Q2 is mistaken and F is correct.

It should also be mentioned that F includes some stage directions, such as "On scuffling they change Rapiers," that suggest it is based on a text prepared for performance—but it also omits many necessary exits and entrances. Perhaps the most we can say about the copy for F is that whoever made it began with Shakespeare's foul papers and added some stage directions and some material—whether by

Shakespeare or by the actors is uncertain—that has come to be part of the play.

The Present Text

Given the fact that Q2 contains about 220 lines not found in F, and that F contains about 80 lines not found in Q2, and that there are hundreds of small differences between these two texts, what text does an editor print? The editors of the Oxford edition of Shakespeare's complete works (1986) chose the Folio as the control text for *Hamlet*, and print the Q2-only passages at the end of the play. This means, to take only one example, that the reader does not encounter the great soliloquy, "How all occasions do inform against me" (4.4.33–66), except out of context, in the appendix. The Oxford decision obviously was considered unsatisfactory by the editors of the Norton Shakespeare (1997), who use the Oxford text, because in the Norton edition the Q2 passages are restored to their appropriate places within the play itself, but (in deference to Oxford?) in a different typeface (italic) and with different numbering, thereby alerting the reader that these passages are, so to speak, stepchildren. In effect the italic typeface causes the passages to stick out; material that Oxford meant to minimize, Norton inadvertently emphasizes.

Harold Jenkins in the excellent Arden edition (1982), on the other hand, uses Q2 as the control text, and he omits F-only passages that he takes to be interpolations by actors. Thus, in the soliloquy known as "O, what a rogue and peasant slave am I" (2.2.560), after the line in which Hamlet says (speaking of Claudius) "Remorseless, treacherous, lecherous, kindless villain!" Jenkins omits the short line that consists only of "O, vengeance" (593). In a footnote he explains: "F's *Oh Vengeance* has all the marks of an actor's addition. Hamlet accuses himself of cursing . . . but not of threats, and his change from self-reproach to the pursuit of retribution occurs only at [600]" (page 272). This reasoning sounds plausible, but let's turn to another excellent edition of *Hamlet*, Philip Edwards's volume in the New Cambridge Shakespeare. Edwards takes F as the control text, and he therefore includes "O vengeance." In a footnote he offers the following comment on the line: "This cry, the great climax of the rant with which Hamlet emulates the Player, exhausts his futile self-recrimination, and he turns, in proper disgust, from a display of verbal histrionics to more practical things. Q2 omits the phrase altogether, and many editors unfortunately follow suit. This short line and the silence after it are the pivot of the speech" (page 142). Edwards, by the way, does include the Q2-only lines within his text, but he encloses them within square brackets.

The lesson that we can learn from these two footnotes is surely this: Editors following F ought not to omit Q2 material simply because their aesthetic sense tells them that Shakespeare must have decided to cut it, nor, if they are following Q2, should they omit F material because their aesthetic sense tells them that an actor must have added it. (An exception to the rule: The present editor could not bear to follow Hamlet's "The rest is silence" with F's "O, o, o, o.")

In the Overview that begins this volume, the general editor comments on the "instability" of the text. No manuscript of a play by Shakespeare survives; we have only printed versions, some perhaps based on his drafts, some perhaps based on prompt copies made for the playhouse by a professional scribe, some perhaps based (this is a relatively new view) on playhouse manuscripts that show Shakespeare's revision of his earlier work. In any case we can be sure only that the printed text is a "socialized" document, the product not only of Shakespeare, but of whoever prepared the copy for the compositors, and of the compositors themselves, who made of the copy what they could. And the product of the editors, too, who (whether they know it or not) make countless decisions that make each text distinctive. In the unattractive idiom of today, a given text, whether Q2 or F or, for that matter, the present edition, is only "a particular instantiation of the play" (David Scott Kastan, in *Shakespeare Studies* 24 [1996], page 35). The great editors early in this century sought to establish a text that revealed "authorial intent," but today, largely under the influence of Michel Foucault's "What Is an Author?" and Roland Barthes's "The Death of the Author," editors are likely to insist that "authorial intent" is a will-o'-the-wisp. Thus, in Kastan's words, editors who give a "socialized" or "theatrical" version of the text can claim to recognize "the very social and material mediations that permit (both authorial and nonauthorial) intentions to be realized in print and in performance" (page 33).

Editors who hold that Q2 and F are two distinct "instantiations" of *Hamlet* rather than two imperfect texts of *Hamlet* argue that if we combine the texts—"conflate" them is the technical term—we accomplish nothing useful and in fact are producing a text that never was printed or staged in Shakespeare's day. Thus, Stanley Wells and Gary Taylor explain in *William Shakespeare: A Textual Companion* (1988), a massive volume that accompanies the Oxford *Complete Works,* that Hamlet's motivation for reconciliation with Laertes differs in the two versions. To combine them, Wells and Taylor argue, is absurd. In the Quarto, and only in the Quarto, an anonymous lord says to Hamlet, "The Queen desires you to use some gentle entertainment to Laertes before you fall to play" (5.2.207–08), whereas in the Folio, and only in the Folio, Hamlet says,

> But I am very sorry, good Horatio,
> That to Laertes I forgot myself.
> For by the image of my cause I see
> The portraiture of his. I'll court his favors.
> But sure the bravery* of his grief did put me
> Into a tow'ring passion. (75–80)

In their *Textual Companion* the Oxford editors say,

> Thus, in Q2 Gertrude tells Hamlet to attempt a reconciliation with Laertes, just before Hamlet attempts such a reconciliation. In F, where this passage does not appear, Gertrude is in no way responsible for prompting this change in Hamlet's behaviour. . . . In F Hamlet himself decides, without the need of any prompting from Gertrude or anyone else, to seek a reconciliation with Laertes. . . . Q2 and F thus give two entirely different motivations for the crucial change in Hamlet's behaviour to Laertes.

*Bravado.

The traditional conflated text, in sorry contrast, instead combines these two explanations, without comment, making the anonymous lord's entrance and his message a wholly superfluous intrusion upon the dramatic progress of the play's final scene. (Page 400)

This is a bit strong. After all, to say that "in Q2 Gertrude tells Hamlet to attempt a reconciliation," when in fact all that we get is an anonymous lord reporting, in one line, a message from the Queen, is to give to one bland line much more weight than is appropriate. Moreover, a conflated text does not produce any contradiction or absurdity; rather, it lets us see Hamlet, entirely on his own, tell Horatio that he will apologize to Laertes, and a little later it lets us hear that the Queen (who, after all, was not privy to the conversation between Hamlet and Horatio) would like Hamlet to apologize. There is not the slightest inconsistency or redundancy.

Given that Wells and Taylor use this instance of conflation as a horrible example, it apparently is a worst-case scenario. Editors (and readers and viewers) must ask themselves which does more violence to *Hamlet*, inclusion of all of the lines of both texts, or omission of passages—some of them consisting of many lines—because either the Q2 or F omitted them. The present editor, with only the mildest of misgivings, has elected to conflate the texts. Readers will find not only Hamlet's statement that he will apologize to Laertes but also Gertrude's expressed wish (through an anonymous lord) that he do so. Readers will also find Hamlet's comment on the conflict between the companies of adult actors and the companies of boy actors in 2.2 (only in F), Hamlet's comment on hoisting enemies with their own petar in 3.4 (only in Q), and dozens of other lines, too, that some editors relegate to an appendix, where of course they are not read within the context of the play.

Finally, truth in packaging requires that readers be reminded that even in reading a conflated text they are not getting all of Shakespeare's words and nothing but those words. Editors must decide, to give only two now-familiar instances out of many instances, whether Hamlet speaks of "solid flesh" or "sallied [i.e. sullied] flesh," and whether he says his father was "interred" or "enurned." Editors try to make intelligent choices, which usually means that they believe they can give good reasons for their choices, but this does not mean that the editor whose decisions are theory-driven necessarily makes the best decisions. Given the facts that no manuscripts of Shakespeare's plays survive, that we do not know how these lost manuscripts were prepared to become texts for the playhouse, and that we can only conjecture about what sorts of copy the printers worked from, informed guesswork must play a role in preparing a modern edition.

The present edition takes the Second Quarto—the longest of the three early versions—as the control text, but, as the preceding discussion indicates, an editor must also make use of the Folio. Neither the First Quarto nor the Second Quarto is divided into scenes; the Folio indicates only 1.1, 1.2, 1.3, 2.1, and 2.2. The Signet Classic edition, to allow for easy reference, follows the traditional divisions of the Globe edition, placing them (as well as indications of locale) within square brackets to indicate that they are editorial, not authorial. Punctuation and spelling are modernized (*and* is given as *an* when if means "if"), obvious typographical errors are corrected, abbreviations are expanded, speech prefixes are regularized, and the positions of stage directions slightly altered where necessary. Other departures from the Second Quarto are listed below. First is given the adopted reading, in italic, and then the Second Quarto reading, in roman. The vast majority of these adopted readings are from the Folio; if an adopted reading is not from the Folio, the fact is indicated by a bracketed remark explaining, for example, that it is drawn from the First Quarto [Q1] or the Second Folio [F2] or an editor's conjecture [ed].

1.1.16 *soldier* souldiers   63 *Polacks* [F has "Pollax"] pollax   68 *my* mine   73 *why* with   73 *cast* cost   88 *those* these   91 *returned* returne   94 *designed* [F2] design   112 *mote* [ed] moth   121 *feared* [ed] feare   138 *you* your   140 *at it* it   142 s.d. *Exit Ghost* [Q2 omits]

1.2.1 s.d. *Councilors* [ed] Counsaile: as   41 s.d. *Exit Voltemand and Cornelius* [Q2 omits]   58 *He hath* Hath   67 *so* so much   77 *good* coold   82 *shapes* [ed; F has "shewes"] chapes   96 *a mind* or minde   132 *self-slaughter* seale slaughter   133 *weary* wary   137 *to this* thus   143 *would* should   175 *to drink deep* for to drinke   178 *to see* to   209 *Where, as* [ed] Whereas   224 *Indeed, indeed, sirs* Indeede Sirs   237 *Very like, very like* Very like   238 *hundred* hundreth   257 *foul* fonde

1.3.3 *convoy is* conuay in   12 *bulk* bulkes   18 *For he himself is subject to his birth* [Q2 omits]   49 *like a* a   68 *thine* thy   74 *Are* Or   75 *be* boy   76 *loan* loue   83 *invites* inuests   109 *Tend'ring* [Q1] Wrong [F has "Roaming"]   115 *springes* springs   123 *parley* parle   125 *tether* tider   131 *beguile* beguide

1.4.1 *shrewdly* shroudly   2 *a nipping* nipping   6 s.d. *go* [ed] goes   19 *clepe* [ed] clip   27 *the* [ed] their   33 *Their* [ed] His   36 *evil* [ed] eale   57 s.d. *Ghost beckons Hamlet* Beckins   69 *my lord* my   70 *summit* [ed] somnet [F has "sonnet"]   82 *artere* [ed] arture [F has "artire"]   87 *imagination* imagion

1.5.47 *what a* what   55 *lust* but   56 *sate* sort   64 *leperous* leaprous   68 *posset* possesse   91 s.d. *Exit* [Q2 omits]   95 *stiffly* swiftly   113 *Horatio and Marcellus (Within)* Enter Horatio and Marcellus [Q2 gives the speech to Horatio]   116 *bird* and   122 *heaven, my lord* heauen   132 *Look you, I'll* I will   170 *some'er* [ed] so mere [F has "so ere"]

2.1. s.d. *Reynaldo* or two   28 *Faith, no* Fayth   38 *warrant* wit   39 *sullies* sallies   40 *i' th'* with   52–53 *at "friend or so," and "gentleman"* [Q2 omits]   112 *quoted* coted

2.2.43 *Assure you* I assure!   57 *o'erhasty* hastie   58 s.d. *Enter Polonius, Voltemand, and Cornelius* Enter Embassadors   90 *since brevity* breuitie   108 s.d. *the letter* [Q2 omits, but has "letter" at side of line 116]   126 *above* about   137 *winking* working   143 *his* her   148 *watch* wath   149 *a lightness* lightnes   151 *'tis this* this   167 s.d. *Enter Hamlet reading on a book* Enter Hamlet   190 *far gone, far gone* far gone   205 *you yourself* your selfe   205 *should be* shall growe   212 *sanity* sanctity   214–15 *and suddenly . . . between him* [Q2 omits]   217 *will* will not   227 *excellent* extent   231 *overhappy* euer happy   232 *cap* lap   240 *but that* but the   243–74 *Let me question . . . dreadfully attended* [Q2 omits]   278 *even* euer   285 *Why anything* Any thing   312 *a piece* peece   318 *woman* women   329 *of me* on me   332–33 *the clown . . . o' th' sere* [from F, but F has "tickled a" for "tickle o' "; Q2 omits]   334 *blank* black   345–70 *Hamlet. How comes . . . load too* [Q2 omits]   350 *berattle* [ed; F has "be-ratled"; Q2 omits]   357 *most like* [ed; F has "like most"; Q2 omits]   381 *lest my* let

me 407–08 *tragical-historical, tragical-comical-historical-pastoral*
[Q2 omits] 434 *By'r Lady* by lady 439 *French falconers* friendly
Fankners 454 *affectation* affection 457 *tale* talke 467 *heraldry* her-
aldy 485 *Then senseless Ilium* [Q2 omits] 492 *And like* Like
506 *fellies* [ed] follies 515 *Mobled queen is good* [F has "Inobled" for
"Mobled"; Q2 omits] 525 *husband's* husband 530 *whe'r* [ed]
where 550–51 *a need* neede 551 *or sixteen lines* lines, or sixteene
lines 556 *till* tell 564 *his visage* the visage 569 *to Hecuba* to
her 571 *the cue* that 590 *ha' fatted* [F has "have fatted"] a
fatted 593 *O, vengeance* [Q2 omits] 595 *father* [Q4; Q2 and F
omit] 599 *scullion* stallion 611 *devil, and the devil* deale, and the deale

3.1.32–33 *myself (lawful espials) Will* myself Wee'le 46 *loneliness*
lowliness 55 *Let's withdraw* with-draw 83 *cowards of us all* cowards
85 *sicklied* sickled 92 *well, well, well* well 107 *your honesty* you
121 *to a nunnery* a Nunry 129 *knaves all* knaues 139 *Go, farewell,*
farewell 146 *lisp* list 148 *your ignorance* ignorance 155 *expectancy*
expectation 160 *that* what 162 *feature* stature 164 [Q2 concludes
the line with a stage direction, "Exit"] 191 *unwatched* vnmatcht

3.2.1 *pronounced* pronound 24 *own feature* feature 28 *the which*
which 31 *praise* praysd 39 *us, sir* vs 47 s.d. *Exit Players*
[Q2 omits] 51 s.d. *Exit Polonius* [Q2 omits] 54 *ho* [F has "hoa"]
howe 91 *detecting* detected 91 s.d. *Rosencrantz . . . Flourish* [Q2
omits] 117–18 *Hamlet. I mean . . . my lord* [Q2 omits] 140 s.d. *sound*
[ed] sounds 140 s.d. *very lovingly* [Q2 omits] 140 s.d. *She kneels . . .
unto him* [Q2 omits] 140 s.d. *Exeunt* [Q2 omits] 142 *is miching*
munching 147 *keep counsel* keepe 161 *ground* the ground 169 *your*
our 174 *In neither* Eyther none, in neither 175 *love* Lord 196 *like*
the 205 *Grief joys* Greefe ioy 225 *An* [ed] And 229 *a* I be a 233
s.d. *sleeps* [Q2 omits] 234 s.d. *Exit* Exeunt 262 *Confederate* Consid-
erat 264 *infected* inuected 266 s.d. *Pours the poison in his ears* [Q2
omits] 272 *Hamlet. What . . . fire* [Q2 omits] 282–83 *two Provincial*
prouinciall 316 *start* stare 325 *my business* busines 366 *and thumb*
& the vmber 375 *the top of my* my 379 *you can* you 394–95 *Polonius . . . friends* Leaue me friends. I will, say so. By and by is easily
said 397 *breathes* breakes 399 *bitter business as the day* buisnes as
the bitter day 404 *daggers* dagger

3.3.19 *huge* hough 22 *ruin* raine 23 *with a* a 50 *pardoned*
pardon 58 *shove* showe 73 *pat* but 79 *hire and salary* base and silly

3.4.5–6 *with him . . . Mother, Mother, Mother* [Q2 omits] 7 *warrant* wait 21 *inmost* most 23 *ho* [F has "hoa"] how 23 *ho* [F has
"hoa"] how 25 s.d. *kills Polonius* [Q2 omits] 53 *That roars . . . index*
[Q2 gives to Hamlet] 60 *heaven-kissing* heaue, a kissing 89 *panders*

pardons   90 *mine eyes into my very soul* my very eyes into my soule   91 *grainèd* greeued   92 *will not* will   98 *tithe* kyth   140 *Ecstasy* [Q2 omits]   144 *And I* And   159 *live* leaue   166 *Refrain tonight* to refraine night   180 *Thus* This   187 *ravel* rouell   216 *foolish* most foolish   218 s.d. *exit Hamlet, tugging in Polonius* Exit

4.1.35 *dragged* dreg'd

4.2.1   s.d. *Enter Hamlet* Enter Hamlet, Rosencraus, and others   2 *Gentlemen. (Within) Hamlet! Lord Hamlet!* [Q2 omits]   4 s.d. *Enter Rosencrantz and Guildenstern* [Q2 omits]   6 *Compounded* Compound   18 *ape* apple   30–31 *Hide fox, and all after* [Q2 omits]

4.3.15 *Ho* [F has "Hoa"] How   43 *With fiery quickness* [Q2 omits]   52 *and so* so   68 *were ne'er begun* will nere begin

4.5.16 *Queen* [Q2 gives line 16 as part of the previous speech]   20 s.d. *Enter Ophelia distracted* Enter Ophelia [placed after line 16]   39 *grave* ground   42 *God* good   52 *clothes* close   57 *Indeed, la* Indeede   73 s.d. *Exit* [Q2 omits]   82 *in their* in   89 *his* this   96 *Queen. Alack, what noise is this* [Q2 omits]   97 *are* is   106 *They* The   142 *swoopstake* [ed] soopstake   152 s.d. *Let her come in* [Q2 gives to Laertes]   157 *Till* Tell   160 *an old* a poore   161–63 *Nature . . . loves* [Q2 omits]   165 *Hey . . . hey nony* [Q2 omits]   181 *O, you must* you may   186 *affliction* afflictions   194 *All flaxen* Flaxen   198 *Christian souls, I pray God* Christians soules   199 *see this* this

4.6.9 *an't* and   23 *good turn* turne   27 *bore* bord   31 *He* So   32 *give you* you

4.7.6 *proceeded* proceede   14 *conjunctive* concliue   20 *Would* Worke   22 *loud a wind* loued Arm'd   24 *And* But   24 *had* haue   36 *How now . . . Hamlet* [Q2 omits]   42 s.d. *Exit Messenger* [Q2 omits]   46 *your pardon* you pardon   47 *and more strange return* returne   48 *Hamlet* [Q2 omits]   56 *shall live* liue   62 *checking* the King   88 *my* me   115 *wick* [ed] weeke   119 *changes* change   122 *spendthrift* [ed] spend thirfts   125 *in deed* [ed] indeede   134 *on* ore   138 *pass* pace   140 *for that* for   156 *ha't* hate   159 *prepared* prefard   167 *hoar* horry   171 *cold* cull-cold

5.1.9 *se offendendo* so offended   12 *Argall* or all   35–38 *Other. Why . . . without arms* [Q2 omits]   44 *that frame* that   56 s.d. *Enter Hamlet and Horatio afar off* Enter Hamlet and Horatio [Q2 places after line 65]   61 *stoup* soope   71 *daintier* dintier   90 *mazzard* massene   107–08 *Is this . . . recoveries* [Q2 omits]   109 *his vouchers* vouchers   110 *double ones* doubles   122 *O* or   123 *For such a guest is meet* [Q2 omits]   144–45 *a gravemaker* Graue-maker   146 *all the days* the dayes   167 *corses now-a-days* corses   174–75 *three and twenty* 23   185 *Let me see* [Q2 omits]   187 *borne* bore   195 *chamber* table   210–11 *as thus* [Q2 omits]   218 *winter's* waters   219 s.d. *Enter King . . . Lords attendant* Enter K. Q. Laertes and the corse   233 *Shards, flints* Flints   248 *treble* double   252 s.d. *Leaps in the grave* [Q2 omits]   263 *and rash* rash   279 *Dost thou* doost   287 *thus* this   300 *shortly* thirtie   301 *Till* Tell

5.2.5 *Methought* my thought   6 *bilboes* bilbo   17 *unseal* vnfold   19 *Ah* [ed; F has "Oh"] A   43 *as's* [F has "assis"] as sir   52 *Subscribed* Subcribe   57 *Why, man . . . employment* [Q2 omits]   68–80 *To quit . . . comes here* [Q2 omits]   78 *court* [ed; F has "count"; Q2 omits]   80 s.d. *Young Osric* [Q2 omits]   81 *Osric* [Q2 prints "Cour" consistently as the speech prefix]   83 *humbly* humble   94 *Put your* your   99 *sultry* sully   99 *for* or   102 *But, my* my   108 *gentleman* [ed] gentlemen   110 *feelingly* [ed] sellingly   142 *his weapon* [ed] this weapon   151 *hangers* [ed] hanger   158 *carriages* carriage   161 *might be* be   164–65 *all impawned, as* all   180 *e'en so* so   184 *Yours, yours. He* Yours   189 *did comply* did   193 *yeasty* histy   194 *fanned* [ed; F has "fond"] prophane   195 *winnowed* trennowed   208 *to Laertes* [ed] Laertes   210 *lose this wager* loose   213 *But thou* thou   217 *gain-giving* gamgiuing   221 *If it be now* if it be   223 *will come* well come   241 *Sir, in this audience* [Q2 omits]   251 *keep my* my   251 *till* all   254 *Come on* [Q2 omits]   264 *bettered* better   266 s.d. *Prepare to play* [Q2 omits]   273 *union* Vnice   281 s.d. *They play* [Q2 omits]   287 *A touch, a touch* [Q2 omits]   301 s.d. *play* [Q2 omits]   303 s.d. *In scuffling they change rapiers* [Q2 omits]   304 *ho* [F has "hoa"] howe   312 *Ho* [ed] how   314 *Hamlet.* Hamlet Hamlet   317 *thy* my   323 s.d. *Hurts the King* [Q2 omits]   326 *murd'rous, damnèd* damned   327 *thy union* the Onixe   328 s.d. *King dies* [Q2 omits]   332 s.d. *Dies* [Q2 omits]   346 *live* I leaue   359 *Dies* [Q2 omits]   362 s.d. *with Drum, Colors, and Attendants* [Q2 omits]   380 *th'* yet yet   384 *forced* for no   393 *on* no   400 *rite* [ed; F has "rites"] right   404 s.d. *marching . . . shot off* [Q2 omits]

The Tragedy of

OTHELLO

The Moor of Venice

Dramatis Personae

Othello, the Moor
Brabantio, father to Desdemona
Cassio, an honorable lieutenant
Iago, a villain
Roderigo, a gulled gentleman
Duke of Venice
Senators
Montano, Governor of Cyprus
Gentlemen of Cyprus
Lodovico and Gratiano, two noble Venetians
Sailors
Clown
Desdemona, wife to Othello
Emilia, wife to Iago
Bianca, a courtesan
[Messenger, Herald, Officers, Gentlemen,
    Musicians, Attendants
        Scene: Venice and Cyprus]

The Tragedy of Othello

ACT 1

Scene 1. [*Venice. A street.*]

Enter Roderigo and Iago.

Roderigo. Tush! Never tell me? I take it much un-
kindly
    That thou, Iago, who hast had my purse
    As if the strings were thine, shouldst know of this.

Iago. 'Sblood,°¹ but you'll not hear me! If ever I did
dream
    Of such a matter, abhor me.

Roderigo.   Thou told'st me   5
    Thou didst hold him in thy hate.

Iago.   Despise me
    If I do not. Three great ones of the city,
    In personal suit to make me his lieutenant,
    Off-capped° to him; and, by the faith of man,
    I know my price; I am worth no worse a place.   10
    But he, as loving his own pride and purposes,
    Evades them with a bombast circumstance,°

---

¹ The degree sign (°) indicates a footnote, which is keyed to the text by the
line number. Text references are printed in **boldface** type; the annotation follows in roman type.   1.1.4 **'Sblood** by God's blood   9 **Off-capped** doffed
their caps—as a mark of respect   12 **bombast circumstance** stuffed, round-
about speech

3

Horribly stuffed with epithets of war;
Nonsuits° my mediators. For, "Certes," says he,
"I have already chose my officer." And what was
15   he?
Forsooth, a great arithmetician,°
One Michael Cassio, a Florentine,
(A fellow almost damned in a fair wife)°
That never set a squadron in the field,
20   Nor the division of a battle knows
More than a spinster; unless the bookish theoric,
Wherein the tonguèd° consuls can propose
As masterly as he. Mere prattle without practice
Is all his soldiership. But he, sir, had th' election;
25   And I, of whom his eyes had seen the proof
At Rhodes, at Cyprus, and on other grounds
Christian and heathen, must be belee'd and calmed
By debitor and creditor. This counter-caster,°
He, in good time, must his lieutenant be,
And I—God bless the mark!—his Moorship's an-
30   cient.°

Roderigo. By heaven, I rather would have been his
    hangman.

Iago. Why, there's no remedy. 'Tis the curse of service:
Preferment goes by letter and affection,°
And not by old gradation,° where each second
35   Stood heir to th' first. Now, sir, be judge yourself,
Whether I in any just term am affined°
To love the Moor.

Roderigo.   I would not follow him then.

14 **Nonsuits** rejects   16 **arithmetician** theorist (rather than practical)   18 **A . . . wife** (a much-disputed passage, which is probably best taken as a general sneer at Cassio as a dandy and a ladies' man. But in the story from which Shakespeare took his plot the counterpart of Cassio is married, and it may be that at the beginning of the play Shakespeare had decided to keep him married but later changed his mind)   22 **tonguèd** eloquent   28 **counter-caster** i.e., a bookkeeper who *casts* (reckons up) figures on a *counter* (abacus)   30 **ancient** standard-bearer; an underofficer   33 **letter and affection** recommendations (from men of power) and personal preference   34 **old gradation** seniority   36 **affined** bound

Iago. O, sir, content you.
    I follow him to serve my turn upon him.
    We cannot all be masters, nor all masters   *40*
    Cannot be truly followed. You shall mark
    Many a duteous and knee-crooking° knave
    That, doting on his own obsequious bondage,
    Wears out his time, much like his master's ass,
    For naught but provender; and when he's old,
        cashiered.   *45*
    Whip me such honest knaves! Others there are
    Who, trimmed in forms and visages of duty,
    Keep yet their hearts attending on themselves,
    And, throwing but shows of service on their lords,
    Do well thrive by them, and when they have lined
        their coats,   *50*
    Do themselves homage. These fellows have some
        soul;
    And such a one do I profess myself. For, sir,
    It is as sure as you are Roderigo,
    Were I the Moor, I would not be Iago.
    In following him, I follow but myself.   *55*
    Heaven is my judge, not I for love and duty,
    But seeming so, for my peculiar° end;
    For when my outward action doth demonstrate
    The native° act and figure of my heart
    In complement extern,° 'tis not long after   *60*
    But I will wear my heart upon my sleeve
    For daws to peck at; I am not what I am.

Roderigo. What a full fortune does the thick-lips owe°
    If he can carry't thus!

Iago.   Call up her father,
    Rouse him. Make after him, poison his delight,   *65*
    Proclaim him in the streets, incense her kinsmen,
    And though he in a fertile climate dwell,
    Plague him with flies; though that his joy be joy,

42 **knee-crooking** bowing   57 **peculiar** personal   59 **native** natural, innate
60 **complement extern** outward appearances   63 **owe** own

Yet throw such chances of vexation on't
70   As it may lose some color.

Roderigo. Here is her father's house. I'll call aloud.

Iago. Do, with like timorous° accent and dire yell
As when, by night and negligence, the fire
Is spied in populous cities.

Roderigo. What, ho, Brabantio! Signior Brabantio,
75   ho!

Iago. Awake! What, ho, Brabantio! Thieves! Thieves!
Look to your house, your daughter, and your bags!
Thieves! Thieves!

        Brabantio above° [*at a window*].

Brabantio. What is the reason of this terrible sum-
        mons?
80   What is the matter there?

Roderigo. Signior, is all your family within?

Iago. Are your doors locked?

Brabantio.   Why, wherefore ask you
        this?

Iago. Zounds, sir, y'are robbed! For shame. Put on
        your gown!
Your heart is burst, you have lost half your soul.
85   Even now, now, very now, an old black ram
Is tupping your white ewe. Arise, arise!
Awake the snorting citizens with the bell,
Or else the devil will make a grandsire of you.
Arise, I say!

Brabantio.   What, have you lost your wits?

Roderigo. Most reverend signior, do you know my
90   voice?

Brabantio. Not I. What are you?

_____

72 **timorous** frightening   78 s.d. **above** (i.e., on the small upper stage above
and to the rear of the main platform stage, which resembled the projecting upper story of an Elizabethan house)

Roderigo. My name is Roderigo.

Brabantio.   The worser welcome!
I have charged thee not to haunt about my doors.
In honest plainness thou hast heard me say
My daughter is not for thee; and now, in madness,   95
Being full of supper and distemp'ring draughts,°
Upon malicious knavery dost thou come
To start° my quiet.

Roderigo. Sir, sir, sir——

Brabantio.   But thou must needs be sure
My spirits and my place° have in their power   100
To make this bitter to thee.

Roderigo.   Patience, good sir.

Brabantio. What tell'st thou me of robbing? This is
    Venice;
My house is not a grange.°

Roderigo.   Most grave Brabantio,
In simple and pure soul I come to you.

Iago. Zounds, sir, you are one of those that will not   105
    serve God if the devil bid you. Because we come
    to do you service and you think we are ruffians,
    you'll have your daughter covered with a Barbary°
    horse, you'll have your nephews° neigh to you,
    you'll have coursers for cousins,° and gennets for   110
    germans.°

Brabantio. What profane wretch art thou?

Iago. I am one, sir, that comes to tell you your daughter
    and the Moor are making the beast with two backs.

Brabantio. Thou art a villain.

Iago.   You are—a senator.   115

Brabantio. This thou shalt answer. I know thee,
    Roderigo.

96 **distemp'ring draughts** unsettling drinks   98 **start** disrupt   100 **place**
rank, i.e., of senator   103 **grange** isolated house   108 **Barbary** Arabian,
i.e., Moorish   109 **nephews** i.e., grandsons   110 **cousins** relations
110–11 **gennets for germans** Spanish horses for blood relatives

Roderigo. Sir, I will answer anything. But I beseech
    you,
  If't be your pleasure and most wise consent,
  As partly I find it is, that your fair daughter,
120 At this odd-even° and dull watch o' th' night,
  Transported, with no worse nor better guard
  But with a knave of common hire, a gondolier,
  To the gross clasps of a lascivious Moor—
  If this be known to you, and your allowance,
125 We then have done you bold and saucy wrongs;
  But if you know not this, my manners tell me
  We have your wrong rebuke. Do not believe
  That from the sense of all civility°
  I thus would play and trifle with your reverence.
130 Your daughter, if you have not given her leave,
  I say again, hath made a gross revolt,
  Tying her duty, beauty, wit, and fortunes
  In an extravagant° and wheeling stranger
  Of here and everywhere. Straight satisfy yourself.
135 If she be in her chamber, or your house,
  Let loose on me the justice of the state
  For thus deluding you.

Brabantio.   Strike on the tinder, ho!
  Give me a taper! Call up all my people!
  This accident° is not unlike my dream.
140 Belief of it oppresses me already.
  Light, I say! Light!   *Exit [above].*

Iago.   Farewell, for I must leave you.
  It seems not meet, nor wholesome to my place,
  To be produced—as, if I stay, I shall—
  Against the Moor. For I do know the State,
145 However this may gall him with some check,°
  Cannot with safety cast° him; for he's embarked
  With such loud reason to the Cyprus wars,

120 **odd-even** between night and morning 128 **sense of all civility** feeling of what is proper 133 **extravagant** vagrant, wandering (Othello is not Venetian and thus may be considered a wandering soldier of fortune) 139 **accident** happening 145 **check** restraint 146 **cast** dismiss

Which even now stands in act,° that for their souls
Another of his fathom° they have none
To lead their business; in which regard,   150
Though I do hate him as I do hell-pains,
Yet, for necessity of present life,
I must show out a flag and sign of love,
Which is indeed but sign. That you shall surely find
    him,
Lead to the Sagittary° the raisèd search;   155 ·
And there will I be with him. So farewell.   *Exit.*

*Enter Brabantio [in his nightgown], with Servants
          and torches.*

Brabantio. It is too true an evil. Gone she is;
    And what's to come of my despisèd time
    Is naught but bitterness. Now, Roderigo,
    Where didst thou see her?—O unhappy girl!—   160
    With the Moor, say'st thou?—Who would be a
        father?—
    How didst thou know 'twas she?—O, she deceives
        me
    Past thought!—What said she to you? Get moe°
        tapers!
    Raise all my kindred!—Are they married, think
        you?

Roderigo. Truly I think they are.   165

Brabantio. O heaven! How got she out? O treason of
        the blood!
    Fathers, from hence trust not your daughters' minds
    By what you see them act.° Is there not charms
    By which the property° of youth and maidhood
    May be abused? Have you not read, Roderigo,   170
    Of some such thing?

Roderigo.   Yes, sir, I have indeed.

Brabantio. Call up my brother.—O, would you had
        had her!—

148 **stands in act** takes place   149 **fathom** ability   155 **Sagittary** (probably
the name of an inn)   163 **moe** more   168 **act** do   169 **property** true nature

Some one way, some another.—Do you know
Where we may apprehend her and the Moor?

175 *Roderigo.* I think I can discover him, if you please
To get good guard and go along with me.

Brabantio. Pray you lead on. At every house I'll call;
I may command at most.—Get weapons, ho!
And raise some special officers of might.—
180 On, good Roderigo; I will deserve your pains.°

Exeunt.

Scene 2. [*A street.*]

Enter Othello, Iago, Attendants with torches.

Iago. Though in the trade of war I have slain men,
Yet do I hold it very stuff° o' th' conscience
To do no contrived murder. I lack iniquity
Sometime to do me service. Nine or ten times
I had thought t' have yerked° him here, under the
5   ribs.

Othello. 'Tis better as it is.

Iago.   Nay, but he prated,
And spoke such scurvy and provoking terms
Against your honor, that with the little godliness
I have
I did full hard forbear him. But I pray you, sir,
10   Are you fast married? Be assured of this,
That the magnifico° is much beloved,
And hath in his effect a voice potential
As double as the Duke's.° He will divorce you,
Or put upon you what restraint or grievance

---

180 **deserve your pains** be worthy of (and reward) your efforts   1.2.2 **stuff**
essence   5 **yerked** stabbed   11 **magnifico** nobleman   12–13 **hath . . . Duke's**
i.e., can be as effective as the Duke

The law, with all his might to enforce it on,   15
Will give him cable.°

Othello.   Let him do his spite.
My services which I have done the Signiory°
Shall out-tongue his complaints. 'Tis yet to know°—
Which when I know that boasting is an honor
I shall promulgate—I fetch my life and being   20
From men of royal siege;° and my demerits°
May speak unbonneted to as proud a fortune
As this that I have reached.° For know, Iago,
But that I love the gentle Desdemona,
I would not my unhousèd° free condition   25
Put into circumscription and confine
For the seas' worth. But look, what lights come
     yond?

> *Enter Cassio, with [Officers and] torches.*

Iago. Those are the raisèd father and his friends.
     You were best go in.

Othello.   Not I. I must be found.
My parts, my title, and my perfect soul°   30
Shall manifest me rightly. Is it they?

Iago. By Janus, I think no.

Othello. The servants of the Duke? And my lieutenant?
The goodness of the night upon you, friends.
What is the news?

Cassio.   The Duke does greet you, general;   35
And he requires your haste-posthaste appearance
Even on the instant.

Othello.   What is the matter, think you?

Cassio. Something from Cyprus, as I may divine.
It is a business of some heat. The galleys

16 **cable** range, scope   17 **Signiory** the rulers of Venice   18 **yet to know** unknown as yet   21 **siege** rank   21 **demerits** deserts   22–23 **May ... reached,** i.e., are the equal of the family I have married into   25 **unhousèd** unconfined   30 **perfect soul** clear, unflawed conscience

40   Have sent a dozen sequent° messengers
       This very night at one another's heels,
       And many of the consuls, raised and met,
       Are at the Duke's already. You have been hotly
          called for.
       When, being not at your lodging to be found,
45   The Senate hath sent about three several° quests
       To search you out.
    Othello.   'Tis well I am found by you.
       I will but spend a word here in the house,
       And go with you.   [*Exit.*]
    Cassio.   Ancient, what makes he here?
    Iago. Faith, he tonight hath boarded a land carack.°
50   If it prove lawful prize, he's made forever.
    Cassio. I do not understand.
    Iago.   He's married.
    Cassio.   To who?

                [*Enter Othello.*]

    Iago. Marry,° to— Come, captain, will you go?
    Othello.   Have with you.
    Cassio. Here comes another troop to seek for you.

    Enter Brabantio, Roderigo, with Officers and torches.

    Iago. It is Brabantio. General, be advised.
       He comes to bad intent.
55   *Othello.*   Holla! Stand there!
    Roderigo. Signior, it is the Moor.
    Brabantio.   Down with him, thief!
                      [*They draw swords.*]
    Iago. You, Roderigo? Come, sir, I am for you.
    Othello. Keep up your bright swords, for the dew will
       rust them.

---

40 **sequent** successive   45 **several** separate   49 **carack** treasure ship   52
Marry By Mary (an interjection)

Good signior, you shall more command with years
Than with your weapons.   *60*

Brabantio. O thou foul thief, where hast thou stowed
    my daughter?
Damned as thou art, thou hast enchanted her!
For I'll refer me to all things of sense,°
If she in chains of magic were not bound,
Whether a maid so tender, fair, and happy,   *65*
So opposite to marriage that she shunned
The wealthy, curlèd darlings of our nation,
Would ever have, t' incur a general mock,°
Run from her guardage to the sooty bosom
Of such a thing as thou—to fear, not to delight.   *70*
Judge me the world if 'tis not gross in sense°
That thou hast practiced° on her with foul charms,
Abused her delicate youth with drugs or minerals
That weaken motion.° I'll have't disputed on;
'Tis probable, and palpable to thinking.   *75*
I therefore apprehend and do attach° thee
For an abuser of the world, a practicer
Of arts inhibited and out of warrant.°
Lay hold upon him. If he do resist,
Subdue him at his peril.

Othello.   Hold your hands,   *80*
Both you of my inclining and the rest.
Were it my cue to fight, I should have known it
Without a prompter. Whither will you that I go
To answer this your charge?

Brabantio.   To prison, till fit time
Of law and course of direct session   *85*
Call thee to answer.

Othello.   What if I do obey?
How may the Duke be therewith satisfied,
Whose messengers are here about my side

---

63 **refer . . . sense** i.e., base (my argument) on all ordinary understanding of
nature 68 **general mock** public shame 71 **gross in sense** obvious 72
practiced used tricks 74 **motion** thought, i.e., reason 76 **attach** arrest
78 **inhibited . . . warrant** prohibited and illegal (black magic)

Upon some present° business of the state
To bring me to him?

90 *Officer.*   'Tis true, most worthy signior.
The Duke's in council, and your noble self
I am sure is sent for.

Brabantio.   How? The Duke in council?
In this time of the night? Bring him away.
Mine's not an idle cause. The Duke himself,
95 Or any of my brothers° of the state,
Cannot but feel this wrong as 'twere their own;
For if such actions may have passage free,
Bondslaves and pagans shall our statesmen be.

                                   Exeunt.

Scene 3. [*A council chamber.*]

*Enter Duke, Senators, and Officers [set at a table,
with lights and Attendants].*

Duke. There's no composition° in this news
That gives them credit.°

First Senator.   Indeed, they are disproportioned.
My letters say a hundred and seven galleys.

Duke. And mine a hundred forty.

Second Senator.   And mine two hundred.
5 But though they jump° not on a just accompt°—
As in these cases where the aim° reports
'Tis oft with difference—yet do they all confirm
A Turkish fleet, and bearing up to Cyprus.

Duke. Nay, it is possible enough to judgment.°
10 I do not so secure me in the error,

89 **present** immediate   95 **brothers** i.e., the other senators   1.3.1 **composition** agreement   2 **gives them credit** makes them believable   5 **jump** agree   5 **just accompt** exact counting   6 **aim** approximation   9 **to judgment** when carefully considered

But the main article I do approve
In fearful sense.°
Sailor. (Within) What, ho! What, ho! What, ho!

Enter Sailor.

Officer. A messenger from the galleys.
Duke.　　　　　　　　　　Now? What's the business?
Sailor. The Turkish preparation makes for Rhodes.
　　So was I bid report here to the State　　　　　　*15*
　　By Signior Angelo.
Duke. How say you by this change?
First Senator.　　　　　　　　　This cannot be
　　By no assay of reason. 'Tis a pageant°
　　To keep us in false gaze.° When we consider
　　Th' importancy of Cyprus to the Turk,　　　　　*20*
　　And let ourselves again but understand
　　That, as it more concerns the Turk than Rhodes,
　　So may he with more facile question° bear it,
　　For that it stands not in such warlike brace,°
　　But altogether lacks th' abilities　　　　　　　*25*
　　That Rhodes is dressed in. If we make thought of
　　　this,
　　We must not think the Turk is so unskillful
　　To leave that latest which concerns him first,
　　Neglecting an attempt of ease and gain
　　To wake and wage a danger profitless.　　　　　*30*
Duke. Nay, in all confidence he's not for Rhodes.
Officer. Here is more news.

Enter a Messenger.

Messenger. The Ottomites, reverend and gracious,
　　Steering with due course toward the isle of Rhodes,
　　Have there injointed them with an after° fleet.　*35*

10–12 **I do . . . sense** i.e., just because the numbers disagree in the reports, I do not doubt that the principal information (that the Turkish fleet is out) is fearfully true　18 **pageant** show, pretense　19 **in false gaze** looking the wrong way　23 **facile question** easy struggle　24 **warlike brace** "military posture"　35 **after** following

First Senator. Ay, so I thought. How many, as you
    guess?

Messenger. Of thirty sail; and now they do restem
    Their backward course, bearing with frank ap-
    pearance
    Their purposes toward Cyprus. Signior Montano,
40 Your trusty and most valiant servitor,
    With his free duty° recommends° you thus,
    And prays you to believe him.

Duke. 'Tis certain then for Cyprus.
    Marcus Luccicos, is not he in town?

45 *First Senator.* He's now in Florence.

Duke. Write from us to him; post-posthaste dispatch.

First Senator. Here comes Brabantio and the valiant
    Moor.

*Enter Brabantio, Othello, Cassio, Iago, Roderigo,
                and Officers.*

Duke. Valiant Othello, we must straight° employ you
    Against the general° enemy Ottoman.
    [*To Brabantio*] I did not see you. Welcome, gentle
50 signior.
    We lacked your counsel and your help tonight.

Brabantio. So did I yours. Good your grace, pardon
    me.
    Neither my place, nor aught I heard of business,
    Hath raised me from my bed; nor doth the general
    care
55 Take hold on me; for my particular grief
    Is of so floodgate and o'erbearing nature
    That it engluts and swallows other sorrows,
    And it is still itself.

Duke.   Why, what's the matter?

Brabantio. My daughter! O, my daughter!

41 **free duty** unlimited respect   41 **recommends** informs   48 **straight** at
once   49 **general** universal

Senators.   Dead?

Brabantio.   Ay, to me.
   She is abused, stol'n from me, and corrupted   60
   By spells and medicines bought of mountebanks;
   For nature so prepost'rously to err,
   Being not deficient, blind, or lame of sense,
   Sans° witchcraft could not.

Duke. Whoe'er he be that in this foul proceeding   65
   Hath thus beguiled your daughter of herself,
   And you of her, the bloody book of law
   You shall yourself read in the bitter letter
   After your own sense; yea, though our proper° son
   Stood in your action.°

Brabantio.   Humbly I thank your Grace.   70
   Here is the man—this Moor, whom now, it seems,
   Your special mandate for the state affairs
   Hath hither brought.

All.   We are very sorry for't.

Duke. [*To Othello*] What in your own part can you
   say to this?

Brabantio. Nothing, but this is so.   75

Othello. Most potent, grave, and reverend signiors,
   My very noble and approved° good masters,
   That I have ta'en away this old man's daughter,
   It is most true; true I have married her.
   The very head and front° of my offending   80
   Hath this extent, no more. Rude am I in my speech,
   And little blessed with the soft phrase of peace,
   For since these arms of mine had seven years' pith°
   Till now some nine moons wasted,° they have used
   Their dearest° action in the tented field;   85
   And little of this great world can I speak

---

64 **Sans** without   69 **proper** own   70 **Stood in your action** were the ac-
cused in your suit   77 **approved** tested, proven by past performance   80
head and front extreme form (*front* = forehead)   83 **pith** strength   84
wasted past   85 **dearest** most important

More than pertains to feats of broils and battle;
And therefore little shall I grace my cause
In speaking for myself. Yet, by your gracious
    patience,
90 I will a round° unvarnished tale deliver
Of my whole course of love—what drugs, what
    charms,
What conjuration, and what mighty magic,
For such proceeding I am charged withal,
I won his daughter—

    Brabantio.   A maiden never bold,
95 Of spirit so still and quiet that her motion
Blushed at herself;° and she, in spite of nature,
Of years, of country, credit, everything,
To fall in love with what she feared to look on!
It is a judgment maimed and most imperfect
100 That will confess perfection so could err
Against all rules of nature, and must be driven
To find out practices of cunning hell
Why this should be. I therefore vouch again
That with some mixtures pow'rful o'er the blood,
105 Or with some dram, conjured to this effect,
He wrought upon her.

    Duke.   To vouch this is no proof,
Without more wider and more overt test
Than these thin habits° and poor likelihoods
Of modern° seeming do prefer against him.

110 *First Senator.* But, Othello, speak.
Did you by indirect and forcèd courses
Subdue and poison this young maid's affections?
Or came it by request, and such fair question°
As soul to soul affordeth?

    Othello.   I do beseech you,
115 Send for the lady to the Sagittary

---

90 **round** blunt   95–96 **her motion/Blushed at herself** i.e., she was so
modest that she blushed at every thought (and movement)   108 **habits** clothing   109 **modern** trivial   113 **question** discussion

And let her speak of me before her father.
If you do find me foul in her report,
The trust, the office, I do hold of you
Not only take away, but let your sentence
Even fall upon my life.

Duke.   Fetch Desdemona hither.   *120*

Othello. Ancient, conduct them; you best know the
    place.

[*Exit Iago, with two or three Attendants.*]

And till she come, as truly as to heaven
I do confess the vices of my blood,
So justly to your grave ears I'll present
How I did thrive in this fair lady's love,   *125*
And she in mine.

Duke.   Say it, Othello.

Othello. Her father loved me; oft invited me;
    Still° questioned me the story of my life
    From year to year, the battle, sieges, fortune
    That I have passed.   *130*
    I ran it through, even from my boyish days
    To th' very moment that he bade me tell it.
    Wherein I spoke of most disastrous chances,
    Of moving accidents by flood and field,
    Of hairbreadth scapes i' th' imminent° deadly
        breach,   *135*
    Of being taken by the insolent foe
    And sold to slavery, of my redemption thence
    And portance° in my travel's history,
    Wherein of anters° vast and deserts idle,°
    Rough quarries, rocks, and hills whose heads touch
        heaven,   *140*
    It was my hint to speak. Such was my process.
    And of the Cannibals that each other eat,
    The Anthropophagi,° and men whose heads

128 **Still** regularly   135 **imminent** threatening   138 **portance** manner of
acting   139 **anters** caves   139 **idle** empty, sterile   143 **Anthropophagi**
man-eaters

Grew beneath their shoulders. These things to hear
145 Would Desdemona seriously incline;
But still the house affairs would draw her thence;
Which ever as she could with haste dispatch,
She'd come again, and with a greedy ear
Devour up my discourse. Which I observing,
150 Took once a pliant hour, and found good means
To draw from her a prayer of earnest heart
That I would all my pilgrimage dilate,°
Whereof by parcels she had something heard,
But not intentively.° I did consent,
155 And often did beguile her of her tears
When I did speak of some distressful stroke
That my youth suffered. My story being done,
She gave me for my pains a world of kisses.
She swore in faith 'twas strange, 'twas passing°
   strange;
160 'Twas pitiful, 'twas wondrous pitiful.
She wished she had not heard it; yet she wished
That heaven had made her such a man. She thanked
   me,
And bade me, if I had a friend that loved her,
I should but teach him how to tell my story,
165 And that would woo her. Upon this hint I spake.
She loved me for the dangers I had passed,
And I loved her that she did pity them.
This only is the witchcraft I have used.
Here comes the lady. Let her witness it.

Enter Desdemona, Iago, Attendants.

170 *Duke.* I think this tale would win my daughter too.
Good Brabantio, take up this mangled matter at the
   best.°
Men do their broken weapons rather use
Than their bare hands.

---

152 **dilate** relate in full   154 **intentively** at length and in sequence   159
passing surpassing   171 **Take . . . best** i.e., make the best of this disaster

Brabantio.   I pray you hear her speak.
  If she confess that she was half the wooer,
  Destruction on my head if my bad blame   *175*
  Light on the man. Come hither, gentle mistress.
  Do you perceive in all this noble company
  Where most you owe obedience?

Desdemona.   •   My noble father,
  I do perceive here a divided duty.
  To you I am bound for life and education;   *180*
  My life and education both do learn me
  How to respect you. You are the lord of duty,
  I am hitherto your daughter. But here's my husband,
  And so much duty as my mother showed
  To you, preferring you before her father,   *185*
  So much I challenge° that I may profess
  Due to the Moor my lord.

Brabantio.   God be with you. I have done.
  Please it your Grace, on to the state affairs.
  I had rather to adopt a child than get° it.
  Come hither, Moor.   *190*
  I here do give thee that with all my heart
  Which, but thou hast already, with all my heart
  I would keep from thee. For your sake,° jewel,
  I am glad at soul I have no other child,
  For thy escape would teach me tyranny,   *195*
  To hang clogs on them. I have done, my lord.

Duke. Let me speak like yourself and lay a sentence°
  Which, as a grise° or step, may help these lovers.
  When remedies are past, the griefs are ended
  By seeing the worst, which late on hopes depended.°   *200*
  To mourn a mischief that is past and gone
  Is the next° way to draw new mischief on.
  What cannot be preserved when fortune takes,

186 **challenge** claim as right   189 **get** beget   193 **For your sake** because
of you   197 **lay a sentence** provide a maxim   198 **grise** step   200 **late on
hopes depended** was supported by hope (of a better outcome) until lately
202 **next** closest, surest

Patience her injury a mock'ry makes.

205 The robbed that smiles, steals something from the
　　　thief;

He robs himself that spends a bootless° grief.

Brabantio. So let the Turk of Cyprus us beguile:

We lose it not so long as we can smile.

He bears the sentence well that nothing bears

210 But the free comfort which from thence he hears;

But he bears both the sentence and the sorrow

That to pay grief must of poor patience borrow.

These sentences, to sugar, or to gall,

Being strong on both sides, are equivocal.

215 But words are words. I never yet did hear

That the bruisèd heart was piercèd° through the ear.

I humbly beseech you, proceed to th' affairs of state.

Duke. The Turk with a most mighty preparation makes

for Cyprus. Othello, the fortitude° of the place is

220 best known to you; and though we have there a

substitute° of most allowed sufficiency,° yet opin-

ion, a more sovereign mistress of effects, throws a

more safer voice on you.° You must therefore be

content to slubber° the gloss of your new fortunes

225 with this more stubborn and boisterous° expedition.

Othello. The tyrant Custom, most grave senators,

Hath made the flinty and steel couch of war

My thrice-driven° bed of down. I do agnize°

A natural and prompt alacrity

230 I find in hardness and do undertake

This present wars against the Ottomites.

---

206 **bootless** valueless　216 **piercèd** (some editors emend to *pieced,* i.e., healed." But *pierced* makes good sense: Brabantio is saying in effect that his heart cannot be further hurt [pierced] by the indignity of the useless, conventional advice the Duke offers him. *Pierced* can also mean, however, "lanced" in the medical sense, and would then mean "treated")　219 **fortitude** fortification　221 **substitute** viceroy　221 **most allowed sufficiency** generally acknowledged capability　221–23 **opinion . . . you** i.e., the general opinion, which finally controls affairs, is that you would be the best man in this situation　224 **slubber** besmear　225 **stubborn and boisterous** rough and violent　228 **thrice-driven** i.e., softest　228 **agnize** know in myself

Most humbly, therefore, bending to your state,
I crave fit disposition for my wife,
Due reference of place, and exhibition,°
With such accommodation and besort   235
As levels with° her breeding.

Duke.   Why, at her father's.

Brabantio. I will not have it so.

Othello.   Nor I.

Desdemona.   Nor would I there reside,
To put my father in impatient thoughts
By being in his eye. Most gracious Duke,
To my unfolding° lend your prosperous° ear,   240
And let me find a charter° in your voice,
T' assist my simpleness.

Duke.   What would you, Desdemona?

Desdemona. That I love the Moor to live with him,
My downright violence, and storm of fortunes,
May trumpet to the world. My heart's subdued   245
Even to the very quality of my lord.°
I saw Othello's visage in his mind,
And to his honors and his valiant parts
Did I my soul and fortunes consecrate.
So that, dear lords, if I be left behind,   250
A moth of peace, and he go to the war,
The rites° for why I love him are bereft me,
And I a heavy interim shall support
By his dear absence. Let me go with him.

Othello. Let her have your voice.°   255
Vouch with me, heaven, I therefore beg it not
To please the palate of my appetite,
Nor to comply with heat°—the young affects°

234 **exhibition** grant of funds 236 **levels with** is suitable to 240 **unfold-ing** explanation 240 **prosperous** favoring 241 **charter** permission
245–46 **My ... lord** i.e., I have become one in nature and being with the man I married (therefore, I too would go to the wars like a soldier) 252 **rites** (may refer either to the marriage rites or to the rites, formalities, of war) 255 **voice** consent 258 **heat** lust 258 **affects** passions

In me defunct—and proper satisfaction;°
260 But to be free and bounteous to her mind;
And heaven defend° your good souls that you think
I will your serious and great business scant
When she is with me. No, when light-winged toys
Of feathered Cupid seel° with wanton° dullness
265 My speculative and officed instrument,°
That my disports corrupt and taint my business,
Let housewives make a skillet of my helm,
And all indign° and base adversities
Make head° against my estimation!°—

270 *Duke.* Be it as you shall privately determine,
Either for her stay or going. Th' affair cries haste,
And speed must answer it.

First Senator.   You must away tonight.

Othello. With all my heart.

Duke. At nine i' th' morning here we'll meet again
275 Othello, leave some officer behind,
And he shall our commission bring to you,
And such things else of quality and respect
As doth import you.

Othello.   So please your grace, my ancient;
A man he is of honesty and trust.
280 To his conveyance I assign my wife,
With what else needful your good grace shall think
To be sent after me.

Duke.   Let it be so.
Good night to every one. [*To Brabantio*] And, noble
signior,
If virtue no delighted° beauty lack,
285 Your son-in-law is far more fair than black.

First Senator. Adieu, brave Moor. Use Desdemona
well.

259 **proper satisfaction** i.e., consummation of the marriage 261 **defend**
forbid 264 **seel** sew up 264 **wanton** lascivious 265 **speculative . . . instrument** i.e., sight (and, by extension, the mind) 268 **indign** unworthy
269 **Make head** form an army, i.e., attack 269 **estimation** reputation 284
delighted delightful

Brabantio. Look to her, Moor, if thou hast eyes to see:
  She has deceived her father, and may thee.

        [Exeunt Duke, Senators, Officers, &c.]

Othello. My life upon her faith! Honest Iago,
  My Desdemona must I leave to thee.   *290*
  I prithee let thy wife attend on her,
  And bring them after in the best advantage.°
  Come, Desdemona. I have but an hour
  Of love, of worldly matter, and direction
  To spend with thee. We must obey the time.   *295*

        Exit [Moor with Desdemona].

Roderigo. Iago?

Iago. What say'st thou, noble heart?

Roderigo. What will I do, think'st thou?

Iago. Why, go to bed and sleep.

Roderigo. I will incontinently° drown myself.   *300*

Iago. If thou dost, I shall never love thee after. Why,
  thou silly gentleman?

Roderigo. It is silliness to live when to live is torment;
  and then have we a prescription to die when death is
  our physician.   *305*

Iago. O villainous! I have looked upon the world for
  four times seven years, and since I could distinguish
  betwixt a benefit and an injury, I never found man
  that knew how to love himself. Ere I would say I
  would drown myself for the love of a guinea hen, *310*
  I would change my humanity with a baboon.

Roderigo. What should I do? I confess it is my shame
  to be so fond, but it is not in my virtue° to amend it.

Iago. Virtue? A fig! 'Tis in ourselves that we are thus,
  or thus. Our bodies are our gardens, to the which *315*
  our wills are gardeners; so that if we will plant
  nettles or sow lettuce, set hyssop and weed up thyme,

292 **advantage** opportunity   300 **incontinently** at once   313 **virtue** strength
(Roderigo is saying that his nature controls him)

supply it with one gender of herbs or distract° it with
many—either to have it sterile with idleness or
320 manured with industry—why, the power and corri-
gible° authority of this lies in our wills. If the balance of our lives had not one scale of reason to poise
another of sensuality, the blood and baseness of
our natures would conduct us to most prepost'rous
325 conclusions.° But we have reason to cool our raging
motions, our carnal stings or unbitted° lusts,
whereof I take this that you call love to be a sect
or scion.°

Roderigo. It cannot be.

330 *Iago.* It is merely a lust of the blood and a permission of
the will. Come, be a man! Drown thyself? Drown
cats and blind puppies! I have professed me thy
friend, and I confess me knit to thy deserving with
cables of perdurable toughness. I could never better
335 stead° thee than now. Put money in thy purse.
Follow thou the wars; defeat thy favor° with an
usurped° beard. I say, put money in thy purse.
It cannot be long that Desdemona should continue
her love to the Moor. Put money in thy purse. Nor
340 he his to her. It was a violent commencement in
her and thou shalt see an answerable° sequestra-
tion—put but money in thy purse. These Moors
are changeable in their wills—fill thy purse with
money. The food that to him now is as luscious as
345 locusts° shall be to him shortly as bitter as coloquintida.° She must change for youth; when she is
sated with his body, she will find the errors of her
choice. Therefore, put money in thy purse. If thou
wilt needs damn thyself, do it a more delicate way
350 than drowning. Make all the money thou canst. If

318 **distract** vary   320–21 **corrigible** corrective   325 **conclusions** ends
326 **unbitted** i.e., uncontrolled   327–28 **sect or scion** offshoot   335 **stead**
serve   336 **defeat thy favor** disguise your face   337 **usurped** assumed
341 **answerable** similar   345 **locusts** (a sweet fruit)   345–46 **coloquintida**
(a purgative derived from a bitter apple)

sanctimony° and a frail vow betwixt an erring°
barbarian and supersubtle Venetian be not too hard
for my wits, and all the tribe of hell, thou shalt enjoy
her. Therefore, make money. A pox of drowning
thyself, it is clean out of the way. Seek thou rather   355
to be hanged in compassing° thy joy than to be
drowned and go without her.

Roderigo. Wilt thou be fast to my hopes, if I depend
on the issue?

Iago. Thou art sure of me. Go, make money. I have   360
told thee often, and I retell thee again and again, I
hate the Moor. My cause is hearted;° thine hath no
less reason. Let us be conjunctive° in our revenge
against him. If thou canst cuckold him, thou dost
thyself a pleasure, me a sport. There are many   365
events in the womb of time, which will be delivered.
Traverse, go, provide thy money! We will have more
of this tomorrow. Adieu.

Roderigo. Where shall we meet i' th' morning?

Iago. At my lodging.   370

Roderigo. I'll be with thee betimes.

Iago. Go to, farewell. Do you hear, Roderigo?

Roderigo. I'll sell all my land.   *Exit.*

Iago. Thus do I ever make my fool my purse;
For I mine own gained knowledge° should profane   375
If I would time expend with such snipe
But for my sport and profit. I hate the Moor,
And it is thought abroad that 'twixt my sheets
H'as done my office. I know not if't be true,
But I, for mere suspicion in that kind,   380
Will do, as if for surety.° He holds me well;
The better shall my purpose work on him.

---

351 **sanctimony** sacred bond (of marriage)   351 **erring** wandering   356
compassing encompassing, achieving   362 **hearted** deep-seated in the heart
363 **conjunctive** joined   375 **gained knowledge** i.e., practical, worldly wisdom   381 **surety** certainty

Cassio's a proper° man. Let me see now:
To get his place, and to plume up my will°
385 In double knavery. How? How? Let's see.
After some time, to abuse Othello's ears
That he is too familiar with his wife.
He hath a person and a smooth dispose°
To be suspected—framed° to make women false.
390 The Moor is of a free and open nature
That thinks men honest that but seem to be so;
And will as tenderly be led by th' nose
As asses are.
I have't! It is engendered! Hell and night
395 Must bring this monstrous birth to the world's light.

                                                 [*Exit.*]

---

383 **proper** handsome   384 **plume up my will** (many explanations have been offered for this crucial line, which in Q1 reads "make up my will." The general sense is something like "to make more proud and gratify my ego") 388 **dispose** manner   389 **framed** designed

ACT 2

Scene 1. [*Cyprus*.]

Enter Montano and two Gentlemen, [one above].°

Montano. What from the cape can you discern at sea?

First Gentleman. Nothing at all, it is a high-wrought
    flood.
  I cannot 'twixt the heaven and the main
  Descry a sail.

Montano. Methinks the wind hath spoke aloud at land;   *5*
  A fuller blast ne'er shook our battlements.
  If it hath ruffianed so upon the sea,
  What ribs of oak, when mountains melt on them,
  Can hold the mortise? What shall we hear of this?

Second Gentleman. A segregation° of the Turkish
    fleet.   *10*
  For do but stand upon the foaming shore,
  The chidden billow seems to pelt the clouds;
  The wind-shaked surge, with high and monstrous
    main,°
  Seems to cast water on the burning Bear
  And quench the guards of th' ever-fixèd pole.°   *15*

2.1. s.d. (the Folio arrangement of this scene requires that the First Gentleman
stand above—on the upper stage—and act as a lookout reporting sights which
cannot be seen by Montano standing below on the main stage) 10 **segrega-
tion** separation 13 **main** (both "ocean" and "strength") 14–15 **Seems . . .
pole** (the constellation Ursa Minor contains two stars which are the *guards,* or
companions, of the *pole,* or North Star)

I never did like molestation view
On the enchafèd flood.

Montano.   If that the Turkish fleet
Be not ensheltered and embayed, they are drowned;
It is impossible to bear it out.

Enter a [third] Gentleman.

20 *Third Gentleman.* News, lads! Our wars are done.
The desperate tempest hath so banged the Turks
That their designment halts. A noble ship of Venice
Hath seen a grievous wrack and sufferance°
On most part of their fleet.

Montano. How? Is this true?

25 *Third Gentleman.*   The ship is here put in,
A Veronesa; Michael Cassio,
Lieutenant to the warlike Moor Othello,
Is come on shore; the Moor himself at sea,
And is in full commission here for Cyprus.

30 *Montano.* I am glad on't. 'Tis a worthy governor.

Third Gentleman. But this same Cassio, though he
speak of comfort
Touching the Turkish loss, yet he looks sadly
And prays the Moor be safe, for they were parted
With foul and violent tempest.

Montano.   Pray heavens he be;
35 For I have served him, and the man commands
Like a full soldier. Let's to the seaside, ho!
As well to see the vessel that's come in
As to throw out our eyes for brave Othello,
Even till we make the main and th' aerial blue
An indistinct regard.°

40 *Third Gentleman.*   Come, let's do so;
For every minute is expectancy
Of more arrivancie.°

---

23 **sufferance** damage   39–40 **the main . . . regard** i.e., the sea and sky become indistinguishable   42 **arrivancie** arrivals

Enter Cassio.

Cassio. Thanks, you the valiant of the warlike isle,
   That so approve° the Moor. O, let the heavens
   Give him defense against the elements,   45
   For I have lost him on a dangerous sea.

Montano. Is he well shipped?

Cassio. His bark is stoutly timbered, and his pilot
   Of very expert and approved allowance;°
   Therefore my hopes, not surfeited to death,°   50
   Stand in bold cure.° (*Within*) A sail, a sail, a sail!

Cassio. What noise?

First Gentleman. The town is empty; on the brow o'
      th' sea
   Stand ranks of people, and they cry, "A sail!"

Cassio. My hopes do shape him for the governor.   55

                                          [*A shot.*]

Second Gentleman. They do discharge their shot of
      courtesy:
   Our friends at least.

Cassio.   I pray you, sir, go forth
   And give us truth who 'tis that is arrived.

Second Gentleman. I shall.   *Exit.*

Montano. But, good lieutenant, is your general wived?   60

Cassio. Most fortunately. He hath achieved a maid
   That paragons° description and wild fame;°
   One that excels the quirks of blazoning pens,°
   And in th' essential vesture of creation°
   Does tire the ingener.°

44 **approve** ("honor" or, perhaps, "are as warlike and valiant as your governor") 49 **approved allowance** known and tested 50 **not surfeited to death** i.e., not so great as to be in danger 51 **Stand in bold cure** i.e., are likely to be restored 62 **paragons** exceeds 62 **wild fame** extravagant report 63 **quirks of blazoning pens** ingenuities of praising pens 64 **essential vesture of creation** i.e., essential human nature as given by the Creator 65 **tire the ingener** (a difficult line which probably means something like "outdo the human ability to imagine and picture")

Enter [Second] Gentleman.

65   How now? Who has put in?

Second Gentleman. 'Tis one Iago, ancient to the
    general.

Cassio. H'as had most favorable and happy speed:
    Tempests themselves, high seas, and howling winds,
    The guttered° rocks and congregated° sands,
70   Traitors ensteeped° to enclog the guiltless keel,
    As having sense° of beauty, do omit
    Their mortal° natures, letting go safely by
    The divine Desdemona.

Montano.   What is she?

Cassio. She that I spake of, our great captain's captain,
75   Left in the conduct of the bold Iago,
    Whose footing° here anticipates our thoughts
    A se'nnight's° speed. Great Jove, Othello guard,
    And swell his sail with thine own pow'rful breath,
    That he may bless this bay with his tall° ship,
80   Make love's quick pants in Desdemona's arms,
    Give renewed fire to our extinct spirits.

Enter Desdemona, Iago, Roderigo, and Emilia.

    O, behold! The riches of the ship is come on shore!
    You men of Cyprus, let her have your knees.
                              [Kneeling.]
    Hail to thee, lady! and the grace of heaven,
85   Before, behind thee, and on every hand,
    Enwheel thee round.

Desdemona.   I thank you, valiant Cassio.
    What tidings can you tell of my lord?

Cassio. He is not yet arrived, nor know I aught
    But that he's well and will be shortly here.

90 **Desdemona.** O but I fear. How lost you company?

69 **guttered** jagged   69 **congregated** gathered   70 **ensteeped** submerged
71 **sense** awareness   72 **mortal** deadly   76 **footing** landing   77 **se'nnight's**
week's   79 **tall** brave

Cassio. The great contention of sea and skies
  Parted our fellowship. (*Within*) A sail, a sail!
  [*A shot.*]
                But hark. A sail!

Second Gentleman. They give this greeting to the
  citadel;
  This likewise is a friend.

Cassio.   See for the news.   *95*
                [*Exit Gentleman.*]
  Good ancient, you are welcome. [*To Emilia*] Wel-
  come, mistress.
  Let it not gall your patience, good Iago,
  That I extend° my manners. 'Tis my breeding°
  That gives me this bold show of courtesy. [*Kisses
  Emilia.*]

Iago. Sir, would she give you so much of her lips   *100*
  As of her tongue she oft bestows on me,
  You would have enough.

Desdemona.   Alas, she has no speech.

Iago. In faith, too much.
  I find it still when I have leave to sleep.°
  Marry, before your ladyship,° I grant,   *105*
  She puts her tongue a little in her heart
  And chides with thinking.

Emilia.   You have little cause to say so.

Iago. Come on, come on! You are pictures° out of
  door,
  Bells in your parlors, wildcats in your kitchens,
  Saints in your injuries,° devils being offended,   *110*

98 **extend** stretch   98 **breeding** careful training in manners (Cassio is considerably more the polished gentleman than Iago, and aware of it)   104 **still**
. . . sleep i.e., even when she allows me to sleep she continues to scold   105
before your ladyship in your presence   108 **pictures** models (of virtue)
110 **in your injuries** when you injure others

Players in your housewifery,° and housewives in
  your beds.

Desdemona. O, fie upon thee, slanderer!

Iago. Nay, it is true, or else I am a Turk:
  You rise to play, and go to bed to work.

Emilia. You shall not write my praise.

115 *Iago.*   No, let me not.

Desdemona. What wouldst write of me, if thou shouldst
  praise me?

Iago. O gentle lady, do not put me to't,
  For I am nothing if not critical.

Desdemona. Come on, assay. There's one gone to the
  harbor?

Iago. Ay, madam.

120 *Desdemona.* [*Aside*] I am not merry; but I do beguile
  The thing I am by seeming otherwise.—
  Come, how wouldst thou praise me?

Iago. I am about it; but indeed my invention
  Comes from my pate as birdlime° does from
    frieze°—
125 It plucks out brains and all. But my Muse labors,
  And thus she is delivered:
  If she be fair° and wise: fairness and wit,
  The one's for use, the other useth it.

Desdemona. Well praised. How if she be black° and
  witty?

130 *Iago.* If she be black, and thereto have a wit,
  She'll find a white that shall her blackness fit.

Desdemona. Worse and worse!

---

111 **housewifery** (this word can mean "careful, economical household management," and Iago would then be accusing women of only pretending to be
good housekeepers, while in bed they are either [1] economical of their favors,
or more likely [2] serious and dedicated workers)   124 **birdlime** a sticky
substance put on branches to catch birds   124 **frieze** rough cloth   127 **fair**
light-complexioned   129 **black** brunette

Emilia. How if fair and foolish?

Iago. She never yet was foolish that was fair,
  For even her folly helped her to an heir.   *135*

Desdemona. These are old fond° paradoxes to make
fools laugh i' th' alehouse. What miserable praise
hast thou for her that's foul and foolish?

Iago. There's none so foul, and foolish thereunto,
  But does foul pranks which fair and wise ones do.   *140*

Desdemona. O heavy ignorance. Thou praisest the
worst best. But what praise couldst thou bestow on
a deserving woman indeed—one that in the authority of her merit did justly put on the vouch of very
malice itself?°   *145*

Iago. She that was ever fair, and never proud;
  Had tongue at will, and yet was never loud;
  Never lacked gold, and yet went never gay;
  Fled from her wish, and yet said "Now I may";
  She that being angered, her revenge being nigh,   *150*
  Bade her wrong stay, and her displeasure fly;
  She that in wisdom never was so frail
  To change the cod's head for the salmon's tail;°
  She that could think, and nev'r disclose her mind;
  See suitors following, and not look behind: *155*
  She was a wight° (if ever such wights were)—

Desdemona. To do what?

Iago. To suckle fools and chronicle small beer.°

Desdemona. O most lame and impotent conclusion.
Do not learn of him, Emilia, though he be thy hus-   *160*
band. How say you, Cassio? Is he not a most profane
and liberal° counselor?

---

136 **fond** foolish   143–45 **one . . . itself** i.e., a woman so honest and deserving that even malice would be forced to approve of her   153 **To . . . tail** i.e.,
to exchange something valuable for something useless   156 **wight** person
158 **chronicle small beer** i.e., keep household accounts (the most trivial of
occupations in Iago's opinion)   162 **liberal** licentious

Cassio. He speaks home,° madam. You may relish
    him more in° the soldier than in the scholar. [*Takes*
    Desdemona's hand.]

165 *Iago.* [*Aside*] He takes her by the palm. Ay, well said,
    whisper! With as little a web as this will I ensnare
    as great a fly as Cassio. Ay, smile upon her, do! I
    will gyve° thee in thine own courtship.—You say
    true; 'tis so, indeed!—If such tricks as these strip
170   you out of your lieutenantry, it had been better you
    had not kissed your three fingers so oft—which now
    again you are most apt to play the sir° in. Very
    good! Well kissed! An excellent curtsy!° 'Tis so,
    indeed. Yet again your fingers to your lips? Would
175   they were clyster pipes° for your sake! [*Trumpets*
    within.] The Moor! I know his trumpet.°

Cassio. 'Tis truly so.

Desdemona. Let's meet him and receive him.

Cassio. Lo, where he comes.

        Enter Othello and Attendants.

Othello. O my fair warrior!

180 *Desdemona.*   My dear Othello.

Othello. It gives me wonder great as my content
    To see you here before me. O my soul's joy!
    If after every tempest come such calms,
    May the winds blow till they have wakened death.
185   And let the laboring bark climb hills of seas
    Olympus-high, and duck again as low
    As hell's from heaven. If it were now to die,
    'Twere now to be most happy; for I fear
    My soul hath her content so absolute
190   That not another comfort like to this
    Succeeds in unknown fate.

163 **speaks home** thrusts deeply with his speech   163–64 **relish him more
in** enjoy him more as   168 **gyve** bind   172 **the sir** the fashionable gentleman   173 **curtsy** courtesy, i.e., bow   175 **clyster pipes** enema tubes   176
his trumpet (great men had their own distinctive calls)

Desdemona.   The heavens forbid
   But that our loves and comforts should increase
   Even as our days do grow.

Othello.   Amen to that, sweet powers!
   I cannot speak enough of this content;
   It stops me here [*touches his heart*]; it is too much
     of joy.   195
   And this, and this, the greatest discords be
                     [*They kiss.*]
   That e'er our hearts shall make!

Iago.   [*Aside*] O, you are well tuned now!
   But I'll set down the pegs° that make this music,
   As honest as I am.

Othello.   Come, let us to the castle.
   News, friends! Our wars are done; the Turks are
     drowned.   200
   How does my old acquaintance of this isle?
   Honey, you shall be well desired in Cyprus;
   I have found great love amongst them. O my sweet,
   I prattle out of fashion, and I dote
   In mine own comforts. I prithee, good Iago,   205
   Go to the bay and disembark my coffers.
   Bring thou the master to the citadel;
   He is a good one, and his worthiness
   Does challenge° much respect. Come, Desdemona,
   Once more well met at Cyprus.   210
     Exit Othello and Desdemona [and all but Iago and
                           Roderigo].

Iago. [*To an Attendant*] Do thou meet me presently
   at the harbor. [*To Roderigo*] Come hither. If thou
   be'st valiant (as they say base men being in love
   have then a nobility in their natures more than is
   native to them), list me. The lieutenant tonight   215
   watches on the court of guard.° First, I must tell thee
   this: Desdemona is directly in love with him.

Roderigo. With him? Why, 'tis not possible.

---

198 **set down the pegs** loosen the strings (to produce discord)   209 **challenge** require, exact   216 **court of guard** guardhouse

Iago. Lay thy finger thus [*puts his finger to his lips*],
220   and let thy soul be instructed. Mark me with what
violence she first loved the Moor but for bragging
and telling her fantastical lies. To love him still for
prating? Let not thy discreet heart think it. Her
eye must be fed. And what delight shall she have to
225   look on the devil? When the blood is made dull with
the act of sport, there should be a game° to inflame
it and to give satiety a fresh appetite, loveliness in
favor,° sympathy in years,° manners, and beauties;
all which the Moor is defective in. Now for want of
230   these required conveniences,° her delicate tender-
ness will find itself abused, begin to heave the
gorge,° disrelish and abhor the Moor. Very nature
will instruct her in it and compel her to some second
choice. Now, sir, this granted—as it is a most preg-
235   nant° and unforced position—who stands so emi-
nent in the degree of this fortune as Cassio does?
A knave very voluble; no further conscionable°
than in putting on the mere form of civil and hu-
mane° seeming for the better compass of his salt°
240   and most hidden loose° affection. Why, none! Why,
none! A slipper° and subtle knave, a finder of
occasion, that has an eye can stamp and counterfeit
advantages, though true advantage never present
itself. A devilish knave. Besides, the knave is hand-
245   some, young, and hath all those requisites in him
that folly and green minds look after. A pestilent
complete knave, and the woman hath found him
already.

Roderigo. I cannot believe that in her; she's full of
250   most blessed condition.

Iago. Blessed fig's-end! The wine she drinks is made of
grapes. If she had been blessed, she would never

---

226 **game** sport (with the added sense of "gamey," "rank")   228 **favor**
countenance, appearance   228 **sympathy in years** sameness of age   230
conveniences advantages   231–32 **heave the gorge** vomit   234–35 **pregnant**
likely   237 **no further conscionable** having no more conscience   238–39
humane polite   239 **salt** lecherous   240 **loose** immoral   241 **slipper** slip-
pery

have loved the Moor. Blessed pudding! Didst thou
not see her paddle with the palm of his hand? Didst
not mark that?   255

Roderigo. Yes, that I did; but that was but courtesy.

Iago. Lechery, by this hand! [*Extends his index finger.*]
An index° and obscure prologue to the history of
lust and foul thoughts. They met so near with their
lips that their breaths embraced together. Villainous   260
thoughts, Roderigo. When these mutualities so
marshal the way, hard at hand comes the master and
main exercise, th' incorporate° conclusion: Pish!
But, sir, be you ruled by me. I have brought you
from Venice. Watch you tonight; for the command,   265
I'll lay't upon you. Cassio knows you not. I'll not be
far from you. Do you find some occasion to anger
Cassio, either by speaking too loud, or tainting°
his discipline, or from what other course you please
which the time shall more favorably minister.   270

Roderigo. Well.

Iago. Sir, he's rash and very sudden in choler,° and
haply may strike at you. Provoke him that he may;
for even out of that will I cause these of Cyprus to
mutiny, whose qualification shall come into no true   275
taste° again but by the displanting of Cassio. So
shall you have a shorter journey to your desires by
the means I shall then have to prefer them; and the
impediment most profitably removed without the
which there were no expectation of our prosperity.   280

Roderigo. I will do this if you can bring it to any
opportunity.

Iago. I warrant thee. Meet me by and by at the citadel.
I must fetch his necessaries ashore. Farewell.

Roderigo. Adieu.   *Exit.*   285

Iago. That Cassio loves her, I do well believe 't;

---

258 **index** pointer   263 **incorporate** carnal   268 **tainting** discrediting   272
choler anger   275–76 **qualification … taste** i.e., appeasement will not be
brought about (wine was "qualified" by adding water)

That she loves him, 'tis apt and of great credit.
The Moor, howbeit that I endure him not,
Is of a constant, loving, noble nature,
290   And I dare think he'll prove to Desdemona
A most dear° husband. Now I do love her too;
Not out of absolute° lust, though peradventure°
I stand accountant for as great a sin,
But partly led to diet° my revenge,
295   For that I do suspect the lusty Moor
Hath leaped into my seat; the thought whereof
Doth, like a poisonous mineral, gnaw my inwards;
And nothing can or shall content my soul
Till I am evened with him, wife for wife.
300   Or failing so, yet that I put the Moor
At least into a jealousy so strong
That judgment cannot cure. Which thing to do,
If this poor trash of Venice, whom I trace°
For his quick hunting, stand the putting on,
305   I'll have our Michael Cassio on the hip,°
Abuse him to the Moor in the right garb°
(For I fear Cassio with my nightcap too),
Make the Moor thank me, love me, and reward me
For making him egregiously an ass
310   And practicing upon° his peace and quiet,
Even to madness. 'Tis here, but yet confused:
Knavery's plain face is never seen till used.   *Exit.*

---

291 **dear** expensive   292 **out of absolute** absolutely out of   292 **peradventure** perchance   294 **diet** feed   303 **trace** (most editors emend to "trash," meaning to hang weights on a dog to slow his hunting; but "trace" clearly means something like "put on the trace" or "set on the track")   306 **right garb** i.e., "proper fashion"   310 **practicing upon** scheming to destroy

Scene 2. [*A street.*]

Enter Othello's Herald, with a proclamation.

Herald. It is Othello's pleasure, our noble and valiant
general, that upon certain tidings now arrived importing the mere perdition° of the Turkish fleet,
every man put himself into triumph. Some to dance,
some to make bonfires, each man to what sport and   5
revels his addition° leads him. For, besides these
beneficial news, it is the celebration of his nuptial.
So much was his pleasure should be proclaimed.
All offices° are open, and there is full liberty of
feasting from this present hour of five till the bell   10
have told eleven. Bless the isle of Cyprus and our
noble general Othello!   *Exit.*

Scene 3. [*The citadel of Cyprus.*]

Enter Othello, Desdemona, Cassio, and Attendants.

Othello. Good Michael, look you to the guard tonight.
Let's teach ourselves that honorable stop,
Not to outsport discretion.

Cassio. Iago hath direction what to do;
But notwithstanding, with my personal eye   5
Will I look to't.

Othello.   Iago is most honest.
Michael, good night. Tomorrow with your earliest
Let me have speech with you. [*To Desdemona*]
Come, my dear love,

2.2.3 **mere perdition** absolute destruction   6 **addition** rank   9 **offices**
kitchens and storerooms of food

The purchase made, the fruits are to ensue,
10 That profit's yet to come 'tween me and you.
Good night.

Exit [*Othello with Desdemona and Attendants*].

Enter Iago.

Cassio. Welcome, Iago. We must to the watch.

Iago. Not this hour, lieutenant; 'tis not yet ten o' th'
clock. Our general cast° us thus early for the love
15 of his Desdemona; who let us not therefore blame.
He hath not yet made wanton the night with her, and
she is sport for Jove.

Cassio. She's a most exquisite lady.

Iago. And, I'll warrant her, full of game.

20 *Cassio.* Indeed, she's a most fresh and delicate creature.

Iago. What an eye she has! Methinks it sounds a parley
to provocation.

Cassio. An inviting eye; and yet methinks right modest.

Iago. And when she speaks, is it not an alarum° to
25 love?

Cassio. She is indeed perfection.

Iago. Well, happiness to their sheets! Come, lieutenant,
I have a stoup° of wine, and here without are a
brace of Cyprus gallants that would fain have a
30 measure to the health of black Othello.

Cassio. Not tonight, good Iago. I have very poor and
unhappy brains for drinking; I could well wish
courtesy would invent some other custom of entertainment.

35 *Iago.* O, they are our friends. But one cup! I'll drink
for you.

Cassio. I have drunk but one cup tonight, and that was
craftily qualified° too; and behold what innovation

2.3.14 **cast** dismissed   24 **alarum** the call to action, "general quarters"   28
stoup two-quart tankard   38 **qualified** diluted

it makes here. I am unfortunate in the infirmity and
dare not task my weakness with any more.   40

Iago. What, man! 'Tis a night of revels, the gallants
desire it.

Cassio. Where are they?

Iago. Here, at the door. I pray you call them in.

Cassio. I'll do't, but it dislikes me.   *Exit.*   45

Iago. If I can fasten but one cup upon him
    With that which he hath drunk tonight already,
    He'll be as full of quarrel and offense
    As my young mistress' dog. Now, my sick fool
      Roderigo,
    Whom love hath turned almost the wrong side out,   50
    To Desdemona hath tonight caroused
    Potations pottle-deep;° and he's to watch.
    Three else° of Cyprus, noble swelling spirits,
    That hold their honors in a wary distance,°
    The very elements of this warlike isle,   55
    Have I tonight flustered with flowing cups,
    And they watch too. Now, 'mongst this flock of
      drunkards
    Am I to put our Cassio in some action
    That may offend the isle. But here they come.

      Enter Cassio, Montano, and Gentlemen.

    If consequence do but approve my dream,   60
    My boat sails freely, both with wind and stream.

Cassio. 'Fore God, they have given me a rouse° already.

Montano. Good faith, a little one; not past a pint, as
I am a soldier.

Iago. Some wine, ho!   65
    [*Sings*] And let me the canakin clink, clink;
        And let me the canakin clink.

---

52 **pottle-deep** to the bottom of the cup   53 **else** others   54 **hold . . . distance** are scrupulous in maintaining their honor   62 **rouse** drink

    A soldier's a man;
    O man's life's but a span,
70   Why then, let a soldier drink.
  Some wine, boys!

Cassio. 'Fore God, an excellent song!

Iago. I learned it in England, where indeed they are
  most potent in potting. Your Dane, your German,
75 and your swag-bellied° Hollander—Drink, ho!—
  are nothing to your English.

Cassio. Is your Englishman so exquisite° in his drinking?

Iago. Why, he drinks you with facility your Dane dead
80 drunk; he sweats not to overthrow your Almain; he
  gives your Hollander a vomit ere the next pottle can
  be filled.

Cassio. To the health of our general!

Montano. I am for it, lieutenant, and I'll do you justice.

85 *Iago.* O sweet England!
  [*Sings*] King Stephen was and a worthy peer;
    His breeches cost him but a crown;
    He held them sixpence all too dear,
    With that he called the tailor lown.°
90   He was a wight of high renown,
    And thou art but of low degree:
    'Tis pride that pulls the country down;
    And take thine auld cloak about thee.
  Some wine, ho!

95 *Cassio.* 'Fore God, this is a more exquisite song than
  the other.

Iago. Will you hear't again?

Cassio. No, for I hold him to be unworthy of his place
  that does those things. Well, God's above all; and
100 there be souls must be saved, and there be souls
  must not be saved.

75 **swag-bellied** hanging 77 **exquisite** superb 89 **lown** lout

Iago. It's true, good lieutenant.

Cassio. For mine own part—no offense to the general,
nor any man of quality—I hope to be saved.

Iago. And so do I too, lieutenant.   *105*

Cassio. Ay, but, by your leave, not before me. The lieutenant is to be saved before the ancient. Let's have
no more of this; let's to our affairs.—God forgive us
our sins!—Gentlemen, let's look to our business.
Do not think, gentlemen, I am drunk. This is my   *110*
ancient; this is my right hand, and this is my left.
I am not drunk now. I can stand well enough, and
I speak well enough.

Gentlemen. Excellent well!

Cassio. Why, very well then. You must not think then *115*
that I am drunk.   *Exit.*

Montano. To th' platform, masters. Come, let's set
the watch.

Iago. You see this fellow that is gone before.
He's a soldier fit to stand by Caesar
And give direction; and do but see his vice.   *120*
'Tis to his virtue a just equinox,°
The one as long as th' other. 'Tis pity of him.
I fear the trust Othello puts him in,
On some odd time of his infirmity,
Will shake this island.

Montano.   But is he often thus?   *125*

Iago. 'Tis evermore his prologue to his sleep:
He'll watch the horologe a double set°
If drink rock not his cradle.

Montano.   It were well
The general were put in mind of it.
Perhaps he sees it not, or his good nature   *130*
Prizes the virtue that appears in Cassio
And looks not on his evils. Is not this true?

---

121 **just equinox** exact balance (of dark and light)   127 **watch . . . set** stay
awake twice around the clock

Enter Roderigo.

Iago. [*Aside*] How now, Roderigo?
    I pray you after the lieutenant, go! [*Exit Roderigo.*]
135 **Montano.** And 'tis great pity that the noble Moor
    Should hazard such a place as his own second
    With one of an ingraft° infirmity.
    It were an honest action to say so
    To the Moor.

Iago.   Not I, for this fair island!
140   I do love Cassio well and would do much
    To cure him of this evil.   (Help! Help! *Within.*)
                 But hark? What noise?

Enter Cassio, pursuing Roderigo.

Cassio. Zounds, you rogue! You rascal!

Montano. What's the matter, lieutenant?

Cassio. A knave teach me my duty? I'll beat the knave
145   into a twiggen° bottle.

Roderigo. Beat me?

Cassio. Dost thou prate, rogue?   [*Strikes him.*]

Montano. Nay, good lieutenant! I pray you, sir, hold
    your hand.

                      [*Stays him.*]

150 **Cassio.** Let me go, sir, or I'll knock you o'er the
    mazzard.°

Montano. Come, come, you're drunk!

Cassio. Drunk?   [*They fight.*]

Iago. [*Aside to Roderigo*] Away, I say! Go out and
155   cry a mutiny!

                  [*Exit Roderigo.*]
    Nay, good lieutenant. God's will, gentlemen!
    Help, ho! Lieutenant. Sir. Montano.
    Help, masters! Here's a goodly watch indeed!
                  [*A bell rung.*]

137 **ingraft** ingrained   145 **twiggen** wicker-covered   151 **mazzard** head

Who's that which rings the bell? Diablo, ho!
The town will rise. God's will, lieutenant,   160
You'll be ashamed forever.

Enter Othello and Attendants.

Othello.   What is the matter here?
Montano. Zounds, I bleed still. I am hurt to the death.
    He dies.   [*He and Cassio fight again.*]
Othello. Hold for your lives!
Iago. Hold, ho! Lieutenant. Sir. Montano. Gentlemen!   165
    Have you forgot all place of sense and duty?
    Hold! The general speaks to you. Hold, for shame!
Othello. Why, how now, ho? From whence ariseth this?
    Are we turned Turks, and to ourselves do that
    Which heaven hath forbid the Ottomites?°   170
    For Christian shame put by this barbarous brawl!
    He that stirs next to carve for his own rage
    Holds his soul light;° he dies upon his motion.
    Silence that dreadful bell! It frights the isle
    From her propriety.° What is the matter, masters?   175
    Honest Iago, that looks dead with grieving,
    Speak. Who began this? On thy love, I charge thee.
Iago. I do not know. Friends all, but now, even now,
    In quarter° and in terms like bride and groom
    Devesting them for bed; and then, but now—   180
    As if some planet had unwitted men—
    Swords out, and tilting one at other's breasts
    In opposition bloody. I cannot speak
    Any beginning to this peevish odds,°
    And would in action glorious I had lost   185
    Those legs that brought me to a part of it!
Othello. How comes it, Michael, you are thus forgot?
Cassio. I pray you pardon me; I cannot speak.
Othello. Worthy Montano, you were wont to be civil;
    The gravity and stillness of your youth   190

170 **heaven ... Ottomites** i.e., by sending the storm which dispersed the
Turks   173 **Holds his soul light** values his soul lightly   175 **propriety**
proper order   179 **In quarter** on duty   184 **odds** quarrel

The world hath noted, and your name is great
In mouths of wisest censure.° What's the matter
That you unlace° your reputation thus
And spend your rich opinion° for the name
195 Of a night-brawler? Give me answer to it.

Montano. Worthy Othello, I am hurt to danger.
Your officer, Iago, can inform you,
While I spare speech, which something now offends°
    me,
Of all that I do know; nor know I aught
200 By me that's said or done amiss this night,
Unless self-charity be sometimes a vice,
And to defend ourselves it be a sin
When violence assails us.

Othello.   Now, by heaven,
My blood begins my safer guides to rule,
205 And passion, having my best judgment collied,°
Assays to lead the way. If I once stir
Or do but lift this arm, the best of you
Shall sink in my rebuke. Give me to know
How this foul rout began, who set it on;
210 And he that is approved in this offense,
Though he had twinned with me, both at a birth,
Shall lose me. What? In a town of war
Yet wild, the people's hearts brimful of fear,
To manage° private and domestic quarrel?
215 In night, and on the court and guard of safety?
'Tis monstrous. Iago, who began't?

Montano. If partially affined, or leagued in office,°
Thou dost deliver more or less than truth,
Thou art no soldier.

Iago.   Touch me not so near.
220 I had rather have this tongue cut from my mouth
Than it should do offense to Michael Cassio.

---

192 **censure** judgment   193 **unlace** undo (the term refers specifically to the dressing of a wild boar killed in the hunt)   194 **opinion** reputation   198 **offends** harms, hurts   205 **collied** darkened   214 **manage** conduct   217 **If ... office** if you are partial because you are related ("affined") or the brother officer (of Cassio)

Yet I persuade myself to speak the truth
Shall nothing wrong him. This it is, general.
Montano and myself being in speech,
There comes a fellow crying out for help,   225
And Cassio following him with determined sword
To execute upon him. Sir, this gentleman
Steps in to Cassio and entreats his pause.
Myself the crying fellow did pursue,
Lest by his clamor—as it so fell out—   230
The town might fall in fright. He, swift of foot,
Outran my purpose; and I returned then rather
For that I heard the clink and fall of swords,
And Cassio high in oath; which till tonight
I ne'er might say before. When I came back—   235
For this was brief—I found them close together
At blow and thrust, even as again they were
When you yourself did part them.
More of this matter cannot I report;
But men are men; the best sometimes forget.   240
Though Cassio did some little wrong to him,
As men in rage strike those that wish them best,
Yet surely Cassio I believe received
From him that fled some strange indignity,
Which patience could not pass.°

Othello.   I know, Iago,   245
Thy honesty and love doth mince° this matter,
Making it light to Cassio. Cassio, I love thee;
But never more be officer of mine.

                    Enter Desdemona, attended.

Look if my gentle love be not raised up.
I'll make thee an example.

Desdemona.   What is the matter, dear.   250

Othello. All's well, sweeting; come away to bed.
   [*To Montano*] Sir, for your hurts, myself will be
      your surgeon.
   Lead him off.   [*Montano led off.*]

245 **pass** allow to pass   246 **mince** cut up (i.e., tell only part of)

Iago, look with care about the town
255 And silence those whom this vile brawl distracted.
Come, Desdemona: 'tis the soldiers' life
To have their balmy slumbers waked with strife.
                    Exit [with all but Iago and Cassio].

Iago. What, are you hurt, lieutenant?

Cassio. Ay, past all surgery.

260 *Iago.* Marry, God forbid!

Cassio. Reputation, reputation, reputation! O, I have
    lost my reputation! I have lost the immortal part of
    myself, and what remains is bestial. My reputation,
    Iago, my reputation.

265 *Iago.* As I am an honest man, I had thought you had
    received some bodily wound. There is more sense°
    in that than in reputation. Reputation is an idle and
    most false imposition,° oft got without merit and
    lost without deserving. You have lost no reputation
270 at all unless you repute yourself such a loser. What,
    man, there are more ways to recover the general
    again. You are but now cast in his mood°—a
    punishment more in policy° than in malice—even
    so as one would beat his offenseless dog to affright
275 an imperious lion. Sue to him again, and he's yours.

Cassio. I will rather sue to be despised than to deceive
    so good a commander with so slight, so drunken,
    and so indiscreet an officer. Drunk! And speak
    parrot!° And squabble! Swagger! Swear! and dis-
280 course fustian° with one's own shadow! O thou
    invisible spirit of wine, if thou hast no name to be
    known by, let us call thee devil!

Iago. What was he that you followed with your sword?
    What had he done to you?

285 *Cassio.* I know not.

Iago. Is't possible?

266 **sense** physical feeling   268 **imposition** external thing   272 **cast in his
mood** dismissed because of his anger   273 **in policy** politically necessary
278–79 **speak parrot** gabble without sense   279–80 **discourse fustian** speak
nonsense ("fustian" was a coarse cotton cloth used for stuffing)

Cassio. I remember a mass of things, but nothing distinctly: a quarrel, but nothing wherefore. O God, that men should put an enemy in their mouths to steal away their brains! that we should with joy, *290* pleasance, revel, and applause transform ourselves into beasts!

Iago. Why, but you are now well enough. How came you thus recovered?

Cassio. It hath pleased the devil drunkenness to give *295* place to the devil wrath. One unperfectness shows me another, to make me frankly despise myself.

Iago. Come, you are too severe a moraler. As the time, the place, and the condition of this country stands, I could heartily wish this had not befall'n; but since *300* it is as it is, mend it for your own good.

Cassio. I will ask him for my place again: he shall tell me I am a drunkard. Had I as many mouths as Hydra, such an answer would stop them all. To be now a sensible man, by and by a fool, and presently *305* a beast! O strange! Every inordinate cup is unblest, and the ingredient is a devil.

Iago. Come, come, good wine is a good familiar creature if it be well used. Exclaim no more against it. And, good lieutenant, I think you think I love *310* you.

Cassio. I have well approved it, sir. I drunk?

Iago. You or any man living may be drunk at a time, man. I tell you what you shall do. Our general's wife is now the general. I may say so in this respect, *315* for that he hath devoted and given up himself to the contemplation, mark, and devotement of her parts° and graces. Confess yourself freely to her; importune her help to put you in your place again. She is of so free, so kind, so apt, so blessed a disposition she *320* holds it a vice in her goodness not to do more than

317 **devotement of her parts** devotion to her qualities

she is requested. This broken joint between you
and her husband entreat her to splinter;° and my
fortunes against any lay° worth naming, this crack
325 of your love shall grow stronger than it was before.

Cassio. You advise me well.

Iago. I protest, in the sincerity of love and honest
kindness.

Cassio. I think it freely; and betimes in the morning I
330 will beseech the virtuous Desdemona to undertake
for me. I am desperate of my fortunes if they check°
me.

Iago. You are in the right. Good night, lieutenant; I
must to the watch.

335 *Cassio.* Good night, honest Iago.   *Exit Cassio.*

Iago. And what's he then that says I play the villain,
When this advice is free° I give, and honest,
Probal to° thinking, and indeed the course
To win the Moor again? For 'tis most easy
340 Th' inclining° Desdemona to subdue
In any honest suit; she's framed as fruitful°
As the free elements.° And then for her
To win the Moor—were't to renounce his baptism,
All seals and symbols of redeemèd sin—
345 His soul is so enfettered to her love
That she may make, unmake, do what she list,
Even as her appetite° shall play the god
With his weak function.° How am I then a villain
To counsel Cassio to this parallel course,
350 Directly to his good? Divinity of hell!
When devils will the blackest sins put on,°
They do suggest at first with heavenly shows,°
As I do now. For whiles this honest fool
Plies Desdemona to repair his fortune,
355 And she for him pleads strongly to the Moor,

323 **splinter** splint   324 **lay** wager   331 **check** repulse   337 **free** generous
and open   338 **Probal to** provable by   340 **inclining** inclined (to be helpful)   341 **framed as fruitful** made as generous   342 **elements** i.e., basic
nature   347 **appetite** liking   348 **function** thought   351 **put on** advance,
further   352 **shows** appearances

I'll pour this pestilence into his ear: ·
That she repeals him° for her body's lust;
And by how much she strives to do him good,
She shall undo her credit with the Moor.
So will I turn her virtue into pitch,   360
And out of her own goodness make the net
That shall enmesh them all. How now, Roderigo?

Enter Roderigo.

Roderigo. I do follow here in the chase, not like a
hound that hunts, but one that fills up the cry.° My
money is almost spent; I have been tonight exceed-   365
ingly well cudgeled; and I think the issue will be,
I shall have so much experience for my pains; and
so, with no money at all, and a little more wit,
return again to Venice.

Iago. How poor are they that have not patience!   370
What wound did ever heal but by degrees?
Thou know'st we work by wit, and not by witch-
craft;
And wit depends on dilatory time.
Does't not go well? Cassio hath beaten thee,
And thou by that small hurt hath cashiered Cassio.   375
Though other things grow fair against the sun,
Yet fruits that blossom first will first be ripe.
Content thyself awhile. By the mass, 'tis morning!
Pleasure and action make the hours seem short.
Retire thee; go where thou art billeted.   380
Away, I say! Thou shalt know more hereafter.
Nay, get thee gone!   *Exit Roderigo.*
                       Two things are to be done:
My wife must move° for Cassio to her mistress;
I'll set her on;
Myself awhile° to draw the Moor apart   385
And bring him jump° when he may Cassio find
Soliciting his wife. Ay, that's the way!
Dull not device by coldness and delay.   *Exit.*

357 **repeals him** asks for (Cassio's reinstatement)   364 **fills up the cry**
makes up one of the hunting pack, adding to the noise but not actually track-
ing   383 **move** petition   385 **awhile** at the same time   386 **jump** at the
precise moment and place

ACT 3

Scene 1. [*A street.*]

Enter Cassio [*and*] *Musicians.*

Cassio. Masters, play here. I will content your pains.°
Something that's brief; and bid "Good morrow,
general." [*They play.*]

[*Enter Clown.*°]

Clown. Why, masters, have your instruments been in
Naples° that they speak i' th' nose thus?

5 *Musician.* How, sir, how?

Clown. Are these, I pray you, wind instruments?

Musician. Ay, marry, are they, sir.

Clown. O, thereby hangs a tale.

Musician. Whereby hangs a tale, sir?

10 *Clown.* Marry, sir, by many a wind instrument that I
know. But, masters, here's money for you; and the
general so likes your music that he desires you,
for love's sake, to make no more noise with it.

Musician. Well, sir, we will not.

15 *Clown.* If you have any music that may not be heard,
to't again. But, as they say, to hear music the
general does not greatly care.

3.1.1 **content your pains** reward your efforts 2 s.d. **Clown** fool 4
Naples (this may refer either to the Neapolitan nasal tone, or to syphilis—rife
in Naples—which breaks down the nose)

Musician. We have none such, sir.

Clown. Then put up your pipes in your bag, for I'll
away. Go, vanish into air, away!　　　　　　　20

　　　　　　　　　　　　　Exit Musicians.

Cassio. Dost thou hear me, mine honest friend?

Clown. No. I hear not your honest friend. I hear you.

Cassio. Prithee keep up thy quillets.° There's a poor
piece of gold for thee. If the gentlewoman that
attends the general's wife be stirring, tell her there's　　25
one Cassio entreats her a little favor of speech.
Wilt thou do this?

Clown. She is stirring, sir. If she will stir hither, I shall
seem to notify unto her.°　　　　　　*Exit Clown.*

　　　　　　　　　Enter Iago.

Cassio. In happy time, Iago.

Iago.　　　　　　　You have not been abed then?　　30

Cassio. Why no, the day had broke before we parted.
I have made bold, Iago, to send in to your wife;
My suit to her is that she will to virtuous Desdemona
Procure me some access.

Iago.　　　　　　　I'll send her to you presently,
And I'll devise a mean to draw the Moor　　　　35
Out of the way, that your converse and business
May be more free.

Cassio. I humbly thank you for 't.　　*Exit [Iago].*
　　　　　　　　　　I never knew
A Florentine° more kind and honest.

　　　　　　　　Enter Emilia.

Emilia. Good morrow, good lieutenant. I am sorry　　40
For your displeasure;° but all will sure be well.
The general and his wife are talking of it,

---

23 **quillets** puns　29 **seem . . . her** (the Clown is mocking Cassio's overly
elegant manner of speaking)　39 **Florentine** i.e., Iago is as kind as if he were
from Cassio's home town, Florence　41 **displeasure** discomforting

And she speaks for you stoutly. The Moor replies
That he you hurt is of great fame in Cyprus
45 And great affinity,° and that in wholesome wisdom
He might not but refuse you. But he protests he loves
   you,
And needs no other suitor but his likings
To bring you in again.

Cassio.   Yet I beseech you,
If you think fit, or that it may be done,
50 Give me advantage of some brief discourse
With Desdemona alone.

Emilia.   Pray you come in.
I will bestow you where you shall have time
To speak your bosom° freely.

Cassio.   I am much bound to you.
                              [*Exeunt.*]

Scene 2. [*The citadel.*]

Enter Othello, Iago, and Gentlemen.

Othello. These letters give, Iago, to the pilot
And by him do my duties to the Senate.
That done, I will be walking on the works;
Repair° there to me.

Iago.   Well, my good lord, I'll do't.

5 *Othello.* This fortification, gentlemen, shall we see't?

Gentlemen. We'll wait upon your lordship.   *Exeunt.*

45 **affinity** family   53 **bosom** inmost thoughts   3.2.4 **Repair** go

Scene 3. [*The citadel.*]

Enter Desdemona, Cassio, and Emilia.

Desdemona. Be thou assured, good Cassio, I will do
  All my abilities in thy behalf.

Emilia. Good madam, do. I warrant it grieves my husband
  As if the cause were his.

Desdemona. O, that's an honest fellow. Do not doubt,
  Cassio,   5
  But I will have my lord and you again
  As friendly as you were.

Cassio.   Bounteous madam,
  Whatever shall become of Michael Cassio,
  He's never anything but your true servant.

Desdemona. I know't; I thank you. You do love my
  lord.   10
  You have known him long, and be you well assured
  He shall in strangeness stand no farther off
  Than in a politic distance.°

Cassio.   Ay, but, lady,
  That policy may either last so long,
  Or feed upon such nice° and waterish diet,   15
  Or breed itself so out of circumstances,°
  That, I being absent, and my place supplied,°
  My general will forget my love and service.

Desdemona. Do not doubt° that; before Emilia here
  I give thee warrant of thy place. Assure thee,   20
  If I do vow a friendship, I'll perform it

3.3.12–13 **He ... distance** i.e., he shall act no more distant to you than is
necessary for political reasons   15 **nice** trivial   16 **Or ... circumstances**
i.e., or grow so on the basis of accidental happenings and political needs   17
supplied filled   19 **doubt** imagine

To the last article. My lord shall never rest;
I'll watch him tame° and talk him out of patience;
His bed shall seem a school, his board a shrift;°
25 I'll intermingle everything he does
With Cassio's suit. Therefore be merry, Cassio,
For thy solicitor shall rather die
Than give thy cause away.

Enter Othello and Iago [at a distance].

Emilia. Madam, here comes my lord.

30 *Cassio.* Madam, I'll take my leave.

Desdemona. Why, stay, and hear me speak.

Cassio. Madam, not now. I am very ill at ease,
Unfit for mine own purposes.

Desdemona. Well, do your discretion.   *Exit Cassio.*

Iago. Ha! I like not that.

35 *Othello.*   What dost thou say?

Iago. Nothing, my lord; or if—I know not what.

Othello. Was not that Cassio parted from my wife?

Iago. Cassio, my lord? No, sure, I cannot think it
That he would steal away so guilty-like,
Seeing your coming.

40 *Othello.*   I do believe 'twas he.

Desdemona. [*Coming to them*] How now, my lord?
I have been talking with a suitor here,
A man that languishes in your displeasure.

Othello. Who is't you mean?

Desdemona. Why, your lieutenant, Cassio. Good my
45   lord,
If I have any grace or power to move you,
His present° reconciliation take.
For if he be not one that truly loves you,

23 **watch him tame** (animals were tamed by being kept awake)   24 **board
a shrift** table (seem) a confessional   47 **present** immediate

That errs in ignorance, and not in cunning,
I have no judgment in an honest face.   50
I prithee call him back.

Othello.   Went he hence now?

Desdemona. I' sooth so humbled
That he hath left part of his grief with me
To suffer with him. Good love, call him back.

Othello. Not now, sweet Desdemon; some other time.   55

Desdemona. But shall't be shortly?

Othello.   The sooner, sweet, for you.

Desdemona. Shall't be tonight at supper?

Othello.   No, not tonight.

Desdemona. Tomorrow dinner then?

Othello.   I shall not dine at home;
I meet the captains at the citadel.

Desdemona. Why then, tomorrow night, on Tuesday
    morn,   60
On Tuesday noon, or night, on Wednesday morn.
I prithee name the time, but let it not
Exceed three days. In faith, he's penitent;
And yet his trespass, in our common reason
(Save that, they say, the wars must make example   65
Out of her best), is not almost a fault
T' incur a private check.° When shall he come?
Tell me, Othello. I wonder in my soul
What you would ask me that I should deny
Or stand so mamm'ring° on. What? Michael Cassio,   70
That came awooing with you, and so many a time,
When I have spoke of you dispraisingly,
Hath ta'en your part—to have so much to do
To bring him in? By'r Lady, I could do much—

Othello. Prithee no more. Let him come when he will!   75
I will deny thee nothing.

66–67 **is ... check** is almost not serious enough for a private rebuke (let
alone a public disgrace)   70 **mamm'ring** hesitating

Desdemona.   Why, this is not a boon;
   'Tis as I should entreat you wear your gloves,
   Or feed on nourishing dishes, or keep you warm,
   Or sue to you to do a peculiar profit°
80   To your own person. Nay, when I have a suit
   Wherein I mean to touch your love indeed,
   It shall be full of poise° and difficult weight,
   And fearful to be granted.

Othello.   I will deny thee nothing!
   Whereon I do beseech thee grant me this,
85   To leave me but a little to myself.

Desdemona. Shall I deny you? No. Farewell, my lord.

Othello. Farewell, my Desdemona: I'll come to thee
   straight.°

Desdemona. Emilia, come. Be as your fancies teach
   you;
   Whate'er you be, I am obedient.   *Exit [with Emilia].*

90 *Othello.* Excellent wretch! Perdition catch my soul
   But I do love thee! And when I love thee not,
   Chaos is come again.

Iago. My noble lord——

Othello.   What dost thou say, Iago?

Iago. Did Michael Cassio, when you wooed my lady,
95   Know of your love?

Othello. He did, from first to last. Why dost thou ask?

Iago. But for a satisfaction of my thought,
   No further harm.

Othello.   Why of thy thought, Iago?

Iago. I did not think he had been acquainted with her.

100 *Othello.* O, yes, and went between us° very oft.

Iago. Indeed?

Othello. Indeed? Ay, indeed! Discern'st thou aught in
   that?

79 **peculiar profit** particularly personal good 82 **poise** weight 87
straight at once   100 **between us** i.e., as messenger

　　Is he not honest?

Iago.　　　　　　　　Honest, my lord?

Othello.　　　　　　　　　　Honest? Ay, honest.

Iago. My lord, for aught I know.

Othello. What dost thou think?

Iago.　　　　　　　　Think, my lord?

Othello.　　　　　　　　　Think, my lord? *105*
　　By heaven, thou echoest me,
　　As if there were some monster in thy thought
　　Too hideous to be shown. Thou dost mean some-
　　　　thing.
　　I heard thee say even now, thou lik'st not that,
　　When Cassio left my wife. What didst not like? *110*
　　And when I told thee he was of my counsel°
　　Of my whole course of wooing, thou cried'st "In-
　　　　deed?"
　　And didst contract and purse thy brow together,
　　As if thou then hadst shut up in thy brain
　　Some horrible conceit.° If thou dost love me, *115*
　　Show me thy thought.

Iago. My lord, you know I love you.

Othello.　　　　　　　　I think thou dost;
　　And, for I know thou'rt full of love and honesty
　　And weigh'st thy words before thou giv'st them
　　　　breath,
　　Therefore these stops° of thine fright me the more; *120*
　　For such things in a false disloyal knave
　　Are tricks of custom;° but in a man that's just
　　They're close dilations,° working from the heart
　　That passion cannot rule.

Iago.　　　　　　　　For Michael Cassio,
　　I dare be sworn, I think that he is honest. *125*

Othello. I think so too.

---

111 **of my counsel** in my confidence　115 **conceit** thought　120 **stops** in-
terruptions　122 **of custom** customary　123 **close dilations** expressions of
hidden thoughts

Iago.   Men should be what they seem;
   Or those that be not, would they might seem none!

Othello. Certain, men should be what they seem.

Iago. Why then, I think Cassio's an honest man.

130 *Othello.* Nay, yet there's more in this?
   I prithee speak to me as to thy thinkings,
   As thou dost ruminate, and give thy worst of
      thoughts
   The worst of words.

Iago.   Good my lord, pardon me:
   Though I am bound to every act of duty,
135 I am not bound to that all slaves are free to.
   Utter my thoughts? Why, say they are vile and false,
   As where's that palace whereinto foul things
   Sometimes intrude not? Who has that breast so pure
   But some uncleanly apprehensions
140 Keep leets and law days,° and in sessions sit
   With meditations lawful?

Othello. Thou dost conspire against thy friend, Iago,
   If thou but think'st him wronged, and mak'st his ear
   A stranger to thy thoughts.

Iago.   I do beseech you—
145 Though I perchance am vicious in my guess
   (As I confess it is my nature's plague
   To spy into abuses, and of my jealousy
   Shape faults that are not), that your wisdom
   From one that so imperfectly conceits
150 Would take no notice, nor build yourself a trouble
   Out of his scattering and unsure observance.
   It were not for your quiet nor your good,
   Nor for my manhood, honesty, and wisdom,
   To let you know my thoughts.

Othello.   What dost thou mean?

155 *Iago.* Good name in man and woman, dear my lord,
   Is the immediate jewel of their souls.

___

140 **leets and law days** meetings of local courts

Who steals my purse steals trash; 'tis something,
    nothing;
'Twas mine, 'tis his, and has been slave to thousands;
But he that filches from me my good name
Robs me of that which not enriches him   *160*
And makes me poor indeed.

Othello. By heaven, I'll know thy thoughts!

Iago. You cannot, if my heart were in your hand;
    Nor shall not whilst 'tis in my custody.

Othello. Ha!

Iago.   O, beware, my lord, of jealousy!   *165*
    It is the green-eyed monster, which doth mock
    The meat it feeds on. That cuckold lives in bliss
    Who, certain of his fate, loves not his wronger;
    But O, what damnèd minutes tells° he o'er
    Who dotes, yet doubts—suspects, yet fondly° loves!   *170*

Othello. O misery.

Iago. Poor and content is rich, and rich enough;
    But riches fineless° is as poor as winter
    To him that ever fears he shall be poor.
    Good God the souls of all my tribe defend   *175*
    From jealousy!

Othello.   Why? Why is this?
    Think'st thou I'd make a life of jealousy,
    To follow still° the changes of the moon
    With fresh suspicions? No! To be once in doubt
    Is to be resolved. Exchange me for a goat   *180*
    When I shall turn the business of my soul
    To such exsufflicate and blown° surmises,
    Matching thy inference. 'Tis not to make me jealous
    To say my wife is fair, feeds well, loves company,
    Is free of speech, sings, plays, and dances;   *185*
    Where virtue is, these are more virtuous.
    Nor from mine own weak merits will I draw
    The smallest fear or doubt of her revolt,

---

169 **tells** counts   170 **fondly** foolishly   173 **fineless** infinite   178 **To follow still** to change always (as the phases of the moon)   182 **exsufflicate and
blown** inflated and flyblown

For she had eyes, and chose me. No, Iago;
190 I'll see before I doubt; when I doubt, prove;
And on the proof there is no more but this:
Away at once with love or jealousy!

Iago. I am glad of this; for now I shall have reason
To show the love and duty that I bear you
195 With franker spirit. Therefore, as I am bound,
Receive it from me. I speak not yet of proof.
Look to your wife; observe her well with Cassio;
Wear your eyes thus: not jealous nor secure.
I would not have your free and noble nature
200 Out of self-bounty° be abused. Look to't.
I know our country disposition well:
In Venice they do let heaven see the pranks
They dare not show their husbands; their best con-
science
Is not to leave't undone, but kept unknown.°

205 *Othello.* Dost thou say so?

Iago. She did deceive her father, marrying you;
And when she seemed to shake and fear your looks,
She loved them most.

Othello.   And so she did.

Iago.   Why, go to then!
She that so young could give out such a seeming
210 To seel° her father's eyes up close as oak°—
He thought 'twas witchcraft. But I am much to
blame.
I humbly do beseech you of your pardon
For too much loving you.

Othello.   I am bound to thee forever.

Iago. I see this hath a little dashed your spirits.

Othello. Not a jot, not a jot.

215 *Iago.*   Trust me, I fear it has.

200 **self-bounty** innate kindness (which attributes his own motives to others)
203–4 **their ... unknown** i.e., their morality does not forbid adultery, but it
does forbid being found out   210 **seel** hoodwink   210 **oak** (a close-grained
wood)

I hope you will consider what is spoke
Comes from my love. But I do see y' are moved.
I am to pray you not to strain° my speech
To grosser issues, nor to larger reach°
Than to suspicion. 220

Othello. I will not.

Iago. Should you do so, my lord,
My speech should fall into such vile success
Which my thoughts aimed not. Cassio's my worthy
friend—
My lord, I see y' are moved.

Othello. No, not much moved.
I do not think but Desdemona's honest. 225

Iago. Long live she so. And long live you to think so.

Othello. And yet, how nature erring from itself——

Iago. Ay, there's the point, as (to be bold with you)
Not to affect many proposèd matches
Of her own clime, complexion, and degree,° 230
Whereto we see in all things nature tends°—
Foh! one may smell in such a will most rank,
Foul disproportions, thoughts unnatural.
But, pardon me, I do not in position°
Distinctly° speak of her; though I may fear 235
Her will, recoiling to her better judgment,
May fall to match° you with her country forms,°
And happily° repent.

Othello. Farewell, farewell!
If more thou dost perceive, let me know more.
Set on thy wife to observe. Leave me, Iago. 240

Iago. My lord, I take my leave. [*Going.*]

---

218 **strain** enlarge the meaning of   219 **reach** meaning   230 **degree** social station   231 **in . . . tends** i.e., all things in nature seek out their own kind   234 **position** general argument   235 **Distinctly** specifically   237 **fall to match** happen to compare   237 **country forms** i.e., the familiar appearances of her countrymen   238 **happily** by chance

Othello. Why did I marry? This honest creature doubt-
    less
    Sees and knows more, much more, than he unfolds.

Iago. [*Returns.*] My lord, I would I might entreat your
    honor
245   To scan this thing no farther. Leave it to time.
    Although 'tis fit that Cassio have his place,
    For sure he fills it up with great ability,
    Yet, if you please to hold him off awhile,
    You shall by that perceive him and his means.
250   Note if your lady strain his entertainment°
    With any strong or vehement importunity;
    Much will be seen in that. In the meantime
    Let me be thought too busy in my fears
    (As worthy cause I have to fear I am)
255   And hold her free, I do beseech your honor.

Othello. Fear not my government.°

Iago.   I once more take my leave.

                                      Exit.

Othello. This fellow's of exceeding honesty,
    And knows all qualities,° with a learnèd spirit
    Of human dealings. If I do prove her haggard,°
260   Though that her jesses° were my dear heartstrings,
    I'd whistle her off and let her down the wind°
    To prey at fortune. Haply for° I am black
    And have not those soft parts° of conversation
    That chamberers° have, or for I am declined
265   Into the vale of years—yet that's not much—
    She's gone. I am abused, and my relief
    Must be to loathe her. O curse of marriage,
    That we can call these delicate creatures ours,
    And not their appetites! I had rather be a toad

---

250 **strain his entertainment** urge strongly that he be reinstated   256 **government** self-control   258 **qualities** natures, types of people   259 **haggard**
a partly trained hawk which has gone wild again   260 **jesses** straps which
held the hawk's legs to the trainer's wrist   261 **I'd . . . wind** I would release
her (like an untamable hawk) and let her fly free   262 **Haply for** it may be
because   263 **soft parts** gentle qualities and manners   264 **chamberers**
courtiers—or perhaps, accomplished seducers

And live upon the vapor of a dungeon   270
Than keep a corner in the thing I love
For others' uses. Yet 'tis the plague to great ones;
Prerogatived are they less than the base.
'Tis destiny unshunnable, like death.
Even then this forkèd° plague is fated to us   275
When we do quicken.° Look where she comes.

Enter Desdemona and Emilia.

If she be false, heaven mocked itself!
I'll not believe't.

Desdemona.   How now, my dear Othello?
Your dinner, and the generous islanders
By you invited, do attend° your presence.   280

Othello. I am to blame.

Desdemona.   Why do you speak so faintly?
And you not well?

Othello. I have a pain upon my forehead, here.°

Desdemona. Why, that's with watching; 'twill away
again.
Let me but bind it hard, within this hour   285
It will be well.

Othello.   Your napkin° is too little;

[*He pushes the handkerchief away, and it falls.*]
Let it° alone. Come, I'll go in with you.

Desdemona. I am very sorry that you are not well.

Exit [with Othello].

Emilia. I am glad I have found this napkin;
This was her first remembrance from the Moor.   290
My wayward husband hath a hundred times
Wooed me to steal it; but she so loves the token

---

275 **forkèd** horned (the sign of the cuckold was horns)   276 **do quicken** are
born   280 **attend** wait   283 **here** (he points to his imaginary horns)   286
napkin elaborately worked handkerchief   287 **it** (it makes a considerable
difference in the interpretation of later events whether this "it" refers to Othello's forehead or to the handkerchief; nothing in the text makes the reference
clear)

(For he conjured her she should ever keep it)
That she reserves it evermore about her
295   To kiss and talk to. I'll have the work ta'en out°
And give't Iago. What he will do with it,
Heaven knows, not I; I nothing° but to please his
    fantasy.°

Enter Iago.

Iago. How now? What do you here alone?

Emilia. Do not you chide; I have a thing for you.

Iago. You have a thing for me? It is a common
300   thing——

Emilia. Ha?

Iago. To have a foolish wife.

Emilia. O, is that all? What will you give me now
For that same handkerchief?

Iago.   What handkerchief?

305 *Emilia.* What handkerchief?
Why, that the Moor first gave to Desdemona,
That which so often you did bid me steal.

Iago. Hast stol'n it from her?

Emilia. No, but she let it drop by negligence,
310   And to th' advantage,° I, being here, took't up.
Look, here 't is.

Iago.   A good wench. Give it me.

Emilia. What will you do with't, that you have been
    so earnest
To have me filch it?

Iago.   Why, what is that to you?

[Takes it.]

Emilia. If it be not for some purpose of import,°
315   Give't me again. Poor lady, she'll run mad
When she shall lack° it.

---

295 **work ta'en out** needlework copied   297 **I nothing** I wish nothing
297 **fantasy** fancy, whim   310 **to th' advantage** being lucky   314 **import**
importance   316 **lack** miss

Iago.   Be not acknown on't.°
   I have use for it. Go, leave me.   *Exit Emilia.*
   I will in Cassio's lodging lose this napkin
   And let him find it. Trifles light as air
   Are to the jealous confirmations strong   320
   As proofs of Holy Writ. This may do something.
   The Moor already changes with my poison:
   Dangerous conceits are in their natures poisons,
   Which at the first are scarce found to distaste,°
   But, with a little,° act upon the blood,   325
   Burn like the mines of sulfur. I did say so.

                    Enter Othello.

   Look where he comes! Not poppy nor mandragora,°
   Nor all the drowsy syrups of the world,
   Shall ever medicine thee to that sweet sleep
   Which thou owedst° yesterday.

Othello.   Ha! ha! False to me?   330

Iago. Why, how now, general? No more of that.

Othello. Avaunt! be gone! Thou hast set me on the
   rack.
   I swear 'tis better to be much abused
   Than but to know't a little.

Iago.   How now, my lord?

Othello. What sense had I of her stol'n hours of lust?   335
   I saw't not, thought it not, it harmed not me;
   I slept the next night well, fed well, was free and
      merry;
   I found not Cassio's kisses on her lips.
   He that is robbed, not wanting° what is stol'n,
   Let him not know't, and he's not robbed at all.   340

Iago. I am sorry to hear this.

316 **Be not acknown on't** forget you ever saw it   324 **are scarce found to distaste** scarcely can be tasted   325 **with a little** in a short time   327 **poppy nor mandragora** (soporifics)   330 **owedst** possessed   339 **wanting** missing

Othello. I had been happy if the general camp,
 Pioners° and all, had tasted her sweet body,
 So I had nothing known. O now, forever
345 Farewell the tranquil mind! Farewell content!
 Farewell the plumèd troops, and the big wars
 That makes ambition virtue! O, farewell!
 Farewell the neighing steed and the shrill trump,
 The spirit-stirring drum, th' ear-piercing fife,
350 The royal banner, and all quality,
 Pride, pomp, and circumstance° of glorious war!
 And O you mortal engines° whose rude throats
 Th' immortal Jove's dread clamors° counterfeit,
 Farewell! Othello's occupation's gone!

355 *Iago.* Is't possible, my lord?

Othello. Villain, be sure thou prove my love a whore!
 Be sure of it; give me the ocular proof;
 Or, by the worth of mine eternal soul,
 Thou hadst been better have been born a dog
 Than answer my waked wrath!

360 *Iago.*   Is't come to this?

Othello. Make me to see't; or at the least so prove it
 That the probation° bear no hinge nor loop
 To hang a doubt on—or woe upon thy life!

Iago. My noble lord——

365 *Othello.* If thou dost slander her and torture me,
 Never pray more; abandon all remorse;
 On horror's head horrors accumulate;
 Do deeds to make heaven weep, all earth amazed;
 For nothing canst thou to damnation add
 Greater than that.

370 *Iago.* O grace! O heaven forgive me!
 Are you a man? Have you a soul or sense?
 God b' wi' you! Take mine office. O wretched fool,
 That lov'st to make thine honesty a vice!
 O monstrous world! Take note, take note, O world,

---

343 **Pioners** (the basest manual laborers in the army, who dug trenches and mines)   351 **circumstance** pageantry   352 **mortal engines** lethal weapons, i.e., cannon   353 **clamors** i.e., thunder   362 **probation** proof

To be direct and honest is not safe.   375
I thank you for this profit, and from hence
I'll love no friend, sith° love breeds such offense.

Othello. Nay, stay. Thou shouldst be honest.

Iago. I should be wise; for honesty's a fool
And loses that it works for.

Othello.   By the world,   380
I think my wife be honest, and think she is not;
I think that thou art just, and think thou art not.
I'll have some proof. My name, that was as fresh
As Dian's° visage, is now begrimed and black
As mine own face. If there be cords, or knives,   385
Poison, or fire, or suffocating streams,
I'll not endure it. Would I were satisfied!

Iago. I see you are eaten up with passion.
I do repent me that I put it to you.
You would be satisfied?

Othello.   Would? Nay, and I will.   390

Iago. And may; but how? How satisfied, my lord?
Would you, the supervisor,° grossly gape on?
Behold her topped?

Othello.   Death and damnation! O!

Iago. It were a tedious° difficulty, I think,
To bring them to that prospect.° Damn them then,   395
If ever mortal eyes do see them bolster°
More than their own! What then? How then?
What shall I say? Where's satisfaction?
It is impossible you should see this,
Were they as prime° as goats, as hot as monkeys,   400
As salt° as wolves in pride,° and fools as gross
As ignorance made drunk. But yet, I say,

---

377 **sith** since   384 **Dian's** Diana's (goddess of the moon and of chastity)
392 **supervisor** onlooker   394 **tedious** hard to arrange   395 **prospect**
sight (where they can be seen)   396 **bolster** go to bed   400–01 **prime, salt**
lustful   401 **pride** heat

    If imputation and strong circumstances
    Which lead directly to the door of truth
405   Will give you satisfaction, you might have't.

Othello. Give me a living reason she's disloyal.

Iago. I do not like the office.°
    But sith I am entered in this cause so far,
    Pricked° to't by foolish honesty and love,
410   I will go on. I lay with Cassio lately,
    And being troubled with a raging tooth,
    I could not sleep.
    There are a kind of men so loose of soul
    That in their sleeps will mutter their affairs.
415   One of this kind is Cassio.
    In sleep I heard him say, "Sweet Desdemona,
    Let us be wary, let us hide our loves!"
    And then, sir, would he gripe° and wring my hand,
    Cry "O sweet creature!" Then kiss me hard,
420   As if he plucked up kisses by the roots
    That grew upon my lips; laid his leg o'er my thigh,
    And sigh, and kiss, and then cry, "Cursèd fate
    That gave thee to the Moor!"

Othello. O monstrous! monstrous!

Iago.   Nay, this was but his dream.

425 *Othello.* But this denoted a foregone conclusion,°
    'Tis a shrewd doubt,° though it be but a dream.

Iago. And this may help to thicken other proofs
    That do demonstrate° thinly.

Othello.   I'll tear her all to pieces!

Iago. Nay, yet be wise. Yet we see nothing done;
430   She may be honest yet. Tell me but this:
    Have you not sometimes seen a handkerchief
    Spotted with strawberries in your wife's hand?

Othello. I gave her such a one; 'twas my first gift.

---

407 **office** duty   409 **Pricked** spurred   418 **gripe** seize   425 **foregone conclusion** consummated fact   426 **shrewd doubt** penetrating guess   428 **demonstrate** show, appear

Iago. I know not that; but such a handkerchief—
  I am sure it was your wife's—did I today   *435*
  See Cassio wipe his beard with.

Othello.   If it be that——

Iago. If it be that, or any that was hers,
  It speaks against her with the other proofs.

Othello. O, that the slave had forty thousand lives!
  One is too poor, too weak for my revenge.   *440*
  Now do I see 'tis true. Look here, Iago:
  All my fond love thus do I blow to heaven.
  'Tis gone.
  Arise, black vengeance, from the hollow hell!
  Yield up, O Love, thy crown and hearted° throne   *445*
  To tyrannous hate! Swell, bosom, with thy fraught,°
  For 'tis of aspics'° tongues.

Iago.   Yet be content.°

Othello. O, blood, blood, blood!

Iago. Patience, I say. Your mind may change.

Othello. Never, Iago. Like to the Pontic Sea,°   *450*
  Whose icy current and compulsive course
  Nev'r keeps retiring ebb, but keeps due on
  To the Propontic and the Hellespont,
  Even so my bloody thoughts, with violent pace,
  Shall nev'r look back, nev'r ebb to humble love,   *455*
  Till that a capable and wide° revenge
  Swallow them up. [*He kneels.*] Now, by yond mar-
    ble heaven,
  In the due reverence of a sacred vow
  I here engage my words.

Iago.   Do not rise yet.

                   [*Iago kneels.*]

  Witness, you ever-burning lights above,   *460*

---

445 hearted seated in the heart **446 fraught** burden **447 aspics'** asps'
447 content patient, quiet **450 Pontic Sea** the Black Sea (famous for the
strong and constant current with which it flows through the Bosporus into the
Mediterranean, where the water level is lower) **456 capable and wide** sufficient and far-reaching

You elements that clip° us round about,
Witness that here Iago doth give up
The execution° of his wit, hands, heart
To wronged Othello's service! Let him command,
465 And to obey shall be in me remorse,°
What bloody business ever.°   [*They rise.*]

Othello.   I greet thy love,
Not with vain thanks but with acceptance boun-
   teous,°
And will upon the instant put thee to't.°
Within these three days let me hear thee say
470 That Cassio's not alive.

Iago. My friend is dead. 'Tis done at your request.
But let her live.

Othello.   Damn her, lewd minx! O, damn her!
   Damn her!
Come, go with me apart. I will withdraw
To furnish me with some swift means of death
475 For the fair devil. Now art thou my lieutenant.

Iago. I am your own forever.   *Exeunt.*

Scene 4. [*A street.*]

Enter Desdemona, Emilia, and Clown.

Desdemona. Do you know, sirrah, where Lieutenant
   Cassio lies?°

Clown. I dare not say he lies anywhere.

Desdemona. Why, man?

5 *Clown.* He's a soldier, and for me to say a soldier lies,
   'tis stabbing.

---

461 **clip** enfold   463 **execution** workings, action   465 **remorse** pity   466
ever soever   467 **bounteous** absolute   468 **to't** i.e., to the work you have
said you are prepared to do   3.4.2 **lies** lodges

Desdemona. Go to. Where lodges he?

Clown. To tell you where he lodges is to tell you where
  I lie.

Desdemona. Can anything be made of this?   *10*

Clown. I know not where he lodges, and for me to
  devise a lodging, and say he lies here or he lies there,
  were to lie in mine own throat.°

Desdemona. Can you enquire him out, and be edified°
  by report?   *15*

Clown. I will catechize the world for him; that is, make
  questions, and by them answer.

Desdemona. Seek him, bid him come hither. Tell him
  I have moved° my lord on his behalf and hope all
  will be well.   *20*

Clown. To do this is within the compass° of man's wit,
  and therefore I will attempt the doing it. *Exit Clown.*

Desdemona. Where should° I lose the handkerchief,
  Emilia?

Emilia. I know not, madam.

Desdemona. Believe me, I had rather have lost my
  purse   *25*
  Full of crusadoes.° And but my noble Moor
  Is true of mind, and made of no such baseness
  As jealous creatures are, it were enough
  To put him to ill thinking.

Emilia.   Is he not jealous?

Desdemona. Who? He? I think the sun where he was
  born   *30*
  Drew all such humors° from him.

Emilia.   Look where he comes.

---

13 **lie in mine own throat** (to lie in the throat is to lie absolutely and completely) 14 **edified** enlightened (Desdemona mocks the Clown's overly
elaborate diction) 19 **moved** pleaded with 21 **compass** reach 23
should might 26 **crusadoes** Portuguese gold coins 31 **humors** characteristics

Enter Othello.

Desdemona. I will not leave him now till Cassio
 Be called to him. How is't with you, my lord?

Othello. Well, my good lady. [*Aside*] O, hardness to
 dissemble!°—
How do you, Desdemona?

35 *Desdemona.*   Well, my good lord.

Othello. Give me your hand. This hand is moist,°
 my lady.

Desdemona. It hath felt no age nor known no sorrow.

Othello. This argues° fruitfulness and liberal° heart.
 Hot, hot, and moist. This hand of yours requires
40 A sequester° from liberty; fasting and prayer;
 Much castigation; exercise devout;
 For here's a young and sweating devil here
 That commonly rebels. 'Tis a good hand,
 A frank one.

Desdemona. You may, indeed, say so;
45 For 'twas that hand that gave away my heart.

Othello. A liberal hand! The hearts of old gave hands,
 But our new heraldry° is hands, not hearts.

Desdemona. I cannot speak of this. Come now, your
 promise!

Othello. What promise, chuck?

Desdemona. I have sent to bid Cassio come speak with
50 you.

Othello. I have a salt and sorry rheum° offends me.
 Lend me thy handkerchief.

---

34 **hardness to dissemble** (Othello may refer here either to the difficulty he
has in maintaining his appearance of composure, or to what he believes to be
Desdemona's hardened hypocrisy) 36 **moist** (a moist, hot hand was taken as
a sign of a lustful nature) 38 **argues** suggests 38 **liberal** free, open (but
also with a suggestion of "licentious"; from here on in this scene Othello's
words bear a double meaning, seeming to be normal but accusing Desdemona
of being unfaithful) 40 **sequester** separation 47 **heraldry** heraldic sym-
bolism 51 **a salt and sorry rheum** a heavy, running head cold

Desdemona.   Here, my lord.

Othello. That which I gave you.

Desdemona.   I have it not about me.

Othello. Not?

Desdemona. No, indeed, my lord.

Othello.   That's a fault.
That handkerchief   55
Did an Egyptian to my mother give.
She was a charmer,° and could almost read
The thoughts of people. She told her, while she
    kept it
'Twould make her amiable° and subdue my father
Entirely to her love; but if she lost it   60
Or made a gift of it, my father's eye
Should hold her loathèd, and his spirits should hunt
After new fancies. She, dying, gave it me,
And bid me, when my fate would have me wived,
To give it her. I did so; and take heed on't;   65
Make it a darling like your precious eye.
To lose't or give't away were such perdition
As nothing else could match.

Desdemona.   Is't possible?

Othello. 'Tis true. There's magic in the web° of it.
A sibyl that had numbered in the world   70
The sun to course two hundred compasses,
In her prophetic fury° sewed the work;
The worms were hallowed that did breed the silk,
And it was dyed in mummy° which the skillful
Conserved of maidens' hearts.

Desdemona.   Indeed? Is't true?   75

Othello. Most veritable. Therefore look to't well.

Desdemona. Then would to God that I had never
    seen't!

57 **charmer** magician   59 **amiable** desirable   69 **web** weaving   72 **prophetic fury** seized by the spirit and able to prophesy   74 **mummy** liquid drained from embalmed bodies

Othello. Ha! Wherefore?

Desdemona. Why do you speak so startingly and rash?

80 *Othello.* Is't lost? Is't gone? Speak, is it out o' th' way?

Desdemona. Heaven bless us!

Othello. Say you?

Desdemona. It is not lost. But what an if it were?

Othello. How?

85 *Desdemona.* I say it is not lost.

Othello. Fetch't, let me see't!

Desdemona. Why, so I can; but I will not now.
This is a trick to put me from my suit:
Pray you let Cassio be received again.

90 *Othello.* Fetch me the handkerchief! My mind misgives.

Desdemona. Come, come!
You'll never meet a more sufficient° man——

Othello. The handkerchief!

Desdemona.   A man that all his time
Hath founded his good fortunes on your love,
95 Shared dangers with you——

Othello. The handkerchief!

Desdemona. I'faith, you are to blame.

Othello. Away!   *Exit Othello.*

Emilia. Is not this man jealous?

100 *Desdemona.* I nev'r saw this before.
Sure there's some wonder in this handkerchief;
I am most unhappy in the loss of it.

Emilia. 'Tis not a year or two shows us a man.
They are all but stomachs, and we all but food;
105 They eat us hungerly, and when they are full,
They belch us.

92 **sufficient** complete, with all proper qualities

Enter Iago and Cassio.

Look you, Cassio and my husband.

Iago. There is no other way; 'tis she must do't.
And lo the happiness! Go and importune her.

Desdemona. How now, good Cassio? What's the news
    with you?

Cassio. Madam, my former suit. I do beseech you   *110*
    That by your virtuous means I may again
    Exist, and be a member of his love
    Whom I with all the office° of my heart
    Entirely honor. I would not be delayed.
    If my offense be of such mortal kind   *115*
    That nor my service past, nor present sorrows,
    Nor purposed merit in futurity,
    Can ransom me into his love again,
    But to know so must be my benefit.°
    So shall I clothe me in a forced content,   *120*
    And shut myself up in some other course
    To fortune's alms.

Desdemona.   Alas, thrice-gentle Cassio,
    My advocation° is not now in tune.
    My lord is not my lord; nor should I know him
    Were he in favor° as in humor altered.   *125*
    So help me every spirit sanctified
    As I have spoken for you all my best
    And stood within the blank° of his displeasure
    For my free speech. You must awhile be patient.
    What I can do I will; and more I will   *130*
    Than for myself I dare. Let that suffice you.

Iago. Is my lord angry?

Emilia.   He went hence but now,
    And certainly in strange unquietness.

Iago. Can he be angry? I have seen the cannon
    When it hath blown his ranks into the air   *135*
    And, like the devil, from his very arm

---

113 **office** duty   119 **benefit** good   123 **advocation** advocacy   125 **favor**
countenance   28 **blank** bull's-eye of a target

Puffed his own brother. And is he angry?
Something of moment° then. I will go meet him.
There's matter in't indeed if he be angry.

Desdemona. I prithee do so.　　　　　　　*Exit [Iago].*
140　　　　　　　　　　　Something sure of state,°
Either from Venice or some unhatched practice°
Made demonstrable here in Cyprus to him,
Hath puddled° his clear spirit; and in such cases
Men's natures wrangle with inferior things,
145　Though great ones are their object. 'Tis even so.
For let our finger ache, and it endues°
Our other, healthful members even to a sense
Of pain. Nay, we must think men are not gods,
Nor of them look for such observancy
150　As fits the bridal. Beshrew me much, Emilia,
I was, unhandsome warrior as I am,
Arraigning his unkindness with my soul;
But now I find I had suborned the witness,
And he's indicted falsely.

Emilia.　　　　　　　　　　Pray heaven it be
155　State matters, as you think, and no conception
Nor no jealous toy° concerning you.

Desdemona. Alas the day! I never gave him cause.

Emilia. But jealous souls will not be answered so;
They are not ever jealous for the cause,
160　But jealous for they're jealous. It is a monster
Begot upon itself, born on itself.

Desdemona. Heaven keep the monster from Othello's
　　mind!

Emilia. Lady, amen.

Desdemona. I will go seek him. Cassio, walk here
　　about.
165　If I do find him fit,° I'll move your suit
And seek to effect it to my uttermost.

---

138 **moment** importance　140 **of state** state affairs　141 **unhatched practice** undisclosed plot　143 **puddled** muddied　146 **endues** leads　156 **toy** trifle　165 **fit** receptive

Cassio. I humbly thank your ladyship.

       Exit [*Desdemona with Emilia*].

       Enter Bianca.

Bianca. Save you, friend Cassio!

Cassio.   What make you from
 home?
 How is't with you, my most fair Bianca?
 I' faith, sweet love, I was coming to your house.   *170*

Bianca. And I was going to your lodging, Cassio.
 What, keep a week away? Seven days and nights?
 Eightscore eight hours? And lovers' absent hours
 More tedious than the dial eightscore times?
 O weary reck'ning.°

Cassio.   Pardon me, Bianca.   *175*
 I have this while with leaden thoughts been pressed,
 But I shall in a more continuate° time
 Strike off this score° of absence. Sweet Bianca,
   [*Gives her Desdemona's handkerchief.*]
 Take me this work out.

Bianca.   O Cassio, whence came this?
 This is some token from a newer friend.   *180*
 To the felt absence now I feel a cause.
 Is't come to this? Well, well.

Cassio.   Go to, woman!
 Throw your vile guesses in the devil's teeth,
 From whence you have them. You are jealous now
 That this is from some mistress, some remembrance. *185*
 No, by my faith, Bianca.

Bianca.   Why, whose is it?

Cassio. I know not neither; I found it in my chamber.
 I like the work well; ere it be demanded,°
 As like enough it will, I would have it copied.
 Take it and do't, and leave me for this time.   *190*

---

175 **reck'ning** addition 177 **continuate** uninterrupted 178 **Strike off this score** i.e., pay this bill (the *score* being the account of drinks kept in a tavern)
188 **demanded** asked for (by the person who lost it)

Bianca. Leave you? Wherefore?

Cassio. I do attend here on the general
  And think it no addition, nor my wish,
  To have him see me womaned.

Bianca.   Why, I pray you?

Cassio. Not that I love you not.

195 *Bianca.*   But that you do not love me!
  I pray you bring° me on the way a little,
  And say if I shall see you soon at night.

Cassio. 'Tis but a little way that I can bring you,
  For I attend here; but I'll see you soon.

200 *Bianca.* 'Tis very good. I must be circumstanced.°
                                    Exeunt omnes.

---

196 **bring** accompany   200 **circumstanced** accept things as they are

ACT 4

Scene 1. [*A street.*]

Enter Othello and Iago.

Iago. Will you think so?

Othello.   Think so, Iago?

Iago.   What,
  To kiss in private?

Othello.   An unauthorized° kiss?

Iago. Or to be naked with her friend in bed
  An hour or more, not meaning any harm?

Othello. Naked in bed, Iago, and not mean harm?   5
  It is hypocrisy against the devil.
  They that mean virtuously, and yet do so,
  The devil their virtue tempts, and they tempt heaven.

Iago. If they do nothing, 'tis a venial slip.
  But if I give my wife a handkerchief——   10

Othello. What then?

Iago. Why, then 'tis hers, my lord; and being hers,
  She may, I think, bestow't on any man.

Othello. She is protectress of her honor too.
  May she give that?   15

Iago. Her honor is an essence that's not seen;
  They have it very oft that have it not.
  But for the handkerchief——

4.1.2 **unauthorized** illicit

Othello. By heaven, I would most gladly have forgot it!

20　　Thou said'st—O, it comes o'er my memory
　　　As doth the raven° o'er the infected house,
　　　Boding to all—he had my handkerchief.

Iago. Ay, what of that?

Othello.　　　　　　　That's not so good now.

Iago. What if I had said I had seen him do you wrong?

25　　Or heard him say—as knaves be such abroad°
　　　Who having, by their own importunate suit,
　　　Or voluntary dotage° of some mistress,
　　　Convincèd or supplied° them, cannot choose
　　　But they must blab——

Othello.　　　　　　　Hath he said anything?

30　*Iago.* He hath, my lord; but be you well assured,
　　　No more than he'll unswear.

Othello.　　　　　　　What hath he said?

Iago. Why, that he did—I know not what he did.

Othello. What? what?

Iago. Lie——

Othello. With her?

35　*Iago.*　　　　　With her, on her; what you will.

Othello. Lie with her? Lie on her?—We say lie on her
　　　when they belie her.—Lie with her! Zounds, that's
　　　fulsome.°—Handkerchief—confessions—handker-
　　　chief!—To confess, and be hanged for his labor—

40　　first to be hanged, and then to confess! I tremble at
　　　it. Nature would not invest herself in such shadow-
　　　ing passion without some instruction.° It is not
　　　words that shakes me thus.—Pish! Noses, ears, and

---

21 **raven** (a harbinger of death)　25 **abroad** i.e., in the world　27 **voluntary dotage** weakness of the will　28 **Convincèd or supplied** persuaded or gratified (the mistress)　38 **fulsome** foul, repulsive · 41–42 **Nature ... instruction** i.e., my mind would not become so darkened (with anger) unless there were something in this (accusation); (it should be remembered that Othello believes in the workings of magic and supernatural forces)

lips? Is't possible?—Confess?—Handkerchief?—O
devil!   *Falls in a trance.*   45

Iago. Work on.
My med'cine works! Thus credulous fools are
    caught,
And many worthy and chaste dames even thus,
All guiltless, meet reproach.° What, ho! My lord!
My lord, I say! Othello!

                    Enter Cassio.
                        How now, Cassio?   50

Cassio. What's the matter?

Iago. My lord is fall'n into an epilepsy.
This is his second fit; he had one yesterday.

Cassio. Rub him about the temples.

Iago. The lethargy° must have his quiet course.   55
If not, he foams at mouth, and by and by
Breaks out to savage madness. Look, he stirs.
Do you withdraw yourself a little while.
He will recover straight. When he is gone,
I would on great occasion° speak with you.   60

                                [Exit Cassio.]
How is it, general? Have you not hurt your head?

Othello. Dost thou mock° me?

Iago.   I mock you not, by heaven.
Would you would bear your fortune like a man.

Othello. A hornèd man's a monster and a beast.

Iago. There's many a beast then in a populous city,   65
And many a civil° monster.

Othello. Did he confess it?

Iago.   Good, sir, be a man.
Think every bearded fellow that's but yoked
May draw° with you. There's millions now alive

49 **reproach** shame   55 **lethargy** coma   60 **great occasion** very important
matter   62 **mock** (Othello takes Iago's comment as a reference to his
horns—which it is)   66 **civil** city-dwelling   69 **draw** i.e., like the horned
ox

70   That nightly lie in those unproper° beds
      Which they dare swear peculiar.° Your case is
         better.
      O, 'tis the spite of hell, the fiend's arch-mock,
      To lip a wanton in a secure couch,
      And to suppose her chaste. No, let me know;
75   And knowing what I am, I know what she shall be.

Othello. O, thou art wise! 'Tis certain.

Iago.   Stand you awhile apart;
      Confine yourself but in a patient list.°
      Whilst you were here, o'erwhelmèd with your
         grief—
      A passion most unsuiting such a man—
80   Cassio came hither. I shifted him away°
      And laid good 'scuses upon your ecstasy;°
      Bade him anon return, and here speak with me;
      The which he promised. Do but encave° yourself
      And mark the fleers,° the gibes, and notable°
         scorns
85   That dwell in every region of his face.
      For I will make him tell the tale anew:
      Where, how, how oft, how long ago, and when
      He hath, and is again to cope your wife.
      I say, but mark his gesture. Marry patience,
90   Or I shall say you're all in all in spleen,°
      And nothing of a man.

Othello.   Dost thou hear, Iago?
      I will be found most cunning in my patience;
      But—dost thou hear?—most bloody.

Iago.   That's not amiss;
      But yet keep time in all. Will you withdraw?

      [*Othello moves to one side, where his remarks are not
                        audible to Cassio and Iago.*]

70 **unproper** i.e., not exclusively the husband's   71 **peculiar** their own
alone   77 **a patient list** the bounds of patience   80 **shifted him away** got
rid of him by a stratagem   81 **ecstasy** trance (the literal meaning, "outside
one-self," bears on the meaning of the change Othello is undergoing)   83 **en-
cave** hide   84 **fleers** mocking looks or speeches   84 **notable** obvious   90
spleen passion, particularly anger

Now will I question Cassio of Bianca,   95
A huswife° that by selling her desires
Buys herself bread and cloth. It is a creature
That dotes on Cassio, as 'tis the strumpet's plague
To beguile many and be beguiled by one.
He, when he hears of her, cannot restrain   100
From the excess of laughter. Here he comes.

Enter Cassio.
As he shall smile, Othello shall go mad;
And his unbookish° jealousy must conster°
Poor Cassio's smiles, gestures, and light behaviors
Quite in the wrong. How do you, lieutenant?   105

Cassio. The worser that you give me the addition°
Whose want even kills me.

Iago. Ply Desdemona well, and you are sure on't.
Now, if this suit lay in Bianca's power,
How quickly should you speed!

Cassio.   Alas, poor caitiff!°   110

Othello. Look how he laughs already!

Iago. I never knew woman love man so.

Cassio. Alas, poor rogue! I think, i' faith, she loves me.

Othello. Now he denies it faintly, and laughs it out.

Iago. Do you hear, Cassio?

Othello.   Now he importunes him   115
To tell it o'er. Go to! Well said, well said!

Iago. She gives it out that you shall marry her.
Do you intend it?

Cassio. Ha, ha, ha!

Othello. Do ye triumph, Roman? Do you triumph?   120

Cassio. I marry? What, a customer?° Prithee bear

---

96 **huswife** housewife (but with the special meaning here of "prostitute")
103 **unbookish** ignorant   103 **conster** construe   106 **addition** title   110
caitiff wretch   121 **customer** one who sells, a merchant (here, a prostitute)

some charity to my wit; do not think it so unwholesome. Ha, ha, ha!

Othello. So, so, so, so. They laugh that win.

125 *Iago.* Why, the cry goes that you marry her.

Cassio. Prithee, say true.

Iago. I am a very villain else.

Othello. Have you scored° me? Well.

Cassio. This is the monkey's own giving out. She is
130 persuaded I will marry her out of her own love and
flattery, not out of my promise.

Othello. Iago beckons me; now he begins the story.

[*Othello moves close enough to hear.*]

Cassio. She was here even now; she haunts me in every
place. I was the other day talking on the sea bank
135 with certain Venetians, and thither comes the
bauble,° and falls me thus about my neck——

Othello. Crying "O dear Cassio!" as it were. His ges-
ture imports it.

Cassio. So hangs, and lolls, and weeps upon me; so
140 shakes and pulls me! Ha, ha, ha!

Othello. Now he tells how she plucked him to my
chamber. O, I see that nose of yours, but not that
dog I shall throw it to.

Cassio. Well, I must leave her company.

145 *Iago.* Before me!° Look where she comes.

Enter Bianca.

Cassio. 'Tis such another fitchew!° Marry a perfumed
one? What do you mean by this haunting of me?

Bianca. Let the devil and his dam haunt you! What did
you mean by that same handkerchief you gave me
150 even now? I was a fine fool to take it. I must take

---

128 **scored** marked, defaced   136 **bauble** plaything   145 **Before me!** (an
exclamation of surprise)   146 **fitchew** polecat, i.e., strong-smelling creature

out the work? A likely piece of work that you should
find it in your chamber and know not who left it
there! This is some minx's token, and I must take
out the work? There! [*She throws down the handkerchief.*] Give it your hobbyhorse.° Wheresoever   *155*
you had it, I'll take out no work on't.

Cassio. How now, my sweet Bianca? How now? how
now?

Othello. By heaven, that should be my handkerchief!

Bianca. If you'll come to supper tonight, you may; if   *160*
you will not, come when you are next prepared
for.°   *Exit.*

Iago. After her, after her!

Cassio. Faith, I must; she'll rail in the streets else.

Iago. Will you sup there?   *165*

Cassio. Yes, I intend so.

Iago. Well, I may chance to see you, for I would very
fain speak with you.

Cassio. Prithee come. Will you?

Iago. Go to, say no more.   [*Exit Cassio.*]   *170*

Othello. [*Comes forward.*] How shall I murder him,
Iago?

Iago. Did you perceive how he laughed at his vice?

Othello. O Iago!

Iago. And did you see the handkerchief?   *175*

Othello. Was that mine?

Iago. Yours, by this hand! And to see how he prizes
the foolish woman your wife! She gave it him, and
he hath giv'n it his whore.

Othello. I would have him nine years a-killing!—A   *180*
fine woman, a fair woman, a sweet woman?

---

155 **hobbyhorse** prostitute   161–62 **next prepared for** next expected—i.e.,
never

Iago. Nay, you must forget that.

Othello. Ay, let her rot, and perish, and be damned
tonight; for she shall not live. No, my heart is turned
185   to stone; I strike it, and it hurts my hand. O, the
world hath not a sweeter creature! She might lie by
an emperor's side and command him tasks.

Iago. Nay, that's not your way.°

Othello. Hang her! I do but say what she is. So deli-
190   cate with her needle. An admirable musician. O, she
will sing the savageness out of a bear! Of so high
and plenteous wit and invention°——

Iago. She's the worse for all this.

Othello. O, a thousand, a thousand times. And then,
195   of so gentle a condition?°

Iago. Ay, too gentle.

Othello. Nay, that's certain. But yet the pity of it,
Iago. O Iago, the pity of it, Iago.

Iago. If you are so fond over her iniquity, give her
200   patent to offend; for if it touch° not you, it comes
near nobody.

Othello. I will chop her into messes!° Cuckold me!

Iago. O, 'tis foul in her.

Othello. With mine officer!

205 *Iago.* That's fouler.

Othello. Get me some poison, Iago, this night. I'll not
expostulate with her, lest her body and beauty unprovide my mind° again. This night, Iago!

Iago. Do it not with poison. Strangle her in her bed,
210   even the bed she hath contaminated.

Othello. Good, good! The justice of it pleases. Very
good!

188 **way** proper course 192 **invention** imagination 195 **gentle a condi-**
tion (1) well born (2) of a gentle nature 200 **touch** affects 202 **messes**
bits 207–08 **unprovide my mind** undo my resolution

Iago. And for Cassio, let me be his undertaker.° You
  shall hear more by midnight.

Othello. Excellent good!   [*A trumpet.*]
                    What trumpet is that same?   *215*

Iago. I warrant something from Venice.

    Enter Lodovico, Desdemona, and Attendants.
                                    'Tis Lodovico.
  This comes from the Duke. See, your wife's with
    him.

Lodovico. God save you, worthy general.

Othello.   With° all my heart, sir.

Lodovico. The Duke and the senators of Venice greet
  you.   [*Gives him a letter.*]

Othello. I kiss the instrument of their pleasures.   *220*

                    [*Opens the letter and reads.*]

Desdemona. And what's the news, good cousin Lodovico?

Iago. I am very glad to see you, signior.
  Welcome to Cyprus.

Lodovico. I thank you. How does Lieutenant Cassio?

Iago.   Lives, sir.

Desdemona. Cousin, there's fall'n between him   and
  my lord   *225*
  An unkind° breach; but you shall make all well.

Othello. Are you sure of that?

Desdemona. My lord?

Othello. [*Reads*] "This fail you not to do, as you
  will——"

Lodovico. He did not call; he's busy in the paper.   *230*
  Is there division 'twixt my lord and Cassio?

213 **undertaker** (not "burier" but "one who undertakes to do something")
218 **With** i.e., I greet you with   226 **unkind** unnatural

Desdemona. A most unhappy one. I would do much
T' atone° them, for the love I bear to Cassio.

Othello. Fire and brimstone!

Desdemona.   My lord?

Othello.   Are you wise?

Desdemona. What, is he angry?

235 *Lodovico.*   May be th' letter moved him;
For, as I think, they do command him home,
Deputing Cassio in his government.°

Desdemona. Trust me, I am glad on't.

Othello.   Indeed?

Desdemona.   My lord?

Othello. I am glad to see you mad.

Desdemona.   Why, sweet Othello—

240 *Othello.* Devil!   [*Strikes her.*]

Desdemona. I have not deserved this.

Lodovico. My lord, this would not be believed in
     Venice,
Though I should swear I saw't. 'Tis very much.
Make her amends; she weeps.

Othello.   O devil, devil!
245 If that the earth could teem° with woman's tears,
Each drop she falls° would prove a crocodile.°
Out of my sight!

Desdemona.   I will not stay to offend you. [*Going.*]

Lodovico. Truly, an obedient lady.
I do beseech your lordship call her back.

Othello. Mistress!

Desdemona.   My lord?

250 *Othello.*   What would you with her, sir?

233 **atone** reconcile 237 **government** office 245 **teem** conceive 246
falls drops 246 **crocodile** (the crocodile was supposed to shed false tears to
lure its victims)

Lodovico. Who? I, my lord?

Othello. Ay! You did wish that I would make her turn.
   Sir, she can turn, and turn, and yet go on
   And turn again; and she can weep, sir, weep;
   And she's obedient; as you say, obedient.   255
   Very obedient. Proceed you in your tears.
   Concerning this, sir—O well-painted passion!
   I am commanded home.—Get you away;
   I'll send for you anon.—Sir, I obey the mandate
   And will return to Venice.—Hence, avaunt!   260

                         [*Exit Desdemona.*]
   Cassio shall have my place. And, sir, tonight
   I do entreat that we may sup together.
   You are welcome, sir, to Cyprus.—Goats and mon-
      keys!   *Exit.*

Lodovico. Is this the noble Moor whom our full Senate
   Call all in all sufficient? Is this the nature   265
   Whom passion could not shake? whose solid virtue
   The shot of accident nor dart of chance
   Could neither graze nor pierce?

Iago.   He is much changed.

Lodovico. Are his wits safe? Is he not light of brain?

Iago. He's that he is; I may not breathe my censure.   270
   What he might be (if, what he might, he is not)
   I would to heaven he were!

Lodovico.   What, strike his wife?

Iago. Faith, that was not so well; yet would I knew
   That stroke would prove the worst.

Lodovico.   Is it his use?°
   Or did the letters work upon his blood°   275
   And new-create his fault?

Iago.   Alas, alas!
   It is not honesty in me to speak
   What I have seen and known. You shall observe
      him,

274 **use** habit   275 **blood** passion

And his own courses° will denote him so
280   That I may save my speech. Do but go after
And mark how he continues.

Lodovico. I am sorry that I am deceived in him.

Exeunt.

Scene 2. [*The citadel.*]

Enter Othello and Emilia.

Othello. You have seen nothing then?

Emilia. Nor ever heard, nor ever did suspect.

Othello. Yes, you have seen Cassio and she together.

Emilia. But then I saw no harm, and then I heard
5   Each syllable that breath made up° between them.

Othello. What, did they never whisper?

Emilia.   Never, my lord.

Othello. Nor send you out o' th' way?

Emilia. Never.

Othello. To fetch her fan, her gloves, her mask, nor
         nothing?

10   *Emilia.* Never, my lord.

Othello. That's strange.

Emilia. I durst, my lord, to wager she is honest,
         Lay down my soul at stake.° If you think other,
         Remove your thought. It doth abuse your bosom.
15   If any wretch have put this in your head,
         Let heaven requite it with the serpent's curse,°
         For if she be not honest,° chaste, and true,

---

279 **courses** actions   4.2.5 **that breath made up** spoken   13 **at stake** as
the wager   16 **serpent's curse** (God's curse on the serpent after the fall in
Eden)   17 **honest** chaste

There's no man happy. The purest of their wives
Is foul as slander.

Othello.　　　　Bid her come hither. Go.

　　　　　　　　　　　　　Exit Emilia.

She says enough; yet she's a simple bawd° 　20
That cannot say as much. This is a subtle whore,
A closet lock and key of villainous secrets,
And yet she'll kneel and pray; I have seen her do't.

　　　　Enter Desdemona and Emilia.

Desdemona. My lord, what is your will?

Othello.　　　　　　Pray you, chuck, come hither.

Desdemona. What is your pleasure?

Othello.　　　　　　Let me see your eyes. 　25
Look in my face.

Desdemona.　　　What horrible fancy's this?

Othello. [*To Emilia*] Some of your function,° mis-
tress:
Leave procreants alone and shut the door;
Cough or cry hem if anybody come.
Your mystery,° your mystery! Nay, dispatch! 　30

　　　　　　　　　　　　　Exit Emilia.

Desdemona. Upon my knee, what doth your speech
　　import?
I understand a fury in your words.°

Othello. Why, what art thou?

Desdemona.　　　　Your wife, my lord; your true
And loyal wife.

Othello.　　　Come, swear it, damn thyself;
Lest, being like one of heaven, the devils themselves 　35
Should fear to seize thee. Therefore be double-
　　damned:
Swear thou art honest.

Desdemona.　　　　Heaven doth truly know it.

20 **bawd** procuress　27 **Some of your function** do your proper work (as the
operator of a brothel)　30 **mystery** trade　32 **words** (Q1 adds to this line,
"But not the words")

Othello. Heaven truly knows that thou art false as hell.

Desdemona. To whom, my lord? With whom? How am
   I false?

40 *Othello.* Ah, Desdemon! Away! Away! Away!

Desdemona. Alas the heavy day! Why do you weep?
   Am I the motive° of these tears, my lord?
   If haply° you my father do suspect
   An instrument of this your calling back,
45 Lay not your blame on me. If you have lost him,
   I have lost him too.

Othello.   Had it pleased heaven
   To try me with affliction, had they rained
   All kinds of sores and shames on my bare head,
   Steeped° me in poverty to the very lips,
50 Given to captivity me and my utmost hopes,
   I should have found in some place of my soul
   A drop of patience. But, alas, to make me
   The fixèd figure for the time of scorn°
   To point his slow and moving finger at.
55 Yet could I bear that too, well, very well.
   But there where I have garnered up my heart,
   Where either I must live or bear no life,
   The fountain from the which my current runs
   Or else dries up—to be discarded thence,
60 Or keep it as a cistern for foul toads
   To knot and gender° in—turn thy complexion there,
   Patience, thou young and rose-lipped cherubin!
   I here look grim as hell!°

Desdemona. I hope my noble lord esteems me honest.

65 *Othello.* O, ay, as summer flies are in the shambles,°
   That quicken even with blowing.° O thou weed,

42 **motive** cause   43 **haply** by chance   49 **Steeped** submerged   53 **The
... scorn** the very image of scorn in our time   61 **knot and gender**
twist in bunches and procreate   61–63 **turn ... hell** (the rough sense
would seem to be, "even Patience would grow pale, turn complexion, at
Desdemona's perfidy, but that Othello looks grimly on")   65 **shambles**
abattoirs   66 **quicken even with blowing** become impregnated as soon as
they lay their eggs

    Who art so lovely fair, and smell'st so sweet,
    That the sense aches at thee, would thou hadst never
      been born!

Desdemona. Alas, what ignorant° sin have I com-
    mitted?

Othello. Was this fair paper, this most goodly book,   70
    Made to write "whore" upon? What committed?
    Committed? O thou public commoner,°
    I should make very forges of my cheeks
    That would to cinders burn up modesty,
    Did I but speak thy deeds. What committed?   75
    Heaven stops the nose at it, and the moon winks;°
    The bawdy wind that kisses all it meets
    Is hushed within the hollow mine of earth
    And will not hear 't. What committed?

Desdemona. By heaven, you do me wrong!   80

Othello. Are not you a strumpet?

Desdemona.   No, as I am a Christian!
    If to preserve this vessel for my lord
    From any other foul unlawful touch
    Be not to be a strumpet, I am none.

Othello. What, not a whore?

Desdemona.   No, as I shall be saved!   85

Othello. Is't possible?

Desdemona. O, heaven forgive us!

Othello.   I cry you mercy° then.
    I took you for that cunning whore of Venice
    That married with Othello. [*Calling*] You, mistress,

          Enter Emilia.

    That have the office opposite to Saint Peter   90
    And keep the gate of hell! You, you, ay, you!
    We have done our course; there's money for your
      pains.   [*Throws her some coins.*]

---

69 **ignorant** unknowing 72 **commoner** prostitute 76 **winks** closes its
eyes (the moon was the symbol of chastity) 87 **cry you mercy** ask your pardon

I pray you turn the key and keep your counsel.

Exit.

Emilia. Alas, what does this gentleman conceive?
95   How do you, madam? How do you, my good lady?

Desdemona. Faith, half asleep.

Emilia. Good madam, what's the matter with my lord?

Desdemona. With who?

Emilia. Why, with my lord, madam.

Desdemona. Who is thy lord?

100   *Emilia.*   He that is yours, sweet lady.

Desdemona. I have none. Do not talk to me, Emilia.
   I cannot weep, nor answers have I none
   But what should go by water.° Prithee tonight
   Lay on my bed my wedding sheets, remember;
   And call thy husband hither.

105   *Emilia.*   Here's a change indeed!

Exit.

Desdemona. 'Tis meet I should be used so, very meet.
   How have I been behaved, that he might stick
   The small'st opinion on my least misuse?°

Enter Iago and Emilia.

Iago. What is your pleasure, madam? How is't with
   you?

Desdemona. I cannot tell. Those that do teach young
   babes
110   Do it with gentle means and easy tasks.
   He might have chid me so; for, in good faith,
   I am a child to chiding.

Iago.   What is the matter, lady?

Emilia. Alas, Iago, my lord hath so bewhored her,

103 **water** tears 107–08 **stick ... misuse** base any doubt on my smallest
fault

Thrown such despite° and heavy terms upon her   *115*
That true hearts cannot bear it.

Desdemona. Am I that name, Iago?

Iago.   What name, fair lady?

Desdemona. Such as she said my lord did say I was.

Emilia. He called her whore. A beggar in his drink
Could not have laid such terms upon his callet.°   *120*

Iago. Why did he so?

Desdemona. I do not know; I am sure I am none such.

Iago. Do not weep, do not weep. Alas the day.

Emilia. Hath she forsook so many noble matches,
Her father and her country, and her friends,   *125*
To be called whore? Would it not make one weep?

Desdemona. It is my wretched fortune.

Iago.   Beshrew° him for 't!
How comes this trick upon him?

Desdemona.   Nay, heaven doth know.

Emilia. I will be hanged if some eternal villain,
Some busy and insinuating rogue,   *130*
Some cogging,° cozening slave, to get some office,
Have not devised this slander. I will be hanged else.

Iago. Fie, there is no such man! It is impossible.

Desdemona. If any such there be, heaven pardon him.

Emilia. A halter pardon him! And hell gnaw his bones!   *135*
Why should he call her whore? Who keeps her com-
pany?
What place? What time? What form? What likeli-
hood?
The Moor's abused by some most villainous knave,
Some base notorious knave, some scurvy fellow.
O heavens, that such companions° thou'dst unfold,°   *140*
And put in every honest hand a whip
To lash the rascals naked through the world
Even from the east to th' west!

115 **despite** abuse   120 **callet** slut   127 **Beshrew** curse   131 **cogging**
cheating   140 **companions** fellows, rogues   140 **unfold** disclose

Iago.   Speak within door.°

Emilia. O, fie upon them! Some such squire° he was
145   That turned your wit the seamy side without
        And made you to suspect me with the Moor.

Iago. You are a fool. Go to.

Desdemona.   Alas, Iago,
        What shall I do to win my lord again?
        Good friend, go to him, for, by this light of heaven,
150   I know not how I lost him. Here I kneel:
        If e'er my will did trespass 'gainst his love
        Either in discourse of thought° or actual deed,
        Or that mine eyes, mine ears, or any sense
        Delighted them in any other form;
155   Or that I do not yet, and ever did,
        And ever will (though he do shake me off
        To beggarly divorcement) love him dearly,
        Comfort forswear me. Unkindness may do much,
        And his unkindness may defeat° my life,
160   But never taint my love. I cannot say "whore."
        It does abhor me now I speak the word;
        To do the act that might the addition earn
        Not the world's mass of vanity could make me.

Iago. I pray you be content. 'Tis but his humor.°
165   The business of the state does him offense.

Desdemona. If 'twere no other.

Iago.   It is but so, I warrant.

                              [*Trumpets within.*]
        Hark how these instruments summon to supper.
        The messengers of Venice stay the meat.°
        Go in, and weep not. All things shall be well.

                    [*Exeunt Desdemona and Emilia.*]
                    Enter Roderigo.
170   How now, Roderigo?

---

143 **within door** more quietly and moderately   144 **squire** (a term of contempt)   152 **discourse of thought** thinking   159 **defeat** destroy   164 **humor** mood   168 **stay the meat** await the meal

Roderigo. I do not find that thou deal'st justly with me.

Iago. What in the contrary?

Roderigo. Every day thou daff'st° me with some device,° Iago, and rather, as it seems to me now,
keep'st from me all conveniency° than suppliest me   *175*
with the least advantage of hope. I will indeed no
longer endure it; nor am I yet persuaded to put up°
in peace what already I have foolishly suffered.

Iago. Will you hear me, Roderigo?

Roderigo. I have heard too much, and your words   *180*
and performances are no kin together.

Iago. You charge me most unjustly.

Roderigo. With naught but truth. I have wasted myself out of my means. The jewels you have had from
me to deliver Desdemona would half have corrupted   *185*
a votarist.° You have told me she hath received
them, and returned me expectations and comforts
of sudden respect° and acquaintance; but I find
none.

Iago. Well, go to; very well.   *190*

Roderigo. Very well? Go to? I cannot go to, man; nor
'tis not very well. Nay, I think it is scurvy, and begin
to find myself fopped° in it.

Iago. Very well.

Roderigo. I tell you 'tis not very well. I will make my-   *195*
self known to Desdemona. If she will return me
my jewels, I will give over my suit and repent my
unlawful solicitation. If not, assure yourself I will
seek satisfaction of you.

Iago. You have said now?   *200*

Roderigo. Ay, and said nothing but what I protest°
intendment of doing.

---

173 **daff'st** put off   173–74 **device** scheme   175 **conveniency** what is
needful   177 **put up** accept   186 **votarist** nun   188 **sudden respect** immediate consideration   193 **fopped** duped   201 **protest** aver

Iago. Why, now I see there's mettle° in thee, and even
from this instant do build on thee a better opinion
205 than ever before. Give me thy hand, Roderigo. Thou
hast taken against me a most just exception;° but
yet I protest I have dealt most directly° in thy
affair.

Roderigo. It hath not appeared.

210 *Iago.* I grant indeed it hath not appeared, and your
suspicion is not without wit and judgment. But,
Roderigo, if thou hast that in thee indeed which I
have greater reason to believe now than ever—I
mean purpose, courage, and valor—this night show
215 it. If thou the next night following enjoy not Desdemona, take me from this world with treachery and
devise engines for° my life.

Roderigo. Well, what is it? Is it within reason and
compass?°

220 *Iago.* Sir, there is especial commission come from
Venice to depute Cassio in Othello's place.

Roderigo. Is that true? Why, then Othello and Desdemona return again to Venice.

Iago. O, no; he goes into Mauritania and taketh away
225 with him the fair Desdemona, unless his abode be
lingered here by some accident; wherein none can
be so determinate° as the removing of Cassio.

Roderigo. How do you mean, removing him?

Iago. Why, by making him uncapable of Othello's
230 place—knocking out his brains.

Roderigo. And that you would have me to do?

Iago. Ay, if you dare do yourself a profit and a right.
He sups tonight with a harlotry,° and thither will I
go to him. He knows not yet of his honorable for-
235 tune. If you will watch his going thence, which I

203 **mettle** spirit 206 **exception** objection 207 **directly** straightforwardly
217 **engines for** schemes against 219 **compass** possibility 227 **determi-
nate** effective 233 **harlotry** female

will fashion to fall out° between twelve and one,
you may take him at your pleasure. I will be near
to second° your attempt, and he shall fall between
us. Come, stand not amazed at it, but go along with
me. I will show you such a necessity in his death   *240*
that you shall think yourself bound to put it on him.
It is now high supper time, and the night grows
to waste. About it.

Roderigo. I will hear further reason for this.

Iago. And you shall be satisfied.   *Exeunt.* *245*

Scene 3. [The citadel.]

*Enter Othello, Lodovico, Desdemona, Emilia, and
Attendants.*

Lodovico. I do beseech you, sir, trouble yourself no
further.

Othello. O, pardon me; 'twill do me good to walk.

Lodovico. Madam, good night. I humbly thank your
ladyship.

Desdemona. Your honor is most welcome.

Othello. Will you walk, sir? O, Desdemona.   *5*

Desdemona. My lord?

Othello. Get you to bed on th' instant; I will be returned forthwith. Dismiss your attendant there.
Look't be done.

Desdemona. I will, my lord.   *10*

           Exit [Othello, with Lodovico and Attendants].

Emilia. How goes it now? He looks gentler than he did.

236 **fall out** occur   238 **second** support

Desdemona. He says he will return incontinent,°
   And hath commanded me to go to bed,
   And bade me to dismiss you.

Emilia.   Dismiss me?

15   *Desdemona.* It was his bidding; therefore, good Emilia,
   Give me my nightly wearing, and adieu.
   We must not now displease him.

Emilia. I would you had never seen him!

Desdemona. So would not I. My love doth so approve
   him
   That even his stubbornness, his checks,° his
20   frowns—
   Prithee unpin me—have grace and favor.

Emilia. I have laid these sheets you bade me on the
   bed.

Desdemona. All's one.° Good Father, how foolish
   are our minds!
   If I do die before, prithee shroud me
   In one of these same sheets.

25   *Emilia.*   Come, come! You talk.

Desdemona. My mother had a maid called Barbary.
   She was in love; and he she loved proved mad
   And did forsake her. She had a song of "Willow";
   An old thing 'twas, but it expressed her fortune,
30   And she died singing it. That song tonight
   Will not go from my mind; I have much to do
   But to go hang my head all at one side
   And sing it like poor Barbary. Prithee dispatch.

Emilia. Shall I go fetch your nightgown?

35   *Desdemona.* No, unpin me here.
   This Lodovico is a proper man.

Emilia. A very handsome man.

Desdemona. He speaks well.

4.3.12 **incontinent** at once   20 **checks** rebukes   23 **All's one** no matter

Emilia. I know a lady in Venice would have walked
  barefoot to Palestine for a touch of his nether lip. 40

Desdemona. [*Sings*]
    "The poor soul sat singing by a sycamore tree,
      Sing all a green willow;
    Her hand on her bosom, her head on her knee,
      Sing willow, willow, willow.
    The fresh streams ran by her and murmured
      her moans; 45
      Sing willow, willow, willow;
    Her salt tears fell from her, and soft'ned the
      stones—
      Sing willow, willow, willow—"
  Lay by these.   [*Gives Emilia her clothes.*]
    "Willow, Willow"—— 50
  Prithee hie° thee; he'll come anon.°
    "Sing all a green willow must be my garland.
    Let nobody blame him; his scorn I approve"——
  Nay, that's not next. Hark! Who is't that knocks?

Emilia. It is the wind. 55

Desdemona. [*Sings*]
    "I called my love false love; but what said he
      then?
      Sing willow, willow, willow:
    If I court moe° women, you'll couch with moe
      men."
  So, get thee gone; good night. Mine eyes do itch.
  Doth that bode weeping?

Emilia.   'Tis neither here nor there. 60

Desdemona. I have heard it said so. O, these men,
  these men.
  Dost thou in conscience think, tell me, Emilia,
  That there be women do abuse their husbands
  In such gross kind?

Emilia.   There be some such, no question

51 **hie** hurry   51 **anon** at once   58 **moe** more

Desdemona. Wouldst thou do such a deed for all the
65   world?

Emilia. Why, would not you?

Desdemona.   No, by this heavenly light!

Emilia. Nor I neither by this heavenly light.
       I might do't as well i' th' dark.

Desdemona. Wouldst thou do such a deed for all the
       world?

70   *Emilia.* The world's a huge thing; it is a great price for
       a small vice.

Desdemona. In troth, I think thou wouldst not.

Emilia. In troth, I think I should; and undo't when I
       had done. Marry, I would not do such a thing for
75   a joint-ring,° nor for measures of lawn,° nor for
       gowns, petticoats, nor caps, nor any petty exhibi-
       tion,° but for all the whole world? Why, who
       would not make her husband a cuckold to make him
       a monarch? I should venture purgatory for't.

80   *Desdemona.* Beshrew me if I would do such a wrong
       for the whole world.

Emilia. Why, the wrong is but a wrong i' th' world;
       and having the world for your labor, 'tis a wrong
       in your own world, and you might quickly make
85   it right.

Desdemona. I do not think there is any such woman.

Emilia. Yes, a dozen; and as many to th' vantage as
       would store° the world they played for.
       But I do think it is their husbands' faults
90   If wives do fall. Say that they slack their duties
       And pour our treasures into foreign° laps;
       Or else break out in peevish jealousies,
       Throwing restraint upon us; or say they strike us,

---

75 **joint-ring** (a ring with two interlocking halves)   75 **lawn** fine linen
76–77 **exhibition** payment   87–88 **to . . . store** in addition as would fill   91
foreign alien, i.e., other than the wife

Or scant our former having in despite°—
Why, we have galls; and though we have some
　grace, 95
Yet have we some revenge. Let husbands know
Their wives have sense like them. They see, and
　smell,
And have their palates both for sweet and sour,
As husbands have. What is it that they do
When they change° us for others? Is it sport? 100
I think it is. And doth affection° breed it?
I think it doth. Is't frailty that thus errs?
It is so too. And have not we affections?
Desires for sport? and frailty? as men have?
Then let them use us well; else let them know, 105
The ills we do, their ills instruct us so.°

Desdemona. Good night, good night. Heaven me such
　uses° send,
Not to pick bad from bad, but by bad mend. *Exeunt.*

---

94 **scant . . . despite** reduce, in spite, our household allowance (?) 100
change exchange 101 **affection** strong feeling, desire 106 **instruct us so**
teach us to do likewise 107 **uses** practices

ACT 5

Scene 1. [*A street.*]

Enter Iago and Roderigo.

Iago. Here, stand behind this bulk;° straight will he
    come.
    Wear thy good rapier bare, and put it home.
    Quick, quick! Fear nothing; I'll be at thy elbow.
    It makes us, or it mars us, think on that,
5   And fix most firm thy resolution.

Roderigo. Be near at hand; I may miscarry in't.

Iago. Here, at thy hand. Be bold, and take thy stand.

                      [*Moves to one side.*]

Roderigo. I have no great devotion to the deed,
    And yet he hath given me satisfying reasons.
10   'Tis but a man gone. Forth my sword! He dies!

Iago. I have rubbed this young quat° almost to the
    sense,°
    And he grows angry. Now, whether he kill Cassio,
    Or Cassio him, or each do kill the other,
    Every way makes my gain. Live Roderigo,
15   He calls me to a restitution large
    Of gold and jewels that I bobbed° from him
    As gifts to Desdemona.
    It must not be. If Cassio do remain,

5.1.1 **bulk** projecting stall of a shop   11 **quat** pimple   11 **to the sense** raw
16 **bobbed** swindled

He hath a daily beauty in his life
That makes me ugly; and besides, the Moor   20
May unfold me to him; there stand I in much peril.
No, he must die. But so, I hear him coming.

           Enter Cassio.

Roderigo. I know his gait. 'Tis he. Villain, thou diest!

                     [*Thrusts at Cassio.*]

Cassio. That thrust had been mine enemy indeed
  But that my coat° is better than thou know'st.   25
  I will make proof of thine.   [*Fights with Roderigo.*]

Roderigo.   O, I am slain!°

Cassio. I am maimed forever. Help, ho! Murder!
  Murder!

          Enter Othello [*to one side*].

Othello. The voice of Cassio. Iago keeps his word.

Roderigo. O, villain that I am!

Othello.   It is even so.

Cassio. O help, ho! Light! A surgeon!   30

Othello. 'Tis he. O brave Iago, honest and just,
  That hast such noble sense of thy friend's wrong!
  Thou teachest me. Minion,° your dear lies dead,
  And your unblest° fate hies.° Strumpet, I come.
  Forth of my heart those charms, thine eyes, are
    blotted.   35
  Thy bed, lust-stained, shall with lust's blood be
    spotted.

                  Exit Othello.

25 **coat** i.e., a mail shirt or bulletproof vest   26 **slain** (most editors add here
a stage direction which has Iago wounding Cassio in the leg from behind, but
remaining unseen. However, nothing in the text requires this, and Cassio's
wound can be given him in the fight with Roderigo, for presumably when Cassio attacks Roderigo the latter would not simply accept the thrust but would
parry. Since Iago enters again at line 46, he must exit at some point after line
22)   33 **Minion** hussy, i.e., Desdemona   34 **unblest** unsanctified   34 **hies**
approaches swiftly

Enter Lodovico and Gratiano.

Cassio. What, ho? No watch? No passage?° Murder! Murder!

Gratiano. 'Tis some mischance. The voice is very direful.

Cassio. O, help!

40 *Lodovico.* Hark!

Roderigo. O wretched villain!

Lodovico. Two or three groan. 'Tis heavy night.
These may be counterfeits. Let's think 't unsafe
To come into the cry without more help.

45 *Roderigo.* Nobody come? Then shall I bleed to death.

Lodovico. Hark!

Enter Iago [with a light].

Gratiano. Here's one comes in his shirt, with light and weapons.

Iago. Who's there? Whose noise is this that cries on murder?

Lodovico. We do not know.

Iago.   Do not you hear a cry?

Cassio. Here, here! For heaven's sake, help me!

50 *Iago.*   What's the matter?

Gratiano. This is Othello's ancient, as I take it.

Lodovico. The same indeed, a very valiant fellow.

Iago. What are you here that cry so grievously?

Cassio. Iago? O, I am spoiled, undone by villains.
55   Give me some help.

Iago. O me, lieutenant! What villains have done this?

Cassio. I think that one of them is hereabout
And cannot make away.

37 **passage** passersby

Iago.   O treacherous villains!
    [*To Lodovico and Gratiano*] What are you there?
      Come in, and give some help.

Roderigo. O, help me there!   60

Cassio. That's one of them.

Iago.   O murd'rous slave! O vil-
    lain!   [*Stabs Roderigo.*]

Roderigo. O damned Iago! O inhuman dog!

Iago. Kill men i' th' dark?—Where be these bloody
    thieves?—
    How silent is this town!—Ho! Murder! Murder!—
    What may you be? Are you of good or evil?   65

Lodovico. As you shall prove us, praise us.

Iago. Signior Lodovico?

Lodovico. He, sir.

Iago. I cry you mercy. Here's Cassio hurt by villains.

Gratiano. Cassio?   70

Iago. How is't, brother?

Cassio. My leg is cut in two.

Iago.   Marry, heaven forbid!
    Light, gentlemen. I'll bind it with my shirt.

Enter Bianca.

Bianca. What is the matter, ho? Who is't that cried?

Iago. Who is't that cried?   75

Bianca. O my dear Cassio! My sweet Cassio!
    O Cassio, Cassio, Cassio!

Iago. O notable strumpet!—Cassio, may you suspect
    Who they should be that have thus mangled you?

Cassio. No.   80

Gratiano. I am sorry to find you thus. I have been to
    seek you.

Iago. Lend me a garter. So. O for a chair
    To bear him easily hence.

Bianca. Alas, he faints! O Cassio, Cassio, Cassio!

85 *Iago.* Gentlemen all, I do suspect this trash
   To be a party in this injury.—
   Patience awhile, good Cassio.—Come, come.
   Lend me a light. Know we this face or no?
   Alas, my friend and my dear countryman
90 Roderigo? No.—Yes, sure.—Yes, 'tis Roderigo!

Gratiano. What, of Venice?

Iago. Even he, sir. Did you know him?

Gratiano.   Know him? Ay.

Iago. Signior Gratiano? I cry your gentle pardon.
   These bloody accidents must excuse my manners
   That so neglected you.

95 *Gratiano.*   I am glad to see you.

Iago. How do you, Cassio?—O, a chair, a chair!

Gratiano. Roderigo?

Iago. He, he, 'tis he! [*A chair brought in.*] O, that's
   well said;° the chair.
   Some good man bear him carefully from hence.
   I'll fetch the general's surgeon. [*To Bianca*] For you,
100 mistress,
   Save you your labor. [*To Cassio*] He that lies slain
   here, Cassio,
   Was my dear friend. What malice was between you?

Cassio. None in the world; nor do I know the man.

Iago. What, look you pale?—O, bear him out o' th'
   air.   [*Cassio is carried off.*]
   Stay you, good gentlemen.—Look you pale, mis-
105 tress?
   Do you perceive the gastness° of her eye?
   Nay, if you stare, we shall hear more anon.
   Behold her well; I pray you look upon her.

98 **well said** well done   106 **gastness** terror

Do you see, gentlemen? Nay, guiltiness will speak,
Though tongues were out of use.°   *110*

[*Enter Emilia.*]

Emilia. Alas, what is the matter? What is the matter,
husband?

Iago. Cassio hath here been set on in the dark
By Roderigo and fellows that are scaped.
He's almost slain, and Roderigo quite dead.

Emilia. Alas, good gentleman! Alas, good Cassio!   *115*

Iago. This is the fruits of whoring. Prithee, Emilia,
Go know of Cassio where he supped tonight.
[*To Bianca*] What, do you shake at that?

Bianca. He supped at my house; but I therefore shake
not.

Iago. O, did he so? I charge° you go with me.   *120*

Emilia. Oh fie upon thee, strumpet!

Bianca. I am no strumpet, but of life as honest
As you that thus abuse me.

Emilia.   As I? Fie upon thee!

Iago. Kind gentlemen, let's go see poor Cassio
dressed.°
[*To Bianca*] Come, mistress, you must tell's another
tale.   *125*
Emilia, run you to the citadel
And tell my lord and lady what hath happed.

                              [*Exit Emilia.*]
Will you go on afore?   *Exeunt* [*all but Iago*].
                    This is the night
That either makes me or fordoes me quite.°   [*Exit.*]

---

110 **tongues were out of use** men no longer spoke   120 **charge** command
124 **dressed** bandaged   129 **fordoes me quite** completely ruins me

Scene 2. [*Desdemona's chamber.*]

Enter Othello [with a light]; and Desdemona
in her bed.

Othello. It is the cause, it is the cause, my soul.
　　Let me not name it to you, you chaste stars.
　　It is the cause. Yet I'll not shed her blood,
　　Nor scar that whiter skin of hers than snow,
5　　And smooth as monumental alabaster.
　　Yet she must die, else she'll betray more men.
　　Put out the light, and then put out the light.
　　If I quench thee, thou flaming minister,°
　　I can again thy former light restore,
10　　Should I repent me; but once put out thy light,
　　Thou cunning'st° pattern of excelling nature,
　　I know not where is that Promethean heat°
　　That can thy light relume.° When I have plucked
　　　　the rose,
　　I cannot give it vital° growth again;
15　　It needs must wither. I'll smell thee on the tree.

　　　　　　　　　　　　　　　　[*He kisses her.*]

　　O balmy breath, that dost almost persuade
　　Justice to break her sword. One more, one more!
　　Be thus when thou art dead, and I will kill thee,
　　And love thee after. One more, and that's the last!
20　　So sweet was ne'er so fatal. I must weep,
　　But they are cruel tears. This sorrow's heavenly;
　　It strikes where it doth love. She wakes.

Desdemona. Who's there? Othello?

Othello.　　　　　　　　　　　　Ay, Desdemona.

5.2.8 **minister** worker, servant　11 **cunning'st** most intricate and skillfully
wrought (by nature excelling itself)　12 **Promethean heat** divine fire
(Prometheus is the Titan who stole fire from heaven and gave it to man)　13
relume relight　14 **vital** living

Desdemona. Will you come to bed, my lord?

Othello. Have you prayed tonight, Desdemon?

Desdemona.　　　　　　　　　　Ay, my lord.　25

Othello. If you bethink yourself of any crime
Unreconciled as yet to heaven and grace,
Solicit for it straight.

Desdemona. Alack, my lord, what may you mean by
that?

Othello. Well, do it, and be brief; I will walk by.°　30
I would not kill thy unprepar èd spirit.
No, heavens forfend! I would not kill thy soul.

Desdemona. Talk you of killing?

Othello.　　　　　　　　　Ay, I do.

Desdemona.　　　　　　　　　Then heaven
Have mercy on me!

Othello.　　　　　Amen, with all my heart.

Desdemona. If you say so, I hope you will not kill me.　35

Othello. Humh.

Desdemona. And yet I fear you; for you're fatal then
When your eyes roll so. Why I should fear I know
not,
Since guiltiness I know not; but yet I feel I fear.

Othello. Think on thy sins.

Desdemona.　　　　　　　They are loves I bear to you.　40

Othello. Ay, and for that thou diest.

Desdemona. That death's unnatural that kills for
loving.
Alas, why gnaw you so your nether lip?
Some bloody passion shakes your very frame.
These are portents; but yet I hope, I hope,　45
They do not point on me.

Othello.　　　　　　　Peace and be still.

30 **by** nearby

Desdemona. I will so. What's the matter?

Othello. That handkerchief which I so loved and gave
    thee,
Thou gav'st to Cassio.

Desdemona.   No, by my life and soul!
Send for the man and ask him.

50 *Othello.*   Sweet soul, take heed,
Take heed of perjury; thou art on thy deathbed.

Desdemona. Ay, but not yet to die.

Othello.   Presently.°
Therefore confess thee freely of thy sin,
For to deny each article° with oath
55 Cannot remove nor choke the strong conception
That I do groan withal. Thou art to die.

Desdemona. Then Lord have mercy on me.

Othello.   I say, amen.

Desdemona. And have you mercy too. I never did
Offend you in my life; never loved Cassio
60 But with such general warranty° of heaven
As I might love. I never gave him token.

Othello. By heaven, I saw my handkerchief in's hand!
O perjured woman! thou dost stone° my heart,
And mak'st me call what I intend to do
65 A murder, which I thought a sacrifice.
I saw the handkerchief.

Desdemona.   He found it then.
I never gave it him. Send for him hither.
Let him confess a truth.

Othello.   He hath confessed.

Desdemona. What, my lord?

Othello. That he hath used thee.

Desdemona.   How? Unlawfully?

52 **Presently** immediately   54 **article** item (of the charge of adultery. Othello makes heavy use of legal terms in this scene)   60 **warranty** allowance
63 **stone** turn to stone

Othello.　　　　　　　　　　　　　Ay.

Desdemona. He will not say so.

Othello.　　　　　　　　　No, his mouth is stopped.
　Honest Iago hath ta'en order for't.°

Desdemona. O, my fear interprets. What, is he dead?

Othello. Had all his hairs been lives, my great revenge
　Had stomach° for them all.　　　　　　　　　　75

Desdemona. Alas, he is betrayed, and I undone!

Othello. Out, strumpet! Weep'st thou for him to my
　face?

Desdemona. O, banish me, my lord, but kill me not!

Othello. Down, strumpet!

Desdemona. Kill me tomorrow; let me live tonight!　　80

Othello. Nay, if you strive——

Desdemona. But half an hour!

Othello.　　　　　　　　Being done, there is no pause.

Desdemona. But while I say one prayer!

Othello.　　　　　　　　　　　It is too late.
　　　　　　　　　　　　　　　Smothers her.
　　　　　　Emilia at the door.

Emilia. [*Calls within.*] My lord, my lord! What, ho, my
　lord, my lord!

Othello. What noise is this? Not dead? Not yet quite
　dead?　　　　　　　　　　　　　　　　　　85
　I that am cruel am yet merciful;
　I would not have thee linger in thy pain.
　So, so.

Emilia. [*Within*] What, ho! My lord, my lord!

Othello.　　　　　　　　　　　Who's there?

Emilia. [*Within*] O, good my lord, I would speak a
　word with you.

---

72 **ta'en order for't** make sure of it　75 **stomach** appetite

90   *Othello.* Yes, 'tis Emilia.—By and by.—She's dead.—
      'Tis like she comes to speak of Cassio's death.
      The noise was high.° Ha! No more moving?
      Still as the grave.—Shall she come in? Were't
          good?—
      I think she stirs again. No.—What's best to do?
95   If she come in, she'll sure speak to my wife.
      My wife! My wife! What wife? I have no wife.
      O, insupportable! O heavy hour!
      Methinks it should be now a huge eclipse
      Of sun and moon, and that th' affrighted globe
      Should yawn° at alteration.

100   *Emilia.*   [*Within*] I do beseech you
      That I may speak with you, O good my lord!

      Othello. I had forgot thee. O, come in, Emilia.
      Soft, by and by.—Let me the curtains draw.—

      [*Draws the bed hangings and then opens the door.*]
      Where art thou?

                              Enter Emilia.
                    What's the matter with thee now?

105   *Emilia.* O my good lord, yonder's foul murders done!

      Othello. What? Now?

      Emilia. But now, my lord.

      Othello. It is the very error° of the moon.
      She comes more nearer earth than she was wont
110   And makes men mad.

      Emilia. Cassio, my lord, hath killed a young Venetian
      Called Roderigo.

      Othello.   Roderigo killed?
      And Cassio killed?

92 **high** loud (Q1 reads "here")   98–100 **Methinks . . . alteration** (the Elizabethans believed that great changes in human affairs were reflected by disorders in nature)   100 **yawn** gape open (as in an earthquake)   108 **error**
wandering out of regular course (disorders in the heavens were believed by
some to cause disorders on earth, as well as vice versa)

Emilia.   No, Cassio is not killed.

Othello. Not Cassio killed? Then murder's out of tune,
  And sweet revenge grows harsh.   *115*

Desdemona. O, falsely, falsely murdered!

Emilia.   O Lord! What cry is that?

Othello. That? What?

Emilia. Out and alas! that was my lady's voice.
  Help! Help, ho! Help! O lady, speak again!
  Sweet Desdemona! O sweet mistress, speak!   *120*

Desdemona. A guiltless death I die.

Emilia. O, who hath done this deed?

Desdemona. Nobody—I myself. Farewell.
  Commend me to my kind lord. O, farewell!
                       [*She dies.*]

Othello. Why, how should she be murd'red?

Emilia.   Alas, who knows? *125*

Othello. You heard her say herself, it was not I.

Emilia. She said so. I must needs report the truth.

Othello. She's like a liar gone to burning hell!
  'Twas I that killed her.

Emilia.   O, the more angel she,
  And you the blacker devil!   *130*

Othello. She turned to folly, and she was a whore.

Emilia. Thou dost belie her, and thou art a devil.

Othello. She was false as water.

Emilia.   Thou art rash as fire to say
  That she was false. O, she was heavenly true!

Othello. Cassio did top her. Ask thy husband else.   *135*
  O, I were damned beneath all depth in hell
  But that I did proceed upon just grounds
  To this extremity. Thy husband knew it all.

Emilia. My husband?

Othello.   Thy husband.

Emilia.   That she was false to wedlock?

140 *Othello.* Ay, with Cassio. Had she been true,
If heaven would make me such another world
Of one entire and perfect chrysolite,°
I'd not have sold her for it.

Emilia.   My husband?

Othello. Ay, 'twas he that told me on her first.
145 An honest man he is, and hates the slime
That sticks on filthy deeds.

Emilia.   My husband?

Othello. What needs this iterance? Woman, I say thy
husband.

Emilia. O mistress, villainy hath made mocks with
love!
My husband say she was false?

Othello.   He, woman.
150 I say, thy husband. Dost understand the word?
My friend, thy husband; honest, honest Iago.

Emilia. If he say so, may his pernicious soul
Rot half a grain a day! He lies to th' heart.
She was too fond of her most filthy bargain.

155 *Othello.* Hah?

Emilia. Do thy worst.
This deed of thine is no more worthy heaven
Than thou wast worthy her.

Othello.   Peace, you were best.°

Emilia. Thou hast not half that pow'r to do me harm
160 As I have to be hurt. O gull! O dolt!
As ignorant as dirt! Thou hast done a deed—
                    [*Othello moves to draw his sword.*]
I care not for thy sword; I'll make thee known,
Though I lost twenty lives. Help! Help! Ho! Help!
The Moor hath killed my mistress! Murder! murder!

142 **chrysolite** topaz   158 **Peace, you were best** i.e., you had better be
silent

Enter Montano, Gratiano, and Iago [and Others].

Montano. What is the matter? How now, general?   165

Emilia. O, are you come, Iago? You have done well,
    That men must lay their murders on your neck.

Gratiano. What is the matter?

Emilia. Disprove this villain, if thou be'st a man.
    He says thou told'st him that his wife was false.   170
    I know thou didst not; thou'rt not such a villain.
    Speak, for my heart is full.

Iago. I told him what I thought, and told no more
    Than what he found himself was apt and true.

Emilia. But did you ever tell him she was false?   175

Iago. I did.

Emilia. You told a lie, an odious damnèd lie!
    Upon my soul, a lie! A wicked lie!
    She false with Cassio? Did you say with Cassio?

Iago. With Cassio, mistress. Go to, charm° your
    tongue.   180

Emilia. I will not charm my tongue; I am bound to
    speak:
    My mistress here lies murdered in her bed.

All. O heavens forfend!

Emilia. And your reports have set the murder on.

Othello. Nay, stare not, masters. It is true indeed.   185

Gratiano. 'Tis a strange truth.

Montano. O monstrous act!

Emilia.   Villainy, villainy, villainy!
    I think upon't—I think I smell't!—O villainy!
    I thought so then.—I'll kill myself for grief.—
    O villainy, villainy!   190

Iago. What, are you mad? I charge you get you home.

Emilia. Good gentlemen, let me have leave to speak.

180 **charm** control

'Tis proper I obey him, but not now.
Perchance, Iago, I will ne'er go home.

Othello. O! O! O!   [*Falls on the bed.*]

195 *Emilia.*   Nay, lay thee down and roar,
For thou hast killed the sweetest innocent
That e'er did lift up eye.

Othello.   O, she was foul!   [*Rises.*]
I scarce did know you, uncle. There lies your niece,
Whose breath, indeed, these hands have newly
    stopped.
200 I know this act shows horrible and grim.

Gratiano. Poor Desdemon! I am glad thy father's dead.
Thy match was mortal to him, and pure grief
Shore his old thread in twain. Did he live now,
This sight would make him do a desperate turn;
205 Yea, curse his better angel from his side,
And fall to reprobation.°

Othello. 'Tis pitiful; but yet Iago knows
That she with Cassio hath the act of shame
A thousand times committed. Cassio confessed it;
210 And she did gratify his amorous works
With that recognizance and pledge of love,
Which I first gave her. I saw it in his hand.
It was a handkerchief, an antique token
My father gave my mother.

215 *Emilia.* O God! O heavenly God!

Iago. Zounds, hold your peace!

Emilia.   'Twill out, 'twill out! I peace?
No, I will speak as liberal as the north.°
Let heaven and men and devils, let them all,
All, all, cry shame against me, yet I'll speak.

Iago. Be wise, and get you home.

220 *Emilia.*   I will not.

                     [*Iago draws and threatens Emilia.*]

---

206 **reprobation** damnation   217 **liberal as the north** freely (and bitingly)
as the north wind blows

Gratiano. Fie! Your sword upon a woman?

Emilia. O thou dull Moor, that handkerchief thou
    speak'st of
  I found by fortune, and did give my husband;
  For often with a solemn earnestness—
  More than indeed belonged to such a trifle—   225
  He begged of me to steal't.

Iago.   Villainous whore!

Emilia. She give it Cassio? No, alas, I found it,
  And I did give't my husband.

Iago.   Filth, thou liest!

Emilia. By heaven, I do not, I do not, gentlemen.
  O murd'rous coxcomb! What should such a fool   230
  Do with so good a wife?

Othello.   Are there no stones° in heaven
  But what serves for the thunder? Precious villain!
  [*The Moor runs at Iago, but is disarmed by Montano.*
                   Iago kills his wife.]

Gratiano. The woman falls. Sure he hath killed his
  wife.

Emilia. Ay, ay. O, lay me by my mistress' side.

                           [*Exit Iago.*]

Gratiano. He's gone, but his wife's killed.   235

Montano. 'Tis a notorious° villain. Take you this
  weapon,
  Which I have recovered from the Moor.
  Come, guard the door without. Let him not pass,
  But kill him rather. I'll after that same villain,
  For 'tis a damnèd slave.

        Exit [*with all but Othello and Emilia*].

Othello.   I am not valiant neither;   240
  But every puny whipster° gets my sword.
  But why should honor outlive honesty?
  Let it go all.

231 **stones** thunderbolts   236 **notorious** out-and-out   241 **puny whipster**
small top-whipping boy (?)

Emilia.   What did thy song bode, lady?
Hark, canst thou hear me? I will play the swan,

245   And die in music. [*Sings*] "Willow, willow, willow."
Moor, she was chaste. She loved thee, cruel Moor,
So come my soul to bliss as I speak true.
So speaking as I think, alas, I die.   [*She dies.*]

Othello. I have another weapon in this chamber;

250   It was a sword of Spain, the ice-brook's temper.
O, here it is.—Uncle, I must come forth.

Gratiano. [*Within*] If thou attempt it, it will cost thee
    dear.
Thou hast no weapon, and perforce must suffer.

Othello. Look in upon me then and speak with me,

255   Or, naked as I am, I will assault thee.

[*Enter Gratiano.*]

Gratiano. What is the matter?

Othello.   Behold, I have a weapon;
A better never did itself sustain
Upon a soldier's thigh. I have seen the day
That with this little arm and this good sword

260   I have made my way through more impediments
Than twenty times your stop. But O vain boast!
Who can control his fate? 'Tis not so now.
Be not afraid, though you do see me weaponed.
Here is my journey's end, here is my butt,°

265   And very seamark of my utmost sail.°
Do you go back dismayed? 'Tis a lost fear.
Man but a rush° against Othello's breast,
And he retires. Where should Othello go?
Now, how dost thou look now? O ill-starred wench!

270   Pale as thy smock! When we shall meet at compt,°
This look of thine will hurl my soul from heaven,
And fiends will snatch at it. Cold, cold, my girl?
Even like thy chastity.
O cursèd, cursèd slave! Whip me, ye devils,

---

264 **butt** target, stopping place   265 **seamark of my utmost sail** marker of my farthest journey   267 **Man but a rush** attack with only a reed   270 **compt** Judgment Day

From the possession of° this heavenly sight!   275
Blow me about in winds! roast me in sulfur!
Wash me in steep-down gulfs of liquid fire!
O Desdemon! Dead Desdemon; dead. O! O!
    Enter Lodovico, Cassio, Montano, and Iago
      [as prisoner,] with Officers.

Lodovico. Where is this rash and most unfortunate
    man?

Othello. That's he that was Othello; Here I am.   280

Lodovico. Where is that viper? Bring the villain forth.

Othello. I look down towards his feet°—but that's a
    fable.
If that thou be'st a devil, I cannot kill thee.

                     [Wounds Iago.]

Lodovico. Wrench his sword from him.

                [Othello is disarmed.]

Iago.   I bleed, sir, but not killed.

Othello. I am not sorry neither. I'd have thee live;   285
For in my sense, 'tis happiness to die.

Lodovico. O thou Othello that was once so good,
Fall'n in the practice° of a cursèd slave,
What shall be said to thee?

Othello.   Why, anything:
An honorable murderer, if you will;   290
For naught I did in hate, but all in honor.

Lodovico. This wretch hath part confessed his villainy.
Did you and he consent in Cassio's death?

Othello. Ay.

Cassio. Dear general, I never gave you cause.   295

Othello. I do believe it, and I ask your pardon.
Will you, I pray, demand that demi-devil
Why he hath thus ensnared my soul and body?

275 **the possession of** being possessed by 282 **towards his feet** i.e., for
his cloven hoofs 288 **practice** plotting

Iago. Demand me nothing. What you know, you know.
300   From this time forth I never will speak word.

Lodovico. What, not to pray?

Gratiano.   Torments will ope your lips.

Othello. Well, thou dost best.

Lodovico. Sir, you shall understand what hath befall'n,
  Which, as I think, you know not. Here is a letter
305   Found in the pocket of the slain Roderigo;
  And here another. The one of them imports
  The death of Cassio to be undertook
  By Roderigo.

Othello. O villain!

Cassio.   Most heathenish and most gross!

310 *Lodovico.* Now here's another discontented paper
  Found in his pocket too; and this, it seems,
  Roderigo meant t' have sent this damnèd villain;
  But that, belike, Iago in the interim
  Came in and satisfied him.

Othello.   O thou pernicious caitiff!
315   How came you, Cassio, by that handkerchief
  That was my wife's?

Cassio.   I found it in my chamber;
  And he himself confessed it but even now
  That there he dropped it for a special purpose
  Which wrought to his desire.

Othello.   O fool! Fool! Fool!

320 *Cassio.* There is besides in Roderigo's letter,
  How he upbraids Iago that he made him
  Brave me upon the watch; whereon it came
  That I was cast; and even but now he spake,
  After long seeming dead—Iago hurt him,
325   Iago set him on.

Lodovico. You must forsake this room and go with
  us.
  Your power and your command is taken off,
  And Cassio rules in Cyprus. For this slave,

If there be any cunning cruelty
That can torment him much and hold him long,   *330*
It shall be his. You shall close prisoner rest
Till that the nature of your fault be known
To the Venetian state. Come, bring away.

Othello. Soft you, a word or two before you go.
I have done the state some service, and they know't. *335*
No more of that. I pray you, in your letters,
When you shall these unlucky deeds relate,
Speak of me as I am. Nothing extenuate,
Nor set down aught in malice. Then must you speak
Of one that loved not wisely, but too well;   *340*
Of one not easily jealous, but, being wrought,
Perplexed in the extreme; of one whose hand,
Like the base Judean,° threw a pearl away
Richer than all his tribe; of one whose subdued
    eyes,
Albeit unusèd to the melting mood,   *345*
Drops tears as fast as the Arabian trees
Their med'cinable gum. Set you down this.
And say besides that in Aleppo once,
Where a malignant and a turbaned Turk
Beat a Venetian and traduced the state,   *350*
I took by th' throat the circumcisèd dog
And smote him—thus.   [*He stabs himself.*]

Lodovico. O bloody period!°

Gratiano.   All that is spoke is marred.

Othello. I kissed thee ere I killed thee. No way but this,
Killing myself, to die upon a kiss.   *355*

            [*He falls over Desdemona and dies.*]

Cassio. This did I fear, but thought he had no weapon;
For he was great of heart.

Lodovico.   [*To Iago*] O Spartan dog,
More fell° than anguish, hunger, or the sea!

343 **Judean** (most editors use the Q1 reading, "Indian," here, but F is clear;
both readings point toward the infidel, the unbeliever) 353 **period** end
358 **fell** cruel

Look on the tragic loading of this bed.
360   This is thy work. The object poisons sight;
Let it be hid.   [*Bed curtains drawn.*]
           Gratiano, keep° the house,
And seize upon the fortunes of the Moor,
For they succeed on you. To you, lord governor,
Remains the censure of this hellish villain,
365   The time, the place, the torture. O, enforce it!
Myself will straight aboard, and to the state
This heavy act with heavy heart relate.   *Exeunt.*

FINIS

361 **keep** remain in

Textual Note

Othello contains some of the most difficult editorial problems of any Shakespearean play. The play was entered in *The Stationer's Register* on 6 October, 1621, and printed in a quarto edition, Q1, by Thomas Walkley in 1622, some eighteen or nineteen years after it was first staged. More curiously, at the time that Walkley printed his quarto edition, the plans for printing the folio edition of Shakespeare's collected works were completed and printing was well along. The Folio, F, appeared in late 1623, and the text of *Othello* included in it differs considerably from Q1. A second quarto, Q2, was printed from F in 1630. The chief differences between the two major texts, Q1 and F, are: (1) There are 160 lines in F that are not in Q1; some of these omissions affect the sense in Q1, but others seem to be either intentional cuts in Q1 or additions in F. (2) There are a number of oaths in Q1 that are not in F; this fact can be interpreted in a number of ways, but all arguments go back to the prohibition in 1606 of swearing on stage—but apparently not in printed editions. (3) The stage directions in Q1 are much fuller than in F. (4) There are a large number of variant readings in the two texts, in single words, in phrases, and in lineation; where Q1, for example, reads "toged" (i.e., wearing a toga), F reads "tongued"; where Q1 reads "Worships," F reads "Moorships."

These may seem petty problems, but they present an editor with a series of most difficult questions about what to print at any given point where the two texts are in disagreement. The usual solution in the past has been for the editor to include all material in F and Q1, and where the two texts are in disagreement to select the reading he prefers. The result is what is known as an eclectic text. But modern bibliographical studies have demonstrated that it is possible to proceed, in some cases at least, in a more precise manner by examining the conflicting texts carefully in order to arrive at something like a reasonable judgment about their relative authority. Shakespearean bibliography has become a most elaborate affair, however, and in most cases it has become necessary to take the word of specialists on these matters. Unfortunately, in the case of *Othello* the experts are not in agreement, and none of their arguments has the ring of certainty. Here is, however, the most general opinion of how the two different texts came into being and how they are related.

After Shakespeare wrote the play, his original draft, usually termed "foul papers," was copied, around 1604, by a scribe and made into what is known as the "promptbook," the official copy of the play used in the theater as the basis for production. This promptbook was the property of the players' company, the King's Men in this case, and remained in their possession to be used, and perhaps revised, whenever they produced *Othello*. Being a repertory company they would present a play for a few performances, then drop it for a time, and then present it again when conditions seemed favorable. At some time around 1620, another copy was made of the original foul papers, or some later copy of them, and this served as the basis for the 1622 Quarto. Later, when the publishers of the Folio got around to printing *Othello*, they took a copy of Q1 and corrected it by the original promptbook, and this corrected copy was then given to the compositors who were setting type for F. There are genuine objections to this theory, the most telling raised by M. R. Ridley, in *The Arden Shakespeare* edition of *Othello*; but the theory does explain certain difficult facts, and most bibliographers seem to accept some version of it.

Since 1964, and Nevill Coghill's *Shakespeare's Professional Skills*, however, editors have increasingly returned to a much earlier view that the successive editions of *Othello* represent not two different versions of a hypothetical original play but are two somewhat differing plays, each complete in itself, though containing errors. This "two-play theory" has been advanced most forcefully for *King Lear*, but the quarto and folio versions of *Othello* have been argued to be different playhouse versions produced by Shakespeare to update and adjust his play in ways thought best for performance. The full argument for this view is presented by E. J. A. Honigman, "Shakespeare's Revised Plays: *King Lear* and *Othello*," *The Library* 6, 4:2 (1982): 142–73.

The end of this line of argument is to establish fairly reasonably the authority of the F text as being the closest either to what Shakespeare wrote originally or to the play as he finally left it after playhouse revisions. This agrees with what most scholars find in reading the two texts. Sir Walter Greg puts this common belief in the superiority of F in the strongest terms: "In the great majority of cases there can be no doubt that F has preserved the more Shakespearean reading." (*The Shakespeare First Folio*, Oxford, 1955, p. 365.) For practical purposes what this means is that where an F reading makes sense, then an editor has no choice but to accept it—even though he "likes" the Q reading better and would have used it if he had *written,* instead of only edited, the play. But while an editor may be aided and comforted by the bibliographers' decision that F is more authoritative than Q1, his problems are by no means solved. There are places where F does not make sense but Q1 does, places where F is deficient in some way and Q is clear and complete, and places where both fail to make sense or seem to point to a common failure to transcribe correctly their original. When this occurs an editor must try to understand how the trouble occurred and then fall back on his judgment. This will force him to try to reconstruct the original manuscript from which we are told Q and F both derive, and he must attempt to deduce the original reading which both scribes mangled or which the typesetters in the different printing houses misread or made a mistake in setting.

This editorial process is endlessly complicated, but the general basis of this edition is as follows: F is taken for the copy text and its readings are preserved wherever they make sense. Oaths and stage directions are, however, taken from Q1, since they were presumably part of the original manuscript, but were deleted by the promptbook transcriber to comply with the prohibition against swearing on stage and because the prompt copy did not require such elaborate stage directions as a reading version—somewhat contrary to common sense, this last, but the bibliographers insist upon it. Where mislineation occurs in F, but Q1 has it correctly, the Q1 lineation is used on the theory that it has a better chance of being the original than any hypothetical reconstruction of my own. Finally, where F and Q1 both produce nonsense, changes, based on the above theory about the transmission of the text and on the work of previous editors, have been made.

Where F is deficient, the reading adopted and printed in this text is given below first in italics; unless otherwise stated it is taken from Q1. The original F reading that has been changed follows in roman. Obvious typographical errors in F, expansions of abbreviations, spelling variants ("murder," "murther"), and changes in punctuation and lineation are not noted. The act and scene divisions are translated from Latin, and the division at 2.3 is from the Globe edition rather than from F; otherwise the divisions of F and the Globe edition are identical. "The Names of the Actors," here printed at the beginning of the play, in F follows the play.

1.1.1 *Tush! Never* Never   4 *'Sblood, but* But   26 *other* others   27 *Christian* Christen'd   30 *God bless* blesse   63 *full* fall *thick-lips* Thicks-lips   83 *Zounds, sir* Sir   105 *Zounds, sir* Sir   111 *germans* Germaines   143 *produced* producted   151 *hell pains* (emendation) hell apines [hells paines Q1]

1.2.33 *Duke* Dukes   37 *Even* enen   49 *carack* (emendation) Carract [Carrick Q1]   50 *he's made* he' made   57 *Come* Cme   67 *darlings* Deareling   74 *weaken* weakens   83 *Whither* Whether   86 *if I do* if do

1.3.53 *nor* hor   74 *your* yonr   99 *maimed* main'd   106 *Duke* [F omits]   107 *overt test* oer Test   110 *First Senator* Sen.   122 *till* tell   138 *travel's* trauellours   140 *rocks, and hills* Rocks, Hills *heads* head   142 *other* others   146 *thence* hence   154 *intentively* instinctively   203 *preserved* presern'd   227 *couch* (emendation) Coach [Cooch Q1]   229 *alacrity* Alacartie   259 *me* my [F and Q1]   273 *First Senator* Sen.   286 *First Senator* Sen.   321–22 *balance* braine   328 *scion* (emendation) Seyen [seyen Q1]   376 *snipe* snpe   379 *H'as* She ha's

2.1.9 *mortise* (emendation) morties [morties Q1]   33 *prays* praye   40 *Third Gentleman* Gent.   53 *First Gentleman* Gent.   56 *Second Gentleman* Gent.   59 *Second Gentleman* Gent.   65 *ingener* Ingeniuer   66 *Second Gentleman* Gent.   94 *Second Gentleman* Gent.   168 *gyve* (emendation) giue [catch Q1]   173 *an* and   175 *clyster* cluster   212 *hither* thither   242 *has* he's   261 *mutualities* mutabilities   299 *wife* wist   307 *nightcap* Night-Cape

2.3.39 *unfortunate* infortunate   57 *to put* put to   61 *God* heauen   72 *God* Heauen   77 *Englishman* Englishmin   93 *thine* thy   95 *'Fore God* Why   99 *God's* heaven's   108 *God forgive* Forgiue   141 *Within . . . help* [F omits; Q1 reads "Helpe, helpe, within"]   142 *Zounds, you* You   156 *God's will* Alas   160 *God's will* Fie, fie   162 *Zounds, I* I   217 *leagued* (emendation) [league F and Q1]   260 *God* Heauen   274 *to* ro   288 *O God* Oh   343 *were 't* were to   362 *enmesh* en-mash   378 *By the mass* In troth

3.1.1s.d   [F includes the Clown]   20 *Exeunt Musicians* Exit Mu.   25 *general's wife* Generall   30 *Cassio* [no speech ascription in F]

3.2.6 *We'll* Well

3.3.74 *By'r Lady* Trust me   94 *you* he   106 *By heaven* Alas   135 *free to* free   136 *vile* vild   139 *But some* Wherein   148 *Shape* (emendation) Shapes   162 *By heaven I'll* Ile   170 *fondly* (emendation) soundly [strongly Q1]   175 *God* heauen   182 *exsufflicate* (emendation) exufflicate (F and Q1) *blown* blowd   217 *my* your   222 *vile* vilde   248 *hold him* him   258 *qualities* Quantities   259 *human* humane   281 *to* too   335 *of* in   347 *make* makes   372 *b' wi'* buy   392 *supervisor* supervision   437 *that was* (Malone's emendation) it was [F and Q1]

3.4.77 *God* Heauen   81 *Heaven* Blesse   97 *I'faith* In sooth   170 *I'faith* Indeed   186 *by my faith* in good troth

4.1.21 *infected* infectious   37 *Zounds, that's* that's   79 *unsuiting* resulting   103 *conster* conserue   109 *power* dowre   113 *i'faith* indeed   124 *win* winnes   132 *beckons* becomes   164 *Faith, I* I   218 *God save* Save   248 *an obedient* obedient

4.2.16 *requite* requit   30 *Nay* May   48 *kinds* kind   154 *in* [Q2] or   168 *stay* stays

4.3.14 *bade* bid   51 *hie* high

5.1.1 *bulk* Barke   22 *hear* heard   34 *hies* highes   35 *Forth* For   50 *heaven's* heaven   104 *out o' th'* o' th'

5.2.13 *the rose* thy Rose   35 *say so* say   57 *Then Lord* O Heauen   100 *Should* Did   116 *O Lord* Alas   126 *heard* heare   206 *reprobation* Reprobance   215 *O God! O heavenly God* O Heauen! Oh heauenly powres   216 *Zounds* Come

The Tragedy of
KING LEAR

[DRAMATIS PERSONAE

Lear, King of Britain
King of France
Duke of Burgundy
Duke of Cornwall, husband to Regan
Duke of Albany, husband to Goneril
Earl of Kent
Earl of Gloucester
Edgar, son to Gloucester
Edmund, bastard son to Gloucester
Curan, a courtier
Oswald, steward to Goneril
Old Man, tenant to Gloucester
Doctor
Lear's Fool
A Captain, subordinate to Edmund
Gentlemen, attending on Cordelia
A Herald
Servants to Cornwall
Goneril ⎫
Regan ⎬ daughters to Lear
Cordelia ⎭
Knights attending on Lear, Officers,
    Messengers, Soldiers, Attendants

Scene: Britain]

The Tragedy of King Lear

ACT 1

Scene 1. [*King Lear's palace.*]

Enter Kent, Gloucester, and Edmund.

Kent. I thought the King had more affected°¹ the Duke
of Albany° than Cornwall.

Gloucester. It did always seem so to us; but now, in
the division of the kingdom, it appears not which of
the dukes he values most, for equalities are so   5
weighed that curiosity in neither can make choice of
either's moiety.°

Kent. Is not this your son, my lord?

Gloucester. His breeding,° sir, hath been at my
charge. I have so often blushed to acknowledge   10
him that now I am brazed° to't.

Kent. I cannot conceive° you.

Gloucester. Sir, this young fellow's mother could;
whereupon she grew round-wombed, and had indeed, sir, a son for her cradle ere she had a hus-   15
band for her bed. Do you smell a fault?

---

¹ The degree sign (°) indicates a footnote, which is keyed to the text by line
number. Text references are printed in **boldface** type; the annotation follows in roman type.
1.1.1 **affected** loved   2 **Albany** Albanacte, whose domain extended "from
the river Humber to the point of Caithness" (Holinshed)   5-7 **equalities . . .
moiety** i.e., shares are so balanced against one another that careful examination by neither can make him wish the other's portion   9 **breeding** up-
bringing   11 **brazed** made brazen, hardened   12 **conceive** understand (pun
follows)

3

Kent. I cannot wish the fault undone, the issue° of it
being so proper.°

Gloucester. But I have a son, sir, by order of law,
20   some year elder than this, who yet is no dearer
in my account:° though this knave° came something saucily° to the world before he was sent for,
yet was his mother fair, there was good sport at his
making, and the whoreson° must be acknowl-
25   edged. Do you know this noble gentleman, Edmund?

Edmund. No, my lord.

Gloucester. My Lord of Kent. Remember him hereafter as my honorable friend.

30   *Edmund.* My services to your lordship.

Kent. I must love you, and sue° to know you better.

Edmund. Sir, I shall study deserving.

Gloucester. He hath been out° nine years, and away he
shall again. The King is coming.

*Sound a sennet.° Enter one bearing a coronet,°
then King Lear, then the Dukes of Cornwall
and Albany, next Goneril, Regan, Cordelia,
and Attendants.*

35   *Lear.* Attend the lords of France and Burgundy,
Gloucester.

Gloucester. I shall, my lord.   *Exit [with Edmund].*

Lear. Meantime we shall express our darker purpose.°
Give me the map there. Know that we have divided
40   In three our kingdom; and 'tis our fast° intent
To shake all cares and business from our age,
Conferring them on younger strengths, while we

---

17 **issue** result (child)   18 **proper** handsome   21 **account** estimation   21
knave fellow (without disapproval)   22 **saucily** (1) insolently (2) lasciviously
24 **whoreson** fellow (lit., son of a whore)   31 **sue** entreat   33 **out** away,
abroad   34 s.d. **sennet** set of notes played on a trumpet, signaling the
entrance or departure of a procession   34 s.d. **coronet** small crown, intended
for Cordelia   38 **darker purpose** hidden intention   40 **fast** fixed

Unburthened crawl toward death. Our son of
  Cornwall,
And you our no less loving son of Albany,
We have this hour a constant will to publish°   *45*
Our daughters' several° dowers, that future strife
May be prevented° now. The Princes, France and
  Burgundy,
Great rivals in our youngest daughter's love,
Long in our court have made their amorous sojourn,
And here are to be answered. Tell me, my daughters   *50*
(Since now we will divest us both of rule,
Interest° of territory, cares of state),
Which of you shall we say doth love us most,
That we our largest bounty may extend
Where nature doth with merit challenge.° Goneril,   *55*
Our eldest-born, speak first.

Goneril. Sir, I love you more than word can wield°
  the matter;
Dearer than eyesight, space° and liberty;
Beyond what can be valued, rich or rare;
No less than life, with grace, health, beauty, honor;   *60*
As much as child e'er loved, or father found;
A love that makes breath° poor, and speech
  unable:°
Beyond all manner of so much° I love you.

Cordelia. [*Aside*] What shall Cordelia speak? Love,
  and be silent.

Lear. Of all these bounds, even from this line to this,   *65*
With shadowy forests, and with champains riched,°
With plenteous rivers, and wide-skirted meads,°
We make thee lady. To thine and Albany's issues°
Be this perpetual.° What says our second daughter,

---

45 **constant will to publish** fixed intention to proclaim 46 **several**
separate 47 **prevented** forestalled 52 **Interest** legal right 55 **nature …**
challenge i.e., natural affection contends with desert for (or lays claim to)
bounty 57 **wield** handle 58 **space** scope 62 **breath** language 62 **unable**
impotent 63 **Beyond … much** beyond all these comparisons 66 **cham-**
pains riched enriched plains 67 **wide-skirted meads** extensive grass-
lands 68 **issues** descendants 69 **perpetual** in perpetuity

70   Our dearest Regan, wife of Cornwall? Speak.

Regan. I am made of that self mettle° as my sister,
And prize me at her worth.° In my true heart
I find she names my very deed of love;°
Only she comes too short, that° I profess
75   Myself an enemy to all other joys
Which the most precious square of sense
         professes,°
And find I am alone felicitate°
In your dear Highness' love.

Cordelia.   [*Aside*] Then poor Cordelia!
And yet not so, since I am sure my love's
80   More ponderous° than my tongue.

Lear. To thee and thine hereditary ever
Remain this ample third of our fair kingdom,
No less in space, validity,° and pleasure
Than that conferred on Goneril. Now, our joy,
85   Although our last and least;° to whose young love
The vines of France and milk° of Burgundy
Strive to be interest;° what can you say to draw
A third more opulent than your sisters? Speak.

Cordelia. Nothing, my lord.

90   *Lear.* Nothing?

Cordelia. Nothing.

Lear. Nothing will come of nothing. Speak again.

Cordelia. Unhappy that I am, I cannot heave
My heart into my mouth. I love your Majesty
95   According to my bond,° no more nor less.

Lear. How, how, Cordelia? Mend your speech a little,
Lest you may mar your fortunes.

71**self mettle** same material or temperament   72 **prize ... worth** value me
the same (imperative)   73 **my ... love** what my love really is (a legalism)   74 **that** in that   76 **Which ... professes** which the choicest
estimate of sense avows   77 **felicitate** made happy   80 **ponderous** weighty
83 **validity** value   85 **least** youngest, smallest   86 **milk** i.e., pastures   87
interest closely connected, as interested parties   95 **bond** i.e., filial obligation

Cordelia.   Good my lord,
    You have begot me, bred me, loved me. I
    Return those duties back as are right fit,°
    Obey you, love you, and most honor you.   *100*
    Why have my sisters husbands, if they say
    They love you all? Haply,° when I shall wed,
    That lord whose hand must take my plight° shall
        carry
    Half my love with him, half my care and duty.
    Sure I shall never marry like my sisters,   *105*
    To love my father all.

Lear. But goes thy heart with this?

Cordelia.   Ay, my good lord.

Lear. So young, and so untender?

Cordelia. So young, my lord, and true.

Lear. Let it be so, thy truth then be thy dower!   *110*
    For, by the sacred radiance of the sun,
    The mysteries of Hecate° and the night,
    By all the operation of the orbs°
    From whom we do exist and cease to be,
    Here I disclaim all my paternal care,   *115*
    Propinquity and property of blood,°
    And as a stranger to my heart and me
    Hold thee from this for ever. The barbarous
        Scythian,°
    Or he that makes his generation messes°
    To gorge his appetite, shall to my bosom   *120*
    Be as well neighbored, pitied, and relieved,
    As thou my sometime° daughter.

Kent.   Good my liege——

Lear. Peace, Kent!

99 Return ... fit i.e., am correspondingly dutiful   **102 Haply** perhaps
103 plight troth plight   **112 mysteries of Hecate** secret rites of Hecate
(goddess of the infernal world, and of witchcraft)   **113 operation of
the orbs** astrological influence   **116 Propinquity and property of blood**
relationship and common blood   **118 Scythian** (type of the savage)   **119
makes his generation messes** eats his own offspring   **122 sometime**
former

Come not between the Dragon° and his wrath.
125   I loved her most, and thought to set my rest°
On her kind nursery.° Hence and avoid my sight!
So be my grave my peace, as here I give
Her father's heart from her! Call France. Who stirs?
Call Burgundy. Cornwall and Albany,
130   With my two daughters' dowers digest° the third;
Let pride, which she calls plainness, marry her.°
I do invest you jointly with my power,
Pre-eminence, and all the large effects
That troop with majesty.° Ourself,° by monthly
        course,
135   With reservation° of an hundred knights,
By you to be sustained, shall our abode
Make with you by due turn. Only we shall retain
The name, and all th' addition° to a king. The sway,
Revènue, execution of the rest,
140   Belovèd sons, be yours; which to confirm,
This coronet° part between you.

Kent.   Royal Lear,
Whom I have ever honored as my king,
Loved as my father, as my master followed,
As my great patron thought on in my prayers——

Lear. The bow is bent and drawn; make from the
145   shaft.°

Kent. Let it fall° rather, though the fork° invade
The region of my heart. Be Kent unmannerly
When Lear is mad. What wouldst thou do, old
        man?
Think'st thou that duty shall have dread to speak

---

124 **Dragon** (1) heraldic device of Britain (2) emblem of ferocity   125 **set my rest** (1) stake my all (a term from the card game of primero) (2) find my rest   126 **nursery** care, nursing   130 **digest** absorb   131 **Let ... her** i.e., let her pride be her dowry and gain her a husband   134-35 **effects/That troop with majesty** accompaniments that go with kingship   134 **Ourself** (the royal "we")   135 **reservation** the action of reserving a privilege (a legalism)   138 **addition** titles and honors   141 **coronet** (the crown which was to have been Cordelia's)   145 **make from the shaft** avoid the arrow   146 **fall** strike   146 **fork** forked head of the arrow

When power to flattery bows? To plainness honor's
   bound   150
When majesty falls to folly. Reserve thy state,°
And in thy best consideration° check
This hideous rashness. Answer my life my
   judgment,°
Thy youngest daughter does not love thee least,
Nor are those empty-hearted whose low sounds   155
Reverb° no hollowness.°

Lear.   Kent, on thy life, no more!

Kent. My life I never held but as a pawn°
   To wage° against thine enemies; nor fear to lose it,
   Thy safety being motive.°

Lear.   Out of my sight!

Kent. See better, Lear, and let me still° remain   160
   The true blank° of thine eye.

Lear. Now by Apollo——

Kent.   Now by Apollo, King,
   Thou swear'st thy gods in vain.

Lear.   O vassal! Miscreant!°
                   [Laying his hand on his sword.]

Albany, Cornwall. Dear sir, forbear!

Kent. Kill thy physician, and the fee bestow   165
   Upon the foul disease. Revoke thy gift,
   Or, whilst I can vent clamor° from my throat,
   I'll tell thee thou dost evil.

Lear.   Hear me, recreant!°
   On thine allegiance,° hear me!
   That thou hast sought to make us break our vows,   170

---

151 **Reserve thy state** retain your kingly authority   152 **best consideration** most careful reflection   153 **Answer . . . judgment** I will stake my life on my opinion   156 **Reverb** reverberate   156 **hollowness** (1) emptiness (2) insincerity   157 **pawn** stake in a wager   158 **wage** (1) wager (2) carry on war   159 **motive** moving cause   160 **still** always   161 **blank** the white spot in the center of the target (at which Lear should aim)   163 **vassal! Miscreant!** base wretch! Misbeliever!   167 **vent clamor** utter a cry   168 **recreant** traitor   169 **On thine allegiance** (to forswear, which is to commit high treason)

Which we durst never yet, and with strained° pride
To come betwixt our sentence° and our power,
Which nor our nature nor our place can bear,
Our potency made good,° take thy reward.

175　Five days we do allot thee for provision°
To shield thee from diseases° of the world,
And on the sixth to turn thy hated back
Upon our kingdom. If, on the tenth day following,
Thy banished trunk° be found in our dominions,

180　The moment is thy death. Away! By Jupiter,
This shall not be revoked.

    Kent. Fare thee well, King. Sith° thus thou wilt appear,
Freedom lives hence, and banishment is here.
[*To Cordelia*] The gods to their dear shelter take
    thee, maid,

185　That justly think'st, and hast most rightly said.
[*To Regan and Goneril*] And your large speeches
    may your deeds approve,°
That good effects° may spring from words of love.
Thus Kent, O Princes, bids you all adieu;
He'll shape his old course° in a country new. *Exit.*

    Flourish.° Enter Gloucester, with France and
      Burgundy; Attendants.

190　*Gloucester.* Here's France and Burgundy, my noble
    lord.

    Lear. My Lord of Burgundy,
We first address toward you, who with this king
Hath rivaled for our daughter. What in the least
Will you require in present° dower with her,
Or cease your quest of love?

195　*Burgundy.*　　　　　　　　　　Most royal Majesty,
I crave no more than hath your Highness offered,

171 **strained** forced (and so excessive)　172 **sentence** judgment, decree
174 **Our potency made good** my royal authority being now asserted　175 **for
provision** for making preparation　176 **diseases** troubles　179 **trunk** body
182 **Sith** since　186 **approve** prove true　187 **effects** results　189 **shape . . .
course** pursue his customary way　189 s.d. **Flourish** trumpet fanfare
194 **present** immediate

Nor will you tender° less.

Lear.   Right noble Burgundy,
When she was dear° to us, we did hold her so;
But now her price is fallen. Sir, there she stands.
If aught within that little seeming substance,°   *200*
Or all of it, with our displeasure pieced,°
And nothing more, may fitly like° your Grace,
She's there, and she is yours.

Burgundy.   I know no answer.

Lear. Will you, with those infirmities she owes,°
Unfriended, new adopted to our hate,   *205*
Dow'red with our curse, and strangered° with our
    oath,
Take her, or leave her?

Burgundy.   Pardon me, royal sir.
Election makes not up° on such conditions.

Lear. Then leave her, sir; for, by the pow'r that made
    me,
I tell you all her wealth. [*To France.*] For you,
    great King,   *210*
I would not from your love make such a stray
To° match you where I hate; therefore beseech° you
T' avert your liking a more worthier way°
Than on a wretch whom nature is ashamed
Almost t' acknowledge hers.

France.   This is most strange,   *215*
That she whom even but now was your best object,°
The argument° of your praise, balm of your age,
The best, the dearest, should in this trice of time
Commit a thing so monstrous to dismantle°

---

197 **tender** offer   198 **dear** (1) beloved (2) valued at a high price   200 **little seeming substance** person who is (1) inconsiderable (2) outspoken   201 **pieced** added to it   202 **fitly like** please by its fitness   204 **owes** possesses   206 **strangered** made a stranger   208 **Election makes not up** no one can choose   211-12 **make such a stray / To** stray so far as to   212 **beseech** I beseech   213 **avert ... way** turn your affections from her and bestow them on a better person   216 **best object** i.e., the one you loved most   217 **argument** subject   219 **dismantle** strip off

220   So many folds of favor. Sure her offense
        Must be of such unnatural degree
        That monsters it,° or your fore-vouched° affection
        Fall into taint;° which to believe of her
        Must be a faith that reason without miracle
        Should never plant in me.°

225 *Cordelia.*   I yet beseech your Majesty,
        If for° I want that glib and oily art
        To speak and purpose not,° since what I well intend
        I'll do't before I speak, that you make known
        It is no vicious blot, murder, or foulness,
230   No unchaste action or dishonored step,
        That hath deprived me of your grace and favor;
        But even for want of that for which I am richer,
        A still-soliciting° eye, and such a tongue
        That I am glad I have not, though not to have it
        Hath lost° me in your liking.

235 *Lear.*   **Better thou**
        Hadst not been born than not t' have pleased me
          better.

        France. Is it but this? A tardiness in nature°
        Which often leaves the history unspoke°
        That it intends to do. My Lord of Burgundy,
240   What say you° to the lady? Love's not love
        When it is mingled with regards° that stands
        Aloof from th' entire point.° Will you have her?
        She is herself a dowry.

        Burgundy.   **Royal King,**
        Give but that portion which yourself proposed,
245   And here I take Cordelia by the hand,
        Duchess of Burgundy.

222 **That monsters it** as makes it monstrous, unnatural   222 **fore-vouched** previously sworn   223 **Fall into taint** must be taken as having been unjustified all along i.e., Cordelia was unworthy of your love from the first   224–25 **reason . . . me** my reason would have to be supported by a miracle to make me believe   226 **for** because   227 **purpose not** not mean to do what I promise   233 **still-soliciting** always begging   235 **lost** ruined   237 **tardiness in nature** natural reticence   238 **leaves the history unspoke** does not announce the action   240 **What say you** i.e., will you have   241 **regards** considerations (the dowry)   241–42 **stands . . . point** have nothing to do with the essential question (love)

Lear. Nothing. I have sworn. I am firm.

Burgundy. I am sorry then you have so lost a father
  That you must lose a husband.

Cordelia.   Peace be with Burgundy.
  Since that respects of fortune° are his love,   250
  I shall not be his wife.

France. Fairest Cordelia, that art most rich being
        poor,
  Most choice forsaken, and most loved despised,
  Thee and thy virtues here I seize upon.
  Be it lawful I take up what's cast away.   255
  Gods, gods! 'Tis strange that from their cold'st
        neglect
  My love should kindle to inflamed respect.°
  Thy dow'rless daughter, King, thrown to my
        chance,°
  Is Queen of us, of ours, and our fair France.
  Not all the dukes of wat'rish° Burgundy   260
  Can buy this unprized precious° maid of me.
  Bid them farewell, Cordelia, though unkind.
  Thou losest here, a better where° to find.

Lear. Thou hast her, France; let her be thine, for we
  Have no such daughter, nor shall ever see   265
  That face of hers again. Therefore be gone,
  Without our grace, our love, our benison.°
  Come, noble Burgundy.

        Flourish. Exeunt [*Lear, Burgundy, Cornwall,
        Albany, Gloucester, and Attendants*].

France. Bid farewell to your sisters.

Cordelia. The jewels of our father,° with washed°
        eyes   270
  Cordelia leaves you. I know you what you are,

250 **respects of fortune** mercenary considerations   257 **inflamed respect**
more ardent affection   258 **chance** lot   260 **wat'rish** (1) with many rivers
(2) weak, diluted   261 **unprized precious** unappreciated by others, and yet
precious   263 **here . . . where** in this place, in another place   267 **benison**
blessing   270 **The jewels of our father** you creatures prized by our father
270 **washed** (1) weeping (2) clear-sighted

And, like a sister,° am most loath to call
Your faults as they are named.° Love well our
    father.
To your professèd° bosoms I commit him.
275 But yet, alas, stood I within his grace,
I would prefer° him to a better place.
So farewell to you both.

Regan. Prescribe not us our duty.

Goneril.   Let your study
Be to content your lord, who hath received you
280 At Fortune's alms.° You have obedience scanted,°
And well are worth the want that you have wanted.°

Cordelia. Time shall unfold what plighted° cunning
    hides,
Who covers faults, at last shame them derides.°
Well may you prosper.

France.   Come, my fair Cordelia.
            Exit France and Cordelia.

285 *Goneril.* Sister, it is not little I have to say of what
    most nearly appertains to us both. I think our father
    will hence tonight.

Regan. That's most certain, and with you; next month
    with us.

290 *Goneril.* You see how full of changes his age is. The
    observation we have made of it hath not been little.
    He always loved our sister most, and with what
    poor judgment he hath now cast her off appears
    too grossly.°

295 *Regan.* 'Tis the infirmity of his age; yet he hath ever
    but slenderly known himself.

---

272 **like a sister** because I am a sister i.e., loyal, affectionate   273 **as they
are named** i.e., by their right and ugly names   274 **professèd** pretending to
love   276 **prefer** recommend   280 **At Fortune's alms** as a charitable be-
quest from Fortune (and so, by extension, as one beggared or cast down by
Fortune)   280 **scanted** stinted   281 **worth . . . wanted** deserve to be denied,
even as you have denied   282 **plighted** pleated, enfolded   283 **Who . . . derides** those who hide their evil are finally exposed and shamed ("He that
hideth his sins, shall not prosper")   294 **grossly** obviously

Goneril. The best and soundest of his time° hath been
   but rash; then must we look from his age to
   receive not alone the imperfections of long-in-
   grafted° condition,° but therewithal° the unruly   300
   waywardness that infirm and choleric years bring
   with them.

Regan. Such unconstant starts° are we like to have
   from him as this of Kent's banishment.

Goneril. There is further compliment° of leave-taking   305
   between France and him. Pray you, let's hit° together; if our father carry authority with such disposition as he bears,° this last surrender° of his will
   but offend° us.

Regan. We shall further think of it.   310

Goneril. We must do something, and i' th' heat.°
                                              Exeunt.

Scene 2.   [*The Earl of Gloucester's castle.*]

Enter Edmund [with a letter].

Edmund. Thou, Nature,° art my goddess; to thy law
   My services are bound. Wherefore should I
   Stand in the plague of custom,° and permit
   The curiosity° of nations to deprive me,
   For that° I am some twelve or fourteen
        moonshines°   5

297 **of his time** period of his life up to now   299–300 **long-ingrafted** im-
planted for a long time   300 **condition** disposition   300 **therewithal** with
them   303 **unconstant starts** impulsive whims   305 **compliment** formal
courtesy   306 **hit** agree   307–8 **carry . . . bears** continues, and in such frame
of mind, to wield the sovereign power   308 **last surrender** recent abdication
309 **offend** vex   311 **i' th' heat** while the iron is hot   1.2.1 **Nature** (Edmund's conception of Nature accords with our description of a bastard as a natural child)   3 **Stand . . . custom** respect hateful convention   4 **curiosity** nice
distinctions   5 **For that** because   5 **moonshines** months

Lag of° a brother? Why bastard? Wherefore base?
When my dimensions are as well compact,°
My mind as generous,° and my shape as true,
As honest° madam's issue? Why brand they us
10 With base? With baseness? Bastardy? Base? Base?
Who, in the lusty stealth of nature, take
More composition° and fierce° quality
Than doth, within a dull, stale, tired bed,
Go to th' creating a whole tribe of fops°
15 Got° 'tween asleep and wake? Well then,
Legitimate Edgar, I must have your land.
Our father's love is to the bastard Edmund
As to th' legitimate. Fine word, "legitimate."
Well, my legitimate, if this letter speed,°
20 And my invention° thrive, Edmund the base
Shall top th' legitimate. I grow, I prosper.
Now, gods, stand up for bastards.

Enter Gloucester.

Gloucester. Kent banished thus? and France in choler
    parted?
And the King gone tonight? prescribed° his pow'r?
25 Confined to exhibition?° All this done
Upon the gad?° Edmund, how now? What news?

Edmund. So please your lordship, none.

Gloucester. Why so earnestly seek you to put up°
    that letter?

30 *Edmund.* I know no news, my lord.

Gloucester. What paper were you reading?

Edmund. Nothing, my lord.

Gloucester. No? What needed then that terrible dis-
    patch° of it into your pocket? The quality of noth-

---

6 **Lag of** short of being (in age) 7 **compact** framed 8 **generous** gallant
9 **honest** chaste 12 **composition** completeness 12 **fierce** energetic 14 **fops**
fools 15 **Got** begot 19 **speed** prosper 20 **invention** plan 24 **prescribed**
limited 25 **exhibition** an allowance or pension 26 **Upon the gad** on the spur
of the moment (as if pricked by a gad or goad) 28 **put up** put away, conceal
33–34 **terrible dispatch** hasty putting away

ing hath not such need to hide itself. Let's see. 35
Come, if it be nothing, I shall not need spectacles.

Edmund. I beseech you, sir, pardon me. It is a letter
from my brother that I have not all o'er-read; and
for so much as I have perused, I find it not fit
for your o'erlooking.° 40

Gloucester. Give me the letter, sir.

Edmund. I shall offend, either to detain or give it. The
contents, as in part I understand them, are to
blame.°

Gloucester. Let's see, let's see. 45

Edmund. I hope, for my brother's justification, he
wrote this but as an essay or taste° of my virtue.

Gloucester. (*Reads*) "This policy and reverence° of
age makes the world bitter to the best of our
times;° keeps our fortunes from us till our oldness 50
cannot relish° them. I begin to find an idle and
fond° bondage in the oppression of aged tyranny,
who sways, not as it hath power, but as it is suffered.° Come to me, that of this I may speak more.
If our father would sleep till I waked him, you 55
should enjoy half his revenue° for ever, and live
the beloved of your brother,   EDGAR."
Hum! Conspiracy? "Sleep till I waked him, you
should enjoy half his revenue." My son Edgar! Had
he a hand to write this? A heart and brain to 60
breed it in? When came you to this? Who brought
it?

Edmund. It was not brought me, my lord; there's the
cunning of it. I found it thrown in at the casement of
my closet.° 65

---

40 **o'erlooking** inspection   44 **to blame** blameworthy   47 **essay or taste**
test   48 **policy and reverence** policy of reverencing (hendiadys)
49–50 **best of our times** best years of our lives (i.e., our youth)   51
relish enjoy   51–52 **idle and fond** foolish   53–54 **who . . . suffered**
which rules, not from its own strength, but from our allowance   56 **revenue** income   64–65 **casement of my closet** window of my room

Gloucester. You know the character° to be your brother's?

Edmund. If the matter were good, my lord, I durst swear it were his; but in respect of that,° I would
70   fain° think it were not.

Gloucester. It is his.

Edmund. It is his hand, my lord; but I hope his heart is not in the contents.

Gloucester. Has he never before sounded° you in this
75   business?

Edmund. Never, my lord. But I have heard him oft maintain it to be fit that, sons at perfect° age, and fathers declined, the father should be as ward to the son, and the son manage his revenue.

80   *Gloucester.* O villain, villain! His very opinion in the letter. Abhorred villain, unnatural, detested,° brutish villain; worse than brutish! Go, sirrah,° seek him. I'll apprehend him. Abominable villain! Where is he?

85   *Edmund.* I do not well know, my lord. If it shall please you to suspend your indignation against my brother till you can derive from him better testimony of his intent, you should run a certain course;° where, if you violently proceed against
90   him, mistaking his purpose, it would make a great gap° in your own honor and shake in pieces the heart of his obedience. I dare pawn down° my life for him that he hath writ this to feel° my affection to your honor, and to no other pretense of
95   danger.°

Gloucester. Think you so?

66 **character** handwriting   69 **in respect of that** in view of what it is
70 **fain** prefer to   74 **sounded** sounded you out   77 **perfect** mature   81 **detested** detestable   82 **sirrah** sir (familiar form of address)   88–89 **run a certain course** i.e., proceed safely, know where you are going   91 **gap** breach   92 **pawn down** stake   93 **feel** test   94–95 **pretense of danger** dangerous purpose

Edmund. If your honor judge it meet,° I will place
you where you shall hear us confer of this, and by
an auricular assurance° have your satisfaction,
and that without any further delay than this very 100
evening.

Gloucester. He cannot be such a monster.

Edmund. Nor is not, sure.

Gloucester. To his father, that so tenderly and entirely loves him. Heaven and earth! Edmund, seek 105
him out; wind me into him,° I pray you; frame° the
business after your own wisdom. I would unstate
myself to be in a due resolution.°

Edmund. I will seek him, sir, presently;° convey°
the business as I shall find means, and acquaint you 110
withal.°

Gloucester. These late° eclipses in the sun and moon
portend no good to us. Though the wisdom of Na-
ture° can reason° it thus and thus, yet Nature
finds itself scourged by the sequent effects.° Love 115
cools, friendship falls off,° brothers divide. In
cities, mutinies;° in countries, discord; in palaces,
treason; and the bond cracked 'twixt son and
father. This villain of mine comes under the prediction,° there's son against father; the King falls 120
from bias of nature,° there's father against child.
We have seen the best of our time.° Machinations,
hollowness,° treachery, and all ruinous disorders
follow us disquietly° to our graves. Find out this

---

97 **meet** fit   99 **auricular assurance** proof heard with your own ears
106 **wind me into him** insinuate yourself into his confidence for me
106 **frame** manage   107–08 **unstate . . . resolution** forfeit my earldom to
know the truth   109 **presently** at once   109 **convey** manage   111 **withal**
with it   112 **late** recent   113–14 **wisdom of Nature** scientific learning
114 **reason** explain   114–15 **yet . . . effects** nonetheless our world is punished with subsequent disasters   116 **falls off** revolts   117 **mutinies** riots
119–20 **This . . . prediction** i.e., my son's villainous behavior is included in
these portents, and bears them out   121 **bias of nature** natural inclination
(the metaphor is from the game of bowls)   122 **best of our time** our best
days   123 **hollowness** insincerity   124 **disquietly** unquietly

125   villain, Edmund; it shall lose thee nothing.° Do it
carefully. And the noble and true-hearted Kent
banished; his offense, honesty. 'Tis strange.

Exit.

Edmund. This is the excellent foppery° of the world,
that when we are sick in fortune, often the surfeits
130   of our own behavior,° we make guilty of our disasters the sun, the moon, and stars; as if we were
villains on° necessity; fools by heavenly compulsion; knaves, thieves, and treachers by spherical
predominance;° drunkards, liars, and adulterers by
135   an enforced obedience of planetary influence;° and
all that we are evil in, by a divine thrusting on.°
An admirable evasion of whoremaster° man, to
lay his goatish° disposition on the charge of a
star. My father compounded° with my mother
140   under the Dragon's Tail,° and my nativity° was
under Ursa Major,° so that it follows I am rough
and lecherous. Fut!° I should have been that° I
am, had the maidenliest star in the firmament twin-
kled on my bastardizing. Edgar——

Enter Edgar.

145   and pat he comes, like the catastrophe° of the old
comedy. My cue is villainous melancholy, with a
sigh like Tom o' Bedlam.°—O, these eclipses do
portend these divisions. Fa, sol, la, mi.°

Edgar. How now, brother Edmund; what serious con-
150   templation are you in?

125 **it . . . nothing** you will not lose by it   128 **foppery** folly   129–30
often . . . behavior often caused by our own excesses   132 **on** of
133–34 **treachers . . . predominance** traitors because of the ascendancy of a
particular star at our birth   134–35 **by . . . influence** because we had to submit
to the influence of our star   136 **divine thrusting on** supernatural compulsion
137 **whoremaster** lecherous   138 **goatish** scivious   139 **compounded** (1)
made terms (2) formed (a child)   140 **Dragon's Tail** the constellation Draco
140 **nativity** birthday   141 **Ursa Major** the Great Bear   142 **Fut!** 's foot
(an impatient oath)   142 **that** what   145 **catastrophe** conclusion   146–47
My . . . Bedlam I must be doleful, like a lunatic beggar out of Bethlehem (Bedlam) Hospital, the London madhouse   148 **Fa, sol, la, mi** (Edmund's hum-
ming of the musical notes is perhaps prompted by his use of the word
"divisions," which describes a musical variation)

Edmund. I am thinking, brother, of a prediction I read
this other day, what should follow these eclipses.

Edgar. Do you busy yourself with that?

Edmund. I promise you, the effects he writes of suc- 155
ceed° unhappily: as of unnaturalness° between the
child and the parent, death, dearth, dissolutions of
ancient amities,° divisions in state, menaces and
maledictions against King and nobles, needless diffidences,° banishment of friends, dissipation of co- 160
horts,° nuptial breaches, and I know not what.

Edgar. How long have you been a sectary astronomical?°

Edmund. Come, come, when saw you my father last?

Edgar. Why, the night gone by. 165

Edmund. Spake you with him?

Edgar. Ay, two hours together.

Edmund. Parted you in good terms? Found you no
displeasure in him by word nor countenance?°

Edgar. None at all. 170

Edmund. Bethink yourself wherein you may have offended him; and at my entreaty forbear his pres-
ence° until some little time hath qualified° the heat
of his displeasure, which at this instant so rageth
in him that with the mischief of your person it 175
would scarcely allay.°

Edgar. Some villain hath done me wrong.

Edmund. That's my fear, brother I pray you have a
continent forbearance° till the speed of his rage
goes slower; and, as I say, retire with me to my 180

155–56 **succeed** follow   157 **unnaturalness** unkindness   158 **amities** friend-
ships   159–60 **diffidences** distrusts   160–61 **dissipation of cohorts** falling
away of supporters   162–63 **sectary astronomical** believer in astrology
169 **countenance** expression   172–73 **forbear his presence** keep away from
him   173 **qualified** lessened   175–76 **with ... allay** even an injury to you
would not appease his anger   178–79 **have a continent forbearance** be restrained and keep yourself withdrawn

lodging, from whence I will fitly° bring you to hear
my lord speak. Pray ye, go; there's my key. If
you do stir abroad, go armed.

Edgar. Armed, brother?

185 *Edmund.* Brother, I advise you to the best. Go armed.
I am no honest man if there be any good meaning
toward you. I have told you what I have seen and
heard; but faintly, nothing like the image and hor-
ror° of it. Pray you, away.

190 *Edgar.* Shall I hear from you anon?°

Edmund. I do serve you in this business.

Exit Edgar.

A credulous father, and a brother noble,
Whose nature is so far from doing harms
That he suspects none; on whose foolish honesty
195 My practices° ride easy. I see the business.
Let me, if not by birth, have lands by wit.
All with me's meet° that I can fashion fit.°   *Exit.*

Scene 3.   [*The Duke of Albany's palace.*]

Enter Goneril, and [*Oswald, her*] *Steward.*

Goneril. Did my father strike my gentleman for chiding of his Fool?°

Oswald. Ay, madam.

Goneril. By day and night he wrongs me. Every hour
5   He flashes into one gross crime° or other

---

181 **fitly** at a fit time   188–89 **image and horror** true horrible picture
190 **anon** in a little while   195 **practices** plots   197 **meet** proper   197 **fashion fit** shape to my purpose   1.3.2 **Fool** court jester   5 **crime** offense

That sets us all at odds. I'll not endure it.
His knights grow riotous,° and himself upbraids us
On every trifle. When he returns from hunting,
I will not speak with him. Say I am sick.
If you come slack of former services,°   10
You shall do well; the fault of it I'll answer.°

                    [*Horns within.*]

Oswald. He's coming, madam; I hear him.

Goneril. Put on what weary negligence you please,
   You and your fellows. I'd have it come to question.°
   If he distaste° it, let him to my sister,   15
   Whose mind and mine I know in that are one,
   Not to be overruled. Idle° old man,
   That still would manage those authorities
   That he hath given away. Now, by my life,
   Old fools are babes again, and must be used   20
   With checks as flatteries, when they are seen
       abused.°
   Remember what I have said.

Oswald.   Well, madam.

Goneril. And let his knights have colder looks among
       you.
   What grows of it, no matter; advise your fellows so.
   I would breed from hence occasions, and I shall,   25
   That I may speak.° I'll write straight° to my sister
   To hold my course. Go, prepare for dinner.

                              Exeunt.

---

7 **riotous** dissolute   10 **come . . . services** are less serviceable to him than
formerly   11 **answer** answer for   14 **come to question** be discussed
openly   15 **distaste** dislike   17 **Idle** foolish   21 **With . . . abused** with re-
straints as well as soothing words when they are misguided   25–26 **breed . . .
speak** find in this opportunities for speaking out   26 **straight** at once

Scene 4.   [*A hall in the same.*]

Enter Kent [disguised].

Kent. If but as well I other accents borrow
That can my speech defuse,° my good intent
May carry through itself to that full issue°
For which I razed my likeness.° Now, banished
    Kent,
If thou canst serve where thou dost stand
    condemned,
So may it come,° thy master whom thou lov'st
Shall find thee full of labors.

    *Horns within.° Enter Lear, [Knights] and
        Attendants.*

Lear. Let me not stay° a jot for dinner; go, get it
ready. [*Exit an Attendant.*] How now, what art
thou?

Kent. A man, sir.

Lear. What dost thou profess?° What wouldst thou
with us?

Kent. I do profess° to be no less than I seem, to
serve him truly that will put me in trust, to love
him that is honest, to converse with him that is wise
and says little, to fear judgment,° to fight when I
cannot choose, and to eat no fish.°

1.4.2 **defuse** disguise   3 **full issue** perfect result   4 **razed my likeness**
shaved off, disguised my natural appearance   6 **So may it come** so may it
fall out   7 s.d. **within** offstage   8 **stay** wait   12 **What dost thou profess**
what do you do   14 **profess** claim   17 **judgment** (by a heavenly or earthly
judge)   18 **eat no fish** i.e., (1) I am no Catholic, but a loyal Protestant (2) I
am no weakling (3) I use no prostitutes

Lear. What art thou?

Kent. A very honest-hearted fellow, and as poor as   20
the King.

Lear. If thou be'st as poor for a subject as he's for a
king, thou art poor enough. What wouldst thou?

Kent. Service.

Lear. Who wouldst thou serve?   25

Kent. You.

Lear. Dost thou know me, fellow?

Kent. No, sir, but you have that in your countenance°
which I would fain° call master.

Lear. What's that?   30

Kent. Authority.

Lear. What services canst thou do?

Kent. I can keep honest counsel,° ride, run, mar a
curious tale in telling it,° and deliver a plain message bluntly. That which ordinary men are fit for, I   35
am qualified in, and the best of me is diligence.

Lear. How old art thou?

Kent. Not so young, sir, to love a woman for singing, nor so old to dote on her for anything. I have
years on my back forty-eight.   40

Lear. Follow me; thou shalt serve me. If I like thee no
worse after dinner, I will not part from thee yet.
Dinner, ho, dinner! Where's my knave?° my Fool?
Go you and call my Fool hither.

                       [Exit an Attendant.]

           Enter Oswald.

   You, you, sirrah, where's my daughter?   45

Oswald. So please you——   *Exit.*

---

28 **countenance** bearing   29 **fain** like to   33 **honest counsel** honorable
secrets   33–34 **mar . . . it** i.e., I cannot speak like an affected courtier ("curious"="elaborate," as against "plain")   43 **knave** boy

Lear. What says the fellow there? Call the clotpoll°
back. [*Exit a Knight.*] Where's my Fool? Ho, I
think the world's asleep.
             [*Re-enter Knight.*]
50   How now? Where's that mongrel?

Knight. He says, my lord, your daughter is not well.

Lear. Why came not the slave back to me when I
called him?

Knight. Sir, he answered me in the roundest° manner,
55   he would not.

Lear. He would not?

Knight. My lord, I know not what the matter is;
but to my judgment your Highness is not enter-
tained° with that ceremonious affection as you
60   were wont. There's a great abatement of kindness
appears as well in the general dependants° as in the
Duke himself also and your daughter.

Lear. Ha? Say'st thou so?

Knight. I beseech you pardon me, my lord, if I be
65   mistaken; for my duty cannot be silent when I
think your Highness wronged.

Lear. Thou but rememb'rest° me of mine own conception.° I have perceived a most faint neglect°
of late, which I have rather blamed as mine own
70   jealous curiosity° than as a very pretense° and
purpose of unkindness. I will look further into't.
But where's my Fool? I have not seen him this two
days.

Knight. Since my young lady's going into France, sir,
75   the Fool hath much pined away.

Lear. No more of that; I have noted it well. Go you

---

47 **clotpoll** clodpoll, blockhead   54 **roundest** rudest   58–59 **entertained**
treated   61 **dependants** servants   67 **rememb'rest** remindest   67–68 **conception** idea   68 **faint neglect** i.e., "weary negligence" (1.3.13)   69–70 **mine
own jealous curiosity** suspicious concern for my own dignity   70 **very
pretense** actual intention

and tell my daughter I would speak with her. Go
you, call hither my Fool.   [*Exit an Attendant.*]
                    Enter Oswald.
O, you, sir, you! Come you hither, sir. Who am I,
sir?   80

Oswald. My lady's father.

Lear. "My lady's father"? My lord's knave, you
  whoreson dog, you slave, you cur!

Oswald. I am none of these, my lord; I beseech your
  pardon.   85

Lear. Do you bandy° looks with me, you rascal?
                                    [*Striking him.*]

Oswald. I'll not be strucken,° my lord.

Kent. Nor tripped neither, you base football° player.
                                    [*Tripping up his heels.*]

Lear. I thank thee, fellow. Thou serv'st me, and I'll
  love thee.   90

Kent. Come, sir, arise, away. I'll teach you differences.° Away, away. If you will measure your lubber's° length again, tarry; but away. Go to!° Have
  you wisdom?° So.°   [*Pushes Oswald out.*]

Lear. Now, my friendly knave, I thank thee. There's   95
  earnest° of thy service.   [*Giving Kent money.*]
                    Enter Fool.

Fool. Let me hire him too. Here's my coxcomb.°
                                    [*Offering Kent his cap.*]

Lear. How now, my pretty knave? How dost thou?

Fool. Sirrah, you were best° take my coxcomb.

Kent. Why, Fool?   100

86 **bandy** exchange insolently (metaphor from tennis)   87 **strucken** struck
88 **football** (a low game played by idle boys to the scandal of sensible men)
91–92 **differences** (of rank)   92–93 **lubber's** lout's   93 **Go to** (expression
of derisive incredulity)   93–94 **Have you wisdom** i.e., do you know what's
good for you   94 **So** good   96 **earnest** money for services rendered
97 **coxcomb** professional fool's cap, shaped like a coxcomb   99 **you were
best** you had better

Fool. Why? For taking one's part that's out of favor.
    Nay, an° thou canst not smile as the wind sits,°
    thou'lt catch cold shortly. There, take my coxcomb.
    Why, this fellow has banished° two on's daughters,
105 and did the third a blessing against his will. If thou
    follow him, thou must needs wear my coxcomb.
    —How now, Nuncle?° Would I had two coxcombs
    and two daughters.

Lear. Why, my boy?

110 *Fool.* If I gave them all my living,° I'd keep my cox-
    combs myself. There's mine; beg another of thy
    daughters.

Lear. Take heed, sirrah—the whip.

Fool. Truth's a dog must to kennel; he must be
115 whipped out, when Lady the Brach° may stand by
    th' fire and stink.

Lear. A pestilent gall° to me.

Fool. Sirrah, I'll teach thee a speech.

Lear. Do.

120 *Fool.* Mark it, Nuncle.
              Have more than thou showest,
              Speak less than thou knowest,
              Lend less than thou owest,°
              Ride more than thou goest,°
125   Learn more than thou trowest,°
              Set less than thou throwest,°
              Leave thy drink and thy whore,
              And keep in-a-door,
              And thou shalt have more
130   Than two tens to a score.°

Kent. This is nothing, Fool.

102 **an** if   102 **smile ... sits** ingratiate yourself with those in
power   104 **banished** alienated (by making them independent)   107 **Nuncle** (contraction of "mine uncle")   110 **living** property   115 **Brach**
bitch   117 **gall** sore   123 **owest** ownest   124 **goest** walkest   125 **trowest**
knowest   126 **Set ... throwest** bet less than you play for (get odds from
your opponent)   129–30 **have ... score** i.e., come away with more than
you had (two tens, or twenty shillings, make a score, or one pound)

Fool. Then 'tis like the breath of an unfeed° lawyer
—you gave me nothing for't. Can you make no use
of nothing, Nuncle?

Lear. Why, no, boy. Nothing can be made out of *135*
nothing.

Fool. [*To Kent*] Prithee tell him, so much the
rent of his land comes to; he will not believe a
Fool.

Lear. A bitter° Fool. *140*

Fool. Dost thou know the difference, my boy, between
a bitter Fool and a sweet one?

Lear. No, lad; teach me.

Fool.

> That lord that counseled thee
> > To give away thy land, *145*
> Come place him here by me,
> > Do thou for him stand.
> The sweet and bitter fool
> > Will presently appear;
> The one in motley° here, *150*
> > The other found out° there.°

Lear. Dost thou call me fool, boy?

Fool. All thy other titles thou hast given away; that
thou wast born with.

Kent. This is not altogether fool, my lord. *155*

Fool. No, faith; lords and great men will not let me.°
If I had a monopoly° out, they would have part
on't. And ladies too, they will not let me have all
the fool to myself; they'll be snatching. Nuncle,
give me an egg, and I'll give thee two crowns. *160*

---

132 **unfeed** unpaid for   140 **bitter** satirical   150 **motley** the drab costume
of the professional jester   151 **found out** revealed   151 **there** (the Fool
points at Lear, as a fool in the grain)   156 **let me** (have all the folly to myself)   157 **monopoly** (James I gave great scandal by granting to his "snatching" courtiers royal patents to deal exclusively in some commodity)

Lear. What two crowns shall they be?

Fool. Why, after I have cut the egg i' th' middle
and eat up the meat, the two crowns of the egg.
When thou clovest thy crown i' th' middle and
165   gav'st away both parts, thou bor'st thine ass on
thy back o'er the dirt.° Thou hadst little wit in thy
bald crown when thou gav'st thy golden one away.
If I speak like myself° in this, let him be whipped°
that first finds it so.
170   [*Singing*] Fools had ne'er less grace in a year,
           For wise men are grown foppish,
       And know not how their wits to wear,
           Their manners are so apish.°

Lear. When were you wont to be so full of songs,
175   sirrah?

Fool. I have used° it, Nuncle, e'er since thou mad'st
thy daughters thy mothers; for when thou gav'st
them the rod, and put'st down thine own breeches,
[*Singing*] Then they for sudden joy did weep,
180   And I for sorrow sung,
       That such a king should play bo-peep°
           And go the fools among.
Prithee, Nuncle, keep a schoolmaster that can teach
thy Fool to lie. I would fain learn to lie.

185 *Lear.* And° you lie, sirrah, we'll have you whipped.

Fool. I marvel what kin thou and thy daughters are.
They'll have me whipped for speaking true; thou'lt
have me whipped for lying; and sometimes I am
whipped for holding my peace. I had rather be any
190   kind o' thing than a Fool, and yet I would not be

165–66 **bor'st ... dirt** (like the foolish and unnatural countryman in Ae-
sop's fable)   168 **like myself** like a Fool   168 **let him be whipped** i.e., let
the man be whipped for a Fool who thinks my true saying to be foolish
170–73 **Fools ... apish** i.e., fools were never in less favor than now, and
the reason is that wise men, turning foolish, and not knowing how to use
their intelligence, imitate the professional fools and so make them unnecessary   176 **used** practiced   181 **play bo-peep** (1) act like a child (2)
blind himself   185 **And** if

thee, Nuncle: thou hast pared thy wit o' both sides
and left nothing i' th' middle. Here comes one o'
the parings.

Enter Goneril.

Lear. How now, daughter? What makes that frontlet°
on? Methinks you are too much of late i' th'   *195*
frown.

Fool. Thou wast a pretty fellow when thou hadst no
need to care for her frowning. Now thou art an O
without a figure.° I am better than thou art now: I
am a Fool, thou art nothing. [*To Goneril.*] Yes,   *200*
forsooth, I will hold my tongue. So your face bids
me, though you say nothing. Mum, mum,
　　He that keeps nor crust nor crum,°
　　Weary of all, shall want° some.

[*Pointing to Lear*] That's a shealed peascod.°   *205*

Goneril. Not only, sir, this your all-licensed° Fool,
But other° of your insolent retinue
Do hourly carp and quarrel, breaking forth
In rank° and not-to-be-endurèd riots. Sir,
I had thought by making this well known unto you   *210*
To have found a safe° redress, but now grow
　　fearful,
By what yourself too late° have spoke and done,
That you protect this course, and put it on
By your allowance;° which if you should, the fault
Would not 'scape censure, nor the redresses sleep,°   *215*
Which, in the tender of° a wholesome weal,°
Might in their working do you that offense,
Which else were shame, that then necessity
Will call discreet proceeding.°

194 **frontlet** frown (lit., ornamental band)   199 **figure** digit, to give value to
the cipher (Lear is a nought)   203 **crum** soft bread inside the loaf   204 **want**
lack   205 **shealed peascod** empty pea pod   206 **all-licensed** privileged
to take any liberties   207 **other** others   209 **rank** gross   211 **safe** sure
212 **too late** lately   213–14 **put . . . allowance** promote it by your approval
214 **allowance** approval   215 **redresses sleep** correction fail to follow
216 **tender of** desire for   216 **weal** state   217–19 **Might . . . proceeding** as I
apply it, the correction might humiliate you; but the need to take action can-
cels what would otherwise be unfilial conduct in me

220 *Fool.* For you know, Nuncle,
       The hedge-sparrow fed the cuckoo° so long
       That it had it head bit off by it° young.
    So out went the candle, and we were left darkling.°

Lear. Are you our daughter?

225 *Goneril.* Come, sir,
       I would you would make use of your good wisdom
       Whereof I know you are fraught° and put away
       These dispositions° which of late transport you
       From what you rightly are.

230 *Fool.* May not an ass know when the cart draws the
    horse? Whoop, Jug,° I love thee!

Lear. Does any here know me? This is not Lear.
       Does Lear walk thus? Speak thus? Where are his
       eyes?
       Either his notion° weakens, or his discernings°
235   Are lethargied°—Ha! Waking? 'Tis not so.
       Who is it that can tell me who I am?

Fool. Lear's shadow.

Lear. I would learn that; for, by the marks of sover-
       eignty,° knowledge, and reason, I should be false°
240   persuaded I had daughters.

Fool. Which° they will make an obedient father.

Lear. Your name, fair gentlewoman?

Goneril. This admiration,° sir, is much o' th' savor°
       Of other your° new pranks. I do beseech you
245   To understand my purposes aright.
       As you are old and reverend, should be wise.
       Here do you keep a hundred knights and squires,

221 **cuckoo** (who lays its eggs in the nests of other birds)   222 **it** its
223 **darkling** in the dark   227 **fraught** endowed   228 **dispositions** moods
231 **Jug** Joan (? a quotation from a popular song)   234 **notion** understanding   234 **discernings** faculties   235 **lethargied** paralyzed   238–39 **marks
of sovereignty** i.e., tokens that Lear is king, and hence father to his daughters
239 **false** falsely   241 **Which** whom (Lear)   243 **admiration** (affected)
wonderment   243 **is much o' th' savor** smacks much   244 **other your** others of your

Men so disordered, so deboshed,° and bold,
That this our court, infected with their manners,
Shows° like a riotous inn. Epicurism° and lust   250
Makes it more like a tavern or a brothel
Than a graced° palace. The shame itself doth speak
For instant remedy. Be then desired°
By her, that else will take the thing she begs,
A little to disquantity your train,°   255
And the remainders° that shall still depend,°
To be such men as may besort° your age,
Which know themselves, and you.

Lear.   Darkness and devils!
Saddle my horses; call my train together.
Degenerate° bastard, I'll not trouble thee: 260
Yet have I left a daughter.

Goneril. You strike my people, and your disordered
     rabble
Make servants of their betters.

Enter Albany.

Lear. Woe, that too late repents. O, sir, are you
     come?
Is it your will? Speak, sir. Prepare my horses. 265
Ingratitude! thou marble-hearted fiend,
More hideous when thou show'st thee in a child
Than the sea-monster.

Albany.   Pray, sir, be patient.

Lear. Detested kite,° thou liest.
My train are men of choice and rarest parts,°   270
That all particulars of duty know,
And, in the most exact regard,° support
The worships° of their name. O most small fault,

248 **deboshed** debauched 250 **Shows** appears 250 **Epicurism** riotous
living 252 **graced** dignified 253 **desired** requested 255 **disquantity
your train** reduce the number of your dependents 256 **remainders** those
who remain 256 **depend** attend on you 257 **besort** befit 260 **Degenerate** unnatural 269 **kite** scavenging bird of prey 270 **parts** accomplish-
ments 272 **exact regard** strict attention to detail 273 **worships** honor

How ugly didst thou in Cordelia show!
Which, like an engine,° wrenched my frame of
275   nature
From the fixed place;° drew from my heart all love,
And added to the gall.° O Lear, Lear, Lear!
Beat at this gate that let thy folly in [*Striking
his head.*]
And thy dear judgment out. Go, go, my people.

280 *Albany.* My lord, I am guiltless, as I am ignorant
Of what hath moved you.

Lear.   It may be so, my lord.
Hear, Nature, hear; dear Goddess, hear:
Suspend thy purpose if thou didst intend
To make this creature fruitful.
285 Into her womb convey sterility,
Dry up in her the organs of increase,°
And from her derogate° body never spring
A babe to honor her. If she must teem,°
Create her child of spleen,° that it may live
290 And be a thwart disnatured° torment to her.
Let it stamp wrinkles in her brow of youth,
With cadent° tears fret° channels in her cheeks,
Turn all her mother's pains and benefits°
To laughter and contempt, that she may feel
295 How sharper than a serpent's tooth it is
To have a thankless child. Away, away!   *Exit.*

Albany. Now, gods that we adore, whereof comes
this?

Goneril. Never afflict yourself to know the cause,
But let his disposition° have that scope
300 As° dotage gives it.

                      Enter Lear.

Lear. What, fifty of my followers at a clap?°

275 **engine** destructive contrivance   274–76 **wrenched ... place** i.e., disordered my natural self   277 **gall** bitterness   286 **increase** childbearing 287 **derogate** degraded   288 **teem** conceive   289 **spleen** ill humor   290 **thwart disnatured** perverse unnatural   292 **cadent** falling   292 **fret** wear 293 **benefits** the mother's beneficent care of her child   299 **disposition** mood 300 **As** that   *301* **at a clap** at one stroke

Within a fortnight?

Albany.   What's the matter, sir?

Lear. I'll tell thee. [*To Goneril*] Life and death,
　　I am ashamed
　　That thou hast power to shake my manhood°
　　　　thus!
　　That these hot tears, which break from me
　　　　perforce,°   *305*
　　Should make thee worth them. Blasts and fogs
　　　　upon thee!
　　Th' untented woundings° of a father's curse
　　Pierce every sense about thee! Old fond° eyes,
　　Beweep° this cause again, I'll pluck ye out
　　And cast you, with the waters that you loose,°   *310*
　　To temper° clay. Yea, is it come to this?
　　Ha! Let it be so. I have another daughter,
　　Who I am sure is kind and comfortable.°
　　When she shall hear this of thee, with her nails
　　She'll flay thy wolvish visage. Thou shalt find   *315*
　　That I'll resume the shape° which thou dost think
　　I have cast off for ever.
　　　　　　　　　　　Exit [*Lear with Kent and Attendants*].

Goneril.   Do you mark that?

Albany. I cannot be so partial, Goneril,
　　To the great love I bear you°──

Goneril. Pray you, content. What, Oswald, ho!   *320*
　　[*To the Fool*] You, sir, more knave than fool,
　　after your master!

Fool. Nuncle Lear, Nuncle Lear, tarry. Take the Fool°
　　with thee.

---

304 **shake my manhood** i.e., with tears   305 **perforce** involuntarily, against
my will   307 **untented woundings** wounds too deep to be probed with a
tent (a roll of lint)   308 **fond** foolish   309 **Beweep** if you weep over
310 **loose** (1) let loose (2) lose, as of no avail   311 **temper** mix with
and soften   313 **comfortable** ready to comfort   316 **shape** i.e., kingly role
318–19 **I cannot … you** i.e., even though my love inclines me to
you, I must protest   322 **Fool** (1) the Fool himself (2) the epithet or
character of "fool"

                    A fox, when one has caught her,
325   And such a daughter,
                    Should sure to the slaughter,
                    If my cap would buy a halter.°
                    So the Fool follows after.°   *Exit.*

Goneril. This man hath had good counsel. A hundred
        knights!
330   'Tis politic° and safe to let him keep
            At point° a hundred knights: yes, that on every
                dream,
            Each buzz,° each fancy, each complaint, dislike,
            He may enguard° his dotage with their pow'rs
            And hold our lives in mercy.° Oswald, I say!

Albany. Well, you may fear too far.

335 *Goneril.*   Safer than trust too far.
            Let me still take away the harms I fear,
            Not fear still to be taken.° I know his heart.
            What he hath uttered I have writ my sister.
            If she sustain him and his hundred knights,
            When I have showed th' unfitness——
                            Enter Oswald.
340   How now, Oswald?
            What, have you writ that letter to my sister?

Oswald. Ay, madam.

Goneril. Take you some company,° and away to
        horse.
            Inform her full of my particular° fear,
345   And thereto add such reasons of your own
            As may compact° it more. Get you gone,
            And hasten your return. [*Exit Oswald.*] No, no,
                my lord,
            This milky gentleness and course° of yours,
            Though I condemn not,° yet under pardon,

───
327–28 **halter, after** pronounced "hauter," "auter"   330 **politic** good policy
331 **At point** armed 332 **buzz** rumor 333 **enguard** protect 334 **in
mercy** at his mercy 337 **Not … taken** rather than remain fearful of being
overtaken by them 343 **company** escort 344 **particular** own 346 **compact** strengthen 348 **milky … course** mild and gentle way (hendiadys) 349 **condemn not** condemn it not

You are much more attasked° for want of wisdom   350
Than praised for harmful mildness.°

Albany. How far your eyes may pierce I cannot tell;
      Striving to better, oft we mar what's well.

Goneril. Nay then——

Albany. Well, well, th' event.°   *Exeunt.* 355

            Scene 5.   [*Court before the same.*]

            Enter Lear, Kent, and Fool.

Lear. Go you before to Gloucester with these letters.
      Acquaint my daughter no further with anything
      you know than comes from her demand out of
      the letter.° If your diligence be not speedy, I shall
      be there afore you.   5

Kent. I will not sleep, my lord, till I have delivered
      your letter.   *Exit.*

Fool. If a man's brains were in's heels, were't° not in
      danger of kibes?°

Lear. Ay, boy.   10

Fool. Then I prithee be merry. Thy wit shall not go
      slipshod.°

Lear. Ha, ha, ha.

Fool. Shalt° see thy other daughter will use thee
      kindly;° for though she's as like this as a crab's°   15
      like an apple, yet I can tell what I can tell.

350 **attasked** taken to task, blamed   351 **harmful mildness** dangerous in-
dulgence   355 **th' event** i.e., we'll see what happens   1.5.3–4 **than ...
letter** than her reading of the letter brings her to ask   8 **were't** i.e., the
brains   9 **kibes** chilblains   11–12 **Thy ... slipshod** your brains shall not
go in slippers (because you have no brains to be protected from chilblains)   14 **Shalt** thou shalt   15 **kindly** (1) affectionately (2) after her kind
or nature   15 **crab** crab apple

Lear. Why, what canst thou tell, my boy?

Fool. She will taste as like this as a crab does to a
crab. Thou canst tell why one's nose stands i' th'
20   middle on's° face?

Lear. No.

Fool. Why, to keep one's eyes of° either side's nose,
that what a man cannot smell out, he may spy
into.

25 *Lear.* I did her wrong.

Fool. Canst tell how an oyster makes his shell?

Lear. No.

Fool. Nor I neither; but I can tell why a snail has a
house.

30 *Lear.* Why?

Fool. Why, to put 's head in; not to give it away to
his daughters, and leave his horns° without a case.

Lear. I will forget my nature.° So kind a father! Be
my horses ready?

35 *Fool.* Thy asses are gone about 'em. The reason why
the seven stars° are no moe° than seven is a pretty°
reason.

Lear. Because they are not eight.

Fool. Yes indeed. Thou wouldst make a good Fool.

40 *Lear.* To take't again perforce!° Monster ingratitude!

Fool. If thou wert my Fool, Nuncle, I'd have thee
beaten for being old before thy time.

Lear. How's that?

Fool. Thou shouldst not have been old till thou hadst
45   been wise.

---

20 **on's** of his   22 **of** on   32 **horns** (1) snail's horns (2) cuckold's horns
33 **nature** paternal instincts   36 **seven stars** the Pleiades   36 **moe** more
36 **pretty** apt   40 **To ... perforce** (1) of Goneril, who has forcibly taken
away Lear's privileges; or (2) of Lear, who meditates a forcible resumption
of authority

Lear. O, let me not be mad, not mad, sweet heaven!
   Keep me in temper;° I would not be mad!

            [*Enter Gentleman.*]

   How now, are the horses ready?

Gentleman. Ready, my lord.

Lear. Come, boy.   50

Fool. She that's a maid now, and laughs at my
         departure,
   Shall not be a maid long, unless things be cut
      shorter.°   *Exeunt*

___

47 **in temper** sane   51–52 **She . . . shorter** the maid who laughs, missing
the tragic implications of this quarrel, will not have sense enough to preserve her virginity ("things" = penises)

ACT 2

Scene 1. [*The Earl of Gloucester's castle.*]

Enter Edmund and Curan, severally.°

Edmund. Save° thee, Curan.

Curan. And you, sir. I have been with your father,
and given him notice that the Duke of Cornwall
and Regan his duchess will be here with him this
5   night.

Edmund. How comes that?

Curan. Nay, I know not. You have heard of the news
abroad? I mean the whispered ones, for they are yet
but ear-kissing arguments.°

10 *Edmund.* Not I. Pray you, what are they?

Curan. Have you heard of no likely° wars toward,°
'twixt the Dukes of Cornwall and Albany?

Edmund. Not a word.

Curan. You may do, then, in time. Fare you well,
15   sir.   *Exit.*

Edmund. The Duke be here tonight? The better!°
    best!

2.1.1 s.d. **severally** separately (from different entrances on stage)   **1 Save**
God save   **9 ear-kissing arguments** subjects whispered in the ear   **11 likely**
probable   11 **toward** impending   16 **The better** so much the better

This weaves itself perforce° into my business.
My father hath set guard to take my brother,
And I have one thing of a queasy question°
Which I must act. Briefness° and Fortune, work!　　20
Brother, a word; descend. Brother, I say!
　　　　　　　Enter Edgar.
My father watches. O sir, fly this place.
Intelligence° is given where you are hid.
You have now the good advantage of the night.
Have you not spoken 'gainst the Duke of Cornwall?　25
He's coming hither, now i' th' night, i' th' haste,°
And Regan with him. Have you nothing said
Upon his party° 'gainst the Duke of Albany?
Advise yourself.°

Edgar.　　　　　　　I am sure on't,° not a word.

Edmund. I hear my father coming. Pardon me:　　30
In cunning° I must draw my sword upon you.
Draw, seem to defend yourself; now quit you° well.
Yield! Come before my father! Light ho, here!
Fly, brother. Torches, torches!—So farewell.
　　　　　　　　　　　　Exit Edgar.
Some blood drawn on me would beget opinion°　　35
　　　　　　　　[*Wounds his arm*]
Of my more fierce endeavor. I have seen drunkards
Do more than this in sport. Father, father!
Stop, stop! No help?
　Enter Gloucester, and Servants with torches.

Gloucester. Now, Edmund, where's the villain?

Edmund. Here stood he in the dark, his sharp sword
　　out,　　　　　　　　　　　　　　　　　40
Mumbling of wicked charms, conjuring the moon
To stand auspicious mistress.

Gloucester.　　　　　　　But where is he?

---

17 perforce necessarily　**19 of a queasy question** that requires delicate handling (to be "queasy" is to be on the point of vomiting)　**20 Briefness** speed　**23 Intelligence** information　**26 i' th' haste** in great haste　**28 Upon his party** censuring his enmity　**29 Advise yourself** reflect　**29 on't** of it　**31 In cunning** as a pretense　**32 quit you** acquit yourself　**35 beget opinion** create the impression

Edmund. Look, sir, I bleed.

Gloucester.   Where is the villain, Edmund?

Edmund. Fled this way, sir, when by no means he
     could——

Gloucester. Pursue him, ho! Go after.
                     [*Exeunt some Servants.*]

45   By no means what?

Edmund. Persuade me to the murder of your lordship;
     But that I told him the revenging gods
     'Gainst parricides did all the thunder bend;°
     Spoke with how manifold and strong a bond
50   The child was bound to th' father. Sir, in fine,°
     Seeing how loathly opposite° I stood
     To his unnatural purpose, in fell° motion°
     With his preparèd sword he charges home
     My unprovided° body, latched° mine arm;
55   But when he saw my best alarumed° spirits
     Bold in the quarrel's right,° roused to th'
        encounter,
     Or whether gasted° by the noise I made,
     Full suddenly he fled.

Gloucester.   Let him fly far.
     Not in this land shall he remain uncaught;
60   And found—dispatch.° The noble Duke my master,
     My worthy arch° and patron, comes tonight.
     By his authority I will proclaim it,
     That he which finds him shall deserve our thanks,
     Bringing the murderous coward to the stake.
65   He that conceals him, death.°

Edmund. When I dissuaded him from his intent,
     And found him pight° to do it, with curst° speech
     I threatened to discover° him. He replied,

48 **bend** aim   50 **in fine** finally   51 **loathly opposite** bitterly opposed
52 **fell** deadly   52 **motion** thrust (a term from fencing)   54 **unprovided** unprotected   54 **latched** wounded (lanced)   55 **best alarumed** wholly aroused
56 **Bold . . . right** confident in the rightness of my cause   57 **gasted** struck
aghast   60 **dispatch** i.e., he will be killed   61 **arch** chief   65 **death** (the
same elliptical form that characterizes "dispatch," 1.60)   67 **pight** determined
67 **curst** angry   68 **discover** expose

"Thou unpossessing° bastard, dost thou think,
If I would stand against thee, would the reposal°   70
Of any trust, virtue, or worth in thee
Make thy words faithed?° No. What I should
   deny—
As this I would, ay, though thou didst produce
My very character°—I'd turn it all
To thy suggestion,° plot, and damnèd practice.°   75
And thou must make a dullard of the world,°
If they not thought° the profits of my death
Were very pregnant° and potential spirits°
To make thee seek it."

Gloucester.   O strange and fastened° villain!
Would he deny his letter, said he? I never got° him.   80

                              Tucket° within.

Hark, the Duke's trumpets. I know not why he
   comes.
All ports° I'll bar; the villain shall not 'scape;
The Duke must grant me that. Besides, his picture I
will send far and near, that all the kingdom
May have due note of him; and of my land,   85
Loyal and natural° boy, I'll work the means
To make thee capable.°

              Enter Cornwall, Regan, and Attendants.

Cornwall. How now, my noble friend! Since I came
   hither,
Which I can call but now, I have heard strange
   news.

Regan. If it be true, all vengeance comes too short   90
Which can pursue th' offender. How dost, my lord?

Gloucester. O madam, my old heart is cracked, it's
   cracked.

---

69 **unpossessing** beggarly (landless)   70 **reposal** placing   72 **faithed** believed   74 **character** handwriting   75 **suggestion** instigation   75 **practice** device   76 **make ... world** think everyone stupid   77 **not thought**
did not think   78 **pregnant** teeming with incitement   78 **potential spirits**
powerful evil spirits   79 **fastened** hardened   80 **got** begot   80 s.d. **Tucket**
(Cornwall's special trumpet call)   82 **ports** exits, of whatever sort
86 **natural** (1) kind (filial) (2) illegitimate   87 **capable** able to inherit

Regan. What, did my father's godson seek your life?
  He whom my father named, your Edgar?

95 *Gloucester.* O lady, lady, shame would have it hid.

Regan. Was he not companion with the riotous knights
  That tended upon my father?

Gloucester. I know not, madam. 'Tis too bad, too bad.

Edmund. Yes, madam, he was of that consort.°

100 *Regan.* No marvel then, though he were ill affected.°
  'Tis they have put° him on the old man's death,
  To have th' expense and waste° of his revenues.
  I have this present evening from my sister
  Been well informed of them, and with such cautions
105 That, if they come to sojourn at my house,
  I'll not be there.

Cornwall.   Nor I, assure thee, Regan.
  Edmund, I hear that you have shown your father
  A childlike° office.

Edmund. It was my duty, sir.

110 *Gloucester.* He did bewray his practice,° and received
  This hurt you see, striving to apprehend him.

Cornwall. Is he pursued?

Gloucester.   Ay, my good lord.

Cornwall. If he be taken, he shall never more
  Be feared of doing° harm. Make your own purpose,
115 How in my strength you please.° For you, Edmund,
  Whose virtue and obedience° doth this instant
  So much commend itself, you shall be ours.
  Natures of such deep trust we shall much need;
  You we first seize on.

Edmund.   I shall serve you, sir,
  Truly, however else.

120 *Gloucester.*   For him I thank your Grace.

99 **consort** company   100 **ill affected** disposed to evil   101 **put** set   102 **expense and waste** squandering   108 **childlike** filial   110 **bewray his practice** disclose his plot   114 **of doing** because he might do   114–15 **Make ... please** use my power freely, in carrying out your plans for his capture   116 **virtue and obedience** virtuous obedience

Cornwall. You know not why we came to visit you?

Regan. Thus out of season, threading dark-eyed night.
    Occasions, noble Gloucester, of some prize,°
    Wherein we must have use of your advice.
    Our father he hath writ, so hath our sister,   125
    Of differences,° which° I best thought it fit
    To answer from° our home. The several
        messengers
    From hence attend dispatch.° Our good old friend,
    Lay comforts to your bosom,° and bestow
    Your needful° counsel to our businesses,   130
    Which craves the instant use.°

Gloucester.   I serve you, madam.
    Your Graces are right welcome.

                                   Exeunt. Flourish.

                    Scene 2.   [*Before Gloucester's castle.*]

                    Enter Kent and Oswald, severally.

Oswald. Good dawning° to thee, friend. Art of this
    house?°

Kent. Ay.

Oswald. Where may we set our horses?

Kent. I' th' mire.   5

Oswald. Prithee, if thou lov'st me, tell me.

Kent. I love thee not.

122 **prize** importance   125 **differences** quarrels   125 **which** (referring not
to "differences," but to the letter Lear has written)   126 **from** away
from·   127 **attend dispatch** are waiting to be sent off   128 **Lay . . . bosom**
console yourself (about Edgar's supposed treason)   129 **needful** needed
131 **craves the instant use** demands immediate transaction   2.2.1 **dawning** (dawn is impending, but not yet arrived)   1–2 **Art of this house** i.e., do
you live here

Oswald. Why then, I care not for thee.

10 *Kent.* If I had thee in Lipsbury Pinfold,° I would make thee care for me.

Oswald. Why dost thou use me thus? I know thee not.

Kent. Fellow, I know thee.

Oswald. What dost thou know me for?

Kent. A knave, a rascal, an eater of broken meats;°
15 a base, proud, shallow, beggarly, three-suited,°
hundred-pound,° filthy worsted-stocking° knave; a
lily-livered, action-taking,° whoreson, glass-gazing,° superserviceable,° finical° rogue; one-trunk-
inheriting° slave; one that wouldst be a bawd in
20 way of good service,° and art nothing but the com-
position° of a knave, beggar, coward, pander, and
the son and heir of a mongrel bitch; one whom I
will beat into clamorous whining if thou deniest the
least syllable of thy addition.°

25 *Oswald.* Why, what a monstrous fellow art thou, thus
to rail on one that is neither known of thee nor
knows thee!

Kent. What a brazen-faced varlet art thou to deny
thou knowest me! Is it two days since I
30 tripped up thy heels and beat thee before the
King? [*Drawing his sword*] Draw, you rogue,
for though it be night, yet the moon shines. I'll
make a sop o' th' moonshine° of you. You whoreson cullionly barbermonger,° draw!

9 Lipsbury Pinfold a pound or pen in which strayed animals are enclosed
("Lipsbury" may denote a particular place, or may be slang for "between my
teeth")   **14 broken meats** scraps of food   **15 three-suited** (the wardrobe per-
mitted to a servant or "knave")   **16 hundred-pound** (the extent of Oswald's
wealth, and thus a sneer at his aspiring to gentility)   **16 worsted-stocking**
(worn by servants)   **17 action-taking** one who refuses a fight and goes to law
instead   **17–18 glass-gazing** conceited   **18 superserviceable** sycophantic,
serving without principle.   **18 finical** overfastidious   **18–19 one-trunk-
inheriting** possessing only a trunkful of goods   **19–20 bawd . . . service** pimp,
to please his master   **20–21 composition** compound   **24 addition** titles
33 sop o' th' moonshine i.e., Oswald will admit the moonlight, and so sop it
up, through the open wounds Kent is preparing to give him   **34 cullionly barbermonger** base patron of hairdressers (effeminate man)

Oswald. Away, I have nothing to do with thee.   35

Kent. Draw, you rascal. You come with letters
against the King, and take Vanity the puppet's° part
against the royalty of her father. Draw, you rogue,
or I'll so carbonado° your shanks. Draw, you rascal. Come your ways!°   40

Oswald. Help, ho! Murder! Help!

Kent. Strike, you slave! Stand, rogue! Stand, you neat°
slave! Strike! [*Beating him*]

Oswald. Help, ho! Murder, murder!

  *Enter Edmund, with his rapier drawn, Cornwall,
    Regan, Gloucester, Servants.*

Edmund. How now? What's the matter? Part!   45

Kent. With you,° goodman boy,° if you please! Come,
I'll flesh° ye, come on, young master.

Gloucester. Weapons? Arms? What's the matter here?

Cornwall. Keep peace, upon your lives.
He dies that strikes again. What is the matter?   50

Regan. The messengers from our sister and the King.

Cornwall. What is your difference?° Speak.

Oswald. I am scarce in breath, my lord.

Kent. No marvel, you have so bestirred° your valor.
You cowardly rascal, nature disclaims in thee.° A   55
tailor made thee.°

Cornwall. Thou art a strange fellow. A tailor make a
man?

Kent. A tailor, sir. A stonecutter or a painter could

37 **Vanity the puppet's** Goneril, here identified with one of the personified
characters in the morality plays, which were sometimes put on as puppet
shows   39 **carbonado** cut across, like a piece of meat before cooking
40 **Come your ways** get along   42 **neat** (1) foppish (2) unmixed, as in "neat
wine"   46 **With you** i.e., the quarrel is with you   46 **goodman boy** young
man (peasants are "goodmen"; "boy" is a term of contempt)   47 **flesh** intro-
duce to blood (term from hunting)   52 **difference** quarrel   54 **bestirred**
exercised   55 **nature disclaims in thee** nature renounces any part in you
55–56 **A tailor made thee** (from the proverb "The tailor makes the man")

60 not have made him so ill, though they had been
    but two years o' th' trade.

Cornwall. Speak yet, how grew your quarrel?

Oswald. This ancient ruffian, sir, whose life I have
    spared at suit of° his gray beard——

65 *Kent.* Thou whoreson zed,° thou unnecessary letter!
    My lord, if you will give me leave, I will tread this
    unbolted° villain into mortar and daub the wall of
    a jakes° with him. Spare my gray beard, you wag-
    tail!°

70 *Cornwall.* Peace, sirrah!
    You beastly° knave, know you no reverence?

Kent. Yes, sir, but anger hath a privilege.

Cornwall. Why art thou angry?

Kent. That such a slave as this should wear a sword,
    Who wears no honesty. Such smiling rogues as
75   these,
    Like rats, oft bite the holy cords° atwain
    Which are too intrince° t' unloose; smooth°
        every passion
    That in the natures of their lords rebel,
    Being oil to fire, snow to the colder moods;
80 Renege,° affirm, and turn their halcyon beaks°
    With every gale and vary° of their masters,
    Knowing naught, like dogs, but following.
    A plague upon your epileptic° visage!
    Smile you° my speeches, as I were a fool?

64 **at suit of** out of pity for   65 **zed** the letter Z, generally omitted in contemporary dictionaries   67 **unbolted** unsifted, i.e., altogether a villain
68 **jakes** privy   68–69 **wagtail** a bird that bobs its tail up and down, and
thus suggests obsequiousness   71 **beastly** irrational   76 **holy cords** sacred
bonds of affection (as between husbands and wives, parents and children)   77 **intrince** entangled, intricate   77 **smooth** appease   80 **Renege**
deny   80 **halcyon beaks** (the halcyon or kingfisher serves here as a type of
the opportunist because, when hung up by the tail or neck, it was supposed
to turn with the wind, like a weathervane)   81 **gale and vary** varying
gale (hendiadys)   83 **epileptic** distorted by grinning   84 **Smile you** do you
smile at

Goose, if I had you upon Sarum Plain,°   *85*
I'd drive ye cackling home to Camelot.°

Cornwall. What, art thou mad, old fellow?

Gloucester. How fell you out? Say that.

Kent. No contraries° hold more antipathy
Than I and such a knave.   *90*

Cornwall. Why dost thou call him knave? What is his fault?

Kent. His countenance likes° me not.

Cornwall. No more perchance does mine, nor his, nor hers.

Kent. Sir, 'tis my occupation to be plain:
I have seen better faces in my time   *95*
Than stands on any shoulder that I see
Before me at this instant.

Cornwall.   This is some fellow
Who, having been praised for bluntness, doth affect
A saucy roughness, and constrains the garb
Quite from his nature.° He cannot flatter, he;   *100*
An honest mind and plain, he must speak truth.
And° they will take it, so; if not, he's plain.
These kind of knaves I know, which in this plainness
Harbor more craft and more corrupter ends
Than twenty silly-ducking observants°   *105*
That stretch their duties nicely.°

Kent. Sir, in good faith, in sincere verity,
Under th' allowance° of your great aspect,°
Whose influence,° like the wreath of radiant fire

---

85 **Sarum Plain** Salisbury Plain   86 **Camelot** the residence of King Arthur (presumably a particular point, now lost, is intended here)   89 **contraries** opposites   92 **likes** pleases   99–100 **constrains ... nature** forces the manner of candid speech to be a cloak, not for candor but for craft   102 **And** if   105 **silly-ducking observants** ridiculously obsequious attendants   106 **nicely** punctiliously   08 **allowance** approval   108 **aspect** (1) appearance (2) position of the heavenly bodies   109 **influence** astrological power

On flick'ring Phoebus' front°——

110 *Cornwall.*   What mean'st by this?

Kent. To go out of my dialect,° which you discommend
    so much. I know, sir, I am no flatterer. He° that
    beguiled you in a plain accent was a plain knave,
    which, for my part, I will not be, though I should
115   win your displeasure to entreat me to't.°

Cornwall. What was th' offense you gave him?

Oswald. I never gave him any.
    It pleased the King his master very late°
    To strike at me, upon his misconstruction;°
120 When he, compact,° and flattering his displeasure,
    Tripped me behind; being down, insulted, railed,
    And put upon him such a deal of man°
    That worthied him,° got praises of the King
    For him attempting who was self-subdued;°
125 And, in the fleshment° of this dread exploit,
    Drew on me here again.

Kent.   None of these rogues and cowards
    But Ajax is their fool.°

Cornwall.   Fetch forth the stocks!
    You stubborn° ancient knave, you reverent°
       braggart,
    We'll teach you.

Kent.   Sir, I am too old to learn.

---

110 **Phoebus' front** forehead of the sun   111 **dialect** customary manner of
speaking   112 **He** i.e., the sort of candid-crafty man Cornwall has been de-
scribing   114–15 **though . . . to't** even if I were to succeed in bringing
your graceless person ("displeasure" personified, and in lieu of the expected
form, "your grace") to beg me to be a plain knave   118 **very late** recently
119 **misconstruction** misunderstanding   120 **compact** in league with the
king   122 **put . . . man** pretended such manly behavior   123 **worthied
him** made him seem heroic   124 **For . . . self-subdued** for attacking a man
(Oswald) who offered no resistance   125 **fleshment** the bloodthirstiness
excited by his first success or "fleshing"   126–27 **None . . . fool** i.e., cowardly rogues like Oswald always impose on fools like Cornwall (who is
likened to Ajax: [1] the braggart Greek warrior [2] a jakes or privy)
128 **stubborn** rude   128 **reverent** old

Call not your stocks for me, I serve the King,   *130*
On whose employment I was sent to you.
You shall do small respect, show too bold malice
Against the grace and person° of my master,
Stocking his messenger.

Cornwall. Fetch forth the stocks. As I have life and
    honor,   *135*
There shall he sit till noon.

Regan. Till noon? Till night, my lord, and all night
    too.

Kent. Why, madam, if I were your father's dog,
You should not use me so.

Regan.   Sir, being his knave, I will.

Cornwall. This is a fellow of the selfsame color°   *140*
Our sister speaks of. Come, bring away° the stocks.
                                   Stocks brought out.

Gloucester. Let me beseech your Grace not to do so.
His fault is much, and the good King his master
Will check° him for't. Your purposed° low
    correction
Is such as basest and contemnèd'st° wretches   *145*
For pilf'rings and most common trespasses
Are punished with.
The King his master needs must take it ill
That he, so slightly valued in° his messenger,
Should have him thus restrained.

Cornwall.   I'll answer° that.   *150*

Regan. My sister may receive it much more worse,
To have her gentleman abused, assaulted,
For following her affairs. Put in his legs.
                    [*Kent is put in the stocks.*]
Come, my good lord, away!
                    [*Exeunt all but Gloucester and Kent.*]

---

133 **grace and person** i.e., Lear as sovereign and in his personal character
140 **color** kind   141 **away** out   144 **check** correct   144 **purposed** intended   145 **contemnèd'st** most despised   149 **slightly valued in** little
honored in the person of   150 **answer** answer for

Gloucester. I am sorry for thee, friend. 'Tis the Duke's
155   pleasure,
    Whose disposition° all the world well knows
    Will not be rubbed° nor stopped. I'll entreat for
    thee.

Kent. Pray do not, sir. I have watched° and traveled
    hard.
    Some time I shall sleep out, the rest I'll whistle.
160   A good man's fortune may grow out at heels.°
    Give° you good morrow.

Gloucester. The Duke's to blame in this. 'Twill be
    ill taken.°   *Exit.*

Kent. Good King, that must approve° the common
    saw,°
    Thou out of Heaven's benediction com'st
165   To the warm sun.°
    Approach, thou beacon to this under globe,°
    That by thy comfortable° beams I may
    Peruse this letter. Nothing almost sees miracles
    But misery.° I know 'tis from Cordelia,
170   Who hath most fortunately been informed
    Of my obscurèd° course. And shall find time
    From this enormous state, seeking to give
    Losses their remedies.° All weary and o'erwatched,
    Take vantage,° heavy eyes, not to behold
175   This shameful lodging. Fortune, good night;
    Smile once more, turn thy wheel.°

                                  Sleeps.

---

156 **disposition** inclination   157 **rubbed** diverted (metaphor from the game of
bowls)   158 **watched** gone without sleep   160 **A . . . heels** even a good man
may have bad fortune   161 **Give** God give   162 **taken** received   163 **approve** confirm   163 **saw** proverb   164–65 **Thou . . . sun** i.e., Lear goes from
better to worse, from Heaven's blessing or shelter to lack of shelter   166 **bea-
con . . . globe** i.e., the sun, whose rising Kent anticipates   167 **comfortable**
comforting   168–69 **Nothing . . . misery** i.e., true perception belongs only to
the wretched   171 **obscurèd** disguised   171–73 **shall . . . remedies** (a possible reading: Cordelia, away from this monstrous state of things, will find occasion to right the wrongs we suffer)   174 **vantage** advantage (of sleep)
176 **turn thy wheel** i.e., so that Kent, who is at the bottom, may climb upward

[Scene 3.   *A wood.*]

Enter Edgar.

Edgar. I heard myself proclaimed,
    And by the happy° hollow of a tree
    Escaped the hunt. No port is free, no place
    That guard and most unusual vigilance
    Does not attend my taking.° Whiles I may 'scape,   5
    I will preserve myself; and am bethought°
    To take the basest and most poorest shape
    That ever penury, in contempt of man,
    Brought near to beast;° my face I'll grime with filth,
    Blanket° my loins, elf° all my hairs in knots,   10
    And with presented° nakedness outface°
    The winds and persecutions of the sky.
    The country gives me proof° and precedent
    Of Bedlam° beggars, who, with roaring voices,
    Strike° in their numbed and mortified° bare arms   15
    Pins, wooden pricks,° nails, sprigs of rosemary;
    And with this horrible object,° from low° farms,
    Poor pelting° villages, sheepcotes, and mills,
    Sometimes with lunatic bans,° sometime with
        prayers,
    Enforce their charity. Poor Turlygod, Poor Tom,°   20
    That's something yet: Edgar I nothing am.°   *Exit.*

2.3.2 **happy** lucky   5 **attend my taking** watch to capture me   6 **am bethought** have decided   8–9 **penury . . . beast** poverty, to show how con-
temptible man is, reduced to the level of a beast   10 **Blanket** cover only
with a blanket   10 **elf** tangle (into "elflocks," supposed to be caused by
elves)   11 **presented** the show of   11 **outface** brave   13 **proof** example
14 **Bedlam** (see 1.2.r. 146–47)   15 **strike** stick   15 **mortified** not alive to
pain   16 **pricks** skewers   17 **object** spectacle   17 **low** humble   18 **pelting** paltry   19 **bans** curses   20 **Poor . . . Tom** (Edgar recites the names a
Bedlam beggar gives himself)   21 **That's . . . am** there's a chance for me in
that I am no longer known for myself

[Scene 4.   *Before Gloucester's castle. Kent in
the stocks.*]

Enter Lear, Fool, and Gentleman.

Lear. 'Tis strange that they should so depart from
    home,
    And not send back my messenger.

Gentleman.   As I learned,
    The night before there was no purpose° in them
    Of this remove.°

Kent.   Hail to thee, noble master.

5   *Lear.* Ha!
    Mak'st thou this shame thy pastime?°

Kent.   No, my lord.

Fool. Ha, ha, he wears cruel° garters. Horses are tied
    by the heads, dogs and bears by th' neck, monkeys
    by th' loins, and men by th' legs. When a man's over-
10   lusty at legs,° then he wears wooden netherstocks.°

Lear. What's he that hath so much thy place mistook
    To set thee here?

Kent.   It is both he and she,
    Your son and daughter.

Lear. No.

15 *Kent.* Yes.

Lear. No, I say.

Kent. I say yea.

2.4.3 **purpose** intention   4 **remove** removal   6 **Mak'st . . . pastime** i.e.,
are you doing this to amuse yourself   7 **cruel** (1) painful (2) "crewel," a
worsted yarn used in garters   9–10 **overlusty at legs** (1) a vagabond (2) ?
sexually promiscuous   10 **netherstocks** stockings (as opposed to knee
breeches or upperstocks)

Lear. No, no, they would not.

Kent. Yes, they have.

Lear. By Jupiter, I swear no!　　　　　　　　　　　　　　20

Kent. By Juno, I swear ay!

Lear.　　　　　　　　　　They durst not do't;
They could not, would not do't. 'Tis worse than
　　murder
To do upon respect° such violent outrage.
Resolve° me with all modest° haste which way
Thou mightst deserve or they impose this usage,　　　25
Coming from us.

Kent.　　　　　　　　My lord, when at their home
I did commend° your Highness' letters to them,
Ere I was risen from the place that showed
My duty kneeling, came there a reeking post,°
Stewed° in his haste, half breathless, panting forth　　30
From Goneril his mistress salutations,
Delivered letters, spite of intermission,°
Which presently° they read; on° whose contents
They summoned up their meiny,° straight took
　　horse,
Commanded me to follow and attend　　　　　　　　35
The leisure of their answer, gave me cold looks,
And meeting here the other messenger,
Whose welcome I perceived had poisoned mine,
Being the very fellow which of late
Displayed° so saucily against your Highness,　　　　40
Having more man than wit° about me, drew;
He raised° the house, with loud and coward cries.
Your son and daughter found this trespass worth°
The shame which here it suffers.

23 **upon respect** (1) on the respect due to the King (2) deliberately
24 **Resolve** inform　24 **modest** becoming　27 **commend** deliver　29 **reeking post** sweating messenger　30 **stewed** steaming　32 **spite of intermission**
in spite of the interrupting of my business　33 **presently** at once　33 **on** on the
strength of　34 **meiny** retinue　40 **Displayed** showed off　41 **more man
than wit** more manhood than sense　42 **raised** aroused　43 **worth** deserving

45 *Fool.* Winter's not gone yet, if the wild geese fly that
         way.°
                    Fathers that wear rags
                         Do make their children blind,°
                    But fathers that bear bags°
50   Shall see their children kind.
                    Fortune, that arrant whore,
                         Ne'er turns the key° to th' poor.
         But for all this, thou shalt have as many dolors° for
         thy daughters as thou canst tell° in a year.

55 *Lear.* O, how this mother° swells up toward my heart!
         Hysterica passio,° down, thou climbing sorrow,
         Thy element's° below. Where is this daughter?

    Kent. With the Earl, sir, here within.

    Lear.   Follow me not;
         Stay here.   *Exit.*

    Gentleman. Made you no more offense but what you
60   speak of?

    Kent. None.
         How chance° the King comes with so small a
              number?

    Fool. And° thou hadst been set i' th' stocks for that
         question, thou'dst well deserved it.

65 *Kent.* Why, Fool?

    Fool. We'll set thee to school to an ant, to teach thee
         there's no laboring i' th' winter.° All that follow

45–46 **Winter's . . . way** i.e., more trouble is to come, since Cornwall and
Regan act so ("geese" is used contemptuously, as in Kent's quarrel with
Oswald, 2.2. 85–6) 48 **blind** i.e., indifferent   49 **bags** moneybags
52 **turns the key** i.e., opens the door   53 **dolors** (1) sorrows (2) dollars
(English name for Spanish and German coins)   54 **tell** (1) tell about
(2) count   55–56 **mother . . . Hysterica passio** hysteria, causing suffocation or choking   57 **element** proper place   62 **How chance** how does it
happen that   63 **And** if   66–67 **We'll . . . winter** (in the popular fable the
ant, unlike the improvident grasshopper, anticipates the winter when none
can labor by laying up provisions in the summer. Lear, trusting foolishly to
summer days, finds himself unprovided for, and unable to provide, now that
"winter" has come)

their noses are led by their eyes but blind men,
and there's not a nose among twenty but can smell
him that's stinking.° Let go thy hold when a great   70
wheel runs down a hill, lest it break thy neck with
following. But the great one that goes upward,
let him draw thee after. When a wise man gives
thee better counsel, give me mine again. I would
have none but knaves follow it since a Fool gives   75
it.
    That sir, which serves and seeks for gain,
        And follows but for form,°
    Will pack,° when it begins to rain,
        And leave thee in the storm.   80
    But I will tarry; the Fool will stay,
        And let the wise man fly.
    The knave turns Fool that runs away,
        The Fool no knave,° perdy.°

Kent. Where learned you this, Fool?   85

Fool. Not i' th' stocks, fool.

        Enter Lear and Gloucester.

Lear. Deny° to speak with me? They are sick, they
    are weary,
They have traveled all the night? Mere fetches,°
The images° of revolt and flying off!°
Fetch me a better answer.

Gloucester.   My dear lord,   90
You know the fiery quality° of the Duke,
How unremovable and fixed he is
In his own course.

Lear.   Vengeance, plague, death, confusion!
Fiery? What quality? Why, Gloucester, Gloucester,
I'd speak with the Duke of Cornwall and his wife.   95

67–70 **All ... stinking** i.e., all can smell out the decay of Lear's fortunes   78 **form** show   79 **pack** be off   83–84 **The ... knave** i.e., the faith-
less man is the true fool, for wisdom requires fidelity. Lear's Fool, who
remains faithful, is at least no knave   84 **perdy** by God (Fr. *par Dieu*)
87 **Deny** refuse   88 **fetches** subterfuges, acts of tacking (nautical metaphor)
89 **images** exact likenesses   89 **flying off** desertion   91 **quality** temperament.

Gloucester. Well, my good lord, I have informed them so.

Lear. Informed them? Dost thou understand me, man?

Gloucester. Ay, my good lord.

Lear. The King would speak with Cornwall. The dear father

    Would with his daughter speak, commands—tends°

100   —service.

    Are they informed of this? My breath and blood!

    Fiery? The fiery Duke, tell the hot Duke that—

    No, but not yet. May be he is not well.

    Infirmity doth still neglect all office

105   Whereto our health is bound.° We are not ourselves

    When nature, being oppressed, commands the mind

    To suffer with the body. I'll forbear;

    And am fallen out° with my more headier will°

    To take the indisposed and sickly fit

110   For the sound man. [*Looking on Kent*] Death on my state!° Wherefore

    Should he sit here? This act persuades me

    That this remotion° of the Duke and her

    Is practice° only. Give me my servant forth.°

    Go tell the Duke and's wife I'd speak with them!

115   Now, presently!° Bid them come forth and hear me,

    Or at their chamber door I'll beat the drum

    Till it cry sleep to death.°

Gloucester. I would have all well betwixt you.

                                Exit.

---

100 **tends** attends (i.e., awaits); with, possibly, an ironic second meaning, "tenders," or "offers"   105 **Whereto ... bound** duties which we are required to perform, when in health   108 **fallen out** angry   108 **headier will** headlong inclination   110 **state** royal condition   112 **remotion** (1) removal (2) remaining aloof   113 **practice** pretense   113 **forth** i.e., out of the stocks   115 **presently** at once   117 **cry ... death** follow sleep, like a cry or pack of hounds, until it kills it

Lear. O me, my heart, my rising heart! But down!

Fool. Cry to it, Nuncle, as the cockney° did to   *120*
the eels when she put 'em i' th' paste° alive. She
knapped° 'em o' th' coxcombs° with a stick and
cried, "Down, wantons,° down!" 'Twas her brother
that, in pure kindness to his horse, buttered his
hay.°   *125*

Enter Cornwall, Regan, Gloucester, Servants.

Lear. Good morrow to you both.

Cornwall.   Hail to your Grace.

                    Kent here set at liberty.

Regan. I am glad to see your Highness.

Lear. Regan, I think you are. I know what reason
I have to think so. If thou shouldst not be glad,
I would divorce me from thy mother's tomb,   *130*
Sepulchring an adultress.° [*To Kent*] O, are you
    free?
Some other time for that. Beloved Regan,
Thy sister's naught.° O Regan, she hath tied
Sharp-toothed unkindness, like a vulture, here.

                    [*Points to his heart.*]

I can scarce speak to thee. Thou'lt not believe   *135*
With how depraved a quality°—O Regan!

Regan. I pray you, sir, take patience. I have hope
You less know how to value her desert
Than she to scant her duty.°

Lear.   Say? how is that?

---

120 **cockney** Londoner (ignorant city dweller) 121 **paste** pastry pie
122 **knapped** rapped 122 **coxcombs** heads 123 **wantons** i.e., playful
things (with a sexual implication) 125 **buttered his hay** i.e., the city
dweller does from ignorance what the dishonest ostler does from craft:
greases the hay the traveler has paid for, so that the horse will not eat
130–31 **divorce … adultress** i.e., repudiate your dead mother as having
conceived you by another man 133 **naught** wicked 136 **quality** nature
137–39 **I … duty** (despite the double negative, the passage means, "I believe
that you fail to give Goneril her due, rather than that she fails to fulfill her
duty")

140 *Regan.* I cannot think my sister in the least
    Would fail her obligation. If, sir, perchance
    She have restrained the riots of your followers,
    'Tis on such ground, and to such wholesome end,
    As clears her from all blame.

Lear. My curses on her!

145 *Regan.*   O, sir, you are old,
    Nature in you stands on the very verge
    Of his confine.° You should be ruled, and led
    By some discretion that discerns your state
    Better than you yourself.° Therefore I pray you
150   That to our sister you do make return,
    Say you have wronged her.

Lear.   Ask her forgiveness?
    Do you but mark how this becomes the house:°
    "Dear daughter, I confess that I am old.

                        [Kneeling.]

    Age is unnecessary. On my knees I beg
155   That you'll vouchsafe me raiment, bed, and food."

Regan. Good sir, no more. These are unsightly tricks.
    Return you to my sister.

Lear.   *[Rising]* Never, Regan.
    She hath abated° me of half my train,
    Looked black upon me, struck me with her tongue,
160   Most serpentlike, upon the very heart.
    All the stored vengeances of heaven fall
    On her ingrateful top!° Strike her young bones,°
    You taking° airs, with lameness.

Cornwall.   Fie, sir, fie!

Lear. You nimble lightnings, dart your blinding flames
165   Into her scornful eyes! Infect her beauty,

146–47 **Nature ... confine** i.e., you are nearing the end of your life
148–49 **some ... yourself** some discreet person who understands your condition more than you do   152 **becomes the house** suits my royal and paternal position   158 **abated** curtailed   162 **top** head   162 **young bones** (the
reference may be to unborn children, rather than to Goneril herself)
163 **taking** infecting

You fen-sucked° fogs, drawn by the pow'rful sun,
To fall and blister° her pride.

Regan.   O the blest gods!
So will you wish on me when the rash mood is on.

Lear. No, Regan, thou shalt never have my curse.
Thy tender-hefted° nature shall not give   *170*
Thee o'er to harshness. Her eyes are fierce, but thine
Do comfort, and not burn. 'Tis not in thee
To grudge my pleasures, to cut off my train,
To bandy° hasty words, to scant my sizes,°
And, in conclusion, to oppose the bolt°   *175*
Against my coming in. Thou better know'st
The offices of nature, bond of childhood,°
Effects° of courtesy, dues of gratitude.
Thy half o' th' kingdom hast thou not forgot,
Wherein I thee endowed.

Regan.   Good sir, to th' purpose.° *180*

                    Tucket within.

Lear. Who put my man i' th' stocks?

Cornwall.   What trumpet's that?

Regan. I know't—my sister's. This approves° her
  letter,
That she would soon be here.

                Enter Oswald.

                    Is your lady come?

Lear. This is a slave, whose easy borrowed° pride
Dwells in the fickle grace° of her he follows.   *185*
Out, varlet,° from my sight.

Cornwall.   What means your Grace?

166 **fen-sucked** drawn up from swamps by the sun   167 **fall and blister**
fall upon and raise blisters   170 **tender-hefted** gently framed   174 **bandy**
volley (metaphor from tennis)   174 **scant my sizes** reduce my allow-
ances   175 **oppose the bolt** i.e., bar the door   177 **offices ... childhood**
natural duties, a child's duty to its parent   178 **Effects** manifestations
180 **to th' purpose** come to the point   182 **approves** confirms   184 **easy
borrowed** (1) facile and taken from another (2) acquired without anything
to back it up (like money borrowed without security)   185 **grace** favor
186 **varlet** base fellow

Lear. Who stocked my servant? Regan, I have good
hope
     Thou didst not know on't.

                    Enter Goneril.

                    Who comes here? O heavens!
     If you do love old men, if your sweet sway
190 Allow° obedience, if you yourselves are old,
     Make it° your cause. Send down, and take my part.
     [*To Goneril*] Art not ashamed to look upon
          this beard?
     O Regan, will you take her by the hand?

Goneril. Why not by th' hand, sir? How have I
     offended?
195 All's not offense that indiscretion finds°
     And dotage terms so.

Lear.   O sides,° you are too tough!
     Will you yet hold? How came my man i' th' stocks?

Cornwall. I set him there, sir; but his own disorders°
     Deserved much less advancement.°

Lear.   You? Did you?

200 *Regan.* I pray you, father, being weak, seem so.°
     If till the expiration of your month
     You will return and sojourn with my sister,
     Dismissing half your train, come then to me.
     I am now from home, and out of that provision
205 Which shall be needful for your entertainment.°

Lear. Return to her, and fifty men dismissed?
     No, rather I abjure all roofs, and choose
     To wage° against the enmity o' th' air,
     To be a comrade with the wolf and owl,
210 Necessity's sharp pinch.° Return with her?
     Why, the hot-blooded° France, that dowerless
          took

---

190 **Allow** approve of   191 **it** i.e., my cause   195 **finds** judges   196 **sides**
breast   198 **disorders** misconduct   199 **advancement** promotion 200 **seem
so** i.e., act weak   205 **entertainment** maintenance   208 **wage** fight
210 **Necessity's sharp pinch** (a summing up of the hard choice he has just
announced)   211 **hot-blooded** passionate

Our youngest born, I could as well be brought
To knee° his throne, and, squirelike,° pension beg
To keep base life afoot. Return with her?
Persuade me rather to be slave and sumpter°   215
To this detested groom. [*Pointing at Oswald.*]

Goneril.   At your choice, sir.

Lear. I prithee, daughter, do not make me mad.
I will not trouble thee, my child; farewell.
We'll no more meet, no more see one another.
But yet thou art my flesh, my blood, my daughter,   220
Or rather a disease that's in my flesh,
Which I must needs call mine. Thou art a boil,
A plague-sore, or embossèd carbuncle°
In my corrupted blood. But I'll not chide thee.
Let shame come when it will, I do not call it.   225
I do not bid the Thunder-bearer° shoot,
Nor tell tales of thee to high-judging° Jove.
Mend when thou canst, be better at thy leisure,
I can be patient, I can stay with Regan,
I and my hundred knights.

Regan.   Not altogether so.   230
I looked not for you yet, nor am provided
For your fit welcome. Give ear, sir, to my sister,
For those that mingle reason with your passion°
Must be content to think you old, and so—
But she knows what she does.

Lear.   Is this well spoken?   235

Regan. I dare avouch° it, sir. What, fifty followers?
Is it not well? What should you need of more?
Yea, or so many, sith that° both charge° and
    danger
Speak 'gainst so great a number? How in one house

---

213 **knee** kneel before   213 **squirelike** like a retainer   215 **sumpter** pack
horse   223 **embossèd carbuncle** swollen boil   226 **Thunder-bearer** i.e.,
Jupiter   227 **high-judging** (1) supreme (2) judging from heaven   233 **mingle . . . passion** i.e., consider your turbulent behavior coolly and reasonably
236 **avouch** swear by   238 **sith that** since   238 **charge** expense

240   Should many people, under two commands,
       Hold° amity? 'Tis hard, almost impossible.

Goneril. Why might not you, my lord, receive attendance
       From those that she calls servants, or from mine?

Regan. Why not, my lord? If then they chanced to slack° ye,
245   We could control them. If you will come to me
       (For now I spy a danger), I entreat you
       To bring but five-and-twenty. To no more
       Will I give place or notice.°

Lear. I gave you all.

Regan.   And in good time you gave it.

250 *Lear.* Made you my guardians, my depositaries,°
       But kept a reservation° to be followed
       With such a number. What, must I come to you
       With five-and-twenty? Regan, said you so?

Regan. And speak't again, my lord. No more with me.

Lear. Those wicked creatures yet do look well-
255   favored°
       When others are more wicked; not being the worst
       Stands in some rank of praise.° [*To Goneril*] I'll go with thee.
       Thy fifty yet doth double five-and-twenty,
       And thou art twice her love.°

Goneril.   Hear me, my lord.
260   What need you five-and-twenty? ten? or five?
       To follow° in a house where twice so many
       Have a command to tend you?

Regan.   What need one?

Lear. O reason° not the need! Our basest beggars

---

241 **hold** preserve   244 **slack** neglect   248 **notice** recognition   250 **depositaries** trustees   251 **reservation** condition   255 **well-favored** handsome   256–57 **not . . . praise** i.e., that Goneril is not so bad as Regan is one thing in her favor   259 **her love** i.e., as loving as she   261 **follow** attend on you   263 **reason** scrutinize

Are in the poorest thing superfluous.°
Allow not nature more than nature needs,°   265
Man's life is cheap as beast's. Thou art a lady:
If only to go warm were gorgeous,
Why, nature needs not what thou gorgeous wear'st,
Which scarcely keeps thee warm.° But, for true
     need—
You heavens, give me that patience, patience I
     need.   270
You see me here, you gods, a poor old man,
As full of grief as age, wretched in both.
If it be you that stirs these daughters' hearts
Against their father, fool° me not so much
To bear° it tamely; touch me with noble anger,   275
And let not women's weapons, water drops,
Stain my man's cheeks. No, you unnatural hags!
I will have such revenges on you both
That all the world shall—I will do such things—
What they are, yet I know not; but they shall be   280
The terrors of the earth. You think I'll weep.
No, I'll not weep.

                    Storm and tempest.

I have full cause of weeping, but this heart
Shall break into a hundred thousand flaws°
Or ere° I'll weep. O Fool, I shall go mad!   285
       Exeunt Lear, Gloucester, Kent, and Fool.

Cornwall. Let us withdraw, 'twill be a storm.

Regan. This house is little; the old man and's people
Cannot be well bestowed.°

Goneril. 'Tis his own blame; hath° put himself from
     rest°
And must needs taste his folly.   290

---

264 **Are ... superfluous** i.e., have some trifle not absolutely necessary
265 **needs** i.e., to sustain life   267–69 **If ... warm** i.e., if to satisfy the
need for warmth were to be gorgeous, you would not need the clothing you
wear, which is worn more for beauty than warmth   274 **fool** humiliate
275 **To bear** as to make me bear   284 **flaws** (1) pieces (2) cracks (3) gusts
of passion   285 **Or ere** before   288 **bestowed** lodged   289 **hath** he hath
289 **rest** (1) place of residence (2) repose of mind

Regan. For his particular,° I'll receive him gladly,
　　But not one follower.

Goneril. 　　　　　So am I purposed.°
　　Where is my Lord of Gloucester?

Cornwall. Followed the old man forth.

　　　　　　　Enter Gloucester.

　　　　　　　　　　　　　He is returned.

Gloucester. The King is in high rage.

295 　*Cornwall.* 　　　　　Whither is he going?

Gloucester. He calls to horse, but will I know not
　　whither.

Cornwall. 'Tis best to give him way, he leads himself.°

Goneril. My lord, entreat him by no means to stay.

Gloucester. Alack, the night comes on, and the high
　　winds
300 　Do sorely ruffle.° For many miles about
　　There's scarce a bush.

Regan. 　　　　　O, sir, to willful men
　　The injuries that they themselves procure
　　Must be their schoolmasters. Shut up your doors.
　　He is attended with a desperate train,
305 　And what they may incense° him to, being apt
　　To have his ear abused,° wisdom bids fear.

Cornwall. Shut up your doors, my lord; 'tis a wild
　　night.
　　My Regan counsels well. Come out o' th' storm.

　　　　　　　　　　　　　Exeunt.

---

291 **his particular** himself personally　292 **purposed** determined
297 **give . . . himself** let him go; he insists on his own way　300 **ruffle** rage
305 **incense** incite　305–06 **being . . . abused** he being inclined to harken
to bad counsel

ACT 3

Scene 1.   [*A heath.*]

*Storm still.° Enter Kent and a Gentleman
severally.*

Kent. Who's there besides foul weather?

Gentleman. One minded like the weather most
   unquietly.°

Kent. I know you. Where's the King?

Gentleman. Contending with the fretful elements;
   Bids the wind blow the earth into the sea,   5
   Or swell the curlèd waters 'bove the main,°
   That things might change,° or cease; tears his white
      hair,
   Which the impetuous blasts, with eyeless° rage,
   Catch in their fury, and make nothing of;
   Strives in his little world of man° to outscorn   10
   The to-and-fro-conflicting wind and rain.
   This night, wherein the cub-drawn° bear would
      couch,°
   The lion, and the belly-pinchèd° wolf
   Keep their fur dry, unbonneted° he runs,

3.1. s.d. **still** continually   2 **minded . . . unquietly** disturbed in mind, like
the weather   6 **main** land   7 **change** (1) be destroyed (2) be exchanged
(i.e., turned upside down) (3) change for the better   8 **eyeless** (1) blind (2)
invisible   10 **little world of man** (the microcosm, as opposed to the universe or macrocosm, which it copies in little)   12 **cub-drawn** sucked dry
by her cubs, and so ravenously hungry   12 **couch** take shelter in its lair
18 **belly-pinchèd** starved   14 **unbonneted** hatless

67

And bids what will take all.°

15 *Kent.*   But who is with him?

Gentleman. None but the Fool, who labors to outjest
    His heart-struck injuries.

Kent.   Sir, I do know you,
    And dare upon the warrant of my note°
    Commend a dear thing° to you. There is division,
20 Although as yet the face of it is covered
    With mutual cunning, 'twixt Albany and Cornwall;
    Who have—as who have not, that° their great
        stars
    Throned° and set high?—servants, who seem no
        less,°
    Which are to France the spies and speculations
25 Intelligent° of our state. What hath been seen,
    Either in snuffs and packings° of the Dukes,
    Or the hard rein which both of them hath borne°
    Against the old kind King, or something deeper,
    Whereof, perchance, these are but furnishings°—
30 But, true it is, from France there comes a power°
    Into this scattered° kingdom, who already,
    Wise in our negligence, have secret feet
    In some of our best ports, and are at point°
    To show their open banner. Now to you:
35 If on my credit you dare build° so far
    To° make your speed to Dover, you shall find
    Some that will thank you, making° just° report
    Of how unnatural and bemadding° sorrow
    The King hath cause to plain.°
40 I am a gentleman of blood and breeding,°

---

15 **take all** (like the reckless gambler, staking all he has left)   18 **warrant
of my note** strength of what I have taken note (of you)   19 **Commend . . .
thing** entrust important business   22 **that** whom   22–23 **stars/Throned**
destinies / have throned   23 **seem no less** seem to be so   24–25
speculations/Intelligent giving intelligence   26 **snuffs and packings**
quarrels and plots   27 **hard . . . borne** close and cruel control they have exercised   29 **furnishings** excuses   30 **power** army   31 **scattered** dis-
united   33 **at point** ready   35 **If . . . build** if you can trust me, proceed
36 **To** as to   37 **making** for making   37 **just** accurate   38 **bemadding**
maddening   39 **plain** complain of   40 **blood and breeding** noble family

And from some knowledge and assurance° offer
This office° to you.

Gentleman. I will talk further with you.

Kent.   No, do not.
For confirmation that I am much more
Than my out-wall,° open this purse and take   *45*
What it contains. If you shall see Cordelia,
As fear not but you shall, show her this ring,
And she will tell you who that fellow° is
That yet you do not know. Fie on this storm!
I will go seek the King.   *50*

Gentleman. Give me your hand. Have you no more to
    say?

Kent. Few words, but, to effect,° more than all yet:
That when we have found the King—in which your
    pain°
That way, I'll this—he that first lights on him,
Holla the other.   *Exeunt [severally].*   *55*

Scene 2.   [*Another part of the heath.*]

Storm still.

Enter Lear and Fool.

Lear. Blow, winds, and crack your cheeks. Rage, blow!
You cataracts and hurricanoes,° spout
Till you have drenched our steeples, drowned the
    cocks.°

41 **knowledge and assurance** sure and trustworthy information   42 **office**
service (i.e., the trip to Dover)   45 **out-wall** superficial appearance   48 **fellow** companion   52 **to effect** in their importance   53 **pain** labor 3.2.2 **hurricanoes** waterspouts   3 **cocks** weathercocks

You sulph'rous and thought-executing° fires,
5   Vaunt-couriers° of oak-cleaving thunderbolts,
Singe my white head. And thou, all-shaking thunder,
Strike flat the thick rotundity° o' th' world,
Crack Nature's molds,° all germains spill° at once,
That makes ingrateful° man.

10   *Fool.* O Nuncle, court holy-water° in a dry house is
better than this rain water out o' door. Good
Nuncle, in; ask thy daughters blessing. Here's a
night pities neither wise man nor fools.

Lear. Rumble thy bellyful. Spit, fire. Spout, rain!
15   Nor rain, wind, thunder, fire are my daughters.
I tax° not you, you elements, with unkindness.
I never gave you kingdom, called you children,
You owe me no subscription.° Then let fall
Your horrible pleasure.° Here I stand your slave,
20   A poor, infirm, weak, and despised old man.
But yet I call you servile ministers,°
That will with two pernicious daughters join
Your high-engendered battles° 'gainst a head
So old and white as this. O, ho! 'tis foul.

25   *Fool.* He that has a house to put 's head in has a good
headpiece.°
                    The codpiece° that will house
                    Before the head has any,
                    The head and he° shall louse:
30   So beggars marry many.°
                    The man that makes his toe

4 **thought-executing** (1) doing execution as quick as thought (2) executing
or carrying out the thought of him who hurls the lightning   5 **Vaunt-
couriers** heralds, scouts who range before the main body of the army   7 **ro-
tundity** i.e., not only the sphere of the globe, but the roundness of gestation
(Delius)   8 **Nature's molds** the molds or forms in which men are made
8 **all germains spill** destroy the basic seeds of life   9 **ingrateful** ungrateful
10 **court holy-water** flattery   16 **tax** accuse   18 **subscription** allegiance,
submission   9 **pleasure** will   21 **ministers** agents   23 **high-engendered
battles** armies formed in the heavens   26 **headpiece** (1) helmet (2) brain
27 **codpiece** penis (lit., padding worn at the crotch of a man's hose)   29 **he**
it   30 **many** i.e., lice   27–30 **The . . . many** i.e., the man who gratifies
his sexual appetites before he has a roof over his head will end up a lousy
beggar

What he his heart should make
Shall of a corn cry woe,
And turn his sleep to wake.°
For there was never yet fair woman but she made   35
mouths in a glass.°

Enter Kent.

Lear. No, I will be the pattern of all patience,
I will say nothing.

Kent. Who's there?

Fool. Marry,° here's grace and a codpiece; that's a   40
wise man and a fool.°

Kent. Alas, sir, are you here? Things that love night
Love not such nights as these. The wrathful skies
Gallow° the very wanderers of the dark
And make them keep° their caves. Since I was man   45
Such sheets of fire, such bursts of horrid° thunder,
Such groans of roaring wind and rain, I never
Remember to have heard. Man's nature cannot
    carry°
Th' affliction nor the fear.

Lear.   Let the great gods
That keep this dreadful pudder° o'er our heads   50
Find out their enemies now.° Tremble, thou wretch,
That hast within thee undivulgèd crimes
Unwhipped of justice. Hide thee, thou bloody hand,
Thou perjured,° and thou simular° of virtue

31–34 **The . . . wake** i.e., the man who, ignoring the fit order of things, elevates what is base above what is noble, will suffer for it as Lear has, in banishing Cordelia and enriching her sisters   35–36 **made mouths in a glass** posed before a mirror (irrelevant nonsense, except that it calls to mind the general theme of vanity and folly)   40 **Marry** by the Virgin Mary   40–41 **here's . . . fool** (Kent's question is answered: The King ["grace"] is here, and the Fool—who customarily wears an exaggerated codpiece. But which is which is left ambiguous, since Lear has previously been called a codpiece)   44 **Gallow** frighten   45 **keep** remain inside   46 **horrid** horrible   48 **carry** endure   50 **pudder** turmoil   51 **Find . . . now** i.e., discover sinners by the terror they reveal   54 **perjured** perjurer   54 **simular** counterfeiter

55   That art incestuous. Caitiff,° to pieces shake,
        That under covert and convenient seeming°
        Has practiced on° man's life. Close° pent-up guilts,
        Rive° your concealing continents° and cry
        These dreadful summoners grace.° I am a man
        More sinned against than sinning.

60 *Kent.*   Alack, bareheaded?
        Gracious my lord,° hard by here is a hovel;
        Some friendship will it lend you 'gainst the
            tempest.
        Repose you there, while I to this hard house
        (More harder than the stones whereof 'tis raised,
65   Which even but now, demanding after° you,
        Denied me to come in) return, and force
        Their scanted° courtesy.

    Lear.   My wits begin to turn.   •
        Come on, my boy. How dost, my boy? Art cold?
        I am cold myself. Where is this straw, my fellow?
70   The art° of our necessities is strange,
        That can make vile things precious. Come, your
            hovel.
        Poor Fool and knave, I have one part in my heart
        That's sorry yet for thee.

    Fool. [*Singing*]
        He that has and a little tiny wit,
75   With heigh-ho, the wind and the rain,
        Must make content with his fortunes fit,°
            Though the rain it raineth every day.

    Lear. True, my good boy. Come, bring us to this hovel.
                                Exit [*with Kent*].

---

55 **Caitiff** wretch   56 **seeming** hypocrisy   57 **practiced on** plotted against
57 **Close** hidden   58 **Rive** split open   58 **continents** containers   58–59 **cry
. . . grace** beg mercy from the vengeful gods (here figured as officers who
summoned a man charged with immorality before the ecclesiastical
court)   61 **Gracious my lord** my gracious lord   65 **demanding after** asking for   67 **scanted** stinted   70 **art** magic powers of the alchemists, who
sought to transmute base metals into precious   76 **Must . . . fit** must
be satisfied with a fortune as tiny as his wit

Fool. This is a brave° night to cool a courtesan. I'll
   speak a prophecy ere I go: 80

   When priests are more in word than matter;
   When brewers mar their malt with water;
   When nobles are their tailors' tutors,
   No heretics burned, but wenches' suitors;°
   When every case in law is right,   85
   No squire in debt nor no poor knight;
   When slanders do not live in tongues;
   Nor cutpurses come not to throngs;
   When usurers tell their gold i' th' field,°
   And bawds and whores do churches build,°   90
   Then shall the realm of Albion°
   Come to great confusion.
   Then comes the time, who lives to see't,
   That going shall be used with feet.°

This prophecy Merlin° shall make, for I live before   95
his time.   *Exit.*

Scene 3. [*Gloucester's castle.*]

Enter Gloucester and Edmund.

Gloucester. Alack, alack, Edmund, I like not this unnatural dealing. When I desired their leave that I
   might pity° him, they took from me the use of mine

79 **brave** fine   81–84 **When . . . suitors** (the first four prophecies are fulfilled already, and hence "confusion" has come to England. The priest does
not suit his action to his words. The brewer adulterates his beer. The nobleman is subservient to his tailor [i.e., cares only for fashion]. Religious
heretics escape, and only those burn [i.e., suffer] who are afflicted with
venereal disease)   89 **tell . . . field** count their money in the open
85–90 **When . . . build** (the last six prophecies, as they are Utopian, are
meant ironically. They will never be fulfilled)   91 **Albion** England
94 **going . . . feet** people will walk on their feet   95 **Merlin** King Arthur's
great magician who, according to Holinshed's **Chronicles,** lived later than
Lear   3.3.3 **pity** show pity to

own house, charged me on pain of perpetual dis-
5   pleasure neither to speak of him, entreat for him,
or any way sustain° him.

Edmund. Most savage and unnatural.

Gloucester. Go to; say you nothing. There is division°
between the Dukes, and a worse° matter than that.
10   I have received a letter this night—'tis dangerous
to be spoken°—I have locked the letter in my
closet.° These injuries the King now bears will be
revenged home;° there is part of a power° already
footed;° we must incline to° the King. I will look°
15   him and privily° relieve him. Go you and maintain
talk with the Duke, that my charity be not of° him
perceived. If he ask for me, I am ill and gone to
bed. If I die for it, as no less is threatened me, the
King my old master must be relieved. There is
20   strange things toward,° Edmund; pray you be careful.   *Exit.*

Edmund. This courtesy forbid° thee shall the Duke
Instantly know, and of that letter too.
This seems a fair deserving,° and must draw me
25   That which my father loses—no less than all.
The younger rises when the old doth fall.

                                              Exit.

3.3.6 **sustain** care for   8 **division** falling out   9 **worse** more serious (i.e.,
the French invasion)   11 **spoken** spoken of   12 **closet** room   13 **home** to
the utmost   13 **power** army   14 **footed** landed   14 **incline to** take the
side of   14 **look** search for   15 **privily** secretly   16 **of** by   20 **toward**
impending   22 **courtesy forbid** kindness forbidden (i.e., to Lear)   24 **fair
deserving** an action deserving reward

Scene 4.   [*The heath. Before a hovel.*]

Enter Lear, Kent, and Fool.

Kent. Here is the place, my lord. Good my lord,
   enter.
  The tyranny of the open night's too rough
  For nature to endure.

                           Storm still.

Lear.   Let me alone.

Kent. Good my lord, enter here.

Lear.   Wilt break my heart?°

Kent. I had rather break mine own. Good my lord,
   enter.   *5*

Lear. Thou think'st 'tis much that this contentious
   storm
  Invades us to the skin: so 'tis to thee;
  But where the greater malady is fixed,°
  The lesser is scarce felt. Thou'dst shun a bear;
  But if thy flight lay toward the roaring sea,   *10*
  Thou'dst meet the bear i' th' mouth.° When the
   mind's free,°
  The body's delicate. The tempest in my mind
  Doth from my senses take all feeling else,
  Save what beats there. Filial ingratitude,
  Is it not as° this mouth should tear this hand   *15*
  For lifting food to't? But I will punish home.°
  No, I will weep no more. In such a night
  To shut me out! Pour on, I will endure.

3.4.4 **break my heart** i.e., by shutting out the storm which distracts
me from thinking 8 **fixed** lodged (in the mind) 11 **i' th' mouth** in the
teeth 11 **free** i.e., from care 15 **as** as if 16 **home** to the utmost

In such a night as this! O Regan, Goneril,
Your old kind father, whose frank° heart gave
20   all—
O, that way madness lies; let me shun that.
No more of that.

Kent.   Good my lord, enter here.

Lear. Prithee go in thyself; seek thine own ease.
This tempest will not give me leave to ponder
25   On things would hurt me more, but I'll go in.
[*To the Fool*] In, boy; go first. You houseless
       poverty°—
Nay, get thee in. I'll pray, and then I'll sleep.

                          Exit [Fool].

Poor naked wretches, wheresoe'er you are,
That bide° the pelting of this pitiless storm,
30   How shall your houseless heads and unfed sides,
Your looped and windowed° raggedness, defend
       you
From seasons such as these? O, I have ta'en
Too little care of this! Take physic, pomp;°
Expose thyself to feel what wretches feel,
35   That thou mayst shake the superflux° to them,
And show the heavens more just.

Edgar. [*Within*] Fathom and half, fathom and half!°
       Poor Tom!

                   Enter Fool.

Fool. Come not in here, Nuncle, here's a spirit. Help
40   me, help me!

Kent. Give me thy hand. Who's there?

Fool. A spirit, a spirit. He says his name's Poor Tom.

Kent. What art thou that dost grumble there i' th'
       straw?
       Come forth.

---

20 **frank** liberal (magnanimous)   26 **houseless poverty** (the unsheltered poor, abstracted)   29 **bide** endure   31 **looped and windowed** full of holes 33 **Take physic, pomp** take medicine to cure yourselves, you great men   35 **superflux** superfluity   37 **Fathom and half** (Edgar, because of the downpour, pretends to take soundings)

Enter Edgar [disguised as a madman].

Edgar. Away! the foul fiend follows me. Through the   45
sharp hawthorn blows the cold wind.° Humh! Go to
thy cold bed, and warm thee.°

Lear. Didst thou give all to thy daughters? And art
thou come to this?

Edgar. Who gives anything to Poor Tom? Whom the   50
foul fiend hath led through fire and through flame,
through ford and whirlpool, o'er bog and quag-
mire; that hath laid knives under his pillow and
halters in his pew,° set ratsbane° by his porridge,°
made him proud of heart, to ride on a bay trotting   55
horse over four-inched bridges,° to course° his
own shadow for° a traitor. Bless thy five wits,°
Tom's a-cold. O, do, de, do, de, do, de. Bless thee
from whirlwinds, star-blasting,° and taking.° Do
Poor Tom some charity, whom the foul fiend vexes.   60
There could I have him now—and there—and there
again—and there.

                               Storm still.

Lear. What, has his daughters brought him to this
pass?°
Couldst thou save nothing? Wouldst thou give 'em
all?

Fool. Nay, he reserved a blanket,° else we had been   65
all shamed.

Lear. Now all the plagues that in the pendulous° air
Hang fated o'er° men's faults light on thy
daughters!

45–46 **Through . . . wind** (a line from the ballad of "The Friar of Orders
Gray")   46–47 **go . . . thee** (a reminiscence of *The Taming of the Shrew*,
Induction, 1.10)   53–54 **knives . . . halters . . . ratsbane** (the fiend tempts
Poor Tom to suicide)   54 **pew** gallery or balcony outside a window
54 **porridge** broth   55–56 **ride . . . bridges** i.e., risk his life   56 **course**
chase   57 **for** as   57 **five wits** i.e., common wit, imagination, fantasy, estimation, memory   59 **star-blasting** the evil caused by malignant stars
59 **taking** pernicious influences   63 **pass** wretched condition   65 **blanket**
i.e., to cover his nakedness   67 **pendulous** overhanging   68 **fated o'er**
destined to punish

Kent. He hath no daughters, sir.

Lear. Death, traitor; nothing could have subdued°
70   nature
To such a lowness but his unkind daughters.
Is it the fashion that discarded fathers
Should have thus little mercy on° their flesh?
Judicious punishment—'twas this flesh begot
75   Those pelican° daughters.

Edgar. Pillicock sat on Pillicock Hill.° Alow, alow,
loo, loo!°

Fool. This cold night will turn us all to fools and madmen.

80   *Edgar.* Take heed o' th' foul fiend; obey thy parents;
keep thy word's justice;° swear not; commit not°
with man's sworn spouse; set not thy sweet heart on
proud array. Tom's a-cold.

Lear. What hast thou been?

85   *Edgar.* A servingman, proud in heart and mind; that
curled my hair, wore gloves in my cap;° served the
lust of my mistress' heart, and did the act of darkness with her; swore as many oaths as I spake
words, and broke them in the sweet face of
90   heaven. One that slept in the contriving of lust,
and waked to do it. Wine loved I deeply, dice
dearly; and in woman out-paramoured the Turk.°
False of heart, light of ear,° bloody of hand; hog
in sloth, fox in stealth, wolf in greediness, dog in
95   madness, lion in prey.° Let not the creaking° of
shoes nor the rustling of silks betray thy poor

---

70 **subdued** reduced 73 **on** i.e., shown to 75 **pelican** (supposed to feed on
its parent's blood) 76 **Pillicock ... Hill** (probably quoted from a nursery
rhyme, and suggested by "pelican." **Pillicock** is a term of endearment
and the phallus) 76–77 **Alow ... loo** (? a hunting call, or the refrain of
the song) 81 **keep ... justice** i.e., do not break thy word 81 **commit not**
i.e., adultery 86 **gloves in my cap** i.e., as a pledge from his mistress
92 **out-paramoured the Turk** had more concubines than the Sultan 93 **light
of ear** ready to hear flattery and slander 95 **prey** preying 95 **creaking**
(deliberately cultivated, as fashionable)

heart to woman. Keep thy foot out of brothels,
thy hand out of plackets,° thy pen from lenders'
books,° and defy the foul fiend. Still through the
hawthorn blows the cold wind; says suum, mun, *100*
nonny.° Dolphin° my boy, boy, sessa!° let him trot
by.

Storm still.

Lear. Thou wert better in a grave than to answer°
with thy uncovered body this extremity° of the
skies. Is man no more than this? Consider him *105*
well. Thou ow'st° the worm no silk, the beast no
hide, the sheep no wool, the cat° no perfume. Ha!
here's three on's° are sophisticated.° Thou art the
thing itself; unaccommodated° man is no more
but such a poor, bare, forked° animal as thou art. *110*
Off, off, you lendings!° Come, unbutton here.

                    [*Tearing off his clothes.*]

Fool. Prithee, Nuncle, be contented, 'tis a naughty°
night to swim in. Now a little fire in a wild° field
were like an old lecher's heart—a small spark, all
the rest on's body, cold. Look, here comes a walk- *115*
ing fire.

         Enter Gloucester, with a torch.

Edgar. This is the foul fiend Flibbertigibbet.° He begins at curfew,° and walks till the first cock.° He
gives the web and the pin,° squints° the eye, and
makes the harelip; mildews the white° wheat, and *120*
hurts the poor creature of earth.

---

98 **plackets** openings in skirts   98–99 **pen . . . books** i.e., do not enter your
name in the moneylender's account book   100–01 **suum, mun, nonny** the
noise of the wind   101 **Dolphin** the French Dauphin (identified by the English
with the devil. Poor Tom is presumably quoting from a ballad)   101 **sessa**
an interjection: "Go on!"   103 **answer** confront, bear the brunt of   104 **extremity** extreme severity   106 **ow'st** have taken from   107 **cat** civet cat,
whose glands yield perfume   108 **on's** of us   108 **sophisticated** adulterated,
made artificial   109 **unaccommodated** uncivilized   110 **forked** i.e., two-
legged   111 **lendings** borrowed garments   112 **naughty** wicked   113 **wild**
barren   117 **Flibbertigibbet** (a figure from Elizabethan demonology)   118
curfew: 9 P.M.   118 **first cock** midnight   119 **web and the pin** cataract
119 **squints** crosses   120 **white** ripening.

Swithold footed thrice the old;°
He met the nightmare,° and her nine fold;°
   Bid her alight°
125   And her troth plight,°
And aroint° thee, witch, aroint thee!

Kent. How fares your Grace?

Lear. What's he?

Kent. Who's there? What is't you seek?

130 *Gloucester.* What are you there? Your names?

Edgar. Poor Tom, that eats the swimming frog, the
toad, the todpole, the wall-newt and the water;°
that in the fury of his heart, when the foul fiend
rages, eats cow-dung for sallets,° swallows the old
135 rat and the ditch-dog,° drinks the green mantle°
of the standing° pool; who is whipped from tithing°
to tithing, and stocked, punished, and imprisoned;
who hath had three suits to his back, six shirts to
his body,
140   Horse to ride, and weapon to wear,
   But mice and rats, and such small deer,°
   Have been Tom's food for seven long year.°
Beware my follower!° Peace, Smulkin,° peace,
thou fiend!

Gloucester. What, hath your Grace no better com-
145 pany?

Edgar. The Prince of Darkness is a gentleman.
Modo° he's called, and Mahu.°

---

122 **Swithold . . . old** Withold (an Anglo-Saxon saint who subdued demons)
walked three times across the open country   123 **nightmare** demon
123 **fold** offspring   124 **alight** i.e., from the horse she had possessed
125 **her troth plight** pledge her word   126 **aroint** be gone   132 **todpole . . .
water** tadpole, wall lizard, water newt   134 **sallets** salads   135 **ditch-dog**
dead dog in a ditch   135 **mantle** scum   136 **standing** stagnant   136 **tithing**
a district comprising ten families   141–42 **But . . . year** (adapted from a popular romance, "Bevis of Hampton")   141 **deer** game   143 **follower** familiar
143, 147 **Smulkin, Modo, Mahu** (Elizabethan devils, from Samuel Harsnett's
Declaration of 1603)

Gloucester. Our flesh and blood, my Lord, is grown
          so vile
     That it doth hate what gets° it.

Edgar. Poor Tom's a-cold.   *150*

Gloucester. Go in with me. My duty cannot suffer°
     T' obey in all your daughters' hard commands.
     Though their injunction be to bar my doors
     And let this tyrannous night take hold upon you,
     Yet have I ventured to come seek you out   *155*
     And bring you where both fire and food is ready.

Lear. First let me talk with this philosopher.
     What is the cause of thunder?

Kent. Good my lord, take his offer; go into th' house.

Lear. I'll talk a word with this same learnèd Theban.°   *160*
     What is your study?°

Edgar. How to prevent° the fiend, and to kill vermin.

Lear. Let me ask you one word in private.

Kent. Importune him once more to go, my lord.
     His wits begin t' unsettle.

Gloucester.   Canst thou blame him?   *165*

                              Storm still.

     His daughters seek his death. Ah, that good Kent,
     He said it would be thus, poor banished man!
     Thou say'st the King grows mad—I'll tell thee,
          friend,
     I am almost mad myself. I had a son,
     Now outlawed from my blood;° he sought my life   *170*
     But lately, very late.° I loved him, friend,
     No father his son dearer. True to tell thee,
     The grief hath crazed my wits. What a night's this!

---

149 **gets** begets   151 **suffer** permit me   160 **Theban** i.e., Greek philosopher   161 **study** particular scientific study   162 **prevent** balk   170 **out-
lawed from my blood** disowned and tainted, like a carbuncle in the
corrupted blood   171 **late** recently

I do beseech your Grace——

Lear.   O, cry you mercy,° sir.
175   Noble philosopher, your company.

Edgar. Tom's a-cold.

Gloucester. In, fellow, there, into th' hovel; keep thee
    warm.

Lear. Come, let's in all.

Kent.   This way, my lord.

Lear.   With him!
    I will keep still with my philosopher.

Kent. Good my lord, soothe° him; let him take the
180   fellow.

Gloucester. Take him you on.°

Kent. Sirrah, come on; go along with us.

Lear. Come, good Athenian.°

Gloucester. No words, no words! Hush.

185 *Edgar.* Child Rowland to the dark tower came;°
    His word was still,° "Fie, foh, and fum,
    I smell the blood of a British man."°   *Exeunt.*

---

174 **cry you mercy** I beg your pardon   180 **soothe** humor   181 **you on**
with you   183 **Athenian** i.e., philosopher (like "Theban")   185 **Child . . .
came** (? from a lost ballad; "child"=a candidate for knighthood; **Rowland**
was Charlemagne's nephew, the hero of *The Song of Roland*)   186 **His . . .
still** his motto was always   186–87 **Fie . . . man** (a deliberately absurd link-
ing of the chivalric hero with the nursery tale of Jack the Giant-Killer)

Scene 5.   [*Gloucester's castle.*]

Enter Cornwall and Edmund.

Cornwall. I will have my revenge ere I depart his
house.

Edmund. How, my lord, I may be censured,° that
nature thus gives way to loyalty, something fears°
me to think of.   5

Cornwall. I now perceive it was not altogether your
brother's evil disposition made him seek his death;
but a provoking merit, set a-work by a reprovable
badness in himself.°

Edmund. How malicious is my fortune that I must   10
repent to be just! This is the letter which he spoke
of, which approves° him an intelligent party°
to the advantages° of France. O heavens, that his
treason were not! or not I the detector!

Cornwall. Go with me to the Duchess.   15

Edmund. If the matter of this paper be certain, you
have mighty business in hand.

Cornwall. True or false, it hath made thee Earl of
Gloucester. Seek out where thy father is, that he
may be ready for our apprehension.°   20

Edmund. [*Aside*] If I find him comforting° the
King, it will stuff his suspicion more fully.—I will
persever° in my course of loyalty, though the conflict be sore between that and my blood.°

3.5.8 **censured** judged   4 **something fears** somewhat frightens   8–9 **a
provoking . . . himself** a stimulating goodness in Edgar, brought into play by
a blamable badness in Gloucester   12 **approves** proves   12 **intelligent
party** (1) spy (2) well-informed person   13 **to the advantages** on behalf of
20 **apprehension** arrest   21 **comforting** supporting (a legalism)   23 **persever** persevere   24 **blood** natural feelings

25 *Cornwall.* I will lay trust upon° thee, and thou
    shalt find a dearer father in my love.   *Exeunt.*

Scene 6.   [*A chamber in a farmhouse
adjoining the castle.*]

Enter Kent and Gloucester.

Gloucester. Here is better than the open air; take it
    thankfully. I will piece out the comfort with what
    addition I can. I will not be long from you.

Kent. All the power of his wits have given way to his
5   impatience.° The gods reward your kindness.
                                Exit [*Gloucester*].

Enter Lear, Edgar, and Fool.

Edgar. Frateretto° calls me, and tells me Nero° is
    an angler in the lake of darkness. Pray, innocent,°
    and beware the foul fiend.

Fool. Prithee, Nuncle, tell me whether a madman be a
10   gentleman or a yeoman.°

Lear. A king, a king.

Fool. No, he's a yeoman that has a gentleman to his
    son; for he's a mad yeoman that sees his son a gen-
    tleman before him.

15 *Lear.* To have a thousand with red burning spits
    Come hizzing° in upon 'em——

---

25 lay trust upon (1) trust (2) advance **3.6.5 impatience** raging
6 Frateretto Elizabethan devil, from Harsnett's *Declaration*   **6 Nero** (who
is mentioned by Harsnett, and whose angling is reported by Chaucer in
"The Monk's Tale")   **7 innocent** fool   **10 yeoman** farmer (just below a
gentleman in rank. The Fool asks what class of man has most indulged
his children, and thus been driven mad)   **16 hizzing** hissing

Edgar. The foul fiend bites my back.

Fool. He's mad that trusts in the tameness of a wolf,
a horse's health, a boy's love, or a whore's oath.

Lear. It shall be done; I will arraign° them straight.°   20
[*To Edgar*] Come, sit thou here, most learned
justice.°
[*To the Fool*] Thou, sapient° sir, sit here. Now,
you she-foxes——

Edgar. Look, where he° stands and glares. Want'st
thou eyes at trial, madam?°
Come o'er the bourn,° Bessy, to me.   25

Fool. Her boat hath a leak,
And she must not speak
Why she dares not come over to thee.°

Edgar. The foul fiend haunts Poor Tom in the voice
of a nightingale.° Hoppedance° cries in Tom's belly   30
for two white herring.° Croak° not, black angel; I
have no food for thee.

Kent. How do you, sir? Stand you not so amazed.°
Will you lie down and rest upon the cushions?

Lear. I'll see their trial first. Bring in their evidence.   35
[*To Edgar*] Thou, robèd man of justice, take
thy place.
[*To the Fool*] And thou, his yokefellow of equity,°
Bench° by his side. [*To Kent*] You are o' th'
commission;°
Sit you too.

Edgar. Let us deal justly.   40

---

20 **arraign** bring to trial   20 **straight** straightaway   21 **justice** justicer,
judge   22 **sapient** wise   23 **he** i.e., a fiend   23–24 **Want'st ... madam**
(to Goneril) i.e., do you want eyes to look at you during your trial? The
fiend serves that purpose   25 **bourn** brook (Edgar quotes from a popular
ballad)   26–28 **Her ... thee** (the Fool parodies the ballad)   30 **nightingale** i.e., the Fool's singing   30 **Hoppedance** Hoberdidance (another devil
from Harsnett's *Declaration*)   31 **white herring** unsmoked (? as against
the black and sulfurous devil)   31 **Croak** rumble (because his belly is
empty)   33 **amazed** astonished   35 **evidence** the evidence of witnesses
against them   37 **yokefellow of equity** partner in justice   38 **Bench** sit on
the bench   38 **commission** those commissioned as king's justices

> Sleepest or wakest thou, jolly shepherd?
>> Thy sheep be in the corn;°
> And for one blast of thy minikin° mouth
>> Thy sheep shall take no harm.°
45 Purr, the cat is gray.°

Lear. Arraign her first. 'Tis Goneril, I here take my oath before this honorable assembly, she kicked the poor King her father.

Fool. Come hither, mistress. Is your name Goneril?

50 *Lear.* She cannot deny it.

Fool. Cry you mercy, I took you for a joint stool.°

Lear. And here's another, whose warped looks proclaim
What store° her heart is made on. Stop her there!
Arms, arms, sword, fire! Corruption in the place!°
55 False justicer, why hast thou let her 'scape?

Edgar. Bless thy five wits!

Kent. O pity! Sir, where is the patience now
That you so oft have boasted to retain?

Edgar. [*Aside*] My tears begin to take his part so much
60 They mar my counterfeiting.°

Lear. The little dogs and all,
Tray, Blanch, and Sweetheart—see, they bark at me.

Edgar. Tom will throw his head at them. Avaunt, you curs.
Be thy mouth or black or° white,

41–44 **Sleepest . . . harm** (probably quoted or adapted from an Elizabethan song)   42 **corn** wheat   43 **minikin** shrill   45 **gray** (devils were thought to assume the shape of a gray cat)   51 **Cry . . . joint stool** (proverbial and deliberately impudent apology for overlooking a person. A joint stool was a low stool made by a joiner, perhaps here a stage property to represent Goneril and in line 52, Regan. "Joint stool" can also suggest the judicial bench; hence Goneril may be identified by the Fool, ironically, with those in power, who judge)   53 **store** stuff   54 **Corruption . . . place** bribery in the court   60 **counterfeiting** i.e., feigned madness   64 **or . . . or** either . . . or

> Tooth that poisons if it bite;   65
> Mastiff, greyhound, mongrel grim,
> Hound or spaniel, brach° or lym,°
> Or bobtail tike, or trundle-tail°—
> Tom will make him weep and wail;
> For, with throwing° thus my head,   70
> Dogs leaped the hatch,° and all are fled.
> Do, de, de, de. Sessa!° Come, march to wakes°
> and fairs and market towns. Poor Tom, thy horn°
> is dry.

Lear. Then let them anatomize Regan. See what breeds   75
    about her heart.° Is there any cause in nature that
    make° these hard hearts? [*To Edgar*] You, sir,
    I entertain° for one of my hundred;° only I do not
    like the fashion of your garments. You will say
    they are Persian;° but let them be changed.   80

Kent. Now, good my lord, lie here and rest awhile.

Lear. Make no noise, make no noise; draw the
    curtains.°
    So, so. We'll go to supper i' th' morning.

Fool. And I'll go to bed at noon.°

Enter Gloucester.

Gloucester. Come hither, friend. Where is the King
    my master?   85

Kent. Here, sir, but trouble him not; his wits are gone.

Gloucester. Good friend, I prithee take him in thy
    arms.

---

67 **brach** bitch   67 **lym** bloodhound (from the liam or leash with which
he was led)   68 **bobtail . . . trundle-tail** short-tailed or long-tailed cur
70 **throwing** jerking (as a hound lifts its head from the ground, the scent
having been lost)   71 **leaped the hatch** leaped over the lower half of a
divided door (i.e., left in a hurry)   72 **Sessa** be off   72 **wakes** feasts attending the dedication of a church   73 **horn** horn bottle which the Bedlam
used in begging a drink (Edgar is suggesting that he is unable to play his
role any longer)   75–76 **Then . . . heart** i.e., if the Bedlam's horn is dry, let
Regan, whose heart has become as hard as horn, be dissected   77 **make**
(subjunctive)   78 **entertain** engage   78 **hundred** i.e., Lear's hundred
knights   80 **Persian** gorgeous (ironically of Edgar's rags)   82 **curtains**
(Lear imagines himself in bed)   84 **And . . . noon** (the Fool's last words)

I have o'erheard a plot of death upon him.
There is a litter ready; lay him in't
And drive toward Dover, friend, where thou shalt
90   meet
Both welcome and protection. Take up thy master.
If thou shouldst dally half an hour, his life,
With thine and all that offer to defend him,
Stand in assurèd loss. Take up, take up,
95   And follow me, that will to some provision°
Give thee quick conduct.°

Kent.   Oppressèd nature sleeps.
This rest might yet have balmed thy broken
     sinews,°
Which, if convenience° will not allow,
Stand in hard cure.° [*To the Fool*] Come, help
     to bear thy master.
Thou must not stay behind.

100 *Gloucester*.   Come, come, away!
                              Exeunt [*all but Edgar*].

Edgar. When we our betters see bearing our woes,
We scarcely think our miseries our foes.°
Who alone suffers suffers most i' th' mind,
Leaving free° things and happy shows° behind;
105 But then the mind much sufferance° doth o'erskip
When grief hath mates, and bearing fellowship.°
How light and portable° my pain seems now,
When that which makes me bend makes the
     King bow.
He childed as I fathered. Tom, away.
110 Mark the high noises,° and thyself bewray°
When false opinion, whose wrong thoughts° defile
     thee,

95 **provision** maintenance   96 **conduct** direction   97 **balmed thy broken
sinews** soothed thy racked nerves   98 **convenience** fortunate occasion
99 **Stand . . . cure** will be hard to cure   102 **our foes** enemies peculiar to
ourselves   104 **free** carefree   104 **shows** scenes   105 **sufferance** suffering   106 **bearing fellowship** suffering has company   107 **portable** able
to be supported or endured   110 **Mark the high noises** observe the rumors
of strife among those in power   110 **bewray** reveal   111 **wrong thoughts**
misconceptions

In thy just proof repeals and reconciles thee.°
What will hap more° tonight, safe 'scape the King!
Lurk,° lurk.   [*Exit.*]

Scene 7.   [*Gloucester's castle.*]

Enter Cornwall, Regan, Goneril, Edmund, and
Servants.

Cornwall. [*To Goneril*] Post speedily to my Lord
your husband; show him this letter. The army of
France is landed. [*To Servants*] Seek out the
traitor Gloucester. [*Exeunt some of the Servants.*]

Regan. Hang him instantly.   5

Goneril. Pluck out his eyes.

Cornwall. Leave him to my displeasure. Edmund,
keep you our sister company. The revenges we are
bound° to take upon your traitorous father are not
fit for your beholding. Advise the Duke where you   10
are going, to a most festinate° preparation. We are
bound to the like. Our posts° shall be swift and
intelligent° betwixt us. Farewell, dear sister; farewell, my Lord of Gloucester.°

Enter Oswald.

How now? Where's the King?   15

Oswald. My Lord of Gloucester hath conveyed him
hence.

112 **In ... thee** on the manifesting of your innocence recalls you from
outlawry and restores amity between you and your father   113 **What ...**
more whatever else happens   114 **Lurk** hide   3.7.9 **bound** (1) forced
(2) purposing to   11 **festinate** speedy   12 **posts** messengers   13 **intelligent**
full of information   14 **Lord of Gloucester** i.e., Edmund, now elevated
to the title

Some five or six and thirty of his knights,
Hot questrists° after him, met him at gate;
Who, with some other of the lords dependants,°
Are gone with him toward Dover, where they
20   boast
To have well-armèd friends.

Cornwall.   Get horses for your mistress.
                              [*Exit Oswald.*]

Goneril. Farewell, sweet lord, and sister.

Cornwall. Edmund, farewell.
                    [*Exeunt Goneril and Edmund.*]
                    Go seek the traitor Gloucester,
Pinion him like a thief, bring him before us.
                    [*Exeunt other Servants.*]
25   Though well we may not pass upon° his life
Without the form of justice, yet our power
Shall do a court'sy to° our wrath, which men
May blame, but not control.

      Enter Gloucester, brought in by two or three.

                              Who's there, the traitor?

Regan. Ingrateful fox, 'tis he.

30 *Cornwall.* Bind fast his corky° arms.

Gloucester. What means your Graces? Good my
      friends, consider
You are my guests. Do me no foul play, friends.

Cornwall. Bind him, I say.

                              [*Servants bind him.*]

Regan.   Hard, hard! O filthy traitor.

Gloucester. Unmerciful lady as you are, I'm none.

Cornwall. To this chair bind him. Villain, thou shalt
35   find——

18 **questrists** searchers   19 **lords dependants** attendant lords (members of
Lear's retinue)   25 **pass upon** pass judgment on   27 **do a court'sy to**
indulge   30 **corky** sapless (because old)

[Regan plucks his beard.°]

Gloucester. By the kind gods, 'tis most ignobly done
　　To pluck me by the beard.

Regan. So white, and such a traitor?

Gloucester.　　　　　　　　　Naughty° lady,
　　These hairs which thou dost ravish from my chin
　　Will quicken° and accuse thee. I am your host.　　　　*40*
　　With robber's hands my hospitable favors°
　　You should not ruffle° thus. What will you do?

Cornwall. Come, sir, what letters had you late° from
　　France?

Regan. Be simple-answered,° for we know the truth.

Cornwall. And what confederacy have you with the
　　traitors　　　　　　　　　　　　　　　　　　　　　*45*
　　Late footed in the kingdom?

Regan. To whose hands you have sent the lunatic
　　King:
　　Speak.

Gloucester. I have a letter guessingly° set down,
　　Which came from one that's of a neutral heart,
　　And not from one opposed.

Cornwall.　　　　　　　　　Cunning.

Regan.　　　　　　　　　　　And false.　　　　　　*50*

Cornwall. Where hast thou sent the King?

Gloucester. To Dover.

Regan. Wherefore to Dover? Wast thou not charged at
　　peril°——

Cornwall. Wherefore to Dover? Let him answer that.

---

35 s.d. **plucks his beard** (a deadly insult)　38 **Naughty** wicked
40 **quicken** come to life　41 **hospitable favors** face of your host　42 **ruffle**
tear at violently　43 **late** recently　44 **simple-answered** straightforward in
answering　48 **guessingly** without certain knowledge　53 **charged at peril**
ordered under penalty

Gloucester. I am tied to th' stake, and I must stand
55   the course.°

Regan. Wherefore to Dover?

Gloucester. Because I would not see thy cruel nails
          Pluck out his poor old eyes; nor thy fierce sister
          In his anointed° flesh rash° boarish fangs.
60   The sea, with such a storm as his bare head
          In hell-black night endured, would have buoyed° up
          And quenched the stellèd° fires.
          Yet, poor old heart, he holp° the heavens to rain.
          If wolves had at thy gate howled that dearn° time,
          Thou shouldst have said, "Good porter, turn the
65   key."°
          All cruels else subscribe.° But I shall see
          The wingèd° vengeance overtake such children.

Cornwall. See't shalt thou never. Fellows, hold the
          chair.
          Upon these eyes of thine I'll set my foot.

Gloucester. He that will think° to live till he be
70   old,
          Give me some help. —O cruel! O you gods!

Regan. One side will mock° another. Th' other too.

Cornwall. If you see vengeance——

First Servant.   Hold your hand, my lord!
          I have served you ever since I was a child;
75   But better service have I never done you
          Than now to bid you hold.

Regan.   How now, you dog?

First Servant. If you did wear a beard upon your chin,

---

55 **course** coursing (in which a relay of dogs baits a bull or bear tied in
the pit)   59 **anointed** holy (because king)   59 **rash** strike with the tusk,
like a boar   61 **buoyed** risen   62 **stellèd** (1) fixed (as opposed to the planets
or wandering stars) (2) starry   63 **holp** helped   64 **dearn** dread   65 **turn
the key** i.e., unlock the gate   66 **All cruels else subscribe** all cruel creatures
but man are compassionate   67 **wingèd** (1) heavenly (2) swift   70 **will
think** expects   72 **mock** make ridiculous (because of the contrast)

I'd shake it° on this quarrel. What do you mean!°

Cornwall. My villain!°

Draw and fight.

First Servant. Nay, then, come on, and take the
chance of anger.   80

Regan. Give me thy sword. A peasant stand up thus?

*She takes a sword and runs at him behind,
kills him.*

First Servant. O, I am slain! my lord, you have one
eye left
To see some mischief° on him. O!

Cornwall. Lest it see more, prevent it. Out, vile jelly.
Where is thy luster now?   85

Gloucester. All dark and comfortless. Where's my son
Edmund?
Edmund, enkindle all the sparks of nature°
To quit° this horrid act.

Regan.   Out, treacherous villain,
Thou call'st on him that hates thee. It was he
That made the overture° of thy treasons to us;   90
Who is too good to pity thee.

Gloucester. O my follies! Then Edgar was abused.°
Kind gods, forgive me that, and prosper him.

Regan. Go thrust him out at gates, and let him smell
His way to Dover.   *Exit [one] with Gloucester.*
How is't, my lord? How look you?°   95

Cornwall. I have received a hurt. Follow me, lady.
Turn out that eyeless villain. Throw this slave
Upon the dunghill. Regan, I bleed apace.

---

78 **shake it** (an insult comparable to Regan's plucking of Gloucester's
beard)   78 **What . . . mean** i.e., what terrible thing are you doing   79 **villain** serf (with a suggestion of the modern meaning)   83 **mischief** injury
87 **enkindle . . . nature** fan your natural feeling into flame   88 **quit** requite
90 **overture** disclosure   92 **abused** wronged   95 **How look you** how
are you

Untimely comes this hurt. Give me your arm.
                                              Exeunt.

100 *Second Servant.* I'll never care what wickedness I do,
        If this man come to good.

     Third Servant.   If she live long,
        And in the end meet the old course of death,°
        Women will all turn monsters.

     Second Servant. Let's follow the old Earl, and get the
        Bedlam
105   To lead him where he would. His roguish madness
        Allows itself to anything.°

     Third Servant. Go thou. I'll fetch some flax and
        whites of eggs
        To apply to his bleeding face. Now heaven help
        him.   [*Exeunt severally.*]

102 **meet . . . death** die the customary death of old age   105–6 **His . . .
anything** his lack of all self-control leaves him open to any suggestion

ACT 4

Scene 1. [*The heath.*]

Enter Edgar.

Edgar. Yet better thus, and known to be contemned,°
　　Than still contemned and flattered. To be worst,
　　The lowest and most dejected° thing of fortune,
　　Stands still in esperance,° lives not in fear:
　　The lamentable change is from the best,　　　　　5
　　The worst returns to laughter.° Welcome then,
　　Thou unsubstantial air that I embrace!
　　The wretch that thou hast blown unto the worst
　　Owes° nothing to thy blasts.

　　　　　Enter Gloucester, led by an Old Man.

　　　　　　　　　　　　But who comes here?
　　My father, poorly led?° World, world, O world!　　10
　　But that thy strange mutations make us hate thee,
　　Life would not yield to age.°

Old Man. O, my good lord, I have been your tenant,
　　and your father's tenant, these fourscore years.

Gloucester. Away, get thee away; good friend, be
　　gone:　　　　　　　　　　　　　　　　15

4.1.1 **known to be contemned** conscious of being despised　3 **dejected**
abased　4 **esperance** hope　6 **returns to laughter** changes for the better
9 **Owes** is in debt for　10 **poorly led** (1) led like a poor man, with only one
attendant (2) led by a poor man　11–12 **But . . . age** we should not agree to
grow old and hence die, except for the hateful mutability of life

95

Thy comforts° can do me no good at all;
Thee they may hurt.°

Old Man.   You cannot see your way.

Gloucester. I have no way and therefore want° no
   eyes;
   I stumbled when I saw. Full oft 'tis seen,
20 Our means secure us, and our mere defects
   Prove our commodities.° Oh, dear son Edgar,
   The food° of thy abusèd° father's wrath!
   Might I but live to see thee in° my touch,
   I'd say I had eyes again!

Old Man.   How now! Who's there?

Edgar. [*Aside*] O Gods! Who is 't can say "I am at
25   the worst"?
   I am worse than e'er I was.

Old Man.   'Tis poor mad Tom.

Edgar. [*Aside*] And worse I may be yet: the worst
      is not
   So long as we can say "This is the worst."°

Old Man. Fellow, where goest?

Gloucester.   Is it a beggar-man?

30 *Old Man.* Madman and beggar too.

Gloucester. He has some reason,° else he could not
      beg.
   I' th' last night's storm I such a fellow saw,
   Which made me think a man a worm. My son
   Came then into my mind, and yet my mind
   Was then scarce friends with him. I have heard
35   more since.
   As flies to wanton° boys, are we to th' gods,

16 **comforts** ministrations   17 **hurt** injure   18 **want** require   20–21 **Our . . .
commodities** our resources make us overconfident, while our afflictions make
for our advantage   22 **food** i.e., the object on which Gloucester's anger
fed   22 **abusèd** deceived   23 **in** i.e., with, by means of   27–28 **the . . . worst**
so long as a man continues to suffer (i.e., is still alive), even greater suffering may await him   31 **reason** faculty of reasoning   36 **wanton** (1) playful
(2) reckless

They kill us for their sport.

Edgar. [*Aside*]   How should this be?°
Bad is the trade that must play fool to sorrow,
Ang'ring° itself and others. Bless thee, master!

Gloucester. Is that the naked fellow?

Old Man.   Ay, my lord.   *40*

Gloucester. Then, prithee, get thee gone: if for my
sake
Thou wilt o'ertake us hence a mile or twain
I' th' way toward Dover, do it for ancient° love,
And bring some covering for this naked soul,
Which I'll entreat to lead me.

Old Man.   Alack, sir, he is mad.   *45*

Gloucester. 'Tis the times' plague,° when madmen
lead the blind.
Do as I bid thee, or rather do thy pleasure;°
Above the rest,° be gone.

Old Man. I'll bring him the best 'parel° that I have,
Come on 't what will.   *Exit.*   *50*

Gloucester. Sirrah, naked fellow——

Edgar. Poor Tom's a-cold. [*Aside*] I cannot daub
it° further.

Gloucester. Come hither, fellow.

Edgar. [*Aside*] And yet I must. —Bless thy sweet
eyes, they bleed.   *55*

Gloucester. Know'st thou the way to Dover?

Edgar. Both stile and gate, horse-way and footpath.
Poor Tom hath been scared out of his good wits.
Bless thee, good man's son, from the foul fiend!
Five fiends have been in Poor Tom at once; of lust,   *60*

37 **How should this be** i.e., how can this horror be?   39 **Ang'ring** offending   43 **ancient** (1) the love the Old Man feels, by virtue of his long tenancy (2) the love that formerly obtained between master and man   46 **times' plague** characteristic disorder of this time   47 **thy pleasure** as you like   48 **the rest** all   49 **'parel** apparel   52–53 **daub it** lay it on (figure from plastering mortar)

as Obidicut;° Hobbididence, prince of dumbness;° Mahu, of stealing; Modo, of murder; Flibbertigibbet, of mopping and mowing;° who since
possesses chambermaids and waiting-women. So,
65   bless thee, master!

Gloucester. Here, take this purse, thou whom the
        heavens' plagues
Have humbled to all strokes:° that I am wretched
Makes thee the happier. Heavens, deal so still!
Let the superfluous° and lust-dieted° man,
70   That slaves° your ordinance,° that will not see
Because he does not feel, feel your pow'r quickly;
So distribution should undo excess,°
And each man have enough. Dost thou know
        Dover?

Edgar. Ay, master.

Gloucester. There is a cliff whose high and bending°
75   head
Looks fearfully° in the confinèd deep:°
Bring me but to the very brim of it,
And I'll repair the misery thou dost bear
With something rich about me: from that place
I shall no leading need.

80   *Edgar.*   *Give me thy arm:*
Poor Tom shall lead thee.   *Exeunt.*

61 **Obidicut** Hoberdicut, a devil (like the four that follow, from Harsnett's
Declaration)   61–62 **dumbness** muteness (like the crimes and afflictions
in the next lines, the result of diabolic possession)   63 **mopping and mowing** grimacing and making faces   67 **humbled to all strokes** brought so
low as to bear anything humbly   69 **superfluous** possessed of super-
fluities   69 **lust-dieted** whose lust is gratified (like Gloucester's)   70 **slaves**
(1) tramples, spurns like a slave (2) ? tears, rends (Old English **slaefan**)
70 **ordinance** law   72 **So . . . excess** then the man with too much wealth
would distribute it among those with too little   75 **bending** overhanging
76 **fearfully** occasioning fear   76 **confinèd deep** the sea, hemmed in below

Scene 2.   [*Before the Duke of Albany's palace.*]

Enter Goneril and Edmund.

Goneril. Welcome, my lord: I marvel our mild husband
  Not met° us on the way.

                    Enter Oswald.

                        Now, where's your master?

Oswald. Madam, within; but never man so changed.
  I told him of the army that was landed:
  He smiled at it. I told him you were coming;   5
  His answer was, "The worse." Of Gloucester's treachery,
  And of the loyal service of his son
  When I informed him, then he called me sot,°
  And told me I had turned the wrong side out:
  What most he should dislike seems pleasant to him;   10
  What like,° offensive.

Goneril. [*To Edmund*] Then shall you go no further.
  It is the cowish° terror of his spirit,
  That dares not undertake:° he'll not feel wrongs,
  Which tie him to an answer.° Our wishes on the way
  May prove effects.° Back, Edmund, to my brother;   15
  Hasten his musters° and conduct his pow'rs.°

4.2.2 **Not met** did not meet   8 **sot** fool   11 **What like** what he should like
12 **cowish** cowardly   13 **undertake** venture   14 **tie him to an answer**
oblige him to retaliate   14–15 **Our . . . effects** our desires (that you might
be my husband), as we journeyed here, may be fulfilled   16 **musters** col-
lecting of troops   16 **conduct his pow'rs** lead his army

I must change names° at home and give the
    distaff°
Into my husband's hands. This trusty servant
Shall pass between us: ere long you are like to hear,
20   If you dare venture in your own behalf,
A mistress's° command. Wear this; spare speech;

                            [*Giving a favor*]

Decline your head.° This kiss, if it durst speak,
Would stretch thy spirits up into the air:
Conceive,° and fare thee well.

Edmund. Yours in the ranks of death.

25   *Goneril.*   My most dear Gloucester!
                            Exit [*Edmund*].

O, the difference of man and man!
To thee a woman's services are due:
My fool usurps my body.°

Oswald.   Madam, here comes my lord.
                                    Exit.

                Enter Albany.

Goneril. I have been worth the whistle.°

Albany.   O Goneril!
30   You are not worth the dust which the rude wind
Blows in your face. I fear your disposition:°
That nature which contemns° its origin
Cannot be bordered certain in itself;°
She that herself will sliver and disbranch°

---

17 **change names** i.e., exchange the name of "mistress" for that of "master"
17 **distaff** spinning stick (wifely symbol)   21 **mistress's** lover's (and also, Albany having been disposed of, lady's or wife's)   22 **Decline your head** i.e.,
that Goneril may kiss him   24 **Conceive** understand (with a sexual implication, that includes "stretch thy spirits," 1. 23; and "death," 1. 25: "to die,"
meaning "to experience sexual intercourse")   28 **My fool usurps my body**
my husband wrongfully enjoys me   29 **I . . . whistle** i.e., once you valued me
(the proverb is implied, "It is a poor dog that is not worth the whistling")
31 **disposition** nature   32 **contemns** espises   33 **bordered . . . itself** kept
within its normal bounds   34 **sliver and disbranch** cut off

From her material sap,° perforce must wither   35
And come to deadly use.°

Goneril. No more; the text° is foolish.

Albany. Wisdom and goodness to the vile seem vile:
Filths savor but themselves.° What have you done?
Tigers, not daughters, what have you performed?   40
A father, and a gracious agèd man,
Whose reverence even the head-lugged bear°
    would lick,
Most barbarous, most degenerate, have you
    madded.°
Could my good brother suffer you to do it?
A man, a prince, by him so benefited!   45
If that the heavens do not their visible spirits°
Send quickly down to tame these vile offenses,
It will come,
Humanity must perforce prey on itself,
Like monsters of the deep.

Goneril.   Milk-livered° man!   50
That bear'st a cheek for blows, a head for wrongs;
Who hast not in thy brows an eye discerning
Thine honor from thy suffering;° that not know'st
Fools do those villains pity who are punished
Ere they have done their mischief.° Where's thy
    drum?   55
France spreads his banners in our noiseless°
    land,
With plumèd helm° thy state begins to threat,°

35 **material sap** essential and life-giving sustenance   36 **come to deadly
use** i.e., be as a dead branch for the burning   37 **text** i.e., on which your ser-
mon is based   39 **Filths savor but themselves** the filthy relish only the taste
of filth   42 **head-lugged bear** bear-baited by the dogs, and hence enraged
43 **madded** made mad   46 **visible spirits** avenging spirits in material form
50 **Milk-livered** lily-livered (hence cowardly, the liver being regarded as the
seat of courage)   52–53 **discerning . . . suffering** able to distinguish between insults that ought to be resented, and ordinary pain that is to be borne
54–55 **Fools . . . mischief** only fools are sorry for criminals whose intended
criminality is prevented by punishment   56 **noiseless** i.e., the drum, signi-
fying preparation for war, is silent   57 **helm** helmet   7 **thy . . . threat**
France begins to threaten Albany's realm

Whilst thou, a moral° fool, sits still and cries
"Alack, why does he so?"

Albany.   See thyself, devil!
60   Proper° deformity seems not in the fiend
So horrid as in woman.

Goneril.   O vain fool!

Albany. Thou changèd and self-covered° thing,
    for shame,
Be-monster not thy feature.° Were 't my fitness°
To let these hands obey my blood,°
65   They are apt enough to dislocate and tear
Thy flesh and bones: howe'er° thou art a fiend,
A woman's shape doth shield thee.

Goneril. Marry,° your manhood mew°——

                Enter a Messenger.

Albany. What news?

Messenger. O, my good lord, the Duke of Cornwall's
70   dead,
Slain by his servant, going to° put out
The other eye of Gloucester.

Albany.   Gloucester's eyes!

Messenger. A servant that he bred,° thrilled with
    remorse,°
Opposed against the act, bending his sword
75   To his great master, who thereat enraged
Flew on him, and amongst them felled° him dead,
But not without that harmful stroke which since

---

58 **moral** moralizing; but also with the implication that morality and folly are
one   60 **Proper** (1) natural (to a fiend) (2) fair-appearing   62 **changèd and
self-covered** i.e., transformed, by the contorting of her woman's face, on
which appears the fiendish behavior she has allowed herself. (Goneril has disguised nature by wickedness)   63 **Be-monster not thy feature** do not change
your appearance into a fiend's   63 **my fitness** appropriate for me   64 **blood**
passion   66 **howe'er** but even if   68 **Marry** by the Virgin Mary   68 **your
manhood mew** (1) coop up or confine your (pretended) manhood
(2) molt or shed it, if that is what is supposed to "shield" me from you   71 **going to** as he was about to   73 **bred** reared   73 **thrilled with remorse** pierced
by compassion   76 **amongst them felled** others assisting, they felled

      Hath plucked him after.°

Albany.   This shows you are above,
   You justicers,° that these our nether° crimes
   So speedily can venge.° But, O poor Gloucester!   *80*
   Lost he his other eye?

Messenger.   Both, both, my lord.
   This letter, madam, craves° a speedy answer;
   'Tis from your sister.

Goneril.   [*Aside*] One way I like this well;
   But being widow, and my Gloucester with her,
   May all the building in my fancy pluck   *85*
   Upon my hateful life.° Another way,°
   The news is not so tart.°—I'll read, and answer.
                                        Exit.

Albany. Where was his son when they did take his
      eyes?

Messenger. Come with my lady hither.

Albany.   He is not here.

Messenger. No, my good lord; I met him back° again.   *90*

Albany. Knows he the wickedness?

Messenger. Ay, my good lord; 'twas he informed
      against him,
   And quit the house on purpose, that their punish-
      ment
   Might have the freer course.

Albany.   Gloucester, I live
   To thank thee for the love thou showed'st the
      King,   *95*
   And to revenge thine eyes. Come hither, friend:
   Tell me what more thou know'st.   *Exeunt.*

78 **plucked him after** i.e., brought Cornwall to death with his servant
79 **justicers** judges   79 **nether** committed below (on earth)   80 **venge**
avenge   82 **craves** demands   85–86 **May . . . life** these things (1.84) may
send my future hopes, my castles in air, crashing down upon the hateful (married) life I lead now   86 **Another way** looked at another way   87 **tart** sour
90 **back** going back

[Scene 3. *The French camp near Dover.*]

Enter Kent and a Gentleman.

Kent. Why the King of France is so suddenly gone
   back, know you no reason?

Gentleman. Something he left imperfect in the
   state,° which since his coming forth is thought of,
5   which imports° to the kingdom so much fear and
   danger that his personal return was most required
   and necessary.

Kent. Who hath he left behind him general?

Gentleman. The Marshal of France, Monsieur La Far.

10 *Kent.* Did your letters pierce° the queen to any dem-
   onstration of grief?

Gentleman. Ay, sir; she took them, read them in my
     presence,
   And now and then an ample tear trilled° down
   Her delicate cheek: it seemed she was a queen
15   Over her passion, who most rebel-like
   Sought to be king o'er her.

Kent.   O, then it moved her.

Gentleman. Not to a rage: patience and sorrow
     strove
   Who should express her goodliest.° You have seen
   Sunshine and rain at once: her smiles and tears
20   Were like a better way:° those happy smilets°
   That played on her ripe lip seemed not to know
   What guests were in her eyes, which parted thence

4.3.3–4 **imperfect in the state** unsettled in his own kingdom   5 **imports** por-
tends   10 **pierce** impel   13 **trilled** trickled   18 **Who ... goodliest** which
should give her the most becoming expression   20 **Were like a better way**
i.e., improved on that spectacle   20 **smilets** little smiles

As pearls from diamonds dropped. In brief,
Sorrow would be a rarity most belovèd,
If all could so become it.°

Kent.   Made she no verbal question? *25*

Gentleman. Faith, once or twice she heaved° the name
   of "father"
Pantingly forth, as if it pressed her heart;
Cried "Sisters! Sisters! Shame of ladies! Sisters!
Kent! Father! Sisters! What, i' th' storm? i' th'
   night?
Let pity not be believed!"° There she shook *30*
The holy water from her heavenly eyes,
And clamor moistened:° then away she started
To deal with grief alone.

Kent.   It is the stars,
The stars above us, govern our conditions;°
Else one self mate and make could not beget *35*
Such different issues.° You spoke not with her
   since?

Gentleman. No.

Kent. Was this before the King returned?

Gentleman.   No, since.

Kent. Well, sir, the poor distressèd Lear's i' th'
   town;
Who sometime in his better tune° remembers *40*
What we are come about, and by no means
Will yield to see his daughter.

Gentleman.   Why, good sir?

Kent. A sovereign° shame so elbows° him: his own
   unkindness

24–25 **Sorrow . . . it** sorrow would be a coveted jewel if it became others as
it does her 26 **heaved** expressed with difficulty 30 **Let pity not be believed** let it not be believed for pity 32 **clamor moistened** moistened
clamor, i.e., mixed (and perhaps assuaged) her outcries with tears 34 **govern our conditions** determine what we are 35–36 **Else . . . issues** otherwise the same husband and wife could not produce such different children
40 **better tune** composed, less jangled intervals 43 **sovereign** overpower-
ing 43 **elbows** jogs his elbow i.e., reminds him

That stripped her from his benediction, turned her
45 To foreign casualties,° gave her dear rights
To his dog-hearted daughters: these things sting
His mind so venomously that burning shame
Detains him from Cordelia.

Gentleman.   Alack, poor gentleman!

Kent. Of Albany's and Cornwall's powers you heard
not?

50 *Gentleman.* 'Tis so;° they are afoot.

Kent. Well, sir, I'll bring you to our master Lear,
And leave you to attend him: some dear cause°
Will in concealment wrap me up awhile;
When I am known aright, you shall not grieve
55 Lending me this acquaintance. I pray you, go
Along with me.   [*Exeunt.*]

[Scene 4.   *The same. A tent.*]

*Enter, with drum and colors, Cordelia, Doctor,
and Soldiers.*

Cordelia. Alack, 'tis he: why, he was met even now
As mad as the vexed sea; singing aloud;
Crowned with rank femiter and furrow-weeds,
With hardocks, hemlock, nettles, cuckoo-flow'rs,
5 Darnel,° and all the idle weeds that grow
In our sustaining corn.° A century° send forth;
Search every acre in the high-grown field,

45 **casualties** chances   50 **'Tis so** i.e., I have heard of them   52 **dear cause**
important reason   4.4.3–5 **femiter . . . Darnel: femiter** fumitory, whose
leaves and juice are bitter; **furrow-weeds** weeds that grow in the furrow; or
plowed land; **hardocks** ? hoar or white docks, burdocks, harlocks; **hemlock**
a poison; **nettles** plants which sting and burn; **cuckoo-flow'rs** identified with
a plant employed to remedy diseases of the brain; **Darnel** tares, noisome
weeds   6 **sustaining corn** life-maintaining wheat   6 **century** ? sentry;
troop of a hundred soldiers

And bring him to our eye [*Exit an Officer.*] What
    can man's wisdom°
In the restoring his bereavèd° sense?
He that helps him take all my outward° worth.   10

Doctor. There is means, madam:
    Our foster-nurse° of nature is repose,
    The which he lacks: that to provoke° in him,
    Are many simples operative,° whose power
    Will close the eye of anguish.

Cordelia.   All blest secrets,   15
    All you unpublished virtues° of the earth,
    Spring with my tears! be aidant and remediate°
    In the good man's distress! Seek, seek for him,
    Lest his ungoverned rage dissolve the life
    That wants the means to lead it.°

Enter Messenger.

Messenger.   News, madam;   20
    The Brittish pow'rs are marching hitherward.

Cordelia.'Tis known before. Our preparation stands
    In expectation of them. O dear father,
    It is thy business that I go about;
    Therefore° great France   25
    My mourning and importuned° tears hath pitied.
    No blown° ambition doth our arms incite,
    But love, dear love, and our aged father's right:
    Soon may I hear and see him!   *Exeunt.*

---

8 **What can man's wisdom** what can science accomplish   9 **bereavèd**
impaired   10 **outward** material   12 **foster-nurse** fostering nurse   13 **provoke** induce   14 **simples operative** efficacious medicinal herbs   16 **unpublished virtues** i.e., secret remedial herbs   17 **remediate** remedial
20 **wants ... it** i.e., lacks the reason to control the rage   25 **Therefore**
because of that   26 **importuned** importunate   27 **blown** puffed up

[Scene 5.   *Gloucester's castle.*]

Enter Regan and Oswald.

Regan But are my brother's pow'rs set forth?

Oswald.   Ay, madam.

Regan. Himself in person there?

Oswald.   Madam, with much ado:°
　Your sister is the better soldier.

Regan. Lord Edmund spake not with your lord at
　home?

5　*Oswald.* No, madam.

Regan. What might import° my sister's letter to him?

Oswald. I know not, lady.

Regan. Faith, he is posted° hence on serious matter.
　It was great ignorance,° Gloucester's eyes being
　out,
10　To let him live. Where he arrives he moves
　All hearts against us: Edmund, I think, is gone,
　In pity of his misery, to dispatch
　His nighted° life; moreover, to descry
　The strength o' th' enemy.

Oswald. I must needs after him, madam, with my
15　letter.

Regan. Our troops set forth tomorrow: stay with us;
　The ways are dangerous.

Oswald.   I may not, madam:
　My lady charged my duty° in this business.

4.5.2 **ado** bother and persuasion   6 **import** purport, carry as its message
8 **is posted** has ridden speedily   9 **ignorance** folly   13 **nighted** (1) darkened, because blinded (2) benighted   18 **charged my duty** ordered me as a
solemn duty

Regan. Why should she write to Edmund? Might not you
    Transport her purposes° by word? Belike,°   *20*
    Some things I know not what. I'll love thee much,
    Let me unseal the letter.

Oswald.   Madam, I had rather——

Regan. I know your lady does not love her husband;
    I am sure of that: and at her late° being here
    She gave strange eliads° and most speaking looks   *25*
    To noble Edmund. I know you are of her bosom.°

Oswald. I, madam?

Regan. I speak in understanding: y'are; I know 't:
    Therefore I do advise you, take this note:°
    My lord is dead; Edmund and I have talked;   *30*
    And more convenient° is he for my hand
    Than for your lady's: you may gather more.°
    If you do find him, pray you, give him this;°
    And when your mistress hears thus much from you,
    I pray, desire her call° her wisdom to her.   *35*
    So, fare you well.
    If you do chance to hear of that blind traitor,
    Perferment° falls on him that cuts him off.

Oswald. Would I could meet him, madam! I should show
    What party I do follow.

Regan.   Fare thee well.   *40*

                        Exeunt.

---

20 Transport her purposes convey her intentions **20 Belike** probably
24 late recently **25 eliads** amorous looks **26 of her bosom** in her confidence **29 take this note** take note of this **31 convenient** fitting
32 gather more surmise more yourself **33 this** this advice **35 call** recall
38 Preferment promotion

[Scene 6.   *Fields near Dover.*]

Enter Gloucester and Edgar.

Gloucester. When shall I come to th' top of that same
   hill?

Edgar. You do climb up it now. Look, how we labor.

Gloucester. Methinks the ground is even.

Edgar.   Horrible steep.
   Hark, do you hear the sea?

Gloucester.   No, truly.

5   *Edgar.* Why then your other senses grow imperfect
   By your eyes' anguish.°

Gloucester.   So may it be indeed.
   Methinks thy voice is altered, and thou speak'st
   In better phrase and matter than thou didst.

Edgar. Y'are much deceived: in nothing am I changed
   But in my garments.

10   *Gloucester.*   Methinks y'are better spoken.

Edgar. Come on, sir; here's the place: stand still. How
   fearful
   And dizzy 'tis to cast one's eyes so low!
   The crows and choughs° that wing the midway air°
   Show scarce so gross° as beetles. Half way down
15   Hangs one that gathers sampire,° dreadful trade!
   Methinks he seems no bigger than his head.
   The fishermen that walk upon the beach
   Appear like mice; and yond tall anchoring° bark
   Diminished to her cock;° her cock, a buoy

4.6.6 **anguish** pain   13 **choughs** a kind of crow   13 **midway air** i.e.,
halfway down the cliff   14 **gross** large   15 **sampire** samphire, an aromatic
herb associated with Dover Cliffs   18 **anchoring** anchored   19 **cock** cock-
boat, a small boat usually towed behind the ship

Almost too small for sight. The murmuring surge   20
That on th' unnumb'red idle pebble° chafes
Cannot be heard so high. I'll look no more,
Lest my brain turn and the deficient sight
Topple° down headlong.

Gloucester.   Set me where you stand.

Edgar. Give me your hand: you are now within a foot   25
Of th' extreme verge: for all beneath the moon
Would I not leap upright.°

Gloucester.   Let go my hand.
Here, friend, 's another purse; in it a jewel
Well worth a poor man's taking. Fairies° and gods
Prosper it with thee! Go thou further off;   30
Bid me farewell, and let me hear thee going.

Edgar. Now fare ye well, good sir.

Gloucester.   With all my heart.

Edgar. [*Aside*] Why I do trifle thus with his despair
Is done to cure it.°

Gloucester.   O you mighty gods!

                              He kneels.

This world I do renounce, and in your sights   35
Shake patiently my great affliction off:
If I could bear it longer and not fall
To quarrel° with your great opposeless° wills,
My snuff° and loathèd part of nature should
Burn itself out. If Edgar live, O bless him!   40
Now, fellow, fare thee well.

                              He falls.

Edgar.   Gone, sir, farewell.

---

21 **unnumb'red idle pebble** innumerable pebbles, moved to and fro by
the waves to no purpose   23–24 **the deficient sight/Topple** my failing
sight topple me   27 **upright** i.e., even up in the air, to say nothing of forward, over the cliff   29 **Fairies** (who are supposed to guard and multiply
hidden treasure)   33–34 **Why . . . if** I play on his despair in order to cure it
37–38 **fall/To quarrel with** rebel against   38 **opposeless** not to be, and not
capable of being, opposed   39 **snuff** the guttering (and stinking) wick of a
burnt-out candle

And yet I know not how° conceit° may rob
The treasury of life, when life itself
Yields to° the theft. Had he been where he thought,
45   By this had thought been past. Alive or dead?
Ho, you sir! friend! Hear you, sir! speak!
Thus might he pass° indeed: yet he revives.
What are you, sir?

Gloucester.   Away, and let me die.

Edgar. Hadst thou been aught but gossamer, feathers,
      air,
50 ‐ So many fathom down precipitating,°
Thou'dst shivered like an egg: but thou dost
      breathe;
Hast heavy substance; bleed'st not; speak'st; art
      sound.
Ten masts at each° make not the altitude
Which thou hast perpendicularly fell:
55   Thy life's° a miracle. Speak yet again.

Gloucester. But have I fall'n, or no?

Edgar. From the dread summit of this chalky bourn.°
Look up a-height;° the shrill-gorged° lark so far
Cannot be seen or heard: do but look up.

60 *Gloucester.* Alack, I have no eyes.
Is wretchedness deprived that benefit,
To end itself by death? 'Twas yet some comfort,
When misery could beguile° the tyrant's rage
And frustrate his proud will.

Edgar.   Give me your arm.
65   Up, so. How is 't? Feel you° your legs? You stand.

Gloucester. Too well, too well.

Edgar.   This is above all strangeness.
Upon the crown o' th' cliff, what thing was that

---

42 **how** but what   42 **conceit** imagination   44 **Yields to** allows   47 **pass**
die   50 **precipitating** falling   53 **at each** one on top of the other   55 **life's**
survival   57 **bourn** boundary   58 **a-height** on high   58 **gorged** throated,
voiced   63 **beguile** cheat (i.e., by suicide)   65 **Feel you** have you any feeling in

Which parted from you?

Gloucester.   A poor unfortunate beggar.

Edgar. As I stood here below, methought his eyes
Were two full moons; he had a thousand noses,   70
Horns whelked° and waved like the enridgèd° sea:
It was some fiend; therefore, thou happy father,°
Think that the clearest° gods, who make them
    honors
Of men's impossibilities,° have preserved thee.

Gloucester. I do remember now: henceforth I'll bear   75
Affliction till it do cry out itself
"Enough, enough," and die. That thing you speak
    of,
I took it for a man; often 'twould say
"The fiend, the fiend"—he led me to that place.

Edgar. Bear free° and patient thoughts.
        *Enter Lear [fantastically dressed with wild
                    flowers].*
                        But who comes here?   80
The safer° sense will ne'er accommodate°
His master thus.

Lear. No, they cannot touch me for coining;° I am
    the King himself.

Edgar. O thou side-piercing sight!   85

Lear. Nature's above art in that respect.° There's
    your press-money.° That fellow handles his bow

---

71 **whelked** twisted   71 **enridgèd** i.e., furrowed into waves   72 **happy father** fortunate old man   73 **clearest** purest   73–74 **who . . . impossibilities**
who cause themselves to be honored and revered by performing miracles
of which men are incapable   80 **free** i.e., emancipated from grief and despair, which fetter the soul   81 **safer** sounder, saner   81 **accommodate**
dress, adorn   83 **touch me for coining** arrest me for minting coins (the
king's prerogative)   86 **Nature's . . . respect** i.e., a born king is superior to
legal (and hence artificial) inhibition. There is also a glance here at the popular Renaissance debate, concerning the relative importance of nature (inspiration) and art (training)   87 **press-money** (paid to conscripted soldiers)

like a crow-keeper;° draw me a clothier's yard.°
Look, look, a mouse! Peace, peace; this piece of
90 toasted cheese will do 't. There's my gauntlet;° I'll
prove it on° a giant. Bring up the brown bills.° O,
well flown,° bird! i' th' clout, i' th' clout:° hewgh!°
Give the word.°

Edgar. Sweet marjoram.°

95 *Lear.* Pass.

Gloucester. I know that voice.

Lear. Ha! Goneril, with a white beard! They flattered
me like a dog,° and told me I had white hairs
in my beard ere the black ones were there.° To
100 say "ay" and "no" to everything that I said! "Ay"
and "no" too was no good divinity.° When the
rain came to wet me once and the wind to make
me chatter; when the thunder would not peace at
my bidding; there I found 'em, there I smelt 'em
105 out. Go to, they are not men o' their words: they
told me I was everything; 'tis a lie, I am not ague-
proof.°

Gloucester. The trick° of that voice I do well remember: Is't not the king?

Lear.   Ay, every inch a king.
110 When I do stare, see how the subject quakes.
I pardon that man's life. What was thy cause?°

88 **crow-keeper** a farmer scaring away crows   88 **clothier's yard** (the
standard English arrow was a cloth-yard long. Here the injunction is to draw
the arrow back, like a powerful archer, a full yard to the ear)   90 **gauntlet**
armored glove, thrown down as a challenge   91 **prove it on** maintain my
challenge even against   91 **brown bills** halberds varnished to prevent rust
(here the reference is to the soldiers who carry them)   92 **well flown**
(falconer's cry; and perhaps a reference to the flight of the arrow)   92 **clout**
the target shot at   92 **hewgh** ? imitating the whizzing of the arrow
93 **word** password   94 **Sweet marjoram** herb, used as a remedy for brain
disease   96 **like a dog** as a dog flatters   98–99 **I . . . there** I was wise before I had even grown a beard   101 **no good divinity** (bad theology, because contrary to the Biblical saying [II Corinthians 1:18], "Our word
toward you was not yea and nay." See also James 5:12 "But let your yea be
yea, and your nay, nay; lest ye fall into condemnation"; and Matthew
5:36–37)   106–07 **ague-proof** secure against fever   108 **trick** intonation
111 **cause** offense

Adultery?
Thou shalt not die: die for adultery! No:
The wren goes to 't, and the small gilded fly
Does lecher° in my sight.　　　　　　　　　　　*115*
Let copulation thrive; for Gloucester's bastard son
Was kinder to his father than my daughters
Got° 'tween the lawful sheets.
To 't, luxury,° pell-mell! for I lack soldiers.°
Behold yond simp'ring dame,　　　　　　　　　　*120*
Whose face between her forks presages snow,°
That minces° virtue and does shake the head
To hear of pleasure's name.°
The fitchew,° nor the soilèd° horse, goes to 't
With a more riotous appetite.　　　　　　　　　*125*
Down from the waist they are Centaurs,°
Though women all above:
But to the girdle° do the gods inherit,°
Beneath is all the fiend's.
There's hell, there's darkness, there is the
　　sulphurous pit,　　　　　　　　　　　　　　*130*
Burning, scalding, stench, consumption; fie, fie, fie!
pah, pah! Give me an ounce of civet;° good apothe-
cary, sweeten my imagination: there's money for thee.

Gloucester. O, let me kiss that hand!

Lear. Let me wipe it first; it smells of mortality.°　　*135*

Gloucester. O ruined piece of nature! This great world
　Shall so wear out to nought.° Dost thou know me?

---

115 **lecher** copulate　118 **Got** begot　119 **luxury** lechery　119 **for . . . sol-diers** i.e., ? (1) whom copulation will supply (2) and am therefore powerless
121 **Whose . . . snow** whose cold demeanor seems to promise chaste behavior ("forks": legs)　122 **minces** squeamishly pretends to　123 **pleasure's name** the very name of sexual pleasure　124 **fitchew** polecat (and slang for "prostitute")　124 **soilèd** put to pasture, and hence wanton with feeding
126 **Centaurs** lustful creatures, half man and half horse　128 **girdle** waist
128 **inherit** possess　132 **civet** perfume　135 **mortality** (1) death (2) existence　136–37 **This . . . nought** i.e., the universe (macrocosm) will decay to nothing in the same way as the little world of man (microcosm)

Lear. I remember thine eyes well enough. Dost thou
squiny° at me? No, do thy worst, blind Cupid;° I'll
140 not love. Read thou this challenge;° mark but the
penning of it.

Gloucester. Were all thy letters suns, I could not see.

Edgar. I would not take° this from report: it is,
And my heart breaks at it.

145 *Lear.* Read.

Gloucester. What, with the case° of eyes?

Lear. O, ho, are you there with me?° No eyes in your
head, nor no money in your purse? Your eyes are
in a heavy case,° your purse in a light,° yet you
150 see how this world goes.

Gloucester. I see it feelingly.°

Lear. What, art mad? A man may see how this world
goes with no eyes. Look with thine ears: see how
yond justice rails upon yond simple° thief. Hark,
155 in thine ear: change places, and, handy-dandy,°
which is the justice, which is the thief? Thou hast
seen a farmer's dog bark at a beggar?

Gloucester. Ay, sir.

Lear. And the creature run from the cur? There thou
160 mightst behold the great image of authority:° a
dog's obeyed in office.°
Thou rascal beadle,° hold thy bloody hand!
Why dost thou lash that whore? Strip thy own
back;
Thou hotly lusts to use her in that kind°

139 **squiny** squint, look sideways, like a prostitute   139 **blind Cupid** the
sign hung before a brothel   140 **challenge** a reminiscence of ll. 89–90
143 **take** believe   146 **case** empty sockets   147 **are . . . me** is that what you
tell me   149 **heavy case** sad plight (pun on l. 146)   149 **light** i.e., empty
151 **feelingly** (1) by touch (2) by feeling pain (3) with emotion   154 **simple**
common, of low estate   155 **handy-dandy** i.e., choose, guess (after the children's game—"Handy-dandy, prickly prandy"—of choosing the right hand)
160 **image of authority** symbol revealing the true meaning of authority
160–61 **a . . . office** i.e., whoever has power is obeyed   162 **beadle** parish
constable   164 **kind** i.e., sexual act

For which thou whip'st her. The usurer hangs the
    cozener.°   *165*
Through tattered clothes small vices do appear;
Robes and furred gowns° hide all. Plate sin with
    gold,
And the strong lance of justice hurtless° breaks;
Arm it in rags, a pygmy's straw does pierce it.
None does offend, none, I say, none; I'll able°
    'em: *170*
Take that° of me, my friend, who have the power
To seal th' accuser's lips. Get thee glass eyes,°
And, like a scurvy politician,° seem
To see the things thou dost not. Now, now, now,
    now.
Pull off my boots: harder, harder: so.   *175*

Edgar. O, matter and impertinency° mixed!
    Reason in madness!

Lear. If thou wilt weep my fortunes, take my eyes.
    I know thee well enough; thy name is Gloucester:
    Thou must be patient; we came crying hither: *180*
    Thou know'st, the first time that we smell the air
    We wawl and cry. I will preach to thee: mark.

Gloucester. Alack, alack the day!

Lear. When we are born, we cry that we are come
    To this great stage of fools. This'° a good block.°   *185*

164–65 **The usurer . . . cozener** i.e., the powerful moneylender, in his
role as judge, puts to death the petty cheat   167 **Robes and furred
gowns** (worn by a judge)   168 **hurtless** i.e., without hurting the sinner
170 **able** vouch for   171 **that** (the immunity just conferred) (l. 170)
172 **glass eyes** spectacles   173 **scurvy politician** vile politic man
176 **matter and impertinency** sense and nonsense   185 **This'** this is
185 **block** (various meanings have been suggested, for example, the
stump of a tree, on which Lear is supposed to climb; a mounting-block,
which suggests "horse" l. 187; a hat [which Lear or another must be made
to wear], from the block on which a felt hat is molded, and which would
suggest a "felt" l. 187. The proposal here is that "block" be taken to denote
the quintain, whose function is to bear blows, "a mere lifeless block"
[*As You Like It*, 1.2.263], an object shaped like a man and used for tilting
practice. See also *Much Ado*, 2.1.246–7, "she misused me past the endurance of a block!" and, in the same passage, the associated reference,
"I stood like a man at a mark [target]" [1.253])

It were a delicate° stratagem, to shoe
A troop of horse with felt: I'll put 't in proof;°
And when I have stol'n upon these son-in-laws,
Then, kill, kill, kill, kill, kill, kill!

    Enter a Gentleman [with Attendants].

190 *Gentleman.* O, here he is: lay hand upon him. Sir,
  Your most dear daughter—

Lear. No rescue? What, a prisoner? I am even
  The natural fool° of fortune. Use me well;
  You shall have ransom. Let me have surgeons;
  I am cut° to th' brains.

195 *Gentleman.*   You shall have anything.

Lear. No seconds?° all myself?
  Why, this would make a man a man of salt,°
  To use his eyes for garden water-pots,
  Ay, and laying autumn's dust.

200 *Gentleman.* Good sir—

Lear. I will die bravely,° like a smug° bridegroom.°
  What!
  I will be jovial: come, come; I am a king;
  Masters, know you that?

Gentleman. You are a royal one, and we obey you.

205 *Lear.* Then there's life in 't.° Come, and you get it,
  you shall get it by running. Sa, sa, sa, sa.°

    Exit [running; Attendants follow].

Gentleman. A sight most pitiful in the meanest wretch,
  Past speaking of in a king! Thou hast one daughter
  Who redeems nature from the general curse
210   Which twain have brought her to.°

186 **delicate** subtle 187 **put't in proof** test it 193 **natural fool** born sport
(with pun on "natural": "imbecile") 195 **cut** wounded 196 **seconds** supporters 197 **man of salt** i.e., all (salt) tears 201 **bravely** (1) smartly attired
(2) courageously 201 **smug** spick and span 201 **bridegroom** whose
"brave" sexual feats are picked up in the pun on "die" 205 **there's life in't**
there's still hope 206 **Sa . . . sa** hunting and rallying cry; also an interjection
of defiance 209–10 **general . . . to** (1) universal condemnation which Goneril
and Regan have made for (2) damnation incurred by the original sin of Adam
and Eve

Edgar. Hail, gentle° sir.

Gentleman.   Sir, speed° you: what's your will?

Edgar. Do you hear aught, sir, of a battle toward?°

Gentleman. Most sure and vulgar:° every one hears that,
Which can distinguish sound.

Edgar.   But, by your favor,
How near's the other army?   *215*

Gentleman. Near and on speedy foot; the main descry
Stands on the hourly thought.°

Edgar.   I thank you, sir: that's all.

Gentleman. Though that the Queen on special cause is here,
Her army is moved on.

Edgar.   I thank you, sir.

                    Exit [Gentleman].

Gloucester. You ever-gentle gods, take my breath from me;   *220*
Let not my worser spirit° tempt me again
To die before you please.

Edgar.   Well pray you, father.

Gloucester. Now, good sir, what are you?

Edgar. A most poor man, made tame° to fortune's blows;
Who, by the art of known and feeling sorrows,°   *225*
Am pregnant° to good pity. Give me your hand,
I'll lead you to some biding.°

Gloucester.   Hearty thanks;

---

211 **gentle** noble   211 **speed** God speed   212 **toward** impending   213 **vulgar** common knowledge   216–17 **the . . . thought** we expect to see the main body of the army any hour   221 **worser spirit** bad angel, evil side of my nature   224 **tame** submissive   225 **art . . . sorrows** instruction of sorrows painfully experienced   226 **pregnant** disposed   227 **biding** place of refuge

The bounty and the benison° of heaven
To boot, and boot.°

Enter Oswald.

Oswald.   A proclaimed prize°! Most happy!°
230 That eyeless head of thine was first framed° flesh
To raise my fortunes. Thou old unhappy traitor,
Briefly thyself remember:° the sword is out
That must destroy thee.

Gloucester.   Now let thy friendly° hand
Put strength enough to 't.

[*Edgar interposes.*]

Oswald.   Wherefore, bold peasant,
235 Dar'st thou support a published° traitor? Hence!
Lest that th' infection of his fortune take
Like hold on thee. Let go his arm.

Edgar. Chill° not let go, zir, without vurther 'casion.°

Oswald. Let go, slave, or thou diest!

240 *Edgar.* Good gentleman, go your gait,° and let poor
volk° pass. And chud ha' bin zwaggered° out of my
life, 'twould not ha' bin zo long as 'tis by a vort-
night. Nay, come not near th' old man; keep out,
che vor' ye,° or I'se° try whether your costard°
245 or my ballow° be the harder: chill be plain with
you.

Oswald. Out, dunghill!

They fight.

---

228 **benison** blessing   229 **To boot, and boot** also, and in the highest degree
229 **proclaimed prize** i.e., one with a price on his head   229 **happy** fortunate (for Oswald)   230 **framed** created   232 **thyself remember** i.e., pray,
think of your sins   233 **friendly** i.e., because it offers the death Gloucester
covets   235 **published** proclaimed   238 **Chill** . . . (Edgar speaks in rustic
dialect)   238 **Chill** I will   238 **vurther 'casion** further occasion   240 **gait**
way   241 **volk** folk   241 **And chud ha' bin zwaggered** if I could have
been swaggered   244 **Che vor' ye** I warrant you   244 **I'se** I shall
244 **costard** head (literally, "apple")   245 **ballow** cudgel

Edgar. Chill pick your teeth,° zir: come; no matter
   vor your foins.°

                         [*Oswald falls.*]

Oswald. Slave, thou hast slain me. Villain, take my
     purse: 250
   If ever thou wilt thrive, bury my body,
   And give the letters which thou find'st about° me
   To Edmund Earl of Gloucester; seek him out
   Upon the English party.° O, untimely death!
   Death!   255

                               He dies.

Edgar. I know thee well. A serviceable° villain,
   As duteous° to the vices of thy mistress
   As badness would desire.

Gloucester.   What, is he dead?

Edgar. Sit you down, father; rest you.
   Let's see these pockets: the letters that he speaks
     of   260
   May be my friends. He's dead; I am only sorry
   He had no other deathsman.° Let us see:
   Leave,° gentle wax;° and, manners, blame us not:
   To know our enemies' minds, we rip their hearts;
   Their papers° is more lawful.   265

                     Reads the letter.

   "Let our reciprocal vows be remembered. You
have many opportunities to cut him off: if your
will want not,° time and place will be fruitfully
offered. There is nothing done, if he return the conqueror: then am I the prisoner, and his bed my 270
jail; from the loathed warmth whereof deliver me,
and supply the place for your labor.
   "Your—wife, so I would° say—affectionate

---

248 **Chill pick your teeth** I will knock your teeth out   249 **foins** thrusts
252 **about** upon   254 **party** side   256 **serviceable** ready to be used
257 **duteous** obedient   262 **deathsman** executioner   263 **Leave** by your
leave   263 **wax** (with which the letter is sealed)   265 **Their papers** i.e., to
rip their papers   267–68 **if . . . not** if your desire (and lust) be not lacking
273 **would** would like to

    servant, and for you her own for venture,°
275   'Goneril.' "
    O indistinguished space of woman's will!°
    A plot upon her virtuous husband's life;
    And the exchange° my brother! Here in the sands
    Thee I'll rake up,° the post unsanctified°
280   Of murderous lechers; and in the mature° time,
    With this ungracious paper° strike° the sight
    Of the death-practiced° Duke: for him 'tis well
    That of thy death and business I can tell.

    Gloucester. The King is mad: how stiff° is my vile
        sense,°
285   That I stand up, and have ingenious° feeling
    Of my huge sorrows! Better I were distract:°
    So should my thoughts be severed from my griefs,
    And woes by wrong imaginations° lose
    The knowledge of themselves.
                            Drum afar off.

    Edgar.   Give me your hand:
290   Far off, methinks, I hear the beaten drum.
    Come, father, I'll bestow° you with a friend.
                                    Exeunt.

Scene 7.   [*A tent in the French camp.*]

    Enter Cordelia, Kent, Doctor, and Gentleman.

    Cordelia. O thou good Kent, how shall I live and
        work,

274 **and ... venture** i.e., and one who holds you her own for venturing (Edmund had earlier been promised union by Goneril, "If you dare venture in your own behalf," 4.2.20). 276 **indistinguished ... will** unlimited range of woman's lust 278 **exchange** substitute 279 **rake up** cover up, bury 279 **post unsanctified** unholy messenger 280 **mature** ripe 281 **ungracious paper** wicked letter 281 **strike** blast 282 **death-practiced** whose death is plotted 284 **stiff** unbending 284 **vile sense** hateful capacity for feeling 285 **ingenious** conscious 286 **distract** distracted, mad 288 **wrong imaginations** delusions 291 **bestow** lodge

    To match thy goodness? My life will be too short,
    And every measure fail me.

Kent. To be acknowledged, madam, is o'erpaid.
    All my reports go° with the modest truth,   *5*
    Nor more nor clipped,° but so.

Cordelia.   Be better suited:°
    These weeds° are memories° of those worser
       hours:
    I prithee, put them off.

Kent.   Pardon, dear madam;
    Yet to be known shortens my made intent:°
    My boon I make it,° that you know me not   *10*
    Till time and I think meet.°

Cordelia. Then be 't so, my good lord. [*To the Doc-tor.*] How does the King?

Doctor. Madam, sleeps still.

Cordelia. O you kind gods!
    Cure this great breach in his abusèd° nature.   *15*
    Th' untuned and jarring senses, O, wind up°
    Of this child-changèd father.

Doctor.   So please your Majesty
    That we may wake the King: he hath slept long.

Cordelia. Be governed by your knowledge, and
       proceed
    I' th' sway of° your own will. Is he arrayed?   *20*

      Enter Lear in a chair carried by Servants.

4.7.5 **go** conform 6 **clipped** curtailed 6 **suited** attired 7 **weeds** clothes
7 **memories** reminders 9 **Yet . . . intent** to reveal myself just yet interferes
with the plan I have made 10 **My boon I make it** I ask this reward 11
meet fitting 15 **abusèd** disturbed 16 **wind up** tune 17 **child-changèd**
changed, deranged (and also, reduced to a child) by the cruelty of his children 20 **I' th' sway of** according to

Gentleman. Ay, madam; in the heaviness of sleep
　　We put fresh garments on him.

Doctor. Be by, good madam, when we do awake him;
　　I doubt not of his temperance.°

Cordelia.　　　　　　　　　　　Very well.

Doctor. Please you, draw near. Louder the music
25　　　there!

Cordelia. O my dear father, restoration hang
　　Thy medicine on my lips, and let this kiss
　　Repair those violent harms that my two sisters
　　Have in thy reverence° made.

Kent.　　　　　　　　　　Kind and dear Princess.

Cordelia. Had you not been their father, these white
30　　　flakes°
　　Did challenge° pity of them. Was this a face
　　To be opposed against the warring winds?
　　To stand against the deep dread-bolted° thunder?
　　In the most terrible and nimble stroke
35　　Of quick, cross° lightning to watch—poor
　　　perdu!°—
　　With this thin helm?° Mine enemy's dog,
　　Though he had bit me, should have stood that night
　　Against my fire; and wast thou fain,° poor father,
　　To hovel thee with swine and rogues° forlorn,
40　　In short° and musty straw? Alack, alack!
　　'Tis wonder that thy life and wits at once
　　Had not concluded all.° He wakes; speak to him.

Doctor. Madam, do you; 'tis fittest.

---

24 **temperance** sanity　29 **reverence** revered person　30 **flakes** hairs (in long strands)　31 **challenge** claim　33 **deep dread-bolted** deep-voiced and furnished with the dreadful thunderbolt　35 **cross** zigzag　35 **perdu** (1) sentry in a forlorn position (2) lost one　36 **helm** helmet (his scanty hair)　38 **fain** pleased　39 **rogues** vagabonds　40 **short** (when straw is freshly cut, it is long, and suitable for bedding, given its flexibility and crispness. As it is used, it becomes musty, shreds into pieces, is "short." In contemporary Maine usage, "short manure" refers to dung mixed with straw that has been broken up; "long manure" to dung mixed with coarse new straw)　42 **concluded all** come to a complete end

Cordelia. How does my royal lord? How fares your
  Majesty?

Lear. You do me wrong to take me out o' th' grave: 45
  Thou art a soul in bliss; but I am bound
  Upon a wheel of fire,° that mine own tears
  Do scald like molten lead.

Cordelia.   Sir, do you know me?

Lear. You are a spirit, I know. Where did you die?

Cordelia. Still, still, far wide.°   50

Doctor. He's scarce awake: let him alone awhile.

Lear. Where have I been? Where am I? Fair daylight?
  I am mightily abused.° I should ev'n die with pity,
  To see another thus. I know not what to say.
  I will not swear these are my hands: let's see;   55
  I feel this pin prick. Would I were assured
  Of my condition.

Cordelia.   O, look upon me, sir,
  And hold your hand in benediction o'er me.
  You must not kneel.

Lear.   Pray, do not mock me:
  I am a very foolish fond° old man,   60
  Fourscore and upward, not an hour more nor less;
  And, to deal plainly,
  I fear I am not in my perfect mind.
  Methinks I should know you and know this man,
  Yet I am doubtful; for I am mainly° ignorant   65
  What place this is, and all the skill I have
  Remembers not these garments, nor I know not
  Where I did lodge last night. Do not laugh at me,
  For, as I am a man, I think this lady
  To be my child Cordelia.

Cordelia.   And so I am, I am.   70

Lear. Be your tears wet? Yes, faith. I pray, weep not.
  If you have poison for me, I will drink it.

47 **wheel of fire** (torment associated by the Middle Ages with Hell, where
Lear thinks he is)   50 **wide** i.e., of the mark (of sanity)   53 **abused** de-
luded   60 **fond** in dotage   65 **mainly** entirely

I know you do not love me; for your sisters
Have, as I do remember, done me wrong.
You have some cause, they have not.

75 *Cordelia.*   No cause, no cause.

Lear. Am I in France?

Kent.   In your own kingdom, sir.

Lear. Do not abuse° me.

Doctor. Be comforted, good madam: the great rage,°
You see, is killed in him: and yet it is danger
80 To make him even o'er° the time he has lost.
Desire him to go in; trouble him no more
Till further settling.°

Cordelia. Will 't please your Highness walk?°

Lear. You must bear with me. Pray you now, forget
85 and forgive. I am old and foolish.

              Exeunt. Mane[n]t° Kent and Gentleman.

Gentleman. Holds it true, sir, that the Duke of Cornwall was so slain?

Kent. Most certain, sir.

Gentleman. Who is conductor of his people?

90 *Kent.* As 'tis said, the bastard son of Gloucester.

Gentleman. They say Edgar, his banished son, is with
the Earl of Kent in Germany.

Kent. Report is changeable.° 'Tis time to look about;
the powers° of the kingdom approach apace.

95 *Gentleman.* The arbitrement° is like to be bloody.
Fare you well, sir.   [*Exit.*]

Kent. My point and period will be throughly
     wrought,°
Or well or ill, as this day's battle's fought.

                             Exit.

---

77 abuse deceive   **78 rage** frenzy   **80 even o'er** smooth over by filling in; and hence, "recollect"   **82 settling** calming   **83 walk** (perhaps in the sense of "withdraw")   **85 s.d. Mane[n]t** remain   **93 Report is changeable** rumors are unreliable   **94 powers** armies   **95 arbitrement** deciding encounter   **97 My . . . wrought** the aim and end, the close of my life would be completely worked out

ACT 5

Scene 1.   [*The British camp near Dover.*]

Enter, with drum and colors, Edmund, Regan,
Gentlemen, and Soldiers.

Edmund. Know° of the Duke if his last purpose hold,°
  Or whether since he is advised° by aught
  To change the course: he's full of alteration
  And self-reproving: bring his constant pleasure.°

                [*To a Gentleman, who goes out.*]

Regan. Our sister's man is certainly miscarried.°   5

Edmund. 'Tis to be doubted,° madam.

Regan.   Now, sweet lord,
  You know the goodness I intend upon you:
  Tell me, but truly, but then speak the truth,
  Do you not love my sister?

Edmund.   In honored° love.

Regan. But have you never found my brother's way   10
  To the forfended° place?

Edmund.   That thought abuses° you.

5.1.1 **Know** learn   1 **last purpose hold** most recent intention (to fight) be
maintained   2 **advised** induced   4 **constant pleasure** fixed (final) decision
5 **miscarried** come to grief   6 **doubted** feared   9 **honored** honorable
11 **forfended** forbidden   11 **abuses** (1) deceives (2) demeans, is unworthy of

127

Regan. I am doubtful that you have been conjunct
   And bosomed with her, as far as we call hers.°

Edmund. No, by mine honor, madam.

15 *Regan.* I shall never endure her: dear my lord,
   Be not familiar with her.

Edmund.   Fear° me not.—
   She and the Duke her husband!

*Enter, with drum and colors, Albany, Goneril
      [and] Soldiers.*

Goneril. [*Aside*] I had rather lose the battle than
      that sister
   Should loosen° him and me.

20 *Albany.* Our very loving sister, well be-met.°
   Sir, this I heard, the King is come to his daughter,
   With others whom the rigor of our state°
   Forced to cry out. Where I could not be honest,°
   I never yet was valiant: for this business,
25 It touches us, as° France invades our land,
   Not bolds the King, with others, whom, I fear,
   Most just and heavy causes make oppose.°

Edmund. Sir, you speak nobly.

Regan.   Why is this reasoned?°

Goneril. Combine together 'gainst the enemy;
30 For these domestic and particular broils°
   Are not the question° here.

Albany.   Let's then determine
   With th' ancient of war° on our proceeding.

Edmund. I shall attend you presently at your tent.

12–13 **I ... hers** I fear that you have united with her intimately, in the
fullest possible way   16 **Fear** distrust   19 **loosen** separate   20 **be-met**
met   22 **rigor ... state** tyranny of our government   23 **honest** honorable
25 **touches us, as** concerns me, only in that   26–27 **Not ... oppose** and not
in that France emboldens the King and others, who have been led, by real
and serious grievances, to take up arms against us   28 **reasoned** argued
30 **particular broils** private quarrels   31 **question** issue   32 **th' ancient
of war** experienced commanders

Regan. Sister, you'll go with us?°

Goneril. No.   35

Regan. 'Tis most convenient;° pray you, go with us.

Goneril. [*Aside*] O, ho, I know the riddle.°—I
  will go.
   Exeunt both the Armies. Enter Edgar [*disguised*].

Edgar. If e'er your Grace had speech with man so
  poor,
Hear me one word.

Albany. [*To those going out*] I'll overtake you. [*To
  Edgar*] Speak.

          Exeunt [*all but Albany and Edgar*].

Edgar. Before you fight the battle, ope this letter.   40
If you have victory, let the trumpet sound
For° him that brought it: wretched though I seem,
I can produce a champion that will prove°
What is avouchèd° there. If you miscarry,
Your business of° the world hath so an end,   45
And machination° ceases. Fortune love you.

Albany. Stay till I have read the letter.

Edgar.   I was forbid it.
When time shall serve, let but the herald cry,
And I'll appear again.

Albany. Why, fare thee well: I will o'erlook° thy
  paper.   *Exit* [*Edgar*].   50
         Enter Edmund.

Edmund. The enemy's in view: draw up your powers.
Here is the guess° of their true strength and
  forces
By diligent discovery;° but your haste

---

34 **us** me (rather than Edmund)   36 **convenient** fitting, desirable   37 **rid-dle** real reason (for Regan's curious request)   41–42 **sound/For** summon   43 **prove** i.e., by trial of combat   44 **avouchèd** maintained   45 **of** in   46 **machination** plotting   50 **o'erlook** read over   52 **guess** estimate   53 **By diligent discovery** obtained by careful reconnoitering

Is now urged on you.

Albany.   We will greet° the time. *Exit.*

55 *Edmund.* To both these sisters have I sworn my love;
      Each jealous° of the other, as the stung
      Are of the adder. Which of them shall I take?
      Both? One? Or neither? Neither can be enjoyed,
      If both remain alive: to take the widow
60   Exasperates, makes mad her sister Goneril;
      And hardly° shall I carry out my side,°
      Her husband being alive. Now then, we'll use
      His countenance° for the battle; which being done,
      Let her who would be rid of him devise
65   His speedy taking off. As for the mercy
      Which he intends to Lear and to Cordelia,
      The battle done, and they within our power,
      Shall never see his pardon; for my state
      Stands on me to defend, not to debate.°   *Exit.*

Scene 2.   [*A field between the two camps.*]

      *Alarum° within. Enter, with drum and colors,
      Lear, Cordelia, and Soldiers, over the stage; and
      exeunt.*
            Enter Edgar and Gloucester.
  Edgar. Here, father,° take the shadow of this tree
      For your good host; pray that the right may thrive.
      If ever I return to you again,
      I'll bring you comfort.
  Gloucester.   Grace go with you, sir.
                                    Exit [Edgar].

54 **greet** i.e., meet the demands of   56 **jealous** suspicious   61 **hardly** with
difficulty   61 **carry . . . side** (1) satisfy my ambition (2) fulfill my bargain
(with Goneril)   63 **countenance** authority   68–69 **for . . . debate** my position requires me to act, not to reason about right and wrong 5.2. s.d.
Alarum a trumpet call to battle   1 **father** i.e., venerable old man (Edgar
has not yet revealed his identity)

Alarum and retreat° within. [Re-]enter Edgar.

Edgar. Away, old man; give me thy hand; away!   5
  King Lear hath lost, he and his daughter ta'en:°
  Give me thy hand; come on.

Gloucester. No further, sir; a man may rot even here.

Edgar. What, in ill thoughts again? Men must endure
  Their going hence, even as their coming hither: 10
  Ripeness° is all. Come on.

Gloucester.   And that's true too.
                            Exeunt.

Scene 3.   [*The British camp near Dover.*]

*Enter, in conquest, with drum and colors, Ed-
mund; Lear and Cordelia, as prisoners; Soldiers,
Captain.*

Edmund. Some officers take them away: good guard,°
  Until their greater pleasures° first be known
  That are to censure° them.

Cordelia.   We are not the first
  Who with best meaning° have incurred the worst.
  For thee, oppressèd King, I am cast down;   5
  Myself could else out-frown false fortune's frown.
  Shall we not see these daughters and these sisters?

Lear. No, no, no, no! Come, let's away to prison:
  We two alone will sing like birds i' th' cage:
  When thou dost ask me blessing, I'll kneel down   10
  And ask of thee forgiveness: so we'll live,
  And pray, and sing, and tell old tales, and laugh

---

4 s.d. **retreat** (signaled by a trumpet) 6 **ta'en** captured 11 **Ripeness** maturity, as of fruit that is ready to fall 5.3.1 **good guard** let there be good guard 2 **their greater pleasures** the will of those in command, the great ones 3 **censure** pass judgment on 4 **meaning** intentions

        At gilded butterflies,° and hear poor rogues
        Talk of court news; and we'll talk with them too,
15   Who loses and who wins, who's in, who's out;
        And take upon's the mystery of things,
        As if we were God's spies:° and we'll wear out,°
        In a walled prison, packs and sects of great ones
        That ebb and flow by th' moon.°

Edmund.   Take them away.

20 *Lear.* Upon such sacrifices, my Cordelia,
        The gods themselves throw incense.° Have I caught
            thee?
        He that parts us shall bring a brand from heaven,
        And fire us hence like foxes.° Wipe thine eyes;
        The good years° shall devour them,° flesh and fell,°
        Ere they shall make us weep. We'll see 'em starved
25   first.
        Come.   [*Exeunt Lear and Cordelia, guarded.*]

Edmund. Come hither, captain; hark.
        Take thou this note: go follow them to prison:
        One step I have advanced thee; if thou dost
30   As this instructs thee, thou dost make thy way
        To noble fortunes: know thou this, that men
        Are as the time is:° to be tender-minded
        Does not become a sword:° thy great employment
        Will not bear question;° either say thou'lt do 't,
        Or thrive by other means.

35 *Captain.*   I'll do 't, my lord.

---

13 **gilded butterflies** i.e., gorgeously attired courtiers, fluttering after nothing   16–17 **take ... spies** profess to read the riddle of existence, as if endowed with divine omniscience   17 **wear out** outlast   18–19 **packs ... moon** intriguing and partisan cliques of those in high station, whose fortunes change every month   20–21 **Upon ... incense** i.e., the gods approve our renunciation of the world   22–23 **He ... foxes** no human agency can separate us, but only divine interposition, as of a heavenly torch parting us like foxes who are driven from their place of refuge by fire and smoke   24 **good years** plague and pestilence ("undefined malefic power or agency," *N.E.D.*)   24 **them** i.e., the enemies of Lear and Cordelia   24 **fell** skin   32 **as the time is** i.e., absolutely determined by the exigencies of the moment   33 **become a sword** befit a soldier   34 **bear question** admit of discussion

Edmund. About it; and write happy° when th' hast
    done.
    Mark; I say, instantly, and carry it so°
    As I have set it down.

Captain. I cannot draw a cart, nor eat dried oats;
    If it be man's work, I'll do 't.   *Exit Captain.*   40

> *Flourish. Enter Albany, Goneril, Regan [another
            Captain, and] Soldiers.*

Albany. Sir, you have showed today your valiant
    strain,°
    And fortune led you well: you have the captives
    Who were the opposites of° this day's strife:
    I do require them of you, so to use them
    As we shall find their merits° and our safety   45
    May equally determine.

Edmund.   Sir, I thought it fit
    To send the old and miserable King
    To some retention and appointed guard;°
    Whose° age had charms in it, whose title more,
    To pluck the common bosom on his side,°   50
    And turn our impressed lances in our eyes°
    Which do command them. With him I sent the
        Queen:
    My reason all the same; and they are ready
    Tomorrow, or at further space,° t' appear
    Where you shall hold your session.° At this time   55
    We sweat and bleed: the friend hath lost his friend;
    And the best quarrels, in the heat, are cursed
    By those that feel their sharpness.°
    The question of Cordelia and her father

---

36 write happy style yourself fortunate   **37 carry it so** manage the affair
in exactly that manner (as if Cordelia had taken her own life)   **41 strain**
(1) stock (2) character   **43 opposites of** opponents in   **45 merits** deserts
48 retention ... guard confinement under duly appointed guard
49 Whose i.e., Lear's   **50 pluck ... side** win the sympathy of the people to
himself   **51 turn ... eyes** turn our conscripted lancers against us   **54 further space** a later time   **55 session** trial   **57–58 the ... sharpness** the
worthiest causes may be judged badly by those who have been affected
painfully by them, and whose passion has not yet cooled

Requires a fitter place.

60 *Albany.*   Sir, by your patience,
I hold you but a subject of° this war,
Not as a brother.

Regan.   That's as we list to grace° him.
Methinks our pleasure might have been demanded,
Ere you had spoke so far. He led our powers,
65 Bore the commission of my place and person;
The which immediacy may well stand up
And call itself your brother.°

Goneril.   Not so hot:
In his own grace he doth exalt himself
More than in your addition.°

Regan.   In my rights,
70 By me invested, he compeers° the best.

Goneril. That were the most,° if he should husband
you.°

Regan. Jesters do oft prove prophets.

Goneril.   Holla, holla!
That eye that told you so looked but a-squint.°

Regan. Lady, I am not well; else I should answer
75 From a full-flowing stomach.° General,
Take thou my soldiers, prisoners, patrimony;°
Dispose of them, of me; the walls is thine:°
Witness the world, that I create thee here
My lord, and master.

Goneril.   Mean you to enjoy him?

80 *Albany.* The let-alone° lies not in your good will.

---

61 **subject of** subordinate in   62 **list to grace** wish to honor   65–67 **Bore . . .
brother** was authorized, as my deputy, to take command; his present status, as
my immediate representative, entitles him to be considered your equal
69 **your addition** honors you have bestowed on him   70 **compeers** equals
71 **most** most complete investing in your rights   71 **husband you** become your husband   73 **a-squint** cross-eyed   75 **From . . . stomach** angrily
76 **patrimony** inheritance   77 **walls is thine** i.e., Regan's person, which Edmund has stormed and won   80 **let-alone** power to prevent

Edmund. Nor in thine, lord.

Albany.   Half-blooded° fellow, yes.

Regan. [*To Edmund*] Let the drum strike, and prove
  my title thine.°

Albany. Stay yet; hear reason. Edmund, I arrest thee
  On capital treason; and in thy attaint°
  This gilded serpent [*pointing to Goneril*]. For
  your claim, fair sister,   85
  I bar it in the interest of my wife.
  'Tis she is subcontracted° to this lord,
  And I, her husband, contradict your banes.°
  If you will marry, make your loves° to me;
  My Lady is bespoke.°

Goneril. .   An interlude!°   90

Albany. Thou art armed, Gloucester: let the trumpet
  sound:
  If none appear to prove upon thy person
  Thy heinous, manifest, and many treasons,
  There is my pledge° [*throwing down a glove*]:
  I'll make° it on thy heart,
  Ere I taste bread, thou art in nothing less   95
  Than I have here proclaimed thee.

Regan.   Sick, O, sick!

Goneril. [*Aside*] If not, I'll ne'er trust medicine.°

Edmund. [*Throwing down a glove*] There's my
  exchange:° what in the world he is
  That names me traitor, villain-like he lies:°
  Call by the trumpet:° he that dares approach,   100

81 **Half-blooded** bastard, and so only half noble   82 **prove . . . thine** prove
by combat your entitlement to my rights   84 **in thy attaint** as a sharer in the
treason for which you are impeached   87 **subcontracted** pledged by a contract which is called into question by the existence of a previous contract
(Goneril's marriage)   88 **contradict your banes** forbid your announced
intention to marry (by citing the precontract)   89 **loves** love-suits   90 **bespoke** already pledged   90 **interlude** play   94 **pledge** gage 94 **make** prove
97 **medicine** poison   98 **exchange** (technical term, denoting the glove Edmund throws down)   99 **villain-like he lies** (the lie direct, a challenge to
mortal combat)   100 **trumpet** trumpeter

On him, on you—who not?—I will maintain
My truth and honor firmly.

Albany. A herald, ho!

Edmund.   A herald, ho, a herald!

Albany. Trust to thy single virtue;° for thy soldiers,
105   All levied in my name, have in my name
Took their discharge.

Regan.   My sickness grows upon me.

Albany. She is not well; convey her to my tent.

                              [*Exit Regan, led.*]

              Enter a Herald.

Come hither, herald. Let the trumpet sound—
And read out this.

110 *Captain.* Sound, trumpet!

              A trumpet sounds.

Herald. (*Reads.*) "If any man of quality or degree°
within the lists° of the army will maintain upon Edmund, supposed Earl of Gloucester, that he is a
manifold traitor, let him appear by the third sound
115   of the trumpet: he is bold in his defense."

Edmund. Sound!

              First trumpet.

Herald. Again!

              Second trumpet.

Herald. Again!

              Third trumpet.

       *Trumpet answers within. Enter Edgar, at the
       third sound, armed, a trumpet before him.*°

Albany. Ask him his purposes, why he appears
Upon this call o' th' trumpet.

120 *Herald.*   What are you?

---

104 **single virtue** unaided valor   111 **quality or degree** rank or position
112 **lists** rolls   118 s.d. **trumpet before him** trumpeter preceding him

Your name, your quality,° and why you answer
This present summons?

Edgar.   Know, my name is lost;
By treason's tooth bare-gnawn and canker-bit:°
Yet am I noble as the adversary
I come to cope.°

Albany.   Which is that adversary?   *125*

Edgar. What's he that speaks for Edmund, Earl of
Gloucester?

Edmund. Himself: what say'st thou to him?

Edgar.   Draw thy sword,
That if my speech offend a noble heart,
Thy arm may do thee justice: here is mine.
Behold it is my privilege,   *130*
The privilege of mine honors,
My oath, and my profession.° I protest,
Maugre° thy strength, place, youth, and eminence,
Despite thy victor sword and fire-new° fortune,
Thy valor and thy heart,° thou art a traitor,   *135*
False to thy gods, thy brother, and thy father,
Conspirant° 'gainst this high illustrious prince,
And from th' extremest upward° of thy head
To the descent and dust below thy foot,°
A most toad-spotted traitor.° Say thou "No,"   *140*
This sword, this arm and my best spirits are bent°
To prove upon thy heart, whereto I speak,°
Thou liest.

Edmund.   In wisdom° I should ask thy name,
But since thy outside looks so fair and warlike,

121 **quality** rank   123 **canker-bit** eaten by the caterpillar   125 **cope** encounter   130–32 **it . . . profession** my knighthood entitles me to challenge
you, and to have my challenge accepted   133 **Maugre** despite   134 **fire-
new** fresh from the forge or mint   135 **heart** courage   137 **Conspirant** con-
spiring, a conspirator   138 **extremest upward** the very top   139 **the . . .
foot** your lowest part (sole) and the dust beneath it   140 **toad-spotted traitor**
spotted with treason (and hence venomous, as the toad is allegedly marked
with spots that exude venom)   141 **bent** directed   142 **whereto I speak**
(Edgar speaks from the heart, and speaks to the heart of Edmund)   143 **wisdom** prudence (since he is not obliged to fight with one of lesser rank)

And that thy tongue some say° of breeding
145   breathes,
What safe and nicely° I might well delay°
By rule of knighthood, I disdain and spurn:
Back do I toss these treasons° to thy head;
With the hell-hated° lie o'erwhelm thy heart;
150   Which for they yet glance by and scarcely bruise,
This sword of mine shall give them instant way,
Where they shall rest for ever.° Trumpets, speak!
          Alarums. [They] fight. [Edmund falls.]

Albany. Save° him, save him!

Goneril.   This is practice,° Gloucester:
By th' law of war thou wast not bound to answer
155   An unknown opposite;° thou are not vanquished,
But cozened and beguiled.

Albany.   Shut your mouth, dame,
Or with this paper shall I stop it. Hold, sir;°
Thou° worse than any name, read thine own evil.
No tearing, lady; I perceive you know it.

160 *Goneril.* Say, if I do, the laws are mine, not thine:
Who can arraign me for 't?

Albany.   Most monstrous! O!
Know'st thou this paper?

Goneril.   Ask me not what I know.
                              Exit.

Albany. Go after her; she's desperate; govern° her.

Edmund. What you have charged me with, that have
          I done;
165   And more, much more; the time will bring it out.
'Tis past, and so am I. But what art thou

145 **say** assay (i.e., touch, sign)   146 **safe and nicely** cautiously and punctiliously   146 **delay** i.e., avoid   148 **treasons** accusations of treason
149 **hell-hated** hated like hell   150–52 **Which . . . ever** which accusations
of treason, since as yet they do no harm, even though I have hurled them
back, I now thrust upon you still more forcibly, with my sword, so that they
may remain with you permanently   153 **Save** spare   153 **practice** trickery
155 **opposite** opponent   157 **Hold, sir** (to Edmund: "Just a moment!")
158 **Thou** (probably Goneril)   163 **govern** control

That hast this fortune on° me? If thou 'rt noble,
I do forgive thee.

Edgar.   Let's exchange charity.°
I am no less in blood° than thou art, Edmund;
If more,° the more th' hast wronged me.   *170*
My name is Edgar, and thy father's son.
The gods are just, and of our pleasant° vices
Make instruments to plague us:
The dark and vicious place° where thee he got°
Cost him his eyes.

Edmund.   Th' hast spoken right, 'tis true;   *175*
The wheel is come full circle; I am here.°

Albany. Methought thy very gait did prophesy°
A royal nobleness: I must embrace thee:
Let sorrow split my heart, if ever I
Did hate thee or thy father!

Edgar.   Worthy° Prince, I know 't.   *180*

Albany. Where have you hid yourself?
How have you known the miseries of your father?

Edgar. By nursing them, my lord. List a brief tale;
And when 'tis told, O, that my heart would burst!
The bloody proclamation to escape°   *185*
That followed me so near—O, our lives' sweetness,
That we the pain of death would hourly die
Rather than die at once!°—taught me to shift
Into a madman's rags, t' assume a semblance
That very dogs disdained: and in this habit°   *190*
Met I my father with his bleeding rings,°
Their precious stones new lost; became his guide,
Led him, begged for him, saved him from despair;

---

167 **fortune on** victory over   168 **charity** forgiveness and love   169 **blood**
lineage   170 **If more** if I am more noble (since legitimate)   172 **of our**
pleasant out of our pleasurable   174 **place** i.e., the adulterous bed   174 **got**
begot   176 **Wheel ... here** i.e., Fortune's wheel, on which Edmund ascended, has now, in its downward turning, deposited him at the bottom,
whence he began   177 **gait did prophesy** carriage did promise   180 **Worthy** honorable   185 **to escape** (my wish) to escape the sentence of death
186–88 **O ... once** how sweet is life, that we choose to suffer death every
hour rather than make an end at once   190 **habit** attire   191 **rings** sockets

　　　　Never—O fault!—revealed myself unto him,
195　　Until some half-hour past, when I was armed,
　　　　Not sure, though hoping, of this good success,
　　　　I asked his blessing, and from first to last
　　　　Told him our pilgrimage.° But his flawed° heart—
　　　　Alack, too weak the conflict to support—
200　　'Twixt two extremes of passion, joy and grief,
　　　　Burst smilingly.

　　Edmund.　　　　This speech of yours hath moved me,
　　　　And shall perchance do good: but speak you on;
　　　　You look as you had something more to say.

　　Albany. If there be more, more woeful, hold it in;
205　　For I am almost ready to dissolve,°
　　　　Hearing of this.

　　Edgar.　　　　This would have seemed a period°
　　　　To such as love not sorrow; but another,
　　　　To amplify too much, would make much more,
　　　　And top extremity.°
210　　Whilst I was big in clamor,° came there in a man,
　　　　Who, having seen me in my worst estate,°
　　　　Shunned my abhorred° society; but then, finding
　　　　Who 'twas that so endured, with his strong arms
　　　　He fastened on my neck, and bellowed out
215　　As he'd burst heaven; threw him on my father;
　　　　Told the most piteous tale of Lear and him
　　　　That ever ear received: which in recounting
　　　　His grief grew puissant,° and the strings of life
　　　　Began to crack: twice then the trumpets sounded,
　　　　And there I left him tranced.°

220 *Albany.*　　　　　　　　But who was this?

　　Edgar. Kent, sir, the banished Kent; who in disguise
　　　　Followed his enemy° king, and did him service
　　　　Improper for a slave.

---

198 **our pilgrimage** of our (purgatorial) journey　198 **flawed** cracked　05 **dissolve** i.e., into tears　206 **period** limit　207–09 **but . . . extremity** just one woe more, described too fully, would go beyond the extreme limit　210 **big in clamor** loud in lamentation　211 **estate** condition　212 **abhorred** abhorrent 218 **puissant** overmastering　220 **tranced** insensible　222 **enemy** hostile

Enter a Gentleman, with a bloody knife.

Gentleman. Help, help, O, help!

Edgar.   What kind of help?

Albany.   Speak, man.

Edgar. What means this bloody knife?

Gentleman.   'Tis hot, it smokes;°   *225*
   It came even from the heart of—O, she's dead!

Albany. Who dead? Speak, man.

Gentleman. Your lady, sir, your lady: and her
   sister
By her is poisoned; she confesses it.

Edmund. I was contracted° to them both: all three   *230*
   Now marry° in an instant.

Edgar.   Here comes Kent.

Albany. Produce the bodies, be they alive or dead.

                              [*Exit Gentleman.*]

   This judgment of the heavens, that makes us
      tremble,
   Touches us not with pity.

                    Enter Kent.

                         O, is this he?
   The time will not allow the compliment°   *235*
   Which very manners° urges.

Kent.   I am come
To bid my king and master aye° good night:
Is he not here?

Albany.   Great thing of° us forgot!
   Speak, Edmund, where's the King? and where's
      Cordelia?
   Seest thou this object,° Kent?   *240*

The bodies of Goneril and Regan are brought in.

Kent. Alack, why thus?

225 **smokes** steams   230 **contracted** betrothed   231 **marry** i.e., unite in
death   235 **compliment** ceremony   236 **very manners** ordinary civility
237 **aye** forever   238 **thing of** matter by   240 **object** sight (the bodies of
Goneril and Regan)

Edmund.   Yet° Edmund was beloved:
The one the other poisoned for my sake,
And after slew herself.

Albany. Even so. Cover their faces.

245 *Edmund.* I pant for life:° some good I mean to do,
Despite of mine own nature. Quickly send,
Be brief in it, to th' castle; for my writ°
Is on the life of Lear and on Cordelia:
Nay, send in time.

Albany.   Run, run, O, run!

250 *Edgar.* To who, my lord? Who has the office?° Send
Thy token of reprieve.°

Edmund. Well thought on: take my sword,
Give it the captain.

Edgar.   Haste thee, for thy life.
                                     [Exit Messenger.]

Edmund. He hath commission from thy wife and me
255 To hang Cordelia in the prison, and
To lay the blame upon her own despair,
That she fordid° herself.

Albany. The gods defend her! Bear him hence awhile.
                                [Edmund is borne off.]

Enter Lear, with Cordelia in his arms [Gentle-
man, and others following].

Lear. Howl, howl, howl, howl! O, you are men of
stones:
260 Had I your tongues and eyes, I'd use them so
That heaven's vault should crack. She's gone for
ever.
I know when one is dead and when one lives;
She's dead as earth. Lend me a looking-glass;
If that her breath will mist or stain the stone,°
Why, then she lives.

241 **Yet** in spite of all   245 **pant for life** gasp for breath   247 **writ** command (ordering the execution)   250 **office** commission   251 **token of reprieve** sign that they are reprieved   257 **fordid** destroyed   264 **stone** i.e.,
the surface of the crystal looking glass

Kent.   Is this the promised end?°   265

Edgar. Or image° of that horror?

Albany.   Fall and cease.°

Lear. This feather stirs; she lives. If it be so,
  It is a chance which does redeem° all sorrows
  That ever I have felt.

Kent.   O my good master.

Lear. Prithee, away.

Edgar.   'Tis noble Kent, your friend.   270

Lear. A plague upon you, murderers, traitors all!
  I might have saved her; now she's gone for ever.
  Cordelia, Cordelia, stay a little. Ha,
  What is 't thou say'st? Her voice was ever soft,
  Gentle and low, an excellent thing in woman.   275
  I killed the slave that was a-hanging thee.

Gentleman: 'Tis true, my lords, he did.

Lear.   Did I not, fellow?
  I have seen the day, with my good biting falchion°
  I would have made them skip: I am old now,
  And these same crosses° spoil me.° Who are you?   280
  Mine eyes are not o' th' best: I'll tell you straight.°

Kent. If Fortune brag of two° she loved and hated,
  One of them we behold.

Lear. This is a dull sight.° Are you not Kent?

Kent.   The same,
  Your servant Kent. Where is your servant Caius?°   285

Lear. He's a good fellow, I can tell you that;
  He'll strike, and quickly too: he's dead and rotten.

Kent. No, my good lord; I am the very man.

265 **promised end** Doomsday   266 **image** exact likeness   266 **Fall and
cease** i.e., let the heavens fall, and all things finish   268 **redeem** make good
278 **falchion** small curved sword   280 **crosses** troubles   280 **spoil me** i.e.,
my prowess as a swordsman   281 **tell you straight** recognize you straightway   282 **two** i.e., Lear, and some hypothetical second, who is also a prime
example of Fortune's inconstancy ("loved and hated")   284 **dull sight**
(1) melancholy spectacle (2) faulty eyesight (Lear's own, clouded by weeping)   285 **Caius** (Kent's name, in disguise)

Lear. I'll see that straight.°

290 *Kent.* That from your first of difference and decay°
    Have followed your sad steps.

Lear.   You are welcome hither.

Kent. Nor no man else:° all's cheerless, dark and
        deadly
    Your eldest daughters have fordone° themselves,
    And desperately° are dead.

Lear.   –   Ay, so I think.

295 *Albany.* He knows not what he says, and vain is it
    That we present us to him.

Edgar.   Very bootless.°

Enter a Messenger.

Messenger. Edmund is dead, my lord.

Albany.   That's but a trifle here.
    You lords and noble friends, know our intent.
    What comfort to this great decay may come°
300   Shall be applied. For us, we° will resign,
    During the life of this old majesty,
    To him our absolute power: [*To Edgar and Kent*]
        you, to your rights;
    With boot,° and such addition° as your honors
    Have more than merited. All friends shall taste
305   The wages of their virtue, and all foes
    The cup of their deservings. O, see, see!

Lear. And my poor fool° is hanged: no, no, no
        life?
    Why should a dog, a horse, a rat, have life,

---

289 **see that straight** attend to that in a moment   290 **your . . . decay** beginning of your decline in fortune   292 **Nor no man else** no, I am not welcome, nor is anyone else   293 **fordone** destroyed   294 **desperately** in
despair   296 **bootless** fruitless   299 **What . . . come** whatever aid may
present itself to this great ruined man   300 **us, we** (the royal "we")
303 **boot** good measure   303 **addition** additional titles and rights
307 **fool** Cordelia ("fool" being a term of endearment. But it is perfectly
possible to take the word as referring also to the Fool)

And thou no breath at all? Thou'lt come no more,
Never, never, never, never, never.   *310*
Pray you, undo this button.° Thank you, sir.
Do you see this? Look on her. Look, her lips,
Look there, look there.

                                        He dies.

Edgar.   He faints. My lord, my lord!

Kent. Break, heart; I prithee, break.

Edgar.   Look up, my lord.

Kent. Vex not his ghost:° O, let him pass! He hates
    him   *315*
    That would upon the rack° of this tough world
    Stretch him out longer.°

Edgar.   He is gone indeed.

Kent. The wonder is he hath endured so long:
    He but usurped° his life.

Albany. Bear them from hence. Our present business   *320*
    Is general woe. [*To Kent and Edgar*] Friends of
        my soul, you twain,
    Rule in this realm and the gored state sustain.

Kent. I have a journey, sir, shortly to go;
    My master calls me, I must not say no.

Edgar. The weight of this sad time we must obey,°   *325*
    Speak what we feel, not what we ought to say.
    The oldest hath borne most: we that are young
    Shall never see so much, nor live so long.

                                Exeunt, with a dead march.

F I N I S

---

311 **undo this button** i.e., to ease the suffocation Lear feels   315 **Vex ... ghost** do not trouble his departing spirit   316 **rack** instrument of torture, stretching the victim's joints to dislocation   317 **longer** (1) in time (2) in bodily length   319 **usurped** possessed beyond the allotted term   325 **obey** submit to

Textual Note

The earliest extant version of Shakespeare's *King Lear* is the First Quarto of 1608. This premier edition is known as the Pied Bull Quarto, after the sign which hung before the establishment of the printer. The title page reads as follows: "M. William Shak-speare: / HIS / True Chronicle Historie of the life and / death of King Lear and his three / Daughters. / *With the vnfortunate life of* Edgar, *sonne* and heire to the Earle of Gloster, and his / sullen and assumed humor of / Tom of Bedlam: / *As it was played before the Kings Maiestie at Whitehall vpon* / S. Stephans *night in Christmas Hollidayes.* / By his Maiesties seruants playing vsually at the Gloabe / on the Bancke-side. / LONDON, / Printed for *Nathaniel Butter,* and are to be sold at his shop in *Pauls* / Church-yard at the signe of the Pide Bull neere / S^t. *Austin's* Gate. 1608." Twelve copies of the First Quarto survive. They are, however, in ten different states, because proofreading, and hence correcting, took place as the play was being printed. The instances (167 in all) in which these copies of Q1 differ from one another have been enumerated by contemporary scholarship.[1] Various theories account for the origin of Q1. Perhaps it is a "reported" text, depending on memorial reconstruction by actors who had performed it, or on a shorthand transcription, or on a conventional but poor transcription of Shakespeare's "foul papers" (rough draft). In *Shakespeare's Revision of "King*

---

[1] W. W. Greg, *The Variants in the First Quarto of "King Lear,"* London, 1940 (for 1939).

Lear" (1980), Steven Urkowitz, disputing suggestions of memorial contaminating, concluded that Q was printed directly from the foul papers, not from a transcript of them.

In 1619 appeared the Second Quarto, known as the N. Butter Quarto, and falsely dated in the same year as the first (the title page reads: "Printed for Nathaniel Butter. 1608"). Actually Q2 was printed by William Jaggard as part of an intended collection of plays by or ascribed to Shakespeare, to be published by Jaggard's friend Thomas Pavier. The source of Q2 was apparently a copy of Q1 in which a number of sheets had been corrected.

Four years later *King Lear* was reprinted once more, this time in the first collection of Shakespeare's works, the First Folio of 1623. The source of the Folio text has been much debated. Some propose a corrected copy of Q1, perhaps collated with the theater's promptbook, a shorter, acting version of the play. Comparative study indicates that Q2 with its corrections was also important for the printing of F, and may have been its principal source. Gary Taylor, analyzing the work of the compositors who set the Folio text, suggested this; others suggested that F's compositors used an MS copy, probably derived from the promptbook, plus a version of Q2. Between the Q and F texts, variations, both accidental and substantive, are frequent. Accidental changes, those of orthography and punctuation, mean little for a modernized edition like this one. Substantive changes, those of words, may alter the sense. F lacks 285 lines that appear in Q1, and adds 115 lines not in Q1, also supplying many different readings and different punctuation and lineation.

Here are some examples of the way the texts differ. In Q's version of Act 1, Scene 2, Gloucester thinks his son Edgar cannot be the monster suggested by Edmund's forged letter. This follows:

Edmund. Nor is not, sure.
Gloucester. To his father, that so tenderly and entirely loves him. Heaven and earth!

(103–5)

F cuts these two brief speeches, speeding up the pace but losing aspects of devious, credulous, and paternal behavior. A little earlier (Act 1, Scene 1), Lear enters for the first time, and Q has him expressing his purpose to divide the kingdom, transferring its ruler's obligations to younger hands. F's version of this passage is more circumstantial. Lear's age is emphasized, also his unbecoming self-indulgence. He will "Unburdened crawl toward death." Highlighting a filial relationship, he addresses "Our son of Cornwall" and "our no less loving son of Albany." Still vigorous, hardly the doting old man of some productions, he stresses his "constant will," and is provident in publicizing his daughters' dowries in order "that future strife may be prevented now." All this Q omits. To the present editor it seems reasonable to conflate the lines omitted in one text and added by the other text, a practice followed by all editors until recently, beginning with Alexander Pope in his edition of 1723–25.

The F text is seldom abridged simply to shorten the play. Its cuts are likely to change our sense of things, and this is true also of its amplifications. To many scholars, that looks like evidence of authorial intervention. Some propose two different versions of the play, each with its own integrity. They think the First Quarto of 1608 represents Shakespeare's initial version, satisfactory to him when he wrote it. He didn't remain satisfied, however, and before his death in 1616 revised this version substantially. His revision is preserved in the First Folio. Editors who think this, like the new *Oxford Shakespeare*'s (Stanley Wells and Gary Taylor, 1986), will offer separate texts of the play. The most forceful statement that *Lear* exists in two separate but equal versions is presented in *The Division of the Kingdom: Shakespeare's Two Versions of "King Lear"* (1983), edited by Gary Taylor and Michael Warren. This collection of essays by eleven scholars argues that Q is more or less the play as Shakespeare wrote it in 1605-06, and that F—with its additions and reassignment of some speeches—is based on a promptbook which represents Shakespeare's own reshaping of the play, perhaps around 1610–11. There is, however, at least one great difficulty with this theory: Even if we grant that F represents a revision, how can we be certain that Shakespeare was the reviser? When the Globe burned in 1613, presumably the promptbook was lost, and the company had to construct a new one, probably without Shakespeare's help, since he had retired to Stratford around 1611. The authors of *The Division of the Kingdom* argue that the omissions in F improve the play, but it is hard, for instance, to see F's omission of the mock trial scene in 3.6 as an improvement, even though one writer in the book assures us that this omission "strengthens the dramatic structure."

John Russell Brown, whose theater criticism is fortified by long experience as a director, is useful on the matter of textual priority. Arguing that the later date of F is no guarantee of Shakespeare's approval, he points out that playwrights, "even the most willful and the most gentle," are often bullied into making expedient changes by the theater people who put the play on stage. When the American poet-turned-playwright Archibald MacLeish gave the director Elia Kazan the text of his new drama, *J.B.*, he thought, said Kazan with amusement, that he had written a play. The director, knowing better, went on to stamp it with his own ideas. Sometimes the actor, especially a star actor, takes over the play, forcing the playwright to build up his part. Sir Henry Irving wouldn't have cared for a bit part. References to France and the French king's invasion of England drop from F, perhaps reflecting the censor's disapproval of allusions to state business in the reign of King James (beginning 1603). Other cuts, though they may be editorial, may as plausibly come from the scribe, or the book-keeper seeking to clarify performance, or may represent a compositor's error. And so on.

There seems no reason, accordingly, to deprive readers of anything Shakespeare wrote at any time. The present text of *King Lear* is therefore an amalgamation of Q and F. It relies chiefly on the Folio, but it turns to the Quarto when the Folio is guilty of an obvious misprinting, or when it omits pertinent material found in the Quarto, or when its version seems to the editor so inferior to the Quarto version as to demand precedence for the latter, or when an emendation, even though perhaps unnecessary (like Edwards' "top th' legitimate"), has been canonized by use and wont.

In the preparation of this text, the spelling of Folio and Quarto has been modernized; punctuation and capitalization have been altered, when alteration seemed suitable; character designations have been expanded or clarified (F "Cor." becomes "Cordelia," F "Bastard" and "Steward" become "Edmund" and "Oswald"); contractions not affecting pronunciation have been eliminated (F "banish'd" becomes "banished"); necessary quotation marks (as in the reading of a letter) have been supplied; as have diacritical marks whenever a syllable that is normally unemphasized must be stressed (as in "oppressèd"). These changes are not recorded.

All other departures from the Folio appearing in this text are recorded here in italic type. Unless specifically noted, these departures derive in every case from the First Quarto [Q]. If some other source is levied on, such as the Second Quarto [Q2] or Second Folio [F2] or the conjecture of an editor (for example, [Theobald]), that source is given, within brackets, immediately after the reading. There follows next, in roman type, the Folio reading which has been superseded. If an editor's emendation has been preferred to both Folio and Quarto readings, the emendation, with its provenance, is followed by the Folio and Quarto readings it replaces.

Stage directions are not given lineation. Reference to them in these notes is determined, therefore, by the line of text they follow. If a stage direction occurs at the beginning of a scene, reference is to the line of text it precedes. On occasion, the stage direction in the present text represents a conflation of Folio and Quarto. In that case, both Folio and Quarto readings are set down in the notes. Stage directions and notations of place, printed within brackets, are, unless otherwise noted, substantially from the Globe edition. The list of Dramatis Personae, first given by Rowe, is taken also from the Globe edition.

1.1. *Act 1 Scene 1* Actus Primus. Scena Prima   5 *equalities* qualities   34 s.d.   *Sound . . . Attendants* Sennet. Enter King Lear, Corn-

wall, Albany, Gonerill, Regan, Cordelia, and attendants [F] Sound
a Sennet, Enter one bearing a Coronet, then Lear, then the Dukes of
Albany, and Cornwall, next Gonerill, Regan, Cordelia, with
followers [Q]   70 *speak* [F omits]   98 *loved me. I* loved me
99 *Return* I return   106 *To love my father all* [F omits]   112 *mysteries* [F2] miseries [F] mistress [Q]   157 *as a pawn* as pawn
158 *nor* nere [i.e., "ne'er"]   165 *the* thy   172 *sentences* sentences
176 *diseases* disasters   190 *Gloucester* Cor[delia]   208 *on* in
216 *best object* object   227 *well* will   235 *Better thou* Better thou
hadst   250 *respects of fortune* respect and Fortunes   268 s.d.
Lear . . . Attendants [Capell] Exit Lear and Burgundy [Q]
283 *shame them derides* with shame derides   291 *hath not been*
hath been   299–300 *ingrafted* ingraffed   306 *let's hit* let us sit

1.2. *Scene 2* Scena Secunda   21 *top th'* [Edwards] to' th' [F] tooth'
[Q]   103–05 *Edmund . . . earth* [F omits]   142 *Fut* [F omits]
144 *Edgar* [F omits]   145 *and pat* [Steevens] Pat [F] and out
[Q]   156–64 *as . . . come* [F omits]   165 *Why, the* The   178 *brother*
[F omits]   185 *Go armed* [F omits]   191 s.d. *Exit Edgar* Exit

1.3. *Scene 3* Scena Tertia   17–21 *Not . . . abused* [F omits]
25–26 *I would . . . speak* [F omits]   27 *Go, prepare* prepare

1.4. *Scene 4* Scena Quarta   1 *well* will   51 *daughter* Daughters   100 *Fool* my Boy   115 *Lady the Brach* [Steevens] the Lady
Brach [F] Ladie oth'e brach [Q]   144–59 *That . . . snatching* [F
omits]   158 *on't* [Q2] [F omits] an't [Q]   158 *ladies* [Q cor-
rected] [F omits] lodes [Q uncorrected]   167 *crown* Crownes
182 *fools* Foole   195 *Methinks* [F omits]   222 *it had* it's
had   225 *Come, Sir* [F omits]   234 *or his* his   237–41 *I . . . father* [F omits]   264 *O . . . come* [F omits]   298 *the cause* more of
it   311 *Yea . . . this* [F omits]   350 *You are* [F2] Your are [F]
Y'are [Q]   350 *attasked for* [Q corrected: "attaskt"] at task for [F]
alapt [Q uncorrected]

1.5. *Scene 5* Scena Quinta   1 s.d. *Enter . . . Fool* [Q2] Enter Lear,
Kent, Gentleman, and Foole   17 *Why . . . boy* What can'st tell Boy

2.1. *Act 2. Scene 1* Actus Secundus. Scena Prima   21 s.d. *Enter
Edgar* [placed by Theobald] [F prints after l. 20]   55 *But*
And   72 *I should* should I   73 *ay* [F omits]   80 *I . . . him*
[F omits]   80 s.d. *Tucket within* [placed by Malone] [F prints af-
ter l. 79]   81 *why* wher   89 *strange news* strangenesse

2.2. *Scene 2* Scena Secunda   23 *clamorous* [Q corrected] clamours
[F] clamarous [Q uncorrected]   44 s.d. *Enter . . . drawn*
Enter Bastard, Cornwall, Regan, Gloster, Servants [F] Enter Ed-
mund with his rapier drawne, Gloster the Duke and Dutchesse
[Q]   77 *too* t'   80 *Renege* Revenge   81 *gale* gall   110 *flick'ring*
[Pope: "flickering"] flicking [F] flitkering [Q]   125 *dread*

dead 132 *respect* respects 141 s.d. *Stocks brought out* [placed by Dyce] [F prints after 1. 139] [Q omits] 143–47 *His . . . with* [F omits] 145 *contemnèd'st* [Capell] [F omits] contaned [Q uncorrected] temnest [Q corrected] 153 *For . . . legs* [F omits] 154 *Come . . . away* [F assigns to Cornwall] 154 *my good Lord* my Lord 154 s.d. *Exeunt . . . Kent* Exit [F] [Q omits] 155 *Duke's* Duke 176 s.d. *Sleeps* [F omits]

2.3. *Scene 3* [Steevens] [F, Q omit] 4 *unusual* unusall 15 *mortified bare arms* mortified Armes 18 *sheepcotes* Sheeps-Cotes

2.4.1 s.d. *Scene 4* [Steevens] [F, Q omit] 2 *messenger* Messengers 6 *thy* ahy 9 *man's* man 18–19 *No . . . have* [F omits] 30 *panting* painting 33 *whose* those 61 *the* the the 75 *have* hause 86 s.d. *Enter . . . Gloucester* [F prints after 1. 84] 130 *mother's* Mother 167 *her pride* [F omits] 183 s.d. *Enter Oswald* [placed by Dyce] [F and Q print after 1. 181] 185 *fickle* fickly 188 s.d. *Enter Goneril* [placed by Johnson] [F and Q print after 1. 186] 282 s.d. *Storm and tempest* [F prints after 1. 283] [Q omits] 285 s.d. *Exeunt . . . Fool* [Q2] Exeunt [F] Exeunt Lear, Leister, Kent, and Foole [Q] 294 s.d. *Enter Gloucester* [F and Q print after 1. 293]

3.1. *Act 3. Scene 1* Actus Tertius. Scena Prima 7–14 *tears . . . all* [F omits] 30–42 *But . . . you* [F omits]

3.2. *Scene 2* Scena Secunda 3 *drowned* drown 71 *That* And 78 *True . . . boy* True boy

3.3. *Scene 3* Scaena Tertia

3.4. *Scene 4* Scena Quarta 7 *skin: so* [Rowe] skinso [F] skin, so [Q] 10 *thy* they 27 s.d. *Exit* [placed by Johnson] [F prints after 1. 26] [Q omits] 38 s.d. *Enter Fool* [Duthie] Enter Edgar, and Foole [F, which prints after 1. 36] [Q omits] 44 s.d. *Enter Edgar* Enter Edgar, and Foole [F, which prints after 1. 36] [Q omits] 46 *blows . . . wind* blow the windes 47 *thy cold bed* thy bed 52 *ford* Sword 57 *Bless* Blisse 58 *Bless* blisse 63 *What, has* Ha's · 91 *deeply* deerely 101 *sessa* [Malone] Sesey [F] caese [Q] cease [Q2] 116 s.d. *Enter . . . torch* [F prints after 1. 111] Enter Gloster [Q, which prints after 1. 116] 117 *foul fiend Flibbertigibbet* foule Flibbertigibbet 118 *till . . . cock* at first Cocke 138 *hath* had hath

3.5. *Scene 5* Scena Quinta 13 *his* this 25 *dearer* deere

3.6. *Scene 6* Scena Sexta 5 s.d. *Exit* [placed by Capell] [F prints after 1. 3] 17–55 *The . . . 'scape* [F omits] 22 *Now* [Q2] [F omits] no [Q] 25 *bourn* [Capell] [F omits] broome [Q] 34 *cushions* [F omits] cushings [Q] 47 *she kicked* [Q2] [F omits] kicked [Q] 53 *made on* [Capell] [F omits] made an [Q] 67 *lym*

[Hanmer] Hym [F] him [Q]   68 *tike, or trundle* tight, or
Troudle   72 *Sessa!* [Malone] sese [F] [Q omits]   84 s.d.   *Enter
Gloucester* [placed by Capell] [F prints after l. 80]   97–100 *Op-
pressèd . . . behind* [F omits]   101–14 *When . . . lurk* [F omits]

3.7. *Scene 7* Scena Septima   21 s.d.   *Exit Oswald* [Staunton] [F
and Q omit]   23 s.d.   *Exeunt . . . Edmund* [Staunton] [F (Exit) and
Q (Exit Gon. and Bast.) print after l. 22]   28 s.d.   *Enter . . . three*
[Q, which prints after "traitor"] Enter Gloucester, and Servants [F,
which prints as here after "control"]   59 *rash* sticke   64 *dearn*
sterne   79 s.d.   *Draw and fight* [F omits]   81 s.d.   *She . . . him*
Killes him [F] Shee . . . behind [Q]   100–108 *I'll . . . him* [F omits]
100 *Second Servant* [Capell] [F omits] Servant [Q]   101 *Third
Servant* [Capell] [F omits] 2 Servant [Q]   104 *Second Servant*
[Capell] [F omits] 1 Ser. [Q]   105 *roguish* [Q2] [Q omits]   107
Third Servant [Capell] [F omits] 2 Ser. [Q]   108 s.d.   *Exeunt severally* [F omits] Exit [Q]

4.1. *Act 4 Scene 1* Actus Quartus. Scena Prima   9 s.d.   *led by an
Old Man* [Q, which prints after l. 12] and an Old man [F, which
places after l. 9, as here]   41 *Then, prithee, get thee gone* Get thee
away   60–65 *Five . . . master* [F omits]   62–63 *Flibbertigibbet*
[Pope] Stiberdigebit [Q]   63 *mopping and mowing* [Theobald]
Mobing, & Mohing [Q]

4.2. *Scene 2* Scena Secunda   1 s.d.   *Enter Goneril and Edmund*
Enter Gonerill, Bastard, and Steward   2 s.d. [after "way"]   *Enter
Oswald* [placed by Theobald] [Q prints after "master," 1.2] [F
omits]   25 s.d.   *Exit Edmund* [placed by Rowe] Exit [F, which
prints after "death"] [Q omits]   28 s.d.   *Exit* [F omits] Exit Stew.
[Q]   31–50 *I . . . deep* [F omits]   32 *its* ith [Q]   45 *benefited* [Q
corrected] benificted [Q uncorrected]   47 *these* [Jennens; Heath
conj.] the [Q uncorrected] this [Q corrected]   49 *Humanity* [Q cor-
rected] Humanly [Q uncorrected]   53–59 *that . . . so* [F omits]
56 *noiseless* [Q corrected] noystles [Q uncorrected]   57 *thy state
begins to threat* [Jennens] thy slayer begin threats [Q uncorrected]
thy state begins threat [Q corrected] thy slaier begins threats [Q2]
58 *Whilst* [Q corrected] Whil's [Q uncorrected]   62–69 *Thou . . .
news* [F omits]   65 *dislocate* [Q3] dislecate [Q2.1,2]   68 *mew* [Q
corrected] now [Q uncorrected]   68 s.d.   *Enter a Messenger* [F
prints after l. 61] Enter a Gentleman   [Q, which prints after l. 69;
and Q2, which prints after l. 68, as here]   75 *thereat enraged*
threat-enrag'd [Q corrected] Iustices [F, Q]   87 s.d.
Exit [F omits]

4.3. *Scene 3* Scena Tertia [for Scene IV]   1 s.d.   *Enter . . . Gentleman* [F omits the entire scene]   12 *sir* [Theobald] say   17 *strove*
[Pope] streme   21 *seemed* [Pope: "seem'd"] seeme   30 *believed*

[Q2] beleeft   32 *moistened* [Capell] moystened her   56 *Exeunt*
[Pope] Exit

4.4. *Scene 4* [Pope] Scena Tertia [F] [Q omits]   1 s.d. *Cordelia,*
Doctor, and Soldiers Cordelia, Gentlemen, and Souldiours [F]
Cordelia, Doctor and others [Q]   3 *femiter* Fenitar   6 *century*
Centery   18 *distress* desires   28 *right* Rite

4.5. *Scene 5* [Pope] Scena Quarta [F] [Q omits]   39 *meet him* meet

4.6. *Scene 6* [Pope] Scena Quinta [Q omits]   17 *walk* walk'd
34 s.d.   *He kneels* [F omits]   41 s.d.   *He falls* [F omits]
71 *whelked* wealk'd   71 *enridgèd* enraged   83 *coining* crying   97 *had white* had the white   166 *Through* Thorough *small*
great   167 *Plate sin* [Theobald] Place sinnes [F] [Q omits]   199
Ay . . . dust [F omits]   200 *Good sir* [Q2] [F and Q omit]   206 s.d.
Exit . . . follow Exit [F] Exit King running [Q]   208 *one*
a   244 *I'se* [Johnson: "Ise"] ice [F] ile [Q]   247 s.d. *They fight*
[F omits]   255 s.d.   *He dies* [F omits]   274 *and . . . venture*
[Q reads "Venter"] [F omits] [This line, from the First Quarto, is
almost universally omitted from editions of the play]   276 *indis-*
tinguished indinguish'd   289 s.d.   *Drum afar off* [F prints after
l. 287] A drum a farre off [Q, which prints as here]

4.7. *Scene 7* Scena Septima   1 s.d.   *Enter . . . Gentleman*
Enter Cordelia, Kent, and Gentleman [F] Enter Cordelia, Kent,
and Doctor [Q]   24 *doubt not* doubt   24–25 *Very . . . there*
[F omits]   32 *warring* iarring   33–36 *To . . . helm* [F omits]
79–80 *and . . . lost* [F omits]   85 s.d.   *Exeunt . . . Gentleman*
Exeunt   86–98 *Holds . . . fought* [F omits]

5.1. *Act 5 Scene 1* Actus Quintus. Scena Prima   11–13 *That . . .*
hers [F omits]   16 *Fear me not* Feare not   18–19 *I . . . me*
[F omits]   23–28 *Where . . . nobly* [F omits]   33 *I . . . tent*
[F omits]   36 *pray you* pray   39 s.d.   *To those going out* [F and Q
omit]   *To Edgar* [F and Q omit]   *Exeunt* [placed by Cambridge edi-
tion] [Q prints after "word," l. 39] [F omits]   46 *love* loues
50 s.d.   *Exit* [placed by Dyce] [F and Q print after l. 49]

5.2. *Scene 2* Scena Secunda

5.3. *Scene 3* Scena Tertia   13 *hear poor rogues* heere (poore
Rogues) [reference in F is to Lear and Cordelia]   26 s.d. *Exeunt . . .*
guarded Exit [F] [Q omits]   39–40 *I . . . do't* [F omits]   40 s.d.
Exit Captain [F prints after l.38] [Q omits]   48 *and appointed*
guard [Q corrected, and Q2] [F and Q omit]   55–60 *At . . . place*
[F omits]   56 *We* [Q corrected, and Q2] mee [Q]   58 *sharpness*
[Q corrected, and Q2] sharpes [Q]   84 *attaint* arrest   85 *sister*
Sisters   98 *he is* hes   103 *Edmund . . . ho, a herald* [F
omits]   108 s.d.   *Enter a Herald* [placed by Hanmer] [F prints
after l. 102] [Q omits]   110 *Sound, trumpet* [F omits]   110 s.d.

A trumpet sounds [F prints after 1. 109] [Q omits] trumpet [F2]
Tumpet   116 *Sound* [F omits]   116 s.d.   *First trumpet* [F prints
after 1. 115] [Q omits]   118 s.d.   *Enter . . . him* Enter Edgar
armed [F] Enter Edgar at the third sound, a trumpet before
him   [Q]   137 *illustrious*   illustirous   145 *some   say* (some
say)   152 s.d.   *fight Fights* [F, which prints after 1. 153,
"him"] [Q omits]   162 *Ask . . . know* [F gives to Edmund]
162 s.d. *Exit* [placed here by Q: "Exit. Gonorill"] [F prints after 1.
161, "for't"]   206–23 *This . . . slave* [F omits]   215 *him* [Theobald]
me [Q] [F omits]   223 s.d.   *Enter . . . knife* Enter a Gentleman [F]
Enter one with a bloudie knife [Q]   234 s.d.   *Enter Kent* [placed
by Q2] [F prints after 1. 231, "Kent"] [Q prints after "allow" in 1.
235]   240 s.d.   *The . . . in* Gonerill and Regans bodies brought out
[F, which prints after 1. 232]   253 s.d.   *Exit Messenger*
[Theobald] [F and Q omit]   259 *Howl, howl, howl, howl* Howle,
howle, howle *you are* your are   279 *them* him   291 *You are* [Q2]
Your   are   [F]   You'r   [Q]   296 s.d.   *Enter a Messenger*
[F, which prints after "him"] Enter Captaine [Q, placed as here]

The Tragedy of
MACBETH

The Tragedy of Macbeth

ACT 1

Scene 1.   [*An open place.*]

Thunder and lightning. Enter Three Witches.

First Witch. When shall we three meet again?
  In thunder, lightning, or in rain?

Second Witch. When the hurlyburly's done,
  When the battle's lost and won.

Third Witch. That will be ere the set of sun.   5

First Witch. Where the place?

Second Witch.   Upon the heath.

Third Witch. There to meet with Macbeth.

First Witch. I come, Graymalkin.° 1

Second Witch. Paddock° calls.

Third Witch.   Anon!°

All. Fair is foul, and foul is fair.   10
  Hover through the fog and filthy air.

                                        Exeunt.

---

¹ The degree sign (°) indicates a footnote, which is keyed to the text by
line number. Text references are printed in **boldface** type; the annotation
follows in roman type.
1.1. 8 **Graymalkin** (the witch's attendant spirit, a gray cat)   9 **Paddock**
toad   9 **Anon** at once

Scene 2. [*A camp.*]

*Alarum within.° Enter King [Duncan], Mal-
colm, Donalbain, Lennox, with Attendants, meeting a bleeding Captain.*

King. What bloody man is that? He can report,
As seemeth by his plight, of the revolt
The newest state.

Malcolm.   This is the sergeant°
Who like a good and hardy soldier fought
5 'Gainst my captivity. Hail, brave friend!
Say to the king the knowledge of the broil°
As thou didst leave it.

Captain.   Doubtful it stood,
As two spent swimmers, that do cling together
And choke their art.° The merciless Macdonwald—
10 Worthy to be a rebel for to that
The multiplying villainies of nature
Do swarm upon him—from the Western Isles°
Of kerns and gallowglasses° is supplied;
And Fortune, on his damnèd quarrel° smiling,
15 Showed like a rebel's whore:° but all's too weak:
For brave Macbeth—well he deserves that name—
Disdaining Fortune, with his brandished steel,
Which smoked with bloody execution,
Like valor's minion° carved out his passage

1.2.s.d. **Alarum within** trumpet call offstage 3 **sergeant** i.e., officer
(he is called, perhaps with no inconsistency in Shakespeare's day,
a captain in the s.d. and speech prefixes. *Sergeant* is trisyllabic)
6 **broil** quarrel 9 **choke their art** hamper each other's doings 12 **Western Isles** Hebrides 13 **Of kerns and gallowglasses** with lightly armed
Irish foot soldiers and heavily armed ones 14 **damnèd quarrel** accursed
cause 15 **Showed like a rebel's whore** i.e., falsely appeared to favor
Macdonwald 19 **minion** (trisyllabic) favorite

Till he faced the slave;   20
Which nev'r shook hands, nor bade farewell to him,
Till he unseamed him from the nave to th' chops,°
And fixed his head upon our battlements.

King. O valiant cousin! Worthy gentleman!

Captain. As whence the sun 'gins his reflection°   25
Shipwracking storms and direful thunders break,
So from that spring whence comfort seemed to come
Discomfort swells. Mark, King of Scotland, mark:
No sooner justice had, with valor armed,
Compelled these skipping kerns to trust their heels   30
But the Norweyan lord, surveying vantage,°
With furbished arms and new supplies of men,
Began a fresh assault.

King.   Dismayed not this
Our captains, Macbeth and Banquo?

Captain.   Yes;
As sparrows eagles, or the hare the lion.   35
If I say sooth,° I must report they were
As cannons overcharged with double cracks;°
So they doubly redoubled strokes upon the foe.
Except° they meant to bathe in reeking wounds,
Or memorize another Golgotha,°   40
I cannot tell—
But I am faint; my gashes cry for help.

King. So well thy words become thee as thy wounds;
They smack of honor both. Go get him surgeons.

                 [*Exit Captain, attended.*]

        Enter Ross and Angus.

Who comes here?

22 **nave to th' chops** navel to the jaws   25 **reflection** (four syllables; the ending *ion*—here and often elsewhere in the play—is disyllabic) 31 **surveying vantage** seeing an opportunity   36 **sooth** truth   37 **cracks** explosives   39 **Except** unless   40 **memorize another Golgotha** make the place as memorable as Golgotha, "the place of the skull"

45 *Malcolm.* The worthy Thane° of Ross.

Lennox. What a haste looks through his eyes! So
    should he look
That seems to° speak things strange.

Ross. God save the king!

King. Whence cam'st thou, worthy Thane?

Ross. From Fife, great King;
Where the Norweyan banners flout the sky
50 And fan our people cold.
Norway° himself, with terrible numbers,
Assisted by that most disloyal traitor
The Thane of Cawdor, began a dismal° conflict;
Till that Bellona's bridegroom, lapped in proof,°
55 Confronted him with self-comparisons,°
Point against point, rebellious arm 'gainst arm,
Curbing his lavish° spirit: and, to conclude,
The victory fell on us.

King. Great happiness!

Ross. That now
Sweno, the Norways' king, craves composition;°
60 Nor would we deign him burial of his men
Till he disbursèd, at Saint Colme's Inch,°
Ten thousand dollars° to our general use.

King. No more that Thane of Cawdor shall deceive
Our bosom interest:° go pronounce his present°
    death,
65 And with his former title greet Macbeth.

Ross. I'll see it done.

King. What he hath lost, noble Macbeth hath won.
Exeunt.

---

45 **Thane** (a Scottish title of nobility) 47 **seems to** seems about to
51 **Norway** the King of Norway 53 **dismal** threatening 54 **Bellona's
. . . proof** the mate of the goddess of war, clad in tested (proved)
armor 55 **self-comparisons** counter-movements 57 **lavish** insolent
59 **composition** terms of peace 61 **Inch** island 62 **dollars** (Spanish and
Dutch currency) 64 **Our bosom interest** my (plural of royalty)
heart's trust 64 **present** immediate

Scene 3.   [*A heath.*]

Thunder. Enter the Three Witches.

First Witch. Where hast thou been, sister?

Second Witch. Killing swine.

Third Witch. Sister, where thou?

First Witch. A sailor's wife had chestnuts in her lap,
    And mounched, and mounched, and mounched.
        "Give me," quoth I.   5
    "Aroint thee,° witch!" the rump-fed ronyon° cries.
    Her husband's to Aleppo gone, master o' th' Tiger:
    But in a sieve I'll thither sail,
    And, like a rat without a tail,
    I'll do, I'll do, and I'll do.   10

Second Witch. I'll give thee a wind.

First Witch. Th' art kind.

Third Witch. And I another.

First Witch. I myself have all the other;
    And the very ports they blow,°   15
    All the quarters that they know
    I' th' shipman's card.°
    I'll drain him dry as hay:
    Sleep shall neither night nor day
    Hang upon his penthouse lid;°   20
    He shall live a man forbid:°
    Weary sev'nights nine times nine
    Shall he dwindle, peak,° and pine:

1.3. 6 **Aroint thee** begone   6 **rump-fed ronyon** fat-rumped scabby creature   15 **ports they blow** harbors to which the winds blow (?)
17 **card** compass card   20 **penthouse lid** eyelid (the figure is of a lean-to)
21 **forbid** cursed   23 **peak** waste away

Though his bark cannot be lost,
25   Yet it shall be tempest-tossed.
Look what I have.

Second Witch. Show me, show me.

First Witch. Here I have a pilot's thumb,
Wracked as homeward he did come.

Drum within.

30   *Third Witch.* A drum, a drum!
Macbeth doth come.

All. The weïrd° sisters, hand in hand,
Posters° of the sea and land,
Thus do go about, about:
35   Thrice to thine, and thrice to mine,
And thrice again, to make up nine.
Peace! The charm's wound up.

Enter Macbeth and Banquo.

Macbeth. So foul and fair a day I have not seen.

Banquo. How far is 't called to Forres? What are these
40   So withered, and so wild in their attire,
That look not like th' inhabitants o' th' earth,
And yet are on 't? Live you, or are you aught
That man may question?° You seem to understand me,
By each at once her choppy° finger laying
45   Upon her skinny lips. You should be women,
And yet your beards forbid me to interpret
That you are so.

Macbeth.   Speak, if you can: what are you?

First Witch. All hail, Macbeth! Hail to thee, Thane of Glamis!

Second Witch. All hail, Macbeth! Hail to thee, Thane of
Cawdor!

---

32 **weïrd** destiny-serving (? Shakespeare's chief source, Holinshed's *Chronicles*,
reports that one common opinion held that the women were "the weird sisters . . .
the goddesses of destiny." The spelling in the First Folio (1623) text of *Macbeth*,
however, is *weyward* here and at 2.1.20; at 3.1.2, 3.4.134, and 4.1.136 it is *weyard*.
The word may glance at *wayward*, and probably is dissyllabic. We use *weïrd* consistently)   33 **Posters** swift travelers   43 **question** talk to   44 **choppy** chapped

Third Witch. All hail, Macbeth, that shalt be King
   hereafter!   50

Banquo. Good sir, why do you start, and seem to fear
   Things that do sound so fair? I' th' name of truth,
   Are ye fantastical,° or that indeed
   Which outwardly ye show? My noble partner
   You greet with present grace° and great prediction   55
   Of noble having° and of royal hope,
   That he seems rapt withal:° to me you speak not.
   If you can look into the seeds of time,
   And say which grain will grow and which will not,
   Speak then to me, who neither beg nor fear   60
   Your favors nor your hate.

First Witch. Hail!

Second Witch. Hail!

Third Witch. Hail!

First Witch. Lesser than Macbeth, and greater.   65

Second Witch. Not so happy,° yet much happier.

Third Witch. Thou shalt get° kings, though thou be
   none.
   So all hail, Macbeth and Banquo!

First Witch. Banquo and Macbeth, all hail!

Macbeth. Stay, you imperfect° speakers, tell me more: 70
   By Sinel's° death I know I am Thane of Glamis;
   But how of Cawdor? The Thane of Cawdor lives,
   A prosperous gentleman; and to be King
   Stands not within the prospect of belief,
   No more than to be Cawdor. Say from whence   75
   You owe° this strange intelligence?° Or why
   Upon this blasted heath you stop our way

---

53 **fantastical** imaginary   55 **grace** honor   56 **having** possession   57 **rapt
withal** entranced by it   66 **happy** fortunate   67 **get** beget   70 **imperfect**
incomplete   71 **Sinel** (Macbeth's father)   76 **owe** own, have   76 **intelligence** information

With such prophetic greeting? Speak, I charge
    you.

                                      Witches vanish.

Banquo. The earth hath bubbles as the water has,
80   And these are of them. Whither are they vanished?

Macbeth. Into the air, and what seemed corporal°
    melted
    As breath into the wind. Would they had stayed!

Banquo. Were such things here as we do speak about?
    Or have we eaten on the insane° root
85   That takes the reason prisoner?

Macbeth. Your children shall be kings.

Banquo.   You shall be King.

Macbeth. And Thane of Cawdor too. Went it not so?

Banquo. To th' selfsame tune and words. Who's here?

                Enter Ross and Angus.

Ross. The King hath happily received, Macbeth,
90   The news of thy success; and when he reads°
    Thy personal venture in the rebels' fight,
    His wonders and his praises do contend
    Which should be thine or his.° Silenced with that,
    In viewing o'er the rest o' th' selfsame day,
95   He finds thee in the stout Norweyan ranks,
    Nothing afeard of what thyself didst make,
    Strange images of death. As thick as tale
    Came post with post,° and every one did bear
    Thy praises in his kingdom's great defense,
    And poured them down before him.

100 *Angus.*   We are sent
    To give thee, from our royal master, thanks;

---

81 **corporal** corporeal   84 **insane** insanity-producing   90 **reads** considers
92–93 **His wonders ... his** i.e., Duncan's speechless admiration, appropriate to him, contends with his desire to praise you (?)   97–98 **As
thick ... post** as fast as could be counted came messenger after messenger

Only to herald thee into his sight,
Not pay thee.

Ross. And for an earnest° of a greater honor,
　He bade me, from him, call thee Thane of Cawdor;　105
　In which addition,° hail, most worthy Thane!
　For it is thine.

Banquo.　　　　What, can the devil speak true?

Macbeth. The Thane of Cawdor lives: why do you dress
　me
　In borrowed robes?

Angus.　　　　Who was the thane lives yet,
　But under heavy judgment bears that life　　　　110
　Which he deserves to lose. Whether he was com-
　　bined°
　With those of Norway, or did line° the rebel
　With hidden help and vantage,° or that with both
　He labored in his country's wrack,° I know not;
　But treasons capital, confessed and proved,　　115
　Have overthrown him.

Macbeth.　　　　[*Aside*] Glamis, and Thane of Cawdor:
　The greatest is behind.° [*To Ross and Angus*] Thanks
　　for your pains.
　[*Aside to Banquo*] Do you not hope your children
　　shall be kings,
　When those that gave the Thane of Cawdor to me
　Promised no less to them?

Banquo.　　　　[*Aside to Macbeth*] That, trusted home,°　120
　Might yet enkindle you unto the crown,
　Besides the Thane of Cawdor. But 'tis strange:
　And oftentimes, to win us to our harm,
　The instruments of darkness tell us truths,
　Win us with honest trifles, to betray 's　　　　125

---

104 **earnest** pledge　106 **addition** title　111 **combined** allied　112 **line** support　113 **vantage** opportunity　114 **wrack** ruin　117 **behind** i.e., to follow　120 **home** all the way

In deepest consequence.°
Cousins,° a word, I pray you.

Macbeth.   [*Aside*] Two truths are told,
As happy prologues to the swelling° act
Of the imperial theme.—I thank you, gentlemen.—

130 [*Aside*] This supernatural soliciting°
Cannot be ill, cannot be good. If ill,
Why hath it given me earnest of success,
Commencing in a truth? I am Thane of Cawdor:
If good, why do I yield to that suggestion

135 Whose horrid image doth unfix my hair
And make my seated° heart knock at my ribs,
Against the use of nature?° Present fears
Are less than horrible imaginings.
My thought, whose murder yet is but fantastical,°

140 Shakes so my single° state of man that function
Is smothered in surmise, and nothing is
But what is not.

Banquo.   Look, how our partner's rapt.

Macbeth. [*Aside*] If chance will have me King, why,
            chance may crown me,
Without my stir.

Banquo.   New honors come upon him,
Like our strange° garments, cleave not to their
145   mold
But with the aid of use.

Macbeth.   [*Aside*] Come what come may,
Time and the hour runs through the roughest day.

Banquo. Worthy Macbeth, we stay upon your leisure.°

Macbeth. Give me your favor.° My dull brain was
            wrought

126 **In deepest consequence** in the most significant sequel   127 **Cousins**
i.e., fellow noblemen   128 **swelling** stately   130 **soliciting** inviting
136 **seated** fixed   137 **Against the use of nature** contrary to my natural
way   139 **fantastical** imaginary   140 **single** unaided, weak (or "entire"?)
145 **strange** new   148 **stay upon your leisure** await your convenience
149 **favor** pardon

With things forgotten. Kind gentlemen, your pains   *150*
Are registered where every day I turn
The leaf to read them. Let us toward the King.
[*Aside to Banquo*] Think upon what hath
          chanced, and at more time,
The interim having weighed it,° let us speak
Our free hearts° each to other.

Banquo.   Very gladly.   *155*

Macbeth. Till then, enough. Come, friends.

                                        Exeunt.

Scene 4.   [*Forres. The palace.*]

*Flourish.° Enter King [Duncan], Lennox,
Malcolm, Donalbain, and Attendants.*

King. Is execution done on Cawdor? Are not
Those in commission° yet returned?

Malcolm.   My liege,
They are not yet come back. But I have spoke
With one that saw him die, who did report
That very frankly he confessed his treasons,   *5*
Implored your Highness' pardon and set forth
A deep repentance: nothing in his life
Became him like the leaving it. He died
As one that had been studied° in his death,
To throw away the dearest thing he owed°   *10*
As 'twere a careless° trifle.

154 **The interim having weighed it** i.e., when we have had time to
think   155 **Our free hearts** our minds freely   1.4.s.d. **Flourish** fanfare
2 **in commission** i.e., commissioned to oversee the execution   9 **studied**
rehearsed   10 **owed** owned   11 **careless** uncared-for

King.   There's no art
To find the mind's construction in the face:
He was a gentleman on whom I built
An absolute trust.

Enter Macbeth, Banquo, Ross, and Angus.

                          O worthiest cousin!
15   The sin of my ingratitude even now
Was heavy on me: thou art so far before,
That swiftest wing of recompense is slow
To overtake thee. Would thou hadst less deserved,
That the proportion° both of thanks and payment
20   Might have been mine! Only I have left to say,
More is thy due than more than all can pay.

Macbeth. The service and the loyalty I owe,
In doing it, pays itself.° Your Highness' part
Is to receive our duties: and our duties
25   Are to your throne and state children and servants;
Which do but what they should, by doing every
     thing
Safe toward° your love and honor.

King.   Welcome hither.
I have begun to plant thee, and will labor
To make thee full of growing. Noble Banquo,
30   That hast no less deserved, nor must be known
No less to have done so, let me enfold thee
And hold thee to my heart.

Banquo.   There if I grow,
The harvest is your own.

King.   My plenteous joys,
Wanton° in fullness, seek to hide themselves
35   In drops of sorrow. Sons, kinsmen, thanes,
And you whose places are the nearest, know,
We will establish our estate° upon
Our eldest, Malcolm, whom we name hereafter

19 **proportion** preponderance   23 **pays itself** is its own reward   27 **Safe toward** safeguarding (?)   34 **Wanton** unrestrained   37 **establish our estate** settle the succession

    The Prince of Cumberland: which honor must
    Not unaccompanied invest him only,   40
    But signs of nobleness, like stars, shall shine
    On all deservers. From hence to Inverness,
    And bind us further to you.

Macbeth. The rest is labor, which is not used for you.°
    I'll be myself the harbinger, and make joyful   45
    The hearing of my wife with your approach;
    So, humbly take my leave.

King.   My worthy Cawdor!

Macbeth. [*Aside*] The Prince of Cumberland! That
        is a step
    On which I must fall down, or else o'erleap,
    For in my way it lies. Stars, hide your fires;   50
    Let not light see my black and deep desires:
    The eye wink at the hand;° yet let that be
    Which the eye fears, when it is done, to see.

                                            Exit.

King. True, worthy Banquo; he is full so valiant,
    And in his commendations° I am fed;   55
    It is a banquet to me. Let's after him,
    Whose care is gone before to bid us welcome.
    It is a peerless kinsman.   *Flourish. Exeunt.*

            Scene 5. [*Inverness. Macbeth's castle.*]

        Enter Macbeth's wife, alone, with a letter.

Lady Macbeth. [*Reads*] "They met me in the day
    of success; and I have learned by the perfect'st

---

44 **The rest … you** i.e., repose is laborious when not employed for
you   52 **wink at the hand** i.e., be blind to the hand's deed   55 **his commendations** commendations of him

report they have more in them than mortal knowledge. When I burned in desire to question them
further, they made themselves air, into which they
vanished. Whiles I stood rapt in the wonder of it,
came missives° from the King, who all-hailed me
'Thane of Cawdor'; by which title, before, these
weïrd sisters saluted me, and referred me to the
coming on of time, with 'Hail, King that shalt
be!' This have I thought good to deliver thee,° my
dearest partner of greatness, that thou mightst not
lose the dues of rejoicing, by being ignorant of
what greatness is promised thee. Lay it to thy heart,
and farewell."

Glamis thou art, and Cawdor, and shalt be
What thou art promised. Yet do I fear thy nature;
It is too full o' th' milk of human kindness°
To catch the nearest way. Thou wouldst be great,
Art not without ambition, but without
The illness° should attend it. What thou wouldst
   highly,
That wouldst thou holily; wouldst not play false,
And yet wouldst wrongly win. Thou'dst have,
   great Glamis,
That which cries "Thus thou must do" if thou have
   it;
And that which rather thou dost fear to do
Than wishest should be undone. Hie thee hither,
That I may pour my spirits in thine ear,
And chastise with the valor of my tongue
All that impedes thee from the golden round°
Which fate and metaphysical° aid doth seem
To have thee crowned withal.°

Enter Messenger.

1.5.   7 **missives** messengers   11 **deliver thee** report to you   18 **milk of human kindness** i.e., gentle quality of human nature   21 **illness** wickedness   29 **round** crown   30 **metaphysical** supernatural   31 **withal** with

　　　　　　　　　　　　　What is your tidings?

Messenger. The King comes here tonight.

Lady Macbeth.　　　　　　　　　Thou'rt mad to say it!
　　Is not thy master with him, who, were 't so,
　　Would have informed for preparation?

Messenger. So please you, it is true. Our thane is
　　　　coming.　　　　　　　　　　　　　　　　　35
　　One of my fellows had the speed of him,°
　　Who, almost dead for breath, had scarcely more
　　Than would make up his message.

Lady Macbeth.　　　　　　　　Give him tending;
　　He brings great news.　　　　　　*Exit Messenger.*
　　　　　　　　　　The raven himself is hoarse
　　That croaks the fatal entrance of Duncan　　　　40
　　Under my battlements. Come, you spirits
　　That tend on mortal° thoughts, unsex me here,
　　And fill me, from the crown to the toe, top-full
　　Of direst cruelty! Make thick my blood,
　　Stop up th' access and passage to remorse,°　　45
　　That no compunctious visitings of nature°
　　Shake my fell° purpose, nor keep peace between
　　Th' effect° and it! Come to my woman's breasts,
　　And take my milk for° gall, you murd'ring ministers,°
　　Wherever in your sightless° substances　　　　50
　　You wait on° nature's mischief! Come, thick night,
　　And pall° thee in the dunnest° smoke of hell,
　　That my keen knife see not the wound it makes,
　　Nor heaven peep through the blanket of the dark,
　　To cry "Hold, hold!"

　　　　　　　　　Enter Macbeth.

　　　　　　　Great Glamis! Worthy Cawdor!　　55
　　Greater than both, by the all-hail hereafter!°

---

36 **had the speed of him** outdistanced him　42 **mortal** deadly　45 **remorse** compassion　46 **compunctious visitings of nature** natural feelings of compassion　47 **fell** savage　48 **effect** fulfillment　49 **for** in exchange for　49 **ministers** agents　50 **sightless** invisible　51 **wait on** assist
52 **pall** enshroud　52 **dunnest** darkest　56 **all-hail hereafter** the third
all-hail (?) the all-hail of the future (?)

Thy letters have transported me beyond
This ignorant° present, and I feel now
The future in the instant.°

Macbeth.   My dearest love,
Duncan comes here tonight.

60 *Lady Macbeth.*   And when goes hence?

Macbeth. Tomorrow, as he purposes.

Lady Macbeth.   O, never
Shall sun that morrow see!
Your face, my Thane, is as a book where men
May read strange matters. To beguile the time,°
65   Look like the time; bear welcome in your eye,
Your hand, your tongue: look like th' innocent
    flower,
But be the serpent under 't. He that's coming
Must be provided for: and you shall put
This night's great business into my dispatch;°
70   Which shall to all our nights and days to come
Give solely sovereign sway and masterdom.

Macbeth. We will speak further.

Lady Macbeth.   Only look up clear.°
To alter favor ever is to fear.°
Leave all the rest to me.   *Exeunt.*

---

58 **ignorant** unknowing   59 **instant** present   64 **To beguile the time** i.e.,
to deceive people of the day   69 **dispatch** management   72 **look up clear**
appear undisturbed   73 **To alter ... fear** to show a disturbed face is
dangerous

Scene 6.   [*Before Macbeth's castle.*]

Hautboys° and torches. Enter King [Duncan],
Malcolm, Donalbain, Banquo, Lennox, Macduff,
Ross, Angus, and Attendants.

King. This castle hath a pleasant seat;° the air
 Nimbly and sweetly recommends itself
 Unto our gentle° senses.

Banquo.   This guest of summer,
 The temple-haunting martlet,° does approve°
 By his loved mansionry° that the heaven's breath   *5*
 Smells wooingly here. No jutty,° frieze,
 Buttress, nor coign of vantage,° but this bird
 Hath made his pendent bed and procreant° cradle.
 Where they most breed and haunt,° I have observed
 The air is delicate.

             Enter Lady [Macbeth].

King.   See, see, our honored hostess!   *10*
 The love that follows us sometime is our trouble,
 Which still we thank as love.° Herein I teach you
 How you shall bid God 'ield° us for your pains
 And thank us for your trouble.

Lady Macbeth.   All our service
 In every point twice done, and then done double,   *15*
 Were poor and single business° to contend
 Against those honors deep and broad wherewith

1.6.s.d. **Hautboys** oboes   1 **seat** site   3 **gentle** soothed   4 **temple-haunting martlet** martin (swift) nesting in churches   4 **approve** prove   5 **mansionry** nests   6 **jutty** projection   7 **coign of vantage** advantageous corner   8 **procreant** breeding   9 **haunt** visit   11–12 **The love ... love** the love offered me sometimes inconveniences me, but still I value it as love   13 **'ield** reward   16 **single business** feeble service

Your Majesty loads our house: for those of old,
And the late dignities heaped up to them,
We rest your hermits.°

20 *King.*   Where's the Thane of Cawdor?
We coursed° him at the heels, and had a purpose
To be his purveyor:° but he rides well,
And his great love, sharp as his spur, hath holp°
    him
To his home before us. Fair and noble hostess,
We are your guest tonight.

25 *Lady Macbeth.*   Your servants ever
Have theirs, themselves, and what is theirs, in
    compt,°
To make their audit at your Highness' pleasure,
Still° to return your own.

King.   Give me your hand.
Conduct me to mine host: we love him highly,
30 And shall continue our graces towards him.
By your leave, hostess.   *Exeunt.*

Scene 7.   [*Macbeth's castle.*]

*Hautboys. Torches. Enter a Sewer,° and diverse Ser-
vants with dishes and service over the stage. Then
enter Macbeth.*

Macbeth. If it were done° when 'tis done, then 'twere
    well
It were done quickly. If th' assassination

___

20 **your hermits** dependents bound to pray for you   21 **coursed** pursued
22 **purveyor** advance-supply officer   23 **holp** helped   26 **Have theirs ...
compt** have their dependents, themselves, and their possessions in trust
28 **Still** always 1.7.s.d. **Sewer** chief butler 1 **done** over and done
with

Could trammel up° the consequence, and catch,
With his surcease,° success;° that but this blow
Might be the be-all and the end-all—here,   5
But here, upon this bank and shoal of time,
We'd jump° the life to come. But in these cases
We still° have judgment here; that we but teach
Bloody instructions, which, being taught, return
To plague th' inventor: this even-handed° justice   10
Commends° th' ingredients of our poisoned
    chalice
To our own lips. He's here in double trust:
First, as I am his kinsman and his subject,
Strong both against the deed; then, as his host,
Who should against his murderer shut the door,   15
Not bear the knife myself. Besides, this Duncan
Hath borne his faculties° so meek, hath been
So clear° in his great office, that his virtues
Will plead like angels trumpet-tongued against
The deep damnation of his taking-off;   20
And pity, like a naked newborn babe,
Striding° the blast, or heaven's cherubin horsed
Upon the sightless couriers° of the air,
Shall blow the horrid deed in every eye,
That° tears shall drown the wind. I have no spur   25
To prick the sides of my intent, but only
Vaulting ambition, which o'erleaps itself
And falls on th' other———

          Enter Lady [*Macbeth*].

                    How now! What news?

Lady Macbeth. He has almost supped. Why have you
    left the chamber?

3 **trammel up** catch in a net 4 **his surcease** Duncan's death(?) the
consequence's cessation(?) 4 **success** what follows 7 **jump** risk 8 **still**
always 10 **even-handed** impartial 11 **Commends** offers 17 **faculties**
powers 18 **clear** spotless 22 **Striding** bestriding 23 **sightless couriers**
invisible coursers (i.e., the winds) 25 **That** so that

   Macbeth. Hath he asked for me?

30   *Lady Macbeth.*   Know you not he has?

   Macbeth. We will proceed no further in this business:
      He hath honored me of late, and I have bought°
      Golden opinions from all sorts of people,
      Which would be worn now in their newest gloss,
      Not cast aside so soon.

35   *Lady Macbeth.*   Was the hope drunk
      Wherein you dressed yourself? Hath it slept since?
      And wakes it now, to look so green° and pale
      At what it did so freely? From this time
      Such I account thy love. Art thou afeard
40   To be the same in thine own act and valor
      As thou art in desire? Wouldst thou have that
      Which thou esteem'st the ornament of life,
      And live a coward in thine own esteem,
      Letting "I dare not" wait upon° "I would,"
      Like the poor cat° i' th' adage?

45   *Macbeth.*   Prithee, peace!
      I dare do all that may become a man;
      Who dares do more is none.

   Lady Macbeth.   What beast was 't then
      That made you break° this enterprise to me?
      When you durst do it, then you were a man;
50   And to be more than what you were, you would
      Be so much more the man. Nor time nor place
      Did then adhere,° and yet you would make both.
      They have made themselves, and that their° fitness
         now
      Does unmake you. I have given suck, and know
55   How tender 'tis to love the babe that milks me:
      I would, while it was smiling in my face,
      Have plucked my nipple from his boneless gums,

---

32 **bought** acquired 37 **green** sickly 44 **wait upon** follow 45 **cat** (who wants fish but fears to wet its paws) 48 **break** broach 52 **adhere** suit 53 **that their** their very

And dashed the brains out, had I so sworn as you
Have done to this.

Macbeth.   If we should fail?

Lady Macbeth.   We fail?
But° screw your courage to the sticking-place,°   60
And we'll not fail. When Duncan is asleep—
Whereto the rather shall his day's hard journey
Soundly invite him—his two chamberlains
Will I with wine and wassail° so convince,°
That memory, the warder° of the brain,   65
Shall be a fume, and the receipt of reason
A limbeck only:° when in swinish sleep
Their drenchèd natures lies° as in a death,
What cannot you and I perform upon
Th' unguarded Duncan, what not put upon   70
His spongy° officers, who shall bear the guilt
Of our great quell?°

Macbeth.   Bring forth men-children only;
For thy undaunted mettle° should compose
Nothing but males. Will it not be received,
When we have marked with blood those sleepy two   75
Of his own chamber, and used their very daggers,
That they have done 't?

Lady Macbeth.   Who dares receive it other,°
As we shall make our griefs and clamor roar
Upon his death?

Macbeth.   I am settled, and bend up
Each corporal agent to this terrible feat.   80
Away, and mock the time° with fairest show:
False face must hide what the false heart doth know.

                                        Exeunt.

60 **But** only   60 **sticking-place** notch (holding the bowstring of a taut
crossbow)   64 **wassail** carousing   64 **convince** overpower   65 **warder**
guard   66–67 **receipt ... only** i.e., the receptacle (*receipt*), which
should collect the distillate of thought—reason—will be a mere vessel
(*limbeck*) of undistilled liquids   68 **lies** lie   71 **spongy** sodden   72 **quell**
killing   73 **mettle** substance   77 **other** otherwise   81 **mock the time** beguile the world

ACT 2

Scene 1.   [*Inverness. Court of Macbeth's
castle.*]

*Enter Banquo, and Fleance, with a torch before
him.*

Banquo. How goes the night, boy?
Fleance. The moon is down; I have not heard the
    clock.
Banquo. And she goes down at twelve.
Fleance.   I take't, 'tis later, sir.
Banquo. Hold, take my sword. There's husbandry° in
    heaven.
5   Their candles are all out. Take thee that too.
    A heavy summons° lies like lead upon me,
    And yet I would not sleep. Merciful powers,
    Restrain in me the cursèd thoughts that nature
    Gives way to in repose!
        Enter Macbeth, and a Servant with a torch.
                                    Give me my sword!
10   Who's there?
    Macbeth. A friend.
    Banquo. What, sir, not yet at rest? The King's a-bed:
        He hath been in unusual pleasure, and
        Sent forth great largess to your offices:°
15   This diamond he greets your wife withal,
        By the name of most kind hostess; and shut up°
        In measureless content.

2.1. 4 **husbandry** frugality   6 **summons** call (to sleep)   14 **largess to
your offices** gifts to your servants' quarters   16 **shut up** concluded

24

Macbeth.   Being unprepared,
  Our will became the servant to defect,°
  Which else should free have wrought.

Banquo.   All's well.
  I dreamt last night of the three weïrd sisters: 20
  To you they have showed some truth.

Macbeth.   I think not of them.
  Yet, when we can entreat an hour to serve,
  We would spend it in some words upon that
        business,
  If you would grant the time.

Banquo.   At your kind'st leisure.

Macbeth. If you shall cleave to my consent, when
        'tis,°   25
  It shall make honor for you.

Banquo.   So° I lose none
  In seeking to augment it, but still keep
  My bosom franchised° and allegiance clear,°
  I shall be counseled.

Macbeth.   Good repose the while!

Banquo. Thanks, sir. The like to you!   30

                    Exit Banquo [with Fleance].

Macbeth. Go bid thy mistress, when my drink is ready,
  She strike upon the bell. Get thee to bed.

                    Exit [Servant].

  Is this a dagger which I see before me,
  The handle toward my hand? Come, let me clutch
        thee.
  I have thee not, and yet I see thee still.   35
  Art thou not, fatal vision, sensible°
  To feeling as to sight, or art thou but
  A dagger of the mind, a false creation,

---

18 **Our ... defect** our good will was hampered by our deficient preparations   25 **cleave ... 'tis** join my cause, when the time comes
26 **So** provided that   28 **franchised** free (from guilt)   28 **clear** spotless
36 **sensible** perceptible

Proceeding from the heat-oppressèd brain?
40 I see thee yet, in form as palpable
As this which now I draw.
Thou marshal'st me the way that I was going;
And such an instrument I was to use.
Mine eyes are made the fools o' th' other senses,
45 Or else worth all the rest. I see thee still;
And on thy blade and dudgeon° gouts° of blood,
Which was not so before. There's no such thing.
It is the bloody business which informs°
Thus to mine eyes. Now o'er the one half-world
50 Nature seems dead, and wicked dreams abuse°
The curtained sleep; witchcraft celebrates
Pale Hecate's offerings;° and withered murder,
Alarumed° by his sentinel, the wolf,
Whose howl's his watch, thus with his stealthy pace,
55 With Tarquin's° ravishing strides, towards his design
Moves like a ghost. Thou sure and firm-set earth,
Hear not my steps, which way they walk, for fear
Thy very stones prate of my whereabout,
And take the present horror from the time,
Which now suits with it.° Whiles I threat, he
60   lives:
Words to the heat of deeds too cold breath gives.

A bell rings.

I go, and it is done: the bell invites me.
Hear it not, Duncan, for it is a knell
That summons thee to heaven, or to hell.

Exit.

---

46 **dudgeon** wooden hilt   46 **gouts** large drops   48 **informs** gives shape
(?)   50 **abuse** deceive   52 **Hecate's offerings** offerings to Hecate (goddess of sorcery)   53 **Alarumed** called to action   55 **Tarquin** (Roman
tyrant who ravished Lucrece)   59–60 **take ... it** remove (by noise) the
horrible silence attendant on this moment and suitable to it (?)

Scene 2. [*Macbeth's Castle.*]

Enter Lady [Macbeth].

Lady Macbeth. That which hath made them drunk hath
    made me bold;
What hath quenched them hath given me fire. Hark!
    Peace!
It was the owl that shrieked, the fatal bellman,
Which gives the stern'st good-night.° He is about it.
The doors are open, and the surfeited grooms   5
Do mock their charge with snores. I have drugged
    their possets,°
That death and nature° do contend about them,
Whether they live or die.

Macbeth.   [*Within*] Who's there? What, ho?

Lady Macbeth. Alack, I am afraid they have awaked
And 'tis not done! Th' attempt and not the deed
Confounds° us. Hark! I laid their daggers ready;   10
He could not miss 'em. Had he not resembled
My father as he slept, I had done 't.

Enter Macbeth.

                        My husband!

Macbeth. I have done the deed. Didst thou not hear a
    noise?

Lady Macbeth. I heard the owl scream and the crickets
    cry.   15
Did not you speak?

Macbeth.   When?

2.2.3–4 **bellman ... good-night** i.e., the owl's call, portending death,
is like the town crier's call to a condemned man 6 **possets** (bedtime
drinks) 7 **nature** natural vitality 11 **Confounds** ruins

Lady Macbeth.   Now.

Macbeth.   As I descended?

Lady Macbeth. Ay.

Macbeth. Hark!
  Who lies i' th' second chamber?

Lady Macbeth.   Donalbain.

20 *Macbeth.* This is a sorry° sight.

Lady Macbeth. A foolish thought, to say a sorry sight.

Macbeth. There's one did laugh in 's sleep, and one
    cried "Murder!"
  That they did wake each other. I stood and heard
    them.
  But they did say their prayers, and addressed them
  Again to sleep.

25 *Lady Macbeth.*   There are two lodged together.

Macbeth. One cried "God bless us!" and "Amen" the
    other,
  As they had seen me with these hangman's° hands:
  List'ning their fear, I could not say "Amen,"
  When they did say "God bless us!"

Lady Macbeth.   Consider it not so deeply.

Macbeth. But wherefore could not I pronounce
30   "Amen"?
  I had most need of blessing, and "Amen"
  Stuck in my throat.

Lady Macbeth.   These deeds must not be thought
  After these ways; so, it will make us mad.

Macbeth. Methought I heard a voice cry "Sleep no
    more!
35   Macbeth does murder sleep"—the innocent sleep,
  Sleep that knits up the raveled sleave° of care,

---

20 **sorry** miserable   27 **hangman's** executioner's (i.e., bloody)   36 **knits
up the raveled sleave** straightens out the tangled skein

The death of each day's life, sore labor's bath,
Balm of hurt minds, great nature's second course,°
Chief nourisher in life's feast——

Lady Macbeth.   What do you mean?

Macbeth. Still it cried "Sleep no more!" to all the
    house: 40
    "Glamis hath murdered sleep, and therefore
        Cawdor
    Shall sleep no more: Macbeth shall sleep no more."

Lady Macbeth. Who was it that thus cried? Why,
        worthy Thane,
    You do unbend° your noble strength, to think
    So brainsickly of things. Go get some water,   45
    And wash this filthy witness° from your hand.
    Why did you bring these daggers from the place?
    They must lie there: go carry them, and smear
    The sleepy grooms with blood.

Macbeth.   I'll go no more.
    I am afraid to think what I have done;   50
    Look on 't again I dare not.

Lady Macbeth.   Infirm of purpose!
    Give me the daggers. The sleeping and the dead
    Are but as pictures. 'Tis the eye of childhood
    That fears a painted° devil. If he do bleed,
    I'll gild° the faces of the grooms withal,   55
    For it must seem their guilt.

                            Exit. Knock within.

Macbeth.   Whence is that knocking?
    How is 't with me, when every noise appalls me?
    What hands are here? Ha! They pluck out mine
        eyes!
    Will all great Neptune's ocean wash this blood
    Clean from my hand? No; this my hand will rather   60

---

38 **second course** i.e., sleep (the less substantial first course is food)
44 **unbend** relax 46 **witness** evidence 54 **painted** depicted 55 **gild** paint

The multitudinous seas incarnadine,°
Making the green one red.°

Enter Lady [Macbeth].

Lady Macbeth. My hands are of your color, but I
    shame
To wear a heart so white. (*Knock.*) I hear a
    knocking
65   At the south entry. Retire we to our chamber.
A little water clears us of this deed:
How easy is it then! Your constancy
Hath left you unattended.° (*Knock.*) Hark! more
    knocking.
Get on your nightgown,° lest occasion call us
70   And show us to be watchers.° Be not lost
So poorly° in your thoughts.

Macbeth. To know my deed, 'twere best not know
    myself. (*Knock.*)
Wake Duncan with thy knocking! I would thou
    couldst!   *Exeunt.*

Scene 3.   [*Macbeth's castle.*]

Enter a Porter. Knocking within.

Porter. Here's a knocking indeed! If a man were
    porter of hell gate, he should have old° turning the
    key. (*Knock.*) Knock, knock, knock! Who's there,

61 **incarnadine** redden   62 **the green one red** (perhaps "the green one"
means "the ocean," but perhaps "one" here means "totally," "uniformly")
67–68 **Your . . . unattended** your firmness has deserted you   69 **nightgown**
dressing-gown   70 **watchers** i.e., up late   71 **poorly** weakly   2.3. 2 **should
have old** would certainly have plenty of

i' th' name of Beelzebub? Here's a farmer, that
hanged himself on th' expectation of plenty.° Come   *5*
in time! Have napkins enow° about you; here you'll
sweat for 't. (*Knock*.) Knock, knock! Who's there,
in th' other devil's name? Faith, here's an equivocator,° that could swear in both the scales against
either scale; who committed treason enough for   *10*
God's sake, yet could not equivocate to heaven. O,
come in, equivocator. (*Knock.*) Knock, knock,
knock! Who's there? Faith, here's an English tailor
come hither for stealing out of a French hose:°
come in, tailor. Here you may roast your goose.°   *15*
(*Knock.*) Knock, knock; never at quiet! What are
you? But this place is too cold for hell. I'll devil-
porter it no further. I had thought to have let in
some of all professions that go the primrose way
to th' everlasting bonfire. (*Knock.*) Anon, anon!   *20*
[*Opens an entrance.*] I pray you, remember the
porter.

Enter Macduff and Lennox.

Macduff. Was it so late, friend, ere you went to bed,
　That you do lie so late?

Porter. Faith, sir, we were carousing till the second   *25*
　cock:° and drink, sir, is a great provoker of three
　things.

Macduff. What three things does drink especially pro-
　voke?

Porter. Marry, sir, nose-painting, sleep, and urine.   *30*
　Lechery, sir, it provokes and unprovokes; it pro-
　vokes the desire, but it takes away the perfor-
　mance: therefore much drink may be said to be an
　equivocator with lechery: it makes him and it mars

4–5 **farmer … plenty** (the farmer hoarded so he could later sell high,
but when it looked as though there would be a crop surplus he hanged
himself)　6 **enow** enough　8–9 **equivocator** i.e., Jesuit (who allegedly
employed deceptive speech to further God's ends)　14 **French hose** tight-
fitting hose　15 **goose** pressing iron　25–26 **second cock** (about 3 a.m.)

35   him; it sets him on and it takes him off; it per-
      suades him and disheartens him; makes him stand
      to and not stand to; in conclusion, equivocates
      him in a sleep, and giving him the lie, leaves him.

Macduff. I believe drink gave thee the lie° last night.

40 *Porter.* That it did, sir, i' the very throat on me: but
      I requited him for his lie, and, I think, being too
      strong for him, though he took up my legs some-
      time, yet I make a shift to cast° him.

Macduff. Is thy master stirring?

                    Enter Macbeth.

45   Our knocking has awaked him; here he comes.

Lennox. Good morrow, noble sir.

Macbeth.   Good morrow, both.

Macduff. Is the king stirring, worthy Thane?

Macbeth.   Not yet.

Macduff. He did command me to call timely° on him:
      I have almost slipped° the hour.

Macbeth.   I'll bring you to him.

50 *Macduff.* I know this is a joyful trouble to you;
      But yet 'tis one.

Macbeth. The labor we delight in physics pain.°
      This is the door.

Macduff.   I'll make so bold to call,
      For 'tis my limited service.°

                                   Exit Macduff.

Lennox. Goes the king hence today?

55 *Macbeth.*   He does: he did appoint so.

---

39 **gave thee the lie** called you a liar (with a pun on "stretched you
out") 43 **cast** (with a pun on "cast," meaning "vomit") 48 **timely**
early 49 **slipped** let slip 52 **The labor . . . pain** labor that gives us
pleasure cures discomfort 54 **limited service** appointed duty

Lennox. The night has been unruly. Where we lay,
   Our chimneys were blown down, and, as they say,
   Lamentings heard i' th' air, strange screams of
     death,
   And prophesying with accents terrible
   Of dire combustion° and confused events   60
   New hatched to th' woeful time: the obscure bird°
   Clamored the livelong night. Some say, the earth
   Was feverous and did shake.

Macbeth.   'Twas a rough night.

Lennox. My young remembrance cannot parallel
   A fellow to it.   65

Enter Macduff.

Macduff. O horror, horror, horror! Tongue nor heart
   Cannot conceive nor name thee.

Macbeth and Lennox.   What's the matter?

Macduff. Confusion° now hath made his masterpiece.
   Most sacrilegious murder hath broke ope
   The Lord's anointed temple, and stole thence   70
   The life o' th' building.

Macbeth.   What is 't you say? The life?

Lennox. Mean you his Majesty?

Macduff. Approach the chamber, and destroy your
     sight
   With a new Gorgon:° do not bid me speak;
   See, and then speak yourselves. Awake, awake!   75

Exeunt Macbeth and Lennox.

   Ring the alarum bell. Murder and Treason!
   Banquo and Donalbain! Malcolm! Awake!
   Shake off this downy sleep, death's counterfeit,°
   And look on death itself! Up, up, and see
   The great doom's image!° Malcolm! Banquo!   80

60 **combustion** tumult 61 **obscure bird** bird of darkness, i.e., the owl
68 **Confusion** destruction 74 **Gorgon** (creature capable of turning be-
holders to stone) 78 **counterfeit** imitation 80 **great doom's image** likeness of Judgment Day

As from your graves rise up, and walk like sprites,°
To countenance° this horror. Ring the bell.

    Bell rings. Enter Lady [Macbeth].

Lady Macbeth. What's the business,
  That such a hideous trumpet calls to parley
  The sleepers of the house? Speak, speak!

85 *Macduff.*   O gentle lady,
  'Tis not for you to hear what I can speak:
  The repetition,° in a woman's ear,
  Would murder as it fell.

    Enter Banquo.

            O Banquo, Banquo!
  Our royal master's murdered.

Lady Macbeth.   Woe, alas!
  What, in our house?

90 *Banquo.*   Too cruel anywhere.
  Dear Duff, I prithee, contradict thyself,
  And say it is not so.

    Enter Macbeth, Lennox, and Ross.

Macbeth. Had I but died an hour before this chance,
  I had lived a blessèd time; for from this instant
95 There's nothing serious in mortality:°
  All is but toys.° Renown and grace is dead,
  The wine of life is drawn, and the mere lees°
  Is left this vault° to brag of.

    Enter Malcolm and Donalbain.

Donalbain. What is amiss?

Macbeth.   You are, and do not know 't.
100 The spring, the head, the fountain of your blood
  Is stopped; the very source of it is stopped.

Macduff. Your royal father's murdered.

81 **sprites** spirits   82 **countenance** be in keeping with   87 **repetition** report   95 **serious in mortality** worthwhile in mortal life   96 **toys** trifles
97 **lees** dregs   98 **vault** (1) wine vault (2) earth, with the sky as
roof (?)

Malcolm.   O, by whom?

Lennox. Those of his chamber, as it seemed, had
    done 't:
    Their hands and faces were all badged° with blood;
    So were their daggers, which unwiped we found   105
    Upon their pillows. They stared, and were
      distracted.
    No man's life was to be trusted with them.

Macbeth. O, yet I do repent me of my fury,
    That I did kill them.

Macduff.   Wherefore did you so?

Macbeth. Who can be wise, amazed,° temp'rate and
    furious,   110
    Loyal and neutral, in a moment? No man.
    The expedition° of my violent love
    Outrun the pauser, reason. Here lay Duncan,
    His silver skin laced with his golden blood,
    And his gashed stabs looked like a breach in nature   115
    For ruin's wasteful entrance: there, the murderers,
    Steeped in the colors of their trade, their daggers
    Unmannerly breeched with gore.° Who could
      refrain,°
    That had a heart to love, and in that heart
    Courage to make 's love known?

Lady Macbeth.   Help me hence, ho!   120

Macduff. Look to° the lady.

Malcolm. [*Aside to Donalbain*] Why do we hold
    our tongues,
    That most may claim this argument for ours?°

Donalbain. [*Aside to Malcolm*] What should be
    spoken here,
    Where our fate, hid in an auger-hole,°

104 **badged** marked   110 **amazed** bewildered   112 **expedition** haste
118 **Unmannerly breeched with gore** covered with unseemly breeches of
blood   118 **refrain** check oneself   121 **Look to** look after   123 **That
most . . . ours?** who are the most concerned with this topic   124 **auger-
hole** i.e., unsuspected place

125   May rush, and seize us? Let's away:
       Our tears are not yet brewed.

Malcolm. [*Aside to Donalbain*] Nor our strong
       sorrow
       Upon the foot of motion.°

Banquo.   Look to the lady.

                    [*Lady Macbeth is carried out.*]

       And when we have our naked frailties hid,°
       That suffer in exposure, let us meet
130   And question° this most bloody piece of work,
       To know it further. Fears and scruples° shake us.
       In the great hand of God I stand, and thence
       Against the undivulged pretense° I fight
       Of treasonous malice.

Macduff.   And so do I.

All.   So all.

135   *Macbeth.* Let's briefly° put on manly readiness,
       And meet i' th' hall together.

All.   Well contented.

              Exeunt [*all but Malcolm and Donalbain*].

Malcolm. What will you do? Let's not consort with
       them.
       To show an unfelt sorrow is an office°
       Which the false man does easy. I'll to England.

140   *Donalbain.* To Ireland, I; our separated fortune
       Shall keep us both the safer. Where we are
       There's daggers in men's smiles; the near in blood,
       The nearer bloody.

Malcolm.   This murderous shaft that's shot
       Hath not yet lighted, and our safest way

126–27 **Our tears . . . motion** i.e., we have not yet had time for tears
nor to express our sorrows in action (?) 128 **naked frailties hid** poor
bodies clothed 130 **question** discuss 131 **scruples** suspicions 133 **un-
divulged pretense** hidden purpose 135 **briefly** quickly 138 **office** function

Is to avoid the aim. Therefore to horse;   ₁₄₅
And let us not be dainty of° leave-taking,
But shift away. There's warrant° in that theft
Which steals itself° when there's no mercy left.

Exeunt.

Scene 4.   [*Outside Macbeth's castle.*]

Enter Ross with an Old Man.

Old Man. Threescore and ten I can remember well:
    Within the volume of which time I have seen
    Hours dreadful and things strange, but this sore°
        night
    Hath trifled former knowings.°

Ross.   Ha, good father,
    Thou seest the heavens, as troubled with man's act,   5
    Threatens his bloody stage. By th' clock 'tis day,
    And yet dark night strangles the traveling lamp:°
    Is 't night's predominance,° or the day's shame,
    That darkness does the face of earth entomb,
    When living light should kiss it?

Old Man.   'Tis unnatural,   10
    Even like the deed that's done. On Tuesday last
    A falcon, tow'ring in her pride of place,°
    Was by a mousing° owl hawked at and killed.

Ross. And Duncan's horses—a thing most strange
        and certain—
    Beauteous and swift, the minions° of their race,   15

146 **dainty of** fussy about   147 **warrant** justification   148 **steals itself**
steals oneself away   2.4.   3 **sore** grievous   4 **trifled former knowings**
made trifles of former experiences   7 **traveling lamp** i.e., the sun   8 **pre-**
dominance astrological supremacy   12 **tow'ring ... place** soaring at
her summit   13 **mousing** i.e., normally mouse-eating   15 **minions** darlings

Turned wild in nature, broke their stalls, flung out,°
Contending 'gainst obedience, as they would make
War with mankind.

Old Man.   'Tis said they eat° each other.

Ross. They did so, to th' amazement of mine eyes,
That looked upon 't.

Enter Macduff.

20   Here comes the good Macduff
How goes the world, sir, now?

Macduff.   Why, see you not?

Ross. Is 't known who did this more than bloody deed?

Macduff. Those that Macbeth hath slain.

Ross.   Alas, the day!
What good could they pretend?°

Macduff.   They were suborned:°
25   Malcolm and Donalbain, the king's two sons,
Are stol'n away and fled, which puts upon them
Suspicion of the deed.

Ross.   'Gainst nature still.
Thriftless° ambition, that will ravin up°
Thine own life's means! Then 'tis most like
30   The sovereignty will fall upon Macbeth.

Macduff. He is already named,° and gone to Scone
To be invested.°

Ross.   Where is Duncan's body?

Macduff. Carried to Colmekill,
The sacred storehouse of his predecessors
And guardian of their bones.

35   *Ross.*   Will you to Scone?

Macduff. No, cousin, I'll to Fife.

---

16 **flung out** lunged wildly 18 **eat** ate 24 **pretend** hope for 24 **suborned** bribed 28 **Thriftless** wasteful 28 **ravin up** greedily devour 31 **named** elected 32 **invested** installed as king

Ross.   Well, I will thither.

Macduff. Well, may you see things well done there.
   Adieu,
   Lest our old robes sit easier than our new!

Ross. Farewell, father.

Old Man. God's benison° go with you, and with those   *40*
   That would make good of bad, and friends of foes!

                              Exeunt omnes.

40 **benison** blessing

ACT 3

Scene 1. [*Forres. The palace.*]

Enter Banquo.

Banquo. Thou hast it now: King, Cawdor, Glamis, all,
　　As the weïrd women promised, and I fear
　　Thou play'dst most foully for 't. Yet it was said
　　It should not stand° in thy posterity,
5　　But that myself should be the root and father
　　Of many kings. If there come truth from them—
　　As upon thee, Macbeth, their speeches shine—
　　Why, by the verities on thee made good,
　　May they not be my oracles as well
10　　And set me up in hope? But hush, no more!

*Sennet° sounded. Enter Macbeth as King, Lady
[Macbeth], Lennox, Ross, Lords, and Attendants*

Macbeth. Here's our chief guest.

Lady Macbeth. 　　　　　　　If he had been forgotten,
　　It had been as a gap in our great feast,
　　And all-thing° unbecoming.

Macbeth. Tonight we hold a solemn° supper, sir,
　　And I'll request your presence.

15　*Banquo.* 　　　　　　　　　　Let your Highness
　　Command upon me, to the which my duties

3.1. 4 **stand** continue   s.d. **Sennet** trumpet call   13 **all-thing** altogether
14 **solemn** ceremonious

40

Are with a most indissoluble tie
For ever knit.

Macbeth. Ride you this afternoon?

Banquo.   Ay, my good lord.

Macbeth. We should have else desired your good advice *20*
(Which still° hath been both grave and
    prosperous°)
In this day's council; but we'll take tomorrow.
Is 't far you ride?

Banquo. As far, my lord, as will fill up the time
'Twixt this and supper. Go not my horse the
    better,°   *25*
I must become a borrower of the night
For a dark hour or twain.

Macbeth.   Fail not our feast.

Banquo. My lord, I will not.

Macbeth. We hear our bloody cousins are bestowed°
In England and in Ireland, not confessing   *30*
Their cruel parricide, filling their hearers
With strange invention.° But of that tomorrow,
When therewithal we shall have cause of state
Craving us jointly.° Hie you to horse. Adieu,
Till you return at night. Goes Fleance with you? *35*

Banquo. Ay, my good lord: our time does call upon 's.

Macbeth. I wish your horses swift and sure of foot,
And so I do commend you to their backs.
Farewell.   *Exit Banquo.*
Let every man be master of his time   *40*
Till seven at night. To make society
The sweeter welcome, we will keep ourself

---

21 **still** always 21 **grave and prosperous** weighty and profitable 25 **Go
. . . better** unless my horse goes better than I expect 29 **are bestowed**
have taken refuge 32 **invention** lies 33–34 **cause . . . jointly** matters of
state demanding our joint attention

Till supper-time alone. While° then, God be with
you!

Exeunt Lords [*and all but Macbeth and a Servant*].

Sirrah,° a word with you: attend° those men
45   Our pleasure?

Attendant. They are, my lord, without° the palace
gate.

Macbeth. Bring them before us.   *Exit Servant.*
To be thus is nothing, but° to be safely thus—
Our fears in° Banquo stick deep,
50   And in his royalty of nature reigns that
Which would° be feared. 'Tis much he dares;
And, to° that dauntless temper° of his mind,
He hath a wisdom that doth guide his valor
To act in safety. There is none but he
55   Whose being I do fear: and under him
My genius is rebuked,° as it is said
Mark Antony's was by Cæsar. He chid the sisters,
When first they put the name of King upon me,
And bade them speak to him; then prophetlike
60   They hailed him father to a line of kings.
Upon my head they placed a fruitless crown
And put a barren scepter in my gripe,°
Thence to be wrenched with an unlineal hand,
No son of mine succeeding. If 't be so,
65   For Banquo's issue have I filed° my mind;
For them the gracious Duncan have I murdered;
Put rancors° in the vessel of my peace
Only for them, and mine eternal jewel°
Given to the common enemy of man,°
70   To make them kings, the seeds of Banquo kings!

---

43 **While** until   44 **Sirrah** (common address to an inferior)   44 **attend**
await   46 **without** outside   48 **but** unless   49 **in** about   51 **would** must
52 **to** added to   52 **temper** quality   56 **genius is rebuked** guardian spirit
is cowed   62 **gripe** grasp   65 **filed** defiled   67 **rancors** bitter enmities
68 **eternal jewel** i.e., soul   69 **common enemy of man** i.e., the Devil

Rather than so, come, fate, into the list,°
And champion me to th' utterance!° Who's there?

Enter Servant and Two Murderers.

Now go to the door, and stay there till we call.

Exit Servant.

Was it not yesterday we spoke together?

Murderers. It was, so please your Highness.

Macbeth.   Well then, now   75
Have you considered of my speeches? Know
That it was he in the times past, which held you
So under fortune,° which you thought had been
Our innocent self: this I made good to you
In our last conference; passed in probation° with
    you,   80
How you were borne in hand,° how crossed;° the
    instruments,°
Who wrought with them, and all things else that
    might
To half a soul° and to a notion° crazed
Say "Thus did Banquo."

First Murderer.   You made it known to us.

Macbeth. I did so; and went further, which is now   85
Our point of second meeting. Do you find
Your patience so predominant in your nature,
That you can let this go? Are you so gospeled,°
To pray for this good man and for his issue,
Whose heavy hand hath bowed you to the grave   90
And beggared yours for ever?

First Murderer.   We are men, my liege.

Macbeth. Ay, in the catalogue ye go for° men;

71 **list** lists 72 **champion me to th' utterance** fight against me to the death 77–78 **held . . . fortune** kept you from good fortune (?) 80 **passed in probation** reviewed the proofs 81 **borne in hand** deceived 81 **crossed** thwarted 81 **instruments** tools 83 **half a soul** a halfwit 83 **notion** mind 88 **gospeled** i.e., made meek by the gospel 92 **go for** pass as

As hounds and greyhounds, mongrels, spaniels,
　　curs,
Shoughs, water-rugs° and demi-wolves, are clept°
95　All by the name of dogs: the valued file°
Distinguishes the swift, the slow, the subtle,
The housekeeper,° the hunter, every one
According to the gift which bounteous nature
Hath in him closed,° whereby he does receive
100　Particular addition, from the bill°
That writes them all alike: and so of men.
Now if you have a station in the file,
Not i' th' worst rank of manhood, say 't,
And I will put that business in your bosoms
105　Whose execution takes your enemy off,
Grapples you to the heart and love of us,
Who wear our health but sickly in his life,°
Which in his death were perfect.

Second Murderer.　　　　　　　　　I am one, my liege,
Whom the vile blows and buffets of the world
110　Hath so incensed that I am reckless what
I do to spite the world.

First Murderer.　　　　　　And I another
So weary with disasters, tugged with fortune,
That I would set° my life on any chance,
To mend it or be rid on 't.

Macbeth.　　　　　　　　　Both of you
Know Banquo was your enemy.

115　*Both Murderers.*　　　　　　　　True, my lord.

Macbeth. So is he mine, and in such bloody distance°
That every minute of his being thrusts
Against my near'st of life:° and though I could

---

94 **Shoughs, water-rugs** shaggy dogs, long-haired water dogs 94 **clept**
called 95 **valued file** classification by valuable traits 97. **housekeeper**
watchdog 99 **closed** enclosed 100 **Particular addition, from the bill**
special distinction in opposition to the list 107 **wear ... life** have
only imperfect health while he lives 113 **set** risk 116 **distance** quarrel
118 **near'st of life** most vital spot

With barefaced power sweep him from my sight
And bid my will avouch° it, yet I must not,   *120*
For° certain friends that are both his and mine,
Whose loves I may not drop, but wail his fall°
Who I myself struck down: and thence it is
That I to your assistance do make love,
Masking the business from the common eye   *125*
For sundry weighty reasons.

Second Murderer.   We shall, my lord,
   Perform what you command us.

First Murderer.   Though our lives——

Macbeth. Your spirits shine through you. Within this
      hour at most
   I will advise you where to plant yourselves,
   Acquaint you with the perfect spy° o' th' time,   *130*
   The moment on 't;° for 't must be done tonight,
   And something° from the palace; always thought°
   That I require a clearness:° and with him—
   To leave no rubs° nor botches in the work—
   Fleance his son, that keeps him company,   *135*
   Whose absence is no less material to me
   Than is his father's, must embrace the fate
   Of that dark hour. Resolve yourselves apart:°
   I'll come to you anon.

Murderers.   We are resolved, my lord.

Macbeth. I'll call upon you straight.° Abide within.   *140*
   It is concluded: Banquo, thy soul's flight,
   If it find heaven, must find it out tonight.   *Exeunt.*

---

120 **avouch** justify   121 **For** because of   122 **wail his fall** bewail his death
130 **perfect spy** exact information (?) (*spy* literally means "observation";
apparently Macbeth already has the Third Murderer in mind)   131 **on 't**
of it   132 **something** some distance   132 **thought** remembered   133 **clearness** freedom from suspicion   134 **rubs** flaws   138 **Resolve yourselves
apart** decide by yourself   140 **straight** immediately

Scene 2.   [*The palace.*]

Enter Macbeth's Lady and a Servant.

Lady Macbeth. Is Banquo gone from court?

Servant. Ay, madam, but returns again tonight.

Lady Macbeth. Say to the King, I would attend his
leisure
For a few words.

Servant.   Madam, I will.   *Exit.*

Lady Macbeth.   Nought's had, all's spent,
5   Where our desire is got without content:
'Tis safer to be that which we destroy
Than by destruction dwell in doubtful joy.

Enter Macbeth.

How now, my lord! Why do you keep alone,
Of sorriest° fancies your companions making,
Using those thoughts which should indeed have
10   died
With them they think on? Things without° all
remedy
Should be without regard: what's done is done.

Macbeth. We have scorched° the snake, not killed it:
She'll close° and be herself, whilst our poor malice°
15   Remains in danger of her former tooth.
But let the frame of things disjoint,° both the
worlds° suffer,
Ere we will eat our meal in fear, and sleep
In the affliction of these terrible dreams

3.2. 9 **sorriest** most despicable 11 **without** beyond 13 **scorched**
slashed, scored 14 **close** heal 14 **poor malice** feeble enmity 16 **frame
of things disjoint** universe collapse 16 **both the worlds** heaven and
earth (?)

    That shake us nightly: better be with the dead,
    Whom we, to gain our peace, have sent to peace,   20
    Than on the torture° of the mind to lie
    In restless ecstasy.° Duncan is in his grave;
    After life's fitful fever he sleeps well.
    Treason has done his° worst: nor steel, nor poison,
    Malice domestic,° foreign levy, nothing,   25
    Can touch him further.

Lady Macbeth.   Come on.
    Gentle my lord, sleek° o'er your rugged° looks;
    Be bright and jovial among your guests tonight.

Macbeth. So shall I, love; and so, I pray, be you:
    Let your remembrance apply to Banquo;°   30
    Present him eminence,° both with eye and tongue:
    Unsafe the while, that we must lave°
    Our honors in these flattering streams
    And make our faces vizards° to our hearts,
    Disguising what they are.

Lady Macbeth.   You must leave this.   35

Macbeth. O, full of scorpions is my mind, dear wife!
    Thou know'st that Banquo, and his Fleance, lives.

Lady Macbeth. But in them nature's copy's° not eterne.

Macbeth. There's comfort yet; they are assailable.
    Then be thou jocund. Ere the bat hath flown   40
    His cloistered flight, ere to black Hecate's summons
    The shard-borne° beetle with his drowsy hums
    Hath rung night's yawning peal, there shall be done
    A deed of dreadful note.

Lady Macbeth.   What's to be done?

---

21 **torture** i.e., rack   22 **ecstasy** frenzy   24 **his** its   25 **Malice domestic**
civil war   27 **sleek** smooth   27 **rugged** furrowed   30 **Let ... Banquo**
focus your thoughts on Banquo   31 **Present him eminence** honor him
32 **Unsafe ... lave** i.e., you and I are unsafe because we must dip
34 **vizards** masks   38 **nature's copy** nature's lease (?) imitation (i.e., a
son) made by nature (?)   42 **shard-borne** borne on scaly wings (?)
dung-bred (?)

Macbeth. Be innocent of the knowledge, dearest
45   chuck,°
Till thou applaud the deed. Come, seeling° night,
Scarf up° the tender eye of pitiful day,
And with thy bloody and invisible hand
Cancel and tear to pieces that great bond°
50   Which keeps me pale! Light thickens, and the crow
Makes wing to th' rooky° wood.
Good things of day begin to droop and drowse,
Whiles night's black agents to their preys do rouse.
Thou marvel'st at my words: but hold thee still;
55   Things bad begun make strong themselves by ill:
So, prithee, go with me.   *Exeunt.*

Scene 3.   [*Near the palace.*]

Enter Three Murderers.

First Murderer. But who did bid thee join with us?

Third Murderer.   Macbeth.

Second Murderer. He needs not our mistrust; since he
    delivers
Our offices and what we have to do
To the direction just.°

First Murderer.   Then stand with us.
5   The west yet glimmers with some streaks of day.
Now spurs the lated° traveler apace
To gain the timely inn, and near approaches
The subject of our watch.

45 **chuck** chick (a term of endearment)   46 **seeling** eye-closing   47 **Scarf up** blindfold   49 **bond** i.e., between Banquo and fate (?) Banquo's lease on life (?) Macbeth's link to humanity (?)   51 **rooky** full of rooks   3.3.   2–4 **He needs ... just** we need not mistrust him (i.e., the Third Murderer) since he describes our duties according to our exact directions   6 **lated** belated

Third Murderer.   Hark! I hear horses.

Banquo. (*Within*) Give us a light there, ho!

Second Murderer.   Then 'tis he. The rest
  That are within the note of expectation°   *10*
  Already are i' th' court.

First Murderer.   His horses go about.

Third Murderer. Almost a mile: but he does usually—
  So all men do—from hence to th' palace gate
  Make it their walk.

          Enter Banquo and Fleance, with a torch.

Second Murderer. A light, a light!

Third Murderer.   'Tis he.

First Murderer.   Stand to 't.   *15*

Banquo. It will be rain tonight.

First Murderer.   Let it come down.

          [*They set upon Banquo.*]

Banquo. O, treachery! Fly, good Fleance, fly, fly, fly!

                    [*Exit Fleance.*]

    Thou mayst revenge. O slave! [*Dies.*]

Third Murderer. Who did strike out the light?

First Murderer.   Was 't not the way?°

Third Murderer. There's but one down; the son is fled.   *20*

Second Murderer. We have lost best half of our affair.

First Murderer. Well, let's away and say how much is
  done.   *Exeunt.*

10 **within the note of expectation** on the list of expected guests   19 **way**
i.e., thing to do

Scene 4.   [*The palace.*]

> *Banquet prepared. Enter Macbeth, Lady [Mac-*
> *beth], Ross, Lennox, Lords, and Attendants.*

Macbeth. You know your own degrees;° sit down:
　　At first and last, the hearty welcome.

Lords. Thanks to your Majesty.

Macbeth. Ourself will mingle with society°
5　　And play the humble host.
　　Our hostess keeps her state,° but in best time
　　We will require° her welcome.

Lady Macbeth. Pronounce it for me, sir, to all our
　　friends,
　　For my heart speaks they are welcome.

> *Enter First Murderer.*

Macbeth. See, they encounter° thee with their hearts'
10　　thanks.
　　Both sides are even: here I'll sit i' th' midst:
　　Be large in mirth; anon we'll drink a measure°
　　The table round. [*Goes to Murderer*] There's
　　blood upon thy face.

Murderer. 'Tis Banquo's then.

15　*Macbeth.* 'Tis better thee without than he within.°
　　Is he dispatched?

Murderer. My lord, his throat is cut; that I did for
　　him.

Macbeth. Thou art the best o' th' cutthroats.

3.4.　1 **degrees** ranks　4 **society** the company　6 **keeps her state** remains
seated in her chair of state　7 **require** request　10 **encounter** meet
12 **measure** goblet　15 **thee without than he within** outside you than
inside him

Yet he's good that did the like for Fleance;
If thou didst it, thou art the nonpareil.   20

Murderer. Most royal sir, Fleance is 'scaped.

Macbeth. [*Aside*] Then comes my fit again: I had
   else been perfect,
Whole as the marble, founded° as the rock,
As broad and general as the casing° air:
But now I am cabined, cribbed,° confined, bound in   25
To saucy° doubts and fears.—But Banquo's safe?

Murderer. Ay, my good lord: safe in a ditch he bides,
With twenty trenchèd° gashes on his head,
The least a death to nature.

Macbeth.   Thanks for that.
   [*Aside*] There the grown serpent lies; the worm°
   that's fled   30
Hath nature that in time will venom breed,
No teeth for th' present. Get thee gone. Tomorrow
We'll hear ourselves° again.   *Exit Murderer.*

Lady Macbeth.   My royal lord,
You do not give the cheer.° The feast is sold
That is not often vouched, while 'tis a-making,   35
'Tis given with welcome. To feed were best at
   home;°
From thence, the sauce to meat° is ceremony;
Meeting were bare without it.

     *Enter the Ghost of Banquo, and sits in
        Macbeth's place.*

Macbeth.   Sweet remembrancer!°
Now good digestion wait on appetite,
And health on both!

23 **founded** firmly based   24 **broad ... casing** unconfined as the sur-
rounding   25 **cribbed** penned up   26 **saucy** insolent   28 **trenchèd** trench-
like   30 **worm** serpent   33 **hear ourselves** talk it over   34 **the cheer** a
sense of cordiality   34–36 **The feast ... home** i.e., the feast seems sold
(not given) during which the host fails to welcome the guests. Mere eat-
ing is best done at home   37 **meat** food   38 **remembrancer** reminder

40 *Lennox.*   May 't please your Highness sit.

Macbeth. Here had we now our country's honor
        roofed,°
    Were the gracèd person of our Banquo present—
    Who may I rather challenge for unkindness
    Than pity for mischance!°

Ross.   His absence, sir,
    Lays blame upon his promise. Please 't your
45   Highness
    To grace us with your royal company?

Macbeth. The table's full.

Lennox.   Here is a place reserved, sir.

Macbeth. Where?

Lennox. Here, my good lord. What is 't that moves
        your Highness?

Macbeth. Which of you have done this?

50 *Lords.*   What, my good lord?

Macbeth. Thou canst not say I did it. Never shake
    Thy gory locks at me.

Ross. Gentlemen, rise, his Highness is not well.

Lady Macbeth. Sit, worthy friends. My lord is often
        thus,
55   And hath been from his youth. Pray you, keep seat.
    The fit is momentary; upon a thought°
    He will again be well. If much you note him,
    You shall offend him and extend his passion.°
    Feed, and regard him not.—Are you a man?

60 *Macbeth.* Ay, and a bold one, that dare look on that
    Which might appall the devil.

Lady Macbeth.   O proper stuff!
    This is the very painting of your fear.
    This is the air-drawn dagger which, you said,

---

41 **our country's honor roofed** our nobility under one roof   43–44 **Who
... mischance** whom I hope I may reprove because he is unkind rather
than pity because he has encountered an accident   56 **upon a thought**
as quick as thought   58 **extend his passion** lengthen his fit

Led you to Duncan. O, these flaws° and starts,
Impostors to° true fear, would well become   65
A woman's story at a winter's fire,
Authorized° by her grandam. Shame itself!
Why do you make such faces? When all's done,
You look but on a stool.

Macbeth.   Prithee, see there!
Behold! Look! Lo! How say you?   70
Why, what care I? If thou canst nod, speak too.
If charnel houses° and our graves must send
Those that we bury back, our monuments
Shall be the maws of kites.°   [*Exit Ghost.*]

Lady Macbeth.   What, quite unmanned in folly?

Macbeth. If I stand here, I saw him.

Lady Macbeth.   Fie, for shame!   75

Macbeth. Blood hath been shed ere now, i' th' olden
     time,
Ere humane statute purged the gentle weal;°
Ay, and since too, murders have been performed
Too terrible for the ear. The times has been
That, when the brains were out, the man would die,   80
And there an end; but now they rise again,
With twenty mortal murders on their crowns,°
And push us from our stools. This is more strange
Than such a murder is.

Lady Macbeth.   My worthy lord,
Your noble friends do lack you.

Macbeth.   I do forget.   85
Do not muse at me, my most worthy friends;
I have a strange infirmity, which is nothing
To those that know me. Come, love and health to
     all!

---

64 **flaws** gusts, outbursts 65 **to** compared with 67 **Authorized** vouched
for 72 **charnel houses** vaults containing bones 73–74 **our ... kites**
our tombs shall be the bellies of rapacious birds 77 **purged the gentle
weal** i.e., cleansed the state and made it gentle 82 **mortal murders on
their crowns** deadly wounds on their heads

Then I'll sit down. Give me some wine, fill full.

Enter Ghost.

90   I drink to th' general joy o' th' whole table,
 And to our dear friend Banquo, whom we miss;
 Would he were here! To all and him we thirst,°
 And all to all.°

Lords.   Our duties, and the pledge.

Macbeth. Avaunt! and quit my sight! Let the earth hide
 thee!
95 Thy bones are marrowless, thy blood is cold;
 Thou hast no speculation° in those eyes
 Which thou dost glare with.

Lady Macbeth.   Think of this, good peers,
 But as a thing of custom; 'tis no other.
 Only it spoils the pleasure of the time.

100 *Macbeth.* What man dare, I dare.
 Approach thou like the rugged Russian bear,
 The armed rhinoceros, or th' Hyrcan° tiger;
 Take any shape but that, and my firm nerves°
 Shall never tremble. Or be alive again,
105 And dare me to the desert° with thy sword.
 If trembling I inhabit then, protest me
 The baby of a girl.° Hence, horrible shadow!
 Unreal mock'ry, hence!   *[Exit Ghost.]*
       Why, so: being gone,
 I am a man again. Pray you, sit still.

Lady Macbeth. You have displaced the mirth, broke the
110 good meeting,
 With most admired° disorder.

Macbeth.   Can such things be,
 And overcome us° like a summer's cloud,

92 **thirst** desire to drink 93 **all to all** everything to everybody (?) let everybody drink to everybody (?) 96 **speculation** sight 102 **Hyrcan** of Hyrcania (near the Caspian Sea) 103 **nerves** sinews 105 **the desert** a lonely place 106–07 **If ... girl** if then I tremble, proclaim me a baby girl 111 **admired** amazing 112 **overcome us** come over us

Without our special wonder? You make me strange
Even to the disposition that I owe,°
When now I think you can behold such sights,   *115*
And keep the natural ruby of your cheeks,
When mine is blanched with fear.

Ross.   What sights, my lord?

Lady Macbeth. I pray you, speak not: he grows worse
    and worse;
    Question enrages him: at once, good night.
    Stand not upon the order of your going,°   *120*
    But go at once.

Lennox.   Good night; and better health
    Attend his Majesty!

Lady Macbeth.   A kind good night to all!

                                        Exeunt Lords.

Macbeth. It will have blood, they say: blood will have
    blood.
    Stones have been known to move and trees to
        speak;
    Augures and understood relations° have   *125*
    By maggot-pies and choughs and rooks brought
        forth°
    The secret'st man of blood. What is the night?°

Lady Macbeth. Almost at odds° with morning, which is
    which.

Macbeth. How say'st thou, that Macduff denies his
    person
    At our great bidding?

Lady Macbeth.   Did you send to him, sir?   *130*

Macbeth. I hear it by the way,° but I will send:

113–14 **You ... owe** i.e., you make me wonder what my nature is
120 **Stand ... going** do not insist on departing in your order of rank
125 **Augures and understood relations** auguries and comprehended reports 126 **By ... forth** by magpies, choughs, and rooks (telltale
birds) revealed 127 **What is the night** what time of night is it
128 **at odds** striving 131 **by the way** incidentally

There's not a one of them but in his house
I keep a servant fee'd.° I will tomorrow,
And betimes° I will, to the weïrd sisters:
135　More shall they speak, for now I am bent° to know
By the worst means the worst. For mine own good
All causes° shall give way. I am in blood
Stepped in so far that, should I wade no more,
Returning were as tedious as go o'er.
140　Strange things I have in head that will to hand,
Which must be acted ere they may be scanned.°

Lady Macbeth. You lack the season of all natures,°
　　sleep.

Macbeth. Come, we'll to sleep. My strange and self-
　　abuse°
Is the initiate fear that wants hard use.°
145　We are yet but young in deed.　　　　　*Exeunt.*

Scene 5.　　[*A Witches' haunt.*]

*Thunder. Enter the Three Witches, meeting
Hecate.*

First Witch. Why, how now, Hecate! you look
　　angerly.

Hecate. Have I not reason, beldams° as you are,
　　Saucy and overbold? How did you dare
　　To trade and traffic with Macbeth
5　　In riddles and affairs of death;

133　**fee'd** i.e., paid to spy　134　**betimes** quickly　135　**bent** determined
137　**causes** considerations　141　**may be scanned** can be examined
142　**season of all natures** seasoning (preservative) of all living creatures
143　**My strange and self-abuse** my strange delusion　144　**initiate ...**
use beginner's fear that lacks hardening practice　3.5. 2　**beldams** hags

And I, the mistress of your charms,
The close contriver° of all harms,
Was never called to bear my part,
Or show the glory of our art?
And, which is worse, all you have done   10
Hath been but for a wayward son,
Spiteful and wrathful; who, as others do,
Loves for his own ends, not for you.
But make amends now: get you gone,
And at the pit of Acheron°   15
Meet me i' th' morning: thither he
Will come to know his destiny.
Your vessels and your spells provide,
Your charms and everything beside.
I am for th' air; this night I'll spend   20
Unto a dismal and a fatal end:
Great business must be wrought ere noon.
Upon the corner of the moon
There hangs a vap'rous drop profound;°
I'll catch it ere it come to ground: 25
And that distilled by magic sleights°
Shall raise such artificial sprites°
As by the strength of their illusion
Shall draw him on to his confusion.°
He shall spurn fate, scorn death, and bear   30
His hopes 'bove wisdom, grace, and fear:
And you all know security°
Is mortals' chiefest enemy.

Music and a song.

Hark! I am called; my little spirit, see,
Sits in a foggy cloud and stays for me.   [*Exit.*]   35
    Sing within, "Come away, come away," &c.

First Witch. Come, let's make haste; she'll soon be
    back again.   *Exeunt.*

---

7 **close contriver** secret inventor   15 **Acheron** (river of Hades)   24 **profound** heavy   26 **sleights** arts   27 **artificial sprites** spirits created by magic arts (?) artful (cunning) spirits (?)   29 **confusion** ruin   32 **security** overconfidence

Scene 6.   [*The palace.*]

Enter Lennox and another Lord.

Lennox. My former speeches have but hit your
            thoughts,°
        Which can interpret farther. Only I say
        Things have been strangely borne.° The gracious
            Duncan
        Was pitied of Macbeth: marry, he was dead.
5   And the right-valiant Banquo walked too late;
        Whom, you may say, if 't please you, Fleance
            killed,
        For Fleance fled. Men must not walk too late.
        Who cannot want the thought,° how monstrous
        It was for Malcolm and for Donalbain
10   To kill their gracious father? Damnèd fact!°
        How it did grieve Macbeth! Did he not straight,
        In pious rage, the two delinquents tear,
        That were the slaves of drink and thralls° of sleep?
        Was not that nobly done? Ay, and wisely too;
15   For 'twould have angered any heart alive
        To hear the men deny 't. So that I say
        He has borne° all things well: and I do think
        That, had he Duncan's sons under his key—
        As, an 't° please heaven, he shall not—they should
            find
20   What 'twere to kill a father. So should Fleance.
        But, peace! for from broad words,° and 'cause he
            failed
        His presence at the tyrant's feast, I hear,

3.6. 1 **My ... thoughts** i.e., my recent words have only coincided
with what you have in your mind 3 **borne** managed 8 **cannot want
the thought** can fail to think 10 **fact** evil deed 13 **thralls** slaves
17 **borne** managed 19 **an 't** if it 21 **for from broad words** because of
frank talk

Macduff lives in disgrace. Sir, can you tell
Where he bestows himself?

Lord.   The son of Duncan,
From whom this tyrant holds the due of birth,°   25
Lives in the English court, and is received
Of the most pious Edward° with such grace
That the malevolence of fortune nothing
Takes from his high respect.° Thither Macduff
Is gone to pray the holy King, upon his aid°   30
To wake Northumberland° and warlike Siward;
That by the help of these, with Him above
To ratify the work, we may again
Give to our tables meat, sleep to our nights,
Free from our feasts and banquets bloody knives,   35
Do faithful homage and receive free° honors:
All which we pine for now. And this report
Hath so exasperate the King that he
Prepares for some attempt of war.

Lennox.   Sent he to Macduff?

Lord. He did: and with an absolute "Sir, not I,"   40
The cloudy° messenger turns me his back,
And hums, as who should say "You'll rue the time
That clogs° me with this answer."

Lennox.   And that well might
Advise him to a caution, t' hold what distance
His wisdom can provide. Some holy angel   45
Fly to the court of England and unfold
His message ere he come, that a swift blessing
May soon return to this our suffering country
Under a hand accursed!

Lord.   I'll send my prayers with him.

                                        Exeunt.

---

25 **due of birth** birthright   27 **Edward** Edward the Confessor (reigned
1042–1066)   28–29 **nothing . . . respect** does not diminish the high respect in which he is held   30 **upon his aid** to aid him (Malcolm)
31 **To wake Northumberland** i.e., to arouse the people in an English
county near Scotland   36 **free** freely granted   41 **cloudy** disturbed
43 **clogs** burdens

ACT 4

Scene 1.   [*A Witches' haunt.*]

Thunder. Enter the Three Witches.

First Witch. Thrice the brinded° cat hath mewed.

Second Witch. Thrice and once the hedge-pig°
    whined.

Third Witch. Harpier° cries. 'Tis time, 'tis time.

First Witch. Round about the caldron go:
5   In the poisoned entrails throw.
    Toad, that under cold stone
    Days and nights has thirty-one
    Swelt'red venom sleeping got,°
    Boil thou first i' th' charmèd pot.

10 *All.* Double, double, toil and trouble;
    Fire burn and caldron bubble.

Second Witch. Fillet° of a fenny° snake,
    In the caldron boil and bake;
    Eye of newt and toe of frog,
15   Wool of bat and tongue of dog,
    Adder's fork° and blindworm's° sting,
    Lizard's leg and howlet's° wing,

4.1.   1 **brinded** brindled   2 **hedge-pig** hedgehog   3 **Harpier** (an attendant spirit, like Graymalkin and Paddock in 1.1)   8 **Swelt'red venom sleeping got** venom sweated out while sleeping   12 **Fillet** slice   12 **fenny** from a swamp   16 **fork** forked tongue   16 **blindworm** (a legless lizard) 17 **howlet** owlet

For a charm of pow'rful trouble,
Like a hell-broth boil and bubble.

All. Double, double, toil and trouble;   20
Fire burn and caldron bubble.

Third Witch. Scale of dragon, tooth of wolf,
Witch's mummy,° maw and gulf°
Of the ravined° salt-sea shark,
Root of hemlock digged i' th' dark,   25
Liver of blaspheming Jew,
Gall of goat, and slips of yew
Slivered in the moon's eclipse,
Nose of Turk and Tartar's lips,
Finger of birth-strangled babe   30
Ditch-delivered by a drab,°
Make the gruel thick and slab:°
Add thereto a tiger's chaudron,°
For th' ingredience of our caldron.

All. Double, double, toil and trouble;   35
Fire burn and caldron bubble.

Second Witch. Cool it with a baboon's blood,
Then the charm is firm and good.

   Enter Hecate and the other Three Witches.

Hecate. O, well done! I commend your pains;
And every one shall share i' th' gains: 40
And now about the caldron sing,
Like elves and fairies in a ring,
Enchanting all that you put in.

   Music and a song: "Black Spirits," &c.

   [*Exeunt Hecate and the other Three Witches.*]

Second Witch. By the pricking of my thumbs,
Something wicked this way comes: 45
   Open, locks,
   Whoever knocks!

---

23 **Witch's mummy** mummified flesh of a witch   23 **maw and gulf**
stomach and gullet   24 **ravined** ravenous   31 **Ditch-delivered by a drab**
born in a ditch of a harlot   32 **slab** viscous   33 **chaudron** entrails

Macbeth. How now, you secret, black, and midnight
    hags!
    What is 't you do?

All.   A deed without a name.

50 *Macbeth.* I conjure you, by that which you profess,
    Howe'er you come to know it, answer me:
    Though you untie the winds and let them fight
    Against the churches; though the yesty° waves
    Confound° and swallow navigation up;
    Though bladed corn be lodged° and trees blown
55   down;
    Though castles topple on their warders' heads;
    Though palaces and pyramids do slope°
    Their heads to their foundations; though the treas-
        ure
    Of nature's germens° tumble all together,
60 Even till destruction sicken,° answer me
    To what I ask you.

First Witch.   Speak.

Second Witch.   Demand.

Third Witch.   We'll answer.

First Witch. Say, if th' hadst rather hear it from our
        mouths,
    Or from our masters?

Macbeth.   Call 'em, let me see 'em.

First Witch. Pour in sow's blood, that hath eaten
65 Her nine farrow;° grease that's sweaten°
    From the murderer's gibbet throw
    Into the flame.

All.   Come, high or low,
    Thyself and office° deftly show!

53 **yesty** foamy   54 **Confound** destroy   55 **bladed corn be lodged** grain
in the ear be beaten down   57 **slope** bend   59 **nature's germens** seeds
of all life   60 **sicken** i.e., sicken at its own work   65 **farrow** young pigs
65 **sweaten** sweated   68 **office** function

Thunder. First Apparition: an Armed Head.

Macbeth. Tell me, thou unknown power————

First Witch.   He knows thy thought:
Hear his speech, but say thou nought.   70

First Apparition. Macbeth! Macbeth! Macbeth! Beware
Macduff!
Beware the Thane of Fife. Dismiss me: enough.

                                        He descends.

Macbeth. Whate'er thou art, for thy good caution
thanks:
Thou hast harped° my fear aright. But one word
more————

First Witch. He will not be commanded. Here's another,   75
More potent than the first.

        Thunder. Second Apparition: a Bloody Child.

Second Apparition. Macbeth! Macbeth! Macbeth!

Macbeth. Had I three ears, I'd hear thee.

Second Apparition. Be bloody, bold, and resolute!
Laugh to scorn
The pow'r of man, for none of woman born   80
Shall harm Macbeth.   *Descends.*

Macbeth. Then live, Macduff: what need I fear of
thee?
But yet I'll make assurance double sure,
And take a bond of fate.° Thou shalt not live;
That I may tell pale-hearted fear it lies,   85
And sleep in spite of thunder.

        *Thunder. Third Apparition: a Child Crowned,
                with a tree in his hand.*

---

74 **harped** hit upon, struck the note of 84 **take a bond of fate** get a
guarantee from fate (i.e., he will kill Macduff and thus will compel
fate to keep its word)

                                              What is this,
     That rises like the issue° of a king,
     And wears upon his baby-brow the round
     And top of sovereignty?°

All.   Listen, but speak not to 't.

Third Apparition. Be lion-mettled, proud, and take
90   no care
     Who chafes, who frets, or where conspirers are:
     Macbeth shall never vanquished be until
     Great Birnam Wood to high Dunsinane Hill
     Shall come against him.   *Descends.*

Macbeth.   That will never be.
95   Who can impress° the forest, bid the tree
     Unfix his earth-bound root? Sweet bodements,°
        good!
     Rebellious dead,° rise never, till the Wood
     Of Birnam rise, and our high-placed Macbeth
     Shall live the lease of nature,° pay his breath
100 To time and mortal custom.° Yet my heart
     Throbs to know one thing. Tell me, if your art
     Can tell so much: shall Banquo's issue ever
     Reign in this kingdom?

All.   Seek to know no more.

Macbeth. I will be satisfied.° Deny me this,
105 And an eternal curse fall on you! Let me know.
     Why sinks that caldron? And what noise° is this?

                             Hautboys.

First Witch. Show!

Second Witch. Show!

Third Witch. Show!

---

87 **issue** offspring 88–89 **round/And top of sovereignty** i.e., crown
95 **impress** conscript 96 **bodements** prophecies 97 **Rebellious dead**
(perhaps a reference to Banquo; but perhaps a misprint for "rebellion's
head") 99 **lease of nature** natural lifespan 100 **mortal custom** natural
death 104 **satisfied** i.e., fully informed 106 **noise** music

All. Show his eyes, and grieve his heart;   *110*
  Come like shadows, so depart!

>   *A show of eight Kings and Banquo, last [King]*
>   *with a glass° in his hand.*

Macbeth. Thou art too like the spirit of Banquo.
      Down!
  Thy crown does sear mine eyelids. And thy hair,
  Thou other gold-bound brow, is like the first.
  A third is like the former. Filthy hags!   *115*
  Why do you show me this? A fourth! Start,° eyes!
  What, will the line stretch out to th' crack of
      doom?°
  Another yet! A seventh! I'll see no more.
  And yet the eighth appears, who bears a glass
  Which shows me many more; and some I see   *120*
  That twofold balls and treble scepters° carry:
  Horrible sight! Now I see 'tis true;
  For the blood-boltered° Banquo smiles upon me,
  And points at them for his. What, is this so?

First Witch. Ay, sir, all this is so. But why   *125*
  Stands Macbeth thus amazedly?
  Come, sisters, cheer we up his sprites,°
  And show the best of our delights:
  I'll charm the air to give a sound,
  While you perform your antic round,°   *130*
  That this great king may kindly say
  Our duties did his welcome pay.

>   *Music. The Witches dance, and vanish.*

Macbeth. Where are they? Gone? Let this pernicious
      hour
  Stand aye accursèd in the calendar!
  Come in, without there!

111.s.d. **glass** mirror 116 **Start** i.e., from the sockets 117 **crack of doom**
blast (of a trumpet?) at doomsday 121 **twofold balls and treble
scepters** (coronation emblems) 123 **blood-boltered** matted with blood
127 **sprites** spirits 130 **antic round** grotesque circular dance

Enter Lennox.

135 *Lennox.*   What's your Grace's will?

Macbeth. Saw you the weïrd sisters?

Lennox.   No, my lord.

Macbeth. Came they not by you?

Lennox.   No indeed, my lord.

Macbeth. Infected be the air whereon they ride,
      And damned all those that trust them! I did hear
140   The galloping of horse.° Who was 't came by?

Lennox. 'Tis two or three, my lord, that bring you
      word
      Macduff is fled to England.

Macbeth.   Fled to England?

Lennox. Ay, my good lord.

Macbeth. [*Aside*] Time, thou anticipat'st° my
      dread exploits.
145   The flighty purpose never is o'ertook
      Unless the deed go with it.° From this moment
      The very firstlings of my heart° shall be
      The firstlings of my hand. And even now,
      To crown my thoughts with acts, be it thought and
      done:
150   The castle of Macduff I will surprise;°
      Seize upon Fife; give to th' edge o' th' sword
      His wife, his babes, and all unfortunate souls
      That trace him in his line.° No boasting like a fool;
      This deed I'll do before this purpose cool:
155   But no more sights!—Where are these gentlemen?
      Come, bring me where they are.   *Exeunt.*

---

140 **horse** horses (or "horsemen")   144 **anticipat'st** foretold   145–46 **The
flighty ... it** the fleeting plan is never fulfilled unless an action accompanies it   147 **firstlings of my heart** i.e., first thoughts, impulses
150 **surprise** attack suddenly   153 **trace him in his line** are of his lineage

Scene 2.   [*Macduff's castle.*]

Enter Macduff's wife, her Son, and Ross.

Lady Macduff. What had he done, to make him fly the
     land?

Ross. You must have patience, madam.

Lady Macduff.   He had none:
     His flight was madness. When our actions do not,
     Our fears do make us traitors.

Ross.   You know not
     Whether it was his wisdom or his fear.   5

Lady Macduff. Wisdom! To leave his wife, to leave his
     babes,
     His mansion and his titles,° in a place
     From whence himself does fly? He loves us not;
     He wants the natural touch:° for the poor wren,
     The most diminutive of birds, will fight,   10
     Her young ones in her nest, against the owl.
     All is the fear and nothing is the love;
     As little is the wisdom, where the flight
     So runs against all reason.

Ross.   My dearest coz,°
     I pray you, school° yourself. But, for your husband,   15
     He is noble, wise, judicious, and best knows
     The fits o' th' season.° I dare not speak much
     further:
     But cruel are the times, when we are traitors
     And do not know ourselves; when we hold rumor
     From what we fear,° yet know not what we fear,   20

4.2.   **7 titles** possessions   **9 wants the natural touch** i.e., lacks natural affection for his wife and children   **14 coz** cousin   **15 school** control   **17 fits
o' th' season** disorders of the time   **19–20 hold rumor/From what we fear**
believe rumors because we fear

But float upon a wild and violent sea
Each way and move. I take my leave of you.
Shall not be long but I'll be here again.
Things at the worst will cease,° or else climb up-
        ward
25 To what they were before. My pretty cousin,
Blessing upon you!

Lady Macduff. Fathered he is, and yet he's fatherless.

Ross. I am so much a fool, should I stay longer,
It would be my disgrace° and your discomfort.
I take my leave at once.   *Exit Ross.*

30 *Lady Macduff.*   Sirrah,° your father's dead:
And what will you do now? How will you live?

Son. As birds do, mother.

Lady Macduff.   What, with worms and flies?

Son. With what I get, I mean; and so do they.

Lady Macduff. Poor bird! thou'dst never fear the net
        nor lime,°
35 The pitfall nor the gin.°

Son. Why should I, mother? Poor birds they are not
        set for.
My father is not dead, for all your saying.

Lady Macduff. Yes, he is dead: how wilt thou do for a
        father?

Son. Nay, how will you do for a husband?

Lady Macduff. Why, I can buy me twenty at any
40   market.

Son. Then you'll buy 'em to sell° again.

Lady Macduff. Thou speak'st with all thy wit, and yet,
        i' faith,
With wit enough for thee.°

24 **cease** i.e., cease worsening   29 **It would be my disgrace** i.e., I would
weep   30 **Sirrah** (here an affectionate address to a child)   34 **lime** birdlime (smeared on branches to catch birds)   35 **gin** trap   41 **sell** betray
43 **for thee** i.e., for a child

Son. Was my father a traitor, mother?

Lady Macduff. Ay, that he was. 45

Son. What is a traitor?

Lady Macduff. Why, one that swears and lies.°

Son. And be all traitors that do so?

Lady Macduff. Every one that does so is a traitor, and must be hanged.

Son. And must they all be hanged that swear and lie? 50

Lady Macduff. Every one.

Son. Who must hang them?

Lady Macduff. Why, the honest men.

Son. Then the liars and swearers are fools; for there are liars and swearers enow° to beat the honest 55 men and hang up them.

Lady Macduff. Now, God help thee, poor monkey! But how wilt thou do for a father?

Son. If he were dead, you'd weep for him. If you would not, it were a good sign that I should quickly 60 have a new father.

Lady Macduff. Poor prattler, how thou talk'st!

Enter a Messenger.

Messenger. Bless you, fair dame! I am not to you
known,
Though in your state of honor I am perfect.°
I doubt° some danger does approach you nearly: 65
If you will take a homely° man's advice,
Be not found here; hence, with your little ones.
To fright you thus, methinks I am too savage;
To do worse to you were fell° cruelty,
Which is too nigh your person. Heaven preserve
you! 70

---

47 **swears and lies** i.e., takes an oath and breaks it 55 **enow** enough
64 **in . . . perfect** I am fully informed of your honorable rank 65 **doubt**
fear 66 **homely** plain 69 **fell** fierce

I dare abide no longer.   *Exit Messenger.*

Lady Macduff.   Whither should I fly?
I have done no harm. But I remember now
I am in this earthly world, where to do harm
Is often laudable, to do good sometime
75 Accounted dangerous folly. Why then, alas,
Do I put up that womanly defense,
To say I have done no harm?—What are these faces?

Enter Murderers.

Murderer. Where is your husband?

Lady Macduff. I hope, in no place so unsanctified
Where such as thou mayst find him.

80 *Murderer.*   He's a traitor.

Son. Thou li'st, thou shag-eared° villain!

Murderer.   What, you egg!

[*Stabbing him.*]

Young fry° of treachery!

Son.   He has killed me, mother:
Run away, I pray you!

[*Dies.*]
Exit [*Lady Macduff*], *crying "Murder!"* [*followed by Murderers*].

Scene 3. [*England. Before the King's palace.*]

Enter Malcolm and Macduff.

Malcolm. Let us seek out some desolate shade, and
there
Weep our sad bosoms empty.

81 **shag-eared** hairy-eared (?), with shaggy hair hanging over the ears
(?)   82 **fry** spawn

Macduff.   Let us rather
Hold fast the mortal° sword, and like good men
Bestride our down-fall'n birthdom.° Each new
    morn
New widows howl, new orphans cry, new sorrows   5
Strike heaven on the face, that° it resounds
As if it felt with Scotland and yelled out
Like syllable of dolor.°

Malcolm.   What I believe, I'll wail;
What know, believe; and what I can redress,
As I shall find the time to friend,° I will.   10
What you have spoke, it may be so perchance.
This tyrant, whose sole° name blisters our tongues,
Was once thought honest:° you have loved him
    well;
He hath not touched you yet. I am young; but
    something
You may deserve of him through me;° and wisdom°   15
To offer up a weak, poor, innocent lamb
T' appease an angry god.

Macduff. I am not treacherous.

Malcolm.   But Macbeth is.
A good and virtuous nature may recoil
In° an imperial charge. But I shall crave your
    pardon;
                                                      20
That which you are, my thoughts cannot
    transpose:°
Angels are bright still, though the brightest° fell:
Though all things foul would wear° the brows of
    grace,
Yet grace must still look so.°

4.3.   3 **mortal** deadly   4 **Bestride our down-fall'n birthdom** protectively
stand over our native land   6 **that** so that   8 **Like syllable of dolor**
similar sound of grief   10 **to friend** friendly, propitious   12 **sole** very
13 **honest** good   15 **deserve of him through me** i.e., earn by betraying
me to Macbeth   15 **wisdom** it may be wise   19–20 **recoil/In** give way
under   21 **transpose** transform   22 **the brightest** i.e., Lucifer   23 **would
wear** desire to wear   24 **so** i.e., like itself

Macduff.   I have lost my hopes.

Malcolm. Perchance even there where I did find my
25   doubts.
Why in that rawness° left you wife and child,
Those precious motives, those strong knots of
      love,
Without leave-taking? I pray you,
Let not my jealousies° be your dishonors,
30   But mine own safeties. You may be rightly just°
Whatever I shall think.

Macduff.   Bleed, bleed, poor country:
Great tyranny, lay thou thy basis° sure,
For goodness dare not check° thee: wear thou thy
      wrongs;
The title is affeered.° Fare thee well, lord:
35   I would not be the villain that thou think'st
For the whole space that's in the tyrant's grasp
And the rich East to boot.

Malcolm.   Be not offended:
I speak not as in absolute fear of you.
I think our country sinks beneath the yoke;
40   It weeps, it bleeds, and each new day a gash
Is added to her wounds. I think withal°
There would be hands uplifted in my right;°
And here from gracious England° have I offer
Of goodly thousands: but, for° all this,
45   When I shall tread upon the tyrant's head,
Or wear it on my sword, yet my poor country
Shall have more vices than it had before,
More suffer, and more sundry ways than ever,
By him that shall succeed.

Macduff.   What should he be?

50   *Malcolm.* It is myself I mean, in whom I know

---

26 **rawness** unprotected condition   29 **jealousies** suspicions   30 **rightly just**
perfectly honorable   32 **basis** foundation   33 **check** restrain   34 **affeered**
legally confirmed   41 **withal** moreover   42 **in my right** on behalf of my
claim   43 **England** i.e., the King of England   44 **for** despite

　All the particulars° of vice so grafted°
That, when they shall be opened,° black Macbeth
Will seem as pure as snow, and the poor state
Esteem him as a lamb, being compared
With my confineless harms.°

Macduff.　　　　　　　　　　　Not in the legions　　　55
Of horrid hell can come a devil more damned
In evils to top Macbeth.

Malcolm.　　　　　　　　　　I grant him bloody,
Luxurious,° avaricious, false, deceitful,
Sudden,° malicious, smacking of every sin
That has a name: but there's no bottom, none,　　　60
In my voluptuousness:° your wives, your daughters,
Your matrons and your maids, could not fill up
The cistern of my lust, and my desire
All continent° impediments would o'erbear,
That did oppose my will. Better Macbeth　　　　65
Than such an one to reign.

Macduff.　　　　　　　　　　Boundless intemperance
In nature° is a tyranny; it hath been
Th' untimely emptying of the happy throne,
And fall of many kings. But fear not yet
To take upon you what is yours: you may　　　70
Convey° your pleasures in a spacious plenty,
And yet seem cold, the time° you may so hoodwink.
We have willing dames enough. There cannot be
That vulture in you, to devour so many
As will to greatness dedicate themselves,　　　75
Finding it so inclined.

Malcolm.　　　　　　　　　With this there grows
In my most ill-composed affection° such

51 **particulars** special kinds　51 **grafted** engrafted　52 **opened** in bloom,
i.e., revealed　55 **confineless harms** unbounded evils　58 **Luxurious** lecherous　59 **Sudden** violent　61 **voluptuousness** lust　64 **continent** restraining
67 **In nature** in man's nature　71 **Convey** secretly manage　72 **time** age,
i.e., people　77 **ill-composed affection** evilly compounded character

A stanchless° avarice that, were I King,
I should cut off the nobles for their lands,
80   Desire his jewels and this other's house:
And my more-having would be as a sauce
To make me hunger more, that I should forge
Quarrels unjust against the good and loyal,
Destroying them for wealth.

Macduff.   This avarice
85   Sticks deeper, grows with more pernicious root
Than summer-seeming° lust, and it hath been
The sword of our slain kings.° Yet do not fear.
Scotland hath foisons to fill up your will
Of your mere own.° All these are portable,°
90   With other graces weighed.

Malcolm. But I have none: the king-becoming graces,
As justice, verity, temp'rance, stableness,
Bounty, perseverance, mercy, lowliness,
Devotion, patience, courage, fortitude,
95   I have no relish of° them, but abound
In the division of each several crime,°
Acting it many ways. Nay, had I pow'r, I should
Pour the sweet milk of concord into hell,
Uproar° the universal peace, confound
All unity on earth.

100 *Macduff.*   O Scotland, Scotland!

Malcolm. If such a one be fit to govern, speak:
I am as I have spoken.

Macduff.   Fit to govern!
No, not to live. O nation miserable!
With an untitled tyrant bloody-sceptered,
105   When shalt thou see thy wholesome days again,

---

78 **stanchless** never-ending   86 **summer-seeming** befitting summer, i.e.,
youthful (?) transitory (?)   87 **sword of our slain kings** i.e., the cause
of death to our kings   88–89 **foisons . . . own** enough abundance of
your own to satisfy your covetousness   89 **portable** bearable   95 **relish
of** taste for (?) trace of (?)   96 **division of each several crime** variations of each kind of crime   99 **Uproar** put into a tumult

Since that the truest issue of thy throne
By his own interdiction° stands accursed,
And does blaspheme his breed?° Thy royal father
Was a most sainted king: the queen that bore thee,
Oft'ner upon her knees than on her feet,   *110*
Died° every day she lived. Fare thee well!
These evils thou repeat'st upon thyself
Hath banished me from Scotland. O my breast,
Thy hope ends here!

Malcolm.   Macduff, this noble passion,
Child of integrity, hath from my soul
Wiped the black scruples,° reconciled my thoughts   *115*
To thy good truth and honor. Devilish Macbeth
By many of these trains° hath sought to win me
Into his power; and modest wisdom° plucks me
From over-credulous haste: but God above   *120*
Deal between thee and me! For even now
I put myself to° thy direction, and
Unspeak mine own detraction; here abjure
The taints and blames I laid upon myself,
For° strangers to my nature. I am yet   *125*
Unknown to woman, never was forsworn,
Scarcely have coveted what was mine own,
At no time broke my faith, would not betray
The devil to his fellow, and delight
No less in truth than life. My first false speaking   *130*
Was this upon myself. What I am truly,
Is thine and my poor country's to command:
Whither indeed, before thy here-approach,
Old Siward, with ten thousand warlike men,
Already at a point,° was setting forth.   *135*
Now we'll together, and the chance of goodness
Be like our warranted quarrel!° Why are you
    silent?

---

107 **interdiction** curse, exclusion   108 **breed** ancestry   111 **Died** i.e., prepared for heaven   116 **scruples** suspicions   118 **trains** plots   119 **modest
wisdom** i.e., prudence   122 **to** under   125 **For** as   135 **at a point** prepared
136–37 **the chance ... quarrel** i.e., may our chance of success equal the
justice of our cause

Macduff. Such welcome and unwelcome things at once
'Tis hard to reconcile.

Enter a Doctor.

Malcolm. Well, more anon. Comes the King forth, I
140 pray you?

Doctor. Ay, sir. There are a crew of wretched souls
That stay° his cure: their malady convinces
The great assay of art;° but at his touch,
Such sanctity hath heaven given his hand,
They presently amend.°

145 *Malcolm.*   I thank you, doctor.

Exit [*Doctor*].

Macduff. What's the disease he means?

Malcolm.   'Tis called the evil:°
A most miraculous work in this good King,
Which often since my here-remain in England
I have seen him do. How he solicits heaven,
150 Himself best knows: but strangely-visited° people,
All swoll'n and ulcerous, pitiful to the eye,
The mere° despair of surgery, he cures,
Hanging a golden stamp° about their necks,
Put on with holy prayers: and 'tis spoken,
155 To the succeeding royalty he leaves
The healing benediction. With this strange virtue°
He hath a heavenly gift of prophecy,
And sundry blessings hang about his throne
That speak° him full of grace.

Enter Ross.

Macduff.   See, who comes here?

160 *Malcolm.* My countryman; but yet I know him not.

---

142 **stay** await   142–43 **convinces/The great assay of art** i.e., defies the
efforts of medical science   145 **presently amend** immediately recover
146 **evil** (scrofula, called "the king's evil" because it could allegedly be
cured by the king's touch)   150 **strangely-visited** oddly afflicted   152 **mere**
utter   153 **stamp** coin   156 **virtue** power   159 **speak** proclaim

Macduff. My ever gentle° cousin, welcome hither.

Malcolm. I know him now: good God, betimes°
   remove
  The means that makes us strangers!

Ross.   Sir, amen.

Macduff. Stands Scotland where it did?

Ross.   Alas, poor country!
  Almost afraid to know itself! It cannot   *165*
  Be called our mother but our grave, where nothing°
  But who knows nothing is once seen to smile;
  Where sighs and groans, and shrieks that rent the
    air,
  Are made, not marked;° where violent sorrow seems
  A modern ecstasy.° The dead man's knell   *170*
  Is there scarce asked for who, and good men's lives
  Expire before the flowers in their caps,
  Dying or ere they sicken.

Macduff.   O, relation
  Too nice,° and yet too true!

Malcolm.   What's the newest grief?

Ross. That of an hour's age doth hiss the speaker;°   *175*
  Each minute teems° a new one.

Macduff.   How does my wife?

Ross. Why, well.

Macduff.   And all my children?

Ross.   Well, too.

Macduff. The tyrant has not battered at their peace?

Ross. No; they were well at peace when I did leave
   'em.

---

161 **gentle** noble   162 **betimes** quickly   166 **nothing** no one   169 **marked**
noticed   170 **modern ecstasy** i.e., ordinary emotion   173–74 **relation/Too
nice** tale too accurate   175 **That . . . speaker** i.e., the report of the
grief of an hour ago is hissed as stale news   176 **teems** gives birth to

180 *Macduff.* Be not a niggard of your speech: how goes 't?

    Ross. When I came hither to transport the tidings,
      Which I have heavily° borne, there ran a rumor
      Of many worthy fellows that were out;°
      Which was to my belief witnessed° the rather,
185   For that I saw the tyrant's power° afoot.
      Now is the time of help. Your eye in Scotland
      Would create soldiers, make our women fight,
      To doff their dire distresses.

    Malcolm.   Be 't their comfort
      We are coming thither. Gracious England hath
190   Lent us good Siward and ten thousand men;
      An older and a better soldier none
      That Christendom gives out.°

    Ross.   Would I could answer
      This comfort with the like! But I have words
      That would° be howled out in the desert air,
      Where hearing should not latch° them.

195 *Macduff.*   What concern they?
      The general cause or is it a fee-grief
      Due to some single breast?°

    Ross.   No mind that's honest
      But in it shares some woe, though the main part
      Pertains to you alone.

    Macduff.   If it be mine,
200   Keep it not from me, quickly let me have it.

    Ross. Let not your ears despise my tongue for ever,
      Which shall possess them with the heaviest sound
      That ever yet they heard.

    Macduff.   Humh! I guess at it.

    Ross. Your castle is surprised;° your wife and babes

---

182 **heavily** sadly   183 **out** i.e., up in arms   184 **witnessed** attested   185
power army   192 **gives out** reports   194 **would** should   195 **latch** catch
196–97 **fee-grief/Due to some single breast** i.e., a personal grief belonging to
an individual   204 **surprised** suddenly attacked

Savagely slaughtered. To relate the manner,   *205*
Were, on the quarry° of these murdered deer,
To add the death of you.

Malcolm.   Merciful heaven!
What, man! Ne'er pull your hat upon your brows;
Give sorrow words. The grief that does not speak
Whispers the o'er-fraught heart,° and bids it break.   *210*

Macduff. My children too?

Ross.   Wife, children, servants, all
That could be found.

Macduff.   And I must be from thence!
My wife killed too?

Ross.   I have said.

Malcolm.   Be comforted.
Let's make us med'cines of our great revenge,
To cure this deadly grief.   *215*

Macduff. He has no children. All my pretty ones?
Did you say all? O hell-kite!° All?
What, all my pretty chickens and their dam
At one fell swoop?

Malcolm. Dispute° it like a man.

Macduff.   I shall do so;   *220*
But I must also feel it as a man.
I cannot but remember such things were,
That were most precious to me. Did heaven look on,
And would not take their part? Sinful Macduff,
They were all struck for thee! Naught° that I am,   *225*
Not for their own demerits but for mine
Fell slaughter on their souls. Heaven rest them now!

Malcolm. Be this the whetstone of your sword. Let
          grief
Convert to anger; blunt not the heart, enrage it.

---

206 **quarry** heap of slaughtered game   210 **Whispers the o'er-fraught heart**
whispers to the overburdened heart   217 **hell-kite** hellish bird of prey
220 **Dispute** counter   225 **Naught** wicked

230 *Macduff.* O, I could play the woman with mine eyes,
    And braggart with my tongue! But, gentle heavens,
    Cut short all intermission;° front to front°
    Bring thou this fiend of Scotland and myself;
    Within my sword's length set him. If he 'scape,
    Heaven forgive him too!

235 *Malcolm.*   This time goes manly.
    Come, go we to the King. Our power is ready;
    Our lack is nothing but our leave.° Macbeth
    Is ripe for shaking, and the pow'rs above
    Put on their instruments.° Receive what cheer you
    may.
240   The night is long that never finds the day.   *Exeunt.*

232 **intermission** interval   232 **front to front** forehead to forehead i.e.,
face to face   237 **Our lack is nothing but our leave** i.e., we need only
to take our leave   239 **Put on their instruments** arm themselves (?)
urge us, their agents, onward (?)

ACT 5

Scene 1.　[*Dunsinane. In the castle.*]

*Enter a Doctor of Physic and a
Waiting-Gentlewoman.*

Doctor. I have two nights watched with you, but can
perceive no truth in your report. When was it she
last walked?

Gentlewoman. Since his Majesty went into the field, I
have seen her rise from her bed, throw her night-　5
gown upon her, unlock her closet,° take forth
paper, fold it, write upon 't, read it, afterwards seal
it, and again return to bed; yet all this while in a
most fast sleep.

Doctor. A great perturbation in nature, to receive at　10
once the benefit of sleep and do the effects of
watching!° In this slumb'ry agitation, besides her
walking and other actual performances,° what, at
any time, have you heard her say?

Gentlewoman. That, sir, which I will not report after　15
her.

Doctor. You may to me, and 'tis most meet° you
should.

Gentlewoman. Neither to you nor anyone, having no
witness to confirm my speech.　20

Enter Lady [*Macbeth*], *with a taper.*

5.1.　6 **closet** chest　11–12 **effects of watching** deeds of one awake
13 **actual performance** deeds　17 **meet** suitable

Lo you, here she comes! This is her very guise,° and, upon my life, fast asleep! Observe her; stand close.°

Doctor. How came she by that light?

25 *Gentlewoman.* Why, it stood by her. She has light by her continually. 'Tis her command.

Doctor. You see, her eyes are open.

Gentlewoman. Ay, but their sense° are shut.

Doctor. What is it she does now? Look, how she rubs
30 her hands.

Gentlewoman. It is an accustomed action with her, to seem thus washing her hands: I have known her continue in this a quarter of an hour.

Lady Macbeth. Yet here's a spot.

35 *Doctor.* Hark! she speaks. I will set down what comes from her, to satisfy° my remembrance the more strongly.

Lady Macbeth. Out, damned spot! Out, I say! One: two: why, then 'tis time to do 't. Hell is murky.
40 Fie, my lord, fie! A soldier, and afeard? What need we fear who knows it, when none can call our pow'r to accompt?° Yet who would have thought the old man to have had so much blood in him?

Doctor. Do you mark that?

45 *Lady Macbeth.* The Thane of Fife had a wife. Where is she now? What, will these hands ne'er be clean? No more o' that, my lord, no more o' that! You mar all with this starting.

Doctor. Go to,° go to! You have known what you
50 should not.

Gentlewoman. She has spoke what she should not, I

---

21 **guise** custom   23 **close** hidden   28 **sense** i.e., powers of sight   36 **satisfy** confirm   42 **to accompt** into account   49 **Go to** (an exclamation)

am sure of that. Heaven knows what she has known.

Lady Macbeth. Here's the smell of the blood still. All
the perfumes of Arabia will not sweeten this little
hand. Oh, oh, oh! 55

Doctor. What a sigh is there! The heart is sorely
charged.°

Gentlewoman. I would not have such a heart in my
bosom for the dignity° of the whole body.

Doctor. Well, well, well—— 60

Gentlewoman. Pray God it be, sir.

Doctor. This disease is beyond my practice.° Yet I
have known those which have walked in their sleep
who have died holily in their beds.

Lady Macbeth. Wash your hands; put on your night- 65
gown; look not so pale! I tell you yet again, Banquo's buried. He cannot come out on 's° grave.

Doctor. Even so?

Lady Macbeth. To bed, to bed! There's knocking at
the gate. Come, come, come, come, give me your 70
hand! What's done cannot be undone. To bed, to
bed, to bed!   *Exit Lady [Macbeth].*

Doctor. Will she go now to bed?

Gentlewoman. Directly.

Doctor. Foul whisp'rings are abroad. Unnatural deeds 75
Do breed unnatural troubles. Infected minds
To their deaf pillows will discharge their secrets.
More needs she the divine than the physician.
God, God forgive us all! Look after her;
Remove from her the means of all annoyance,° 80
And still° keep eyes upon her. So good night.

---

57 **charged** burdened   59 **dignity** worth, rank   62 **practice** professional skill   67 **on 's** of his   80 **annoyance** injury   81 **still** continu-
ously

My mind she has mated° and amazed my sight:
I think, but dare not speak.

Gentlewoman.   Good night, good doctor.

                                        Exeunt.

Scene 2.   [*The country near Dunsinane.*]

Drum and colors. Enter Menteith, Caithness,
Angus, Lennox, Soldiers.

Menteith. The English pow'r° is near, led on by
    Malcolm,
    His uncle Siward and the good Macduff.
    Revenges burn in them; for their dear° causes
    Would to the bleeding and the grim alarm
    Excite the mortified man.°

5 *Angus.*   Near Birnam Wood
    Shall we well meet them; that way are they coming.

Caithness. Who knows if Donalbain be with his
    brother?

Lennox. For certain, sir, he is not. I have a file°
    Of all the gentry: there is Siward's son,
10 And many unrough° youths that even now
    Protest° their first of manhood.

Menteith.   What does the tyrant?

Caithness. Great Dunsinane he strongly fortifies.
    Some say he's mad; others, that lesser hate him,
    Do call it valiant fury: but, for certain,

82 **mated** baffled   5.2.   1 **pow'r** army   3 **dear** heartfelt   4–5 **Would . . .**
man i.e., would incite a dead man (or "a paralyzed man") to join the
bloody and grim call to battle   8 **file** list   10 **unrough** i.e., beardless
11 **Protest** assert

He cannot buckle his distempered° cause   *15*
Within the belt of rule.°

Angus.   Now does he feel
His secret murders sticking on his hands;
Now minutely revolts upbraid° his faith-breach.
Those he commands move only in command,
Nothing in love. Now does he feel his title   *20*
Hang loose about him, like a giant's robe
Upon a dwarfish thief.

Menteith.   Who then shall blame
His pestered° senses to recoil and start,
When all that is within him does condemn
Itself for being there?

Caithness.   Well, march we on,   *25*
To give obedience where 'tis truly owed.
Meet we the med'cine° of the sickly weal,°
And with him pour we, in our country's purge,
Each drop of us.°

Lennox.   Or so much as it needs
To dew° the sovereign° flower and drown the
weeds.   *30*
Make we our march towards Birnam.

                         Exeunt, marching.

Scene 3.   [*Dunsinane. In the castle.*]

Enter Macbeth, Doctor, and Attendants.

Macbeth. Bring me no more reports; let them fly all!
Till Birnam Wood remove to Dunsinane
I cannot taint° with fear. What's the boy Malcolm?

---

15 **distempered** swollen by dropsy   16 **rule** self-control   18 **minutely
revolts upbraid** rebellions every minute rebuke   23 **pestered** tormented
27 **med'cine** i.e., Malcolm   27 **weal** commonwealth   29 **Each drop of
us** i.e., every last drop of our blood (?)   30 **dew** bedew, water (and
thus make grow)   30 **sovereign** (1) royal (2) remedial   5.3.   3 **taint**
become infected

Was he not born of woman? The spirits that know
All mortal consequences° have pronounced me
5   thus:
"Fear not, Macbeth; no man that's born of woman
Shall e'er have power upon thee." Then fly, false
    thanes,
And mingle with the English epicures.
The mind I sway° by and the heart I bear
10   Shall never sag with doubt nor shake with fear.

Enter Servant.

The devil damn thee black, thou cream-faced loon!°
Where got'st thou that goose look?

Servant. There is ten thousand————

Macbeth.   Geese, villain?

Servant.   Soldiers, sir.

Macbeth. Go prick thy face and over-red° thy fear,
15   Thou lily-livered boy. What soldiers, patch?°
Death of° thy soul! Those linen° cheeks of thine
Are counselors to fear. What soldiers, whey-face?

Servant. The English force, so please you.

Macbeth. Take thy face hence.   [*Exit Servant.*]
                    Seyton!—I am sick at heart,
20   When I behold—Seyton, I say!—This push°
Will cheer me ever, or disseat° me now.
I have lived long enough. My way of life
Is fall'n into the sear,° the yellow leaf,
And that which should accompany old age,
25   As honor, love, obedience, troops of friends,
I must not look to have; but, in their stead,
Curses not loud but deep, mouth-honor, breath,
Which the poor heart would fain deny, and dare not.
Seyton!

---

5 **mortal consequences** future human events 9 **sway** move 11 **loon**
fool 14 **over-red** cover with red 15 **patch** fool 16 **of** upon 16 **linen**
i.e., pale 20 **push** effort 21 **disseat** i.e., unthrone (with wordplay on
"cheer," pronounced "chair") 23 **sear** withered

Enter Seyton.

Seyton. What's your gracious pleasure?

Macbeth.   What news more?   30

Seyton. All is confirmed, my lord, which was reported.

Macbeth. I'll fight, till from my bones my flesh be
      hacked.
   Give me my armor.

Seyton.   'Tis not needed yet.

Macbeth. I'll put it on.
   Send out moe° horses, skirr° the country round.   35
   Hang those that talk of fear. Give me mine armor.
   How does your patient, doctor?

Doctor.   Not so sick, my lord,
   As she is troubled with thick-coming fancies
   That keep her from her rest.

Macbeth.   Cure her of that.
   Canst thou not minister to a mind diseased,   40
   Pluck from the memory a rooted sorrow,
   Raze out° the written troubles of the brain,
   And with some sweet oblivious° antidote
   Cleanse the stuffed bosom of that perilous stuff
   Which weighs upon the heart?

Doctor.   Therein the patient   45
   Must minister to himself.

Macbeth. Throw physic° to the dogs, I'll none of it.
   Come, put mine armor on. Give me my staff.
   Seyton, send out.—Doctor, the thanes fly from
      me.—
   Come, sir, dispatch.° If thou couldst, doctor, cast   50
   The water° of my land, find her disease
   And purge it to a sound and pristine health,
   I would applaud thee to the very echo,

---

35 **moe** more   35 **skirr** scour   42 **Raze out** erase   43 **oblivious** causing
forgetfulness   47 **physic** medical science   50 **dispatch** hurry   50–51 **cast/
The water** analyze the urine

That should applaud again.—Pull 't off, I say.—
55   What rhubarb, senna, or what purgative drug,
    Would scour these English hence? Hear'st thou of
      them?

Doctor. Ay, my good lord; your royal preparation
  Makes us hear something.

Macbeth.   Bring it° after me.
  I will not be afraid of death and bane°
60   Till Birnam Forest come to Dunsinane.

Doctor. [*Aside*] Were I from Dunsinane away
    and clear,
  Profit again should hardly draw me here.   *Exeunt.*

Scene 4.   [*Country near Birnam Wood.*]

*Drum and colors. Enter Malcolm, Siward, Mac-
duff, Siward's Son, Menteith, Caithness, Angus,
and Soldiers, marching.*

Malcolm. Cousins, I hope the days are near at hand
  That chambers will be safe.°

Menteith.   We doubt it nothing.°

Siward. What wood is this before us?

Menteith.   The Wood of Birnam.

Malcolm. Let every soldier hew him down a bough
5   And bear 't before him. Thereby shall we shadow
    The numbers of our host, and make discovery°
    Err in report of us.

Soldiers.   It shall be done.

---

58 **it** i.e., the armor 59 **bane** destruction 5.4. 2 **That chambers will
be safe** i.e., that a man will be safe in his bedroom 2 **nothing** not at
all 6 **discovery** reconnaissance

Siward. We learn no other but° the confident tyrant
　　Keeps still in Dunsinane, and will endure°
　　Our setting down before 't.

Malcolm.　　　　　　　　　　　'Tis his main hope,　　　10
　　For where there is advantage to be given°
　　Both more and less° have given him the revolt,
　　And none serve with him but constrainèd things
　　Whose hearts are absent too.

Macduff.　　　　　　　　　　Let our just censures
　　Attend the true event,° and put we on　　　　　15
　　Industrious soldiership.

Siward.　　　　　　　　The time approaches,
　　That will with due decision make us know
　　What we shall say we have and what we owe.°
　　Thoughts speculative their unsure hopes relate,
　　But certain issue strokes must arbitrate:°　　　20
　　Towards which advance the war.°

　　　　　　　　　　　　Exeunt, marching.

Scene 5.　　[*Dunsinane. Within the castle.*]

*Enter Macbeth, Seyton, and Soldiers, with drum
and colors.*

Macbeth. Hang out our banners on the outward walls.
　　The cry is still "They come!" Our castle's strength
　　Will laugh a siege to scorn. Here let them lie
　　Till famine and the ague° eat them up.
　　Were they not forced° with those that should be
　　　ours,　　　　　　　　　　　　　　　　　　5

8 **no other but** nothing but that　9 **endure** allow　11 **advantage to
be given** afforded an opportunity　12 **more and less** high and low
14–15 **just censures/Attend the true event** true judgment await the actual
outcome　18 **owe** own (the contrast is between "what we shall say we
have" and "what we shall really have")　20 **certain issue strokes must
arbitrate** the definite outcome must be decided by battle　21 **war** army
5.5.　4 **ague** fever　5 **forced** reinforced

We might have met them dareful,° beard to beard,
And beat them backward home.

        A cry within of women.

                        What is that noise?

Seyton. It is the cry of women, my good lord.   [*Exit.*]

Macbeth. I have almost forgot the taste of fears:
10   The time has been, my senses would have cooled
     To hear a night-shriek, and my fell° of hair
     Would at a dismal treatise° rouse and stir
     As life were in 't. I have supped full with horrors.
     Direness, familiar to my slaughterous thoughts,
     Cannot once start° me.

            [*Enter Seyton.*]

15   Wherefore was that cry?

Seyton. The Queen, my lord, is dead.

Macbeth. She should° have died hereafter;
     There would have been a time for such a word.°
     Tomorrow, and tomorrow, and tomorrow
20   Creeps in this petty pace from day to day,
     To the last syllable of recorded time;
     And all our yesterdays have lighted fools
     The way to dusty death. Out, out, brief candle!
     Life's but a walking shadow, a poor player
25   That struts and frets his hour upon the stage
     And then is heard no more. It is a tale
     Told by an idiot, full of sound and fury
     Signifying nothing.

            Enter a Messenger.

     Thou com'st to use thy tongue; thy story quickly!

30 *Messenger.* Gracious my lord,
     I should report that which I say I saw,
     But know not how to do 't.

    Macbeth.   Well, say, sir.

---

6 **met them dareful** i.e., met them in the battlefield boldly   11 **fell** pelt
12 **treatise** story   15 **start** startle   17 **should** inevitably   would   (?)
18 **word** message

Messenger. As I did stand my watch upon the hill,
    I looked toward Birnam, and anon, methought,
    The wood began to move.

Macbeth.   Liar and slave!   35

Messenger. Let me endure your wrath, if 't be not so.
    Within this three mile may you see it coming;
    I say a moving grove.

Macbeth.   If thou speak'st false,
    Upon the next tree shalt thou hang alive,
    Till famine cling° thee. If thy speech be sooth,°   40
    I care not if thou dost for me as much.
    I pull in resolution,° and begin
    To doubt° th' equivocation of the fiend
    That lies like truth: "Fear not, till Birnam Wood
    Do come to Dunsinane!" And now a wood   45
    Comes toward Dunsinane. Arm, arm, and out!
    If this which he avouches° does appear,
    There is nor flying hence nor tarrying here.
    I 'gin to be aweary of the sun,
    And wish th' estate° o' th' world were now undone.   50
    Ring the alarum bell! Blow wind, come wrack!
    At least we'll die with harness° on our back.

                                        Exeunt.

Scene 6.   [*Dunsinane. Before the castle.*]

*Drum and colors. Enter Malcolm, Siward,
    Macduff, and their army, with boughs.*

Malcolm. Now near enough. Your leavy° screens
    throw down,
    And show like those you are. You, worthy uncle,

40 **cling** wither   40 **sooth** truth   42 **pull in resolution** restrain confidence
43 **doubt** suspect   47 **avouches** asserts   50 **th' estate** the orderly condition   52 **harness** armor   5.6.   1 **leavy** leafy

Shall, with my cousin, your right noble son,
Lead our first battle.° Worthy Macduff and we°
5 Shall take upon 's what else remains to do,
According to our order.°

Siward.   Fare you well.
Do we° but find the tyrant's power° tonight,
Let us be beaten, if we cannot fight.

Macduff. Make all our trumpets speak; give them all
        breath.
10 Those clamorous harbingers of blood and death.

Exeunt. Alarums continued.

Scene 7.   [*Another part of the field.*]

Enter Macbeth.

Macbeth. They have tied me to a stake; I cannot fly,
But bearlike I must fight the course.° What's he
That was not born of woman? Such a one
Am I to fear, or none.

Enter Young Siward.

Young Siward. What is thy name?

5 *Macbeth.*   Thou'lt be afraid to hear it.

Young Siward. No; though thou call'st thyself a hotter
        name
Than any is in hell.

Macbeth.   My name's Macbeth.

4 **battle** battalion 4 **we** (Malcolm uses the royal "we") 6 **order** plan
7 **Do we** if we do 7 **power** forces 5.7. 2 **course** bout, round (he has
in mind an attack of dogs or men upon a bear chained to a stake)

Young Siward. The devil himself could not pronounce
  a title
  More hateful to mine ear.

Macbeth.   No, nor more fearful.

Young Siward. Thou liest, abhorrèd tyrant; with my
  sword   *10*
  I'll prove the lie thou speak'st.

     Fight, and Young Siward slain.

Macbeth.   Thou wast born of woman.
  But swords I smile at, weapons laugh to scorn,
  Brandished by man that's of a woman born.

                    Exit.

     Alarums. Enter Macduff.

Macduff. That way the noise is. Tyrant, show thy face!
  If thou be'st slain and with no stroke of mine,   *15*
  My wife and children's ghosts will haunt me still.
  I cannot strike at wretched kerns,° whose arms
  Are hired to bear their staves.° Either thou,
    Macbeth,
  Or else my sword, with an unbattered edge,
  I sheathe again undeeded.° There thou shouldst
    be;   *20*
  By this great clatter, one of greatest note
  Seems bruited.° Let me find him, Fortune!
  And more I beg not.   *Exit. Alarums.*

     Enter Malcolm and Siward.

Siward. This way, my lord. The castle's gently
  rend'red:°
  The tyrant's people on both sides do fight;   *25*
  The noble thanes do bravely in the war;
  The day almost itself professes° yours,
  And little is to do.

---

17 **kerns** foot soldiers (contemptuous)   18 **staves** spears   20 **undeeded**
i.e., having done nothing   22 **bruited** reported   24 **gently rend'red** sur-
rendered without a struggle   27 **itself professes** declares itself

Malcolm.　　　　　　We have met with foes
　　That strike beside us.°

Siward.　　　　　　　　Enter, sir, the castle.

　　　　　　　　　　　　　　　Exeunt. Alarum.

　　　　　[Scene 8.　　*Another part of the field.*]

　　　　　　　　　Enter Macbeth.

Macbeth. Why should I play the Roman fool, and die
　　On mine own sword? Whiles I see lives,° the gashes
　　Do better upon them.

　　　　　　　　　Enter Macduff.

Macduff.　　　　　　Turn, hell-hound, turn!

Macbeth. Of all men else I have avoided thee.
5　　But get thee back! My soul is too much charged°
　　With blood of thine already.

Macduff.　　　　　　I have no words:
　　My voice is in my sword, thou bloodier villain
　　Than terms can give thee out!°

　　　　　　　　　Fight. Alarum.

Macbeth.　　　　　　　Thou losest labor:
　　As easy mayst thou the intrenchant° air
10　　With thy keen sword impress° as make me bleed:
　　Let fall thy blade on vulnerable crests;
　　I bear a charmèd life, which must not yield
　　To one of woman born.

29 **beside us** i.e., deliberately miss us (?) as our comrades (?) 5.8.
2 **Whiles I see lives** so long as I see living men 5 **charged** burdened
8 **terms can give thee out** words can describe you 9 **intrenchant** incapable
of being cut 10 **impress** make an impression on

Macduff.   Despair° thy charm,
And let the angel° whom thou still hast served
Tell thee, Macduff was from his mother's womb   *15*
Untimely ripped.

Macbeth. Accursèd be that tongue that tells me so,
For it hath cowed my better part of man!°
And be these juggling fiends no more believed,
That palter° with us in a double sense;   *20*
That keep the word of promise to our ear,
And break it to our hope. I'll not fight with thee.

Macduff. Then yield thee, coward,
And live to be the show and gaze o' th' time:°
We'll have thee, as our rarer monsters° are,   *25*
Painted upon a pole,° and underwrit,
"Here may you see the tyrant."

Macbeth.   I will not yield,
To kiss the ground before young Malcolm's feet,
And to be baited° with the rabble's curse.
Though Birnam Wood be come to Dunsinane,   *30*
And thou opposed, being of no woman born,
Yet I will try the last. Before my body
I throw my warlike shield. Lay on, Macduff;
And damned be him that first cries "Hold,
     enough!"   *Exeunt, fighting. Alarums.*

     [*Re-*]*enter fighting, and Macbeth slain.* [*Exit
     Macduff, with Macbeth.*] *Retreat and flour-
     ish.*° *Enter, with drum and colors, Malcolm,
     Siward, Ross, Thanes, and Soldiers.*

Malcolm. I would the friends we miss were safe
     arrived.   *35*

Siward. Some must go off;° and yet, by these I see,
So great a day as this is cheaply bought.

---

13 **Despair** despair of   14 **angel** i.e., fallen angel, fiend   18 **better part
of man** manly spirit   20 **palter** equivocate   24 **gaze o' th' time** spectacle
of the age   25 **monsters** freaks   26 **Painted upon a pole** i.e., pictured
on a banner set by a showman's booth   29 **baited** assailed (like a bear
by dogs)   34 s.d. **Retreat and flourish** trumpet call to withdraw, and
fanfare   36 **go off** die (theatrical metaphor)

Malcolm. Macduff is missing, and your noble son.

Ross. Your son, my lord, has paid a soldier's debt:
40   He only lived but till he was a man;
  The which no sooner had his prowess confirmed
  In the unshrinking station° where he fought,
  But like a man he died.

Siward.   Then he is dead?

Ross. Ay, and brought off the field. Your cause of
     sorrow
45   Must not be measured by his worth, for then
  It hath no end.

Siward.   Had he his hurts before?

Ross. Ay, on the front.

Siward.   Why then, God's soldier be he!
  Had I as many sons as I have hairs,
  I would not wish them to a fairer death:
  And so his knell is knolled.

50 *Malcolm.*   He's worth more sorrow,
  And that I'll spend for him.

Siward.   He's worth no more:
  They say he parted well and paid his score:°
  And so God be with him! Here comes newer
     comfort.

     Enter Macduff, with Macbeth's head.

Macduff. Hail, King! for so thou art: behold, where
     stands
55   Th' usurper's cursèd head. The time is free.°
  I see thee compassed° with thy kingdom's pearl,
  That speak my salutation in their minds,
  Whose voices I desire aloud with mine:
  Hail, King of Scotland!

All.   Hail, King of Scotland!

---

42 **unshrinking station** i.e., place at which he stood firmly   52 **parted well and paid his score** departed well and settled his account   55 **The time is free** the world is liberated   56 **compassed** surrounded

Flourish.

Malcolm. We shall not spend a large expense of time   60
     Before we reckon with your several loves,°
     And make us even with you. My thanes and
        kinsmen,
     Henceforth be earls, the first that ever Scotland
     In such an honor named. What's more to do,
     Which would be planted newly with the time°—   65
     As calling home our exiled friends abroad
     That fled the snares of watchful tyranny,
     Producing forth the cruel ministers°
     Of this dead butcher and his fiendlike queen,
     Who, as 'tis thought, by self and violent° hands   70
     Took off her life—this, and what needful else
     That calls upon us,° by the grace of Grace
     We will perform in measure, time, and place:°
     So thanks to all at once and to each one,
     Whom we invite to see us crowned at Scone.   75

Flourish. Exeunt Omnes.

FINIS

61 **reckon with your several loves** reward the devotion of each of you
64–65 **What's more ... time** i.e., what else must be done which should
be newly established in this age   68 **ministers** agents   70 **self and violent** her own violent   72 **calls upon us** demands my attention   73 **in measure, time, and place** fittingly, at the appropriate time and place

Textual Note

Macbeth, never printed during Shakespeare's lifetime, was first printed in the Folio of 1623. The play is remarkably short, and it may be that there has been some cutting. That in 1.5 Lady Macbeth apparently proposes to kill Duncan and that later in the play Macbeth kills him is scarcely evidence that a scene had been lost, but the inconsistent stage directions concerning Macbeth's death (one calls for him to be slain on stage, another suggests he is both slain and decapitated off stage) indicate some sort of revision. Nevertheless, when one reads the account of Macbeth in Holinshed (Shakespeare's source) one does not feel that the play as it has come down to us omits anything of significance. If, as seems likely, the play was presented at court, its brevity may well be due to King James's known aversion to long plays. On the other hand, it is generally believed that Hecate is a non-Shakespearean addition to the play (she dominates 3.5 and has a few lines in 4.1), but the evidence is not conclusive, although the passages (along with 4.1.125–32) sound un-Shakespearean.

The present division into acts and scenes is that of the Folio except for 5.8, a division added by the Globe editors. The present edition silently modernizes spelling and punctuation, regularizes speech prefixes, and translates into English the Folio's Latin designations of act and scene. Other departures from the Folio are listed below. The reading of the present text is given first, in italics, and then the reading of the Folio (F) in roman.

1.1.9 *Second Witch . . . Anon* [F attributes to "All," as part of the ensuing speech]

1.2.13 *gallowglasses* gallowgrosses   14 *quarrel* Quarry   26 *thunders break* Thunders   33–34 *Dismayed . . . Banquo* [one line in F] 33–35 *Dismayed . . . lion* [three lines in F, ending: Banquoh, Eagles, Lyon]   42 *But . . . faint* [F gives to previous line]   46 *So . . . look* [F gives to next line]   59 *Sweno . . . king* [F gives to previous line]

1.3.5 *Give . . . I* [F prints as a separate line]   32 *weïrd* weyward [also at 1.5.9; 2.1.20; "weyard" at 3.1.2; 3.4.134; 4.1.136]   39 *Forres* Soris   78 *Speak . . . you* [F prints as a separate line]   81–82 *Into . . . stayed* [three lines in F, ending: corporall, Winde, stay'd]   98 *Came* can   108 *why . . . me* [F gives to next line]   111–14 *Which . . . not* [five lines in F, ending: loose, Norway, helpe, labour'd, not]   131 *If ill* [F gives to next line]   140–42 *Shakes . . . not* [F's lines end: Man, surmise, not]   143 *If . . . crown me* [two lines in F, ending: King, crown me]   149–53 *Give . . . time* [seven lines in F, ending: fauour, forgotten, registred, Leafe, them, vpon, time]   156 *Till . . . friends* [two lines in F, ending: enough, friends]

1.4.1 *Are not* Or not [given in F to next line]   2–8 *My . . . died* [seven lines in F, ending: back, die, hee, Pardon, Repentance, him, dy'de]   23–27 *In . . . honor* [six lines in F, ending: selfe, Duties, State, should, Loue, Honor]

1.5.23–24 *And yet . . . have it* [three lines in F, ending: winne, cryes, haue it]

1.6.1 *the air* [F gives to next line]   4 *martlet* Barlet   9 *most* must   17–20 *Against . . . hermits* [F's lines end: broad, House, Dignities, Ermites]

1.7.6 *shoal* Schoole [variant spelling]   47 *do* no   58 *as you* [F gives to next line]

2.1.4 *Hold . . . heaven* [two lines in F, ending: Sword, Heauen]   7–9 *And . . . repose* [F's endings: sleepe, thoughts, repose]   13–17 *He . . . content* [F's endings: Pleasure, Offices, withall, Hostesse, content]   25 *when 'tis* [F gives to next line]   55 *strides* sides   56 *sure* sowre   57 *way they* they may

2.2.2–6 *What . . . possets* [6 lines in F, ending: fire, shriek'd, good-night, open, charge, Possets]   13 s.d. *Enter Macbeth* [F places after "die" in 1.8]   14 *I . . . noise* [two lines in F, ending: deed, noyse]   18–19 *Hark . . . chamber* [one line in F]   22–25 *There's . . . sleep* [F's endings: sleepe, other, Prayers, sleepe]   32 *Stuck . . . throat* [F gives to previous line]   64–65 *To wear . . . chamber* [three lines in F, ending: white, entry, Chamber]   68 *Hath . . . knocking* [two lines in F, ending: vnattended, knocking]   72–73 *To . . . couldst* [four lines in F, ending: deed, my selfe, knocking, could'st. The s.d. "Knock" appears after "deed"]

2.3.25–27 *Faith . . . things* [two lines of verse in F, the second beginning "And"]   44 s.d. *Enter Macbeth* [F places after 1.43]   53–54 *I'll . . . service* [one line of prose in F]   56–63 *The night . . . shake* [10 lines in F, ending: vnruly, downe, Ayre, Death, terrible, Euents, time, Night, feuorous, shake]   66 *Tongue nor heart* [F gives to next line]   88–89 *O . . . murdered* [one line in F] 137–43 *What . . . bloody* [nine lines in F, ending: doe, them, Office, easie, England, I, safer, Smiles, bloody]

2.4.14 *And . . . horses* [F prints as a separate line] 17 *make* [F gives to next line] 19 *They . . . so* [F prints as a separate line]

3.1.34–35 *Craving . . . with you* [three lines in F, ending: Horse, Night, you] 42–43 *The sweeter . . . you* [three lines in F, ending: welcome, alone, you] 72 *Who's there* [F prints as a separate line] 75–82 *Well . . . might* [ten lines in F, ending: then, speeches, past, fortune, selfe, conference, with you, crost, them, might] 85–91 *I . . . ever* [nine lines in F, ending: so, now, meeting, predominant, goe, man, hand, begger'd, euer] 111 *I do* [F gives to previous line] 114–15 *Both . . . enemy* [one line in F] 128 *Your . . . most* [two lines in F, ending: you, most]

3.2.16 *But . . . suffer* [two lines in F, ending: dis-ioynt, suffer] 22 *Duncan . . . grave* [F prints as a separate line] 43 *there . . . done* [F gives to next line] 50 *and . . . crow* [F gives to next line]

3.3.9 *The rest* [F gives to next line] 17 *O . . . fly, fly, fly* [two lines in F, the first ending: Trecherie] 21 *We . . . affair* [two lines in F, ending: lost, Affaire]

3.4.21–22 *Most . . . perfect* [four lines in F, ending: Sir, scap'd, againe, perfect] 49 *Here . . . Highness* [two lines in F, ending: Lord, Highness] 110 *broke . . . meeting* [F gives to next line] 122 s.d. *Exeunt* Exit 123 *blood will have blood* [F prints as a separate line] 145 *in deed* indeed

3.5.36 *back again* [F prints as a separate line]

3.6.1 *My . . . thoughts* [two lines in F, ending: Speeches, Thoughts] 24 *son* Sonnes 38 *the* their

4.1.46–47 *Open . . . knocks* [one line in F] 59 *germens* Germaine 71 *Beware Macduff* [F prints as a separate line] 79 *Laugh to scorn* [F prints as a separate line] 86 *What is this* [F gives to next line] 93 *Dunsinane* Dunsmane 98 *Birnam* Byrnan [this F spelling, or with *i* for *y* or with a final *e*, occurs at 5.2.5, 31; 5.3.2, 60; 5.4.3; 5.5.34, 44; 5.8.30] 119 *eighth* eight 133 *Let . . . hour* [F prints as a separate line]

4.2.27 *Fathered . . . fatherless* [two lines in F, ending: is, Father-lesse] 34 *Poor bird* [F prints as a separate line] 36–43 *Why . . . for thee* [ten lines in F, ending: Mother, for, saying, is dead, Father, Husband, Market, againe, wit, thee] 48–49 *Every . . . hanged* [two lines of verse in F, ending: Traitor, hang'd] 57–58 [two lines of verse in F, ending: Monkie, Father] 77 *What . . . faces* [F prints as a separate line]

4.3.4 *down-fall'n* downfall 15 *deserve* discerne 25 *where . . . doubts* [F prints as a separate line] 102 *Fit to govern* [F gives to next line] 107 *accursed* accust 133 *thy* they 140 *I pray you* [F prints as a separate line]   173 *O relation* [F gives to next line]   211–12 *Wife . . . found* [one line in F]   212–13 *And . . . too* [one line in F]

5.3.39 *Cure her* Cure   55 *senna* Cyme

5.6.1 *Your . . . down* [F prints as a separate line]

5.8.54 *behold . . . stands* [F prints as a separate line]

Suggested References

The number of possible references is vast and grows alarmingly. (The *Shakespeare Quarterly* devotes one issue each year to a list of the previous year's work, and *Shakespeare Survey*—an annual publication—includes a substantial review of biographical, critical, and textual studies, as well as a survey of performances.) The vast bibliography is best approached through James Harner, *The World Shakespeare Bibliography on CD-Rom: 1900–Present.* The first release, in 1996, included more than 12,000 annotated items from 1990–93, plus references to several thousand book reviews, productions, films, and audio recordings. The plan is to update the publication annually, moving forward one year and backward three years. Thus, the second issue (1997), with 24,700 entries, and another 35,000 or so references to reviews, newspaper pieces, and so on, covered 1987–94.

Though no works are indispensable, those listed below have been found especially helpful. The arrangement is as follows:

1. Shakespeare's Times
2. Shakespeare's Life
3. Shakespeare's Theater
4. Shakespeare on Stage and Screen
5. Miscellaneous Reference Works
6. Shakespeare's Plays: General Studies
7. The Comedies
8. The Romances
9. The Tragedies
10. The Histories
11. *Hamlet*
12. *Othello*
13. *King Lear*
14. *Macbeth*

The titles in the first five sections are accompanied by brief explanatory annotations.

1. Shakespeare's Times

Andrews, John F., ed. *William Shakespeare: His World, His Work, His Influence,* 3 vols. (1985). Sixty articles, dealing not only with such subjects as "The State," "The Church," "Law," "Science, Magic, and Folklore," but also with the plays and poems themselves and Shakespeare's influence (e.g., translations, films, reputation).

Byrne, Muriel St. Clare. *Elizabethan Life in Town and Country* (8th ed., 1970). Chapters on manners, beliefs, education, etc., with illustrations.

Dollimore, John, and Alan Sinfield, eds. *Political Shakespeare: New Essays in Cultural Materialism* (1985). Essays on such topics as the subordination of women and colonialism, presented in connection with some of Shakespeare's plays.

Greenblatt, Stephen. *Representing the English Renaissance* (1988). New Historicist essays, especially on connections between political and aesthetic matters, statecraft and stagecraft.

Joseph, B. L. *Shakespeare's Eden: The Commonwealth of England 1558–1629* (1971). An account of the social, political, economic, and cultural life of England.

Kernan, Alvin. *Shakespeare, the King's Playwright: Theater in the Stuart Court 1603–1613* (1995). The social setting and the politics of the court of James I, in relation to *Hamlet, Measure for Measure, Macbeth, King Lear, Antony and Cleopatra, Coriolanus,* and *The Tempest.*

Montrose, Louis. *The Purpose of Playing: Shakespeare and the Cultural Politics of the Elizabethan Theatre* (1996). A poststructuralist view, discussing the professional theater "within the ideological and material frameworks of Elizabethan culture and society," with an extended analysis of *A Midsummer Night's Dream.*

Mullaney, Steven. *The Place of the Stage: License, Play, and Power in Renaissance England* (1988). New Historicist analysis, arguing that popular drama became a cultural institution "only by . . . taking up a place on the margins of society."

Schoenbaum, S. *Shakespeare: The Globe and the World* (1979). A readable, abundantly illustrated introductory book on the world of the Elizabethans.

Shakespeare's England, 2 vols. (1916). A large collection of scholarly essays on a wide variety of topics, e.g., astrology, costume, gardening, horsemanship, with special attention to Shakespeare's references to these topics.

2. Shakespeare's Life

Andrews, John F., ed. *William Shakespeare: His World, His Work, His Influence,* 3 vols. (1985). See the description above.

Bentley, Gerald E. *Shakespeare: A Biographical Handbook* (1961). The facts about Shakespeare, with virtually no conjecture intermingled.

Chambers, E. K. *William Shakespeare: A Study of Facts and Problems,* 2 vols. (1930). The fullest collection of data.

Fraser, Russell. *Young Shakespeare* (1988). A highly readable account that simultaneously considers Shakespeare's life and Shakespeare's art.

————. *Shakespeare: The Later Years* (1992).

Schoenbaum, S. *Shakespeare's Lives* (1970). A review of the evidence and an examination of many biographies, including those of Baconians and other heretics.

————. *William Shakespeare: A Compact Documentary Life* (1977). An abbreviated version, in a smaller format, of the next title. The compact version reproduces some fifty documents in reduced form. A readable presentation of all that the documents tell us about Shakespeare.

————. *William Shakespeare: A Documentary Life* (1975). A large-format book setting forth the biography with facsimiles of more than two hundred documents, and with transcriptions and commentaries.

3. Shakespeare's Theater

Astington, John H., ed. *The Development of Shakespeare's Theater* (1992). Eight specialized essays on theatrical companies, playing spaces, and performance.

Beckerman, Bernard. *Shakespeare at the Globe, 1599–1609* (1962). On the playhouse and on Elizabethan dramaturgy, acting, and staging.

Bentley, Gerald E. *The Profession of Dramatist in Shakespeare's Time* (1971). An account of the dramatist's status in the Elizabethan period.

————. *The Profession of Player in Shakespeare's Time, 1590–1642* (1984). An account of the status of members of London companies (sharers, hired men, apprentices, managers) and a discussion of conditions when they toured.

Berry, Herbert. *Shakespeare's Playhouses* (1987). Usefully emphasizes how little we know about the construction of Elizabethan theaters.

Brown, John Russell. *Shakespeare's Plays in Performance* (1966). A speculative and practical analysis relevant to all of the plays, but with emphasis on *The Merchant of Venice, Richard II, Hamlet, Romeo and Juliet*, and *Twelfth Night*.

————. *William Shakespeare: Writing for Performance* (1996). A discussion aimed at helping readers to develop theatrically conscious habits of reading.

Chambers, E. K. *The Elizabethan Stage*, 4 vols. (1945). A major reference work on theaters, theatrical companies, and staging at court.

Cook, Ann Jennalie. *The Privileged Playgoers of Shakespeare's London, 1576–1642* (1981). Sees Shakespeare's audience as wealthier, more middle-class, and more intellectual than Harbage (below) does.

Dessen, Alan C. *Elizabethan Drama and the Viewer's Eye* (1977). On how certain scenes may have looked to spectators in an Elizabethan theater.

Gurr, Andrew. *Playgoing in Shakespeare's London* (1987). Something of a middle ground between Cook (above) and Harbage (below).

————. *The Shakespearean Stage, 1579–1642* (2nd ed., 1980). On the acting companies, the actors, the playhouses, the stages, and the audiences.

Harbage, Alfred. *Shakespeare's Audience* (1941). A study of the size and nature of the theatrical public, emphasizing the representativeness of its working class and middle-class audience.

Hodges, C. Walter. *The Globe Restored* (1968). A conjectural restoration, with lucid drawings.

Hosley, Richard. "The Playhouses," in *The Revels History of Drama in English*, vol. 3, general editors Clifford Leech and T. W. Craik (1975). An essay of a hundred pages on the physical aspects of the playhouses.

Howard, Jane E. "Crossdressing, the Theatre, and Gender Struggle in Early Modern England," *Shakespeare Quarterly* 39 (1988): 418–40. Judicious comments on the effects of boys playing female roles.

Orrell, John. *The Human Stage: English Theatre Design, 1567–1640* (1988). Argues that the public, private, and court playhouses are less indebted to popular structures (e.g., innyards and bear-baiting pits) than to banquet-ing halls and to Renaissance conceptions of Roman amphitheaters.

Slater, Ann Pasternak. *Shakespeare the Director* (1982). An analysis of theatrical effects (e.g., kissing, kneeling) in stage directions and dialogue.

Styan, J. L. *Shakespeare's Stagecraft* (1967). An introduction to Shakespeare's visual and aural stagecraft, with chapters on such topics as acting conventions, stage groupings, and speech.

Thompson, Peter. *Shakespeare's Professional Career* (1992). An examination of patronage and related theatrical conditions.

———. *Shakespeare's Theatre* (1983). A discussion of how plays were staged in Shakespeare's time.

4. Shakespeare on Stage and Screen

Bate, Jonathan, and Russell Jackson, eds. *Shakespeare: An Illustrated Stage History* (1996). Highly readable essays on stage productions from the Renaissance to the present.

Berry, Ralph. *Changing Styles in Shakespeare* (1981). Discusses productions of six plays (*Coriolanus*, *Hamlet*, *Henry V*, *Measure for Measure*, *The Tempest*, and *Twelfth Night*) on the English stage, chiefly 1950–1980.

———. *On Directing Shakespeare: Interviews with Contemporary Directors* (1989). An enlarged edition of a book first published in 1977, this version includes the seven interviews from the early 1970s and adds five interviews conducted in 1988.

Brockbank, Philip, ed. *Players of Shakespeare: Essays in Shakespearean Performance* (1985). Comments by twelve actors, reporting their experiences with roles. See also the entry for Russell Jackson (below).

Bulman, J. C., and H. R. Coursen, eds. *Shakespeare on Television* (1988). An anthology of general and theoretical essays, essays on individual productions, and shorter reviews, with a bibliography and a videography listing cassettes that may be rented.

Coursen, H. P. *Watching Shakespeare on Television* (1993). Analyses not only of TV versions but also of films and videotapes of stage presentations that are shown on television.

Davies, Anthony, and Stanley Wells, eds. *Shakespeare and the Moving Image: The Plays on Film and Television* (1994). General essays (e.g., on the comedies) as well as essays devoted entirely to *Hamlet*, *King Lear*, and *Macbeth*.

Dawson, Anthony B. *Watching Shakespeare: A Playgoer's Guide* (1988). About half of the plays are discussed, chiefly in terms of decisions that actors and directors make in putting the works onto the stage.

Dessen, Alan. *Elizabethan Stage Conventions and Modern Inter-

pretations (1984). On interpreting conventions such as the representation of light and darkness and stage violence (duels, battles).

Donaldson, Peter. *Shakespearean Films/Shakespearean Directors* (1990). Postmodernist analyses, drawing on Freudianism, Feminism, Deconstruction, and Queer Theory.

Jackson, Russell, and Robert Smallwood, eds. *Players of Shakespeare 2: Further Essays in Shakespearean Performance by Players with the Royal Shakespeare Company* (1988). Fourteen actors discuss their roles in productions between 1982 and 1987.

———. *Players of Shakespeare 3: Further Essays in Shakespearean Performance by Players with the Royal Shakespeare Company* (1993). Comments by thirteen performers.

Jorgens, Jack. *Shakespeare on Film* (1977). Fairly detailed studies of eighteen films, preceded by an introductory chapter addressing such issues as music, and whether to "open" the play by including scenes of landscape.

Kennedy, Dennis. *Looking at Shakespeare: A Visual History of Twentieth-Century Performance* (1993). Lucid descriptions (with 170 photographs) of European, British, and American performances.

Leiter, Samuel L. *Shakespeare Around the Globe: A Guide to Notable Postwar Revivals* (1986). For each play there are about two pages of introductory comments, then discussions (about five hundred words per production) of ten or so productions, and finally bibliographic references.

McMurty, Jo. *Shakespeare Films in the Classroom* (1994). Useful evaluations of the chief films most likely to be shown in undergraduate courses.

Rothwell, Kenneth, and Annabelle Henkin Melzer. *Shakespeare on Screen: An International Filmography and Videography* (1990). A reference guide to several hundred films and videos produced between 1899 and 1989, including spinoffs such as musicals and dance versions.

Sprague, Arthur Colby. *Shakespeare and the Actors* (1944). Detailed discussions of stage business (gestures, etc.) over the years.

Willis, Susan. *The BBC Shakespeare Plays: Making the Televised Canon* (1991). A history of the series, with interviews and production diaries for some plays.

5. Miscellaneous Reference Works

Abbott, E. A. *A Shakespearean Grammar* (new edition, 1877). An examination of differences between Elizabethan and modern grammar.

Allen, Michael J. B., and Kenneth Muir, eds. *Shakespeare's Plays in Quarto* (1981). One volume containing facsimiles of the plays issued in small format before they were collected in the First Folio of 1623.

Bevington, David. *Shakespeare* (1978). A short guide to hundreds of important writings on the subject.

Blake, Norman. *Shakespeare's Language: An Introduction* (1983). On vocabulary, parts of speech, and word order.

Bullough, Geoffrey. *Narrative and Dramatic Sources of Shakespeare*, 8 vols. (1957–75). A collection of many of the books Shakespeare drew on, with judicious comments.

Campbell, Oscar James, and Edward G. Quinn, eds. *The Reader's Encyclopedia of Shakespeare* (1966). Old, but still the most useful single reference work on Shakespeare.

Cercignani, Fausto. *Shakespeare's Works and Elizabethan Pronunciation* (1981). Considered the best work on the topic, but remains controversial.

Dent, R. W. *Shakespeare's Proverbial Language: An Index* (1981). An index of proverbs, with an introduction concerning a form Shakespeare frequently drew on.

Greg, W. W. *The Shakespeare First Folio* (1955). A detailed yet readable history of the first collection (1623) of Shakespeare's plays.

Harner, James. *The World Shakespeare Bibliography*. See head-note to Suggested References.

Hosley, Richard. *Shakespeare's Holinshed* (1968). Valuable presentation of one of Shakespeare's major sources.

Kökeritz, Helge. *Shakespeare's Names* (1959). A guide to pronouncing some 1,800 names appearing in Shakespeare.

———. *Shakespeare's Pronunciation* (1953). Contains much information about puns and rhymes, but see Cercignani (above).

Muir, Kenneth. *The Sources of Shakespeare's Plays* (1978). An account of Shakespeare's use of his reading. It covers all the plays, in chronological order.

Miriam Joseph, Sister. *Shakespeare's Use of the Arts of Language* (1947). A study of Shakespeare's use of rhetorical devices, reprinted in part as *Rhetoric in Shakespeare's Time* (1962).

The Norton Facsimile: The First Folio of Shakespeare's Plays (1968). A handsome and accurate facsimile of the first collection (1623) of Shakespeare's plays, with a valuable introduction by Charlton Hinman.

Onions, C. T. *A Shakespeare Glossary*, rev. and enlarged by R. D. Eagleson (1986). Definitions of words (or senses of words) now obsolete.

Partridge, Eric. *Shakespeare's Bawdy*, rev. ed. (1955). Relatively brief dictionary of bawdy words; useful, but see Williams, below.

Shakespeare Quarterly. See headnote to Suggested References.

Shakespeare Survey. See headnote to Suggested References.

Spevack, Marvin. *The Harvard Concordance to Shakespeare* (1973). An index to Shakespeare's words.

Vickers, Brian. *Appropriating Shakespeare: Contemporary Critical Quarrels* (1993). A survey—chiefly hostile—of recent schools of criticism.

Wells, Stanley, ed. *Shakespeare: A Bibliographical Guide* (new edition, 1990). Nineteen chapters (some devoted to single plays, others devoted to groups of related plays) on recent scholarship on the life and all of the works.

Williams, Gordon. *A Dictionary of Sexual Language and Imagery in Shakespearean and Stuart Literature*, 3 vols. (1994). Extended discussions of words and passages; much fuller than Partridge, cited above.

6. Shakespeare's Plays: General Studies

Bamber, Linda. *Comic Women, Tragic Men: A Study of Gender and Genre in Shakespeare* (1982).

Barnet, Sylvan. *A Short Guide to Shakespeare* (1974).

Callaghan, Dympna, Lorraine Helms, and Jyotsna Singh. *The Weyward Sisters: Shakespeare and Feminist Politics* (1994).

Clemen, Wolfgang H. *The Development of Shakespeare's Imagery* (1951).

Cook, Ann Jennalie. *Making a Match: Courtship in Shakespeare and His Society* (1991).

Dollimore, Jonathan, and Alan Sinfield. *Political Shakespeare: New Essays in Cultural Materialism* (1985).

Dusinberre, Juliet. *Shakespeare and the Nature of Women* (1975).

Granville-Barker, Harley. *Prefaces to Shakespeare*, 2 vols. (1946–47; volume 1 contains essays on *Hamlet, King Lear, Merchant of Venice, Antony and Cleopatra*, and *Cymbeline*; volume 2 contains essays on *Othello, Coriolanus, Julius Caesar, Romeo and Juliet, Love's Labor's Lost*).

————. *More Prefaces to Shakespeare* (1974; essays on *Twelfth Night, A Midsummer Night's Dream, The Winter's Tale, Macbeth*).

Harbage, Alfred. *William Shakespeare: A Reader's Guide* (1963).

Howard, Jean E. *Shakespeare's Art of Orchestration: Stage Technique and Audience Response* (1984).

Jones, Emrys. *Scenic Form in Shakespeare* (1971).

Lenz, Carolyn Ruth Swift, Gayle Greene, and Carol Thomas Neely, eds. *The Woman's Part: Feminist Criticism of Shakespeare* (1980).

Novy, Marianne. *Love's Argument: Gender Relations in Shakespeare* (1984).

Rose, Mark. *Shakespearean Design* (1972).

Scragg, Leah. *Discovering Shakespeare's Meaning* (1994).

————. *Shakespeare's "Mouldy Tales": Recurrent Plot Motifs in Shakespearean Drama* (1992).

Traub, Valerie. *Desire and Anxiety: Circulations of Sexuality in Shakespearean Drama* (1992).

Traversi, D. A. *An Approach to Shakespeare,* 2 vols. (3rd rev. ed, 1968–69).

Vickers, Brian. *The Artistry of Shakespeare's Prose* (1968).

Wells, Stanley. *Shakespeare: A Dramatic Life* (1994).

Wright, George T. *Shakespeare's Metrical Art* (1988).

7. The Comedies

Barber, C. L. *Shakespeare's Festive Comedy* (1959; discusses *Love's Labor's Lost, A Midsummer Night's Dream, The Merchant of Venice, As You Like It, Twelfth Night*).

Barton, Anne. *The Names of Comedy* (1990).

Berry, Ralph. *Shakespeare's Comedy: Explorations in Form* (1972).

Bradbury, Malcolm, and David Palmer, eds. *Shakespearean Comedy* (1972).

Bryant, J. A., Jr. *Shakespeare and the Uses of Comedy* (1986).

Carroll, William. *The Metamorphoses of Shakespearean Comedy* (1985).

Champion, Larry S. *The Evolution of Shakespeare's Comedy* (1970).

Evans, Bertrand. *Shakespeare's Comedies* (1960).

Frye, Northrop. *Shakespearean Comedy and Romance* (1965).

Leggatt, Alexander. *Shakespeare's Comedy of Love* (1974).

Miola, Robert S. *Shakespeare and Classical Comedy: The Influence of Plautus and Terence* (1994).

Nevo, Ruth. *Comic Transformations in Shakespeare* (1980).

Ornstein, Robert. *Shakespeare's Comedies: From Roman Farce to Romantic Mystery* (1986).

Richman, David. *Laughter, Pain, and Wonder: Shakespeare's Comedies and the Audience in the Theater* (1990).

Salingar, Leo. *Shakespeare and the Traditions of Comedy* (1974).

Slights, Camille Wells. *Shakespeare's Comic Commonwealths* (1993).

Waller, Gary, ed. *Shakespeare's Comedies* (1991).

Westlund, Joseph. *Shakespeare's Reparative Comedies: A Psychoanalytic View of the Middle Plays* (1984).

Williamson, Marilyn. *The Patriarchy of Shakespeare's Comedies* (1986).

8. The Romances (*Pericles, Cymbeline, The Winter's Tale, The Tempest, The Two Noble Kinsmen*)

Adams, Robert M. *Shakespeare: The Four Romances* (1989).

Felperin, Howard. *Shakespearean Romance* (1972).

Frye, Northrop. *A Natural Perspective: The Development of Shakespearean Comedy and Romance* (1965).

Mowat, Barbara. *The Dramaturgy of Shakespeare's Romances* (1976).

Warren, Roger. *Staging Shakespeare's Late Plays* (1990).

Young, David. *The Heart's Forest: A Study of Shakespeare's Pastoral Plays* (1972).

9. The Tragedies

Bradley, A. C. *Shakespearean Tragedy* (1904).

Brooke, Nicholas. *Shakespeare's Early Tragedies* (1968).

Champion, Larry. *Shakespeare's Tragic Perspective* (1976).

Drakakis, John, ed. *Shakespearean Tragedy* (1992).

Evans, Bertrand. *Shakespeare's Tragic Practice* (1979).

Everett, Barbara. *Young Hamlet: Essays on Shakespeare's Tragedies* (1989).

Foakes, R. A. *Hamlet versus Lear: Cultural Politics and Shakespeare's Art* (1993).

Frye, Northrop. *Fools of Time: Studies in Shakespearean Tragedy* (1967).

Harbage, Alfred, ed. *Shakespeare: The Tragedies* (1964).

Mack, Maynard. *Everybody's Shakespeare: Reflections Chiefly on the Tragedies* (1993).

McAlindon, T. *Shakespeare's Tragic Cosmos* (1991).

Miola, Robert S. *Shakespeare and Classical Tragedy: The Influence of Seneca* (1992).

——. *Shakespeare's Rome* (1983).

Nevo, Ruth. *Tragic Form in Shakespeare* (1972).

Rackin, Phyllis. *Shakespeare's Tragedies* (1978).

Rose, Mark, ed. *Shakespeare's Early Tragedies: A Collection of Critical Essays* (1995).

Rosen, William. *Shakespeare and the Craft of Tragedy* (1960).

Snyder, Susan. *The Comic Matrix of Shakespeare's Tragedies* (1979).

Wofford, Susanne. *Shakespeare's Late Tragedies: A Collection of Critical Essays* (1996).

Young, David. *The Action to the Word: Structure and Style in Shakespearean Tragedy* (1990).

——. *Shakespeare's Middle Tragedies: A Collection of Critical Essays* (1993).

10. The Histories

Blanpied, John W. *Time and the Artist in Shakespeare's English Histories* (1983).

Campbell, Lily B. *Shakespeare's "Histories": Mirrors of Elizabethan Policy* (1947).

Champion, Larry S. *Perspective in Shakespeare's English Histories* (1980).

Hodgdon, Barbara. *The End Crowns All: Closure and Contradiction in Shakespeare's History* (1991).

Holderness, Graham. *Shakespeare Recycled: The Making of Historical Drama* (1992).

——, ed. *Shakespeare's History Plays: "Richard II" to "Henry V"* (1992).

Leggatt, Alexander. *Shakespeare's Political Drama: The History Plays and the Roman Plays* (1988).

Ornstein, Robert. *A Kingdom for a Stage: The Achievement of Shakespeare's History Plays* (1972).

Rackin, Phyllis. *Stages of History: Shakespeare's English Chronicles* (1990).

Saccio, Peter. *Shakespeare's English Kings: History, Chronicle, and Drama* (1977).

Tillyard, E. M. W. *Shakespeare's History Plays* (1944).
Velz, John W., ed. *Shakespeare's English Histories: A Quest for Form and Genre* (1996).

11. *Hamlet*

In addition to the titles mentioned in Section 4, Shakespeare on Stage and Screen, and those mentioned in Section 9, The Tragedies, the following may be consulted.

For information concerning textual problems in *Hamlet*, consult the editions by Harold Jenkins (1982), Philip Edwards (1985), and G. R. Hibbard (1985), and an essay by Paul Werstine, "The Textual Mystery of *Hamlet*," in *Shakespeare Quarterly* 39 (1988): 1–26. See also Stanley Wells and Gary Taylor, *William Shakespeare: A Textual Companion* (1987). The three earliest texts of *Hamlet* are assembled in *The Three-Text "Hamlet": Parallel Texts of the First and Second Quartos and First Folio,* ed. Paul Bertram and Bernice W. Kliman (1991).

Alexander, Nigel. *Poison, Play and Duel: A Study of "Hamlet"* (1971).
Bamber, Linda. *Comic Women, Tragic Men* (1982).
Belsey, Catherine. "The Case of Hamlet's Conscience." *Studies in Philology* 76 (1979): 127–48.
Bevington, David, ed. *Twentieth Century Interpretations of "Hamlet"* (1968).
Booth, Stephen. "On the Value of *Hamlet*," in *Reinterpretations of Elizabethan Drama*. Ed. Norman Rabkin (1969), pp. 137–76.
Brown, John Russell, and Bernard Harris, eds. *Stratford-upon-Avon Studies 5: "Hamlet"* (1963).
Charney, Maurice. *Style in "Hamlet"* (1969).
Clayton, Thomas, ed. *The "Hamlet" First Published* (1992).
Conklin, Paul. *A History of "Hamlet" Criticism, 1601–1821* (1947).
Ewbank, Inga-Stina. "*Hamlet* and the Power of Words." *Shakespeare Survey* 30 (1977): 85–102.
Frye, Roland Mushat. *The Renaissance "Hamlet": Issues and Responses in 1600* (1984).
Granville-Barker, Harley. *Preface to "Hamlet"* (1936).
Hattaway, Michael. *Hamlet* (1987).
Honigman, E.A.J. *Shakespeare: Seven Tragedies* (1976).
Jones, Ernest. *Hamlet and Oedipus* (1949).

Kastan, David Scott, ed. *Critical Essays on Shakespeare's "Hamlet"* (1995).

Kernan, Alvin. *Shakespeare, The King's Playwright: Theater in the Stuart Court* (1995).

Levin, Harry. *The Question of "Hamlet"* (1959).

Mercer, Peter. *"Hamlet" and the Acting of Revenge* (1987).

Showalter, Elaine. "Representing Ophelia: Women, Madness and the Responsibilities of Feminist Criticism," in *Shakespeare and the Question of Theory*. Eds. Patricia Parker and Geoffrey Hartman (1985), pp. 77–94.

Slights, Camille Wells. *The Casuistical Tradition* (1981).

Walker, Roy. *The Time Is Out of Joint: A Study of "Hamlet"* (1948).

Wilson, J. Dover. *What Happens in "Hamlet."* 3rd ed. (1951).

Wright, George T. "Hendiadys and *Hamlet*." *PMLA* 96 (1981): 168–93.

12. *Othello*

In addition to the items listed in Section 9, The Tragedies, consult the following:

Barthelemy, Anthony Gerard, ed. *Critical Essays on Shakespeare's* Othello (1994).

Calderwood, James L. *The Properties of* Othello (1989).

Colie, Rosalie. *Shakespeare's Living Art* (1974).

Goldman, Michael. *Acting and Action in Shakespearean Tragedy* (1985).

Granville-Barker, Harley. *Prefaces to Shakespeare*, vol. 2. (1947).

Greenblatt, Stephen. *Renaissance Self-Fashioning* (1983).

Heilman, Robert B. *Magic in the Web, Action & Language in* Othello (1956).

Honigmann, E. A. J. *Shakespeare: Seven Tragedies* (1976).

———. *The Texts of* Othello *and Shakespearean Revision* (1996).

Knight, G. Wilson. *The Wheel of Fire*, 5th rev. ed. (1957).

McPherson, David. *Shakespeare, Jonson, and the Myth of Venice* (1990).

Neill, Michael. "Unproper Beds: Race, Adultery, and the Hideous in *Othello*," *Shakespeare Quarterly* 40 (1989): 383–412.

Vaughan, Virginia Mason. Othello: *A Contextual History* (1994).

13. *King Lear*

In addition to the readings listed above in Section 9, The Tragedies, see the following: for material concerning the texts of the play, see (in addition to the items by Peter Blaney, Michael Warren, and Rene Weis) page 146 of *King Lear* in this edition.

Armstrong, Philip. "Uncanny Spectacles: Psychoanalysis and the texts of *King Lear*." *Textual Practice* 8 (1994): 414–34.

Blaney, Peter. *The Texts of "King Lear" and Their Origins* (1982).

Bonheim, Helmut, ed. *The Lear Perplex* (1960).

Bradley, A. C. *Shakespearean Tragedy* (1904).

Campbell, Lily B. *Shakespeare's Tragic Heroes* (1930).

Colie, Rosalie, and F. T. Flahiff, eds. *Some Facets of "King Lear"* (1974).

Cunningham, J. V. *Woe and Wonder* (1951).

Danby, John F. *Shakespeare's Doctrine of Nature* (1949).

Fraser, Russell A. *Shakespeare's Poetics in Relation to "King Lear"* (1962).

Granville-Barker, Harley. *Prefaces to Shakespeare*. 2 vols. (1946–47); part of the material is reprinted above.

Halio, Jay, ed. *The Tragedy of King Lear* (1992).

Heilman, Robert B. *This Great Stage: Image and Structure in "King Lear"* (1948).

Holland, Norman N., and Sidney Homan and Bernard J. Paris, eds. *Shakespeare's Personality* (1989).

Kahn, Coppélia. "The Absent Mother in *King Lear*." *Rewriting the Renaissance: The Discourses of Sexual Difference in Early Modern Europe*. Ed. Margaret Ferguson, Maureen Quilligan, and Nancy J. Vickers (1986); pp. 33–49.

Lamb, Charles. "On Shakespeare's Tragedies" (1808); rptd. in *Lamb's Criticism*, ed. E.M.W. Tillyard (1923), pp. 43–48.

Lothian, John Maule. *"King Lear": A Tragic Reading of Life* (1950).

Mack, Maynard. *"King Lear" in Our Time* (1965); part of the material is reprinted above.

Moulton, Richard G. *Shakespeare as a Dramatic Artist* (1897).

Novy, Marianne. *Love's Argument: Gender Relations in Shakespeare* (1984).

———. *Women's Re-Visions of Shakespeare: On the Responses of Dickinson, Woolf, Rich, H.D., George Eliot, and Others* (1990).

Perrett, Wilfred. *The Story of King Lear from Geoffrey of Monmouth to Shakespeare* (1904).

Rosen, William. *Shakespeare and the Craft of Tragedy* (1960).

Sewall, Richard B. *The Vision of Tragedy* (1959).

Shakespeare Studies 13 (1960; devoted to *King Lear*).

Stoll, E. E. *Art and Artifice in Shakespeare* (1933).

Taylor, Gary, and Michael Warren, eds. *The Division of the Kingdom: Shakespeare's Two Versions of "King Lear"* (1983).

Thompson, Ann. "Are There Any Women in *King Lear?*" *The Matter of Difference: Materialist Feminist Criticism of Shakespeare.* Ed. Valerie Wayne (1991), pp. 117–28.

Warren, Michael. *The Complete "King Lear" 1608–1623* (1989); unbound photographic facsimiles of Q1, Q2, and F, as well as a bound version of the next title listed.

———. *The Parallel "King Lear" 1608–23* (1989); photographic facsimiles of Q1 and F, in parallel columns, and, in the outer margins, reproductions of corrected states of Q and F.

Weis, René, ed. *"King Lear": A Parallel Text Edition* (1993); prints Q on the left-hand page, F on the right, both in modernized spelling.

Wilson, Richard. *Will Power* (1993).

14. *Macbeth*

In addition to the items listed in Section 9, The Tragedies, and the items concerning stage productions listed in Section 4 above, consult the following:

Adelman, Janet. *Suffocating Mothers: Fantasies of Maternal Origin in Shakespeare's Plays, "Hamlet" to "The Tempest"* (1992).

Berger, Harry. "The Text Against Performance in Shakespeare: The Example of *Macbeth.*" *The Power of Forms in the English Renaissance.* Ed. Stephen Greenblatt (1982), pp. 49-79.

Bradley, A. C. *Shakespearean Tragedy* (1904). Part of the material is reprinted above.

Brown, John Russell, ed. *Focus on "Macbeth"* (1982).

Kahn, Coppélia. *Man's Estate: Masculine Identity in Shakespeare* (1981).

Kimbrough, Robert. "Macbeth: The Prisoner of Gender." *Shakespeare Studies* 16 (1983): 175-90.

Long, Michael. *Macbeth* (1989).

Mack, Maynard. "The Jacobean Shakespeare: Some Observations on the Construction of the Tragedies." *Stratford-upon-Avon Studies 1: Jacobean Theatre* (1960); reprinted in the Signet Classic edition of *Othello.*

Muir, Kenneth, ed. *Shakespeare Survey* 19 (1966).

Sinfield, Alan. *Faultlines: Cultural Materialism and the Politics of Dissident Reading* (1992); part of the chapter on *Macbeth* is reprinted above.

——, ed. *Macbeth* (1992; twelve recent essays).

Turner, John. *Macbeth* (1992).

Walker, Roy. *The Time Is Free* (1949).

Wheeler, Thomas. *"Macbeth": An Annotated Bibliography* (1990).